WRITING BUSINESS LETTERS & REPORTS

Second Edition

Carmella E. Mansfield, Ph.D.
Professor of Business Education and Office Administration
Ball State University

Margaret Hilton Bahniuk, Ed.D.
Associate Professor of Business Administration
The Cleveland State University

Glencoe Publishing Company
Bobbs-Merrill Division
Mission Hills, California

Send all inquiries to:
Glencoe Publishing Company
15319 Chatsworth Street
Mission Hills, CA 91345

Printed in the United States of America

ISBN 0-02-682970-3

1 2 3 4 5 6 7 8 9 91 90 89 88 87

Contents

APPENDIXES

Preface

TO THE TEACHER

The 1981 edition of *Writing Business Letters and Reports* was designed to help readers become skilled writers of letters and reports. The text language was clear and simple; the content, practical, rather than theoretical. The book was primarily written for the learner, not the teacher whose vocabulary and knowledge of the subject matter are more advanced.

Objectives

Even though advancements in technology have changed the business environment so that automated equipment is generally available for communicating, the principles of communication have not changed. Electronic and electromagnetic equipment and software can be considered partners in the communication process. They can help handle routine and complex communication tasks with speed and efficiency—especially the formatting, editing, sending, storing, and retrieving of communications. Messages can be transmitted in traditional envelopes, with electronic equipment, or through a combination of the traditional and technological.

This edition retains all the qualities of the first edition while updating content and incorporating new information that reflects current developments in the business world. We have employed simple step-by-step procedures that range from simple to complex communications and have selected research-based, realistic, and current examples to illustrate business forms, letters, and reports.

In addition to providing us with up-to-date information, representatives from 170 Fortune 500 companies advised us about:

1. The types of communications that should be taught in college classrooms.
2. The communication methods and documents that should be given the most emphasis.
3. The weaknesses reflected in communication documents (e.g., memorandums, letters, and written reports).
4. Content information for resumes, employment letters, and other business-related communications.

Most of the respondents believed that teachers should instruct students on oral presentations, letter writing, report writing, attentive listening, electronic communication, and telephone communications. This edition, therefore, covers such information, in addition to providing numerous examples and ideas to strengthen students' knowledge and ability.

Because nonverbal communication affects the effectiveness of oral presentations and listening, a chapter on nonverbal communication has been added. And, as recommended, we are also emphasizing interoffice memorandums, oral presentations, persuasive requests, and reports (particularly informal, summary, and analytical). Oral communication and written memorandums are crucial forms of business communication and appear to be growing in importance. Consequently, this edition includes new chapters on these forms of communication, in addition to minor emphasis in other chapters. Letter and report writing chapters include new ideas, as well as the helpful and pertinent old ideas. The importance of employment interviews merited a separate chapter in the text this time, rather than a list of selected ideas, which appears in an appendix in the first edition.

Quality of writing was a major concern to the Fortune 500 companies we contacted. The most common writing faults they mentioned were, in order of importance: hazy or unclear objectives; wordiness; poor organization; excessive length; incorrect spelling, punctuation, and grammar; outdated terminology; writing in the passive voice; excessive formality; careless corrections; uninteresting writing; incomplete and incorrect information; writer-centered thinking; offensive letter salutations; and insufficient illustrations, charts, and graphs in reports. To strengthen students' ability to write English, we have added a language arts chapter emphasizing writing skill development. In addition, numerous editing and language skills exercises have been added.

Organization

The text is conveniently divided into six major divisions:

Part 1 Basic Concepts of Communication
Part 2 Basic Mechanics of Writing
Part 3 Application of Writing Ideas—Letters, Memoranda, Etc.
Part 4 Application of Writing Ideas—Reports
Part 5 Oral and Nonverbal Communication
Part 6 Career Applications

The comprehensive appendixes include valuable information to help learners conveniently use the dictionary, thesaurus, and library; increase their spelling vocabulary; punctuate properly; understand proofreaders' marks for editing business communications; and differentiate between words frequently misused. We have also included selected pages of a formal report.

The book is divided into chapters that should provide a logical and progressive study from the basic concepts of communication and the fundamentals of writing to specialized areas of communications. To make the book as understandable and practical as possible, we have identified the important facets of nonverbal and oral (speaking, listening, dictating) communication. Also, we have identified and explained each part of effective written communications—selecting an appropriate format and the mechanics of constructing an attractively typewritten page; developing clear, concise, and correct sentences, and preparing a topic outline and business documents that instill a positive, reader-oriented tone. Often, these components overlap; an attractive communication contributes to clarity as well as to positivism, for example. All components work together to create successful communications that project a favorable image for the writer and aid in achieving and maintaining employee morale or good public relations.

TO THE LEARNERS

This book was written for college students, but all adults can use it as a guide to improve and develop their communication skills. Communication skills include not only the ability to get along well with others but also the ability to speak and write effectively. These skills are gateways to success in business.

The examples in this book should help you improve your communication skills by providing ideas. They are not to be copied, since effective communicators individualize their communications. They consider the human element—their audience—in all their communications. As you make oral presentations or write your memos, letters, reports, or other business communications, consider the nonverbal messages you may be communicating. What does your communication say about you?

We encourage you to follow the procedure for writing effective communications, including the preparation of a brief, written preliminary topic outline detailing what you want to say in logical order. Then, prepare a rough draft and revise it until your final communication is reader-centered and in accordance with the elements of effective communications. To be certain, check your work with the Checksheet for Writing Effective Communications.

End-of-chapter questions and activities should challenge your skills, as well as enable you to analyze your understanding of the topic and apply the principles of effective communication studied in that chapter and in previous chapters. The editing and language skills exercises will help you improve your ability to write well. In addition, the appendixes should help with your writing, as well as provide selected readings that offer greater dimensions for expanding your knowledge and ability to communicate.

THANK YOU

We dedicated the first edition to our husbands—Walt and Gene. This edition is also dedicated to them. We appreciate their patience and inspiration.

We thank the teachers and students who used the first edition. They encouraged us with their valuable comments and ideas for improvement and with their support. We also thank the many individuals and companies who aided us with our research or granted us permission to reprint information.

WRITING BUSINESS LETTERS & REPORTS

Basic Concepts of Communication

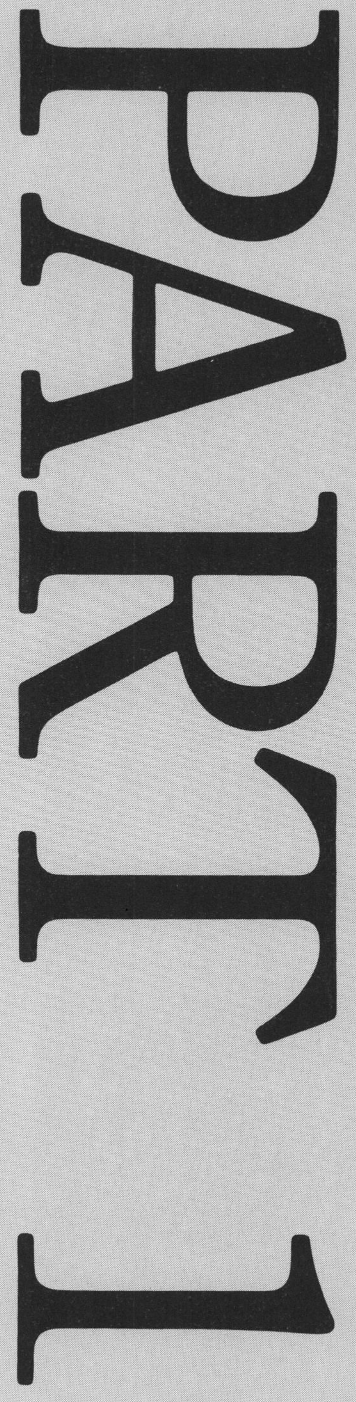

1 An Overview of Communication

After studying Chapter 1, you should be able to:

- Describe the communication process
- Recognize a communications model
- Distinguish between verbal and nonverbal communications
- Distinguish between formal and informal organizational communications
- Distinguish between internal and external organizational communications
- Describe the many different forms communications take in the business world today
- Recognize an effective communication
- Set personal communication goals

Writers have defined "communication" in words, while others have explained it with pictures or communication models. Basically, **communication** is several things:

1. A process for transmitting a message
2. A social experience or two-way interaction between sender(s) and receiver(s)
3. The actual message

Communications in the business world are classified as either verbal or nonverbal, informal or formal, and internal or external. Internal communications can be upward, downward, or horizontal.

Advancements in technology have automated communication in the modern business world. Telecommunication and teleconferencing (including electronic mail) are now common means of communicating information. Advanced technology can be your partner in the communication process. It has simplified and expedited formatting and editing written communications, as well as sending and receiving all kinds of messages. Regardless of equipment and materials used to communicate, the principles of communication have not changed; you must adhere to them to communicate effectively in business.

Written communications provide writers and readers with a permanent record; they are a valuable means of spelling out exact information and for complying with the law when written data are required.

EXPLANATION OF COMMUNICATION

The one widely held idea about communication is that a universal explanation is illusive. For centuries, writers and thinkers in many disciplines have provided us with definitions or explanations. Some explanations are rather complex.

According to *Webster's Third New International Dictionary*,* "communication" comes from the Latin verb *communicare*, which means the act or action of imparting or transmitting something in common (*communis*). The key word here is *common*. For genuine communication to take place, mutual understanding must exist between sender and receiver. Effective communication is reader-centered (showing sincere concern for the reader's needs), complete, clear, concise, concrete, correct, coherent (logically organized), courteous, and positive.

We do know that communication is a **process**. Meanings are exchanged between or among individuals through a common system of symbols (e.g., language, signs, or gestures). In an organiza-

---

**Webster's Third New International Dictionary, Unabridged*. Springfield, Mass.: G. & C. Merriam Company Publishers, 1981, page 460.

tion, communication may actually be a communication **system**—the devices for conveying messages (for example, computer, telephone, or radio).

It is also a **social function**. This is said because much communication is two-way: a message proceeds from sender to receiver and a return message goes from receiver to sender (feedback). The message is influenced by the perceptions, background, beliefs, and other personal characteristics of the communicators. For genuine communication, the receiver must understand the message sent and communicate this fact to the sender.

Finally, communication may be the **message** itself: the talk, the letter, or the report.

Communication Process

The communication process involves several steps. First, the sender (transmitter) must have a specific **purpose for communicating**. In other words, the message to be relayed must be clear to the sender. Without this, the sender would find it difficult to translate or **encode the idea** into the appropriate symbols, the second step in the process. The symbols chosen must fit the situation and the individuals involved: their backgrounds, experiences, culture, customs, beliefs, biases, emotions, mentality, physical characteristics, attitudes, perceptions, verbal and nonverbal skills, and language understanding. Common symbols include an idea, word, sound, gesture, picture, letter, report, and silence.

The chosen symbol will affect the third step of the communication process: **selecting the channel** or medium for transmitting the message. For example, if gestures (the symbol) are chosen to encode the message, then telephone lines would be an inappropriate channel. The message could not be communicated to the receiver. If a supervisor must communicate a message quickly (for example, a rush request), the telephone lines would be a more appropriate channel than second-class mail delivery. Employees who have access to a computer network can use the system to transmit messages at their convenience—even if the receiver is not present.

Other channels in the communication process include sight, sound, touch, radio waves, electric impulses, coaxial cables (underground or under the ocean communication lines), and satellites (relay stations positioned thousands of miles above the earth).

Noise, anything that distracts the receiver's attention, will affect the message transmitted. If noise is present, the message may be altered or even stopped. Common communication noises include language barriers, spelling errors, unintentional sounds or silences, and inappropriate or unattractive format. Thus, if a sender uses an unknown technical word, the word may confuse or distract the receiver long enough to inhibit, and possibly destroy, the intended message. Too many "uhs" and "okays," a spelling error, or sloppy correction in an otherwise well-written message may lead the receiver to believe the sender is careless, incompetent, uncaring, or uninformed, none of which are messages the sender intended. The interviewee who distracts the interviewer may change the interviewer's perception that the applicant is a good candidate for the job vacancy. Thus, noises are barriers to communication.

The fourth step in the communication process is the **decoding/receiving action.** Here, the receiver takes meaning from the symbols transmitted by the sender. No matter how effective and cooperative the receiver is, the message is subject to misinterpretation because of conditions inherent in the communication process. The receiver is influenced by the symbols and media used, as well as any noise that occurs. In addition, the message may be changed because of the recipient's characteristics, beliefs, skills, emotions, attitude, and so on.

The fifth and final step is the **receiver's action**. The receiver may either accept and file the message or reject and discard it. On the other hand, **two-way communication** may require feedback in the form of a reply using appropriate symbols. This reply might be a gesture, a single word, or many words in the form of a letter or report or other business document. Thus, the communication process resumes with the receiver becoming the sender and the sender, the receiver.

One-way communication, on the other hand, takes place when the sender and receiver are the same person. This happens when a person reads and responds to a letter, report, or other document she or he has written. It also happens when a person listens and responds to her or his recorded voice.

Communication Models

Communication is often defined with a **communication model** (a pictorial, line drawing). Examples of well-known models include the Shannon–Weaver Communication Model (1949), which represented communication as a one-way process to illustrate electronic communication; the Schramm Communication Model (1971), which depicted communication as a two-way process; and the

Berlo Communication Model (1960), which emphasized the importance of human behavior in the two-way process.*

The communication model in Figure 1-1 illustrates the important elements in the communication process and other factors that influence senders and receivers and, ultimately, the message sent and received.

CLASSIFICATIONS OF COMMUNICATION

Communication is classified in various ways. All communication is generally classified as verbal or nonverbal. Organizational communications can be divided several ways:

1. By degree of formality—formal or informal
2. By area of application—internal or external
3. Within the organization—upward, downward, or horizontally

Verbal and Nonverbal

Although some people consider verbal communication as nothing more than oral communication, it is much more. **Verbal** communication involves words; therefore, it includes not only speaking, but listening, thinking, reading, and writing as well. All other communication methods are **nonverbal**; words are not used.

Informal and Formal

Much oral communication is informal; it has little or no structure. Person-to-person conversations, telephone conversations, and the grapevine (employee gossip) are examples of **informal oral communications**.

Probably half of what employees learn about a company is communicated through the grapevine. This type of gossip seems to feed on several basic human needs: to be part of a team, to be recognized as an individual, to share information and ideas, to feel secure, to think well of oneself, and to be a success. These social needs may vary from individual to individual and depend on the specific situation. As a result, gossip in the grapevine may start as a secret one employee tells another. Barriers to speaking and listening skills may alter the secret as it is retold. Surprisingly, however, the grapevine is generally accurate.

---

*If you are interested in reading more about these communication models, please refer to: Berlo, D. K., *The Process of Communication*. New York: Holt, Rinehart, and Winston, 1960; Shannon, C. E., and Weaver, W. *The Mathematical Theory of Communication*. Urbana, Illinois: The University of Illinois Press, 1949; Bello, F. "The Information Theory," *Fortune*, December, 1953; and Schramm, W., and Roberts, D. F., eds. *The Process and Effects of Mass Communication*. Urbana, Illinois: The University of Illinois Press, 1971.

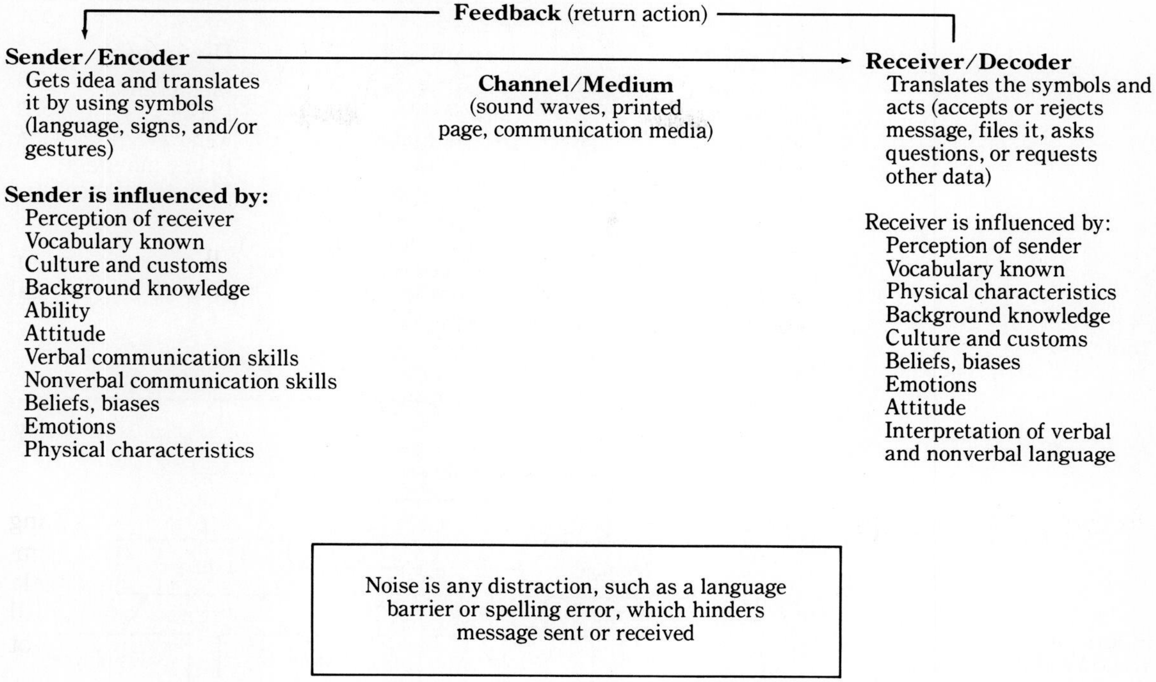

Feedback (return action)

Sender/Encoder
Gets idea and translates it by using symbols (language, signs, and/or gestures)

Channel/Medium
(sound waves, printed page, communication media)

Receiver/Decoder
Translates the symbols and acts (accepts or rejects message, files it, asks questions, or requests other data)

Sender is influenced by:
Perception of receiver
Vocabulary known
Culture and customs
Background knowledge
Ability
Attitude
Verbal communication skills
Nonverbal communication skills
Beliefs, biases
Emotions
Physical characteristics

Receiver is influenced by:
Perception of sender
Vocabulary known
Physical characteristics
Background knowledge
Culture and customs
Beliefs, biases
Emotions
Attitude
Interpretation of verbal and nonverbal language

Noise is any distraction, such as a language barrier or spelling error, which hinders message sent or received

Figure 1-1
A Communication Model

Frequently management must transmit official information quickly. Since the formal communication channels of an organization are often very slow, some managers *use* the grapevine. They "feed" it information by filtering an announcement through the grapevine at the right moment and to the "proper" person, rather than delaying and processing the information through the usual formal procedure.

Formal oral communications include interviews, conferences, meetings, and dictation (see Chapter 25). In each different situation, structure, general and specific knowledge about individuals, and the situation are important. To use formal oral communications effectively, good communication skills are a must.

Informal written communications include memoranda, bulletin board notices, and notes for suggestion boxes. Letters and reports are **formal written communications**.

Internal and External

All communication within the organization is **internal communication**. Table 1-1 gives examples of popular internal written communications, as well as communication directions. Some

Table 1-1
Internal Written Communications—Typical Divisions

Upward	Downward	Horizontal
Notes for suggestion boxes	Bulletin board notices	Memoranda
Memoranda	Inserts in pay envelopes	Letters
Letters	Company magazines	Reports
Reports	Company manuals	Policy manuals
	Minutes of meetings	Minutes of meetings
	Newsletters	
	Memoranda	
	Letters	
	Reports	

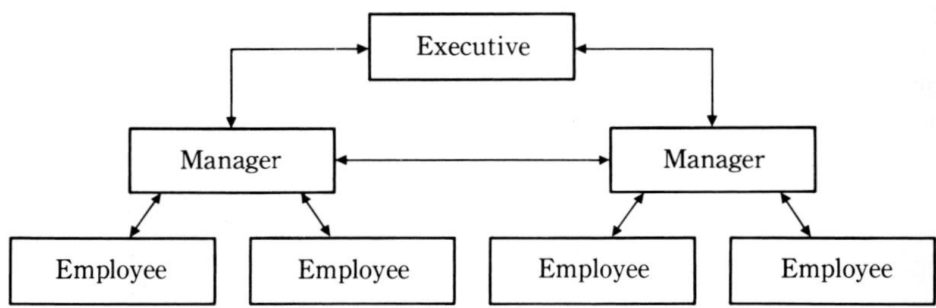

Figure 1-2
Vertical and Horizontal Communication

internal communications (e.g., memoranda) are important throughout the organization; others have limited uses.

Some consider upward communications (e.g., communications going from Treasurer up to President) as the most important internal communications. This is not completely true. Even though upward communications are the basis for managerial decisions that initiate action, communications going downward (for example, from Manager to Assistant Manager) or horizontally (for example, from Director of Operations to Director of Sales) are very important. At all levels and within all functions of the company, individuals and groups must communicate effectively and work toward corporate rather than individual goals. An individual or group that puts personal goals before company goals creates undue stress that may result in a breakdown in communication. Figure 1-2 depicts desirable communication at various organizational levels. Everyone acts like a team, communicating with each other.

All communication directed to individuals or groups outside the organization is **external communication**. The greatest volume of external communication are letters, but reports (e.g., annual reports) can be both internal and external communication. Because memoranda are easy to format and save time and money, they are becoming more useful as informal external communications.

COMMUNICATION IN THE MODERN BUSINESS WORLD

Even though the way in which communication is explained and classified has remained relatively constant, the symbols and channels of communication have become more sophisticated. Office routines are more challenging.

Communication Equipment and Methods

Earlier in the 20th century, standard office communication equipment consisted of items such as manual and electric typewriters, telephones, calculators, and dictation machines. The communicator sat behind a desk and used the devices to format, send, and receive verbal messages. Many office tasks were time-consuming (for example, typing duplicate copies, filing numerous copies, and correcting errors on originals and carbon copies). Since errors had to be corrected individually, some errors slipped by without correction. The result was miscommunication and ultimately loss of time and goodwill, as well as increased costs.

Communication in a modern office is accomplished with sophisticated technology (for example, electronic typewriters, electronic message services, telephone networks, and computer systems). Computers are used to create documents such as letters and reports. Preparing these documents is made easier with software or computer programs that perform such routine tasks as correcting keyed spelling errors; adding and deleting a word, several words, or even pages; and establishing margins and pages. With this software, communicators can revise visual text much faster than they can using either an electric or electronic typewriter. They can also prepare and exchange information (for example, memoranda and letters) very rapidly.

In addition to storing information for later retrieval, computer systems are used to communicate with other employees, with individuals representing other organizations, and with society. Computers and electronic message services help management personnel reach logical decisions quickly because they make quick feedback possible. Accounting, manufacturing, and production workers also use computers to make and assemble products, control inventories, and schedule shipments. Current communication equipment and methods, therefore, encourage teamwork, increase office productivity, and office morale.

Both telecommunication and telephone and computer teleconferencing are important advances in communication equipment. Telecommunication is used frequently in the business world.

Computer teleconferencing is relatively new, but telephone teleconferencing has been available for many years.

Telecommunication

Telecommunication is the transfer of information by electromagnetic means. Telephone lines, computers, and satellites are basic channels of communication in a telecommunication system. The symbols used to input the data would include the voice, printed word, pictures, graphs, typewriter keyboard, magnetic tape, and CRT (cathode ray tube) terminal. Telephone lines are often the common link in the telecommunication network. When participants have access to either personal computers or large centralized computer systems, computer telecommunication is possible.

Teleconferencing

Teleconferencing refers to the interaction of individuals involved in the communication network.

Telephone teleconferencing. Two or more persons can participate in a **telephone teleconference**, even though the individuals may be in different locations and many miles apart. It is a relatively fast and convenient communication method. Since the communication involves one telephone call, it is usually more convenient and less expensive than making a long-distance telephone call to each individual or writing and mailing the information. In addition, all parties hear the same message. Users of telephone telecommunication should be skilled telephone users and oral communicators; otherwise, the communication method can be costly and/or ineffective. (Chapter 25 includes tips for telephone users.)

Computer teleconferencing. **Computer teleconferencing** uses the features of electronic mail coupled with computer terminals to allow several people in various locations to access data simultaneously. Thus, information housed in a central area can be shared. Effective communication requires interaction and feedback; therefore, participants in the computer teleconference should have keyboarding, computing, and editing skills.

Audio teleconferencing. Microphones and a computer network are needed for audio teleconferences. The computers are joined with a cable so that the users in the network can communicate with each other using the microphones. Data stored in the auxiliary storage of one computer are accessed and transferred electronically to another computer in the network. Using electronic mail software, messages (such as letters) can be sent to others in the network. The message can be displayed on a CRT, and the recipient can reply immediately if desired. This type of shared information should be carefully planned.

The advantages for holding electronic audio teleconferences rather than the traditional face-to-face group meetings are the greater possibilities for:

1. Participating in out-of-state and international meetings
2. Going to the "meeting" when convenient, since not all participants need to be present at the same time
3. Using time productively because you can plan documents and data when convenient and attend the meeting when convenient
4. Saving travel time and costs
5. Saving money for paper and for labor to store and retrieve data

On the other hand, participants in an electronic audio teleconference cannot rely on nonverbal language, as they can with face-to-face meetings and video teleconferencing.

Video teleconferencing. The **video teleconference** is the most complex and expensive form of teleconferencing. In its most common form, a central satellite station is used to transmit images of a speaker. Participants can talk to speakers through a telephone or satellite hookup.

In addition to saving travel time and costs, video conferencing allows individuals from various locations to talk, discuss, and share complex information in a near face-to-face situation. Another advantage may be the ability to attract a speaker who is not willing (or unable) to attend a traditional face-to-face meeting.

Video conferencing, however, is complex and expensive, and its success depends on the verbal and nonverbal communication skills of speakers and listeners. In addition, participants must plan their presentations and graphic displays carefully.

IMPORTANCE OF WRITTEN COMMUNICATIONS

Written communications are a vital part of every business. They provide readers and writers with:

1. A permanent record for later referral
2. A basis for providing detailed and/or complex information, thereby making it easier for senders to convey some messages and reduce the risk of misinterpretation
3. A way to confirm previous agreements or decisions, providing reassurance to the communicants

4. A dated record of business transactions
5. The record required by law, since certain information must be in writing to be legal

Written communications can be powerful business devices. Business persons and public officials often acknowledge that timely and well-written letters and reports helped them get prompt action, influence decisions, change policies and practices, and get and maintain goodwill. Written communications can express goodwill through congratulations, thanks, sympathy, praise, and welcome. They can also help the communicator secure employment, information or materials, adjustments for claims, merchandise or service, credit, payment of current and past-due amounts, and sales.

Written communications are ineffective if they use incorrect grammar, punctuation, or format or are difficult to read or understand. Incorrect or unclear written communications cause needless delays; they waste energy, time, and money. As a result, business and goodwill may be lost.

QUALITIES OF THE EFFECTIVE COMMUNICATOR

The effective communicator must possess multiple skills to communicate the intended message. An accomplished writer must be skilled in communicating verbally, whereas the effective speaker must be skilled in communicating verbally and nonverbally. Both must understand humans and their behavior. They must give their primary consideration to the receivers—their basic and special needs, desires, interests, beliefs, emotions, and verbal and nonverbal skills. Unless this is done, the intended message may be misunderstood or rejected. Messages must be formatted with language that is edited for reader-centeredness, clarity, correctness, conciseness, completeness, coherence, courtesy, concreteness, and positivism.

Effective communicators know their subject matter well enough to talk or write about it with confidence and care. They must be able to determine the appropriate and best way to communicate various messages. They know that the basic criteria for selecting a communication method are:

1. *Availability of equipment, materials, and personnel in order to use the communication method.* The best method may not always be available.
2. *Knowledge and skills of individuals involved in the process.* The message must be conveyed and understood if the purpose for the communication is to be achieved.

3. *Cost for communicating.* Cost is generally considered relative to other desirable criteria (for example, necessary speed and purpose). Choose the least expensive way to get the job done effectively.
4. *Speed.* This criteria is sometimes more important than cost, for example. How soon must the message be conveyed?
5. *Impact desired.* A greater impact is possible if a change is made in the usual communication method. For example, if an interoffice memorandum is usually used, a personal visit, telephone call, or letter may create a greater impact on the receiver.
6. *Purpose of the communication.* Some communications must be in writing to comply with the law, to be understood, or to be conveyed; others must be oral or nonverbal. Should a business form, memorandum, letter, or report be written? Which type? Would a face-to-face meeting be more convincing because nonverbal communication can be readily observed?
7. *Feedback desired.* Nonverbal communication is difficult or impossible in some cases (for example, a telephone telecommunication). Feedback can be a different communication method. In other words, a telephone call might be used to answer a letter, a report may be necessary to answer a telephone message, and so on.

Although technology may change communication methods in business, the criteria for an effective communicator will not change. They have been and will remain constant. This book is dedicated to helping individuals improve their communication skills so that they can become effective communicators.

GOALS FOR COMMUNICATORS

How do you rate as an effective communicator? As you use this book, set appropriate goals for yourself. We suggest that your goals include:

1. To gain confidence as a communicator.
2. To strive for excellence in communicating.
3. To expand your knowledge of effective verbal and nonverbal communication (including listening), particularly as it applies to business situations.
4. To put yourself in the place of the intended receiver and then speak, listen, write, or act respecting the individual's specific needs, interests, beliefs, feelings, and emotions.
5. To get all the necessary facts before communicating.
6. To develop your ability to use verbal and nonverbal language—appropriately and accurately.

7. To plan your communications so that they will be professional, pleasing to the receivers, complete, clear, correct, concise, concrete, coherent, courteous, positive, and sincere.
8. To write letters, reports, and other business communications that are appropriate, polished, and professional in appearance and text.
9. To apply the guidelines for writing effective business communications.
10. To use the following procedures for writing effective business communications:
    a. Decide purpose for the communication.
    b. Reflect on the purpose to determine type of communication needed to achieve it and the best writing approach.
    c. Make a brief outline detailing what to say in logical order.
    d. Prepare a rough draft from the outline.
    e. Revise the draft as often as necessary using the checksheet in Chapter 4 (see Figure 4–2) as a guide.
    f. Prepare a neat, correct, and properly executed final copy.
    g. Distribute copies as necessary and desirable.

CHAPTER SUMMARY

Although "communication" has several meanings, it is basically considered a two-way process involving at least one sender and one receiver who transmit ideas with symbols through a channel or medium. The symbol is encoded and transmitted through the medium. Any noise (distraction) might alter or stop the message. The receiver decodes the message and provides feedback with the same or different symbols and in the same or different channels. Because the two-way process involves the interaction of people, communication is considered a social process. Communication is also the actual message (for example, letter, memo, or report) transmitted.

Researchers have used the communication model to define communications graphically.

Communications are generally classified as either verbal or nonverbal. Organizational communications can be formal or informal, internal or external.

Written communications, a type of verbal communication, are necessary business devices. In addition to communicating various messages, written communications, some of which are highly technical, provide communicants with permanent, dated records of information. Some communications must be in writing to be recognized by law.

Technology has transformed the business office and communication methods (not the principles of effective communication), challenging business people at all organizational levels to use the software and rapidly changing electronic and electromagnetic equipment for formatting, editing, sending, storing, and retrieving communications. In skilled hands, routine and complex tasks can be done quickly, possibly resulting in better time management, higher productivity, reduced costs, goodwill and good employee morale.

Since communication involves people, the people factor in communicating should not be ignored. Skilled communicators use their knowledge of human relations for selecting appropriate communication methods and for preparing receiver-centered messages. They use their language skills to produce communications that are courteous, clear, complete, correct, concise, coherent, and concrete. The latest technology can help them create, edit, transmit, store, and retrieve their effective verbal communications.

Anyone can be a better communicator by setting communication goals based on the guidelines for effective communication and then working to achieve those goals.

STUDY QUESTIONS

1. Why is communication generally understood as a process? Why is it a social process?
2. What vocabulary terms are associated with the communication process? Define each.
3. Besides those listed in the text, what other "noises" would you consider barriers to communication? Explain.
4. What is the purpose of a communication model?
5. What is verbal communication? What is nonverbal communication?
6. Why is the grapevine considered an informal organizational communication? Why does the grapevine exist?
7. What is the difference between an internal organizational communication and an external organizational communication? Cite examples in each category.
8. How does the business office of today differ from the office of 1960? How do you believe the changes will affect your communication methods and skills? Do you foresee other changes? Explain.
9. What are the characteristics of a skilled communicator?

ACTIVITIES

1. Prepare your own definition or explanation for communication using words or a communication model.
2. As accurately as you can, for one week, keep a daily record of the time you spend reading, writing, speaking, and listening. Total the hours in each category and determine to the nearest percent what part of each day you spend in each activity. Are you surprised at the results?
3. Explain why you believe each of the following might be a good or poor communication practice:
   a. Telephoning several office workers to explain that the building is on fire
   b. Telephoning office workers to give details on a meeting next month
   c. Writing a letter to say that a meeting is tomorrow
   d. Correcting an employee before other co-workers
   e. Correcting an employee in a face-to-face conversation
   f. Confirming a real estate transaction on the telephone
   g. Arranging a video teleconference to which a well-known speaker has been invited
   h. Using the computer system to communicate with a co-worker in another building across town
4. Explain the method of communication you would use to:
   a. Send a copy of a catalog
   b. Send a message to a co-worker who works on your floor
   c. Convey the results of a survey (to your superior)
   d. Invite a well-known speaker to a professional meeting
   e. Report the results of a meeting
   f. Reserve hotel/motel rooms for employees attending a meeting

Principles of Written Communication

After studying Chapter 2, you should be able to:

- Describe how written communications are prepared
- Decide on the purpose of the communication
- Develop an outline
- Distinguish between the deductive approach and the inductive approach
- Prepare a rough draft and revise, edit, and proofread it
- Recognize and use a readable writing style

As discussed in Chapter 1, communication is a two-way process. Receivers give verbal and nonverbal feedback (for example, printed information, questions, comments, and gestures). This feedback allows senders to clarify their messages with words, detailed illustrations, or nonverbal cues.

Written communications, on the other hand, require senders or writers to play a major role in the communication process. Writers must anticipate the reader's interests, needs, and problems and use the language skillfully. They must also prepare the message in an appropriate and acceptable format. Written communications that are poorly organized, formatted, or written give readers cause to question the writer's knowledge about the subject; the writer's ability to communicate successfully; and the writer's desire to inform, please, or consider the reader. Readers may lose confidence in such writers.

Skillful writers, therefore, understand human nature; are adept with verbal and nonverbal language; choose the best communication vehicle (for example, standard business form, memorandum, letter, or report); and format appropriate, reader-centered messages. Even with written communications, effective communicators are aware of nonverbal messages.

To develop written communication skill, determine the best communication form to achieve the purpose or reason for writing. Then prepare a good topic outline; make a rough draft of the communication; and revise, edit, and proofread the communication so that the final copy will follow the elements of good writing. You can develop a readable writing style by choosing your words carefully, using various types of sentences and sentence lengths, and adhering to traditional formats. A readability formula can help you check the reading level of communications intended for employees and the public.

WRITE WITH A PURPOSE

The written business communication is the means to an end. Before writing anything, determine the **purpose**—the dominant reason for writing. Then choose the best communication form to achieve the intended result. This form might be an invoice, purchase order, statement of account, memorandum, letter, report, or other common business document.

Business letters are frequently written to request information or materials, answer requests, express goodwill, promote or sell goods and services, discuss or adjust complaints, acknowledge orders, grant credit, and encourage payment of accounts. The letter written to request information is different from the letter written to request a claim or to sell a product. Interoffice memoranda are commonly used for business messages within an organization. The purpose of the communication might suggest writing an informal report (such as a memorandum report) or a formal report which includes supplemental parts (such as a table of contents or bibliography).

DEVELOP AN OUTLINE

Once you have determined the type of letter, report, or other document needed, you are ready to prepare an appropriate outline. An **outline** is your preliminary guide for writing letters and reports. Think of the finished outline as a table of contents. The working outline is actually a list of ideas to include in the communication.

Until you can write an outline with relative ease, start by listing all data pertinent to your communication. After listing the ideas, ask yourself:

Is the purpose specified clearly?
Are the facts complete and correct?
What information is unnecessary?
Have I considered the readers' needs, interests, and beliefs?

Revise your list as needed and arrange the ideas psychologically, so that your plan is in logical order and reflects the correct approach for the reader (direct or indirect).

Communications beginning with the most important idea are written in the **direct** or **deductive approach**. This is the most common arrangement and is used for communicating routine or pleasant messages. If the main idea is delayed (de-emphasized) by being placed in the middle of the communication, the **indirect** or **inductive approach** is being used. This indirect arrangement is helpful when writing refusals or persuasive communications. In either case, there should be a natural transition from sentence to sentence and from paragraph to paragraph. The end of the letter is almost as important as the beginning: The last paragraph should strengthen the writer's position and inspire action. Meaningless repetition should be avoided.

DRAFT YOUR COMMUNICATION

After you have prepared a good outline that has the appropriate approach and logical order, you are ready to draft the letter or report. Using your outline, prepare a **rough draft** of the communication. In the first writing, do not worry unnecessarily if the words do not seem the best or if the spelling, grammar, or punctuation is incorrect. Just continue developing the ideas in your outline. After the complete rough draft is written, revise it as often as necessary so as to produce the desired message in a readable writing style.

REVISE, EDIT, AND PROOFREAD

Like other forms of communication, written communication is a process. It requires the writer to revise, edit, and proofread. Although the communication process can be simple and fast for some written communications (for example, simple requests for information or materials), most communications require careful and periodic attention over an extended period—several days or a week or more. This procedure is especially helpful, for example, when writing a complex letter or report, a complaint letter, or employment communications.

Writer's need time to:

1. Make certain that the appropriate communication device and format have been chosen
2. Consider the reader's needs, interests, and beliefs
3. Investigate and gather all pertinent facts
4. Arrange ideas in proper and logical order
5. Revise and edit the document so that it has correct spelling, grammar, and punctuation and will achieve its purpose

In addition, time may be needed to "cool down" (become calmer), particularly when writing a complaint letter. The first rough draft may be very negative; however, the last revision should emphasize the facts with positive words and tone and request a fair adjustment.

Before mailing or distributing your communication, revise, edit, and proofread it until it complies with the elements of professional writing. Good writing is:

1. *Complete.* Are all facts included so that the reader can determine who is involved, what is involved, why, when, where, and how?
2. *Clear.* Is the language readily understood by the reader?
3. *Concise.* Are only necessary words and ideas used?
4. *Concrete.* Is the language expressive, rather than dull and lifeless?
5. *Correct.* Are all facts accurate? Is the written English (spelling, punctuation, and grammar) accurate?
6. *Coherent.* Is the purpose specifically stated? Does the language flow smoothly throughout the communication?
7. *Courteous.* Is the tone considerate of the beliefs, feelings, and needs of the reader? Is the communication attractive?
8. *Positive.* Is the subject treated with positive ideas and words, eliminating the negative as much as possible?
9. *Effective beginning.* Is the approach logical for the situation—direct (for favorable or routine messages) or indirect (for unfavorable or persuasive messages)?

10. *Effective ending.* Is the ending convincing and active, rather than stereotyped and repetitive?

Chapter 4 discusses each of these characteristics in more detail.

Part 2 explains and illustrates traditional letter parts and styles; Parts 3, 4, and 6 give specific principles for various communications and provide opportunities to apply basic (detailed in Part 1) and specific principles for writing appropriate messages.

DEVELOP A READABLE WRITING STYLE

Readable writing is simple, expressive writing that can be understood by the reader and logically organized into an attractive and appropriate format. Business people have neither the desire nor time to wade through poorly organized, overly long, difficult to understand, unattractive or inappropriate communications. Written business communications should be **readable**—easy to read and understand.

Short Words Are Best

Simple writing is not necessarily childish writing. The effective business writer will consider the feelings, beliefs, and needs of the reader and will never verbally or nonverbally "talk down" to the reader. The chosen words should be simple, but not immature. For example, you can write *ask* rather than *interrogate*, *insert* instead of *interpose*, *explain* rather than *illuminate*, and *improve* rather than *ameliorate*. The most expressive and understandable terms are usually short words familiar to the reader.

Active Verbs Are Expressive

Whenever possible, the reader should be able to visualize the action. This is possible by using active verbs, rather than passive verbs. The passive form includes a helper—a form of the "to be" verb—and produces awkward, dull, and long sentences. In active writing, the subject acts. It is better to write the active *we believe* instead of the inactive *it is believed*. *Ms. Smith received the letter* is an active sentence. The reader can quickly grasp the correct details. On the other hand, *The letter was received by Ms. Smith* is an inactive sentence. It includes the passive verb phrase *was received* and an unnecessary prepositional phrase. The subject of the sentence is lifeless (*letter*). *Ms. Smith* is just the object of the preposition rather than the instigator of the action. Chapters 3 and 4 contain additional information and examples.

Unnecessary Words Add Length

Every written word should contribute to the message. Avoid add-on terms, which merely contribute length. You should write *assemble* rather than *assemble together*. *Assemble* means to gather into a group. *Please write the report* is preferable to *Please write up the report*. Reports are written neither up nor down. Write *The consensus is that he will be the keynote speaker* instead of *The consensus of opinion is that he will be the keynote speaker.* Consensus means agreement of opinion.

Prepositional phrases may encourage redundancy. For example, *He is an American by birth* should be written, *He was born in America.* The prepositional phrases, *at 11:00 a.m. in the morning* should be shortened to *at 11 a.m.* Chapter 4 includes numerous illustrations to help you write concisely.

Readability Formulas Determine Reading Ease

Effective communicators will adapt their writing style and writing vocabulary to fit the knowledge and language level of the reader. Generally, short sentences and paragraphs are more readable and understandable than long ones. No one wants to struggle through long sentences and paragraphs when short ones are possible. Actually, business communications should contain a variety of sentence types, sentence lengths, and paragraph lengths. Each sentence should contain one basic thought.

Readability formulas are tools to determine reading ease (*but not the quality*) of communications. The formulas (see Chapter 24) are based on average sentence and word length—not whether what is being tested exhibits characteristics of good writing.

Readability was popularized by Rudolph Flesch after much research.* Flesch stressed the desirability of short to average-length sentences; a variety of sentence structures; and simple terminology. The Gunning Fog Index† is probably the most widely used readability formula. It is based on average sentence length and percentage of difficult (three or more syllables) words in a 100-word sample. Much business writing is between the eighth grade and eleventh grade reading level.

Critics of readability formulas complain that the formulas are not accurate measures of readability levels and that they lower language quality and destroy writing style. Nonetheless, used as intended, the formulas help writers determine language difficulty.

Written communications for employees and the public should be prepared in language they understand. Some government publications, insurance policies, financial reports, and annual reports are prepared in a simplified format and written in easy-to-understand, reader-centered language understood by the public. The communications are clear, concise, and coherent.

---

*Rudolph Flesch, *The Art of Readable Writing.* New York: Harper & Row, 1949.
†Robert Gunning, *The Technique of Clear Writing.* New York: McGraw-Hill, 1968.

Technical writing is for people who understand the specialized language. Communications to doctors, for example, may include medical terms, but they should not include technical legal terminology without explanations. On the other hand, lawyers should not be expected to understand the doctor's special vocabulary.

Communications written in language above or below the level understood by the intended readers nonverbally indicate a disregard for the readers—a negative tone. Tone is the writer's attitude nonverbally communicated by the verbal language. Thus, if readers consider the language elementary, they may believe the writer considers them unknowledgeable and inferior and may feel insulted. Goodwill or employee morale may suffer. If the language level is difficult, readers will not understand the message and may resent asking for clarification. The communication objective may not be accomplished.

Uniform Format Aids Readability

Using traditional formats for memorandums, letters, reports, purchase orders, invoices, and other business communications increases readability and efficiency. The writer can routinize repeated messages; the reader can recognize the communication and not waste valuable time determining the basic purpose. You should deviate from tradition only if that deviation will help you better achieve your purpose.

CHAPTER SUMMARY

Written communications are more difficult than other forms of verbal communication because in addition to human relation and language skills, the writer must know the appropriate format for the message and avoid negative nonverbal messages.

After deciding the purpose for your communication, determine the appropriate written communication to achieve the purpose and develop a good topic outline. Prepare a rough draft and revise, edit, and proofread it until it is readable and easy to understand (using a readability formula) and adheres to elements of effective writing. Your communications should be complete, clear, concise, concrete, coherent, courteous, and positive, and the beginning and ending should state the correct approach and be reader-centered.

STUDY QUESTIONS

1. Compared to other verbal communication methods, what special traits does the writer need to communicate successfully?
2. What are the steps for writing effective communications? Explain each.
3. What are the characteristics of good writing? How does each one help you prepare professional and effective communications?
4. What can you do to cultivate a readable writing style?
5. How do readability formulas determine reading ease?
6. Why are readability formulas an inappropriate means to evaluate the *quality* of writing? Explain.

ACTIVITIES

1. Copy 100 consecutive words from a current periodical or book. Show the steps (and calculations) as you determine the reading level using the SMOG Index or FOG Index. (See Chapter 24 for help.)
2. For each of the following, substitute, using a dictionary if necessary, a shorter or more appropriate expression:
   a. altercation
   b. luxuriant
   c. secession
   d. terminate
   e. unencumbered
   f. complimentary
   g. encompass the park
   h. precocious person
   i. fatuous person
3. For each of the following, eliminate the unnecessary word:
   a. sending along
   b. first priority
   c. complete monopoly
   d. free gift
   e. most excellent
4. Revise these paragraphs until they are clear, concise, concrete, correct, coherent, courteous, positive, and reader-centered.

   Precocious employees will avoid altercations with superiors. They will strive to get along well and willingly with co-workers and with management and with customers.

   When workers terminate their employment with the company before Christmas, they should not expect to receive complimentary Christmas gifts after they resign their jobs. Are you agreeable with this statement?

5. Rewrite the following passive sentences:
   a. The tree was struck by lightning.
   b. Mr. Smith was advised of his legal rights by his lawyer.
6. For each of the following situations, state the purpose of your answer and the appropriate communication form needed (letter, report, telegram, and so on):
   a. You receive a request for a free catalog.
   b. Your supervisor requests detailed information and recommendations to remedy parking problems. You have made a comprehensive study of the situation.
   c. A customer complains about a company product and asks for a refund. You agree that a refund and an explanation are appropriate.
7. Outline the important points for writing a letter to request a subscription to a magazine for one year. Include a statement saying how you plan to pay for the order: a postal money order for $25. Arrange the ideas in logical order.

3 Development of Language Skill

After studying Chapter 3, you should be able to:

- Recognize and write a simple, compound, complex, and compound-complex sentence
- Eliminate sentence fragments, run-on sentences, and dangling and misplaced modifiers from your writing
- Avoid sex bias in your business communications
- Recognize and compose an effective paragraph
- Determine where emphasis will be placed in sentences and paragraphs

Written communications require the application of language—selecting and combining words to convey thoughts. For the combinations to be effective, the writer must carefully form them into sentences and paragraphs. This requires basic knowledge about sentence structure and paragraphing. Although this chapter touches on some techniques that may help you improve some of the more common writing problems, you may want to consult a comprehensive business English handbook for more information.

Writing is a process that requires extensive reorganization of ideas and editing to produce communications designed to achieve the intended purpose. You should reorganize and edit your communications until they convey your message with words and in a tone that will be understood and accepted by the readers.

WRITING SENTENCES

Sentences are fundamental to effective written communication. Each sentence should contain one basic idea. It can consist of only one word (commands) or many words because of the addition of explanatory and descriptive words and phrases.

Definition

A sentence always has a **subject**, the actor or the starting point of the action, and a **predicate**, a declaration about the subject. The subject is always a **noun** or **pronoun** (or **noun phrase** functioning as a noun or pronoun); the predicate is a **verb** or **verb phrase**. Most sentences state the subject first, then the predicate, and finally the objects (if there are any).

A complete sentence may consist of just two words:

We believe.	Sales increased.	You write.
This is.	John wrote.	Helen ordered.

In some cases where the subject *you* is omitted, a sentence may consist of one word, the verb or predicate. (The only subject you can omit writing is *you*.) This kind of sentence is a **command** and is rarely used in business communications. These one-word statements (with *you* as the understood subject) are complete sentences:

Write. **Meaning**: *You* write.	Order. **Meaning**: *You* order.	Adjust. **Meaning**: *You* adjust.

Always specify the subject if the subject is a noun or any other pronoun besides *you*.

Generally, sentences consist of more than two words. Adjectives, adverbs, phrases, and clauses complete the meaning of the sentence and add expression to it. **Adjectives** modify (explain, describe, limit) nouns or pronouns; **adverbs** modify verbs, adjectives, or other adverbs. Adjectives generally precede the nouns they modify, whereas adverbs usually follow their predicate or are positioned near the words they describe. A **phrase** is a group of words that complete the sentence meaning but that do not have a subject and predicate. Adjectives, adverbs, and phrases cannot stand as a sentence because they do not contain a subject and predicate and, as a result, cannot form a complete thought. A **clause** is a group of words that has both a subject and a predicate. An **independent clause** can stand alone as a sentence; the meaning is complete in itself. A **dependent clause** cannot stand alone; it depends on the rest of the sentence to give it meaning.

The following statements illustrate how adjectives, adverbs, and phrases can be used to add expression and broader meaning to a simple sentence.

Subject Predicate Object
Careers are available.

Adjective
Many careers are available.

Prepositional Phrase
Many careers are available **for men and women**.

Prepositional Phrase — Adverb
Many careers **in data processing** are **easily** available for men and women.

Adjective — Adjective — Noun
Many **challenging** careers in the data-processing **field** are easily available for **energetic** men and women.
Adjective

These five sentences are *all* simple sentences. (An explanation of a simple sentence follows under Classification.)

Classification

The four classes of sentences are simple, compound, complex, and compound-complex. Classification is determined by independent clauses (clauses than can stand alone as a sentence) and/or dependent clauses (cannot stand alone). The number of modifiers does not influence sentence classification.

Simple: One independent clause.

Compound: Two or more independent clauses connected either by a comma and a coordinating conjunction *or* by a semicolon.

Complex: One independent clause and at least one dependent clause.

Compound-Complex: Two or more independent clauses and at least one dependent clause. Avoid using compound-complex sentences in your business communications. They often add to reading difficulty.

A simple sentence can be long and complicated, whereas compound or complex sentences can be relatively short and easy to understand. Sentence length, therefore, does not indicate sentence classification or difficulty.

Subject Predicate

Simple: Cash **sales increased** during July and August, the warmest months.

Subject Predicate

Simple: **We are complying** with your request

Predicate

and **will make** the necessary changes to your record.

Subject Predicate

Compound: Cash **sales increased** during July and

Subject Predicate

August, but **they decreased** in September.

Subject Subject Predicate

Complex: Because **July** and **August are** very

DEPENDENT CLAUSE

INDEPENDENT CLAUSE

Subject Predicate

warm, cash **sales increased.** (This is a complex sentence. It has one dependent clause and one independent clause.)

Subject Predicate

Compound-Complex: **Sales are** important to business
INDEPENDENT CLAUSE

Subject Predicate

organizations, for when **sales rise**,
DEPENDENT CLAUSE

Subject Predicate

employers can raise salaries.
INDEPENDENT CLAUSE

Variety and Readability

Effective communicators vary the type and length of sentences used. Simple sentences that convey the intended meaning are best, but a communication with only simple sentences is too elementary for most readers. Such readers will be bored and possibly offended. Instead, use a combination of simple, compound, and complex sentences, each with one basic idea. Choose the type of sentence that conveys your message clearly and maintains harmonious relations with your reader. In addition, be sure your sentences are not fragments or run-ons. They should also be accurately worded and punctuated.

For business communications, the average sentence length is generally between 17 and 20 words, but the message is more important than the exact number of words.

See the section entitled "Writing Paragraphs" in this chapter. It illustrates the many combinations of different types of sentences that will provide interesting and logical reading.

Emphasis

Place words and ideas to achieve the emphasis you desire. If you want to emphasize a word, place it at the beginning or at the end of the sentence. Short sentences are best.

Enclosed is a personal check for $55.80.
Placing words in prepositional phrases de-emphasizes them.
A **$55.80 check** is enclosed.

We would appreciate **immediate delivery**.

I wrote the **report**.

Mary wrote the transmittal letter for the report.

You can also emphasize by using specific, descriptive words and the active (rather than the passive) voice.

To draw attention away from an idea (such as a negative), place it in the dependent clause of a complex sentence. Dependent clauses often begin with subordinating conjunctions and adverbs as well as participial or gerund phrases. Some more common examples of subordinating conjunctions and adverbs are *after*, *as soon as*, *although*, *because*, *before*, *if*, *otherwise*, *since*, *than*, *that*, *though*, *until*, *when*, and *while*, although there are many others. Most *ing* words and many *ed* words are participles or gerunds. Several examples include *having written the report*, *exhausted by the heavy routine*, and *joining the group*.

Other techniques for de-emphasizing are:

- Use general terms
- Place nouns in prepositional phrases
- Use the passive voice
- Phrase the idea as a question

> Since Mary wrote the transmittal letter, I wrote the report.
> *This complex sentence takes away from what Mary did.*
>
> Mary wrote the transmittal letter. I wrote the report.
> or
> Mary wrote the transmittal letter; I wrote the report.
> *Mary's role is on an equal footing with the writer's role here.*
>
> Because your payment was received after the ten-day discount period, the $30.25 unearned cash discount has been charged to your account.
> *This long and complex sentence de-emphasizes the negative.*
>
> Having written the report, I asked Mary to write the transmittal letter.
> I asked *is emphasized more than Mary or the report.*
>
> A request for an explanation of the charges was made by the Account Supervisor.
> *This simple sentence uses several prepositional phrases and passive voice to de-emphasize.*
>
> The Account Supervisor asked for an explanation of the charges.
> *This sentence is written in the active voice.*
>
> Will you please explain the charges?
> *Asking a question softens the negative idea.*

Chapter 4 includes explanations and examples to help you write sentences that are reader-centered, complete, clear, concise, concrete, correct, coherent, courteous, and positive—the elements of effective writing.

PURSUING SENTENCE CLARITY

Not only must sentences contain one idea, but they must also be written clearly enough that a reader can understand, without any questions, what the writer has said.

Sentence Fragments

A **sentence fragment** is a phrase or dependent clause that cannot be considered a sentence because it has no meaning by itself. In the preceding illustrations, the following phrases and clauses are sentence fragments—not sentences.

> During July and August, the warmest months
>
> Because sales increased during July and August
>
> For when sales rise

They have no meaning without the accompanying independent clauses.

Run-On Sentences

A **run-on sentence** (also called a **fused sentence**) is:

1. Two sentences without punctuation separating them
2. Two independent clauses with only a comma separating them, which is also called a **comma fault** or **comma splice**

The following statements are run-on sentences and are, therefore, incorrect:

> The accountant corrected the computer records some were incorrect.
>
> The accountant corrected the computer records, some were incorrect.

The following examples show how to avoid writing run-on sentences:

> The accountant corrected the computer records. Some (records) were incorrect.
> *Separate into two sentences.*
>
> The accountant corrected the computer records; some were incorrect.
> *Connect the two independent thoughts with a semicolon.*
>
> The accountant corrected the computer records, for some were incorrect
> *Make the sentences into complex sentences. Use a comma and a coordinate conjunction to join the thoughts. Common coordinate conjunctions are* and, or, but, for, nor.
>
> The accountant corrected the computer records, some of which were incorrect.
> *Change wording and punctuation to make one clause subordinate to the other.*

Subject–Predicate Agreement

The subject and its predicate must agree in number. A single subject takes a single predicate; a plural subject takes a plural predicate.

Singular Subject — Singular Predicate

The **letter is** a written communication.

Compound Subject — Plural Predicate

Letters and **reports are** important management tools.

Singular Subject — Singular Predicate

Martha Houston, author of both reports, **writes** textbooks.

When determining the sentence subject and its predicate, ignore prepositional phrases **except** when the subject is *more, some, part, most,* or fractions and percentages followed by an *of* prepositional phrase. In such cases, refer to the object of the preposition. If it is singular, use a singular predicate. If it is plural, use a plural predicate.

> **Most** *of the sales managers* **have increased** sales.
> *Since the object* managers *is plural, use a plural predicate.*

> **Part** *of the annual report* **is** ready now.
> *Since* report *is singular, use a singular predicate.*

> **One-fifth** *of the workers* **have** at least ten years' service.
> *Since* workers *is plural, use a plural predicate.*

Collective nouns, or nouns singular in form but plural in meaning, are singular when they act as a single unit.

> The Perkins Mfg. Company imports items manufactured in West Germany.
> *The singular predicate is used because* The Perkins Mfg. Company *is considered one unit.*

Examples of other collective nouns include: *army, class, club, crew, crowd, committee, data, humanity, jury, orchestra,* and *public.* As a general rule, treat these collective nouns as singular subjects unless the individual members are acting separately. If they are, use a plural predicate.

> The committee is preparing the budget for next year.
> *Committee is working as a single unit; it requires a single predicate.*

> The committee are analyzing the budget items.
> *Members of the committee are acting as individuals; therefore, plural predicate is needed. This sentence actually says:*
> Committee members are analyzing the budget items.

> Fenner, Fenner, and Carter is interested in serving you; *we* have offices in New York, Chicago, and Indianapolis.
> *Although* it *would be the correct pronoun, using* we *personalizes the otherwise impersonal company name. Writers may prefer this deviation from the usual.*

Other examples of singular subjects that may cause some confusion include: *each*, *everyone*, *someone*, *somebody*, *anybody*, *anyone*, *everybody*, *anything*, *either*, *one*, and *no one*. Use singular predicates with these singular pronouns.

Singular Subject — Singular Predicate

Each person **is invited** to make comments about the proposal.

Singular Subject — Singular Predicate

Either is invited to make comments about the report.

The name of a publication or topic is also considered a single unit and requires a single predicate.

"Writing Sales Letters" is a chapter title.

Numbers can also cause confusion. They are singular when they represent a whole; however, they are plural when considered as individual items. When considered a single unit, use a singular predicate. When considered individual items, use a plural predicate.

One million dollars is the price for the movie star's house.
All of the dollars are considered as one unit and, therefore, require a singular predicate.

Ten thousand automobiles were produced last month.
Each automobile is a unit; therefore, the subject is plural and requires a plural predicate.

When *number* is the sentence subject, choose the predicate based on the preceding word. *The number* requires a singular predicate; whereas, *a number* requires a plural predicate:

The number of persons writing effective reports **is** increasing.

A number of people **are** attending communication workshops.

When *or* or *nor* connects two subjects, refer to the **second** subject to determine the predicate. If the second subject is singular, use a singular predicate. If the second subject is plural, use a plural predicate.

Your **note** or **letter is** due before March 1.
The second subject—letter—*is singular.*

The **note** or **letters are** due before March 1.
The second subject—letters—*is plural.*

The conjunctions *either* and *neither* cannot be used as subjects; however, the nouns or pronouns following them can be sentence subjects. Always use *or* with *either* (*either . . . or . . .*) and *nor* with *neither* (*neither . . . nor . . .*).

Either the **clerks** or the **customer is** available for consultation.
*The second subject—*customer*—is singular.*

Either the **customer** or the **clerks are** available for consultation.
*The second subject—*clerks*—is plural.*

Neither the **man** nor the **woman has understood** all the instructions.
*The second subject—*woman*—is singular.*

You always requires a plural predicate.

You know that **you were elected** president of the organization.

Active and Passive Voice

Effective business communications are generally written in the active rather than the passive voice. As noted in Chapter 2, the active voice provides sentence vigor, readability, clarity, and reader interest.

In the active voice, the subject acts so that the writing depicts energy, life, motion. Sentences written in the active voice are usually shorter than those written in the passive; therefore, active sentences are easier to understand.

In the passive voice, the subject is acted upon; it receives the action. The reader has to read the entire sentence to determine the action. The predicate is often longer, requiring more helping verbs than the active voice. Prepositional phrases are often used and add unnecessary length to the sentence.

Active: Mary **wrote** the letter to the university president.
8 words
Passive: The letter **was written** by Mary to the university president.
10 words

Active: This report **contains** the City Council's recommendations on the proposed jail complex.
12 words
Passive: The City Council's recommendations on the proposed jail complex **are contained** in this report.
14 words

Even though most of your writing should be in the active voice, the passive voice can be effectively used to soften a negative tone, thereby aiding morale or goodwill.

Active: Mr. Smithe made ten errors in the report.
Passive: Ten errors were found in the report written by Mr. Smithe.

Chapter 4, in its treatment of concreteness, contains further discussion of the active and passive voices.

Parallel Structure

Parallel construction provides logical order within sentences, keeping all similar parts on the same level. The relationship of the subject to the rest of the sentence will be equal. Thus, the reader can apply correctly the first part of the sentence to each individual part at the end.

> We are enclosing **blank** forms, **white** cards, and **legal-size** envelopes.
> *This is a parallel sentence because each enclosure is preceded by the same type word, an adjective. The parts of the predicate are equal. The sentence is saying:* **We are enclosing blank forms. We are enclosing white cards. We are enclosing legal-size envelopes.**
>
> We are enclosing **blank** forms, cards, and **legal-size** envelopes.
> *This sentence is not parallel since the parts of the predicate are not equal. Each noun in the predicate is not preceded by an adjective.*
>
> Our medical personnel would be pleased **to offer** suggestions on treating local reactions and **(to) assist** you.
> *This sentence is parallel because* **to offer** *and* **(to) assist** *are both infinitives.*
>
> Students should carefully observe how their instructors **conduct** experiments and when the results **are recorded**.
> *This sentence is not parallel because* **conduct** *and* **are recorded** *are not the same verb form.*
>
> John F. Kennedy said: "Let every nation know . . . we shall **meet** any hardship, **support** any friend, **oppose** any foe. . . ."
> *This sentence is parallel because each series item begins with a verb in the same tense:* **meet**, **support**, *and* **oppose.**
>
> Abe Lincoln believed that government should be **of** the people, **by** the people, and **for** the people.
> *This sentence is parallel because the series items begin with prepositions:* **of**, **by**, *and* **for**.

It is better to be repetitive (e.g., use the same adjective or same preposition several times) than to write a statement that is not parallel.

Information stated in columns must also be parallel. The following list is parallel because each item functions as a predicate adjective in the sentence.

> The following traits describe John Doe:
>
> 1. industrious
> 2. well-organized
> 3. careful
> 4. self-reliant
> 5. energetic
> 6. well-informed

Parallel construction is especially important to the reader of an outline, table of contents, or report. Parallel subdivisions help readers grasp the relationship between ideas. See, for example, the Table of Contents for the formal report in Chapter 23 or the outline in Chapter 21. The Contents for this text is also parallel and provides an excellent example.

Parallel construction is discussed again in Chapter 4 as an element of "coherence."

Dangling or Misplaced Modifiers

Modifiers should be placed near the words they limit, explain, or describe. To do otherwise may change the sentence meaning or make the meaning more difficult to understand without repeated readings.

Unclear: After returning to the office, the letter was written.
This sentence states that the letter *returned to the office.*

Better: After returning to the office, *the* secretary wrote the letter.
The revised sentence is in the active voice, is easier to understand, and eliminates the misplaced modifier.

Awkward: Please mail the report to Mr. Jones with your corrections.

Improved: Please mail the report with your corrections to Mr. Jones.

Better: Please correct the report and mail it to Mr. Jones.

The placement of one word can change the sentence meaning.

Just Miss Jones wrote that the items were received.
Miss Jones *just* wrote that the items were received.
Miss Jones wrote *just* that the items were received.
Miss Jones wrote that *just* the items were received.
Miss Jones wrote that the items *just* were received.

Chapter 4 provides more examples of misplaced modifiers in the section entitled "Clarity."

WRITING NONSEXIST EXPRESSIONS

A **sexist expression** casts men and women in predetermined roles. Thus, it commits an individual's social and business roles to a particular sex. Generally, women are stereotyped into negative or inferior or subordinate roles. However, men are also treated unjustly. Sexual bias is not only unjust, it is offensive, destroys goodwill and morale, and may be illegal.

Over the last decade, we have seen a growing trend to avoid sexism in business communications. To increase your effectiveness in communicating and promoting morale and goodwill, commit yourself verbally and nonverbally to using **nonsexist terminology**, which is free from sexual bias.

Chapter 5 continues this discussion. It notes that traditional letter parts are leaning toward nonsexist and courteous wording. For example, *Gentlemen* has been replaced by *Ladies and Gentlemen* or *Gentlepersons*, and *Presiding Officer* has taken the place of *Dear Chairman*. Women can choose to use Ms. as their courtesy title, rather than the customary *Miss* or *Mrs.*

Interorganizational memoranda have traditionally directed messages to specific individuals without including their courtesy titles. In Chapter 14, "Luis Rivera" and "Dana Martinez" are used instead of "Mr. Luis Rivera" and "Mrs. Dana Martinez".

Avoid sex bias in your verbal and nonverbal communications by:

1. Using nonsexist terminology whenever possible
2. Using plural nouns instead of singular nouns
3. Using both male and female pronouns
4. Alternating the position of male and female words so that one gender is not always in the superior or emphatic position
5. Using female expressions to refer to **specific** females; male expressions to **specific** males
6. Rewording sentences

Use Nonsexist Terminology

Using nonsexist terminology is one of the first steps toward avoiding sexual bias. The following examples give alternatives to what were once fairly common sexist terms.

Nonsexist	**Sexist**
chairperson, chair, presiding officer	chairman
businessperson, business executive	businessman, businesswoman
member of Congress, legislator	congressman
police officer	policeman, policewoman
salesperson	salesman, saleswoman
flight attendant	stewardess, steward
writer, reporter, novelist	author, authoress
pilot	aviator, aviatrix
humanity, society	mankind
supervisor, manager, employer	foreman
mail carrier	mailman, mailwoman
labor time	man hours
homemaker	housewife
administrative assistant	secretary

In general, avoid words ending in *man*, *ess*, *ix*, *ette*.

Sex bias is evident in social or career roles. For example, a nurse, employee, baby sitter, grade school teacher, typist, stenographer, secretary, cook, and follower are usually females. On the other hand, a president, pilot, professor, administrator, executive, chef, engineer, and leader are stereotyped as males. You can avoid such generalizations by using plurals, the individual's proper name, or other rewording.

Sex bias has permeated our language and traditions. Until recently, tornadoes and hurricanes were always given female names (e.g., Arlene, Barbara, and Carla). Today, female and male names are alternately assigned (e.g., Arlene, Bradley, Carla, Donald). Nature is generally referred to as *Mother Nature*. The minister may say *man and wife*, instead of *husband and wife*. Men are *men*, but a woman may be called a *girl* or *honey*. Heads of households are usually males, seldom females. A salesperson often wants to speak to the *man of the house*. Even when present, the woman may be ignored.

Sexism is also evident in gender order. *Bride* always appears before *groom* (as in *bride and groom*); yet, *husband* appears before *wife* (as in *husband and wife*). Try reversing the order some time and pay attention to the reactions you get.

Use Plural Nouns Instead of Singular Nouns

To eliminate the use of *he* or *she*, use plural nouns so that the plural pronouns can also be used. This small change will help you avoid sex bias in communicating.

Sexist: The nurse is an important member of the medical team; she helps the doctor with his office patients.
Nonsexist: Nurses are important members of the medical team; they help doctors attend to office patients.

Sexist: A supervisor should delegate his duties to his subordinates.
Nonsexist: Supervisors should delegate duties to their subordinates.

Use Both Male and Female Pronouns

Including pronouns that refer to both sexes is an alternative to using plural nouns and pronouns; however, such writing can make reading tedious and boring. Use this alternative **sparingly.**

Sexist: He will supervise his office staff.
Less sexist: He or She will supervise his or her office staff.

Sexist: Legally, a person can check his credit records.
Less sexist: Legally, a person can check his or her credit records.

Alternate the Pronoun Position

Reversing the usual pronoun positions is only slightly better than using both pronouns in traditional order. This alternative should also be used **sparingly**.

Sexist: As president, he can attend the board meetings.
Less Sexist: As president, she or he can attend the board meetings.

Sexist: The elementary teacher plans projects for his students.
Less Sexist: The elementary teacher plans projects for his or her students.

Use Specific Individuals

You can refer to each individual by name and use the appropriate noun or pronoun.

Sexist: An accountant should be trained professionally to analyze his client's financial records.
Nonsexist: John Tucker, an accountant, is trained professionally to analyze his client's financial records.

Use sexist terms only when they apply directly. For example, "Liz Taylor is a well-known actress" is more appropriate than "Liz Taylor is a well-known actor."

Reword Sentences

Reword your sentence if you are tempted to use a sexist term (or have used the male-female pronouns too often). Such nonsexist terms as *you*, *your*, *person*, *one*, *a*, *an*, *the*, and *it* can be very useful.

Sexist: A supervisor should delegate his duties to his subordinates.
Nonsexist: **The** supervisor is a **person** who delegates duties to subordinates.

Sexist: Legally, a person can check his or her credit records.
Nonsexist: Legally, **you** can check **your** credit records.

Sexist: She or He will supervise her or his office staff.
Nonsexist: **The** office manager will supervise **an** office staff.
Nonsexist: **It** is the office manager who supervises **an** office staff.

Sexist: As president, she or he can attend the board meetings.
Nonsexist: As president, **one** can attend board meetings.

Resolve to remove sex bias from your business communications. The preceding discussion provides several guidelines. When you encounter a sexist idea, check the guidelines for alternatives. By doing so, you should achieve your purpose without offending anyone or hindering goodwill.

WRITING PARAGRAPHS

Sentences are combined to form paragraphs. Effective writers vary the types of sentences they use. They also organize and divide paragraphs to reveal information clearly and coherently. Paragraphs differ in length depending on the idea discussed, but each paragraph contains only one major idea.

Definition

A **paragraph** is a subdivision or distinct section of a communication and usually deals with one specific point. Each paragraph begins on a new line so that it is clearly separate from the preceding paragraph. Depending on the format chosen, paragraphs may or may not be indented from the left margin. For example, the first line of paragraphs in most double-spaced documents should be indented five to ten spaces.

Length

As with sentences, paragraphs are not classified by length. The writer will want to vary paragraph length so that the meaning is clear, the major ideas are emphasized, and the paragraphs are visually appealing to readers. One-sentence paragraphs (perhaps one to four typewritten lines) can be used to emphasize data. These very short paragraphs are best placed at the beginning or end of letters or reports. Middle paragraphs are generally longer. If a paragraph is more than eight typewritten lines, look for a natural break in ideas to form a new paragraph.

Development

The typical paragraph includes one basic idea—generally positioned in either the first or last sentence—and additional sentences as necessary to support, explain, or discuss that basic idea. Coherence within sentences, between sentences, and between paragraphs is necessary.

Stating the major idea first in the paragraph provides readers with immediate insight. They can comprehend the reason for each detail more easily as one flows into the next. This method represents the **deductive (direct) approach** (discussed in Chapter 1) and is best for stating routine or pleasant information. On the other hand, if the details or supporting information precedes the major idea, readers are more apt to accept a negative or argumentative topic. This method represents the **inductive (indirect) approach** (discussed in Chapter 1). Choose the method that will help you achieve your purpose while maintaining a harmonious relationship with the reader. To aid the reader, be consistent; use either deductive or inductive paragraphs throughout the communication.

Several different techniques can be used to make paragraphs work as a whole. Sentences within a paragraph can be joined logically by repeating part of the previous sentence, usually the last part.

> Thank you for your gift to the College of Business Alumni fund. **This fund** is used to . . .
>
> or
>
> Thank you for your gift to the College of Business Alumni fund. **Your gift** will be used to . . .

You can also achieve this cohesion between sentences by starting with a pronoun instead of a noun.

> Thank you for your gift to the College of Business Alumni Fund. **It** is the largest fund available for supporting . . .

Another method that will help the idea of one sentence flow into the next is to use coordinating or adverbial conjunctions.

> Thank you, Mr. Smith, for supporting the College of Business Alumni Fund. **Because** of you and other generous alumni, we are able to support activities which are expected of an excellent university.

The preceding paragraph might be followed by the next two paragraphs.

> Our quest for **excellent** students and faculty is promoted by **alumni gifts** for scholarship and nonscholarship activities. By far the largest percentage of **alumni dollars**—65 percent— go to **excellent** students who need monetary help.
>
> **Alumni dollars** are used to support faculty activities for which state money or student fees cannot be used. Last year, six instructors were able to attend important business seminars to update their business knowledge and skill. The faculty must attend such meetings if our university is to pursue **excellence**.

Notice that important words and ideas are emphasized by repetition (*alumni dollars, alumni gifts, excellence*). Transitional words and phrases help achieve a smooth flow of thought within sentences, between sentences, or between paragraphs: *as a result, and, because, besides, but, consequently, finally, for, furthermore, he, hence, however, in addition, in conclusion, it, moreover, on the other hand, she, that, therefore, these, this, thus, those, they, we,* and *you*.

Choose your words carefully so that your message is clear; emphasis is properly placed; writing is reader-centered; and nouns, verbs, and modifiers add energy and excitement to your writing.

Emphasis

As with words in a sentence, the position of a paragraph within a document is important. Generally, the first paragraph of a letter or report is the most important. It sets the stage. If the approach is incorrect, the writer may be wasting valuable space. Even more importantly, the reader may resent the message and possibly may refuse to read it. Consequently, effective writers always start with a positive, reader-centered idea.

A one-sentence paragraph at the beginning of a letter gives the thought the most emphasis.

The last paragraph is also a position of emphasis. Effective writers use this space to tie up loose ends and give unity to the message. Whenever possible, they will end with appropriate action statements.

The in-between paragraphs complete the message. How these paragraphs are organized depends on the purpose of the document. For help in organizing ideas, see specific letter- and report-writing chapters.

For the in-between paragraphs, emphasis is determined by the amount of space given an idea. The more space you give an idea, the more emphasis you give it. Nevertheless, divide the paragraphs so that no one paragraph is unusually long or overpowering.

CHAPTER SUMMARY

Business forms, memoranda, letters, and reports rely on the sentence and the paragraph to be effective.

Sentences are the heart of effective communication. They consist of words and punctuation marks, correctly chosen and placed to produce the desired message. Sentences in business communications should vary in size and complexity and use the active, rather than passive, voice. The average sentence has 17 to 20 words and may be classified as either a simple, a compound, a complex, or a compound-complex statement. Sentence fragments, run-on sentences, and dangling and misplaced modifiers occur frequently in poorly written business communications. Other signs of poor writing are nonparallel constructions and subjects and predicates that disagree in tense, number, or gender.

The tendency today is to avoid sex bias in business communications. It can be avoided by using nonsexist terms, plurals, male and female pronouns, or specific names; by alternating pronouns, and by rewording sentences. Sexist writing is not psychologically sound; it may offend the reader and dampen any goodwill that had already been established.

Paragraphs vary in length to achieve the desired purpose. However, short paragraphs stand out and are basically used at either the beginning or end of the document. The more space devoted to a topic, the more emphasis it receives. A complete paragraph may consist of only one sentence. Paragraphs with more than eight typewritten lines can distract and overwhelm readers. Look for natural breaks to divide such paragraphs.

Emphasis can be achieved by carefully conceived placement. In general, the first and last paragraphs within a document are most important, whereas the beginning and end of each sentence and paragraph can be used for emphasis. Ideas to be emphasized should be placed in short, simple sentences with concrete words and the active voice. Ideas to be de-emphasized can be placed in complex or compound-complex sentences or written in abstract terms and the passive voice.

Sentences and paragraphs must be coherently joined. This can be done by repeating part of the previous sentence, using pronouns to replace specific nouns, and using conjunctions to add unity to thoughts.

STUDY QUESTIONS

1. How can you tell if a statement is a complete sentence or a fragment?
2. What are the various types of sentences? Explain the differences.
3. Does the number of modifiers affect sentence classification?
4. What is a run-on or fused sentence? Give an example. Correct the example.
5. What is the basic rule for subject and predicate agreement? Illustrate this principle with sentences containing:
   a. At least two prepositional phrases
   b. A specific percentage as a subject
   c. A collective noun as a subject
   d. A specific number as a subject
6. Why should the items within sentences, outlines, and tables of contents be parallel? Illustrate.
7. What is a dangling or misplaced modifier? Illustrate a sentence with a dangling modifier. Correct the example.
8. What are the six ways you can emphasize words and ideas?
9. What can you do to de-emphasize or draw attention away from words and ideas?
10. What is the difference between a deductive and an inductive paragraph?

11. What can you do to achieve coherence within a sentence, between sentences, and between paragraphs?
12. Why should you strive to avoid sex bias in business communications?
13. When applied to males, "aggressive" is considered positive; however, an aggressive woman is a negative idea. Why?

ACTIVITIES

1. From the following statements, (1) distinguish between the fragmented statements and complete sentences and (2) identify whether the sentences are simple, compound, complex, and compound-complex.
   a. The Administrative Management Society reported that 64 percent of the U.S. firms work a 40-hour week.
   b. While the 37½-hour week is second at 17 percent.
   c. Published in the 1983–1984 *Office Salaries Directory*.
   d. The position requires a knowledge of company policy, company procedure, and administrative skills.
   e. According to the Administrative Management Society, most American employers hire workers for 40 hours weekly.
   f. Some employers hire workers for 40 hours a week; some, for 37½ hours a week.
   g. Some employers hire workers for 40 hours a week, but some employers hire workers for fewer hours.
   h. Work with management.
   i. If your employer asks you to work overtime, she may be required to pay you time-and-a-half wages, and you can expect more money.
   j. You can work for more than one employer, but you will have less leisure time.
   k. Working for more than one employer, you will earn more money but you will have less leisure time.
   l. The ability to speak well can help increase income, develop poise and confidence, and educate others.
   m. Some listeners may be unconcerned about your topic, or they may disagree with your viewpoint, but if your introduction is spoken with understanding and conviction, their minds should be open to you.
   n. Love you.
   o. Would you like to be an executive?
2. Edit each sentence to determine its weakness; then rewrite to eliminate the identified weakness (inaccuracy).
   a. The manager delegates duties this is a manager's responsibility.

b. None of the district representatives are in Los Angeles, California.
c. Forty percent of the electricians writes sales letters.
d. Other information reported in the surveys were available for researchers.
e. Included in the report is information about cashiers, clerks, and salespeople for the first time.
f. Please keep a copy of the agenda for easy reference close by.
g. The Eli Lilly and Company produce Elizabeth Arden cosmetics.
h. The number of employees interested in stock purchases have increased to 20,000.
i. Neither the boys nor Sally want a copy of the report.
j. My work experience includes district manager of sales, supervision, senior foreman, house painting.
k. As district manager, I managed efficiently $1.8 million worth of grain products, specialized in disease detection, effectively coordinated operations, and was responsible for training work crews.

3. Choose the writing ideas that will emphasize your words or ideas.
   a. Place word at beginning of sentence
   b. Place word at end of sentence
   c. Repeat the word or idea throughout
   d. Place word or idea in a simple sentence
   e. Use short sentences
   f. Use short paragraphs
   g. Place idea in an independent clause
   h. Use active voice
   i. Avoid repeating the word or idea
   j. Use specific and concrete words
   k. Place paragraph at end of the communication
   l. Use abstract or vague words
   m. Use passive voice
   n. Place word or idea in a dependent clause
   o. Place sentence at beginning of paragraph
   p. Place word or idea in a complex sentence
   q. Place idea in a middle paragraph
   r. Write much about the idea
   s. Place idea in middle of a long paragraph
   t. Use a thing as the doer of the action
   u. Place sentence at end of paragraph
   v. Place paragraph at beginning of the communication
4. From the choices in Activity 3, select those writing ideas that will de-emphasize or draw attention away from a word or idea.

5. Underline the emphasized words in each of the following sentences. Notice how slight changes in wording can change the emphasis.
   a. Remember that the anniversary sale for preferred customers will be on June 1 and 2, 19__.
   b. The anniversary sale for preferred customers will be on June 1 and 2, 19__.
   c. June 1 and 2, 19__ are the dates for the anniversary sale for preferred customers.
   d. Although the anniversary sale is June 1 and 2, 19__, you can order now.
   e. You, a preferred customer, are invited to the anniversary sale.
   f. The plumber will replace the water heater today.
   g. The water heater will be replaced by the plumber today.
   h. This is the water heater which the plumber replaced today.
6. Underline the words emphasized in the following paragraphs:

   I am very pleased that your sales record points to you as "Insurance Salesman of the Year." Congratulations on persuading so many people to buy insurance!

   Can you join me for lunch on Friday, March 10? Please telephone me at my office, 212-5742.

7. Rewrite the first note in Activity 6 so as to eliminate the beginning *I*. Instead, stress *you* and *congratulations* and change *salesman* to *salesperson*.
8. Write a paragraph emphasizing the following words and phrases: *congratulations*, *promotion to professor*, *professional*, *quality education*.
9. Edit these sexist terms and sentences:
   a. Gentlemen
   b. Man and wife
   c. Cameraman
   d. Chorus girl
   e. Brotherly love
   f. The committee chairman called the meeting to order.
   g. The accountant should check his records to be sure he has correct data.
   h. She or he must do his or her jobs promptly.
   i. A secretary takes minutes of the meetings and reads her report at the next meeting.
   j. The working man and his wife and kids are here.
   k. Diamonds are a girl's best friend.

4 Adherence to the Elements of Effective Writing

After studying Chapter 4, you should be able to:

- State a basic purpose of your business communications
- Present a reader-centered message
- Apply the elements of effective writing (completeness, clarity, conciseness, concreteness, correctness, coherence, courtesy, and positivism)
- Organize your message
- Distinguish between deductive and inductive approaches
- Describe the importance of beginning and ending paragraphs

The effective letter achieves its purpose. To achieve this purpose, it must be **reader-centered**. It must reflect a sincere interest in the reader's needs, interests, wants, and feelings. Reader-centered messages are carefully planned. They are logically organized to include the necessary facts completely, clearly, concisely, concretely, correctly, coherently, courteously, and positively. In addition, the letter should be attractive and neatly and appropriately placed on good quality stationery.

APPLYING THE ELEMENTS OF EFFECTIVE WRITING

The effective letter:

1. States the basic purpose specifically and clearly
2. Is reader-centered, rather than writer-centered
3. Uses language the intended reader will consider complete, clear, concise, concrete, correct, coherent, courteous, and positive.

Statement of the Purpose

For communication to take place, the letter should have *one* purpose that is clearly understood by both writer and reader. Poetry, fiction, and other literary works may entertain. inspire, or educate on a number of levels. A letter must have one main goal; it is effective only if it achieves that goal.

Many business people complain of receiving letters with "hazy" objectives. They must either guess the purpose or follow up with another communication—telephone call, letter, or wire—which incurs loss of time, as well as expense. The person who communicates effectively and efficiently through written correspondence is likely to gain favor with the reader. The following introductory paragraph obscures the purpose of the letter:

> Your university is so beautiful with its large rolling campus filled with tall trees and stylish buildings. I imagine that no one ever tires of the view. I have compared your campus with others, but when it comes to beauty and spaciousness, none even comes close to yours. I would like to be part of such a campus.

The following paragraph, on the other hand, concisely states the purpose:

> Please mail me an application for admission. I plan to pursue a Bachelor of Arts degree, majoring in English.

Reader Awareness

Each letter you write should present a reader-centered message that clearly conveys the purpose but reflects the individuality of the reader. The greater the writer's understanding of human behavior, the more likely the message will be reader-centered.

Since every individual is unique, an individual treated as somebody special is likely to strive to be outstanding. The same individual treated as mediocre may appear unimaginative or even dull. Hence, the tone with which you approach people is certain to influence their reaction to your correspondence.

Effective communicators learn all they can about their intended readers. The time spent doing this research is time spent advantageously. If they can learn little or nothing about their readers, they must assume their readers' needs, interests, and feelings based on general knowledge of human relations. What do the readers need and want and how should the writers reveal their interest and sincerity?

Completeness

A communication is **complete** if it contains all information the reader needs to respond to the purpose of the letter. You can achieve completeness by:

1. Analyzing the facts in the specific situation
2. Answering the who, what, why, when, where, and how

Before writing, analyze all the facts and include all information needed to achieve the purpose. Anything less than this would be wasteful and might adversely affect goodwill. On the other hand, providing unnecessary information may create confusion and weaken the message.

The following examples illustrate how statements can be strengthened by supplying complete information:

Incomplete: Your order will receive our early attention.
When is that?
Better: We will ship by June 5 the automobile parts requested in your purchase order No. 1356.

Incomplete: Our goods are not expensive.
Expensive by whose standards?
Better: We sell refrigerators at less than the suggested retail price.

Incomplete: The meeting will be on February 18 from 7:00 to 9:00 p.m.
Where?
Better: The sales meeting will be on February 18 in room 123 of City Hall, 7:00 to 9:00 p.m.
Better: The sales meeting will be on Monday, February 18 in City Hall room 123, 7:00 to 9:00 p.m.

Incomplete: The shoes are not satisfactory.
Why not?
Better: The shoes are size 6N instead of 7N.

When you need help finding facts, consult the library. Most libraries house numerous reference books and directories about business and industrial firms; governmental units; educational institutions; labor unions; and religious, charitable, and civic organizations. (See specific sources in the "Appendix II—How to Use the Library.)

Clarity

Another characteristic essential to presenting ideas effectively is **clarity**. You can achieve clarity by:

1. Using simple words to convey a specific thought
2. Using language understood by the reader
3. Structuring sentences accurately
4. Having one main idea per paragraph

Use language that will be understood. Long words do not necessarily create an impressive letter. The impressive letter uses well-chosen words—preferably words that convey action, stimulate interest, and create a specific mental image. For this, simple words are frequently best. However, they often have many different usages and must be used to create a specific image. For example, *walk* can be used as a noun or a verb.

The path used for walking: a **walk**
The distance walked: an hour's **walk**
The pace of one who walks: at a **walk**
The manner of walking: her **walk**
A manner of advancement: to **walk**
A manner of conduct: **walk** in silence
A way to get to first base in baseball: a **walk** to first

Each synonym for *walk* creates a different mental image. What do these synonyms for *walk* suggest to you: *step, stride, stroll, saunter, ambulate, march, promenade, tramp, hike, constitutional*? Simple words, too, must be chosen carefully.

Contrast the phrases in Table 4-1. Those in the left-hand column are frequently used but can have general meanings. Notice how the expressions in the right-hand column give a specific picture.

Use trade terms only when you are certain they will be understood and appreciated by your audience. The sportscaster's vocabulary is generally understood and accepted by fans: shut out, edged, belted, whipped, singled, and sliced. In any other context, many of the expressions would have different meanings.

Professional workers often use technical words that are traditionally accepted and used by members of the specialized group,

Table 4–1
General Expressions and Their Specific Counterparts

General or vague	Specific or clear
Drop in	Please visit
Let us hear	Please write
Inexpensive goods	Umbrellas for only $8
Pursuant to your desires	As you wish
Deem it advisable	Believe
Decrease monetary expenditures	Cut costs by 10 percent
We will mail the order soon	We will mail the books by May 1
Thank you for your recent letter	Thank you for your letter of June 1
Please send us a few copies	Please mail us three copies
The above-mentioned shareholder	Leonard A. Lincoln
The weather is bad here	The weather is cold and rainy here
It was hot on Sunday	The temperature reached 100°F on Sunday
Come over anytime	Please visit us on Monday or Tuesday
Due to operational conditions, the books are unobtainable	The library books are checked out
The writer feels that you would be good on the job	I believe that you would be a successful manager

as in medicine or law. But the average person is not likely to recognize terms such as *B and G*, *H_2O*, *hemostat*, *L.S.*, *p.r.n.*, *witness my hand*, *per diem*, *loculation*, in situ, *thoraco*, and *electromotive force*. Confusion may also result when the trade term is a word commonly used in many contexts. *Appeal*, *acknowledgment*, *consideration*, *crucifiers*, *damages*, *diamond*, *dummy*, and *plant* hold radically different meanings in different professions; thus, they must be defined by the subject matter.

Acronyms, or letters taken from a longer word or phrase, are growing in popularity but can be confusing. Sometimes these groups of letters have more than one meaning, and the reader must determine their meaning from the context. For example, *AM* can refer to *airmail*, *air marshall*, *anno mundi*, *amplitude modulation*, *ante meridiem* (morning), *associate member*, *Ave Maria*, or *American* (as in Pan Am). *DA* can refer to *days after acceptance*, *deposit account*, *direct action*, *discharge afloat*, *district attorney*, *documentary bill for acceptance*, *documents against acceptance*, *documents for acceptance*, or *documents attached*.

Ad (advertisement)	Know what I mean?
A lot (much, many)	Like you say
A lot better	Mad (angry)
Auto (automobile)	Math (mathematics)
Awfully (very)	Phone (telephone)
Bank on (rely on)	Prof (Professor)
Be taken in (convinced)	Quite the thing
Brothers (fraternity brothers)	Right on
Bunch of people (many people)	Rip-off
Cab (taxi cab)	Show (movie)
Come in handy (useful)	Sisters (sorority sisters)
Corny	Stat (statistics)
Cute, cutey	Swell
Do away with (delete, omit)	Terribly (very)
Far and wide (broad)	Terrific
Fellow	Text (textbook)
Gal	Through thick and thin
Guy	Turn off
Flunked (failed)	Turn on
Hard and fast	Week in and week out
Kids (children)	You know . . .

Table 4–2
Expressions to Avoid in Business Communications

Consult a reliable reference source to determine whether the capital letters should be followed by periods, diagonals, or blank spaces:

> M.A. (Master of Arts)
> M. Sgt. or M/Sgt. (Master Sergeant)
> S O S (the standard distress signal)

At times the writer may choose whether to include punctuation marks:

> CPA or C.P.A. (Certified Public Accountant)
> AAA or A.A.A. (Agricultural Adjustment Administration, American Automobile Association, or Automobile Association of America)

However, if you have a choice when using any alphabetic designations in communications, state the complete names the first time:

> He was a member of the Society for Prevention of Cruelty to Animals (S.P.C.A.).

For the sake of clarity, avoid idioms, slang expressions, or shortened words (Table 4–2). Use standard abbreviations only when absolutely necessary—and only in correct form. Avoid abbreviations such as *etc.*, *e.g.*, and *i.e.* and contractions such as *I'll*, *we'll*, *can't*, *don't*, *won't*, *you're*, and *it's* in business letters. Besides adding clarity, spelling out words or phrases is courteous.

Good sentence structure also adds clarity. The way words are put together affect the meaning of the sentence. In the following examples, notice the different meanings resulting from slight changes in placement of words.

Unclear: We would like you for dinner Wednesday evening. *As the entree?*
Clear: We would like you to come for dinner on Wednesday evening.

Unclear: She saw the bus walking down the street. *Strange bus!*
Clear: While walking down the street, she saw a bus.

Unclear: Running from the scene, Henry saw the suspect. *Henry was running?*
Clear: Henry saw the suspect running from the scene.

Other examples are included in Chapter 3 in the section entitled "Dangling or Misplaced Modifiers."

Confusion may also result if a paragraph has more than one main idea. The following short paragraph with three different thoughts lacks clarity.

> We are pleased that you are interested in our company. Perhaps you can invite Mr. Mark Oliver to speak. He is well known for his many lectures. Thank you for your informative letter.

The following changes give improved clarity:

> Thank you for telling us how much you like our new *City Directory*. Your well-written letter was so encouraging that we plan to provide each salesperson with a copy of it.
>
> May we recommend Mr. Mark Oliver, our distinguished consultant, as your banquet speaker. He is well known for his informative and interesting lectures. You can telephone Mr. Oliver at 198-5456, extension 226.

Conciseness

Conciseness is also essential to effective writing. Many business people bemoan the lack of conciseness in letters they receive. The following comments reflect common complaints:

1. Many executives think they write good letters, but they are verbose, use poor sentence structure, and make grammatical errors. It is important to learn good sentence structure and to avoid clichés.
2. When a company recruiter must answer 500 letters a month in addition to performing many other duties, it is frustrating to read overly clever, wordy, or uninteresting letters.

3. Many of the letters we get are handwritten by young people, but they are constructed fairly well. It is the sophisticated college graduate whose letter lacks clarity or conciseness. It is *too* long and unorganized.

A letter is concise when it has been trimmed down to the essential language. Effective letters should have no **clichés** (stereotyped or meaningless expressions), no extra words, and no unnecessary information to confuse or bore the reader. Its sentences and paragraphs should not be excessively long or short, neither should the letter look cumbersome or choppy. In other words, you can achieve conciseness by:

1. Including only necessary information
2. Using essential words and phrases (avoiding useless words)
3. Using up-to-date expressions (avoiding stereotyped words)
4. Avoiding cumbersome sentences and paragraphs

Generally, a few short paragraphs can relate the essential facts. But when substantial data are needed, make the letter as long as necessary to accomplish its purpose. Eliminating necessary information merely leads to the need for supplementary letters and additional expense. And if word economy results in curtness, goodwill may be lost.

The following opening paragraph for an order letter lacks conciseness in that it includes inappropriate (personal and private) information.

> I would like to order the chair advertised in the Cleveland News. This chair would be an ideal birthday gift for my sixty-year old father who will retire soon from the Brass Foundry Company. I am sure his family room has ample space for your lovely chair.

The following opening statement would have been better:

> Please deliver one No. GR501A chair as advertised in this morning's Cleveland News to:

Some writers continue using stereotyped and useless expressions, such as "permit me to state." Obviously, you need not ask for permission to state the purpose of the letter. Table 4-3 comments on some other stereotyped and useless expressions to avoid in business letters.

Some common everyday expressions may sound meaningful in conversation, but are useless and vague in written correspondence. Consider, for example, *in the near future.* When is the near future? Instead, as mentioned in Tables 4-1 and 4-3, state a definite time or date: *next Thursday, July 10* or *before July 10* or *by July 10.*

Stereotyped expressions	Comments
According to our records	Doesn't information usually come from records? Omit this phrase.
As a matter of fact	State the fact instead.
As per my letter	Say, "As I wrote you."
As soon as possible	Give a definite time or date (*within 20 days*).
As you know	If the reader knows, why repeat?
At an early date	Give a definite date (*on September 25*).
Better than ever	A comparative phrase that needs clarification.
By return mail	This phrase actually means *in the next mail.* Use instead, *mail now* or *mail today* or *mail immediately.*
Hoping to hear from you	Think of a better way to end letter than with a participle and a negative suggestion.
I am sorry	Say this only if you mean it!
If our records are correct	Why imply records may not be correct? Omit this phrase.
In reply we wish to state	Omit and state the fact instead.
May we take the liberty	State your point instead.
Our records show	Tell instead what the records indicate.
Permit me to say	Omit! You cannot wait for permission.
Self-addressed envelope	Say *addressed envelope*; an envelope could never address itself.
Soon	Give a definite time or date (*by June 30*).
Thanking you in advance	Never thank in advance; it is not polite. Think of a better ending for letter. After favor is granted, you can write a letter of appreciation.
The privilege of serving you	Think of something more original.
The writer	Use *I* or *We*.
This is to inform you that	This is obvious; omit it.
Under separate cover	This actually means *separately*, an unnecessary expression. Instead, tell how and when sent—*mailed today.*
Usual	What is usual? Give specific information.
You are advised that	Give the advice instead.
Your attention is directed to	Use *Please see . . . .*
Your earliest convenience	Give a definite date (*before January 31*).
Your kind letter	Omit *kind*; only people can be kind or unkind.

Table 4–3
Stereotyped Expressions to Avoid in Business Correspondence

Wordy	Concise
Acknowledging your letter	Thank you for your letter
Along the lines of	Like
As a result	Consequently
At all times	Always
Attached hereto is	Here is, Attached is
At the present time	Now
Be kind enough	Please
Call off	Discontinue, Cancel
Despite the fact that	Although
Due to the fact that	Because
Enclosed herewith	Here is, Enclosed is, I am enclosing
Enclosed please find	Here is, Enclosed is, I am enclosing
Every now and then	Sometimes
I am of the opinion	I think, I believe
I am sending along	I am sending
I would like to take this opportunity to thank you	Thank you for
Inasmuch as	Since
In a position	Able, Can
In the amount of	For
In the city of Chicago	In Chicago
In the event that	If
In the month of June	In June
In regards to	About, Regarding
In view of the fact that	Because, Since
It is our understanding	We understand
It would be greatly appreciated if you would send us your check	Please mail us your check
Kindly advise	Please tell us, Please advise
Make an adjustment in	Adjust
Prior to	Before
Right away	Immediately, Now
Seldom ever	Seldom
Subsequent to	After
Under date of	Dated, On
Until such time as	When
Whether or not	Whether
Wish to advise you	Tell you, Advise

Table 4–4
Achieving Conciseness

Often a group of words can be shortened to one simple, concise word with the same meaning. In Table 4–4, prepositional phrases are frequently eliminated or reduced to achieve conciseness. If your business correspondence contains more than two prepositional phrases per sentence, it probably lacks conciseness.

As you learned in Chapter 3, repetition may be useful to achieve coherence and the emphasis you desire. However, unnecessary repetition or **redundancy** hinders conciseness. Can you add any redundant expressions to those listed in Table 4–5?

Redundant expressions	Concise expressions
Adequate enough	Adequate
And etc.	Etc.
Basic fundamental	Basic, Fundamental
Brown in color	Brown
Capitol building	Capitol
Circle around	Circle
Close proximity	Close, Near
Complete monopoly	Monopoly
Complimentary gift	Gift
Consensus of opinion	Consensus
Doctorate degree	Doctorate
End result	Result
Entirely complete	Complete
Exact same	Same
Exactly identical	Identical
First priority	Priority
Free gift	Gift
In the state of confusion	Confused
In the state of Tennessee	In Tennessee
In the year of 1988	In 1988
Join together	Join
Passing fad	Fad
Past history	History
Personal opinion	Opinion
Round in shape	Round
Sending along	Sending, Mailing
Small in size	Small
Teacher by profession	Teacher
True facts	Facts
Widow woman	Widow
Young infant	Infant
5:00 p.m. in the evening	5:00 p.m.
9:00 a.m. in the morning	9:00 a.m.

Table 4–5
Substitutions for Redundant Words

Avoid writing **expletives** (meaningless words) at the beginning of a sentence. *There* and *it* are sometimes used as expletives. Eliminating expletives will improve your writing so that it will be more concise.

Vague: *There* is a copy of his sales report in the office.
Better: A copy of his sales report is in the office.
There *can never be the subject of the sentence.*

Vague: *It is* obvious that the report is current.
Better: The report is obviously current.
Unlike there, *the word* it *can be a sentence subject, but sometimes the word is used incorrectly. The reader cannot tell—or incorrectly assumes—what* it *refers to.*

Concreteness

A concrete communication is one that conveys a clear and definite picture to the reader. You can achieve **concreteness** by:

1. Using specific, rather than general or abstract, words
2. Using the active, rather than the passive, voice
3. Emphasizing people rather than things

Notice how the following general expressions are improved by substituting specific language.

Vague: It has been suggested that certain holidays be changed so that four-day holidays will be possible.
Better: The legislators suggested that Washington's birthday and Columbus Day be changed to permit four-day holidays.

Vague: We are in receipt of same.
Better: We received your report.
Better: Thank you for your report.

Vague: The cereal is better than ever.
Better: We have added Vitamins B1 and B2 to Wheat Flakes.

Vague: Your contract will be effective as of August 1.
Better: Your employment contract begins August 1.

Whenever possible, use the active voice, rather than the passive. The active voice asserts; it brings the writing to life. A verb in the passive voice lies lifeless and dull. In the active voice, the subject acts; in the passive, the subject is being acted upon.

Passive: Your report was received by Mr. Jones.
Active: Mr. Jones received your report.

Passive: A request for an explanation of the charges was made by the president.
Active: The president requested an explanation of the charges.

Passive: Delays in this office are caused by employees who take long coffee breaks.
Active: The employees who take long coffee breaks cause delays in this office.

Occasionally, general or inactive language may be useful to avoid a discourteous tone:

Passive: Several typographical errors were noticed in the report. *Nonaccusatory*
Active: The secretary made ten typing errors in the report. *Poor secretary!*

Passive: Opposition to the proposal was voiced.
Active: The Ohio Senators opposed the proposal.

Sentences cast in active voice are usually more concise and clearer than those written in passive voice.

Correctness

A communication is correct if all the facts are included without error or bias, if proper language is used to express those facts, and if the parts and framework for the communication are properly presented. You can achieve **correctness** by:

1. Using appropriate and accurate letter mechanics
2. Including true and unbiased pertinent facts
3. Applying the rules of English grammar, spelling, and punctuation

An executive who receives numerous telephone calls and letters from the general public said, "The degree of illiteracy is appalling. Bad grammar and poor spelling complicate our job of answering. It is sad that in this wealthy country, we do not learn the basics of good English." Perhaps with concentrated effort, we can improve the quality of writing exhibited by our written communications.

Errors are human, and costly. One small error may cause a range of problems from unpleasantness and loss of goodwill to serious delays, heightened expenses, and even an action for libel. The following errors may be humorous but they are also embarrassing.

> I would enjoy having you for dinner Wednesday evening.
> *The writer intends to invite the guest to eat dinner, but technically is inviting the guest to be eaten.*
>
> They saw a bus running down the street.
> *The mental picture is a bus with legs!*

Spelling correctly is also very important. Not only must all the words within the body of the letter be spelled correctly but the receiver's name and address must be accurate. Misspelling the addressee's name may alienate the reader. Letters without a readable, correct, and complete address end up in the dead letter office of the United States Postal Service. It is difficult to estimate the unhappiness created by such mistakes, but they cost business and industry millions of dollars annually. So spell correctly, and use the most complete dictionary available.

Using correct punctuation is just as important as using correct spelling. The following sentences illustrate how punctuation alters the meaning of a sentence:

> The diamond, valued at $1000, was placed in the safe.
> The diamond was placed in the safe, valued at $1000.
>
> The driver of the car said the man was in the building.
> "The driver of the car," said the man, "was in the building."

Coherence

When a letter has coherence, the thoughts flow from the first to the last sentence. You can achieve **coherence** by:

1. Making logical connections within a sentence
2. Making logical connections between sentences
3. Making logical connections between paragraphs

Parallel construction gives logical order within sentences, keeping all parts on the same level.

Parallel: John and Mary went shopping and sightseeing.
Parallel: John and Mary went to the grocery store and to the Art Museum.
Not Parallel: John and Mary went shopping and to the Art Museum.

Parallel: I can type, file, and record data.
Parallel: I can do filing, typing, and recording of data.
Not Parallel: I can type, some filing, some recording.

Parallel: Mr. Martin wanted to pay cash immediately rather than (to) charge the sale.
Not Parallel: Mr. Martin wanted to pay cash immediately rather than charging the sale.

The following examples illustrate how to relate sentences to each other. In the first example, the second sentence is about to explain the idea introduced in the first sentence. It makes an unmistakable connection by repeating the last part of the previous sentence.

> The Village Branch of the American Bank can provide you with a variety of services. **These services** include . . .

In the second example, a pronoun and a conjunction (*it* and *however*) help achieve coherence.

> The Village Branch of the American Bank can provide you with a variety of services. **It** is already known for its convenient U.S. Post Office; **however**, did you also know that one-step banking is possible?

In the third example, the listing of services available explains how one-stop banking is possible at American Bank.

> One-stop banking is possible at American Bank. For your use, we have safety deposit boxes at low yearly rental rates, savings account paying 8% or more interest, mortgage loans for 12%, . . .

Finally, in the fourth example, the second sentence picks up an idea from the first sentence (*familiar with*). In addition, this example emphasizes you—very effective in sales letters:

> Are you **familiar with** all of the services provided by our Village Branch of American Bank? You are **probably familiar with** our convenient U.S. Post Office Substation, but did you know that we have safe deposit boxes. . . .

Although these illustrations relate sentences to each other, the same techniques can be used to tie paragraphs together.

The following words and phrases help to achieve a smooth transition within sentences, between sentences, or between paragraphs: *as a result*, *besides*, *finally*, *furthermore*, *consequently*, *in addition*, *in conclusion*, *it*, *he*, *hence*, *moreover*, *on the other hand*, *she*, *that*, *therefore*, *these*, *this*, *thus*, *those*, *they*, *we*, *you*. For more ideas, see the sections entitled "Parallel Structure" and "Writing Paragraphs—Development" in Chapter 3.

Courtesy

A courteous letter not only considers the reader's needs, wants, wishes, and beliefs, but also uses positive terminology and polite words, such as *please*, *may I*, and *thank you* to create a pleasing tone. Address the reader as he or she prefers. The reader who prefers Ms. to Miss or Mrs. should be addressed as Ms. regardless of your personal beliefs or preferences. You can achieve **courtesy** by:

1. Using polite words
2. Creating a polite tone
3. Considering the needs, wants, wishes, and beliefs of the reader

Courtesy contributes to goodwill, and goodwill contributes to good human relations, good consumer relations, and good public relations. Goodwill encourages sales, sales increase profits, and profits make owners and stockholders happy.

The customers who have a choice between companies will deal with the company whose personnel—all other things being equal—convey courteous consideration of their ideas. As Ralph Waldo Emerson said in his essay, "Social Aims," "Life is not so short but that there is always time enough for courtesy."

Positivism

Well-organized and well-written letters using positive terminology give a positive impact. The fact that a letter achieves its purpose is a positive outcome in itself. You can encourage **positive thinking** by:

1. Using cheerful and positive words
2. Organizing your letter to achieve the purpose

The words that are used in any business communication control the tone of the letter's impact. Some words inherently possess a positive quality:

bonus
congratulations
convenient
excellent
friend
generous
glad
good
honest
immediately
I will
like
of course
pleasant
pleasing
pleasure
pretty
qualified
right
safe
sale
satisfactory
sweet
thank you
vacation
yes

Other words or expressions stimulate negative thoughts:

Negative: Mr. Smith hoarded.
Positive: Mr. Smith bought in anticipation of needs.

Negative: We cannot comply because of company policy.
Positive: We honor requests for money from qualified charitable organizations.

Negative: It is not likely that the contract will be ready before Tuesday.
Positive: The contract should be ready by Tuesday.

When possible, avoid using negative words. Instead of apologizing, tell the reader what you can do. The following terms should be avoided because they suggest the negative:

alone
anger
apologize
at a loss
bad
broken
cannot
careless
cheap
cheat
delay
difficult
disappointed
displeased
doubt
error
fail to understand
failure
hate
horrible
I hope
impossible
inconvenient
incorrect
inferior
I trust
lie
lost
luck
mistake
terrible
trouble
unfortunately
unsatisfactory
wrong
you claim
you misunderstood
you must
you say
you state

Other means of creating a positive impression are:

- Using attractive stationery
- Typing the letter on good quality bond paper
- Enclosing, when needed, an addressed and stamped envelope, a simplified form to complete, an order blank, or a reply form.

Purpose →

Details to support purpose →

Will you please speak at our September 4 dinner meeting in the banquet room of Doyle's Smorgasbord? Dinner will begin at 6:30 p.m.; your talk should begin near 7:30 p.m. We can pay you $500 and transportation expenses.

Please explain how the diamond came to be the traditional gem for brides. Do you see any changes in this tradition? How can we recognize a flawless diamond? These and other questions have been asked by the thirty members of the Young Singles.

The Young Singles are acquainted with your research, lectures, and guest appearances on television. We believe your talks are enlightening and entertaining.

. . .

Deductive (Direct)

Figure 4–1A
Application of the Deductive (Direct) Approach

Explanatory information to prepare reader for purpose →

"Courting Customs Are Curious." Who could disagree after reading your comments in the Harpersville News, February 25?

In 19--, six people started the Young Singles Club, which now has thirty members whose interests and occupations are very diversified. Their common interest is a desire to be with other young singles for fun and relaxation.

The Young Singles are acquainted with your research, lectures, and guest appearances on television. Your talks are enlightening and entertaining.

Purpose and details →

Will you please attend our September 4 or October 7 dinner meeting and tell us more about the relationship between gems and weddings? Dinner will begin at 6:30 p.m.

. . .

Inductive (Indirect)

Figure 4–1B
Application of the Inductive (Indirect) Approach

ORGANIZING THE MESSAGE

As indicated in Chapters 2 and 3, paragraphs may be deductive or inductive. Deductive paragraphs introduce the main idea immediately; inductive paragraphs delay the main topic until the end of the paragraph.

Deductive or Inductive Approach

Letters, too, use either the deductive (direct) or inductive (indirect) approach. Figures 4–1A and 4–1B illustrate letters using both of these approaches.

Most letters should use the **direct approach** so that the busy reader immediately knows why the letter is being written.

Direct approach	Indirect approach	Persuasive letters*
Routine requests	Refusal letters	Persuasive requests
Reservation letters		Persuasive letters to Congress
Nonpersuasive letters to Congress		Persuasive claim letters
Routine claim letters		Unsolicited sales letters
Letters answering "yes"		Collection inquiry letters
Positive adjustment letters		Collection appeal letters
Order acknowledgments		Collection ultimatum letters
Order letters		Collection notices for freight
Letters of appreciation		Collection notices for unearned discount
Letters of congratulation		Persuasive reference letters
Letters of condolence		Application letter
Welcome letters		
Solicited sales letters		
Credit requests		
Collection reminders		
Letters to collection agencies		
Interoffice memoranda		
News releases		
Letters accepting employment		
Letters of resignation		
Follow-up employment letters		
Nonpersuasive reference letters		

*Persuasive letters typically begin with an indirect approach.

Table 4–6
Guide for Determining Best Approach for Typical Communications

This includes letters requesting or giving routine or pleasant information. Here the writer states the purpose immediately.

Letter writers should not annoy readers seeking routine information by making them wait until late in the letter to find out what information is desired. Only writers of literature can afford the luxury of encouraging reader imagination or playing a guessing game. The kinds of letters that typically begin with the direct approach are listed in Table 4–6.

If the writer's purpose is to persuade the reader or give negative information, the **indirect approach** is generally best. The statement of purpose is not stated immediately; instead, the beginning paragraphs explain the circumstances or persuade the reader. The implied or expressed refusal statement or special request would follow the explanations or persuasive data supporting the purpose of the letter. The kinds of letters that typically begin with the indirect approach are listed in Table 4–6. Those letters that require persuasive information are listed separately.

Table 4–6 suggests typical approaches for various business letters; however, you can change the approach when the circumstances warrant it. The list should be used as a *guide*, rather than an absolute statement of the exclusive beginning for specific letters. Your letters should communicate your message rather than follow rigid guidelines.

Preliminary Outline

After establishing the purpose and best approach, it is time to plan the actual letter. However, even before you write one sentence, you should develop a carefully prepared outline. For most letters, a written outline is necessary.

The written outline will help you organize your communications so that details are complete and presented in the best order and with the proper emphasis. If you use an outline, the reader will recognize that you are well informed. Your correspondence will not ramble and will include all important points. The relationships discussed within your correspondence will be obvious. In the long run, you will save time, but, more importantly, using an outline will help you communicate effectively and promote good human relations.

The following outline might be the basis for a letter persuading the reader to attend a meeting. Because the reader must be persuaded, the purpose requires an inductive beginning.

I. Get reader's attention and persuade him or her
    A. Introduce testimonial on flying (by A. L. Baker)
    B. Tell about Central State Flying Club
        1. Organized September 15, 19__
        2. Has 15 active members
        3. Study principles of flying
        4. Fly to nearby cities

II. Invite to meeting and give details
    A. Wednesday, April 30
    B. Student Union, B-2
    C. Open meeting
    D. Purpose to discuss membership particulars

III. Provide easy action, confident ending
    A. Barbara Smith, contact
    B. 515-1207

Instead of using this formal outline, the following abbreviated outline could be used satisfactorily:

1. Attention and Persuasion
   introduce testimonial (A. L. Baker)
   organized 9/15/__
   15 actives
   study principles
   fly nearby
2. Purpose—invite to meeting
   Wed., 4/30
   B-2
   open meeting
   membership particulars
3. Action
   Barbara Smith, contact
   515-1207

For some writers, the outline can be further reduced to a listing of points in proper order:

1. Introduce testimonial, A. L. Baker
2. 9/15/__
3. 15 members
4. study principles
5. fly nearby
6. Meeting, Wed., 4/30, B-2 (open)
7. Membership ideas
8. Barbara Smith
9. 515-1207

Although preparing an outline takes time, it will help you recall specific ideas and list them coherently.

The preliminary outline forces writers to organize their thoughts, include all relevant facts, and exclude all unnecessary information. It allows them to identify the beginning, middle, and ending topics. The advantages for preparing a specific outline for each letter far outweigh the time it takes to write one.

Effective Beginnings

The **first paragraph** is the most important paragraph of any letter. If the opening statement does not get the reader's attention and interest, the rest of the message may be ignored. Like the cornerstone, the beginning statement is the foundation for the letter. It sets the stage and tone for the message that follows.

The opening statement should emphasize the reader's interests and should use a reader-centered approach. If possible, avoid referring to yourself in the first paragraph, particularly in letters attempting to persuade. You can have an **effective beginning** by:

1. Using reader-centered statements involving the basic letter purpose:
    a. Deductive approach—state purpose immediately, concisely, and clearly.
    b. Inductive approach—delay statement of purpose until you believe reader is in a favorable and receptive frame of mind; avoid writer-centered words and ideas in the first paragraph.
2. Avoiding clichés and overused expressions, debatable thoughts, unrealistic ideas, obvious flattery, and negative words or tone.

The following examples draw the reader into the letter by stating (deductive approach) or suggesting (inductive approach) the purpose of the letter using positive, helpful, and interesting language. They are examples of effective opening ideas. See the specific letter-writing chapters for other ideas.

Deductive: Please mail one-year subscriptions to *Viva America* to these persons:

Deductive: Thank you, Mr. Nieman, for completing the employment survey form, which I mailed you in May. Here are the basic results of that survey:

Deductive: Enclosed is a $195.50 check to cover your June 8, 19__, invoice for replacement of an ABC appliance still under warranty.

Deductive: Please complete and return the enclosed application for credit.

Deductive: Your letter of August 2 encouraged us to take another look at the Gallant XL-119.

Inductive: How long should it take to replace an A. B. Erlander PEC-52 water heater?

Inductive: Cliff Rigsby, the famous trumpet player, said this about flying:

> Flying makes it possible for me to see many far-away, exciting places; to escape the boredom of everyday life; to meet the public and famous personalities. I wish everyone could share my enthusiasm.

Note that the examples seldom use *I* or other writer-centered words, stereotyped expressions, or flattery to get the reader's attention and interest. An effective beginning paragraph can consist of just one or two sentences, begin with a question, or lead into a short or long quotation.

Effective Endings

The end of the letter is almost as important as the beginning. Use the **last paragraph** to strengthen your position and inspire action, not for redundant, meaningless, negative, or stereotyped expressions. The end should leave the reader with a good feeling.

You can have an **effective ending** by:

1. Using a convincing statement that requires action
2. Writing a positive and meaningful statement
3. Avoiding stereotyped endings (for example, *It will be a privilege to serve you.*)
4. Leaving the reader with a good feeling

Never end your letter with a participial phrase, a doubtful expression, or a "thank you" for the past or future actions. The following poor endings are inappropriate because they

1. Are not complete sentences
2. Express doubt and are, therefore, negative ideas
3. Thank the reader twice for the same thing
4. Presumptuously thank the reader beforehand, implying demand for compliance.

Poor ending	**Better ending**
Hoping to hear from you soon, I remain, *This is a participial phrase, not a sentence.*	May I come in for an interview? You can telephone me at 162-8171 between 10:00 a.m. and 4:00 p.m.
Trusting that we may have an early reply, we are,	Please check your answer on the enclosed form and return it by March 31.
I hope you will mail us your order soon.	For your first order, you can use the handy order blank attached to the back cover of the catalog, or telephone us at 1-800-157-7208.
I trust this will be satisfactory.	Please write us your reaction to the proposal.
Thank you again for your order.	Enclosed is an order form for your next purchase. (One thank you is adequate, and it should be in the first sentence only.)

Thank you.

This is a fragment, not a complete sentence. The complete sentence would be: I thank you.

Thank you for your cooperation

Thanking you in advance, I remain,

These statements reveal that the writer expects the reader to comply with her or his request. This attitude is not fair to the reader.

The following examples illustrate appropriate, courteous, and positive ways to conclude a message. See the specific letter-writing chapters for other examples.

> Please telephone Miss Tracy Johnson at 218-5327 for additional information.
>
> Here is a $46 check to pay for the subscriptions.
>
> Please take five minutes to complete the enclosed form and return it in the addressed and stamped envelope.
>
> I would welcome an opportunity to discuss my qualifications with you. You can reach me by telephoning (219) 414-3116.

Since the final paragraph is your last chance to convince the reader or to sell the product or idea, the space should be used to reinforce your point. Do not spoil it by writing stereotyped, meaningless, doubtful, or discourteous sentences or fragments.

CHECKSHEET FOR WRITING EFFECTIVE COMMUNICATIONS

Figure 4–2 is a checksheet for analyzing your outlines, rough drafts, and letters for effectiveness.

Check your outline against the checksheet to ensure that the:

1. Purpose is specifically and clearly stated
2. Plan considers reader's needs, interests, feelings, etc.
3. Approach is correct (deductive or inductive as needed)
4. Order is logical
5. Facts are complete and correct
6. Ending is convincing, active, positive

If necessary, correct the outline before writing the first rough draft. Using your outline, write a rough draft of the letter. At this stage, you need not be overly concerned that you have chosen the best words, or that spelling, English, or grammar are correct. Use the checksheet to help you revise each rough draft until the final letter adheres to the elements of effective writing. In the end, your letter should:

1. State the purpose specifically and clearly
2. Use language and tone that are reader-centered

CHECKSHEET FOR WRITING EFFECTIVE COMMUNICATIONS

1. **Purpose**
   a. State one specific purpose
   b. State the purpose clearly
2. **Psychological considerations (reader-centeredness)**
   a. Consider the feelings and philosophy of reader
   b. Make it interesting to reader
   c. Show sincerity
3. **Completeness**
   a. Include all necessary facts
   b. Answer: Who? What? Why? When? Where? How?
4. **Clarity and conciseness**
   a. Use simple words that convey the specific idea
   b. Use language the reader will understand—avoid slang, shortened words, contractions, English idioms, overused and outdated expressions, redundant expressions
   c. Place words and phrases correctly
   d. Limit each paragraph to one idea
   e. Include only the necessary information
   f. Trim the sentences down to essential words and phrases
   g. Use short—but not choppy—sentences and paragraphs
5. **Concreteness**
   a. Use words with specific, rather than general or abstract, meaning
   b. Use active, rather than passive, writing
   c. Emphasize people, rather than things
6. **Correctness**
   a. Use only true and unbiased facts
   b. Employ appropriate and accurate letter mechanics
   c. Use accurate English—grammar, spelling, and punctuation
7. **Coherence**
   a. Word each sentence to make sense to the reader
   b. Use logical sentence sequence
   c. Use logical paragraph divisions
   d. Use logical paragraph sequence
8. **Courtesy**
   a. Select polite words
   b. Instill a polite, tactful tone
9. **Positivism**
   a. Choose cheerful and positive words
   b. Organize letter to achieve purpose
10. **Effective beginning**
    a. Determine the best approach—inductive or deductive as required
    b. Establish a you-centered approach
    c. Avoid stereotyped expressions, debatable or negative ideas, unrealistic ideas, and obvious flattery
11. **Effective ending**
    a. Summarize with positive and complete sentences—no negatives or fragments
    b. Conclude with an active or convincing thought
    c. Avoid redundancies or thank-you expressions

Figure 4–2
Checksheet for Writing Effective Communications

3. Follow the correct and appropriate communication format
4. Be edited for correct English, grammar, punctuation, and factual information
5. Eliminate unnecessary data
6. Use simple words that convey the message, are cheerful, and express a positive tone
7. Be logically organized from beginning to end
8. Have complete information

The checksheet is your guide to writing effective communications.

CHAPTER SUMMARY

You can be certain you have written an effective letter if it meets these standards:

1. It must have one basic purpose the reader can readily understand.
2. It must show consideration for the interests and philosophy of the reader.
3. It must speak to the reader in simple, correct language that is complete, clear, concise, concrete, correct, coherent, courteous, and positive.
4. It must progress logically; it should begin with a paragraph that positively gets the reader's attention and end with a paragraph that positively encourages the reader.

STUDY QUESTIONS

1. What are the ten basic guidelines for effective writing? Explain each one.
2. Which types of letters usually use the inductive approach? Which use deductive?
3. Why is it necessary to plan and write communications that recognize the individuality of the reader?
4. Which paragraph is the most important paragraph of your letter? Why?
5. Why are the following statements inappropriate for ending your letter:
   a. Thanking you in advance, I am,
   b. I hope you will write soon.
   c. Thank you for cooperating with us.

ACTIVITIES

1. Using a current dictionary, determine the basic differences between these commonly interchanged or confused words:
   a. Adapt
      Adept
   b. Advice
      Advise
   c. Affect
      Effect
   d. Anxious
      Eager
   e. All ready
      Already
   f. Altar
      Alter
   g. Among
      Between
   h. Believe
      Feel
   i. Can
      May
   j. Capital
      Capitol
   k. Cite
      Sight
      Site
   l. Compliment
      Complement
   m. Correspondence
      Correspondent
   n. Imply
      Infer
   o. Postal card
      Post card
   p. Principal
      Principle
   q. Receive
      Receipt
   r. Respectfully
      Respectively
   s. Weather
      Whether
2. Without in-depth thinking, list those words that create pleasant or positive thoughts for you (Allow 5 minutes for this activity.)
3. Without in-depth thinking, list those words that create negative or unpleasant thoughts for you (Allow 5 minutes for this activity.)
4. For each of the following words or phrases, substitute either a word or an expression that is more correct, clear, or concise:
   a. Soon
   b. Let us hear from you
   c. I wish to thank you
   d. The writer
   e. As per my letter
   f. Self-addressed
   g. Recent date
   h. The goods
   i. Drop in and see me
   j. Come any time
   k. Kind letter
   l. Kindly advise
   m. Within the next five days
   n. Enclosed herewith
   o. In the city of Eaton
   p. As soon as possible
   q. Seldom ever
   r. It would be greatly appreciated
   s. I feel
   t. 7 in the morning
   u. At your earliest convenience
   v. By return mail
   w. Under separate cover

5. Rewrite the following sentences so that they will be clear and coherent (weak phrases are italicized):
   a. *Drop in soon.*
   b. *Your kind* letter of May 12 *was received.*
   c. *Let us hear* from you *in regards to* this plan.
   d. *I wish* to thank you for your letter of *recent date.*
   e. Are you eating *more* and enjoying *it* less?
   f. *Upon returning* to the office, a new photostat *was issued* to replace the lost one.
   g. The *goods* are *inexpensive.*
   h. *As per my letter* of October 12, the shoes *are not satisfactory.*
   i. Write *soon.*
6. Rewrite the following sentences so that they will comply with the elements of effective writing (weak phrases are italicized):
   a. *Kindly advise* when I can come to your office.
   b. I shall be happy to visit your store *within the next ten days.*
   c. *The writer is of the opinion* that you are *in a position* to do the *work.*
   d. *Enclosed herewith* is my check *in the amount of* $175 to cover rent *for the month of June.*
   e. *May I take the liberty of* sending you a sample bar of Clean soap?
   f. *Due to the fact that I will be in the city of Pittsburgh early next month,* I would appreciate an interview *during that time.*
   g. *If our records are correct,* the balance of your account is now *two months past due.* (Make a positive statement.)
   h. The *Winchester Dormitory,* located just *five minutes* from the campus, is now taking *applications* for the *next school year.*
   i. The *service* you have given me is *not very good.*
7. Rewrite these sentences so that they will comply with the elements of effective writing (weak phrases are italicized):
   a. Thank you *for taking the time* to write me *in regards to* the *job opening.*
   b. Please *send* your reply *by return mail.*
   c. You are *in a position* to speak with authority.
   d. This information is *of a confidential nature.*
   e. *We are pleased to report* that a copy of your book *was received* yesterday.
   f. *Seldom ever do I come* to visit you *in the month of* July.
   g. *In the event that* you are not well, you can remain at home.

   h. *I would like to take this opportunity* to congratulate you on your *new job.*
   i. The books *are being sent under separate cover.*

8. Rewrite the following sentences so that they will comply with the elements of effective writing (weak phrases are italicized):
   a. Please *send* us the reply card *at your earliest convenience.*
   b. I owe you, *as a matter of fact, a total of* $195.90, covering March and April purchases.
   c. *Your attention is directed to* paragraph two of our letter.
   d. The job is *along the lines of* your present job.
   e. *In regards to your letter of April 14, I wish to state that* I have scheduled an appointment for Monday, May 10, at 10 *o'clock in the morning.*
   f. *It would be greatly appreciated* if you would pay your *past-due amount.*
   g. *This will acknowledge receipt of your letter* regarding a job at Good Center.
9. Rewrite the following sentences so that they will comply with the elements of effective writing (weak phrases are italicized):
   a. *Irregardless* of the salary, I am interested in working for you.
   b. The cereal is *better than it ever was.*
   c. The repair costs on this model are *less than usual.*
   d. *Enclosed herewith* you will find a copy of our *brochure.*
   e. *Thanking you in advance, I remain,* Yours truly (Substitute a possible ending for the letter.)
   f. We are enclosing a *self-addressed* and stamped envelope *for your convenience.*
   g. *Enclosed find* our *recent* catalog *on women's clothing.*
   h. *Attached hereto* is a copy of our letter.
   i. *Trusting this will be satisfactory, we remain,* Sincerely yours (Substitute a possible ending for the letter.)
10. Rewrite the following sentences so that they will comply with the elements of effective writing (weak phrases are italicized):
    a. *Don't put off* until tomorrow what you can do today.
    b. *If you don't explain the charges to my satisfaction,* how can you expect me to pay your bill for $195.10?
    c. *At the present time, I cannot* speak to the membership.
    d. We *hope* that you will answer *yes.*
    e. We *trust, to avoid unpleasantness* for all concerned, you will arrange to *submit* your check *in the amount of* $125.75 *by return mail.*
    f. *It is unlikely* that I will be able to complete the report before a *week from today.*
    g. *Obviously,* you have *overlooked* my letter of May 10.

h. *Because of the strike, I am sorry* that we *cannot* ship your order as scheduled.
i. *Acknowledging your letter of May 12, we cannot send your order* until May 31.

11. Rewrite the following sentences so that they will be clear and concrete (weak phrases are italicized):
    a. *There has been* opposition to the law *on the part of the lobbyists.*
    b. *It is evident that* a *substantial number* of persons *will not* be able to attend the party.
    c. He *was told* that he was *not appointed* Manager of the San Francisco branch.
    d. The *completion of your report* is due before the *report on further progress* can be made.
12. Why is this note accompanying a check inappropriate? Rewrite the note.

    Enclosed is a check for $95.75. I am deeply sorry that I did not pay my bill on time. Please forgive me. This will not happen again.

EDITING

Correct the grammar, spelling, and punctuation in the following sentences. If necessary, refer to information in Chapters 3 and 4 and the appendix.

1. Please, accept this free gift.
2. Things I found that needed worked on are my creative ability and self confidence.
3. There is in the library a list of periodicals available which contain career information.
4. Pat saw a bicycle built for two walking down the street.
5. It is my personnel opinion that you should hire me for the job.
6. The correspondence has wrote his advise on a post card.
7. A lot of people belong to professional organizations, however, my friend don't.
8. For assistant in finding, and using, periodical indexes, consult a librarian.
9. Often a group of words can be shortened to one simple concise word with the same meaning.
10. he is well-known, for his many lectures.
11. Your well written letter, was very encouraging.
12. Good will contributes to human relations good consumer relations and good public relations.
13. Another valuable tool was the book The English Handbook.

IN-BASKET SIMULATIONS

1. Rewrite these letter statements—letter beginnings—so that they comply with our guidelines for writing effective letters:
   a. Just a note to thank you for joining us in our community of Valley View Acres.
   b. This affirms the intent of the named individual to comply with the requirements of the Indiana Control Law.
   c. In behalf of her many friends and associates over the years, we wish to thank Susan Peters for her many years of reporting society events in our city through the Hamilton Press.
   d. I hope you will send us your subscription renewal instructions today.
   e. We are asking for your help in providing us with your Social Security number. A postage-paid reply postcard is enclosed for your convenience. A place has been provided for your new address, if you moved recently. Thank you for your help.
   f. I received your check today and wanted to thank you for your gift. It will be used in the fight against cancer.
   g. We have received your letter and sincerely regret the trouble you encountered with our flashlamps.
   h. Enclosed please find the 19__ ABC renewal statement for membership renewal fees.
   i. We, the members of the Service to People Club, wish to thank you for your support of our programs. The recent tree sale was one of these. Your money was put to good use, the bulk of it going to support programs for crippled and retarded children. Five hundred dollars will go to the local Feed-the-Babies Program. One hundred percent of any money raised by us is used as contributions. Thank you again.
   j. We regret to inform you that News and Quotes will no longer be published.
   k. We are pleased to welcome you as a charge customer of our stores and hope you will avail yourself of this service often.
   l. I am writing this letter to inform you of what I consider an unfair practice which I feel typifies the computerized manner in which your bank handles its depositors.
   m. I am seeking a position in the field of Personnel and Industrial Relations. I am in the process of completing requirements for the Master of Arts degree in Industrial Relations at the University of Lafayette. I have finished

all of the course work. And am currently working on papers. This research may be completed at my own pace and I am available immediately.

2. Rewrite the following letter endings so that they comply with the guidelines for writing effective letters:
   a. With warm personal regards, I remain, Sincerely,
   b. So for your 15-day FREE REVIEW, mail the enclosed card today. You don't even need postage.
   c. I have enclosed a copy of the Last Will and Testament and I obtained your address from your brother.
   d. May I ask that you send in the order form now—while you're thinking about it . . . and while it's conveniently at hand? I've also enclosed a postage-paid envelope, so you can just drop everything in the mail today.
   e. We hope to see you in Topeka in February.
   f. Under separate cover we are sending you a package of flashlamps which we trust will give you complete satisfaction. If we can be of further service, please do not hesitate to contact us.
   g. Would you please take ten minutes of your time and complete the enclosed questionnaire and return it to us at your earliest convenience. An envelope is enclosed for your use. We would appreciate it very much.
   h. We would appreciate hearing from you on this important issue and we hope you will continue to share your concerns with us.
   i. We are sorry for any inconvenience this procedure may cause. We sincerely hope that you will renew your membership subscription for 19__, and greatly appreciate your cooperation in helping make this organization function as efficiently as possible.
   j. The undersigned first obtained knowledge that checks were being wrongfully dishonored on or about February 3, 19__ when a check was mailed to his residence with a notice attached that said checks had not been paid.
   k. The interview schedule for pharmaceutical firms at Lincoln University is quite meager so I hope that my letter will not be ignored and that an inverview could be arranged. Thank you, in advance, for any consideration given this request.
3. Rewrite the following middle paragraphs so that they comply with the guidelines for writing effective letters:
   a. Enclosed is a self-addressed label so that you may send the broken pipe back to us. We will send you a new pipe.

b. It is time to renew your membership in MBE, the marketing teacher's gold. Enclosed you will find the NEW membership form. This form is being used for M.B.E., ABC, and CDE and all affiliates. Please look at this form very carefully, decide which organizations you wish to enjoy and complete the form accordingly.
c. So, Mr. President, I'm withdrawing everything out of both accounts. I'm in sales and have an expense account and my wife and I have a joint account. Also, I'll see if I can make arrangements to get the money and pay off the loan so then I'll have NOTHING TO DO with this kind of bank.
d. In accordance with your request, we have cancelled your signed contract and are enclosing herewith a refund of your deposit.
e. And yet, most of us are often too busy to dream. We're too concerned with reality. Making ends meet. Saving up for our vacations.
f. Your last membership application card is enclosed. Please give it a good home with a friend or colleague, or both.
g. Enclosed are gift tags and information about the gift program. More of these tags may be obtained at any office. The gifts can be left at any Thompson Market before December 2. Please share the information with your friends, and encourage them to help us help others.

Basic Mechanics of Writing

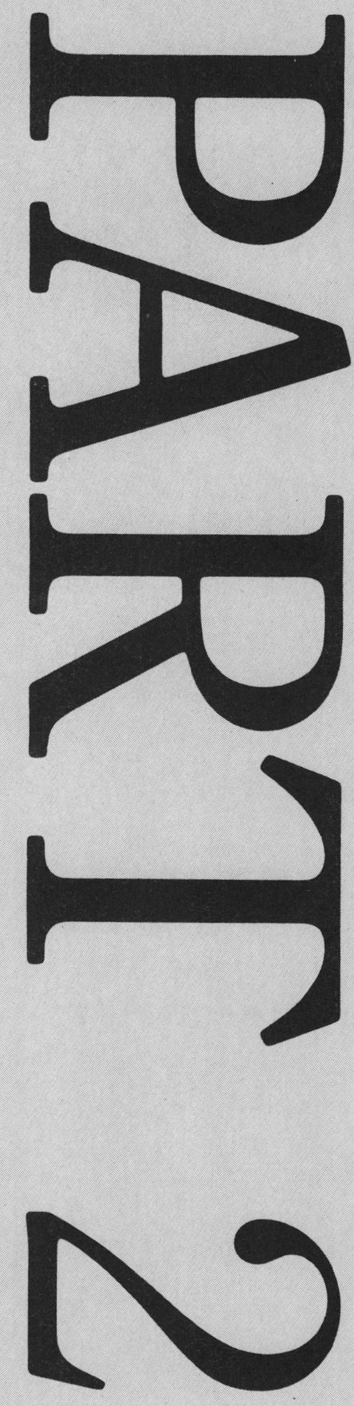

5 Selecting the Parts of the Letter

After studying Chapter 5, you should be able to:

- Describe how the appearance of your letters communicates nonverbally with the reader
- Identify the traditional and optional parts of a letter
- Use each part of a letter effectively in your correspondence
- Format a multiple-page letter

Quite simply, the letter parts have evolved from the needs of businesses—to provide information in an easily identifiable format. There are traditional practices that you can follow, but you should always keep in mind your audience, the purpose of the letter, and the image you wish to project. Only then should you select the appropriate parts and alter them to fit the needs of the specific situation.

If you are familiar with the basic and special letter parts and use them frequently, you will have at your fingertips a communication giant in the business world—a polished, professional, and effective letter.

TRADITIONAL LETTER PARTS

Almost every business letter has at least these eight traditional parts: the letterhead or return address, date, inside address, salutation, body, complimentary close, typed name of writer, and signature. These basic parts contain the information needed to reach your audience, inform your audience, and identify yourself as the writer.

Each letter part is important. Give careful consideration to each so that your letters give the necessary information in an appropriate and effective style.

Letterhead

As an employee, you will probably have access to company letterhead for business correspondence. **Letterhead** eliminates the need for typing a return address, since it includes the address. If you are asked to design or purchase letterhead stationery, there are guidelines you may follow.

Every letterhead should include the company name, address, and telephone number (including the area code), as well as the nature of the business. Often, the type of business is inferred by the company's name; for example, Baxter Pest Control. If the name of the company is The H and H Company, include some descriptive or additional data in the letterhead. A slogan, "If invented, it can be rented," would tell the reader that H and H is a rental store. The street address is sometimes omitted, but the city and state designations should be used, including the ZIP code.

Optional information might include a cable address, names of officers, names of subsidiaries, names of products, and any other information the organization believes should be part of the letterhead (such as *Serving Detroit since 1900*).

A good letterhead design is a work of art. It should be distinctive and use space simply and without crowding. Use colors sparingly—if at all.

Even the most impressive letterhead design requires good quality printing to have a good appearance. The design should be printed on the front or felt side of the paper (you can read the watermark design or words correctly on the front side). Good bond paper is usually substance 20 with at least 25 percent rag content.

Figure 5–1 illustrates actual letterheads for several large companies. Note that the illustrated letterheads specify the firm's name, address, and telephone number. The nature of the business is specifically stated or implied by the firm's name. Other information can include logos, slogans, names of divisions or employees, names of trade associations and their insignias, and Telex number. In these four samples, information is limited to the tops and bottoms of the paper, but it may also be found on the sides of the paper. Horizontal or vertical lines, as well as color or shading are sometimes incorporated in letterhead design.

Date

Place the **date** at least a double space below the letterhead. Position it appropriately for the chosen letter style.

Always type or write the complete date. The date should not show an abbreviation for the month, a figure for the month, an apostrophe for the year, or suffixes such as *st*, *nd*, *rd*, or *th*.

Use: February 10, 1988
Do Not use: 2/10/88 or 2-10-88

Use: December 20, 1988
Do Not use: December 20th, 1988 or Dec. 20th, 1988

Use: March 1, 1988
Do Not use: March 1, '88

Some business offices prefer the military style for writing the date, reversing the month and the day and omitting the comma. Instead of writing January 25, 1988, they write 25 January 1988.

Return Address and Date

The only business letter requiring a **return address** is the personal-business style (illustrated in Chapter 6). A return address is not used if letterhead is used.

Begin the return address at the approximate center of the writing line, or backspace from the right margin and begin the return address so that the longest line of the address and the letter end at the right margin. Type the date immediately below (single-spaced) and flush with the beginning of the return address at the bottom line of the return address.

Figure 5-1
Different Approaches to Letterhead Styles

Firestone

Ball Corporation
345 South High Street, Muncie, Indiana 47302 (317) 747-6100

GENERAL MOTORS CORPORATION
General Motors Building • 767 Fifth Avenue, New York, New York 10153

Telephone
(212) 486-5000

BAXTER PEST CONTROL
2691 NICHOL AVE. ANDERSON, IND. 46011
(313) 644-2533
Able Pest Control, Dayton, Ohio • Able Pest Control, Springfield, Ohio • Able Pest Control, Piqua, Ohio • Able Pest Control, Milford, Ohio
Rogers Pest Control, Richmond, Indiana • American Pest Control, Muncie, Indiana

If the street address is relatively long, use the approved abbreviations (as defined in the U.S. Postal Service list) for words like *Street*, *Avenue*, *Road*, *Boulevard*, *Apartment*, *Building*. One or two blank spaces should precede the ZIP code. For details on the proper state identification initials and ZIP codes, see Chapter 7. The typical return address and date has three lines:

Line 1: Number and street address of writer
Line 2: City or town, state identification initials, and ZIP code
Line 3: Current date

111 Jackson Street
Cleveland, OH 44124
January 10, 19--

According to the U.S. Postal Service, the number of an apartment, room, suite, or other small unit should appear to the right of the line above the city, state, and ZIP code. An example of a street address with the small unit (*apartment* may be abbreviated because of long line length) follows:

111 Jackson Street, Apt. 109
Cleveland, OH 44124
January 10, 19--

If a building name is part of the street address, it should be shown *above* the street address, but the unit number should immediately follow the street address:

Plymouth Building
111 Jackson Street, Room 909
Cleveland, OH 44124
January 10, 19--

If the building name takes the place of the street name, the return address and date would be written as follows:

Plymouth Building, Room 909
Cleveland, OH 44124
January 10, 19--

A rural road, which may be abbreviated, and its box number should be written as follows:

R. R. No. 1, Box 196
Cleveland, OH 44124
January 10, 19--

However, if a station name is included in the address, it should be written *after* the box number:

Box 101, Monroe Station
Cleveland, OH 44124
January 10, 19--

Notice that in every case the date is single-spaced below the return address. The complete date is typed according to the same rules used for typing the date on the letterhead; it should be the current date—the day's actual calendar date.

Inside Address and Courtesy Title

The **inside address** is part of every business letter and is always placed at the left margin. Place the number of an apartment, room, or other small unit exactly as you would for a return address. The postal rule is the same for all addresses. However, the content of the inside address differs. The typical inside address consists of the following three lines:

Line 1: Name of person(s) or company to receive letter
Line 2: Number and street address of person(s) or company
Line 3: City or town, state identification initials, and ZIP code

The following are typical inside addresses:

Mr. John Jones
181 Euclid Avenue
Cleveland, OH 44111

Teledyne, Inc.
1901 Avenue of the Stars
Los Angeles, CA 90067

Other illustrations are included throughout this chapter.

If the letter is being sent to an individual, an appropriate **courtesy title** should precede the name. Common permissible courtesy titles include Mr., Mrs., Ms., and Dr. Table 5-1 explains and illustrates how some common courtesy titles are used in correspondence. Do not use two titles with the same basic meaning.

Use: Dr. Roberta Myers
Use: Doctor Roberta Myers
Do Not Use: Dr. Roberta Myers, M.D.
M.D. designates type of doctor

Use: The Reverend William Keane
Use: The Reverend Dr. William Keane
two different titles
Do Not Use: The Reverend Dr. William Keane, D.D.
Dr. *and* **D.D.** *are similar*

Use: Professor Albert Daily
Use: Dr. Albert Daily
Do Not Use: Professor Dr. Albert Daily
Do Not Use: Dr. Albert Daily, Ph.D.

Courtesy title	Typical use	Example
Mr.	All males, except adolescents	Mr. William Prosse
Ms.*	Females who prefer *Ms.*; females whose preference is not known	Ms. Sally Huntersy
Miss	Females who use *Miss* professionally; females who prefer to use *Miss* to indicate marital status; females age 13 and under	Miss Martha Truax
Mrs.	Females who prefer to indicate status of being married or widowed	Mrs. John Adams
Doctor or Dr.	Person with doctoral degree	Doctor Judith Massey or Dr. Judith Massey
The Honorable	Most federal officials; some state officials: Governor, Judge, Mayor, State Senator, Representative, Member of Congress, Supreme Court Justice	The Honorable May Arn The Honorable J. Sand
The President	Special title for the U.S. President	The President
The Vice-President	Special title for the U.S. Vice-President	The Vice-President
The Reverend	Priest or minister	The Reverend John A. Smithe
The Reverend Dr.	Clergy with doctorate	The Reverend Dr. James Carter
Father	Roman Catholic priest	Father David Soule or The Reverend David Soule
Rabbi	Rabbi	Rabbi Solomon Goldberg
The Right Reverend Monsignor	Roman Catholic monsignor	The Right Reverend Monsignor E. J. Cyr

*Ms. is now accepted as the courtesy title for all females regardless of marital status.

Table 5–1
Common Courtesy Titles

You can write to a person whose mailing address you do not know by addressing the correspondence in care of someone who will forward the mail:

Ms. Mary Ann Close
In care of Mr. and Mrs. William Close
1120 White River Boulevard
Atlanta, GA 30301

Do not, however, use *c/o* for *In care of* or an ampersand (&) for *and.*

To contact someone at his or her business address, be sure to include the company name in the address.

Mr. A. Jackson Howell
National American Bank
305 Madison Avenue
Rochester, NY 14650

If the inside address includes a business or professional title, place it after the person's name. Correct placement of the title depends on the length of the title; place short titles on the same line and longer titles on the next line. If an individual's name and title together are about the same length as the company name, then the person's name and business title would be on the same line; the company name, next. Never place a business title on the same line as the name of the company.

Use: Mr. Matthew Acre, Manager
Richmond Supply Company
103 Madison Street, N.W.
La Porte, IN 46350

Do Not Use: Mr. Matthew J. Bakersville, Jr.
Manager, General Mfg. Co.
619 East Main Street
Chicago, IL 60607

Use separate lines when the individual's name or the business title are out of balance with the company name:

Ms. Martha Mullen
Vice President in Charge of Sales
Aluminum Co. of America
1501 Alcoa Building
Pittsburgh, PA 15219

Spell and write the business firm's name as shown in its letterhead or formal reports. If a firm uses an ampersand (&) in its official name, use an ampersand. If, instead, it uses *and*, use *and*. Some corporations, namely retail stores and universities, use *The* as part of their names. In such cases, include *The*. Other words that may be spelled out or abbreviated include *Incorporated*, *Limited*, *Company*, *Corporation*, *Brothers*. Use names, initials, periods, hyphens, apostrophes, and other marks as the named individual or organization desires:

The Halle Bros. Co.
Women's Federal Savings & Loan Association
Link, Link, and Jones
Harvard University
The University of Akron
I. E. Jones
J Marshall Hannan
Mary-Margaret O'Neil

Famous people, too, should be addressed by their public or professional names, rather than their legal names:

Doris Day (legally, Doris Dukinfield)
Harry Houdini (legally, Ehrich Weiss)
Dean Martin (legally, Dino Crocetti)
O Henry (legally, William Sydney Porter)

In very formal and official letters, a few business firms show the inside address about ½ in. below the business title of the writer. For example:

Respectfully yours

A. J. Newsome

A. J. Newsome
Sales Manager

Dr. Robert Baker
President
Acme Developmental Co.
111 Burgandy Place
Detroit, MI 48231

cb

Salutation

The function of a **salutation** is to greet the reader in a way that specifies the audience, suggests the degree of formality, and sets a positive tone by addressing the reader in a way that will meet with his or her approval and help to make him or her receptive to the message that follows.

The salutation of a letter is sometimes called its greeting. It is important to select the appropriate salutation for each letter by determining first:

1. name, occupation, and number of readers
2. relationship between writer and reader
3. degree of formality desired

Many of the salutations used traditionally are being reevaluated to avoid specifying gender or marital status, which no longer seem to be appropriate designations in business letters. In the past, writers often addressed correspondence to the masculine gender (*Gentlemen* or *Sirs*), even when they intended it to be read by both men and women. This usage has come to us quite naturally; the business, industrial, and professional worlds used to employ only males. Now that this practice has become antiquated, some revisions are in order.

In arriving at salutations that comfortably address both men and women, many companies have experienced confusion and awkwardness. Some have even resorted to the noncommital *To Whom it May Concern*. Obviously, they have not found a more personal or specific salutation they can feel comfortable with which avoids gender but addresses the reader with dignity and the desired degree of formality.

These changing times present an ideal opportunity for trying out alternatives. If some of these alternatives seem awkward upon first try, remember that all new mannerisms become familiar with repeated usage. However, you should choose the salutation you feel most comfortable with for the particular situation. It is probable that out of the alternatives being offered today, a favorite will emerge in the business world.

One immediate possibility is the AMS Simplified style (see Chapter 6), which uses a subject line and omits the salutation and complimentary close entirely. It is easy to see why this style may become more popular; it provides a comfortable solution to awkward salutations.

The following priority guidelines were established to determine appropriate salutations. You may consider them all to be acceptable alternatives, depending upon your audience, the degree of formality of your letter, and your relationship with the reader. In addition, Table 5-2 categorizes acceptable salutations according to reader and formality and indicates an acceptable complimentary close.

1. Choose a salutation that considers the relationship you wish to establish with the reader—formal or informal.

	Salutation	Best complimentary close	Degree of formality
Singular forms			
First name	Dear Mary Dear John	Sincerely or Cordially series*	Least Formal
Last name (most business letters)	Dear Mr. Brown Dear Ms. Brown Dear Mrs. Brown Dear Miss Brown	Yours truly series† (but use the Sincerely series with persuasive and goodwill letters)	Typical
Male (name unknown)	Dear Sir	Yours truly series†	Typical
Female (name unknown)	Dear Madam	Yours truly series†	Typical
Sex and name unknown	Dear Sir or Madam Dear (occupation)	Yours truly series†	Typical
Male	Sir	Respectfully series ††	Most formal (for male)
Female	Madam	Respectfully series††	Most formal (for female)
Plural forms			
Two or more males	Gentlemen	Yours truly series†	Typical
Two or more females	Ladies	Yours truly series†	Typical
One male and one female	Dear Ms. (Miss or Mrs.) Jones and Mr. Brown	Yours truly series†	Typical
An organization	Ladies and Gentlemen Dear Manufacturer	Yours truly series†	Typical

**Sincerely yours*; *Very sincerely yours*; *Cordially*; *Cordially yours*; *Very cordially yours*—use any one of these when an informal complimentary close is desired.
†*Yours truly*; *Yours very truly*; *Very truly yours*—use any one with typical business letters.
††*Respectfully*; *Yours respectfully*; *Respectfully yours*—use any one when a very formal complimentary close is desired.

Table 5-2
Salutations and Complimentary Closes

2. Whenever possible in greeting a single person, use the person's name. *Dear Mr. Shaw:* or *Dear Ms. Shaw:* is more personal than *Dear Madam:*.
3. When addressing a reader whose name or job title you do not know, there are a number of alternatives you might use. The AMS Simplified style employs a subject line and omits the salutation and complimentary close. If, however, you still feel the need to use a salutation, choose one that will be appropriate for either sex: *Dear Friend:*, *Dear Reader:*, *Dear Sir or Madam:*, or *Dear Representative:*. If you know the position the reader is likely to hold, you may substitute a descriptive job title, such as *Dear Editor:*, *Dear Credit Manager:*, or *Dear Committee Member:*.
4. When addressing a collective group including both men and women, use a plural form that avoids gender: *Ladies and Gentlemen:*, *Dear Educators:*, *Dear Administrators:*, *Dear Credit Officers:*, *Dear Members of the Board:*, *Dear Rotarians:*, *Dear Sales Representatives:*, and so on. Choose such a salutation carefully so that the readers understand that you are addressing them collectively but with respect and dignity.
5. Use either the person's first or last name in the salutation; never use both.

Use: Dear Sally:
Dear Mr. Goodman:

Do Not Use: Dear Sally Mason:
Dear Mr. John Goodman:

6. Use a colon after all salutations in business correspondence (except open-punctuation styles and very informal letters).

Use: Dear Mr. Jones:
Friends:

Use the first line of the inside address to help you determine an appropriate salutation, since the attention line has no effect on the salutation choice. Below are examples of inside addresses with acceptable salutations. Consult a dictionary or other reference source to determine appropriate salutations for members of the clergy, elected and appointed public officials, members of royalty, and so on.

Executive Board of Directors
Procter & Gamble Co.
301 East Sixth Street
Cincinnati, OH 45202

Dear Members of the Board:

Ms. L. E. Foster
Personnel Manager
Procter & Gamble Co.
301 East Sixth Street
Cincinnati, OH 45202

Dear Ms. Foster:

Manager for Product Development
Procter & Gamble
301 East Sixth Street
Cincinnati, OH 45202

Dear Sir or Madam:

Production Supervisor
Procter & Gamble Co.
301 East Sixth Street
Cincinnati, OH 45202

Dear Supervisor:

Procter & Gamble Co.
301 East Sixth Street
Cincinnati, OH 45202

Attention: Manager for Product Development

Ladies and Gentlemen:

Professor Phillip Moore
Head of Music Department
Eastern College
New York, NY 14603

Dear Professor Moore:

The President
The White House
Washington, DC 20425

My dear Mr. President:

The Honorable Margaret Chase
U. S. Senate
Washington, DC 20510

Madam: or My dear Senator:

Finally, there seems to be a growing tendency to include the addressee's name in the first paragraph of the letter, thereby omitting the need for a salutation. The following form lends itself to many letters:

> Mr. Gerald A. Moss, Sales Manager
> Globe Manufacturing Company, Inc.
> 2024 Lazy Creek Road
> Rochester, NY 14650
>
> Thank you, Mr. Moss, for mailing me a copy of your catalog showing current fashions.
>
> or
>
> Thank you, Mr. Moss,
>
> for mailing me a copy of your catalog showing current fashions. The catalog is just what I needed.

Body

The **body** or the message constitutes the biggest part of the letter. Its physical make-up should appeal to the reader's eyes. These factors negatively influence a reader:

Long paragraphs
Many short paragraphs
Excessive use of a specific technique: capital letters, underlining, dashes, or color
Successive end-of-the-line word divisions
Out-of-balance margins
Sloppy typewriting

An addressee may ignore the uninviting letter, associating its image with the writer. Especially when you are unfamiliar to the reader, your letter reflects your character, ability, and appearance.

If you adhere to the following guidelines, your letters may have more eye-appeal for readers.

1. *Margins.* Since the margins frame the letter, they should be balanced. Generally, the top and bottom margins should be approximately equal with each other, as should the left and right margins. Lines that are too short or too long throw the letter off balance.
2. *Spacing.* The body of the letter usually is single-spaced. However, one-paragraph letters on standard size stationery may be double-spaced. Regardless of whether you use single or double spacing, always double space between paragraphs. Always indent paragraphs of the double-spaced letter.

3. *Paragraphing.* Divide the message into paragraphs which promote eye-appeal and reflect logical changes in thought. Limit each paragraph to one major thought. Generally, the first and last paragraphs should have up to four typewritten lines; the remaining paragraphs, ten. Short, one-sentence paragraphs in succession give a choppy look to the letter. On the other hand, long paragraphs are overwhelming. If a paragraph has more than eight typewritten lines, consider shortening it. Five paragraphs, with the longest one in the middle, should be enough to convey the message to the reader, although sales letters may require more paragraphs.
4. *Syllabication.* To balance side margins, divide words at the end of the writing line. However, take care to avoid awkward divisions. Follow the established rules for correct word division and avoid more than three word divisions per page.
5. *Typewriting.* The letter should be free from typographical errors, strikeovers, visible corrections, smudges, streaks, and other distractions. Retype, rather than mail, a sloppy letter or report.

Complimentary Close

The complimentary close—the goodbye—should agree in formality with the salutation. In other words, an informal salutation requires an informal complimentary close; a formal salutation, a formal close. (See Table 5–2.)

Capitalize only the first word in the complimentary close. The most commonly used complimentary closes are listed and explained in Table 5–2.

Yours in a complimentary close carries no more significance than does *Dear* in a salutation. Neither term should be taken to mean special affection. Avoid complimentary closes such as *Faithfully* and *Love* in business letters.

Typed Name of Writer and Signature

Your pen-written signature adds a personal touch, as well as affixing responsibility for your statements. If the company name is typed above a signature, the responsibility may be lessened.

When signing your name, omit the courtesy title. Otherwise, sign the letter exactly as your name appears at the bottom of the document.

Yours truly,

John L. Jones

John L. Jones

Yours truly,

Jane Adams

Miss Jane Adams

Yours truly,

A. Mary Smith

Ms. A. Mary Smith

Generally, a woman uses her first name in business letters; however, socially she may use her husband's name.

Typical business situation: Yours truly,

Jane Adamson

Mrs. Jane Adamson

Social situation: Yours truly,

Jane Adamson

Mrs. Jane Adamson (Mrs. Peter)

If two people are to sign the letter, follow this example:

Yours truly,

← **1 blank line**

ARTHUR G. McKEE & COMPANY

John S. Sloan ← **3 blank lines**

John S. Sloan
Purchasing Agent ← **0 blank lines**

H. S. Caldemeyer ← **3 blank lines**

H. S. Caldemeyer
Director of Purchases ← **0 blank lines**

SPECIAL LETTER PARTS

As letters grow in complexity (or when you wish to give them special help in reaching their destinations in large organizations), there are features you can add. These commonly used features are optional, but valuable.

Special parts that are frequently used include mail notation, attention line, subject line, company name, business title of writer, reference initials, enclosure notation, copy notation, and postscript. The following information will help you better understand the letter parts and how to use them correctly.

Mail Notation

A **mail notation** is an indication of how a letter was sent. If it is desired, place it at the left margin a double space below the date and a double space above the inside address. Type it in all capital letters.

December 1, 19--

PRIORITY MAIL

Miracle Water Refining
321 Walnut Avenue
Portland, OR 97213

Attention Line

If you want to address the letter to an individual, include the person's name as the first line of the inside address. If you want to direct your letter to a company, but desire a particular individual or department to read the letter, address your letter to the company and use an **attention line.** Generally, mail goes immediately to the name or department indicated in the attention line, so the attention line should also appear on the envelope.

Always precede the individual's name with an appropriate courtesy title and, if you know it, include the business title and department after the name. The attention line usually appears a double space below the inside address, flush with the left margin. This is a common method of showing an attention line in a letter:

Adamson Steel Company, Inc.
125 South La Salle Street
Chicago, IL 60603

Attention: Mr. John P. Smithe, Office Manager

Dear Manufacturer:

There are numerous acceptable ways for formatting the attention line. The word "Attention" may be followed by the word "of," a colon and two blank spaces, one blank space, or a dash and no blank spaces:

Attention of Ms. Jane Davis, President

Attention: Ms. Jane Davis, President

Attention Ms. Jane Davis

Attention: Purchasing Department

Attention--Ms. Jane Davis, President

Subject Line

The **subject line** indicates the topic of the letter in a few well-chosen words. Although this letter part is optional for business letters, it is a traditional part of the AMS simplified style (discussed in Chapter 6). Generally, the subject line appears a double space below the salutation.

Mr. John P. Shaw, President
American Typewriter Company
277 Park Avenue
New York, NY 10017

Dear Mr. Shaw:

Subject: Whole Life and Major Medical Benefits

Ms. A. A. Simpson
Director of Sales
CPC International, Inc.
International Plaza
Englewood Cliffs, NJ 07632

Dear Ms. Simpson:

YOUR LETTER OF MAY 1, 19--

In every subject line, if capital letters are not used throughout, the first word of the subject and every other important word—not prepositions or articles—begins with a capital letter. No period follows the subject line. You can place the subject line at the left margin or center it with or without the word "subject." *Subject* is frequently underscored or typed in all capital letters. Just as often, however, it is followed by a colon or a dash. A few different treatments of the subject line follow:

Subject: Your Order of May 1, 19--

SUBJECT: Contract No. M-6008

Subject—Credit Terms for Current Orders

SALES MEETING IN CHICAGO, SEPTEMBER 12, 19--

Some writers use *Re* or *In Re* instead of *Subject.*

It is not necessary to have both an attention line and a subject line in the same letter, but you may choose to include either, neither, or both. Double spacing is traditional between these parts when used.

Company Name

If your company desires it, repeat the company name in the closing section of the letter, even if the name is printed in the letterhead. The typed company name—in all capital letters and a double space below the complimentary close—usually implies that you, as the writer, are acting as an agent of the company. Word the name exactly as shown in the letterhead, using abbreviations only as given in the letterhead.

Writer's Name and Signature

Every letter needs a pen-written **signature**. Typing the writer's name is not necessary, but it helps the reader. A male writer should not type *Mr.* before his name; it is obvious that he should be addressed as mister. However, women have various courtesy titles and should specify one to assist the reader. Moreover, the typed name helps clarify the signature.

Business Title of Writer

You may add your **business title** immediately after your typewritten name. Either precede it with a comma or single space and type your title directly beneath your typewritten name.

A few examples of the closing section showing company name, signature, typed name, and business title of the writer follow:

Yours truly,

BOEING CO.

J. A. Jacob

Ms. J. A. Jacob

Very truly yours,

SMITH, SMITH, & SMITH

Melvin A. Smith

Melvin A. Smith, Treasurer

Yours truly,

BORDEN, INC.

John L. Small

John L. Smith
Supervisor of Customer Relations

A few writers prefer typing their names at the left margin rather than in the closing section. The typist's reference initials should follow.

Very truly yours,

COMBUSTION ENGINEERING, INC.

Marvella E. Jackson

Production Engineer

Miss Marvella E. Jackson:mle

Reference Initials

Reference initials simply identify persons involved with getting the letter written—usually a writer or dictator and a typist. If you are both writer and typist, include no reference initials.

Reference initials appear a double space below the business title of the writer and at the left margin. Commonly, a colon (:) or diagonal (/) separates the two sets of initials, but a dash (--) also may be used. Because it is easier, reference initials can be typed either in all capital letters, all lowercase letters, or a combination of the two. Always show the writer or dictator's initials first:

JLS:CEN	JLS/CEN	JLS--CEN
JLS:cen	JLS/cen	JLS--cen
jls:cen	jls/cen	jls--cen

If the employer prefers it, the typist may be identified by a number or just a single initial: JLS:8 or JLS:c.

If the dictator or writer's name appears in the closing section, only the typist's initials (lowercase) need to appear in the reference position (left margin). This is often done. If you think it will add balance to the letter or if you need to conserve space, you may space the initials on the same line as the business title:

Very truly yours,

AMERICAN BRANDS, INC.

Alice J. Thompson

Mrs. Alice J. Thompson
bav Public Relations Director

Enclosure Notation

An **enclosure notation** refers to one or more items mailed with the letter. It helps to remind the sender to include the items, it documents that the items were sent, and it provides a quick reference for the receiver. It usually appears at the left margin and a double space below the reference initials. *Enclosure* may be spelled in full or abbreviated *Enc.* or *Encl.* If more than one item is to be enclosed, either the number of enclosures or a description of them should be stated. Here are some variations of the enclosure notations:

Enclosure	Enclosures--2	Encl.
Enclosures: 2	Encl. 2	Enc.
Enclosures: Check for $100 Current Price List	Enc. 2	

Note that nothing extra is added if only one enclosure is enclosed.

The specific enclosures *must* be mentioned in the body of the letter even though the enclosure notation may repeat the data.

Copy Notation

Copy notation indicates to whom business persons mail copies of the original letter. This practice helps transmit the same message and saves the time and cost of writing and typing another letter. When sending copies to other people, make sure that a copy notation has been added so that the reader knows who has received copies of the letter.

The copy notation appears at the left margin, usually a double space below the enclosure notation (if there is one). Otherwise, it appears a double space below the reference initials. Before the advent of photocopy machines in business offices, most copies were carbon copies. Therefore, it was appropriate to always use terms such as *carbon copy*, *carbon copy to*, *carbon copies*, or *cc* to designate these extra copies. Today, it would probably be more accurate to indicate copies by using, *copy to*, *copies to*, *photocopy*, or *photocopies*. Use the initials *pc* to refer to a photocopy. The names of persons receiving the copies would follow the words or initials. Here are some examples:

Copy to Mr. A. L. Jones

Copies to: Mr. A. L. Jones, Apex Industries, Akron, OH 44129
Ms. Carla Adams, National Auto Sales, Dallas, TX 75222

Photocopy: Mr. A. L. Jones
Apex Industries
Akron, OH 44129

pc Ms. Carla Adams

If you do not want the reader to know that copies are being distributed, you may include the notation on the copies only. Use a blind copy notation, so that the notation appears on the copies only.

Blind Photocopy: Mr. A. L. Jones

Blind Copy Ms. Carla Adams

bpc: Ms. Jane Oliver, Personnel Department, Case Industries

When the copies are truly carbon copies, use as appropriate: *blind carbon copy*, *blind carbon copies*, or *bcc* before the name or names.

Note: Include the person's business title and address if such data helps either the writer or the reader.

Postscript

The **postscript** is a note added to the end of a letter. Use it only when you wish to emphasize a point. The postscript is a useful advertising device. It can be used effectively, for example, in the sales letter. Never use it to supply data that should have been in the body of the letter. Instead, rewrite the letter and include the pertinent information.

If you include a postscript, make it the last item in the letter. It may or may not be preceded by the initials *P.S.* As far as form is concerned, consider the postscript as a paragraph of the letter. If the letter has indented paragraphs, indent the postscript a like number of spaces; otherwise, begin the postscript at the left margin. Single space postscripts.

JLS:cen

Enclosure

Copy to: Mr. A. L. Jones

Remember that the Anniversary Sale for Preferred Customers will be on June 1 and 2, 19--.

cen

Encl.

Photocopy: Miss Susan Minute, J & S Sales

P.S. Remember that the Anniversary Sale for Preferred Customers will be on June 1 and 2, 19--.

JLS/cen

pc: Miss Susan Minute, J & S Sales

Remember that the Anniversary Sale for Preferred Customers will be on June 1 and 2, 19--.

ALL LETTER PARTS

If any one letter were to include all possible parts—essential and elective—the parts would be in the following order:

Letterhead **or** return address
Date
Mail notation
Inside address
Attention line
Salutation
Subject line
Body
Complimentary close
Company name
Signature
Typed name of writer
Business title of writer
Reference initials
Enclosure notation
Copy notation
Postscript

Figure 5-2 illustrates the placement and usual spacing between all parts described in this chapter. Note, however, that not all parts illustrated should appear in one letter.

MULTIPLE-PAGE LETTERS

Try to confine most of your business letters to one page. Multiple-page letters often lack conciseness and clarity. However, when multiple pages are necessary, you should observe several practices.

Use letterhead stationery only for the first page of the letter. Type additional pages on plain stationery, identical to the quality, color, and size of the letterhead paper. Each additional page needs a typewritten heading for identification. Because letter pages are not stapled together, it is relatively easy to misplace or lose part of the multiple-page letter.

The proper heading includes the name (same as the first line of the inside address), the page number, and the date of the letter. Begin the heading 1 in. from the top of the sheet at the left margin:

Ms. Holly Ann Oberstar --2-- June 10, 19--

Nuccio and McDonald, Inc.
Page 2
June 10, 19--

Baker Supply Co.
Attention: Mr. Marc Raymond, Sales Manager
2
June 10, 19--

Letterwriter Services, Inc. 654 Olive Grove Place San Diego, CA 92114 619-716-4938 "Our forms give you style"	← Letterhead** or
One Main Street Newark, NJ 07103	← Return address*
July 5, 19--	← Date**
PRIORITY MAIL	← Mail notation**
Lafayette Products Co. P.O. Box 2193 Columbus, GA 31902	← Inside address**
Attention of Miss Cheryl Lind, Accounting Department	← Attention line**
Ladies/Gentlemen	← Salutation**
Subject: All Letter Parts and Spacing	← Subject line**
This letter is meant to show you the placement of all letter parts--if a letter had all the parts possible. All margins should be at least one inch. The shorter the letter, the wider the margins. This guide is helpful for determining side margins: Short letter - approximately 2" side margins Average letter - approximately 1½" side margins Long letter - approximately 1" side margins	← Body**
Yours truly	← Complimentary close**
LETTERWRITER SERVICES, INC.	← Company name****
James A. Taylor (signature)	← Signature****
James A. Taylor	← Typed name of writer*
President	← Business title of writer**
JAT:ceb	← Reference initials**
Enclosure	← Enclosure notation**
Copy to: Mr. Mark Peterson, Accounting	← Copy notation**
If no mail notation is shown, leave three or more blank lines after the date.	← Postscript

The *'s following each letter part are guides to the typical spacing requirement: * no blank line follows; ** one blank line follows; *** three or more blank lines follow; and **** three or more blank lines for signature.

Figure 5-2
Typical Spacing for Business Letters (All Parts Shown)

After typing the heading, space down three lines (triple space) and continue your letter. The concluding page should have at least four typewritten lines *of the message*. If fewer lines remain, you may wish to rewrite in more concise language and end the letter on the preceding page. Figure 5-3 illustrates the second page of a two-page letter to Mr. A. L. English. The side margins should be the same as those for the first page—usually 1 in. for multiple-page letters.

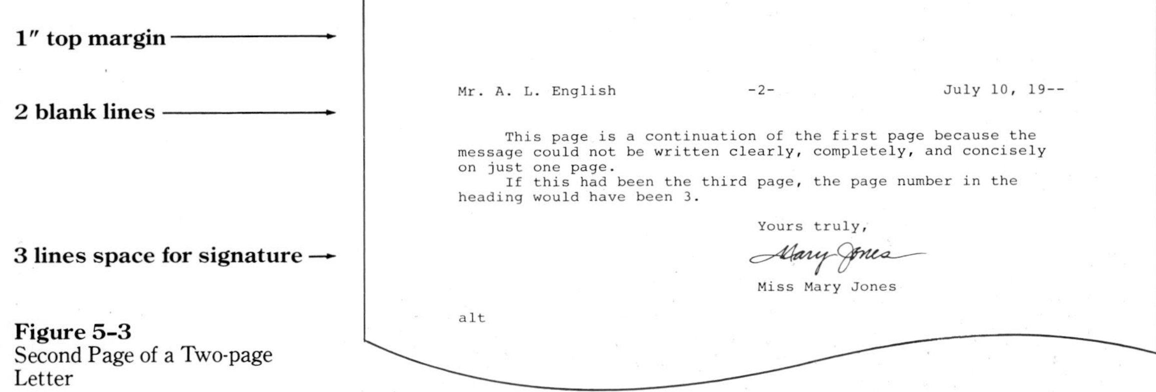
1″ top margin
2 blank lines
3 lines space for signature
Mr. A. L. English -2- July 10, 19--
This page is a continuation of the first page because the message could not be written clearly, completely, and concisely on just one page.
If this had been the third page, the page number in the heading would have been 3.
Yours truly,
Mary Jones
Miss Mary Jones
alt

Figure 5-3
Second Page of a Two-page Letter

CHAPTER SUMMARY

The appearance of your letter tells the reader instantly whether you have given careful consideration to your work. The traditional parts of a letter are expected. Use them in appropriate style, language, and format. Done properly, they add a professional and polished look to the letter, as well as provide convenience and pleasure for the reader.

Type all business letters on good letterhead stationery. Personal-business letters belong on plain stationery, since the letter is not representing a particular organization. Then choose the appropriate date, inside address, salutation, body, and complimentary close. Be sure to include your typewritten name and pen-written signature.

If you need to alert the reader to any special information that may not be readily apparent in the traditional parts of the letter, use one of the many devices that do not appear in all letters but are, nonetheless, common in business correspondence. These devices may expedite delivery of the letter to the appropriate person, facilitate the reader's comprehension of the material, or help to clarify what is included and who should receive copies of the message. Specifically, the devices are mail notation, attention line, subject line, company name, business title of writer, reference initials, enclosure notation, copy notation, and postscript. Use the postscript only to emphasize a point, as in an advertising sales letter; never use it to tack on information that belongs elsewhere in the letter.

Use a multiple-page letter only when the message cannot be said clearly, completely, or concisely on one page. Additional pages must include a heading that consists of the addressee's name, the page number, and the date.

Choose the salutation and complimentary close carefully, giving consideration to the intended reader. Your decision should be based on information in the inside address, the relationship between writer and reader, and the formality desired.

STUDY QUESTIONS

1. List the essential letter parts. Explain their purposes.
2. List the optional letter parts. Explain their purposes.
3. What basic information must all letterheads have?
4. When is a return address used instead of letterhead?
5. What is the specific U.S. Postal Service rule regarding placement of small unit numbers in addresses?
6. What is the best courtesy title in letters to a:
   a. Governor
   b. Judge
   c. Member of Congress
   d. Reverend
   e. President of the United States
7. When should you include *The* or & with a company name?
8. What factors are important to determine the best salutation? What effect does an attention line have on a salutation?
9. What factors are important to determine the best complimentary close?
10. List all letter parts in their proper order. Include the usual spacing requirements.
11. How much space must precede and follow the heading on a second page?
12. At least how many lines of the body must you continue on the concluding page of the multiple-page letter?

ACTIVITIES

1. Letterheads may be as distinctive as a company desires; however, all letterheads should contain certain features. In the list below, write *must* next to the items that should be a part of every letterhead. Next to those which may be appropriate for letterhead, write *okay*. Next to those items that should not be a part of letterhead, write *no*.
   a. Name of company
   b. Names of officers
   c. Names of stockholders
   d. Department names
   e. Names of products
   f. Identification initials
   g. Street address
   h. Cable address

i. ZIP code
j. Postal zone
k. Titles of officers
l. Printing at sides
m. Printing at bottom
n. Two colors
o. Three or more colors
p. City or town
q. Current date
r. Telephone numbers
s. Pictures of products
t. Pictures of offices or factories
u. Names of branches or subsidiaries
v. Location of show rooms
w. Registered trademarks
x. Business slogan
y. Watermark
z. Cartoons
aa. Blind embossing
ab. Executive size

2. Write your return address using current postal regulations.
3. Give the best courtesy title for each of the following individuals:
   a. A 25-year-old male
   b. A 10-year-old female
   c. A female who uses her title to indicate unmarried status
   d. A person with a master's degree
   e. A person with a doctorate
   f. A female who uses her title to indicate married status
   g. A female—You do not know which courtesy title she prefers
   h. The governor
   i. A member of the House of Representatives
4. For each situation, write an inside address, an appropriate salutation, and the best complimentary close. Supply missing information.
   a. A woman who uses her title to indicate unmarried status (informal correspondence)
   b. A woman who uses her title to indicate unmarried status (formal correspondence)
   c. A woman who uses her title to indicate married status
   d. A woman who uses her husband's name (social name) in all correspondence
   e. A man (informal correspondence)
   f. A man (formal correspondence)

   g. A woman who does not indicate marital status in her courtesy title
   h. A professional person with a master's degree
   i. A professional person with a doctor's degree (indicate business address)
5. For each of the following situations, write the inside address, an appropriate salutation, and a complimentary close.
   a. B.F. Goodrich Co., 500 South Main Street, Akron, Ohio 44318
   b. Minnesota Mining & Mfg. Co., 3M Center, St. Paul, Minnesota 55101, attention of Miss A. L. Longsworth, Engineering Department
   c. Ms. Elizabeth A. Peterson, President of Eaton Corporation at 100 Erieview Plaza in Cleveland, Ohio 44114
   d. Vice President of Production (assume name and sex not known), Litton Industries, 360 North Crescent Drive, Beverly Hills, California 90210
6. For each of the following situations, write the inside address, an appropriate salutation, and the best complimentary close. Supply any necessary information.
   a. Man at his place of business. Give him a long title.
   b. Woman at her place of business. Give her a short title.
   c. Member of the Protestant clergy. Include the name of the church.
   d. Roman Catholic priest. Include the name of the church.
   e. President of the United States
   f. Member of Congress—Senator or Representative
7. Indicate the best complimentary close for each of the following salutations:
   a. Dear Susan
   b. Dear Sir or Madam
   c. Dear Mrs. Smith
   d. Dear Madam
   e. Dear Editor
   f. Madam
   g. Dear Chairman
   h. Dear Mr. Andrews
8. Indicate the best complimentary close for each of the following salutations:
   a. Dear Joseph
   b. Dear Sir
   c. Sir
   d. Madam
   e. Dear Sir or Madam
   f. Dear Members of the Board
   g. Dear Misses O'Brien
   h. Dear Ms. Adams
   i. Dear Doctor Spencer
   j. Ladies/Gentlemen

9. Illustrate the use of an attention line; include an inside address, salutation, and complimentary close.
10. What is the usual spacing between the following letter parts:
    a. Date and inside address
    b. Inside address and attention line
    c. Inside address and salutation
    d. Salutation and subject line
    e. Salutation and body of letter
    f. Between paragraphs
    g. Before complimentary close
    h. Between complimentary close and typed name of writer
    i. Between company name and typed name of writer
    j. Between business title of writer and reference initials
    k. Between reference initials and enclosure notation
    l. Between enclosure notation and copy notation
11. Using all information given, illustrate closings for each of the following situations beginning with the complimentary close.
    a. A letter written by a man
    b. A letter written by a woman
    c. A letter written by a woman indicating she is married
    d. A letter written by William Eastern, Assistant Manager
    e. A letter written by E. A. Hughes, Buyer for Sears, Roebuck and Co.
    f. A letter written by Virginia Jennings (indicating unmarried status), Assistant Professor of Marketing, Southern Kentucky University
12. Condense the following information into an appropriate subject line: This letter gives the changes that are being made with personnel at another plant, Plant No. 3. Show the line in two traditional ways.
13. Properly format the following information in a letter: Addressed to Lange Publishing Company located in room 209 of the Publishers Bldg. at 1310 Avenue of the Americas in New York, NY 10021; attention of Marlene Taylor, Senior Editor. The letter states revisions to Chapter 2. Include the inside address, attention line, salutation, subject, and complimentary close.
14. Using the following information, show the reference initials in three traditional ways:

    Lawrence C. Carter, the dictator of letter
    Samuel A. Jackson, the typist

15. Show the enclosure notation in two traditional ways (one specifying that the enclosures are an addressed and stamped envelope and a booklet entitled "Word Power.")

16. Illustrate both a copy notation and a blind copy notation. Explain the reason for the difference.
17. Rewrite the following postscript for a letter with blocked paragraphs:

    The reader and a guest are welcome to attend an open house scheduled for April 5 through 12.

18. Illustrate the heading for the third page of a letter addressed to Acme Products Company, attention of Ms. Helen Lawrence.

EDITING

Correct the following letter parts:

1. Sept. 18th, 19--

2. Mister Raymond Monroe
   1 East One Hundred Ten St.
   Dallas, Texas 75200

3. American Industries
   Attention of: Mrs. Tracy Steele
   Production Supervisor
   1010 Common Street
   Oklahoma City, OK 73125

   Dear Mrs. Steele

4. District Sales Manager
   Northwest Industries
   Richmond, VA. 232610

   Dear Sir

   Respectfully yours,

5. Honorable Senator Richard Armstrong
   Republican Senatorial Committee
   406 C Street, N.E.
   Washington, D. C. 200002

   Dear Honorable Senator

   Truly yours

6. Mr. & Mrs. Richard Dayton
   Park Plaza, Apt. 18C
   2400 Madison Street
   Orange, Calif. 92668

7. Page 2
   March 25, 19--
   Land O'Lakes Corp.
   Attn. George Diamond

8. Yours Truly:

   Shamrock Corp.

   Miss Patricia Lorden
   Manager of Advertising

   deb:pl

   Copy to: Anthony J. Lawyer, Benton Advertising Co.

9. Subject: The Renewal of Your Advertising Campaign For
   the 19-- Year

10. deb

    Enclosed: Booklet, "Word Usage"

11. P.S. Enclosed is your copy of the information you
    requested in your letter of 10/12/87

Return address

12. Marvin Campbell
    Sears Towers Apt. 213
    Arden Hills, Minn. 55713
    7 july 19--

IN-BASKET SIMULATIONS

Background data. Waltere Supermarkets, Inc., has two divisions: the supermarket operations and the convenience market operations. Waltere Supermarkets, Inc., began as a small corner grocery store in 1950. Under the skillful direction of Raymond Waltere, President, the business expanded to become a chain of 20 large units within seven years. In 1970, the first convenience store was opened. A contest among employees to name the convenience stores resulted in their being called Mini Mart. Today,

Waltere Supermarkets, Inc., has 50 large retail units and 120 convenience stores in 38 communities in Indiana. Two warehouses serve the stores.

The corporate headquarters is at 220 Michigan Avenue (P.O. Box 1785), Indianapolis, Indiana 46206. Officers of the corporation are:

President: Mr. Raymond Waltere
Vice-President and General Manager: Mr. Peter Waltere
Controller: Mr. Marc R. Page
Treasurer: Mrs. Ruth Cynthia Munson
Vice-President, Director of Sales: Mr. P. David Summer
Vice-President, Director of Operations: Mr. Joseph Anthony

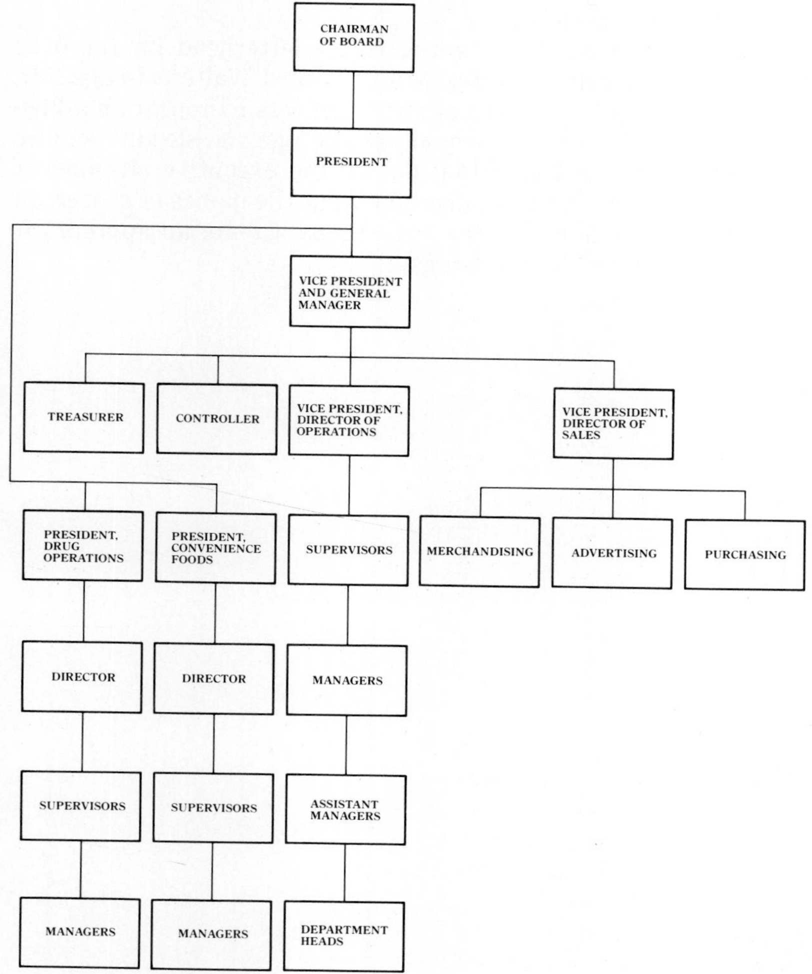

Organizational Chart for Waltere Supermarkets, Inc.

The organizational chart shows how these offices interrelate.

Waltere will soon open a drug store adjacent to a large retail unit.

1. Raymond Waltere authorized Thomas Leonard, president of Drug Operations to delve into ways to promote the new drug division. Leonard wrote a speed letter (similar to an interoffice memorandum) to Joe Marion, Director of Drug Operations, asking him to begin researching possibilities. He asked the following kinds of questions: What kind of advertising should we use? When? Where? Costs? Should we give the drug stores a special name, as was done with the convenience markets? Should we design a special logo and/or slogan? Mr. Marion has requested your ideas. Design an appropriate logo (trade character to be used with all company advertisements) and a possible slogan.
2. Raymond Waltere has authorized a letterhead for the drug division. The drug stores will be named Waltere Drugs. Mr. Waltere would like the corporate address to appear on all letterheads. The officers would like the logo and slogan included on the regular letterhead (not on the executive stationery). The Board of Directors does not want the names of officers or divisions included on the letterheads. Create an appropriate letterhead for Waltere Drugs.

Selecting and Formatting the Professional Letter Style

6

After studying Chapter 6, you should be able to:

- Describe the acceptable styles of letters (personal-business, full-block, AMS simplified, modified block with and without paragraph indentations, official)
- Know when to use each style
- Place a letter attractively on the page
- Distinguish the different punctuation patterns (open, mixed, closed)

Just as letter parts have become traditional in businesses, some letter styles are widely used. These styles display the specific parts discussed in Chapter 5 and require attention to placement on the page, consistent spacing, and a uniform punctuation style. Adhering to a prescribed style lends consistency, which in turn suggests reliability. It gives a neat, attractive, and easily identifiable appearance to the letter.

ACCEPTABLE STYLES

When do you use each style? And why? Typical business styles include the personal-business, full-block, AMS simplified, modified block with or without paragraph indentions, and official. (These styles are sometimes known by other names.) The personal-business style is limited to personal business—not company or group business. Some offices and writers prefer one business style over another simply to establish a routine or because of increased efficiency.

The most efficiently typed letters are the full-block and the AMS simplified. Nevertheless, some business people prefer less severe styles, even though they take longer to type. Many use the modified block style with or without paragraph indentions because they appear informal. Additionally, there are various adaptations of these styles which work well for special letters—such as sales letters. They can show uniqueness and creativity. Many of them are reproduced in large quantities. The official style is available for very formal, official letters to prominent persons.

The best style is the one best suited for the message. Think of the letter style as a frame and vehicle for the message. What is the effect you wish to achieve? For business letters, choose the full-block style to communicate nonverbally the desire to save time and increase efficiency; the AMS simplified to communicate high efficiency; the modified block styles to convey less formality; and the official style to acknowledge the highly formal, official status of the reader.

Personal-Business Style

The **personal-business style** should be used for personal-business correspondence, when the message is from an individual acting solely for herself/himself, rather than as a member of a club, fraternity, or business. Because this style does not involve business, letterhead stationery would be inappropriate. The personal-business style is routinely used for application and other employment letters and for inquiries, complaints, and goodwill messages from individuals to other individuals or to business people.

The personal-business style resembles the modified block style letter with paragraph indentions; however, the personal-business style has a return address instead of a letterhead. Reference initials are not appropriate because the writer and typist should be the same person.

The top and bottom margin should be at least 1 in., whereas the side margins are usually 1½ in. The letter should be centered vertically on plain, white stationery, which is usually 8½ in. × 11 in.

Begin the return address, which is single-spaced, at the approximate centerpoint between the left and right margins. The date immediately follows the return address, as part of the return address. (Return addresses are illustrated and discussed in Chapter 5.) Allow three or more blank lines between the date and the first line of the inside address. (See Figure 6–1.)

Full-Block Style

The **full-block style**, also known as a strict block or extreme block, is considered practical because of its ease in typing. Writers who want to communicate speed and efficiency may choose this letter style; however, some readers consider it cold and impersonal.

Every line of the full-block style begins at the left margin; no parts are indented or centered. Letterhead is used for the first page. (See Figure 6–2.)

AMS Simplified Style

The **AMS simplified style**, like the full-block style, saves typewriting time because each line starts at the left margin. In addition, the salutation and complimentary close and company name are always omitted, which makes this style particularly attractive as an alternative to awkward salutations. The subject line should be typed in capital letters, with two blank line spaces above and below it. Insert at least three blank line spaces below the date and after the body. Unlike other styles, the writer's name and business title are typed in all capital letters. Letterhead is used for the first page. (See Figure 6–3.)

The AMS simplified style was created and is promoted by the Administrative Management Society, Willow Grove, Pennsylvania. It was previously known as the NOMA (pronounced *no-ma*) letter when the Association's name was the National Office Management Association. The AMS style was introduced as an alternative to the other letter styles, which take more time to type and include parts considered unnecessary.

1″ or more for top and bottom margins (center letter attractively)

Return address →

Date →

Inside address (begin inside address on fourth line after the date) →

Salutation →

Indented paragraphs →

Body →

1½″ side margins (average length letter)

Complimentary close →

Signature →

Typed name of writer →

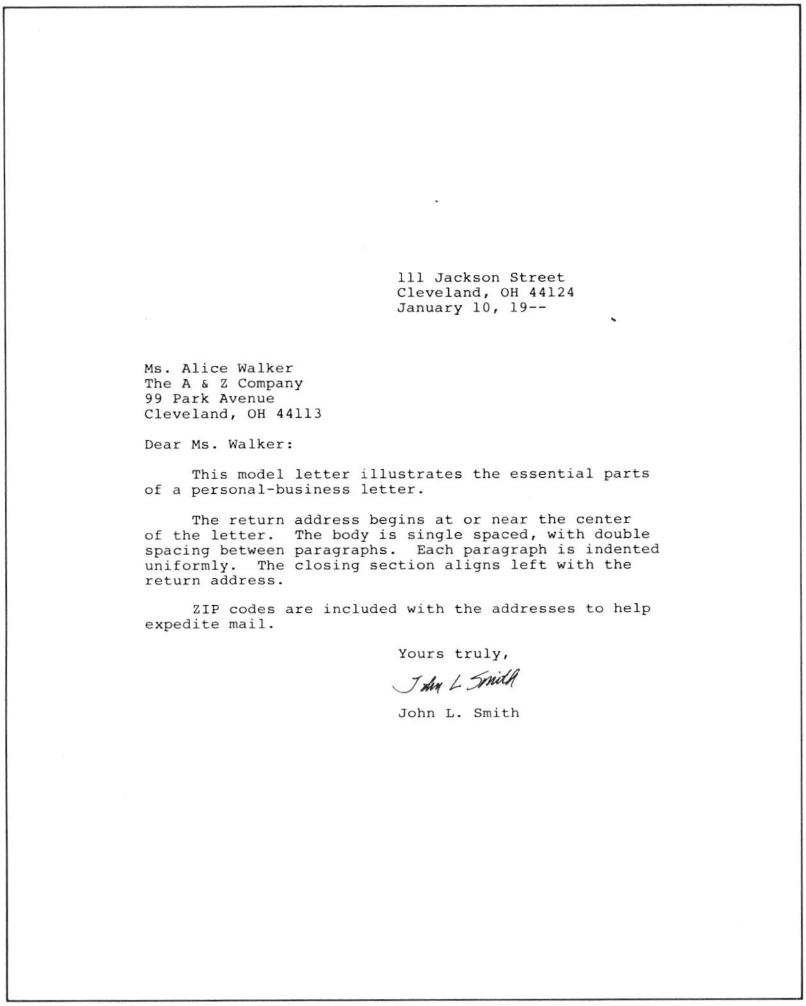

```
                                    111 Jackson Street
                                    Cleveland, OH 44124
                                    January 10, 19--



Ms. Alice Walker
The A & Z Company
99 Park Avenue
Cleveland, OH 44113

Dear Ms. Walker:

     This model letter illustrates the essential parts
of a personal-business letter.

     The return address begins at or near the center
of the letter.  The body is single spaced, with double
spacing between paragraphs.  Each paragraph is indented
uniformly.  The closing section aligns left with the
return address.

     ZIP codes are included with the addresses to help
expedite mail.

                                    Yours truly,

                                    John L. Smith

                                    John L. Smith
```

Figure 6–1
Personal-business Letter Style

Modified Block Style without Paragraph Indentions

The **modified block style without paragraph indentions** is a modification of the full-block style. Since some lines do not start at the left margin, the letter style communicates efficiency but with less formality and more personality than the other styles.

All lines start at the left margin—except the date and the closing section (namely, the complimentary close, company name, signature, typed name of writer, and business title of writer). The date and closing section should begin near the center of the page. Letterhead is used for the first page. Other names for this letter style include semiblock without paragraph indentions or modified block style with block paragraphs. (See Figure 6–4.)

Book Club Associates
915 Railroad Street
Boulder,CO 80302
303-313-4400

BCA

August 4, 19-- ← Date

Big Company, Inc.
P.O. Box 3158
Austin, TX 78710 ← Inside address

Attention: Mr. Michael T. Allen, Purchasing Agent ← Attention line

Dear Manufacturer ← Salutation

Subject: Full-Block Letter Style ← Subject line

This example depicts the full-block letter style, one known for its ease in typing and formal structure.

Basic letter parts include letterhead, date, inside address, salutation, complimentary close, signature, typed name of writer, business title of writer, and reference initials. Special parts can be added as desired and necessary. ← Body

All letter parts begin at the left margin; therefore, no extra typewriter manipulations are necessary. The letter can be typed quickly with minimum space.

Double space between all parts, except:

(1) after the date, leave three or more blank lines

(2) for the signature, allow three or more blank lines

(3) between the typed name of writer and business title of writer, single space.

Single space the lines of the inside address and the body of the letter.

You can choose the full-block letter style when speed and efficiency are important, you prefer it, or company policy requires it.

Yours truly ← Complimentary close

Colleen A. Sullivan ← Signature

Miss Colleen A. Sullivan ← Typed name of writer
Director of Public Relations ← Business title of writer

CAS:abc ← Reference initials

Figure 6-2
Full-block Letter Style

Modified Block Style With Paragraph Indentions

The **modified block style with paragraph indentions** is similar to the personal-business letter, except that letterhead is used rather than a return address. (See Figure 6-5.) Since this letter style is very informal and requires more typing time than other formal business letter styles, it can communicate little need for speed and efficiency.

The first line of each new paragraph is indented a like number of spaces—usually five. Paragraph indentions may be five, six, seven, or more spaces, depending on the writer's wishes. This popular style may also be called the semiblock style with paragraph indentions.

Date →
Inside address →
Attention line →
Subject line →
Body →
Signature →
Typed name and business title of writer →
Reference initials →

Letterwriter Services, Inc.

654 Olive Grove Place
San Diego, CA 92114
619-716-4938

"Our forms give you style"

August 4, 19--

Big Company, Inc.
P.O. Box 3158
Austin, TX 78710

Attention: Mr. Michael T. Allen, Purchasing Agent

AMS SIMPLIFIED LETTER STYLE

Like the full-block letter style, the AMS simplified letter style is relatively easy to type and very formal looking. It has several distinct features.

The AMS simplified letter style:

(1) always includes a subject line in all capital letters and without the word "subject" to identify it. Two blank lines precede and follow the subject line.

(2) often includes enumerated items. One blank line is between the items.

(3) never includes a salutation.

(4) never includes a complimentary close.

(5) always includes the typed name of writer and business title of writer in all capital letters.

The letter may also include special letter parts as needed and desired. Spacing requirements are the same as those for the full-block letter.

You can choose the AMS simplified letter style when speed and high efficiency are important, you believe salutations and complimentary closes are unnecessary, you prefer it, or company policy requires it.

Jack Spencer

JACK SPENCER, PUBLIC RELATIONS

elg

Figure 6-3
AMS Simplified Letter Style

Official Letter Style

The **official letter style** should be saved for the very formal and official message, which is usually directed to a prominent person. It is an adaptation of the modified block style with paragraph indentions. The placement of the inside address is the single variation. It is positioned at the left margin three lines below the writer's typewritten name and business title—instead of below the date. Reference initials appear a double space below the inside address:

Letterwriter Services, Inc.

654 Olive Grove Place
San Diego, CA 92114
619-716-4938

"Our forms give you style"

August 4, 19-- ← Date

Big Company, Inc.
P.O. Box 3158
Austin, TX 78710 ← Inside Address

Attention: Mr. Michael T. Allen
Purchasing Agent ← Attention line

Dear Manufacturer ← Salutation

Subject: Modified Block Style Letter
with Block Paragraphs ← Subject

This example depicts the modified block style letter without paragraph indentions. It is a popular letter style, but it is less formal looking than either the full-block or AMS simplified styles. It also takes longer to type.

The basic letter parts are those included for the full-block style; spacing requirements are also the same. Any special letter part can be added as needed and desired.

When typing this letter style, begin the date and closing section at the horizontal center of the paper. As all letter styles require, begin reference initials, enclosure notations, copy notations, and postscripts at the left margin. ← Body

You can choose the modified block style letter without paragraph indentions when you want less formality than the full-block letter suggests, you prefer it, or company policy requires it.

Yours truly ← Complimentary close

LETTERWRITER SERVICES, INC. ← Company name

Gerald O. Creme ← Signature

Gerald O. Creme ← Typed name of writer
Public Relations ← Business title of writer

GOC:lb ← Reference initials

Figure 6–4
Modified Block Letter Style
without Paragraph Indentions

Respectfully yours,

Stephen A. Mills

Stephen A. Mills

The Honorable Timothy G. Russell
American Ambassador
Paris, France

SAM:cem

Letterwriter Services, Inc.

654 Olive Grove Place
San Diego, CA 92114
619-716-4938

"Our forms give you style"

Date → August 4, 19--

Inside address →
Big Company, Inc.
P.O. Box 3158
Austin, TX 78710

Attention line → Attention: Mr. Michael T. Allen, Purchasing Agent

Salutation → Dear Manufacturer

Subject line →
MODIFIED BLOCK STYLE LETTER WITH
PARAGRAPH INDENTIONS

Body →

This example depicts the modified block style letter with paragraph indentions. It is informal and requires more typing time than the other formal business letter styles.

The only difference between this letter and the modified block letter with block paragraphs is the paragraph indentions. This letter style indents the paragraphs five, six, or seven spaces, as desired by the writer.

You can choose the modified block style letter with paragraph indentions when speed is not the most important consideration, you prefer it, or company policy requires it.

Complimentary close → Yours truly

Company name → LETTERWRITER SERVICES, INC.

Signature → Gerald O. Creme

Typed name of writer → Gerald O. Creme

Business title of writer → Public Relations

Reference initials → lb

Figure 6-5
Modified Block Letter Style with Paragraph Indentions

Other Adaptations

Some writers want to attract the readers' attention by formatting unusual letters and/or using special features. For example, a sales letter may have hanging indented paragraphs. Here, the first line of each paragraph starts at the left margin, the other lines of the paragraph are indented a like number of spaces (five or more) from the margin:

> Tight-fitting lids lock in the food's natural moisture and keep
> it from escaping in steam. This allows foods to cook in
> their own flavorful juices, preserving their goodness.

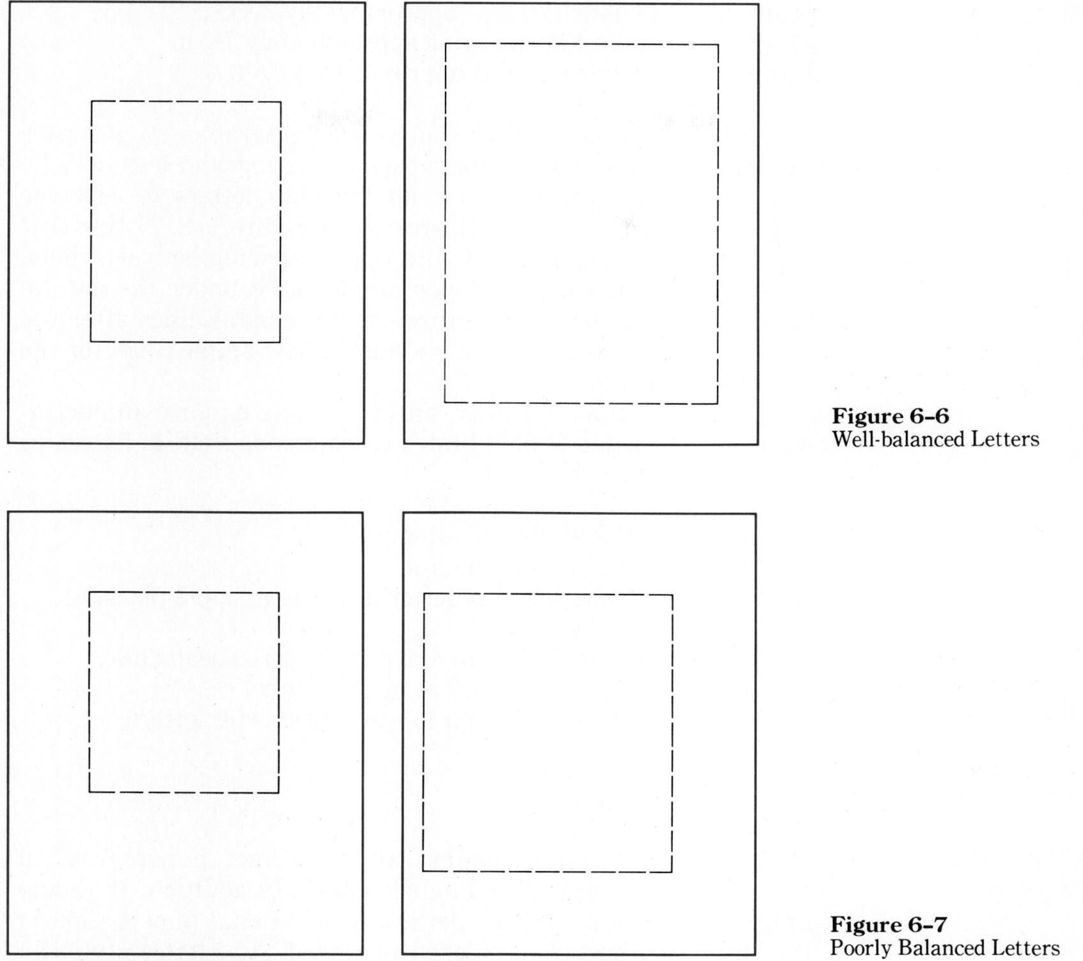

Figure 6–6
Well-balanced Letters

Figure 6–7
Poorly Balanced Letters

ATTRACTIVE LETTER SPACING

Where the personal-business letter is placed on the page will greatly affect its appearance. (See Figures 6–6 and 6–7.) Plan your letter so that the top and bottom margins are equal or approximately equal, although the top margin may be slightly smaller than the bottom margin. No letter should look top heavy or bottom heavy.

Business letters must also be positioned attractively on the page. The letterhead should not interfere. The date should be placed a double space below the letterhead, although this placement can be varied slightly. The left and right side margins should also be fairly equal.

Short letter: Side margins approximately 2 in.
Medium letter: Side margins approximately 1½ in.
Long letter: Side margins approximately 1 in.

Unless the letter is very short—one paragraph—single space the body of the letter. Double space one-paragraph letters only. The spacing requirements for all business letters (except the AMS simplified style) are illustrated in Figure 5–2. Notice that most parts are single spaced with double spacing between them. Three blank line spaces provide ample space under the date to help balance the letter. The three or more blank lines after the complimentary close or company name allow ample room for the writer's signature.

Figure 6–8 from 3M illustrates the way a major manufacturing company in the United States recommends that its letters be typed. Notice that the letter:

1. Illustrates the full-block letter style
2. Illustrates mixed punctuation
3. Emphasizes placement of letter to create a "more pleasing visual effect" by:
   a. Setting left margin to line up with letterhead data
   b. Lining up date with base of 3M symbol
   c. Modifying margins for longer and shorter letters

PUNCTUATION PATTERNS

Every business letter should exhibit correct punctuation in accordance with standard English usage. In addition, it should follow a particular style or pattern of additional punctuation in the salutation and closing: open or mixed. Any letter style can have the open punctuation pattern just as any letter style can have the mixed punctuation pattern. The punctuation style is a matter of preference and has no effect on punctuation within the letter. Correct English and punctuation are always necessary in communications

A glance at the inside address, salutation, or closing section of any letter should reveal the punctuation style used:

Open Punctuation

Open punctuation is very popular. It requires no punctuation after the salutation and complimentary close. (See Figure 6–9.) Standard English punctuation within the body of the letter is required.

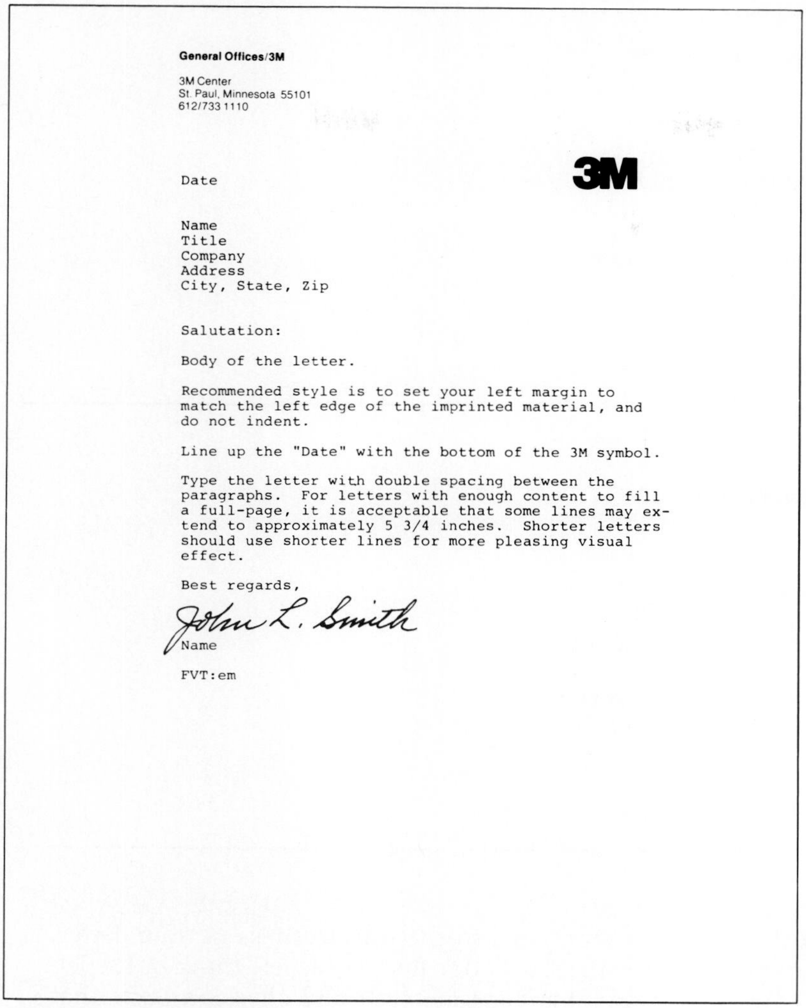

General Offices/3M

3M Center
St. Paul, Minnesota 55101
612/733 1110

3M

Date

Name
Title
Company
Address
City, State, Zip

Salutation:

Body of the letter.

Recommended style is to set your left margin to match the left edge of the imprinted material, and do not indent.

Line up the "Date" with the bottom of the 3M symbol.

Type the letter with double spacing between the paragraphs. For letters with enough content to fill a full-page, it is acceptable that some lines may extend to approximately 5 3/4 inches. Shorter letters should use shorter lines for more pleasing visual effect.

Best regards,

John L. Smith

Name

FVT:em

Figure 6-8
Letter Style Recommended by One Company
Courtesy of 3M, St. Paul, MN

Mixed Punctuation

Mixed punctuation is also popular. It features two additional punctuation marks: one after the salutation and one after the complimentary close. (See Figure 6-10.) To use the mixed punctuation style, add a colon (:) after the salutation and a comma (,) after the complimentary close. For very informal letters, you can substitute a comma for the colon after the salutation.

Closed Punctuation

Closed punctuation is rarely used in this country today, but other countries frequently employ it. It is illustrated in Figure 16-3, where we discuss international communications.

January 10, 19--

A & Z Company
99 Park Avenue
Cleveland, OH 44113

Dear Manufacturer

Very truly yours

Figure 6-9
Open Punctuation

January 10, 19--

A & Z Company
99 Park Avenue
Cleveland, OH 44113

Dear Manufacturer:

Very truly yours,

Figure 6-10
Mixed Punctuation

CHAPTER SUMMARY

The letter style contributes to the effectiveness of your letter. Since you are writing your letter for the reader, think of the letter style as a frame for your message and choose a style that conveys your message appropriately, neatly, attractively, and economically. Business people have accepted several traditional letter styles. Deviate from tradition only if that deviation will help you better achieve your purpose.

Some business firms specify that their employees use certain acceptable letter styles—to establish a routine or to increase efficiency. Such companies usually have style manuals and often specify either the full-block or modified block styles, using either open or mixed punctuation.

The personal-business style is appropriate *only* for personal business and should be typed or written on plain paper (no letterhead).

STUDY QUESTIONS

1. How can letter style affect letter effectiveness?
2. When should you use the personal-business style? When should you use the other letter styles?
3. What is the difference between the full-block and modified block letter styles?
4. How does AMS simplified letter style differ from the full-block style?
5. What are the advantages of the AMS simplified style?
6. When is a letter well-balanced? Poorly-balanced?
7. What are the common punctuation styles used for business letters? Explain the differences.
8. What side margins should you use for the short letter? Medium letter? Long letter?
9. Generally, how many blank lines are used between most letter parts?

ACTIVITIES

1. From memory, make a line layout for each of the following letter styles, label each part, and indicate spacing between parts:
   a. Personal-business
   b. Full-block
   c. Modified block without paragraph indentions
   d. Modified block with paragraph indentions
2. Refer to the text material and carefully check the accuracy of your work for Problem 1. Analyze the differences (if any). If you made a minor error, correct it. If you made a serious error (for example, omitting a part, placing it incorrectly, or labeling it incorrectly) consider redoing all or part of Problem 1.
3. Using the line layouts made for Problem 1, illustrate the following styles:
   a. Full-block letter with open punctuation
   b. Modified block with paragraph indentions with mixed punctuation
   c. Personal-business letter with mixed punctuation.
4. Correct the following information for an AMS simplified letter style:

   Rainbow Roofing Company
   Attention: Mr. Paul Bradley, Acctg. Dept.
   800 South East Street
   Martinsville, IN 46151

   Subject: Invoice No. 2134, October 1, 19--

   Ladies and Gentlemen

   Refer to Chapter 5 if necessary.

5. Correct the following closing section for a modified block style letter:

   Yours truly,

   Miss A. C Newsom

   Miss A. C. Newsom

   acn
   Enclosed is a copy of our letter of April 10, 19--.
   Copy to: Mr. Marvin Stabler, Consultant

6. Correct the following closing sections for full-block letters:

   a. Yours truly

      Miss Michelle Swanson

      Michelle Swanson

   b. Sincerely

      Eric Collins

      Mrs. Eric Collins

   c. Very truly yours
      Brown & Culligan, Inc.

      Thomas Hamilton

      Mr. Thomas Hamilton
      Vice President

   d. Respectfully:

      Harold Jackson

      Mrs. Harold Jackson
      Century Glass Co., Inc.
      Purchasing Agent

EDITING

Correct the following sentences for grammar, punctuation, and sentence construction.

1. This letterhead design is an attractive one, simplistic in design, and represents' Waltere's.
2. The personal-business letter style shows a return address on plain bond stationery, the modified block, letterhead.
3. The AMS simplified letter includes a subject line typed in all capital letters some have attention lines.

4. 1 percent of the letters is written in the AMS style.
5. The open punctuation style requires no additional punctuation, according to tradition.
6. A letter is well balanced when the top and bottom margins are about equal and the side margins are about equal.
7. If margins vary a great deal the letter is poorly-balanced.
8. John typed the AMS letter slow, because he had to check the illustration often.
9. Miss Koo will show slides of her work at 11 o'clock in the morning in Korea.
10. I hope you will attend the stockholders meeting scheduled for the next month.

IN-BASKET SIMULATIONS

1. Secure two current business letters—except sales letters—and analyze each letter in terms of the following points:
   a. Identify basic letter style
   b. Identify punctuation style
   c. Determine whether letter style is correct and appropriate
   d. Critique the letterhead
2. Write a letter to Joe Marion, Director of Drug Operations, submitting a letterhead you propose for the drug division of Waltere Supermarkets, Inc.
3. Write a letter recommending a particular letter style for all Waltere Supermarkets, Inc., correspondence. State specific reasons for your choice. Write your letter to Joe Marion in accordance with the elements of effective writing.

Sending Communications

After studying Chapter 7, you should be able to:

- Distinguish between traditional and electronic mail and use each as appropriate
- Address envelopes for optical scanning and include the proper information on the envelope
- Fold and insert letters properly

Efficiency in business correspondence does not stop with the appropriately formatted, effectively organized and worded, and attractively prepared letter. The message must be transmitted. Messages can be sent **traditionally** in standard business envelopes or **electronically**. At times, a combination of traditional and electronic methods are used.

Even though electronic mail is increasing, most business communications are delivered by the U.S. Postal Service in standard business envelopes. The front of every envelope should include the complete name and address of both sender and receiver, stamps or permits, and special notations for the addressee or postal employees. It is important to address envelopes completely and correctly so that high-speed optical scanning equipment can be used to process mail with minimum handling time, relatively low costs, and few sorting errors. Automated processing requires using acceptable business envelopes and printing the mailing address in the OCR (optical character recognition) area and in accordance with postal regulations. Business firms will find it profitable to use bar coding and facing identification marks for volume mail.

Some organizations use window envelopes—envelopes with a transparent area for the addressee's name and address. This type of envelope is economical for mailing routine and standard business forms such as invoices and statements. At least ¼-in. blank space should border the sides and bottom of the window area.

Electronic mail is convenient and relatively easy to transmit quickly. It can be delivered even on holidays. Depending on the type chosen and its destination, the message can be received within a few minutes, few hours, or two or three days. Some messages are displayed on a video screen and stored for later retrieval; others are delivered in standard business envelopes.

Electronic mail can save the cost of lengthy telephone calls, paper, and labor for traveling, formatting, filing, and retrieving documents. Although paper documents are often the output, electronic mail is contributing to the "paperless office" concept.

Variations of electronic mail include: telegram, mailgram, cablegram, Telex/TWX, computer-based message systems (voice mail and computer letter), communicating word processing systems, and facsimile (FAX).

TRADITIONAL MAILING

Formatting Envelope Data

Although business envelopes come in various sizes and colors, they should be compatible in quality and color with the letterhead. Two popular sizes are:

Size No. 6¾: Measures 3⅝ in. × 6½ in.
Size No. 10: Measures 4⅛ in. × 9½ in.

Sender information belongs in the upper-left corner of the envelope; the envelope flap is not the proper place. Most companies use printed or engraved return information, but it can also be handwritten or typed. A typical return address for envelopes consists of these three lines:

Line 1: Sender's complete name
Line 2: Sender's street address
Line 3: Sender's city or town, Postal Service abbreviation and ZIP code.

See envelope illustrations in this chapter.

Postal employees try to return to senders all mail they cannot deliver to the addressee. However, they deliver undeliverable mail to the only place possible—the Dead Letter Office. Undeliverable mail is mail without a return address or mail with an incomplete return address or mail with an incorrect return or mailing address. Unfortunately, many thousands of undeliverable mailings arrive daily at the Dead Letter Office. Financial losses are tremendous, but the grief and frustration created by undelivered mail cannot be measured.

Postal Service abbreviations. The Postal Service state abbreviations are two capitalized alphabetic letters used to represent the states and possessions of the United States and provinces and territories of Canada. The initials are not to be confused with the standard English abbreviations for the areas. For example, the standard abbreviation for Indiana is Ind.; the Postal Service abbreviation for Indiana is IN (two capital letters without a period following). Instead of spelling out or abbreviating the area's name on envelopes, use the Postal Service abbreviation, as shown in Table 7–1.

ZIP code. The **Zoning Improvement Plan (ZIP) code** quickly identifies the designated mail area. Mail without ZIP codes requires several manual handlings, whereas ZIP coded mail can be sorted rapidly and efficiently with high-speed automated equipment. Presently, over 97% of all mail processed contains a ZIP code.

The original ZIP Code system,* initiated July 1, 1963, has expanded to **ZIP + 4**, a unique system that sorts mail for one side of a city block or both sides of a particular street, one floor in a large building, a cluster of mail boxes, one post office box or

---

*Details on how the five-digit ZIP code originated and developed into the ZIP + 4 are included in the *History of the U. S. Postal Service 1775–1982*, Publication 100, April, 1983, pp. 7, 8, 28, and 29.

Table 7-1
Postal Service Abbreviations

United States (and territories)

Alabama	AL	Montana	MT
Alaska	AK	Nebraska	NE
Arizona	AZ	Nevada	NV
Arkansas	AR	New Hampshire	NH
California	CA	New Jersey	NJ
Canal Zone	CZ	New Mexico	NM
Colorado	CO	New York	NY
Connecticut	CT	North Carolina	NC
Delaware	DE	North Dakota	ND
District of Columbia	DC	Ohio	OH
Florida	FL	Oklahoma	OK
Georgia	GA	Oregon	OR
Guam	GU	Pennsylvania	PA
Hawaii	HI	Puerto Rico	PR
Idaho	ID	Rhode Island	RI
Illinois	IL	South Carolina	SC
Indiana	IN	South Dakota	SD
Iowa	IA	Tennessee	TN
Kansas	KS	Texas	TX
Kentucky	KY	Utah	UT
Louisiana	LA	Vermont	VT
Maine	ME	Virgin Islands	VI
Maryland	MD	Virginia	VA
Massachusetts	MA	Washington	WA
Michigan	MI	West Virginia	WV
Minnesota	MN	Wisconsin	WI
Mississippi	MS	Wyoming	WY
Missouri	MO		

Canadian provinces (and territories)

Alberta	AB	Nova Scotia	NS
British Columbia	BC	Ontario	ON
Labrador	LB	Prince Edward Island	PE
Manitoba	MB	Quebec	PQ
New Brunswick	NB	Saskatchewan	SK
Newfoundland	NF	Yukon Territory	YT
Northwest Territories	NT		

Note: Postal Service abbreviations should be followed with the correct ZIP code. Do not use the abbreviations unless you include the ZIP code.

group of boxes, or other similar limited geographic locations. The ZIP + 4 system was implemented for optional use beginning October 1, 1983. Businesses using the ZIP + 4 enjoy a postage rate discount. An estimated 20 percent of all first-class mail can qualify for ZIP + 4 rates.

To use the ZIP + 4, type the initial five-code ZIP number, a hyphen, and the additional numbers; for example: 11803-9990.

Addressing envelopes for automated equipment. The minimum size envelope for machine processing is 3½ in. high by 5 in. wide; the maximum size is 6⅛ in. high by 11½ in. wide.* These sizes correspond very well with the No. 6¾ and No. 10 business envelopes.

The U. S. Postal Service is using bar coding, facing identification marks, and optical scanning to sort mail faster and more accurately. With **bar coding**, the mailing address on a business reply or business return envelope is translated into a series of vertical bars representing ones and zeros and then printed in the lower-right corner of an envelope. An area ⅝ in. high by 4½ in. long must be kept free for the bar code. **Facing identification marks (FIM)** are placed to the left of the postage area of reply cards and envelopes. They are used on both bar and nonbar business envelopes. According to the U. S. Postal Service, coding permits identification and sorting through special equipment at a much faster rate than can be achieved by manual sorting.† (See Figure 7-1.)

OCR equipment optically scans the envelope address, especially the street name, city or town, state, and ZIP code. The scanner will reprint the ZIP code information as a bar code. Then, letter sorting machines will read automatically the bar code on envelopes being processed.

The OCR read area (see Figure 7-1) should include only address information. To use OCR equipment, do not include underlines, boxes, advertising, computer punch holes, or similar nonprint information. The OCR equipment cannot read italic forms and artistic or script-like writing. Also, characters or numbers within a word or ZIP code should not touch or overlap.

The OCR address area begins no less than 1 in. from the left edge of the envelope in an area 2⅜ in. high × 8 in. wide and within ⅝ in. up from the bottom of the envelope. Thus, you can begin the address near the center of the envelope. For a four- or five-line address, begin slightly higher than the center and to the left of the centerpoint. The bottom ⅝-in. portion is reserved for bar coding. Instruction to postal officials (for example, "Special Delivery" or "Registered") should be noted below the postage stamp or imprint.

**Modern Mailroom Practices*, United States Postal Service Publication 62, February, 1981, p. 4.

†Technical guidelines for bar code and facing identification marks are contained in U. S. Postal Service *Bar Code and FIM Printing Guidelines*, Bulletin 12, March, 1984. The Postal Service Customer Service Representative will aid firms desiring to use bar coding by providing the bar code negatives and working closely with company personnel and their envelope printer.

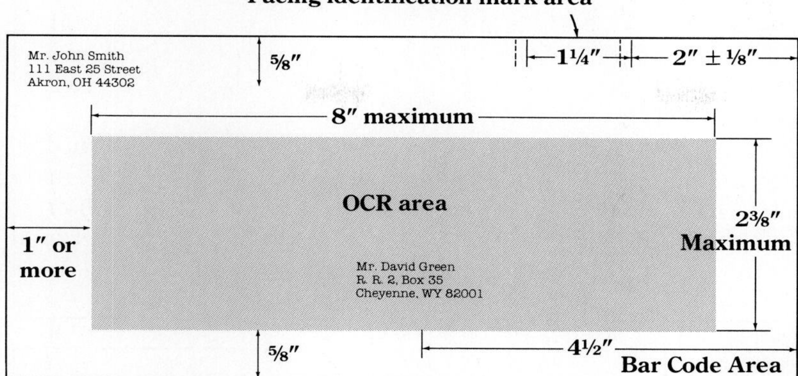

Figure 7-1
Addressed Envelope

The envelope address generally corresponds with the letter's inside address. However, for OCR equipment, the envelope address must be single-spaced and in block style only. Envelopes may be addressed using all capital letters and omitting punctuation marks. Most street addresses consist of the following three lines:

Line 1: Complete name of addressee
Line 2: Space number and street name, followed by necessary unit (apartment, room, office, or suite number)
Line 3: City or town, Postal Service abbreviation, and ZIP code.

Any nonaddress data, such as account numbers or dates, should be placed above the first line of the mailing address. For example:

XYZ 2200-1-2-3-04
GENERAL MFG CORP
ATTN MR ALAN WHITE
500 N ADAMS ST RM 219
WASHINGTON DC 20004-6789

Company logos may appear in the OCR area, but must not fall on or below the delivery address line.

The Postal Service has approved **dual addressing**, the arrangement of both a street address and a box number on different lines. However, mail will be delivered to the lower of the two address lines. For example:

The A & Z Company
1114 Avenue of the Americas
Post Office Box 55
New York, NY 10036

The A & Z Company
Post Office Box 55
1114 Avenue of the Americas
New York, NY 10036

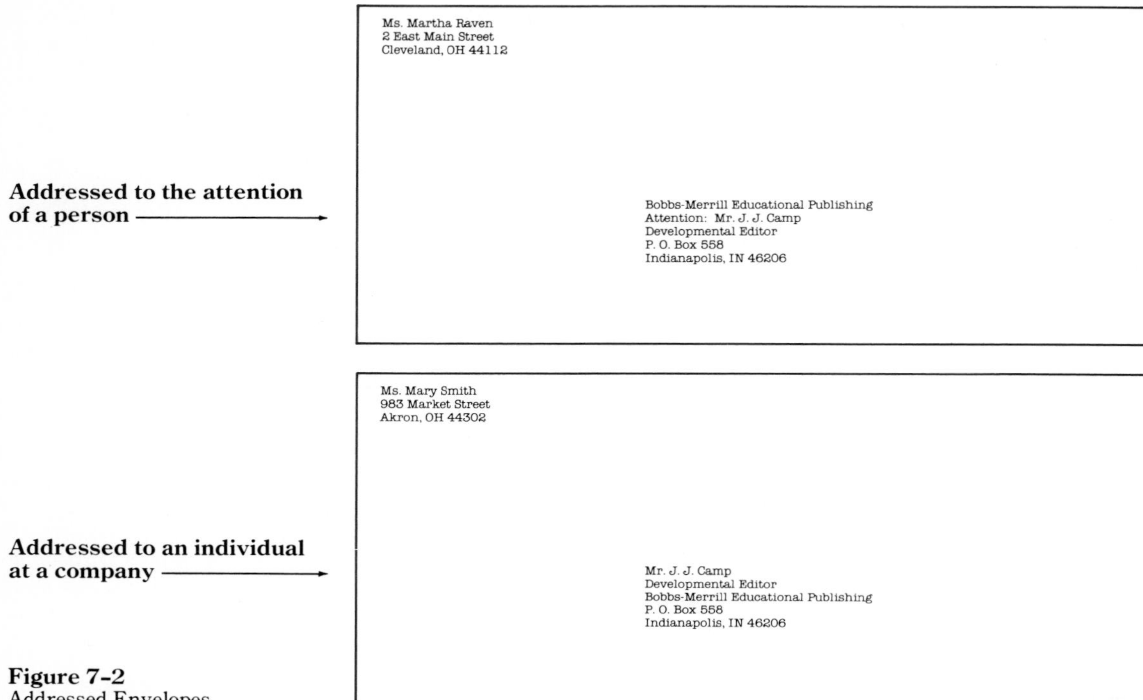

Ms. Martha Raven
2 East Main Street
Cleveland, OH 44112
Addressed to the attention of a person
Bobbs-Merrill Educational Publishing
Attention: Mr. J. J. Camp
Developmental Editor
P. O. Box 558
Indianapolis, IN 46206
Ms. Mary Smith
983 Market Street
Akron, OH 44302
Addressed to an individual at a company
Mr. J. J. Camp
Developmental Editor
Bobbs-Merrill Educational Publishing
P. O. Box 558
Indianapolis, IN 46206

Figure 7-2
Addressed Envelopes

When addressing foreign mail, the country name must appear in full and in capital letters as the last line of the address:

ITALY FRANCE MEXICO

Figures 7-2 and 7-3 illustrate envelopes addressed properly for handling by OCR equipment.

A letter's attention line should be included in the envelope's address. Place the attention line below the firm's name—usually the third line from the bottom. (Recall that the attention line for a letter appears a double space below the inside address.) Note the placement of the attention line on an envelope in Figure 7-2.

For machine processing, the U. S. Postal Service accepts envelopes addressed in all capital letters *and* without punctuation marks. See, for example, the two envelopes in Figure 7-3. However, using automated equipment limits the line length for any one line of an address. U.S. Postal Service publications 65 and 65-A (*National ZIP Code and Post Office Directories*, 1984) lists three sets of abbreviations:

1. Abbreviations for names of streets, roads, and general instructions

MRS. J. C. KELLEY
7605 EAST WALNUT STREET
FALLS CHURCH, VA 22042

LTV CORP
P O BOX 5003
DALLAS TX 75222

← **All capitals, no punctuation, addressed to company box number**

Mr. Walter Bates
4000 Palm Street
New York, NY 10017

PERSONAL

REGISTERED

Doctor A. D. Dunne, Chairman
Music Department
Ball State University
Music Bldg., Room 103
Muncie, IN 47306

← **University building as street address**

Mrs. J. E. Perez
575 Rosehill Drive
Simonton, TX 77476

Mr. Joseph Zappia
14 via Veneto
Rome, ITALY

← **Foreign mail—country name in all capitals**

Mr. Jack Henderson
254 North Hamilton Avenue
Camby, IN 46113

Miss Mae C. Boothe
In care of Mr. and Mrs. J. Boothe
345 Maine Avenue, N.W.
Glenville, IL 60025

← **In care of**

Figure 7-3
Addressed Envelopes

2. Abbreviations for cities, towns, and specific places
3. Abbreviations for states

In line with these publications, Palos Verdes Peninsula, California can be abbreviated PLS VRD PNSLA CA. A few of the abbreviated forms that can be used to shorten long lines in the mailing address are listed below:

APT	for Apartment	N	for North
ATTN	for Attention	R	for Rural
BLVD	for Boulevard	RM	for Room
E	for East	RT	for Route
EXPY	for Expressway	RV	for River
HTS	for Heights	STA	for Station
HOSP	for Hospital	TPKE	for Turnpike
INST	for Institute	VLG	for Village

Folding and Inserting Letters into Envelopes

Proper folding of communications saves reader handling time. How to fold the letter depends upon the size and type of envelope you use.

No. 10 envelope. Standard stationery requires two folds:

1. Fold the lower portion about one third of the way up and crease neatly
2. Bring top portion down leaving about ¼ in. free (for a thumb nail to slip under when unfolding the letter) and crease neatly

To insert folded letter into the envelope, hold envelope in your left hand with the gummed flap to your right, then enclose folded letter with your right hand so that open edge of letter is inserted last. Figure 7-4 illustrates how to fold and insert a letter into a No. 10 envelope.

No. 6¾ envelope. Standard stationery requires three folds:

1. Fold the lower portion to about ¼ in. to the top of the letter and crease neatly
2. Fold right section to the left about one-third of the width and crease neatly
3. Fold left part to within ¼ in. of right edge and crease neatly

Place folded letter into the envelope so that open edge of letter is inserted last. Figure 7-5 illustrates how to fold and insert a letter into a No. 6¾ envelope.

Window envelope. When window envelopes are used, the inside address of the communication is positioned to match the

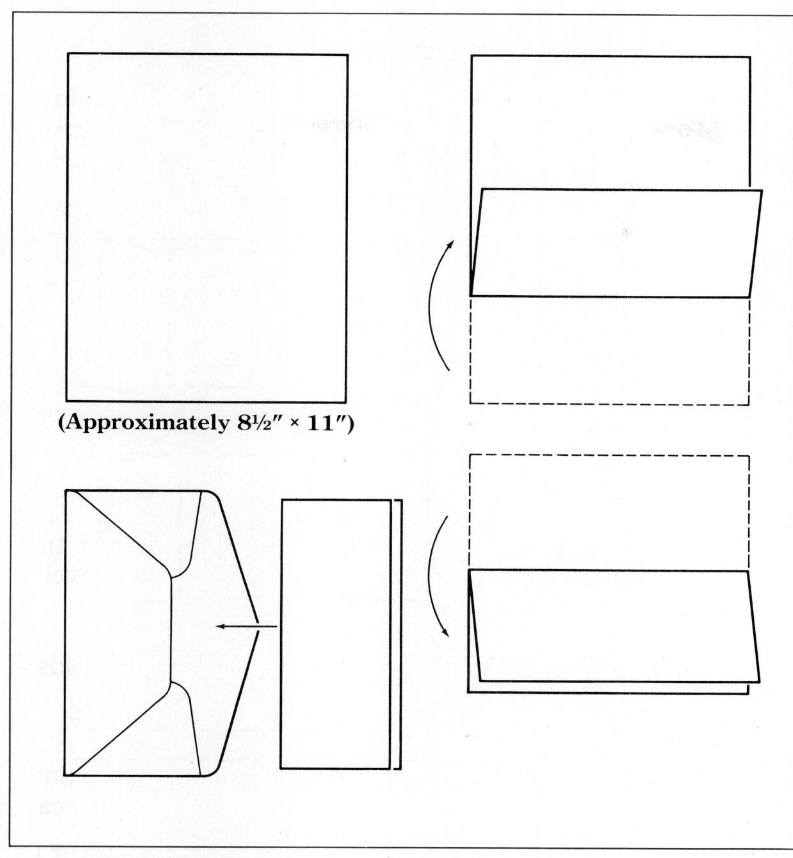

Step 1: **Place the page before you so that you can easily read it.**

Step 2: **Fold up the lower portion to slightly less than one-third of the entire sheet. Crease the fold neatly.**

Step 3: **Fold down the top portion to within ¼″ of the previous fold. Crease the fold neatly.**

Step 4: **Hold the envelope in your left hand so that the gummed flap points to the right. With your right hand, insert the folded pages into the envelope—last fold first.**

Figure 7–4
Folding and Inserting Letter into a No. 10 Envelope (4⅛ in. × 9½ in.)

location of the window. Fold communication for window envelopes so that the mailing address appears through the transparent area with at least a ¼-in. blank space around the bottom and sides of the window area. Standard size stationery requires two folds:

1. Fold the lower portion about one-third of the way up and crease neatly
2. Fold, with inside address facing you, the top portion under toward the first fold and crease neatly so that the inside address is on top

Place folded letter into envelope so that the inside address will appear in the window area (Figure 7–6).

Window envelopes are often used for sending out large quantities of routine business mail—bills, invoices, purchase orders, statements, and even report cards. Some communications require no folding or only one fold before insertion.

Step 1: Place the page before you so that you can easily read it.

Step 2: Fold up the lower portion to within 1/4″ of top of the entire sheet. Crease the fold neatly.

Step 3: Fold (to the left) the right-hand part of the page to slightly less than one-third of the width. Crease the fold neatly.

Step 4: Fold left part to within 1/4″ of the edge. Crease the fold neatly.

Step 5: Hold the envelope in your left hand so that the gummed flap points to the right. With your right hand, insert the folded pages into the envelope—last fold first.

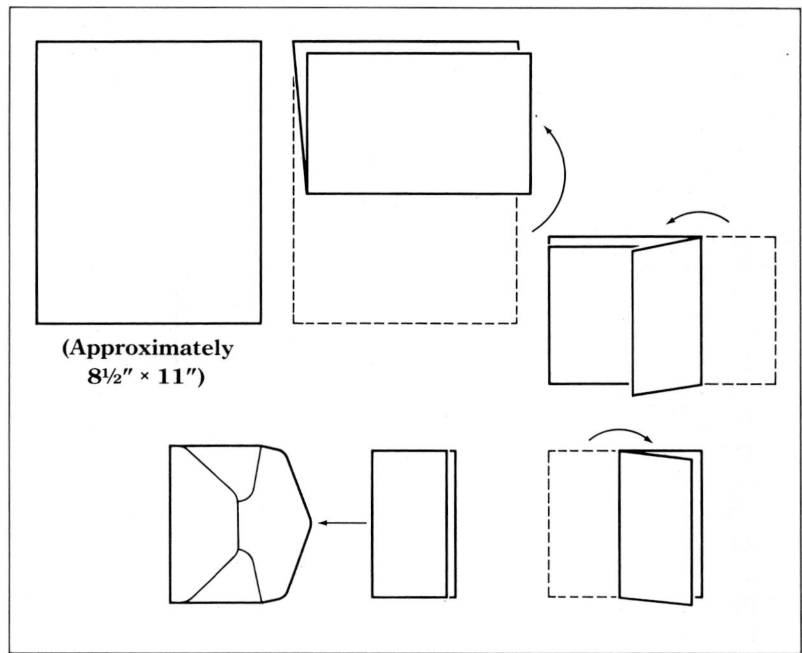

Figure 7-5
Folding and Inserting Letter into a No. 6¾ Envelope (6½ in. × 3⅝ in.)

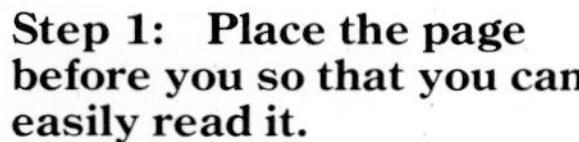

Step 1: Place the page before you so that you can easily read it.

Step 2: Fold up the lower portion to slightly less than one-third of the entire sheet. Crease neatly.

Step 3: Fold top portion back about one-third. Turn over letter. Inside address should be visible. Crease neatly.

Step 4: Hold the envelope in your left hand with the window on top. With your right hand, insert the folded pages into the envelope keeping address on top.

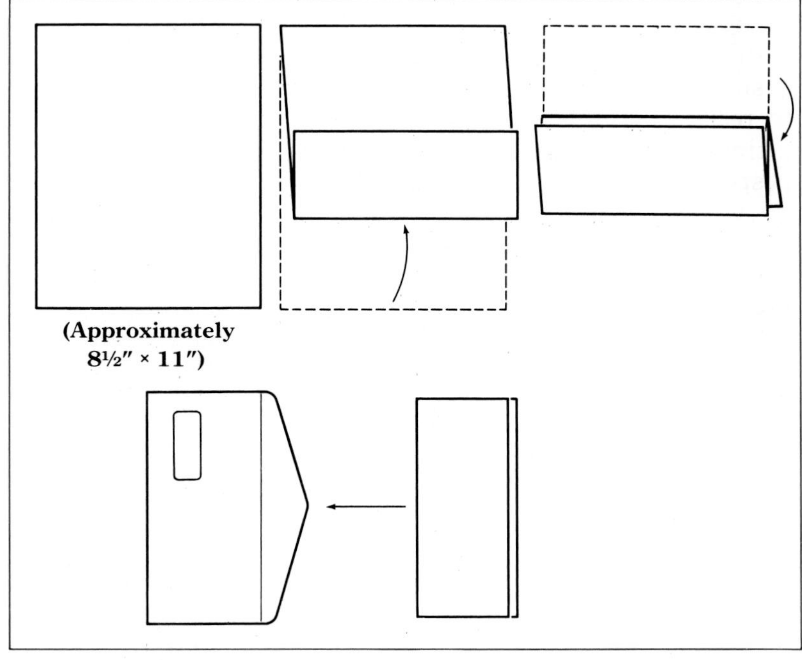

Figure 7-6
Folding and Inserting Letter into a No. 10 Window Envelope (9½ in. × 3⅛ in.)

ELECTRONIC MAIL

An Explanation

Electronic mail is a way to send written or printed information by electronic means (for example, a computer, word processor, typewriter, telephone, or Telex/TWX). It is often considered faster, more efficient, more convenient, and more reliable than other traditional mailing.

The wide acceptance of electronic mail is the result of the widespread and increased use of computers and word-processing equipment and the necessary **software** or computer programs, a series of instructions of what to do and when that are stored in the main memory unit of the computer. The technology and expertise to transmit, process, and display information have also played a major role in the growing use of electronic mail. Regardless of the destination, the terminal-to-terminal message arrives in minutes. In addition, the sender has complete control over where (and sometimes, when) the message is received. Both sender and receiver have written records of their correspondence.

Business, government, and society have been demanding all kinds of information quickly. Thus, electronic message systems with electronic filing capabilities are vital in today's offices. The computer can store pages of information on an **auxiliary storage unit** (diskette or hard disk). A hard disk can store 10 million or more characters, which can be retrieved when convenient. Besides encouraging time management, the computer saves paper, which can be expensive, and filing, storage, and retrieval costs.

Electronic mail correspondents must learn to access common electronic mail commands. Specific features will vary with the system. Nonetheless, many business people are looking for ways to reduce time spent on text-document related activities. It is estimated that approximately 25 percent of a professional's time is spent creating or waiting for information.

Electronic Mail Systems

Common electronic mail includes the telegram, mailgram,* cablegram, Telex/TWX, computer-based message systems, communicating word-processing systems, and facsimile messages.

Telegram. The Western Union Telegraph Company has provided electronic message service with the telegram for more than a century. The **telegram** is a short, concise message sent by telephone or Telex to any domestic location. Telephone telegrams can be confirmed later with a hardcopy. To save money, words for telegrams should be kept to a minimum and chosen carefully.

---

*Mailgram is a registered trademark of Western Union Corporation.

Mailgram. The **mailgram** is an electronic communication service offered by Western Union and the U. S. Postal Service. One or thousands of written messages can be sent overnight for early morning delivery in the United States and other countries. Western Union provides a toll-free telephone network throughout the United States, so senders can telephone Western Union, dictate messages, and be assured that their messages will be delivered. However, mailgrams can also be sent over Telex terminals, by direct computer connection with Western Union, or by submitting a computer magnetic tape. If an answer is needed quickly, a **business reply message** can be sent in a specially marked envelope.

Cablegram. Like the mailgram, a **cablegram** (an international telegram) can be sent overnight through Western Union—to an overseas correspondent. Telegrams, mailgrams, and cablegrams can be transmitted even if the recipient does not have a Telex terminal.

Telex. Western Union's **Telex** (a teletypewriter network) terminals transmit and receive messages quickly and easily throughout the United States and many foreign countries. Subscribers can send messages any time—even when the receiving terminal is not attended. Telex costs are based on transmission time, so it is important to plan messages.

To send a Telex message, the message is entered on teletype equipment, which, in turn, punches a tape. The message is sent as soon as the operator is sure it is formatted correctly. The sender can get an automatic confirmation that the correct person at the receiving terminal picked up the message. This is called **answer-back**; it guards against sending your message to an incorrect receiver.

When speed and a written record are important, Telex may be the best way to send a message. A hardcopy of the message is received at the terminal as soon as it is sent. Messages can be transmitted in a few minutes.

If a mailing list is to be used repeatedly, it should be stored in the Western Union computer. Thus, messages can be automatically addressed without retyping addresses, cutting down errors and typing time.

International Telex. **International Telex** is usually less expensive than a telephone call, and it can be more convenient to communicators. Since messages can be received when the Telex terminal is unattended, international Telex is especially useful for solving time-zone communication problems.

Computer-based message systems. **Computer-based message systems** are designed to handle short, typed messages. Message input and output can be from keyboard-type terminals or word processors. A video screen can display the electronic message. Senders can transmit messages at their convenience; receivers can accept or "read" their electronic messages at their convenience. Thus, the messages can be received immediately, a few hours later, or even days later—unlike telephone conversations, which require simultaneous communication. In addition, individuals can access their **electronic mailboxes** either from public terminals, which are available in major cities, or with their own portable terminals.

Voice mail is a computer-based message system that uses the telephone for input and output. Messages can be stored for later retrieval.

Computer letters are computer-generated letters mailed with supporting materials such as printed forms or printed publications. Within approximately three days, the receiver can receive the data.

The computer letter may be sent with brochures describing new products or services, annual reports to stockholders, direct mail advertising literature to potential and present customers, fund-raising information to potential donors, and other data to whomever the sender chooses.

Communicating word-processing systems. **Communicating word-processing systems** can be used to prepare and transmit letters and other business documents. The sender can type, review, and revise the document until it is ready to be transmitted on a video screen or reproduced in printed form. An average page can be communicated in just a few seconds for much less than Telex or telephone costs. A chief disadvantage is the relatively high cost for equipment and software; however, if a firm plans to transmit thousands of items monthly, the expenditure may be justified. The equipment can also be rented. With a personal computer network, a supervisor can communicate a message to all subordinates at her or his convenience with the assurance that the message will arrive at its destination. The receiver can display all messages at one time.

Facsimile messages. **Facsimile (FAX)** transmits and receives reproductions of a page, by means of a special light that scans the original material and converts the images into electronic pulses. The pulses travel over conventional telephone lines and are then converted into the original visual image. This communication method is best to communicate difficult material in a hurry and when only one copy is required by the receiver. Facsimile-produced materials do not copy well. Typewritten material, photographs, complicated charts and graphs, and neat black ballpoint pen or heavy lead pencil drawings transmit well. Data can be transmitted in a few minutes. Because a FAX is sent over telephone lines, charges are similar to those for telephone calls. Therefore, the longer it takes to transmit the document, the more expensive it will be. Facsimile message service is useful for sending orders, invoices, legal documents, financial statements, customs documents, drawings, and various other business papers.

International FAX messages. **International FAX** message service is available between the United States and several foreign countries. The original document and a transmittal form are scanned by a facsimile reader and transmitted by satellite. A black and white image of the document is printed in the destination country, placed in an envelope, and delivered.

CHAPTER SUMMARY

Your message deserves careful and proper handling whether it is mailed in an envelope or sent electronically or a combination of both.

If you decide to send your communications in traditional envelopes, select an appropiate business envelope and address it completely and correctly so that it reaches its destination (rather than the Dead Letter Office) without delay. Following basic mail procedures can speed delivery and cut costs.

To accommodate automated equipment (such as Optical Character Recognition equipment), use standard-size business envelopes and address them according to postal stipulations: single spaced, block style, printed or typed, complete and accurately placed information, Postal Service abbreviations and ZIP codes.

Businesses sending large-volume mail should consider using ZIP + 4, bar coding, and facing identification marks. The vertical bars placed in the lower right-hand corner (bar coding) or near top-right corner (FIM) of business reply envelopes and cards enable automatic and quick mail sorting, saving time and money for both the U.S. Postal Service and the business using its service.

Properly folding and inserting your letters into appropriate size and style envelopes makes it easier for readers to unfold the letter quickly. This routine will translate as a professional, efficient, and courteous finishing touch to all mailed communications.

Messages can be sent electronically by using the company's office equipment or the services of private business firms including Western Union and the United States Postal Service. The electronic transmission of messages can be as common as the telephone and Telex terminals or as sophisticated as computer terminals and satellites.

Electronic mail can be delivered relatively quickly and conveniently anywhere in the United States and in many foreign countries. Communications can be routine (such as invoices) or personalized for the individual receiver. The message may be displayed on a video screen, stored for later retrieval, or received in a standard business envelope.

STUDY QUESTIONS

1. Why is it important to choose the best way to transmit messages?
2. Why is the proper selection of transmitting messages important to letterwriters?
3. Where should each of the following be placed on an envelope:
   a. Sender's (return) name and address
   b. Addressee's name and address
   c. Postage stamp
   d. Mailing instructions
   e. Instructions to addressee
   f. Attention line
   g. Apartment number
   h. Bar code
   i. FIM
4. Why does the United States Postal Service recommend using Postal Service abbreviations for states and territories, special abbreviations, and the ZIP code in the mailing address?
5. Explain each of the following and how they help letterwriters:
   a. ZIP code
   b. ZIP + 4
   c. Bar coding and FIM
   d. Optical scanning
6. In what format must the addressee's name and address be typed for processing by OCR equipment?
7. What is electronic mail? Explain why you should plan messages sent by Telex.
8. How is the computer used for sending electronic mail?
9. Describe the facsimile (FAX) message service.
10. Which electronic form would you use to forward an annual report?

ACTIVITIES

1. On a plain sheet of paper, draw a rectangle to represent a No. 10 envelope. Label the "envelope" to show placement of:
   a. Sender's address area
   b. OCR area
   c. Bar code read area
   d. Facing identification mark area
   e. Postage area
2. Properly address an envelope for optical scanning to the B. F. Goodrich Co., 500 South Main Street, Akron, Ohio 44318. Remember to include your complete return address.
3. Address envelopes for each of the following situations so that they can be read and sorted by automated equipment.
   a. Individual living in Apartment 208, 2020 East Tenth Avenue, Southfield, Michigan 48077, Registered Mail
   b. Individual living in Apt. 201 of the University Center Apartments in Stamford, Connecticut 06902
   c. Individual living in a rural community with rural route and box number
   d. Married couple living at 141 Spring Street, New York City, 10016
   e. Friend whose current address you do not have (address envelope to him or her in care of parents)
4. Address envelopes for optical scanning for each of the following situations:
   a. Minnesota Mining & Mfg. Co., 3M Center, St. Paul, Minnesota 55101
   b. Mrs. Marianne Sultan at Minnesota Mining & Mfg. Co. (Include Mrs. Sultan's business title, Personnel Director)
   c. Minnesota Mining & Mfg. Co., attention of Mrs. Marianne Sultan, Personnel Director
   d. Minnesota Mining & Mfg. Co., attention of Engineering Department
   e. Vice-President (you do not know exact name), Litton Industries, 360 North Crescent Drive, Beverly Hills, California 90210
   f. Mr. John A. Reyburn, President of Eaton Corporation, 100 Erieview Plaza, Cleveland, Ohio 44114, Special Delivery
   g. Dr. M. B. Colter, Assistant Dean of the School of Business at Indiana State University, Terre Haute, Indiana
   h. Ms. Mary A. Martin; Hotel Americana; 360 Main Street, N.W.; Los Angeles, California 90042; Hold for Arrival
5. Using paper 8½ in. × 11 in. to represent letterhead, fold it for a No. 6¾ envelope.

6. Using paper 8½ in. × 11 in. to represent letterhead, fold it for a No. 10 envelope.
7. Using paper 8½ in. × 11 in. to represent letterhead, fold it for a No. 10 window envelope so that the mailing address would appear in the window area.
8. Using paper 8½ in. × 5½ in. to represent an invoice ready for mailing, fold it for a window envelope so that the mailing address would appear in the window area.
9. Visit a main post office in your area and request complimentary literature such as:
   a. Local ZIP code list
   b. State identification initials and special abbreviations list
   c. Bar coding information
   d. Information on addressing envelopes for OCR equipment
   e. Information on ZIP + 4
   f. Information on FIM

EDITING

Correct the following envelope addresses so that they can be read and sorted by automated equipment:

1. Mr. & Mrs. Jane Andrews
One Main Street
Utica Building, Apart. 231
Portland, OR 97213
2. Basic Products Company 300 East
Tenth Avenue Salt Lake
City, Utah 84104
3. OFFICE OF OPERATIONS
US POSTAL SERVICE
WASHINGTON, D.C. 20260-7140
4. *Miller Mfg. Co., Inc.*
213 Main Street
Augusta, Ga 30903
5. Mr. Gerald Brooks
Memorial Hospital, Room 813B
55 Riverside Avenue
Racine, Wisconsin
53405
6. Ms. Mary Elizabeth Tucker
Lakeview Apartments
Apartment 164
Raleigh, *NC* 27608
7. Mrs. Sandra Wilson
Audio-Systems, Inc.
Accounting Department
918 North 12th Street
Providence, RI 02904

8. Please respond immediately
   Mrs. Margaret Liston
   Holiday travel Lodge
   P.O. Box 525, Rt. 1
   New Orleans, Louisiana 70813
9. Dr. Mary Ellen Dance, Ph. D.
   Professor of Biology
   City University
   219 College Avenue, North West
   Montgomery, AL 36103
10. Vice President and General Manager
    Regent Paper Industries
    Attention of Mr. John J. Hendricks
    2190 M Street
    Kansas City, KN 66104

SPECIAL READINGS

A Consumer's Directory of Postal Services and Products. Washington, D.C.: United States Postal Service, Publication 201, November, 1983.

Addressing for Automation. Washington, D.C.: United States Postal Service, Notice 221, July, 1983.

Addressing for Optical Character Recognition. Washington, D.C.: United States Postal Service, Notice 165, July, 1982.

Bar Code and FIM Printing Guidelines. Washington, D.C.: United States Postal Service, Publication 12, March, 1984.

Converting Your Address Files to ZIP + 4 Codes. Washington, D.C.: United States Postal Service, Notice 260, January, 1984.

Four Services. Washington, D.C.: United States Postal Service, Notice 220, June, 1983.

Guide to Addressing. Washington, D.C.: United States Postal Service, Notice 23-A, July, 1982.

History of the U.S. Postal Service, 1775-1982. Washington, D.C.: United States Postal Service, Publication 100, April, 1983.

INTELPOST—International Electronic Post. Washington, D.C.: United States Postal Service, Publication 252, October 1, 1981.

Mailer's Guide. Washington, D.C.: United States Postal Service, Publication 19, May, 1982.

Modern Mailroom Practices. Washington, D.C.: United States Postal Service, Publication 62, February, 1981.

National ZIP Code and Post Office Directory. Washington D.C.: United States Postal Service, Publications 65 and 65-A, January, 1984.

ZIP + 4 What's In It for Business Mailers. Washington, D.C.: United States Postal Service, Notice 186, January, 1982.

Applications of Writing Ideas—Letters, Memoranda, Etc.

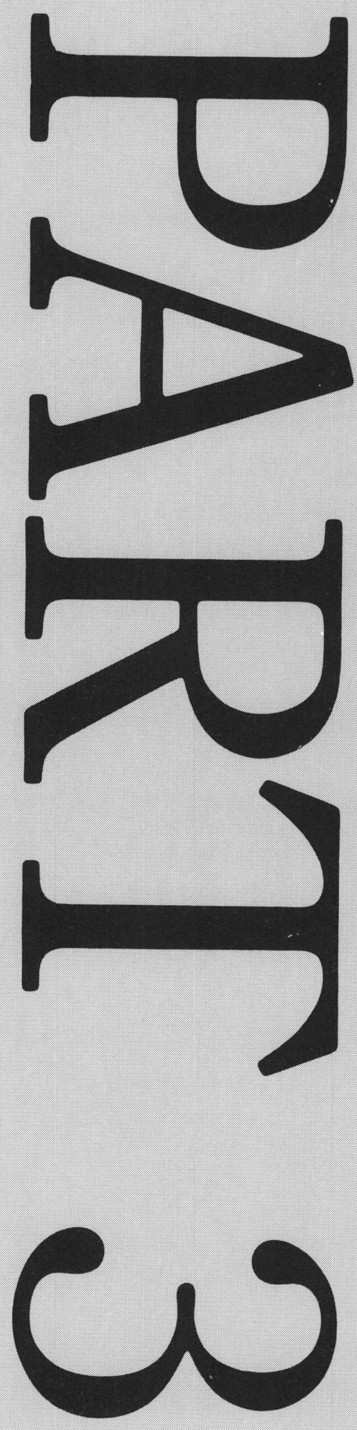

8 Writing Routine Requests, Claims, and Positive Responses

After studying Chapter 8, you should be able to:

- Write effective routine requests and claims
- Write positive responses
- Determine when to use form statements, paragraphs, and letters

Everyone at some time needs to write letters requesting information, materials, or service; letters seeking adjustments; or letters supplying information or materials. Most letters involve routine situations; however, some do require considerable persuasive language to achieve the purpose.

Businesses and governmental offices expect to receive routine inquiries and requests. They also expect consumers to notify them when service is below normal expectations or when products do not perform as designed or expected with normal use. In addition, they realize that letterwriters expect answers to their requests and complaints and helpful information for using products or services. Most organizations are eager to comply to help educate the public, build goodwill, and promote their own interests.

Routine requests can be answered with direct replies. All answers, however, should be personal, courteous, and complete. It is possible to devise form paragraphs or form letters that exhibit these qualities. But when standardized paragraphs do not sufficiently answer the request, an original reply must be constructed.

The general principles of letter writing apply to letters involving routine business situations. However, there are specific techniques for getting prompt results: using a direct approach; giving all the facts briefly, concisely, and courteously in language understood and accepted by the reader; and requesting a fair adjustment for claims.

REQUESTS AND CLAIMS

Requests for Routine Information

Routine inquiry letters ask for information about prices or payments, products or services, people or places. Routine request letters ask for literature, copies of catalogs, booklets, and other products. When writing the **routine request or inquiry letter**:

1. *State the purpose of the letter immediately*. A direct approach provides a convenience to the reader and a guard against misunderstandings. Flattery or complimentary remarks may distract or confuse the reader and do not belong in routine business letters.
2. *Give all necessary facts so that the reader can understand and act accordingly*. Do not expect the reader to telephone or write you for explanatory information. Mention the reason for your inquiry if appropriate.
3. *Make the letter short.* Prepare two or three concise paragraphs addressed to a specific person or department responsible for fulfilling the request.
4. *Write tactfully and courteously* even when you expect the reader to welcome your interest in the products or services.

111 Weir Drive
Indianapolis, IN 46201
January 3, 19--

Director of Admissions
Center State University
190 North Drive
Cleveland, OH 44101

Dear Director of Admissions:

Purpose and facts → Please mail me an application blank for admission to the Master of Arts program in Business Education.

Action → I would like to begin graduate studies in Fall Semester, 19--.

Yours truly,

Mary Doe

Ms. Mary Doe

Figure 8–1
Routine Request for Application Blank

111 Weir Drive
Indianapolis, IN 46201
January 3, 19--

Registrar
Ball State University
Muncie, IN 47306

Dear Registrar:

Purpose → Please mail a certified transcript of my college credits to:

Facts →
Director of Admissions
Center State University
190 North Drive
Cleveland, OH 44101

Action → I would like to begin graduate studies in Fall Semester, 19--.

Yours truly,

Mary Doe

Ms. Mary Doe

Figure 8–2
Routine Request for College Transcript

111 Weir Drive
Indianapolis, IN 46201
January 13, 19--

Miss Kathleen A. Edwards
Director of Admissions
Center State University
190 North Drive
Cleveland, OH 44101

Dear Miss Edwards:

May I begin graduate studies in Fall Semester, 19--? ← **Purpose**

Here are my check for $5 and an application for admission to the Master of Arts program in Business Education. ← **Facts**

Ball State University will be mailing you an official copy of my transcript of credits. ← **Action**

Very truly yours,

Mary Doe

Ms. Mary Doe

Enclosures: 2

Figure 8–3
Routine Request for Admission to University

5. *Close with a courteous, confident statement,* but do not thank in advance. To do so implies that you are making a demand, rather than a request or inquiry.

Suppose that after careful study of several graduate programs, an individual decides to enroll in the Master of Arts program at Center State University. A recent catalog for the university indicated: (1) applications for graduate studies should be requested from the Director of Admissions; (2) application blank must be submitted with a $5 application fee; and (3) applicant should request the registrar of each college or university from which he or she has graduated to send a transcript of credits directly to the Office of Admissions.

The application process should begin with three routine letters: one requesting an application blank (Figure 8–1); one requesting a transcript (Figure 8–2); and one requesting admission (Figure 8–3). If the college/university stipulates a fee for

---

Reservations Manager
Vacation Motor-Inn Corporation
99 Center Street
Memphis, TN 38101

Dear Reservation Manager:

Purpose, necessary facts, and action. →

Please mail us instructions for Phone-A-Reservation and a copy of the free directory as advertised in the January issue of Telephone News.

Yours truly,

Figure 8-4
Routine Request for Printed Information

Mrs. Marianne Adams
Superior Products Company
91 East 71 Street
Peru, IN 46970

Dear Mrs. Adams:

Purpose → Please complete the enclosed credit questionnaire and return it in the addressed and stamped envelope.

Details → In reviewing your file, we notice that we lack current bank, trade, and financial data and would appreciate your helping us update this information.

Action → As always, all information will be kept confidential in the Credit Department.

Sincerely yours,

M.B. Walker

M.B. Walker, Credit

cb

Enclosures: Credit Questionnaire
Envelope

Figure 8-5
Routine Request to Complete Credit Form

---

certified transcripts, a check for the correct amount should be enclosed with the letter that asks for the transcript. If a fee is charged, the letter in Figure 8-3 should have included (after the mailing information) a statement similar to: "Enclosed is a $2 check for the transcript." Notice that each letter states the request, then follows with the necessary details. Each is short

February 25, 19--

Mr. J.W. Hartley
Hayes Regional Aboretum
Richmond, IN 47374

Dear Jay

Please identify the soft-bodied insects and examine the corrugated paper which I am mailing to you. The insects appear to be Collembola, but the background information is rather puzzling. ← **Purpose**

The items were supplied by Eleanor Walter. Her husband, who is in the pest control business, obtained the material in the general area of Butte. She mentioned that the corrugated paper had come from Japan. ← **Facts**

Will you please give us your expert opinion regarding the identification of the insects? Can we assume that the presence of these insects involves risk of damage to furniture, rugs, and so on? ← **Reason**

Please telephone me if you need additional information. ← **Action**

Sincerely yours

Richard E. Silversmith

Richard E. Silversmith, Director
Public Health Entomology Laboratory

jld

Copy to: Mrs. Eleanor Walter

Figure 8–6
Routine Inquiry for Expert Information from a Friend

and complete and written in personal-business letter form.

Routine requests take many forms. A routine request letter may be similar to the double-spaced, one-paragraph letter shown in Figure 8–4. The writer need not specifically explain why he or she wants the instructions and the free directory. The letter in Figure 8–5 illustrates a routine request for financial data in order to bring a customer's file up to date. Readers are more apt to supply credit information if it is to be kept confidential. The letter in Figure 8–6 illustrates a letter requesting an expert opinion from a friend. Notice that the salutation is very informal—the reader's nickname. Therefore, the action requested, "Please telephone *me*," is better than, "Please telephone *us*," even though letterhead is used.

Mr. Silversmith plans to give a copy of the letter to Mrs. Elizabeth Walter, the other person concerned. This procedure saves time and costs for communicating directly with Mrs. Walter to tell her the action taken. To expedite a reply, Mr. Silversmith might also enclose a duplicate letter and ask Mr. Hartley to make comments on the bottom of the copy and return it in the addressed and stamped envelope, also enclosed.

Requests for Hotel/Motel Reservations

While it is faster to make hotel or motel reservations by telephone, some hotels may require mail reservations. **Letters requesting room reservations** follow a plan similar to the plan for routine request letters:

1. *Use a definite reservations statement in the first sentence* (deductive approach). This statement might begin, "Please reserve a room. . . ."
2. *Include all the particulars about the reservation.* Indicate the names of people involved, type of room(s), and dates desired. If the arrival time may be after check-in-time, request "late arrival" and state the expected arrival time. Otherwise, the room may not be available when desired. Some hotels and motels require advance payment to hold rooms. To do so, enclose a check, or specify a credit card name and number.
3. *State group affiliation*, if attending a group meeting at the hotel/motel. Sometimes special arrangements or special prices are available to conference participants staying at the host hotel or motel.
4. *Ask for a written confirmation of the request.* A confirmation is simply an acknowledgment of the reservation. The confirmation does not guarantee you a reservation, but it helps. Payment in advance is a better guarantee of the reservation.

The letter in Figure 8–7 illustrates a complete, brief, and specific reservation letter.

If the reservation is no longer desired, telephone or write a cancellation (Figure 8–8). As in making the reservation, the letter cancelling it should immediately state the purpose using a deductive (direct) approach.

Requests to Members of Congress (Nonpersuasive)

Members of Congress are eager to hear from their constituents. For the **congressional representative who does not need to be persuaded** to the writer's point of view, the writer can follow these principles:

SUBJECT: RESERVATIONS

Please reserve a room with twin beds for Dr. Sally Smith and me for the nights of February 14 and 15. We would appreciate the least expensive room with these accommodations. ← **Purpose** ← **Facts**

Since we shall be attending the National Association for Conservationists Convention, we expect to arrive at 7:00 p.m. on February 14. ← **Reason** ← **Facts**

Please mail us a written confirmation. ← **Action**

Very truly yours,

Figure 8-7
Letter Making Hotel Reservations

Please cancel my reservation for a room with twin beds for the nights of February 14 and 15. Neither Dr. Sally Smith nor I will be needing the reservation. ← **Purpose** ← **Facts**

Figure 8-8
Letter Cancelling Reservations

1. *Address the letter correctly.* (Chapter 5 gives typical addresses.)
2. *Include a return address*—even if no reply is expected.
3. *Identify yourself*—voter, taxpayer, citizen, constituent.
4. *Identify the subject,* preferably with the House or Senate bill number and name. This can be done with a subject line and/or in the body of the letter.
5. *State the purpose specifically and immediately* (direct approach).
6. *Express thoughts and conclusions briefly and concisely.*
7. *Write when legislation is pending in committee,* rather than waiting until a roll call vote is imminent.

The letter in Figure 8-9 encourages a senator to continue supporting an amendment—to continue present actions. Thus, the writer can use the direct approach. When writer and reader have opposing views, the writer must use an indirect approach and supply convincing data to persuade the reader. Chapter 12 explores the principles for persuasive letters.

Routine Claim Letters

An organization could not stay in business if its goods or services were furnished in a slipshod manner. Usually, customers of successful business enterprises are pleased with their purchases. When something goes wrong, the customer seeks an adjustment from the company.

One Parke Avenue
Portland, OR 97209
December 21, 19--

Dear Senator Pasternak:

Purpose →

Please continue your opposition to the gun control law by supporting Amendment S 0000.

I agree with this statement in your letter to voters dated December 18:

Facts →

> The purpose of S 0000 was in no way designed to jeopardize law enforcement efforts or punishment for deeds which bring destruction, pain, suffering, or loss of life. Amendment S 0000 proposes to remove the rather significant burden imposed on sportsmen and others who are using gun powder for wholesome recreational and cultural purposes.

Action →

Citizens, like me, who use guns in a healthy, competitive situation urge your continued support of Amendment S 0000.

Respectfully yours,

Figure 8-9
Routine Request to Member of Congress

Business people receive **claim notes and letters** (communications that request adjustments) in various forms. Customers have written claim notices on backs of envelopes, on the bottom or back of the original letter received, and on scratch pieces of paper. Sometimes the message is written in incorrect English. Stated clearly, the message is more likely to be answered promptly and with keen consideration for the claimant's feelings. This humanistic policy is followed by many business people responsible for answering claim letters.

If you expect an adjustment simply by pointing out the problem, write a routine claim letter. The message may be written in three or four paragraphs, depending on the number of details needed by:

1. *Stating the desired adjustment in the first sentence* (deductive approach). Be sure the adjustment is fair.
2. *Explaining the facts to support the claim.* Assume that the adjustment is needed as a result of human error and then write the facts clearly, completely, correctly and present them without sarcasm. Enclose copies of documents supporting the claim.

3. *Closing with a courteous statement.* This statement might express appreciation, but as with all letters, it should not end with a "thank you," even if the thank you just means, "thank you for reading this letter." Readers do not expect thanks for reading correspondence.

The following additional suggestions will help consumers write effective claim letters:

1. *Write the letter promptly* while an adjustment can be made. Regardless of how busy they may be, business executives appreciate hearing complaints promptly so that suitable adjustments can be made. Delays create mounting problems, loss of goodwill, and loss of customers.
2. *Keep a copy of all correspondence and a record of any telephone calls.*
3. *Write or, preferably, type your letter on 8½ in. × 11 in. stationery.* Smaller-size stationery can be lost, attached to other papers, or misfiled. If the letter is sent by certified mail with a return receipt as proof of delivery, the sender will have a record of who signed for the letter and the date it was delivered.
4. *Include your complete name and return address.*
5. *Address your letter to the proper place and individual.* Product labels, product warranty notices, and library references can provide correct information.
6. *Avoid writing humorous complaint letters.* Humor is sometimes considered sarcasm.
7. *Enclose neat and clear copies of all documents mentioned.* A photocopy of the letter may be sent to an interested consumer agency, business concern, or governmental unit.
8. *Enclose a copy of your previous letter* and politely indicate a date by which action is expected—if a second complaint letter is needed.

The nature and monetary value of the claim need not be significant. Many businesses are interested in maintaining quality standards and good relationships; therefore, they want to know when something is wrong no matter how trivial the problem. Employees who serve as consumer affairs or public relation specialists are responsible for assisting consumers by answering their letter or telephone questions, providing information or explanations, granting adjustments, and promoting goodwill between the company and the public.

The short claim letter in Figure 8–10 was based on a relatively insignificant complaint—shortage of four teaspoons of sugar substitute—with a value of less than fifty cents. Nonetheless, the

214 East 110 Street
Marquette, MI 49825
August 10, 19--

Sugar Substitute Consumer Affairs
P.O. Box 3317
Chicago, IL 60680

Ladies and Gentlemen

Fair adjustment → **Supporting facts** →

Please reimburse me the value of four sugar packets. Empty packets were included in a 50-count box of Sugar Substitute purchased on August 5 for $1.99.

Supporting facts →

Enclosed are the empty packets: three sealed without sugar inside and one unsealed but obviously never containing the product.

Desired action →

I would appreciate either a monetary reimbursement or four sugar packets.

Sincerely

Terry Turner

Mrs. Terry Turner

Enclosures: Four packets

Figure 8–10
Routine Claim for Product Shortage

company acknowledged the complaint with an explanatory letter and trade coupons worth $2 at a local store. The consumer had the satisfaction of knowing that the company appreciated the communication and cared enough to act fairly. Since the product label included the mailing address for consumers seeking information or reporting complaints, the customer wrote a routine claim letter. She used the direct approach and furnished necessary details.

The claim letter in Figure 8–11 was written to the original supplier who guaranteed the trees, rather than to the group selling them to make money.

The Chicago Meat Packing Company shipped an incorrect order to its customer, Waltere Supermarkets, Inc. Instead of returning the shipment, Waltere Supermarkets wrote a routine claim letter requesting a credit for the cost difference between the price of the meat ordered and the price of the meat received. The routine claim letter is illustrated in Figure 8–12.

1010 Market Street
Lafayette, IN 47901
September 10, 19--

Manager
Able Farm Nursery
P.O. Box 225
McMinnville, TN 37110

Dear Manager:

Please send us two red maple and one tulip tree to replace the trees guaranteed to thrive if planted correctly. ← **Fair adjustment**

We purchased the trees as part of a fund-raising campaign for the Junior League, received them in May, and planted them according to your directions. None of the trees are living now. ← **Supporting facts**

Since we purchased the trees based on your guarantee, we would appreciate your sending us the replacements at the proper planting time. ← **Desired action**

Sincerely,

Figure 8-11
Routine Claim for Replacement Trees

POSITIVE RESPONSES

Informative Letter to a Customer

The **informative letter** supplies the reader with needed information. The letter in Figure 8-13 provides the customer with necessary information to comply with government regulations.

Answer to an Inquiry

Before **answering an inquiry**, put yourself in the place of the reader: what would the reader look for in the letter? First, the reader would seek **personalism** (no one likes to be treated like one of many); second, **positivism** (even saying "no" can be done in a positive, considerate way).

The "yes" is a pleasant reply, which should be graciously and enthusiastically written. Although the word "yes" is seldom used, the first statement of the communication should indicate a "yes" reply to the inquiry or request:

1. *Grant the request in the first statement* (deductive approach). This will be good news to the reader.
2. *Explain any pertinent details*—completely, correctly, concisely, and so on.
3. *Close with a convincing goodwill statement.* It might refer to the next action.

Waltere Supermarkets, Inc.
220 Michigan Avenue • P.O. Box 1785
Indianapolis, IN 46206 • 317-115-3502

August 11, 19--

Mr. Charles Sims
Chicago Meat Packing Company
213 Milton Drive
Chicago, IL 60631

Dear Mr. Sims:

Subject: Our Order No. B-31589, Mislabeled Boxes

Fair adjustment →

Please credit our account for $60 to cover the cost difference between meat received and meat ordered on our Order No. B-31589.

Supporting facts →

On August 1, we ordered eight boxes of boneless round roasts; however, your August 7 shipment consisted of four boxes of boneless and four boxes of semi-boneless roasts.

Action →

We would appreciate your correcting our account immediately.

Sincerely,

Roberta Eliot

Miss Roberta Eliot
Buyer

alc

Figure 8-12
Informative Letter Explaining Legal Requirements

The routine request letter for a free directory and instructions using Phone-a-Reservation (Figure 8-4) might have been answered with the brief letter illustrated in Figure 8-14. Notice that the writer helped the reader by emphasizing pages that would interest her and by stating the purpose directly and specifically.

The letter in Figure 8-15 represents an appropriate yes to a writer's request for help with research. Mr. Matthews will read the good news immediately and know that he must furnish data for sixteen participants.

Dear Customer:

If a government representative should visit you and request the names of pesticides used in your pest control service, the attached list will furnish the information. All of the listed pesticides are approved for the mentioned pests. We will, when possible, vary the pesticides in order to obtain maximum control with minimum use of chemicals. The chemicals listed are just part of the arsenal we use to provide our customers with effective pest control service. Many of the chemicals can be applied as emulsions, solutions, and dusts.

← **Purpose**

← **Facts**

The choice of chemical and application method is determined by the trained technician after considering your complete pest control problem. More detailed information on any chemical and application technology will be given you upon request.

Through university training schools and industrial publications, we have kept informed of the latest governmental regulations and scientific developments on insecticides and rodenticides. We are licensed and certified to own, manage, and perform pest control service in this state.

Please retain this letter so that you can furnish this pesticide information to the government agent requesting it.

← **Action**

Sincerely yours,

Figure 8-13
Routine Claim for Credit to Account

The letter in Figure 8-16 represents an answer for information on insulin injections for the diabetic. In addition to a booklet, the reader is given other pertinent information and an offer to furnish consultation services to the reader's doctor. However, the writer worded the communication carefully so that the reader would act prudently and seek his physician's advice concerning treatment.

An individual accepting a group's invitation to speak might do so with the short letter illustrated in Figure 8-17. The acceptance letter should confirm the meeting date, time, place, and topic. The speaker may request specific information; for example, availability of visual aids, characteristics and number of persons in the expected audience, transportation facilities, and so on.

Figure 8-18 answers a request for prices on professional service. Its language should be easily understood by the reader; it states the good news at the beginning of the letter, furnishes needed data, and encourages the reader. In addition, the writer promotes goodwill by guaranteeing service.

Vacation Motor-Inn Corporation

99 Center Street
Memphis, TN 38101
901-187-4580

Toll-free number for residents of Tennessee for making reservations: **1-800-182-7732**
Toll-free number for making reservations: **1-800-211-7732**

February 2, 19--

Ms. Mary Doe
111 Weir Drive
Indianapolis, IN 46201

Dear Ms. Doe:

"Yes" answer and details → Here are the instructions for Phone-a-Reservation and a copy of our current directory. You should find pages 9 to 15 especially helpful.

Goodwill statement → We would be pleased to help you make reservations for staying at any Vacation Motor-Inn.

Sincerely yours,

VACATION MOTOR-INN CORPORATION

Mary Applegate

Mrs. Mary Applegate

rl

Enclosures: 2

Figure 8-14
Answering "Yes" to Furnishing Information Requested in Figure 8-4

Adjustment Letters

Letters answering claims are called **adjustment letters**. The adjustment letter granting the customer's request is good news to the reader; therefore, it follows a pattern similar to the one for routine letters:

1. *Tell the good news immediately* (deductive approach).
2. *Explain the circumstances* so that the reader will be convinced that the problem was the result of a mistake. Readers will want explanations for what might have gone wrong and reasonable assurance that the problem will not happen again.
3. *Close on an optimistic note* to maintain good customer relations.

Dear Mr. Matthews

The Ohio State University student teachers have agreed to participate in your study to determine significant student teaching problems. You chose a timely topic; the results should be enlightening and useful to college supervisors, student teachers, and secondary school teachers. ← **"Yes" answer**

Since the student teaching term ends on December 17, please mail the materials and complete instructions within two weeks. I will need data for 16 student teachers. ← **Details**

May I have a copy of the summary of results. ← **Goodwill action**

Sincerely

Figure 8-15
Answering "Yes" to Participate in Research

Dear Mr. Bowers:

Here is a copy of our booklet, "A Guide for Helping the Diabetic." You should find this publication informative and useful. ← **"Yes" answer**

In answer to your inquiry about insulin reactions, we estimate that between twenty and fifty percent of the patients receiving insulin for the first time will respond with a local reaction. Fortunately, the condition will subside spontaneously in many instances. ← **Explanations**

For the person developing a local reaction to insulin, first be sure that the proper injection technique has been followed, including the use of isopropyl alcohol (preferably 91 percent). Pages 41 and 42 of the enclosed booklet describe the correct method for administering insulin to diabetics.

If an error in injection technique has been ruled out, the physician may want to consider using an oral antihistamine preparation or another preparation of insulin. Since such measures may be instituted by the physician, we recommend that you discuss the matter with your physician if you continue to have a reaction to the insulin injection.

Our medical personnel would be pleased to offer your doctor suggestions on treating local reactions and assist in any way possible. The doctor can telephone or write us. ← **Goodwill**

Cordially yours,

Figure 8-16
Answering "Yes" with Detailed Information and Advice

"Yes" answer → Yes, Mrs. Manners, I will be pleased to attend your November 9 meeting at 7:30 p.m. and give tips on successful business writing. Your students sound like an enthusiastic and enjoyable group.

Details → The topic I have chosen is "Formatting Application Letters." Will you arrange to have a chalkboard and an overhead projector available? These will help my presentation.

Goodwill → I will telephone you from the Carter Hotel, where I should arrive by 5:00 p.m.

Figure 8-17
Answering "Yes" to Being Guest Speaker

Dear Ms. Conrad:

"Yes" answer → Thank you for the opportunity to submit the following bid for pest control service:

Details →

M&M Market at 1010 Main Street--$25 a month

M&M Market at 2025 Paul Street--$22 a month

M&M Market at 11 River Blvd.--$20 a month

Monthly service will include the control of rats, mice, and roaches. If signs of any activity appear between monthly service dates, we will make call-backs at no extra charge.

All service will be performed according to state laws, which make it mandatory for all pest control companies to be licensed and certified. In addition, all services will be supervised and directed by a graduate entymologist.

Goodwill → If you accept this offer, we will give you proof of insurance and a list of the approved pesticides and rodenticides that will be used to service the accounts.

Sincerely yours

Figure 8-18
Answering "Yes" to a Request for Prices and Service Information

---

If a decision is made to grant the request, it should be done in a positive way. The reader should not be made to feel inferior or that a claim is being granted under protest. Writers acknowledging the company's mistakes in a tone pleasing to the readers strengthen the firm's good reputation. Customers will often continue doing business with the organization believing that it will stand by its products or services. Their faith in the company's desire to do the "right" thing increases.

Dear Mrs. Smith:

As requested in your letter of February 12, we are: ← **"Yes" answer**

> crediting your account for the $5 insufficient funds charge and writing both Federal Home Corporation and National Bank explaining that your account was not overdrawn and that we erred in marking your check insufficient funds. A copy of each letter is enclosed. ← **Explanations**

We apologize, Mrs. Smith, for the embarrassment, expense, and inconvenience our bank teller's error caused you. The error was a human one. Such mistakes occur in spite of all our precautions.

The next time you visit us, please introduce yourself to Mrs. Marsha White, your personal banker. She will see personally that your bank transactions are handled quickly and correctly. ← **Goodwill**

Sincerely,

Walter C. Milton

Walter C. Milton
Senior Vice President

WCM: ab

Enclosures: 2

Figure 8-19
Answering "Yes" to Correcting Clerical Errors (An Adjustment Letter)

Many organizations use adjustment letters to promote their services or products. Along with the explanation of what happened, they have an opportunity to explain quality control procedures and provide consumers with relevant information to enhance the reader's perception of their products or services.

The letter in Figure 8-19 is an answer to an angry consumer's complaint. Even though the consumer's checking account had sufficient funds to cover the checks she wrote, a bank clerk did not honor her checks to two banks and charged her a $5 insufficient funds charge. Thus, the consumer was penalized unjustly, inconvenienced unnecessarily, and embarrassed unduly.

The adjustment letter grants the consumer's request to credit her checking account and to write explanatory letters to the banks. To convince the reader that the bank error will not recur, the writer emphasizes that the reader's account will have special attention.

May 10, 19--

Dear Ms. Anderson:

"Yes" answer ⟶ We are sending a technician to inspect your Parker range, Model KS 111 RXAO, purchased about three years ago.

Explanations ⟶ All Parker appliances are produced using the highest quality parts and reliability control. Parts are pretested for durability, and we attempt to give our customers the best product available. Sometimes the product fails.

Goodwill ⟶ Please contact Mr. Gordon Silvers, Parker Products Co., 1010 West 12 Street, Indianapolis, IN 46202, telephone no. (317) 217-8364, if you should have any other problems or questions.

Sincerely,

Bette E. Wilson

Ms. Bette E. Wilson
Manager of Consumer Relations

fjc

Copy to: Mr. Gordon Silvers

Figure 8-20
Answering "Yes" to Claim Letter on Defective Product (An Adjustment Letter)

In Figure 8-20, a prominent appliance company acknowledges its responsibility for a defective range. The writer explains that appliances sometimes fail in spite of company efforts to maintain quality. As an act of goodwill, the writer conveys the name and telephone number of a company representative available to the reader.

Figure 8–21 is the answer to the customer who complained about a product shortage (Figure 8–10). The writer, Supervisor of Consumer Affairs, enclosed a $2 trade certificate redeemable at a store convenient to the reader. The company representative explained how the shortage occurred and how the company minimizes the problem. He included a toll-free telephone number to reassure the customer that prompt attention would be given to any future inquiries.

Since the carton product met the stipulated net weight, the company could have refused the claim. Granting the request, however, encouraged the reader to keep buying the product.

Dear Mrs. Turner:

As requested in your letter, we are enclosing a complimentary certificate redeemable at your local store for $2. ← **"Yes" answer**

Although we maintain a system of rigid quality controls to protect our customers from receiving less than the labeled amount of product, we realize that an occasional error may occur.

Every carton of Sugar Substitute powder is weighed. Any carton not meeting minimum weight standards is removed from the packaging line and filled packets are added to attain the declared net weight. As a result, a few cartons may contain some empty or nearly empty packets in addition to the minimum number of full packets required to meet the net weight requirement. ← **Explanations**

Sugar Substitute is packaged by highly sophisticated machinery operating at very high speeds. Recently, we instituted additional quality controls to further minimize the occurrence of any empty packets in the carton. We will continue our efforts to meet the highest quality standards possible.

Please feel free to use our toll-free telephone number—1-800-123-0973. We will be happy to help you further and answer your questions about Sugar Substitute. ← **Action**

Sincerely yours,

Lawrence B. Levingworth

Lawrence B. Levingworth
Supervisor of Consumer Affairs

cb

Enclosure: Certificate A8-35

Figure 8-21
Answering "Yes" to Claim Letter on Product Shortage Discussed in Figure 8-10 (An Adjustment Letter)

Form Statements, Paragraphs, or Letters

When answering the same requests again and again, save time by writing standardized data that answer the question. Be certain, however, that the wording carries a personalized tone so that the reader feels that he or she has been given individual consideration. Many business people recommend using personalized statements in the beginning and ending paragraphs of form letters. Computerized word-processing systems produce form letters that look and read like personalized, original communications.

Our Quality Control Division has requested a sample of the defective item for examination by our research technicians. We will refund the postage cost.

Figure 8-22
Standard Paragraph for answering Inquiries

Your concern about the increase in the price you are paying for ___**Name of product**___ is understandable. We appreciate this opportunity to discuss the reasons for it.

Like so many others, our company has experienced significant increases in both raw material and manufacturing costs. We have attempted to absorb additional costs through production efficiencies. However, in some cases, it has been necessary to combine production savings with increases in product prices. Even so, the overall prices for ___**Name of product**___ have not kept pace with the rise in the general cost of living as illustrated by the enclosed document.

Figure 8-23
Standard Paragraphs Explaining Need for Price Increase

A finance charge will be applied to the average daily balance when any part of the amount due is not paid by the stipulated due date. The average daily balance and the finance charge are to be calculated as follows:

1. The balance at the beginning of each day is added to new purchases added to your account that day. From this sum, we subtract payments, credits, and previously assessed finance charges. The result is the daily balance.
2. The average daily balance is determined by adding the daily balances for the billing cycle and then dividing by the number of days in the billing cycle.
3. The average daily balance on the monthly statement (including current transactions) is the amount assessed by a finance charge.
4. The finance charge is computed by applying the periodic rate (established by State law) to the average daily balance of your account.

You can avoid finance charges by sending the entire amount due so it reaches us by the due date.

Figure 8-24
Form Paragraphs to Advise Basis for Finance Charge

Dear Customer:

"Yes" answer → We are complying with your letter of ___**Date**___ and will make the necessary changes to your record.

Explanations → Since it will take a few weeks to correct our computer records, please ignore any additional incorrect invoices.

Goodwill → We are enclosing an order form for future purchases.

Sincerely yours,

Figure 8-25
Answering Inquiries with a Form Adjustment Letter

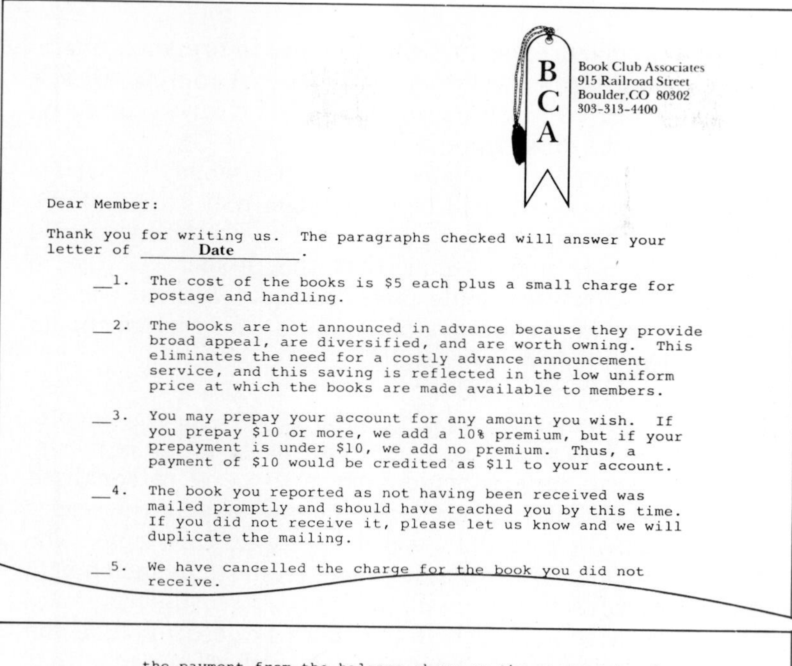

B C A

Book Club Associates
915 Railroad Street
Boulder, CO 80302
303-313-4400

Dear Member:

Thank you for writing us. The paragraphs checked will answer your letter of ___Date___.

__1. The cost of the books is $5 each plus a small charge for postage and handling.

__2. The books are not announced in advance because they provide broad appeal, are diversified, and are worth owning. This eliminates the need for a costly advance announcement service, and this saving is reflected in the low uniform price at which the books are made available to members.

__3. You may prepay your account for any amount you wish. If you prepay $10 or more, we add a 10% premium, but if your prepayment is under $10, we add no premium. Thus, a payment of $10 would be credited as $11 to your account.

__4. The book you reported as not having been received was mailed promptly and should have reached you by this time. If you did not receive it, please let us know and we will duplicate the mailing.

__5. We have cancelled the charge for the book you did not receive.

the payment from the balance shown on the statement and remit only the remaining balance--if any.

__11. We have adjusted our records so that they will agree with your records. If the next statement you receive does not indicate that this adjustment has been made, it will be shown on your next month's statement.

__12. When your remittance dated ________ was received, the charge for ___Order identification___ was still open and the payment was applied to a previous charge.

__13. Your account
. is now in balance
. shows a balance of $______ in your favor
. shows a balance of $______ due for______
Order identification

__14. In addition to the free book, we have sent you ________ monthly books at a total charge of $ ________. We received payment totaling $ ________, leaving a balance due of $______.

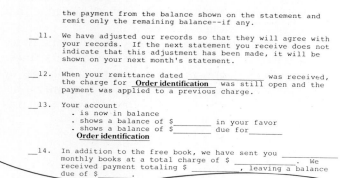

Figure 8–26
Answering Inquiries with a Two-page Form Letter to Book Club Members

Quality control is very important to most firms. The paragraph in Figure 8–22 illustrates the desire to produce and sell good quality merchandise. The paragraphs in Figure 8–23 explain the need for higher product prices, while those in Figure 8–24 advise customers of the basis for calculating finance charges on credit accounts.

Figure 8–25 is a form letter that answers a complaint for an incorrect billing, and Figure 8–26 is a two-page form letter for queries from book club members. Since these letters answer complaints and request adjustments, they are adjustment letters. Many adjustment letters have standardized paragraphs. Nonetheless, the letters should be personalized whenever possible.

CHAPTER SUMMARY

Routine inquiries and requests help to secure information, materials, or services that are routinely furnished. A routine request can be most effective if the purpose is stated clearly, correctly, and concisely, and a direct approach is used.

A routine claim letter should be written when the writer believes a fair adjustment will be made upon notification of the problem. The writer should not claim anything; he or she should just write promptly and assume that the problem is due to human error. Claimants should state the facts without accusations and ask for fair adjustments. An accusatory letter should never be mailed; it only delays results.

Answering inquiries and requests is a common business practice. Letters should be answered promptly. Form statements, paragraphs, and letters can be used to answer routine requests; however, the form letter should appear to be a personalized typewritten letter. Put yourself in the mental mood of the reader and ask yourself: How would I feel if I received this reply? The effective writer can answer inquiries and requests in such a way that the reader can sense goodwill.

Use a deductive approach if the news is good; include the facts necessary to accomplish the purpose, reflecting a tone that the reader will consider pleasing and reassuring.

Letters answering claims are called adjustment letters. Since most firms willingly grant requests for fair adjustments, these letters should state the adjustment or purpose first, followed by the explanation in words that encourage good customer relations. Adjustment letters can be useful communications for promoting sales and goodwill.

STUDY QUESTIONS

1. What approach (direct or indirect) should you use when writing typical:
   a. Routine inquiry or request letters
   b. Routine claim letters
   c. Request for hotel/motel reservations
   d. Positive answer letters
   e. Adjustment letter granting a claim request
2. Why should you avoid thanking the reader in advance?
3. Why might you mail your inquiry letter in duplicate?
4. What information should you include in a routine letter to a member of Congress?
5. Why should you write a nonantagonistic and polite claim letter?
6. Why should you mail claim letters promptly?

7. Why is it important to answer inquiries and requests with personalized and positive letters?
8. What pointers would you give to the writer of a "yes" letter?
9. When are form statements, paragraphs, or letters appropriate in answering inquiries? In addition to the examples in the text, find other examples of form statements and/or paragraphs.
10. What is the purpose for writing an adjustment letter? Why is it included in this chapter on routine letters?

ACTIVITIES

1. Why is the following opening unsatisfactory for a routine request letter:

   Your university is so beautiful with its large rolling campus filled with tall trees and stylish buildings. I imagine that no one ever tires of the view. I have compared your campus with others, but when it comes to beauty and spaciousness, none even comes close to yours.

2. Assume that you will be graduating soon with a Bachelor of Science degree. You have a major in Management and a minor in English. You would like to work toward a Master of Business Administration degree at the University of Colorado, Boulder, Colorado in Fall Semester 19__. Write to A.B. Tryling (fictitious name), Director of Admissions, to determine whether your degree will be acceptable and to advise that a transcript of your college credits will be mailed. Choose your words carefully and prepare an attractive, complete, and mailable letter.
3. Write a letter to a member of Congress expressing your beliefs on a current issue. Ask him or her for an opinion. Some key issues involve unemployment, inflation, taxes, business and labor, medical care, energy consumption, environment, military spending, education, housing, mass transportation, the cities, the right to life, the right to die, international arms sales, control of the government by unions, misuse of taxpayers' money, and equal rights.
4. The Student Conservation Association has volunteer jobs available for college-age men and women in its park and forest assistants program for the winter months. Volunteers are needed to assist in various national parks and national forest agencies to enable them to offer additional visitor services and to accomplish conservation projects they otherwise could not offer. Programs are being offered at Arches National Park, Canyonlands National Park, and Natural Bridges National Monument in Utah; Grand Canyon National Park in Arizona; and Glacier National Park in

Montana. Write for information and an application blank to the Student Conservation Association, P.O. Box 550, Charlestown, NH 03603.

5. Write and mail an inquiry or request letter to the company of your choice. You can request information or available booklets or pamphlets.
6. Write a letter accepting this invitation from a high school guidance counselor:

Invitation from High School Guidance Counselor

Dear ____________________:

Adams High School will be holding Career Day on October 8. If you will remember, a speaker on another Career Day helped you decide on a career in economics. He spent twenty minutes explaining the opportunities and advantages in being an economist.

Will you do the same thing for this year's high school students? Will you visit us on Career Day and tell why you became an economist and why it is an interesting career?

Since Career Day begins at 9 a.m., I would appreciate your being on the program soon after 10 a.m., but I can change this hour if doing so will make it possible for you to be here.

Please let me have your comments this month.

7. Your employer gave you the following card and asked you to write Mr. O'Neil enclosing a free copy of the 32-page booklet and explaining that a representative will contact him in a few days to analyze his current financial situation and recommend steps to make his future more secure.

Reply Card

COVINGTON ASSURANCE CO. P.O. Box 32
St. Louis, MO 63188

Please mail this reply card so that you can receive your *free* 32-page booklet, *Sensible Planning*.

I want to prove to myself that planning can help me achieve my financial goals. Please see that I receive my free booklet.

Name DONALD O'NEIL
(Please Print)

Address 3108 RIVERSIDE AVENUE

City SEDALIA State MO ZIP 65301

8. As Circulation Manager for a publishing firm, you have been asked to quote prices for the booklet "Speaking Effectively." Write a letter indicating that one copy is free; 10 copies are 70 cents each, 11 to 99 copies are 60 cents each, and 100 copies or more are 50 cents each. The postage is included. Give the names of several other booklets available for prompt mailing at the same prices. (For easy reading, show the prices in tabular form.)
9. Answering the letter in Figure 8-11, write a letter to Mr. and Mrs. Bill Castle telling them that the trees requested will be sent to them in October.
10. Answering the letter in Figure 12-5, tell Janice Smith Harper that you will gladly replace the broken pipe—no charge. Enclose an advertising brochure illustrating various styles of Mastercraft pipes and tell her to choose the correct one or one similar to the broken pipe. Send some promotional literature.
11. Develop a form statement that can be used to answer requests for "Speaking Effectively" (see Activity 8) and other booklets your firm stocks.

EDITING

Revise each sentence to eliminate the weaknesses and to represent correct and effective sentences for letters.

1. I would appreciate your sending me a application blank and info on "Arches National Park," "Grand Canyon National Park," and "Glacier National Park."
   (*First sentence in routine request letter*)
2. Since you will be receiving an official transcript of my college credits from Central State University, please evaluate the transcript and let me know if I can pursue grad work for an MBA.
   (*Opening sentence in routine request letter*)
3. After reading your request, Madison Supply Co. bolts can be purchased for $.25 each.
4. Please write back to me and I will send letters I have on file.
   (*Ending statement*)
5. Please send me a copy of the booklet *Effective Business Letters* at your convenience.
   (*Ending statement*)
6. Keep the good work up and contact me if something comes up again.
   (*Ending statement*)
7. Please telephone me at (212) 181-4700, Monday through Friday, 12 pm to 5 pm.
   (*Ending statement*)

8. This letter is to congratulate you on your choice of topics for the March 15 conference.
9. Mr. Michael Carter, he is our sales rep, will contact you by April 2nd.
10. Use the enclosed self-addressed and stamped envelope to advice the equipment you will need so that we can prepare them for your presentation.
11. Him and her will be fantastic managers for Plant 3.
12. As per your recent request, I'm returning the questionnaire completed as you requested.
13. Your letter of July 2, was given to me for reply; we will credit your account for $63.25.
14. Rewrite the following letter, which thanks the reader and states progress on a study:

    I have read with interest your study referring to the articulation of typewriting instruction. Thanks a lot. I have taken the liberty to make a photocopy for me and I'm returning, therefore, your copy to you.

    The study now being conducted at Central State University is in its final process and should be completed this summer. I'll forward a copy of the summary of results to you. Thanks you again.

IN-BASKET SIMULATIONS

1. Write a letter to Mrs. Ruth Cynthia Munson, Treasurer of Waltere Supermarkets, Inc. Request a copy of the current annual report. You are considering purchasing common stock available to employees.
2. Assume that you are private secretary to Mr. Jeffrey J. Jackson, President of Convenience Foods. Write to a hotel/motel and inquire about arrangements for a conference for Friday and Saturday, April 20 and 21, 9 a.m. to 3 p.m.

   You will need one conference room—to accommodate 75 people—with a lectern, microphone, chalkboard, overhead projector, and screen. You will also need three smaller rooms, each with 5 large tables and 25 chairs. No other facilities will be needed in the smaller rooms. Ask for menus and prices so that you can plan two luncheons and coffee hours. Also request room rates.
3. Sometimes the pouring spout for Waltere's private label of pancake syrup (Econo) works beautifully; sometimes not. You were very embarrassed one Sunday morning when your guest poured the syrup and the spout came out gushing forth with the sticky syrup. It was everywhere—or so it seemed. The syrup spilled onto the tablecloth, the carpeting, and the guest's clothes. You paid for cleaning the carpeting and the guest's suit. Write a claim letter.

4. As Mrs. Eric Evans, customer of Waltere Supermarkets, Inc., write a letter complaining about a turkey you purchased at one of their supermarkets. Although you and your guests ate almost all of the turkey, it had a peculiar taste. Enclose the product label and state the price paid. Since you are not sure to whom you should complain, address your letter to the corporate headquarters in Indianapolis.
5. As Mrs. John Cleveland, customer of Waltere Supermarkets, Inc., you had an upsetting experience. You have been a long-time customer and have been very satisfied with the company's services. One week ago, you purchased a package of pork chops at your neighborhood Waltere Supermarket. You came home and immediately put the meat in your freezer. Several days later, you cooked the pork chops. How surprised your husband was when he saw a worm on his dinner plate! You returned the uneaten meat with the worm in it to your local store and the meat manager dutifully refunded your money. You believe the matter should be brought to the attention of the main office. Write corporate headquarters and tell your story. You and your husband have had no side effects from eating the meat. You hope no other Waltere customers will have a similar unappetizing and unpleasant experience.
6. Use form statements a–q to answer In-Basket Simulation 7. Form letters from Waltere Supermarkets, Inc., look very much like original letters; therefore, personalize your answer to In-Basket Simulation 7 as much as possible.
   a. Dear ____________
   b. Dear Customer
   c. Thank you for your letter of ____________.
   d. Thank you for your letter requesting ____________.
   e. Thank you for your letter of ____________ requesting a copy of ____________.
   f. Thank you for your letter of ____________ explaining ____________.
   g. For your information, we are enclosing a copy of our booklet, "____________."
   h. The enclosed copy of our booklet, "____________," should answer your question on ____________.
   i. Our representative will contact you within ____________ days.
   j. The booklet, "____________," is no longer in print.
   k. We are enclosing a copy of ____________.

l. We have had so many requests for ________________ that our stock has been depleted.
m. We do not have any current literature relative to ________________.
n. The information you requested is explained thoroughly in our publication, ________________.
o. Please let us know if we can help you further.
p. An addressed and stamped envelope is enclosed for your reply.
q. __Name of publication__ should contain answers to your questions on ________________. A copy is being mailed to you __Specify date__.

7. For Ms. Tracy Thomas, Public Relations Director, Waltere Supermarkets, Inc., write a letter to employee Carl Grant thanking him for his confidence in Waltere's management, and enclosing a copy of the current annual report and booklets he requested.
8. As the Meat Buyer for Waltere Supermarkets, Inc., answer Mrs. Evans (In-Basket Simulation 4) explaining the action taken regarding her purchase. Tell her that Waltere's will refund her money if the poultry supplier does not and enclose a photocopy of your letter to the supplier. Ask her to let you know if she has not heard from the meat supplier within three weeks.
9. As the Meat Buyer for Waltere's, answer Mrs. Cleveland (In-Basket Simulation 5) explaining that Waltere's makes every effort to procure the finest products available and that all products are U.S.D.A. government inspected selected products. You cannot explain what happened, but assure Mrs. Cleveland that you will make every effort to prevent a recurrence of the situation.

Placing Orders and Writing Acknowledgments

9

After studying Chapter 9, you should be able to:

- Place specific, complete, and correct orders using either forms or letters
- Recognize the importance of acknowledging orders
- Write effective acknowledgments for orders

Orders for goods or services are special types of direct requests—usually welcomed by the receiver. Businesses appreciate orders that are specific, complete, and accurate. Order forms, designed to accomplish these goals, often are available. But when they are not, you must prepare a brief detailed letter stating all information completely, correctly, and clearly.

Although the order letter can be one of the simplest to write, often it is written poorly. Writers omit necessary information (for example, quantities, catalog numbers, and necessary descriptions), give incorrect data (for example, wrong numbers, sizes, and prices), forget to include a necessary check, or forget to sign it. The poorly written order may not be filled, or it may be misinterpreted and incorrectly completed. Unnecessary delay, expense, or even legal complications may result.

ORDER FORMS

The mail order form and the purchase order facilitate the ordering of merchandise. Order forms often include specific columns or spaces for information needed to fill the order: complete name and address of purchaser, quantity desired, catalog and page number, description of item, unit price, extended price, total price for merchandise, shipping weight, shipping and handling costs, sales tax, and total cost of order. To ensure that the order is filled promptly and correctly, the sender should follow the instructions and enter all information accurately. Business firms that accept mail orders usually supply potential customers with descriptive brochures, catalogs, and explicit order forms.

Many firms have purchasing departments whose main responsibility is locating sources and getting the best prices for quality merchandise or service. Purchasing agents often negotiate by using a simplified **purchase order form**. Like the mail order form, the purchase order (Figure 9-1) provides for exact placement of pertinent data so that the order can be filled promptly and correctly.

ORDER LETTER

When order forms are unavailable or inappropriate, compose an **order letter** that requests the desired goods or services. Make the letter straightforward, specific, complete, and correct so that the order can be filled promptly and correctly.

Errors in order letters occur so frequently that many firms use a lengthy form letter listing all possible reasons why an order cannot be processed. The seller simply places check marks next to the appropriate comments and mails the form to the intended purchaser with a request to supply the missing data on the form. This procedure accomplishes the task, saves the cost of writing original letters, and expedites the order.

No.

ABOVE ORDER NO. MUST APPEAR ON ALL PAPERS AND PACKAGES RELATIVE TO THIS ORDER.

PURCHASE ORDER

TO

SHIP TO

DATE	SHIP VIA	ROUTING	DATE REQUIRED	TERMS	REQUISITION NO.
/ /			/ /		

QUANTITY		PLEASE ENTER OUR ORDER FOR GOODS LISTED BELOW:		UNIT PRICE	TOTAL
ORDERED	RECEIVED	STOCK NUMBER	DESCRIPTION		

PLEASE SEND _____ COPIES OF YOUR INVOICE WITH ORIGINAL BILL OF LADING

IMPORTANT
PLEASE NOTIFY US IMMEDIATELY IF YOU ARE UNABLE TO SHIP COMPLETE ORDER BY DATE SPECIFIED.

PURCHASING AGENT

RECEIVED BY DATE RECEIVED / /

1S158 Rediform®

POLY PAK (50 SETS) 1P158

Figure 9-1
Purchase Order Form

There are eight steps you can take to ensure that your order letter accomplishes its goal:

1. Use a definite order statement in the first sentence (deductive approach)
2. Give complete and correct addresses—where to deliver, where to send invoice
3. Give quantity and specific description for each item ordered
4. Give complete and correct price information
5. State manner of payment
6. State method of shipment—if applicable
7. Give desired delivery date, but be realistic
8. Close with confident expectation of delivery as specified

Order Statement

You should begin your order letter with a definite **order statement**:

> Please enter my order for . . .
>
> Please ship the following office equipment as advertised in your current Office Equipment catalog:

A reference to a specific advertisement helps to clarify: ". . . advertised on page 18 of *Travel*, April 19__ issue." In addition, such statements help readers determine the effectiveness of their advertising programs. Avoid vague statements, such as:

> I am interested in the chair . . .
>
> Your advertisement in the Press illustrated . . .
>
> I'd like to order the office supplies . . .

The preceding statements are not order statements. They represent unnecessary or "fill in" information.

Complete Information

The supplier needs to know (1) where to deliver the goods or services and (2) where to send the bill or invoice. The usual procedure is to send the order and bill to the same person or company; but if you list two addresses or names, be sure to specify what goes where. All addresses must be correct and complete—including ZIP code designations.

Sometimes a catalog number represents a complete description—model number, size, color, style, finish, and even the price—and the orderer must supply the exact catalog number and exact quantity desired. When the catalog number does not include a complete description, the orderer must specify the catalog number, the required information describing the items, and the exact quantity. The supplier should know *exactly* what is being ordered. However, do not include unnecessary details that might confuse the reader. For example, "This equipment is exactly what we need to produce the hardware items our customers desire" is neither interesting nor helpful to suppliers. You would obviously order items you need.

The order letter should include complete price information—unit prices, extended totals, and total cost of the order. The unit may be a piece, a foot, a yard, a pair, a dozen, a ream, a gross, an ounce, a box, a pound, one, a liter, a kilogram, a meter. When ordering more than one unit, indicate both the unit prices and the total price for each item in the order. Specifically state the amounts for costs such as shipping charges, handling fees, postage, or sales tax when appropriate.

Sometimes prices are shown **f.o.b. (free on board) destination** or **f.o.b. shipping point**. In the first instance, the supplier pays the shipping costs; in the second instance, the purchaser pays the shipping costs. A notation "f.o.b. Chicago" means that transportation costs to Chicago will be paid by the supplier. If the final destination is to be New York, the supplier would pay shipping costs to Chicago; the purchaser would pay the costs from Chicago to New York. There are also some legal implications involving title to goods connected with the f.o.b. point specified.

When enclosing payment, indicate whether it is in the form of coins, personal check, money order, or cashier's check. Use a small coin envelope or coin mailing card for mailing coins. Because coins in the mail might encourage interception of the order, it is better to use an acceptable paper money form for all mail payments even those under one dollar.

Unless there is a specific understanding as to how the order is to be sent, clearly state instructions for shipment: parcel post (a class of mail), United Parcel Service (UPS), truck, rail, freight, air freight, express, steamship, air mail, bus, or other acceptable method. If you stipulate no shipping information with the order, the sender may elect the method or may request specific instructions.

You may designate RUSH or delivery by a certain time. You may even indicate that you will refuse delivery after a certain date. But be realistic in your demands. Some orders can be shipped immediately; others cannot be shipped for days, weeks, or months. If no specific delivery date is noted, your order will be sent as soon as is practical. It is unlikely that any long-standing company would deliberately delay shipment without good reason.

Figure 9–2 illustrates a very short, but complete, order letter. Notice that it includes:

1. Complete names and addresses
2. A definite order statement
3. Quantity and necessary description of item ordered
4. Complete price information
5. The manner of payment
6. A legible signature

This one-paragraph letter could have been double-spaced.

Figure 9–3 illustrates a situation in which the same item is to be sent to two people. For clarity, the names and addresses appear prominently centered and tabulated.

If your letter covers several items, list them in tabular form without columnar headings (Figures 9–4 and 9–5). Notice that itemizing information and prices makes reading easier. When

Purchaser's address and date →

8 Avenue M
Washington, DC 20404
April 1, 19--

Supplier's name and address →

Science Publishing Company
One Broad Street
New York, NY 10004

Dear Publisher:

SUBJECT: Subscription to The Environment

Order statement and necessary details →

Please enter my order for a one-year subscription to The Environment for which I am enclosing a postal money order for $16.

Yours truly,

Legible signature →

Mara Oliver

Miss Mara Oliver

Enclosure

Figure 9-2
Complete Order Letter for Periodical Subscription

Please mail one-year subscriptions for The Environment to each of the following persons:

Names and addresses of receivers →

Mr. Troy Christopher
99 East Adams Street
Topeka, KS 66603

Mrs. Elaine Murphy
2119 East 18 Street
Vicksburg, MS 39180

I am accepting your special offer--$16 for the first subscription, $10 for each additional subscription. Please charge the $26 to my account.

Special instructions →

Since this order is being placed before January 1, each subscription should begin with the special guidebook on pollution.

Figure 9-3
Order Letter for Periodicals That Will Be Sent to Different Locations

---

ordering different quantities of the items listed, tabulate the individual and extended prices and the special charges and additions. (Figure 9-6 illustrates an order letter for service.)

See additional order letters in Chapter 13.

Please send me by insured parcel post the following lightweight luggage, which is described in your Spring catalog: ← **Order statement**

Two	No. 10021	41″ Garment Bags	$39.95 ea.	$ 79.90
One	No. 10027	25″ Pullman	29.95 ea.	29.95
One	No. 10030	21″ Weekender	24.95 ea.	24.95
				$134.80
		Shipping and handling		9.00
		Total Cost		$143.80

← **Tabulated list of items ordered**

Here is my personal check for $143.80. ← **Payment**

Because the luggage is intended as a graduation gift, I would like it by April 30. Please let me know if you cannot meet this date. ← **Delivery**

Figure 9-4
Tabulated Order Letter (Various Quantities)

Please furnish the following items as specified in your quotation dated October 10: ← **Order statement**

1	Model B-7932	Copier	$1,975.50 List
1	Model B 21X	Calculator	150.50 List
1	Model 3156	Stapler	22.95 List
			$2,148.95
	Less Trade Discount--20%		429.79
	Net Cost of Order		$1,719.16

← **Tabulated list of items ordered**

We understand that a cash discount of 1% is available to us if we pay for this order within ten days after date of invoice. ← **Payment**

As agreed, please process this order immediately so that we can anticipate delivery by November 30. ← **Delivery**

Figure 9-5
Tabulated Order Letter (One Each Item)

Please furnish the following service as outlined in your letter of May 10: ← **Order statement**

Pest control service at south end of Wickes warehouse ← **Service ordered**

Labor and materials--$450 with six-month guarantee

Necessary reapplications made at no charge

Payment will be made within thirty days after service. ← **Delivery and payment**

Figure 9-6
Order Letter for Service

TELEPHONE ORDERS

Some customers prefer to telephone their orders to suppliers. Using the telephone can be more economical than using the mail since many business firms have automatic dialing equipment and some suppliers provide toll-free telephone numbers for customers. In addition, the telephone order request is immediately received; thus, delivery of goods or services can be expedited.

Telephone orders can be filled promptly and correctly if specific, complete, and correct data are accurately received by the supplier. Therefore, telephone buyers must adhere to the principles for writing orders and be effective oral communicators. Not all orders can be placed over the telephone. Complicated orders should be in writing. The law also requires that some orders, such as real estate transactions, be in writing. It is sometimes wise to follow up oral purchases with written confirmations. The letter becomes part of the written record.

MAIL ORDERS AND THE LAW

The Federal Trade Commission's Mail Order Merchandise Rule protects customers who place mail orders. Under this rule, the seller must either send merchandise within thirty days after the order is received or by a promised delivery date. The seller must also notify the customer when an order cannot be sent as promised and must specify the new shipping date. The customer can agree to the new shipping date or request a complete refund.

If merchandise arrives damaged or not as ordered, the customer can write a complaint letter to the seller. The buyer may also want to notify the U.S. Postal Service (when mail delivery service is used) or the company delivering the merchandise.

Customers ordering by mail should take precautions just in case something goes wrong. The following safeguards will protect most buyers:

1. *Order early* to anticipate delivery by date desired.
2. *Keep a copy of the order.* This copy should indicate exactly what was ordered, the date the order was placed, the supplier's name and address, the delivery requirements, the method of payment, and other pertinent order information.
3. *Keep a copy of the advertisement*, or at least a record of the delivery or shipping time stated in the notice and the seller's return policy. It is wise to know the return policy before ordering.
4. *Keep the cancelled checks as proof of payment.*

ACKNOWLEDGING ORDERS

All buyers appreciate acknowledgments advising that their orders have been received. Such communications not only tell them that their order is being processed but also let them know that their business is important.

Order acknowledgments offer other opportunities to promote business: to welcome new customers; advise when service, shipment, or delivery can be expected; and promote other service or products available. In the case of large or special accounts, you may give extra attention to the acknowledgment—to encourage future business.

Acknowledge all orders promptly, whether you can complete all, part, or no part of the order. It helps to build good customer relations. Your reply should express your appreciation as personally and positively as possible:

1. Indicate receipt of order with a thank-you statement. If you are communicating with a new customer, welcome him or her (deductive approach).
2. *Repeat significant details about the goods or services ordered and give the order number*—if there is one.
3. *Give delivery details.* Note when, where, and how materials will be shipped or the service rendered.
4. *Inspire customer confidence.* Tell the customer when to expect the desired order.
5. *Include sales-promotional ideas whenever the reader might be receptive to them.* Sales-promotional material is information on other available related items and/or services you want to sell to the customer.

You may acknowledge routine or small orders with postal cards. These cards usually contain the company name and address and possibly a trademark or slogan. The message may be a computerized form message (Figures 9–7 through 9–11). Notice that these standardized acknowledgments indicate the purchased items and are written in a spirit of goodwill. To make them stand out, some acknowledgments are printed on tinted, rather than white, paper stock.

Figure 9–12 illustrates a personalized order acknowledgment typed on good quality, standard-sized stationery. The letter expresses appreciation for the purchase and inspires reader confidence. Figure 9–13 shows a two-part acknowledgment on good quality note paper folded to 3½ in. × 3½ in. The top states the basic message, thank you; the inside contains the actual acknowledgment with additional sales information.

Chapter 10 includes additional illustrations of order acknowledgments.

Dear Customer:

Thank you → Thank you for your Order No. ________ for

Purchase → ______________ **Items** ______________.

Shipment → You can expect parcel post shipment by

______________ **Date** ______________.

Confidence → If you wish to write us about this order, please refer to our Order No. ________.

Sincerely,

Ray Foster

Figure 9-7
Standardized Acknowledgment for Typical Order (Postal Card)

Dear Customer:

Acknowledgment →
Confidence →

It is a pleasure to fill your request for plastic reproductions of poisonous plants. We believe you will find them a very useful educational aid.

Carol James

Ms. Carol James
Public Relations

Figure 9-8
Standardized Acknowledgment for Request for Reproductions (Postal Card)

Dear Customer:

Acknowledgment → The nursery firm from which you ordered your trees is no longer in business; however, we have agreed to replace your order for:

Purchase → ______________________________

Shipment → This replacement will be shipped in ________, the proper planting time for your order.

Sincerely,

Thomas Mavek

MAVEK FARM NURSERY
P.O. Box 0001
McMinnville, TN 37110

Figure 9-9
Standardized Acknowledgment for Tree Replacements—Figure 8-11 (Postal Card)

Dear ______________

Thank you for your interest in the booklet ← **Acknowledgment**

____. ← **Purchase**
Because of the great demand, our supply is temporarily exhausted.

Additional booklets are now being printed and will be sent by March 31. ← **Shipment**

Sincerely,

Jane McConnel

Figure 9-10
Standardized Acknowledgment for Booklets (Postal Card)

Dear ______________

Thank you for your order. We know you will enjoy your new cool-smoking Masterson. ← **Acknowledgment**

Please tell your friends about Masterson pipes. Better still, mail their orders to us, and we will send YOU a second pipe for half price. This is our way of saying thanks for recommending Masterson pipes. ← **Promotional data**

Sincerely,

Elizabeth A. Manners

Figure 9-11
Standardized Acknowledgment for Pipe Orders with Promotional Data (Postal Card)

Dear Mr. O'Neil:

Thank you for ordering Great Publisher's books and educational materials. ← **Thank you**

Shipments should reach you within three weeks. Sometimes large orders are shipped in several packages; all packages may not arrive at the same time. Let us know if you do not receive orders promptly. ← **Details**

As a new customer, you should know about our special buying plan: Buy $200 or more of materials annually and receive a discount. Of course, you can spread your purchases throughout the year.

If at any time you have questions or wish to discuss an order, please write or telephone us. Be sure to refer to our order number in all communications. ← **Confidence**

We are pleased to serve you.

Sincerely,

Allen Mathews

Figure 9-12
Acknowledgment and Welcome to New Customers

Top →

THANK YOU

Inside →

THANK YOU FOR YOUR NEW ACCOUNT . . .

You will like our personalized checking account service, as well as the various realistic savings programs we have available.

We welcome opportunities to discuss financial requirements or programs with you from personal and auto loans through retirement and estate planning.

For your added convenience, our bank has several conveniently located branch offices plus 24-hour-a-day, 7-day-a-week automatic tellers.

Ed Spencer

President

Figure 9-13
Two-part Acknowledgment for New Client

CHAPTER SUMMARY

Orders and acknowledgments are routine business communications. Both are easy to write; however, orders must be specific, complete, and accurate to be effective. Improperly placed orders can affect office efficiency and ruin goodwill.

Suppliers often provide order forms to make it more convenient for you to place a written order and easier for them to fill it. Forms have a space for everything the supplier needs to know to fill an order.

To enable the supplier to fill your order letter completely and efficiently, provide specific and accurate information: delivery address, invoice address (if different), quantity, description, prices, manner of payment, method of shipment, and desired delivery date. Most firms assign an order number and request purchasers to include the appropriate number on all correspondence.

Customers who order by telephone must adhere to the principles for written orders. When desirable and/or necessary, they should confirm the oral request in writing.

The Federal Trade Commission's Mail Order Merchandise Rule requires sellers to ship orders within thirty days or by a promised delivery date. Customers can request complete refunds from sellers who do not comply with delivery specifications.

Acknowledging orders promotes good business and provides opportunities to include sales-promotional material (data on other available related items or services).

Routine orders can be acknowledged with either preprinted or computerized cards or letters with adequate space for fill-in information. You might want to write an original letter to acknowledge special or large accounts. Whether you mail a printed form or an original letter, be certain to express appreciation in a personal and positive tone.

STUDY QUESTIONS

1. What is the difference between a mail order form and a purchase order? When do you use each?
2. What information does a supplier need from a customer to send the customer's order promptly and correctly?
3. What is the significance of an f.o.b. point?
4. Why is an acknowledgment important to the buyer? Why is it important to the seller?
5. Which approach (deductive or inductive) is typical for order letters and acknowledgments? Can the alternate approach ever be used? Explain.

6. What other descriptive information is needed before the following item can be sent to the purchaser:

   One pair Shelby Shoes, Size 8, $44.95

Activities

1. The following acknowledgment is writer-centered, uses outdated expressions, and lacks sales-promotional ideas. Rewrite the letter.

   As you requested in your letter of May 5, we are mailing to you, under separate cover, a complimentary copy of our current spring catalog featuring women's clothing. Also enclosed, you will find order blanks to assist you in ordering any items you care to order from this catalog. Thank you very much.

2. Rewrite the following order letter:

   Please ship me:

   6 double roll wallpaper bolts @ $17.98
   No. A30X4817

   10 double roll wallpaper bolts @ $25.95
   No. A31X3817

   4 double roll bolts of vinyl wallpaper @ $18.95
   No. V30X5715

   Enclosed is a check for $500.00 to cover all of the above charges plus $4.22 for taxes and $19.50 for transportation. Please ship by National Freight Lines. We would like to have these items shipped by March 15.

3. Using the following advertisement, write a letter ordering a resume kit:

   RESUME KIT—Newly revised resume kit by experienced placement executive. This kit includes sample resumes, full instructions and ample work sheets. Your money back if you are not satisfied. Send $19.95 to KIT, Dept. IWSN, 17806 Tellemeader Blvd., Jacksonville, Florida 32211. Allow 4 to 6 weeks for delivery.

4. Today is November 10, 19—. You have decided to do your Christmas shopping early. With this thought in mind, you scan various catalogs for ideas. You read an advertisement for children's watches and believe that Jimmy, Sally, and Henry would each enjoy receiving one. Therefore, you write an

itemized order letter for the watches you believe the children would prefer. Include a seventy-five cent handling charge for each watch. Ask for delivery to you. Here is a summary of the advertisement:

CHICAGO SALES
CHICAGO, IL 60607

James Bond Super Spy Watch has secret sighting lens and tells time anywhere with World Time Guide.
45 T-241 Only $9.99

G.I. Joe Watch has unique fold-up sighting lens, compass, luminous hands, hour indicators, and compass. It tells military time, too!
45 T-242 Only $9.99

Bradley Teaching Time Watch helps make learning to tell time easy. Swiss movements. Leather bands.
45 T-243—chrome case Only $8.44
45 T-244—yellow case Only $9.44

Barbie's Portrait Watch is a little girl's favorite. Swiss movements. Pink leather band.
45 T-245 Only $9.44

Ballerina Watch is a graceful, Swiss movement watch.
45 T-246 Only $9.44

5. Single copies of "A Working Woman's Guide to Her Job Rights" are free upon request. Order a copy from the Women's Bureau, U.S. Department of Labor, Washington, DC 20210.
6. Write a letter ordering a popular magazine for yourself and a friend. Arrange the mailing information in tabular form. Enclose a check for both subscriptions.
7. Examine a mail order catalog. Using the order form, order any item you choose. Be sure to include all information required so that your order can be processed promptly and accurately.
8. Write a purchase order to Farm Fleet, Inc., R.R. 3, Gary, Indiana 46401, covering shipment of the following filters to you. Supply an order number and request parcel post delivery.

D-107 Filter Discs 6″ Size Five at $1.37 each.
D-109 Filter Discs 6½″ Size Ten at $1.44 each.

9. The following order form was so well received that delivery will be made in 45 days, rather than the 30 days specified. Acknowledge the order with a form letter that can be sent to

the many people who will have to wait until a new shipment of closet lights is available.

Send check or money order to:

SPACE LIGHT CLOSET LIGHT PLEASE PRINT
P.O. Box 439
Farmingdale, NY 11735

Please rush ______ Space Light Closet Light(s) at $5.95 each. Add 50¢ postage and handling fee to each order.

Total amount enclosed $__________

Miss/Mrs./Mr. ______________________________

Street ______________________________

City ____________________ State __________ ZIP __________

Money Back Guarantee: If not completely satisfied, return in 30 days for full refund. Offer good only in Continental U.S.

Allow 30 days for delivery.

Order Form

EDITING

1. Rewrite these statements acknowledging orders:
   a. This is to inform you that we have received your order for the garden tools.
   b. Your order for the household appliances has been received.
2. Rewrite these beginning statements for order letters:
   a. I saw your advertisement for Handsome shoes in the brochure you sent me.
   b. Please send the goods to me at the above address:
3. Rewrite these statements so that they will be better ending statements for order letters:
   a. Thank you for sending this order to us soon; we look forward to receiving it.
   b. Please deliver the merchandise by November 10, 19—.

IN-BASKET SIMULATIONS

1. Miss Margaret Jean Baker, Assistant to the Treasurer of Waltere Supermarkets, Inc., left the following handwritten note on your desk. The copier was Model 3179G, priced at $1500 less 20 percent trade discount, f.o.b. shipping point. Write the order, supplying all necessary information.

> Please order this copy machine (description attached) addressing letter to Ms. Patricia A. Schafer at Allied Business Machines.
>
> MJB

Handwritten Note

2. Write a letter to Mr. James Russell at Western Packing Company advising that the cost of promotional advertising from May 1 through June 3 was $995.98. Sign your letter as a Produce Buyer of Waltere Supermarkets, Inc.
3. Waltere Supermarkets, Inc., furnished the Elton Corporation in Peru, Indiana 46970 with 220 semi-boneless hams for the Christmas season. The total weight for these hams was 3200 lbs. at a price of $1.80/lb. Write a letter to Mr. Timothy Miller at Elton Corporation advising the total cost of the order and requesting that the check be mailed to Waltere Supermarkets, Inc., P.O. Box 1785, Indianapolis, IN 46206, attention of Ms. Tracy Lewis.
4. On July 25, Waltere Supermarkets, Inc., ordered beef flank steaks from the Chicago Beef Center, 913 East Main Street, Suite 105, Chicago, IL 60019. One of the packages received on August 1 was marked, "Beef Flank Steaks"; however, the package contained beef briskets. Write a letter to the attention of Mr. Dennis Cooper at the Chicago Beef Center explaining that the company received the wrong product and request a credit for $127.99—the difference between the cost of the flanks and the briskets.
5. One of Waltere's customers has requested a custom order of flowers for a 50th wedding anniversary celebration: a large floral arrangement (yellow roses and baby's breath) for the head table and a yellow rose in a bud vase (glass) for each of the twelve guest tables. Waltere's controls the quality of plants to be grown for them at 18 greenhouses which provide them with cut flowers, bedding plants, and potted plants.

Thirty Waltere Supermarkets have floral designers who create beautiful arrangements, corsages, and other special orders for Waltere's customers. Thus, Waltere customers are assured of quality and freshness and can select from a variety of products as complete as most floral shops. Customers can purchase all their floral needs with the shopping convenience of a one-stop supermarket. Write an order acknowledgment letter, including some sales-promotional ideas.

6. Prepare a standardized acknowledgment form for Waltere Supermarkets, Inc., to use for acknowledging and thanking customers for recent orders. Your acknowledgment form should include statements concerning approximate delivery data and other pertinent shipping data.
7. Write an acknowledgment to Fisher's Restaurant, One Circle Parkway, Indianapolis, IN 46210. Thank the owner for his recent order and advise that the order will be shipped by Waltere's truck on a date next week. Mr. Elton Fisher ordered 10 prime pork loins approximately 14 lb. each at \$1.95/lb. The standard acknowledgment form can be used.

Writing Letters That Promote Goodwill

10

After studying Chapter 10, you should be able to:

- Distinguish among letters expressing congratulations, appreciation, sympathy, and welcome
- Identify the importance of goodwill letters
- Write effective goodwill messages

Perhaps the most appreciated communications are those which extend a personal wish. We write them by choice, as gestures of goodwill. Cards, notes, and letters all may express congratulations, sympathy, or welcome.

These notices serve many purposes. They provide recognition for a specific event. They lend support to and encourage good relationships with other people in the business world. And they help to preserve humanity in our business world.

EXPRESSING CONGRATULATIONS

Writing a **letter of congratulations** reveals that you are aware that something special has happened to someone and that you care enough to express your pleasure with a personalized note or letter. The congratulatory message is not a necessity, but it is an ego booster to the recipient and, therefore, a builder of good human relations.

You should express congratulations with enthusiasm and without terms such as *good luck*, since such expressions imply chance or good fortune rather than achievement. (Of course, if you are congratulating the reader because her or his name was picked to win a grand prize, then *luck* would seem to be an appropriate term.) Handwriting adds a special personal touch, but typewritten messages are more common among business associates. Use a simple, deductive approach:

1. Give the good news—congratulations—immediately.
2. State the reasons for the congratulations using personalized and informal language.
3. Close with a goodwill statement, avoiding words which symbolize chance.

The manager of a bank peruses the daily newspaper for special happenings to local citizens, then mails a short, congratulatory message enclosing a copy of the news story permanently sealed in plastic. This public-relations gesture not only creates goodwill but also helps promote business.

An employer expresses interest in the personal welfare of employees by sending a personalized note or letter similar to that in Figure 10–1. The note in Figure 10–2 illustrates simple, but sincere, congratulations from one friend to another. The note could have been part of a longer letter. The letters in Figures 10–3 through 10–5 illustrate congratulatory messages to express pleasure for promotions granted to friends, colleagues, or business associates.

You can mix business with pleasure by incorporating congratulations or other goodwill messages within a typical business letter (Figure 10–6). The letter might have been an answer to the letter illustrated in Figure 12–2.

Congratulations, Mr. Smith! ← **Good news**

We saw the enclosed news item about your daughter's marriage in this morning's STAR and thought you might like an extra copy. ← **Reasons**

Please accept this copy with our very best wishes. ← **Goodwill**

Sincerely,

Figure 10-1
Letter of Congratulations Enclosing Newspaper Notice

Dear Millie,

How exciting! You have written a soon-to-be published book. ← **Good news** ← **Reasons**
What a wonderful accomplishment on top of what you have already achieved. You deserve it!

All of us wish you the very best with this project. ← **Goodwill**

Sincerely,

Kathy

Figure 10-2
Letter of Congratulations to New Author

DORSCH TOOL AND ENGINEERING COMPANY
3419 Georgetown Road • Indianapolis, Indiana 46224
Phone: A.C. 317 / 293-6722

December 11, 19--

Mr. Paul A. Edwards
2171 Farmington Avenue
St. Louis, MO 63155

Good News → Congratulations, Mr. Edwards!

Reason → You very much deserve the promotion to District Supervisor for the Los Angeles area of Preston Manufacturing and Engineering Company. This promotion reflects your intelligence and enthusiasm and your ability to work well with salespersons and customers. With your supervision, sales in Los Angeles and vicinity are sure to increase.

Goodwill → When you return to this area, please be sure to visit us. We will be eager to hear the latest news.

Sincerely,

Margaret Williams

Mrs. Margaret Williams
Purchasing Department

MW:dl

Goodwill → You may want to visit Mr. Robert B. Meyers at Schuster Manufacturing Company. He can give you several leads.

Figure 10-3
Letter of Congratulations for Promotion

Dear Ellen,

Congratulations on your recent promotion to Associate Professor. Since most instructors wait much longer than you have for this promotion, your colleagues obviously have recognized your professional attributes.

I am certain you will continue to contribute much to the advancement of quality higher education at U. of A.

Cordially,

Figure 10-4
Letter of Congratulations for Early Promotion

"Insurance Salesperson of the Year!" That's you! Congratulations on persuading so many people to buy life insurance. ← **Good news** ← **Reason**

On the lighter side, Jack, can you join me for lunch Friday or Monday? Please telephone me at my office, 212-8907, so that we can set a definite date. ← **Goodwill**

Figure 10-5
Letter of Congratulations to a Super Salesperson

Congratulations on your choice of topic for your study. Your research should provide useful information for educators. I would appreciate a copy of the summary of results. ← **Good news** ← **Reason**

Since the quarter ends on December 17, please mail me the materials and complete instructions within two weeks. I will need papers for 16 student teachers. ← **Details**

Incidentally, Margy Adams told me that you will be a recorder at the NCATE Conference in Chicago this February. That is great! You will enjoy the sessions and will meet some very interesting and enthusiastic educators. ← **Goodwill**

Figure 10-6
Letter of Congratulations to Researcher

Thank you for your subscription to World News. We are pleased to have you as our customer. ← **Thank you**

If you should move, all your magazine subscriptions can follow you to your new address. Simply send us a list of your magazines--four to six weeks before you actually move--even if you did not order them from us. ← **Personalized help**

Remember that you can write or telephone us whenever you have comments about your subscription or the contents of World News. ← **Confidence**

Figure 10-7
Letter of Appreciation for Periodical Subscription

EXPRESSING APPRECIATION

An oral thank you is polite, but a written thank you makes a special and personal impression. Plan your letter **expressing appreciation** to:

1. Say thank you, usually at the beginning of the letter (deductive approach)
2. Add sincere, personalized comments
3. Close on a strong note (The end of the letter should convey a more productive thought than "Thank you again for. . . .")

Letters of appreciation may be brief, as Figures 10-7 through 10-14 indicate. Figures 10-7 through 10-9 illustrate communica-

Dear Mr. and Mrs. Young:

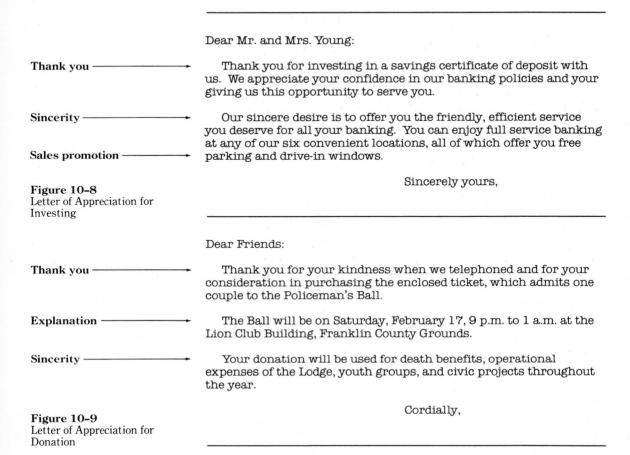

Thank you → Thank you for investing in a savings certificate of deposit with us. We appreciate your confidence in our banking policies and your giving us this opportunity to serve you.

Sincerity → Our sincere desire is to offer you the friendly, efficient service you deserve for all your banking. You can enjoy full service banking at any of our six convenient locations, all of which offer you free

Sales promotion → parking and drive-in windows.

Sincerely yours,

Figure 10–8
Letter of Appreciation for Investing

Dear Friends:

Thank you → Thank you for your kindness when we telephoned and for your consideration in purchasing the enclosed ticket, which admits one couple to the Policeman's Ball.

Explanation → The Ball will be on Saturday, February 17, 9 p.m. to 1 a.m. at the Lion Club Building, Franklin County Grounds.

Sincerity → Your donation will be used for death benefits, operational expenses of the Lodge, youth groups, and civic projects throughout the year.

Cordially,

Figure 10–9
Letter of Appreciation for Donation

tions from business people thanking the readers for subscribing to a periodical, investing in a savings certificate of deposit, and donating funds, respectively. The letters in Figures 10–10 through 10–12 illustrate special thank you's to personal friends and are handwritten. Figure 10–10 illustrates a reply to a note of congratulations. Figures 10–11 and 10–12 thank the reader for a pleasant visit and for a gift, respectively. A thank-you message for those teacher educators who participated in the study of student teaching problems (see Figure 12–2) might have read similar to Figure 10–13. Notice that the writer of Figure 10–13 enclosed a copy of the summary offered in his persuasive inquiry letter. The letter in Figure 10–14 illustrates a thank you to Dr. Adams who had written a letter of recommendation for the writer. (See Chapter 9 for communications acknowledging orders.)

Dear Caron and Walt,

Many thanks for taking the time to notice the newspaper picture, cut it out, and mail us a copy. We really appreciate it! ← **Thank you**

My concern remains high over the trend we seem to follow of heading for bigness—big government, big business, and big unions. Sometimes bigness makes it rather difficult for the little guys and gals to be heard. ← **Personal comment**

Cordially,

Figure 10-10
Letter of Appreciation for Newspaper Clipping

Dear Marc and Cindy,

Thank you for making my Marion visit such a great one! It was so rewarding to return to so many friends and share good laughs together! ← **Thank you**

Do have a happy summer, God bless you both. ← **Personal comment**

Sincerely,

Figure 10-11
Letter of Appreciation to Host and Hostess

Dear Emily and Bill,

Thank you for the lovely and practical wedding gifts. ← **Thank you** I have used the silver platter several times and expect to use it often. ← **Sincerity**

Sincerely,

Figure 10-12
Letter of Appreciation for a Gift

Thank you ⟶ Thank you, Dr. Mosini, for helping me complete my study, which was possible because of your cooperation and the cooperation of student teachers and college supervisors.

Sincerity ⟶ Here is a copy of the summary of findings and conclusions. This summary should be helpful for analyzing problems faced by your student teachers.

Action ⟶ Please write or telephone me at 114-5541 if you would like additional information.

Cordially yours,

Figure 10-13
Letter of Appreciation for Participating in Research (See Figure 12-2)

Thank you ⟶ Thank you, Dr. Adams, for your informative letter of recommendation to Mr. Allen Jones, Personnel Manager of Electronics, Inc. Mr. Jones was very impressed with your comments. Your letter helped me to get the junior accountant job.

Sincerity ⟶ I will do my best to live up to your recommendation.

Sincerely yours,

Figure 10-14
Letter of Appreciation for Letter of Recommendation

Imagine the great pleasure the unsolicited testimonial in Figure 10-15 would give to the distributor of a city directory. The letter could become part of a sales kit for *New City Directory* salespersons. It could be shown to business people who deal with credit accounts with the hope of increasing sales for the directory.

EXPRESSING SYMPATHY

The message of condolence also has a place in business communications. It tells the receiver that you know about the personal grief and are lending support during a difficult time. Because of uncertainty about the person's feelings, many people find it easier to mail a sympathy card rather than express their personal feelings. A personalized message, however, is remembered and appreciated more than any printed message.

Approach the message in simple, honest thoughts that refer directly to the reader's loss but do not dwell on the unpleasantness by:

1. Referring to the situation and individuals involved using natural phrases and words which remind the reader of pleasant—rather than unpleasant—events or things (deductive approach)

DORSCH TOOL AND ENGINEERING COMPANY
3419 Georgetown Road • Indianapolis, Indiana 46224
Phone: A.C. 317 / 293-6722

March 10, 19--

Mr. Warren Clifford
B. L. Smith & Company
25 Washington Boulevard
Taylor, MI 48180

Dear Mr. Clifford:

It was a pleasure meeting you when you visited to ask us to reorder the New City Directory. ← **Good news**

We have been a yearly customer for the New City Directory since 1936. It has helped us collect thousands and thousands of dollars in charge account "skips" because of being able to make crosschecks. For example, we teach our office workers that even if a person's name is not listed as living on a particular street, the individual might be rooming with people listed in the street section of the book. The employee will check. ← **Indirect thanks**

We plan to be a customer for the New City Directory for as long as we are in business. The Directory pays for itself over and over again. ← **Sincerity**

Cordially yours,

Annette S. Clary

Miss Annette S. Clary
Credit Department

ASC:dlj

Figure 10-15
Letter of Praise (Testimonial)

2. Ending with an encouraging reference to the future or with a gesture of goodwill

Although letters should be written with concrete words—words which convey a clear and definite picture—the letter of condolence should avoid words that encourage the reader to relive an unpleasant experience. Use neutral terminology.

There is nothing wrong with using the word "death" in a note expressing sympathy, but never describe the death. Avoid details or "editorializing" at the expense of the reader's feelings.

Dear Mr. Johnson:

Agreeable statement → Although I did not know Mrs. Johnson, I am sure that she will not be forgotten by those who loved and needed her.

Goodwill → Please accept my heartfelt sympathy in these days of sadness following your great loss.

Sincerely,

Figure 10-16
Letter of Condolence (Employment Relationship)

The reader does not wish to reexperience the frightening incident and does not need to be reminded of how shocking or unnecessary the death seemed to be.

Express sorrow with dignity and with respect. End on a realistic but uplifting note that the reader will appreciate:

> Ellen's death has brought sadness to us, but we will always remember her as a warm and friendly person.

The overused phrase, "I am sorry," can sound hollow, insufficient, and insensitive in expressing human grief. Only if your message is worded genuinely and personally and only if you do, indeed, feel personal sorrow should you use the phrase. The context of the message and your relationship with the person will determine whether the phrase expresses a genuine feeling or is a substitute for sincere words.

> Words never quite convey our deepest feeling when a close friend and associate has unexpectedly been taken from us. I want you to know that I am very sorry and will do all I can to help you.

> We shared many happy times with John. The good feelings his presence brought will continue with us, as I know they will with you.

Whether to write in longhand or type the message becomes a personal choice. Either is acceptable for business or employment relations (Figures 10-16 and 10-17). Typewriting may introduce a feeling of impersonality for personal or social relationships; therefore, handwriting is preferred (Figures 10-18 and 10-19).

Death need not be the only occasion for sending expressions of sympathy. Condolences are appropriate also for other situations that create unhappiness for the person. Offer assistance whenever you can (Figure 10-20).

Waltere Supermarkets, Inc.
220 Michigan Avenue • P.O. Box 1785
Indianapolis, IN 46206 • 317-115-3502

June 1, 19--

Mrs. Sandra Bridges
15 White Circle Boulevard
Indianapolis, IN 46209

Dear Mrs. Bridges:

At such a sad time, words seem rather meaningless, but we at Waltere's want you to know how much we liked Carl and how great his loss will be to all of us. When any of us needed a boost from a friend, he was there. ← **Agreeable statement**

We know that the memory you cherish of the many years you shared together will help comfort you in the immediate days ahead. ← **Encouragement**

Please consider us your friends and telephone us if we can be helpful. You can count on us--like we counted on Carl. ← **Goodwill**

Sincerely,

Marvella Shane

Mrs. Marvella Shane
Accounting Department

MS:tsp

Several of us will be visiting you next week.

Figure 10-17
Letter of Condolence (Employment Relationship)

EXPRESSING WELCOME

Banking institutions and other service-oriented organizations often send letters to welcome newcomers to the city. Sometimes the letters are mailed weeks before the individual moves to the new location. These letters not only promote goodwill, they also may introduce brief descriptions of company policy or services. Letters may also welcome a new business, a new employee, or a new member. Make the welcome letter a genuine greeting, rather than a strong sales pitch by:

1. Welcoming the newcomer with an agreeable statement (deductive approach)

Agreeable statement →

Encouragement →

Goodwill →

Dear Mrs. Burns:

Please accept the deep sympathy of all the Fraternity members.

We had the privilege of knowing John for many years, and we valued his good judgment and many contributions to the Club. He will be remembered by everyone who knew him.

If we can do anything for you, now or in the future, you can count on us as willing friends

Very sympathetically,

Figure 10-18
Letter of Condolence (Social Relationship)

Agreeable statement →

Encouragement →

Goodwill →

Dear Henry,

John and I just learned about your great loss. We know how much Ellen meant to you and our hearts are filled with sorrow.

Will you please let us know if there is anything we can do to help you.

Cordially yours,

Figure 10-19
Letter of Condolence (Personal Relationship)

Waltere Supermarkets, Inc.
220 Michigan Avenue • P.O. Box 1785
Indianapolis, IN 46206 • 317-115-3502

November 20, 19--

Miss Marie Adams
219 Crestwood Court
Indianapolis, IN 46209

Dear Miss Adams:

Your mother telephoned this morning to explain your emergency surgery last evening. She assured us that you are recovering well, which we are all delighted to hear! ← **Agreeable statement**

Since your co-workers and I want you to be your hale and hearty self again, we do not want you to think about your work here. Of course we miss you but are revising our routines to carry on until the doctor says that you are ready and until you feel well enough to return. ← **Encouragement**

In the meantime, perhaps you may feel like reading some of the books Mrs. Jones is bringing you today. We will be thinking about you. ← **Goodwill**

Sincerely,

John Smith

John Smith

oc

Figure 10-20
Letter of Condolence (Employee Illness)

2. Introducing yourself (if necessary) and briefly explaining your policy or services.
3. Offering your assistance (goodwill)

The letter in Figure 10-21 welcomes a new member to a professional organization. It explains briefly the privileges of membership. The letter in Figure 10-22 stresses the importance of the potential customer by enclosing an identification card and an offer to extend credit. The letter in Figure 10-23 acknowledges the purchase of two residential lots and welcomes the readers to Forest Hills, a new housing development.

Dear T.E.A. Member:

Agreeable statement → Welcome to charter membership in the Teacher Educators Association.

Explanation and assistance → Your membership entitles you to all of the rights and privileges under our constitution. Several publications, including position papers, pamphlets, the Teacher's Quarterly, and other publications, are under consideration for mailing to all members. If you have any suggestions regarding publication, please advise an officer or a member of the Publications Committee. The members' names are listed in the attached leaflet.

Goodwill → We look forward to seeing you at various meetings and events.

Cordially yours,

Figure 10-21
Welcome Letter to Charter Member

Agreeable attention getter → IT'S A GENUINE PLEASURE, MRS. ENDICOTT,

to have you as a holder of one of our Country House Identification Cards.

Explanation and assistance → You can use your identification card in all departments of the store and at our Super Gas Service Station.

Are you interested in a weekly, 30-day, or budget account? The enclosed brochure describes the special features of each open account. Mrs. Kimberly Cleaver in our Credit Department (111-3418) will be happy to talk with you about our credit accounts.

Goodwill → We will do our best to help you enjoy shopping and buying at Country House.

Sincerely yours,

COUNTRY HOUSE

Jane McConnel

Miss Jane McConnel
Customer Relations

ear

Enclosures

Figure 10-22
Welcome Letter to New Customer

June 21, 19--

Mr. and Mrs. Steve Marshall
3597 Lindhurst Drive
Knoxville, TN 37115

Dear Helen and Steve:

Thank you for joining our community of Forest Hills. We are looking forward to a continued relationship with you. ← **Thank you and welcome**

We enjoyed getting you started with your purchase of two residential lots--Lots 1 and 2, Block 22, Unit 3, Subdivision 2, Township 45S, Range 26E. ← **The purchase**

If we can be of further assistance to you, your family, or your friends, please write or telephone us. ← **Confidence**

Sincerely yours,

Shirlee Rosen

Miss Shirlee Rosen
Vice-President of Customer Relations

SR/df

Figure 10-23
Acknowledgment and Welcome to New Residents

CHAPTER SUMMARY

Some letters have the special objective of pleasing the reader. These goodwill communications may express congratulations, thanks, sympathy, or welcome. They begin with a direct (deductive) approach and always focus on the reader's esteem. Goodwill letters can boost personal relations, customer or public relations, or employee morale.

Write the message by hand if it requires an extra soft and personal touch. You may type the message if you are writing it as a business person, even though you are expressing personal feelings.

Always convey sincerity by avoiding standardized and impersonal phrases and by not exaggerating your feelings. End on a strong and positive note, even when the note concerns unhappy occasions.

STUDY QUESTIONS

1. Why are goodwill communications important? What are the types of goodwill communications?
2. Which approach—inductive or deductive—should you use when writing goodwill communications? Why?
3. Why should you avoid:
   a. The term "good luck" in a congratulatory message?
   b. Descriptive details in a letter of condolence?
   c. The term "I am sorry"?
   d. The term "thank you again" in the last paragraph of a letter of appreciation?
4. What are the occasions for writing a message of condolence?
5. To whom are letters of welcome sent?

ACTIVITIES

1. Mary Jane Johnson has just been appointed Editor of the college newspaper. This is the first time that a woman has held this position. Although you did not get to know her very well, Mary Jane was a classmate in Journalism 123. Write her a congratulatory note.
2. Assume you are the director of the County Soil and Water Conservation Area. Write a congratulatory letter to Michael Hilton, who has received two honors. This was the newspaper account:

   > Farmer Michael Hilton was named Conservationist of the Year and elected to the board of supervisors for the County Soil and Water Conservation Area. Melvin Tree, County Extension Agent, presented the two honors at the 20th annual banquet at the Rustic Cabin.
   >
   > The Conservationist of the Year award is presented to landowners who conserve soil and land by participating in programs that are beneficial for the county's agricultural and nonagricultural lands.
   >
   > Organization members owning more than ten acres of land selected Hilton for the Board.

3. One of your former teachers has written a letter of recommendation for you. You believe that the letter was a crucial factor in your getting the position. Write the teacher a thank-you letter.
4. Write a letter of appreciation to a stranger who has completed a questionnaire for you, thus enabling you to get the information you needed for some informal research, a thesis, or a dissertation. If you like, you can thank Dr. Bowers, the leader in Business Education, who selected and ranked fifteen major issues in the field (Activity 4, Chapter 12).
5. As Sales Director for a relatively new company, write a letter welcoming a new customer, New Haven Supply Company,

and expressing your appreciation. You can use the communication as an opportunity to sell additional products or to explain sales policies, but remember the basic intent of the letter.

6. The wife of your co-worker has died as a result of injuries caused by an automobile accident. The accident was two weeks ago; the woman died yesterday. Although you did meet Mrs. Clyde at a dinner honoring retired employees, you know little about her. Write Mr. Clyde a letter of condolence.
7. Assume you are the president of Ontario Sales, a company that takes special interest in events affecting its employees. You learn that an employee's son is serving as Navy Master Chief Machinist's Mate aboard the submarine tender *U.S.S. Proteus.* The ship, a 574-ft "floating repair shop" is home-ported in Apra Harbor, Guam. The *Proteus* is specially equipped and designed to provide complete service for nuclear-powered fleet ballistic submarines. Write the employee a goodwill message.
8. Write a thank-you letter to a member of Congress who supported your viewpoint—the bill passed. Encourage the reader to continue supporting similar legislation.
9. Write a thank-you note to friends who shared their vacation cottage with you. It did not cost you anything—just a few groceries.
10. You and a co-worker applied for the same job transfer. Your friend got the job. Write him an encouraging note.

EDITING

1. Revise these statements for goodwill messages:
   a. Your invited to a birthday party.
   b. I was delighted to receive the special teaching materials you so thoughtfully sent to me.
   c. It is a real pleasure for me to write this letter of congratulations on your twentieth anniversary, for it gives me an opportunity to thank you for your contributions to our success.
   d. We are pleased to invite you to be our guest at the recognition dinner at the Holiday Travel Inn on August 5th.
2. As Gerald Baker, revise the following acceptance into an *informal* acceptance:

   Mr. Gerald Baker accepts with pleasure the kind invitation of the Associates Club to attend a tea on Saturday, July the tenth at three o'clock.

3. The Beals invited you, the Pinkertons, to dinner. Before analyzing the situation, you drafted a formal refusal. Revise the following formal refusal into an *informal* refusal:

   Mr. and Mrs. Jason Pinkerton regret that a previous engagement prevents their accepting the kind invitation to dinner at the home of Mr. and Mrs. James Beal on Saturday, the fifth of June.

4. Rewrite this brief (too brief) thank-you note:

   Your speech to my business students was very much appreciated. You're a top notch speaker. Thank you very much.

IN-BASKET SIMULATIONS

1. Waltere Supermarkets, Inc., has just hired you as Personnel Relations Director. One of Waltere's employees, Joe Williams, is a very proud father. His son, Jeffrey, a senior at a local high school, was appointed to the Air Force Academy. This is an honor, since the entrance requirements are stringent and require an appointment by a member of Congress. Jeff will serve four years as a cadet at the Air Force Academy. If he then serves five years as an aeronautical engineer, he may some day become a general! Write Joe and his wife Kathy a congratulatory message.
2. A friend of yours has congratulated you on your new position as Personnel Relations Director. Write and thank your friend for the pleasant and encouraging message.
3. Whenever a key employee dies, it is the policy of Waltere to show sympathy in any of the following ways:

   a. Send flowers to the funeral home
   b. Arrange for masses or prayers for the deceased
   c. Send a donation to a charity designated by the survivor's spouse

   In addition, Waltere's employee benefits plan allows a cash payment to the survivor and/or dependents. Greg Martin, a manager of one of the convenience stores, died in a motorcycle accident. Mr. Martin was well liked by his customers and co-workers. He was married and had two young children. Write Mrs. Martin a sympathetic note.
4. Research revealed that an increasing number of Waltere's customers purchase ready-made, home-style cooking. Thus, Waltere's began a catering service for special functions.

   Even though it is not your job, you were asked to help write the format for a welcome letter to new customers who want catering service on a fairly regular basis. Write the letter welcoming the new customer and explaining how he, she, or the company represented can profit from the service.

Writing Negative Responses

After studying Chapter 11, you should be able to:

- Write a tactful letter answering "no" to requests for adjustments, credit, and information, products, and services
- Determine when to use form statements, paragraphs, and letters in negative replies

Chapter 8 gave pointers for answering letters with a positive response. However, some inquiries and requests must be refused. Writing a negative reply need not be a dreaded task; it becomes less awesome when you assume a positive attitude and compose your message recognizing the reader's needs, interests, and emotions. The reader can be refused without using the word "no" and without sacrificing goodwill. The effective letter conveys a disappointing message with tact. It explains the circumstances and what can be done, and it may include sales-promotional data. The letter should end pleasantly and without trite statements.

ANSWERING "NO" TO A REQUEST FOR ADJUSTMENT

Letters that refuse requests follow several basic guidelines:

1. *Begin with a neutral statement with which you and the reader can agree.* Be as positive as you can without leading the reader to believe that a "yes" answer follows (inductive approach).
2. *Give pertinent facts*—completely, clearly, concisely, concretely, correctly, coherently, courteously, and positively. If done effectively, the reader may be receptive to the refusal. Generally, explanations are more lengthy than refusal statements.
3. *De-emphasize the refusal.* Sometimes the refusal can be implied. Whether implied or expressly stated, the reader should realize that the claim is not being granted. Chapter 3 includes ideas on de-emphasizing (for example, using positive language, writing in passive or impersonal language, placing the refusal in a de-emphatic position in the sentence or paragraph, or giving minimum space to the refusal statement).
4. *Say what you can do, instead of apologizing and making excuses.* Statements such as, "I am sorry but we cannot grant your request" are negative and insincere. The apology is merely a figure of speech, a handy excuse, and the reader will know it.
5. *Add sales-promotional data whenever possible.* Like letters granting claims, the refusal adjustment letter is an opportunity to include ideas that lead to future sales. Many companies have standardized form paragraphs that serve this purpose.
6. *Close on an optimistic note.* Before the last paragraph, the reader must be convinced that the writer is being sincere and fair. Avoid trite statements and use positive words.

As with all business letters, the first sentence should get the reader's attention. An immediate refusal at the beginning of the letter is unnecessary and may hinder goodwill. On the other hand, to suggest a "yes" reply would be unfair and tactless. An appropriate beginning—although not very original—might be to thank the reader for the letter or the topic of the letter.

In all refusal letters, the first paragraph should act as a **buffer** (an idea to lessen the shock). In addition to thanking the reader, the buffer can express other neutral and agreeable thoughts: compliments, assurances, or pleasures. You can compliment readers for something they have done, their interest in your product or services, or for their requests. Readers can be assured that the facts are being carefully considered, or you can express pleasure or agreement with reader actions.

It is inappropriate to end a reply to an unhappy customer with, "We are sure that future orders will meet with your complete satisfaction." The statement is a reminder that past orders have been unsatisfactorily filled or handled. It shows no genuine reader interest. It would be better to switch to a related subject. Sales-promotional information is a possibility. If the writer is enclosing a brochure or catalog, mention it and refer the customer to appropriate merchandise that is available for quick delivery or at competitive prices.

The following message would antagonize the reader and is not a good example for a letter refusing an adjustment:

> Thank you for your letter of May 11 about the wig you wish to return for credit. We cannot grant your request because of company policy. If we can help further, please write us.

The refusal is so curt that the customer would feel a "brush off." In addition, readers care little about "company policy," particularly if the policy is contrary to their wishes. Using company policies or practices as an excuse to say "no" damages public and customer relations. "If we can help further" inaccurately implies that the writer has been helpful. In reality, the writer is saying that the request could not be granted and that similar treatment could be expected in the future. The letter in Figure 11–1 is a better refusal. It courteously offers a possible solution: suggests that Mr. Sampson could help refit the wig so that it would become a useful purchase. To alert Mr. Sampson, the writer can mail him a copy of the letter. Mr. Sampson could then anticipate a telephone call or visit from the customer (Ms. Grant).

The letter in Figure 11–2 is the answer to a consumer who had problems with an appliance, now out of warranty. Note that the first paragraph assures Mr. Johnson that all the facts were carefully considered. The company repaired the appliance without charge to the consumer but refused to reimburse the consumer for previous work because the work order was not authorized by a company agent. The refusal is de-emphasized; sales-promotional information is included and a personalized contact is included.

Neutral statement → Thank you, Ms. Grant, for your letter of May 11 requesting the return of a wig you recently purchased.

Pertinent details → Generally, we accept return of all merchandise that is in resalable condition and in compliance with state and federal laws. Wigs fall under governmental health regulations and cannot be accepted for resale.

What can be done now → Mr. Sampson at the Beauty Palace (1110 Madison Street) will adjust your wig to fit you properly for a nominal fee. You purchased one of the best wigs available, so it would be worth your time to contact

Optimism → Mr. Sampson at 184-3408. With his help, you will have a wig you can wear proudly.

Cordially yours,

Figure 11-1
Answering "No" to a Purchase Return (Adjustment)

Dear Mr. Johnson:

Neutral statement regarding claim → Thank you for your recent letter concerning Parker range, Model KS 111 RXAO, Serial No. KRD 01001. Mr. G. Wade, Service Supervisor, reviewed the history and service charges for this range.

Explanation leading to a positive refusal and stating what can be done → Since a Parker Products service technician replaced the left rear burner switch and repaired a broken wire on another switch, we understand that the Parker range is now working properly. We were pleased to service the range at no expense to you. Previous work, however, was performed by an unauthorized agent. We can only be responsible for work done by our agents.

Sales promotion → Parker appliances are produced using the highest quality parts and reliability control. All parts are pretested for durability. Our desire is to give customers the best products available.

Goodwill action → Please contact Mr. Gordon Silvers at our Indianapolis address, or telephone him at 317-217-3727, if you desire help in the future.

Sincerely,

Figure 11-2
Letter Refusing Reimbursement for Unauthorized Repairs

ANSWERING "NO" TO A REQUEST FOR CREDIT

Letters that refuse credit follow guidelines similar to those for saying "no" to granting adjustments:

1. *Begin with a neutral statement* (inductive approach).
2. *Give explanations leading to the credit refusal, using positive and tactful language.* Although persons who have been denied credit can request the reasons why, writers should limit explanations so as not to lecture on credit guidelines, talk down to, or accuse the reader. The refusal should be a natural outcome of the explanation.

3. *Offer an alternative to credit purchases.* Remember that sales are welcome, but the company cannot afford to take credit risks. Offer to sell on some form of cash basis (money order, certified check, etc.).
4. *Provide incentives for cash purchases* (cash discounts, special prices, or desirable merchandise).
5. *Include sales-promotional data*—information on products and services, detailed and illustrated brochures and catalogs, order forms, and ready-to-use envelopes. In addition, names, addresses, and telephone numbers of specific individuals encourage readers to buy quickly and make it easier for them to do so.
6. *Close on an optimistic note*, preferably an action that leads to an immediate order.

Writers of credit refusals should ask themselves, "What can I write that will favorably impress the reader and avoid antagonism?" "What ideas should I use to encourage the reader to buy on a cash basis?"

The letter in Figure 11–3 refuses credit to the reader but offers incentives for cash purchases (cash discount, catalog, immediate shipment, special sale prices, a ready-to-use envelope, and the toll-free telephone number to contact a company sales representative).

Retail credit may be refused because the applicant has not supplied complete information:

> Your credit application did not contain sufficient information for us to open a 30-day charge account in your name. Do you have other favorable information? Please let us know these facts so that we can reconsider your application.

Retail credit may be refused without stating any specific reason, but by stating the factors used to evaluate credit applications:

> Several factors are considered before we accept credit accounts; for example, the applicant's age, income, employment record, credit references, and ability to pay past and current obligations.

Other factors include:

Failure to supply specific information requested on the credit application form
Insufficient time on current job
Unemployment
History of late-payment
Insufficient current assets
Too many current obligations
No bank or savings account

Dear Mr. Walsh:

Neutral statement →

Your order letter for Herrington furniture and request for credit is sincerely appreciated.

Explanation leading to positive refusal and stating what can be done →

In order to offer our customers the lowest prices possible for quality items, we have established a limited credit policy. Through experience, we have learned that we must extend credit only to customers with very high credit ratings. Therefore, we ask that your purchase be on a cash basis (certified check or money order) or, if you prefer, on a cash-on-delivery basis. As a bonus, a 1% cash discount will be available to you. This discount represents a $1 savings for every $100 purchase, excluding shipping costs and state taxes.

Sales promotional information →

Enclosed is a copy of our current catalog illustrating the fine furniture we stock for immediate shipment. You will notice that many well-known brand names are available to you, several of them at very special prices until February 28.

Quick, confident action →

To send your check, Mr. Walsh, please use the enclosed addressed and stamped envelope. If you like, you can telephone our toll-free number 800-171-6704, and we will ship your order c.o.d. You will be pleased with your purchase.

Sincerely,

Figure 11-3
Letter Refusing Credit Purchases

The specific reason for the refusal is sometimes stated in the credit refusal letter:

> Since you are under the legal age limit, you can understand our hesitation in granting you credit now. Things will be different in several years.

Although not always best, some businesses refuse credit without giving a specific reason or any reasons why credit is refused:

> After carefully considering your credit application, we believe it would be better for you to purchase on a cash basis.

Sometimes business firms must refuse credit to other business firms after examining the applicant's financial statements and checking with credit references and/or credit rating agencies (for example, Dun and Bradstreet). The specific reason is usually stated in the credit refusal letter. Nonetheless, the letter should be tactful and as positive as possible. Alternatives should be offered (for example, cash sales, the opportunity for cash discount privileges, the advantages for buying smaller quantities and more

Dear Miss Reynolds

Your interest in our plastic reproductions of poisonous plants is appreciated. ← **Neutral statement**

It is true that we have been providing the leaves without charge. However, due to a limited supply, there are some restrictions in the distribution. The plastic replicas have been furnished primarily to educational areas, such as schools, children's camps, Boy Scouts, Girl Scouts, and similar groups. ← **Explanation**

If you will explain how you plan to use the plastic leaves, we shall be glad to give further consideration to your request. A note at the bottom of this letter would be fine. If possible, we will then forward the reproductions. ← **What can be done—optimism**

Cordially

Figure 11–4
Answering "No" to Request for Special Items

frequently [less money tied up in inventory, up-to-date items available for customers, cash flow possibilities, and so on], local financing possibilities, and special assistance).

ANSWERING "NO" TO REQUESTS FOR INFORMATION, PRODUCTS, OR SERVICES

Sometimes, public officials and business people must refuse requests for information, materials, or services. To refuse such requests:

1. Begin with a neutral statement (inductive approach)
2. Give explanations for the refusal
3. Imply or state the refusal
4. Say what can be done
5. Include sales-promotional data when applicable
6. Close with optimism

The letter in Figure 11–4 is a brief, but sincere, refusal that suggests how the reader might receive plastic reproductions not otherwise available to her. The limited supply restricts distribution, but with an adequate explanation of intended usage, the reader can receive the desired items. To show good faith, the writer suggests that *a note at the bottom of this letter would be fine*.

The letter in Figure 11–5 is a refusal to participate in a survey because of company policy. Instead of using the term "company policy," the writer explains why the company cannot grant the request: no survey forms or questionnaires are answered. Note too that the first paragraph compliments Ms. Parsons.

Dear Ms. Parsons:

Neutral statement → We are sincerely complimented by your interest in our corporation, its products, and its operations.

Explanation and refusal → Like countless other companies, we receive a great many requests to participate in surveys, and in most cases we must devote an uneconomic amount of time to fact-finding and analysis for the information to be truly representative and useful. Frequently, we cannot cooperate because data are not available on the subject of inquiry.

What can be done—optimism → Enclosed is your survey form so that you can submit it to another business firm in your area.

Sincerely,

Figure 11-5
Answering "No" to All Requests for Survey Information

Dear Mr. Watkins

Neutral statement → We appreciate your interest in Sea Shore Products as evidenced by your letter of December 1.

Explanation → Sea Shore Products Co. is a highly decentralized and diversified company with no hiring done at the corporate level for any of its operating divisions. We are, therefore, not able to respond to your survey.

What can be done—optimism → Since you might be able to use your survey form elsewhere, we are returning it to you.

Sincerely

Figure 11-6
Answering "No" Because All Information is Not Available

The letter in Figure 11-6 is similar to the one in Figure 11-5, but the refusal is based on an individual situation rather than a blanket policy of refusing to complete every survey or questionnaire. In this case, the company does not have the information needed to comply with the writer's request.

The letter in Figure 11-7 is a tactful, goodwill-building refusal to speak to executive trainees. In the first paragraph the writer agrees with what the reader is doing. Then, instead of merely stating, *I have another commitment* or *I am busy at that time*, the writer explains the implied refusal. In addition, he names a capable individual as an alternative suggestion. Notice that the writer does not state, *I have asked Miss Hamilton to speak. . . .* Since he does not have the authority to plan the program, it would be presumptuous of him to choose the speakers. Instead, the writer

Dear Mr. Sundae

Your invitation to speak at the management seminar came as a pleasant surprise. Since a similar training session helped me develop my managerial skills, I know how beneficial the experience can be to executive trainees. ← **Neutral, related statement**

The management seminar and Nationwide's in-service training program are scheduled for the same week. In fact, I am presiding over several training sessions. Naturally, my first responsibility is to my employer. ← **Explanation and refusal**

If you would like a suggestion, you might contact M. Dale Hamilton, management consultant for Perfection Company and for International Communications. She has the knowledge and skill necessary to communicate effectively to the seminar participants. Dale and I were classmates at ISU; she has been a consultant for ten years and is well-respected for her work. The enclosed card includes Dale's address and telephone number. ← **Suggestion**

With you in charge, Mr. Sundae, I am sure the seminar will be very productive. You are doing a great job. ← **Goodwill**

Sincerely

Figure 11-7
Answering "No" to a Speaking Engagement

provided the information needed to contact Miss Hamilton. The goodwill statement expresses confidence in the reader.

Some requests for products or information must be refused temporarily. This is the situation in Figure 11-8. Vacation Motor-Inn Corporation wrote Mary Doe that because of high demand the information she requested cannot be sent now; however, she can expect it within twenty days. In the meantime, Ms. Doe can use the toll-free telephone number to make motel reservations. Although brief, Mrs. Applegate's refusal letter is reader-centered, tactful, and positive. The letter reflects the writer's sincerity and goodwill.

STANDARDIZED STATEMENTS AND PARAGRAPHS

Whether your reply is "yes" or "no," save time by writing standardized data for your letters. Form statements or paragraphs similar to those included in Chapter 8 can be used in refusal letters to answer common requests, explain company policies, or provide sales-promotional data. It is especially important that refusal letters look and read like original communications. To maintain goodwill, the consumer must believe that the company has considered carefully the reader's request and is acting fairly.

Vacation Motor-Inn Corporation

99 Center Street
Memphis, TN 38101
901-187-4580

Toll-free number for residents of Tennessee
for making reservations: **1-800-182-7732**
Toll-free number for making reservations: **1-800-211-7732**

February 2, 19--

Ms. Mary Doe
111 Weir Drive
Indianapolis, IN 46201

Neutral Statement →

Thank you, Ms. Doe, for your letter of January 25, indicating your interest in the new Phone-a-Reservation procedure.

Explanation and what can be done →

We have received so many requests for the directory that it is now in its third printing. However, you should receive the directory and instructions for Phone-a-Reservation before February 22.

Goodwill action →

In the meantime, feel free to telephone us at 1-800-211-7732 for help in making reservations for any Vacation Motor-Inn.

Sincerely yours,

VACATION MOTOR-INN CORPORATION

Mary Applegate

Mrs. Mary Applegate

rl

Figure 11-8
Answering the Letter in Figure 8-4 with a Temporary Negative

CHAPTER SUMMARY

Regardless of the topic, the "no" should be tactfully written so that the reader will be convinced that the writer is sincere and fair. Consider the reader's needs, interests, and emotions; then write a letter that conveys sincerity, fairness, and goodwill. Emphasize the explanation; de-emphasize the refusal. Save form statements and paragraphs to use for routine data. Stress the positive so that the negative letter does not appear uncaring or routine.

STUDY QUESTIONS

1. Why is it especially important to compose a "no" letter that is reader-centered or psychologically oriented toward the reader?
2. What pointers would you give to the writer who must refuse an adjustment request?
3. What pointers would you give to the writer refusing a request for credit?
4. Why is the indirect approach best for most refusal letters?
5. Why should refusal letters end optimistically?
6. What techniques can writers use to de-emphasize?
7. Why are form paragraphs sometimes used in refusal letters?
8. Why should you avoid the following statements in "no" letters:
   a. "If we can help further . . ."
   b. "Our company policy is . . ."
   c. "We regret to say . . ."

ACTIVITIES

1. Write a letter refusing this invitation from a high school guidance counselor:

Dear ________________:

Adams High School will be holding Career Day on October 8. If you will remember, a speaker on another Career Day helped you decide on a career in economics. He spent twenty minutes explaining the opportunities and advantages in being an economist.

Will you do the same thing for this year's high school students? Will you visit us on Career Day and tell why you became an economist and why it is an interesting career?

Since Career Day begins at 9:00 a.m., I would appreciate your being on the program soon after 10:00 a.m., but I can change this hour if doing so will make it possible for you to be here.

Please let me have your comments this month.

Sincerely,

Invitation from High School Guidance Counselor

2. You have been the Credit Manager for a large import-export firm for five years. The company sells high-quality crystal and china. Each credit request is thoroughly checked, and credit is available to businesses with good credit ratings. A ¼ percent cash discount encourages buyers to pay purchases within the ten-day cash discount period.

Today, you received a pleasant letter from two people from your home town: Mr. and Mrs. Jerry Silvers, owners of Silvers Gift Shoppe. They requested a credit purchase. An investigation reveals that their credit rating is not good. They are late in making payments; some purchases are never paid.

Write a tactful letter refusing the credit-purchase request. Encourage cash purchases and provide sales-promotional material.

3. Before moving out of town, a friend habitually borrowed your belongings (books, clothes, furniture, equipment, just about anything). You willingly lent everything, even though you usually had to ask for the return of the article. Yesterday, you received a letter requesting your copy of *My Favorite Poetry*. This copy was personally autographed by the well-known author. You are reluctant to part with it. Write a letter refusing the request tactfully. You do not want to hurt your friend's feelings.
4. Write a refusal letter to Allen Mathews (refer to Figure 12–2) explaining that you cannot ask the student teachers to participate in the study because they are very busy working on another project. Assume that you are Dr. Mosini and compliment Mr. Mathews on his choice of topic. If it would help him, you are willing to complete a Q-sort, but you will need complete data and instructions before October 10. Ask for a copy of the summary of results.
5. You are the General Manager of a local automobile club. Write a tactful refusal letter to Arthur Perry, a member who has requested reimbursement of towing expenses. Under the terms of the policy (towing is covered only after an accident situation), Mr. Perry is not entitled to the reimbursement. Return the bill stating the $50 towing expense. You might quote the pertinent data from the service booklet, or send a copy to Mr. Perry.

EDITING

Revise each sentence to eliminate the weaknesses and to represent effective statements in letters.

1. I thank you for the invitation to speak at your conference meeting of March 15th, two o'clock in the afternoon.
2. We do hope you will understand our position and that you will be successful in finding a replacement.
3. Unfortunately, we don't sell directly to consumers, but you can contact your nearest dealer.
4. We regret to inform you that no liability exists for the insurance claim reported in your letter of November 5. *Beginning statement*

5. Thank you for your continued interest in our products, Miss Hollman.
   Ending statement
6. Feel welcome to come in any day between 9:00 am and 5 pm.
   Ending statement
7. It is a policy of our company to promptly address any complaints and to thoroughly explain our viewpoint.
   Sentence in letter refusing to refund $69 for a pair of shoes that have obviously been worn many times by the customer
8. We appreciate your efforts to bring your personal objectives to our attention but trust you will understand our position. Thank you.
   Ending sentence—Substitute an ending that reflects a positive action. You should have already explained the situation and convinced the reader to purchase again.

IN-BASKET SIMULATIONS

Using the form statements a–q, write letters 1 and 2 below. Personalize the letters as much as possible.

a. Dear ______________________
b. Dear Customer
c. Thank you for your letter of ______________________.
d. Thank you for your letter requesting ______________________.
e. Thank you for your letter of ______________________ requesting a copy of ______________________.
f. Thank you for your letter of ______________________ explaining ______________________.
g. For your information, we are enclosing a copy of our booklet, "______________________."
h. The enclosed copy of our booklet, "______________________," should answer your question on ______________________.
i. Our representative will contact you within ______________________ days.
j. The booklet, "______________________," is no longer in print.
k. We are enclosing a copy of ______________________.
l. We have had so many requests for ______________________ that our stock has been depleted.
m. We do not have any current literature relative to ______________________.
n. The information you requested is explained thoroughly in our publication ______________________.

o. Please let us know if we can help you further.
p. An addressed and stamped envelope is enclosed for your reply.
q. (name of publication) should contain answers to your questions on ________________________. A copy is being mailed to you (specify date).

1. As Ms. Tracy, write a letter to Miss Deborah Collins explaining that the booklet, "Consumer Tips," is out of stock because so many people requested copies of it. Suggest other alternatives.
2. Mr. Thomas Leonard, President of Drug Operations, Waltere Drugs, received a letter from Mrs. Kathryn Owens who lives in Baltimore, Maryland. Mrs. Owens requested literature relative to tetanus immunization. With the help of appropriate form statements, write a letter explaining that you do not have any literature relative to tetanus immunization but that the U.S. Public Health Service recommends adults be immunized against tetanus every ten years after the initial immunization procedure during childhood. For information on tetanus booster shots, suggest that she write to the Public Health Services Advisory Committee on Immunization Practices, Center for Disease Control, Atlanta, Georgia.
3. Mr. Peter Waltere received a letter from a college senior requesting copies of financial reports. As Mr. Waltere's assistant, send the student some information on company operations. Do not send the detailed information; it is confidential.
4. Mr. Summer, Vice President, Director of Sales, received a letter requesting an appointment to discuss merchandising operations at Waltere's. The letter did not give complete details. Mr. Summer will be out of town all month visiting various Mini Marts. He has asked you to write a tactful letter of refusal.
5. You work in the Credit Department at Waltere's. Write a letter refusing credit to William Jamison whose application for credit shows that he is not a good credit risk now. You can list the facts considered and encourage him to buy fewer items on a cash basis now and reapply later if circumstances change (for example, when his income increases substantially). Mr. Jamison may want to take advantage of buying brand name products from the automatic merchandising machines at his local store. Enclose a copy of the catalog. Remember to be tactful.

Writing Persuasive Requests and Claims

12

After studying Chapter 12, you should be able to:

- Cite the differences between a routine request and a persuasive request
- Understand the importance of tone in a persuasive letter
- Use the attention-getter to your own advantage
- Write an effective persuasive letter making it easy for the reader to take an action

The communications discussed in Chapters 8 through 10 involved routine business transactions and pleasant news (for example, requests or inquiries about company products or services, claims for products under warranty, letters sending information or materials, order acknowledgments and letters, and goodwill messages). Writers of routine and good news communications do not have to convince readers to say or do anything. The readers are pleased or expect such messages. Since the purpose of the letter can be accomplished by stating it immediately, writers use the deductive or direct approach.

There are, however, occasions when the information communicated is not routine or pleasant (for example, refusals, which are discussed in Chapter 11; special requests; unusual claims; credit and collections; and sales). To convey such messages, writers must furnish pertinent information or explanations **before** stating the purpose of the letter—an inductive or indirect approach. Readers are more likely to accept unpleasant messages if persuasion precedes the purpose of the letter.

Although the guidelines for writing effective credit, collection, and sales communications are similar to those for persuasive requests and persuasive claims, they are given special attention in Chapters 13 and 14. This chapter covers persuasive request and persuasive claim letters.

THE PERSUASIVE REQUEST LETTER

The **persuasive request letter** asks for special, rather than routine, information or favors. Hence, this communication must be given special attention to achieve its purpose. The persuasive request letter should be directed to the correct person, or at least to the correct specific department. Use this plan for writing the persuasive request letter:

1. *Get the reader's attention* with a statement that interests the reader. Especially in the first paragraph, use reader-centered ideas and avoid a tone or words (for example, *I*, *we*, *us*, or your own name) that reflect self-interest.
2. *State the persuasive information.* Since the reader may not be interested or may resist the message, the persuasion must motivate the reader to continue reading the communication, accept the explanation or information, and act as you wish. Use a central theme and withhold the main point (the request) until you have presented your case. Then, the reader is most apt to grant the request.
3. *State the request clearly and concisely.*
4. *Specify the details necessary to comply with the request.*
5. *Close tactfully and with confidence.*

It takes considerable communication skill to write persuasive letters. The effective writer will prepare a preliminary written outline and write a reader-centered letter with an indirect approach that follows the characteristics of effective letters discussed in Chapter 4: reader-awareness, completeness, clarity, conciseness, concreteness, correctness, coherence, courtesy, and positivism.

Writers who make it difficult, impossible, or impractical for readers to act as requested may defeat their purpose. All necessary materials and instructions should be given to readers asked to complete cards, forms, questionnaires, or other papers enclosed with the communication. Writers should suggest a toll-free or collect call and include the complete telephone number when asking readers to telephone long distance. Readers of persuasive messages should not be expected to provide the envelopes, mailing labels, postage, or other items needed to comply with the writer's request.

The letter in Figure 12-1 invites a well-known person to speak at a meeting. In this situation, the writer can offer a nominal speaking fee; therefore, a persuasive request letter is in order. The reader is challenged by the **attention-getter**—the letter begins with a topic related to the subject, but interesting to the reader. The writer chose the reader's published words, although other possibilities might have been excerpts from the reader's speeches, research, or other professional activities. As with all business correspondence, writers of persuasive messages should learn all they can about the intended readers before writing. Such knowledge makes it easier to choose an appropriate attention-getter and other data, which they can use to persuade.

After the attention-getter, the writer conveys details about the group and its enthusiasm for the topic (writing successful business letters), believing that the information will help persuade the reader.

Only after the writer presents the persuasive data is the purpose of the letter stated. The choice of two possible speaking dates increases the reader's opportunity to agree to the request. Speaking dates should be several months later; the prominent person may have little or no free time in the immediate future. In addition, avoid inconvenient dates (for example, days when the reader is likely to have commitments or national or religious holidays) and offer fees without apologies; therefore, do not write *only $50*.

Not all details are needed in the invitation; the reader needs only the details necessary to make a realistic decision and respond. Subsequent communications can provide additional information.

Dr. Joseph Wright
Public Relations
Communication, Inc.
4312 Celice Avenue
Chicago, IL 60608

Dear Dr. Wright:

Attention-getter related to topic →

Your comments in the current issue of Communicator are very timely and thought-provoking, especially these excerpts:

Start of persuasion →

> Business letters written in just one week transmit more ideas than the works of fiction convey in an entire year.
>
> Letters stimulate intense emotions: faith, hope, joy, sorrow, love, anger, and so on.
>
> Letters convey the rationale that inspires decisions affecting every man, woman, and child.

Obviously, written communications serve all persons and influence countless social and business transactions. Letter-writing skills should be a top priority for every individual, particularly every businessperson.

The University Communications Club consists of fifty undergraduate students who are eager to write successful business letters. Many members will be formatting application letters and data sheets this year. We want to write reader-centered and effective letters.

Request and details →

Would you please speak to us about successful business writing at our November 9 or December 8 meeting? Your informal talk would begin at 7:30 p.m.; we can offer you a $50 honorarium.

Confident action →

Please telephone 317-181-1023 collect to give us your response. As soon as we hear from you, we will begin planning for your visit.

Respectfully,

Figure 12-1
Persuasive Letter to Invite Speaker

Since the writer of Figure 12-1 does not have a toll-free telephone number, a collect call is suggested. This method of answering should produce a faster reply than one by mail; however, the reader might have been given the choice of writing or telephoning. A postal card or addressed and stamped envelope could have been enclosed for the reply.

Figure 12-2 is a letter written to gather data for a class project. It was written with the reader in mind even though the writer's interests are served primarily. The boldface numbers in Figure 12-2 show the following carefully conceived plan that Allen Mathews used:

2020 White Avenue
Marion, IN 46952
September 1, 19--

Dr. Carmen Mosini 1
Department of Education
The Ohio State University
Columbus, OH 43210

Your name, Dr. Mosini, was suggested by ten or more economic 2 ← **Attention-getter**
teachers as a leader in teacher education.

Presently, I am collecting data for a comparative study of
student-teaching problems as viewed by student teachers and
college supervisors. Since no known studies have made these group 3 ← **Persuasion**
comparisons, you will find the results helpful in working with your
student teachers and their secondary school supervisors. I will be 4
pleased to share the results with you.

To determine the most significant problems, the Q-sort--a method 5
of sorting cards from most to least important characteristic--will be
used. Would you please assist the project by ← **Request and details**

completing a Q-sort for each of your student teachers; 6

requesting each student teacher to complete a Q-sort for
herself or himself.

All instructions, materials, and postage will be furnished to you ← **Easy action**
promptly. The data will be treated confidentially as only group 7
comparisons will be made.

You can use the addressed and stamped envelope for your reply, 8
which I would appreciate having before September 25. ← **Confidence**

Respectfully yours,

Figure 12-2
Persuasive Letter to Participate in Research

1. He addressed the letter to a specific individual, Dr. Mosini.
2. He used a sincere, complimentary fact about the reader to secure her interest and attention. Flattery would have been out of place had he chosen to use it.
3. He suggested how the reader would benefit. He does not imply that the reader must participate so that he can complete the study needed for a class project.
4. He mentioned that he would reciprocate by sending a copy of the final results if desired—a persuasive idea.
5. He presented the specific request after he believed he had persuaded Dr. Mosini to at least consider the project.

6. He clearly stated what she would have to do if she agreed to participate.
7. He assured Dr. Mosini that she would remain anonymous and not have to use her own supplies if she decided to participate.
8. He enclosed an addressed and stamped envelope to expedite the reply.

PERSUASIVE LETTERS TO CONGRESS

Members of Congress may support or reject pending legislation on the basis of persuasive communications. The following suggestions will help you write effective letters to your congressional representatives:

1. *Address the letter correctly* (see Chapter 5).
2. *Include a return address*—even if you expect no reply.
3. *Research the facts before writing* (Libraries have copies of the *Congressional Record*, *World Almanac*, and other data sources).
4. *Identify the subject*, preferably with the House or Senate bill number and name. This can be done with a subject line and/or in the body of the letter.
5. *Identify yourself*—voter, citizen, taxpayer, constituent.
6. *Express briefly and concisely your thoughts or conclusions*. You can explain how passage or nonpassage of the bill will affect you, your family, your community, or the country. Be objective and support your conclusions with *facts*.
7. *Write a positive and polite letter*, omitting stereotyped phrases, gripes, or any threats, such as "not vote for you unless. . . ." Individual letters are more convincing than numerous form letters, identically worded messages, or petitions.
8. *State your request clearly*. For example, you might request the member of Congress to vote for, vote against, make a statement for the *Congressional Record*, reply stating her or his position, propose a bill, get a bill out of committee, or get a bill through Congress.
9. *Write when legislation is pending in committee, rather than waiting until a roll call vote is imminent*. Letters written too soon or too late are not effective.
10. *Remember that every issue has at least two sides and that congressional representatives represent varied interests and numerous people*. After weighing all the facts, the congressional representative may not agree with your viewpoint on a particular issue.

71712 West Meranda Street
Yardley, PA 19067
April 2, 19--

The Honorable Keith McConnell
U.S. Senate
Washington, DC 20510

Dear Senator McConnell

BILL S 0001--NONRETURNABLE CANS AND BOTTLES

American consumers have benefited from the passage of Bills S 01 and S 001, which you vigorously supported. ← **Attention-getter**

America is being exposed to the ugly burden of litter on its highways. According to a study reported in the October 19-- issue of ENVIRONMENT, for every mile of highway almost 100 pounds of trash are collected. An estimate of the litter content reveals that 55 percent of the trash is in the form of nonreturnable cans and bottles. The other 45 percent is in various forms of paper, plastic, and glass. ← **Persuasive facts**

Please support Bill S 0001, introduced before the Senate on March 15. Because the bill prohibits the sale of nonreturnable cans and bottles, it should help remedy a serious environmental problem. In addition, the bottle deposit should encourage consumers to return containers to the grocery store rather than throw them foolishly on our highways, our beaches, and our private property. ← **Purpose and writer's views**

May I have your comments. ← **Action desired**

Respectfully

Hilda Albertson

Ms. Hilda Albertson

Figure 12-3
Persuasive Letter to Member of Congress

Figure 12-3 is a persuasive letter written to a senator out of concern for the environment. The letterwriter supports her viewpoint with a related research report, rather than self-centered or emotional ideas. Ms. Albertson's letter to Senator McConnell expresses her thoughts briefly, concisely, and courteously. An overly long letter or a form letter signed by many petitioners might not have been as productive as Ms. Albertson's individual and sincere communication.

THE PERSUASIVE CLAIM LETTER

Most claims are considered routine; the company does not expect persuasion to grant the adjustment requests. Sometimes companies grant claims even though the facts do not support this action. This may be done to encourage future business when costs to remedy the problem are insignificant.

When you doubt that the claim will be granted by immediately asking for the fair adjustment, write a **persuasive claim letter**. You must prove to the reader that he or she is responsible and that a company adjustment is in order.

The following complaint letter does not give the reader an opportunity to remedy the situation; the writers reveal their negative attitude. Therefore, both consumer and supplier were losers. The company lost an account and goodwill with the consumers, and the consumers lost the opportunity to allow the company to grant a fair adjustment and continue to serve them. This letter, therefore, is an unsatisfactory way to remedy problems:

> We did not think the enclosed Santagram was very humorous. We know we are behind in our Christmas Club payments, but we <u>will</u> have the total amount in by November 1.
>
> Since the Christmas Club account is entirely voluntary and not an installment loan account, we believe payments should be allowed at any time so long as the entire amount is paid before Christmas.
>
> Next year, you need not mail us a card reminding us to activate the Christmas Club. We will be happy to take our Christmas savings elsewhere.

To write an appropriate persuasive claim letter:

1. *Get the reader's attention by using an agreeable statement* (inductive approach).
2. *Tell the complete story using facts and avoiding any sarcasm.* Assume that the problem resulted from error, not from an attempt to antagonize you. Write a courteous and positive-sounding letter. Enclose copies of documents to support your claim.
3. *State what you consider to be a fair adjustment.* Remember that the legitimate company strives to treat its customers fairly; maintain goodwill relations; and honor advertisements, guarantees, and warranties.
4. *Close with confidence.*

Write your claim letter when you can do so calmly, accurately, and politely. Businesses usually delay responding to antagonistic letters; they frequently set them aside for later action. It may be a long time later! To relieve tension, an angry customer might write a claim letter venting frustrations, but the letter

Parkview Apartment No. 25A
Houston, TX 77022
December 18, 19--

Senior Vice-President
American Bank
P.O. Box 315
Houston, TX 77002

Dear Vice-President:

Recently, I had the following experience with American Bank. ← **Reader's attention**

I mailed you a $4000 deposit, which was stamped received on December 10. On this same date, a bank teller returned a check to the Federal Home Corporation marked insufficient funds. My deposit was more than enough to cover the $2000 check. ← **Facts**

My bank statement indicates that the $4000 deposit was made on December 11. This is not true. ← **Adjustment**

As a result of this error, I was charged $5 for insufficient funds and suffered embarrassment with the Federal Home corporation and with its bank--National.

I believe that you should:

1. Refund me the $5 charge for insufficient funds.

2. Write Federal Home Corporation explaining that my account was not overdrawn.

3. Write National Bank explaining that my account was not overdrawn.

4. Send me copies of your letters to Federal Home Corporation and the National Bank.

I will be waiting for your comments. ← **Confidence**

Sincerely,

Figure 12–4
Persuasive Claim Letter to Remedy Errors

should not be mailed. After a cooling-down period, the claimant should create and mail a reader-centered, positive, and logical claim letter.

The claim letter in Figure 12–4 was written by an individual who had suffered embarrassment and expense because of a bank teller's mistake. A senior vice-president of that bank believed the adjustment requested was fair; he complied with the customer's request.

Attention → "Mastercraft pipes are great!" This is my husband's opinion of your cool-smoking pipes.

Facts → Last December, I ordered three Mastercraft pipes under the name of Janice Smith (212 Main Street) as an intended wedding gift for my future husband, whom I married June 1. Yesterday, one pipe fell to the ground and broke.

Request → Will you please replace this pipe?

Confident action → Please give me mailing instructions.

Figure 12-5
Routine Claim for Replacing Product After Warranty Term

Dear Mr. Henry

Attention-getter → Your large sign says, "Customer satisfaction is our business."

Facts and evidence → Believing your slogan, I brought my car in to have a tune-up, oil change, and chassis lubrication before leaving for a trip west. The mechanic charged me $74 for the job.

After traveling just 350 miles, I learned that seals were incorrectly installed. This error cost me a 24-hour delay, $42 for a room at the Traveler's Motel, and $55.39 for auto service at the local dealer. Enclosed is a copy of each paid bill.

Adjustment confidence → Since I believe you are responsible for the added expense, I would appreciate your check for $97.39.

Figure 12-6
Persuasive Claim Letter to Automobile Dealer

The persuasive claim letter in Figure 12-5 was written after the warranty period; therefore, the writer tactfully requested a replacement and mailing instructions for a broken pipe. Since companies sometimes have special instructions for returns, customers should request instructions before returning items. In this situation, the company replaced the pipe as a goodwill gesture.

The writer of the persuasive claim letter in Figure 12-6 appealed to an automobile dealer's policy of pleasing customers. This customer was inconvenienced for 24 hours because a mechanic erred in servicing his automobile. The writer tactfully explained what happened, enclosed the paid bills as evidence of the added expense because of the error, and requested reimbursement. Acknowledging the claim, the dealer mailed a $97.39 check to his customer and apologized. He assured the customer that he would personally supervise future service work on the customer's automobile.

SUBJECT: PARKER RANGE MODEL KS 111 RXAO
SERIAL NO. KRD 01001

"You can be sure if you have a Parker product" was once a fairly accurate appraisal of Parker products, but apparently this statement is no longer true.

← **Attention-getter**

When our Parker range was less than two years old, it required repairs amounting to $123.69. A copy of the paid bill is enclosed. While waiting for the necessary parts, I had the use of just two burners, then only one. The repairman was not sure what caused the problem. Most of the cost was for replacement parts: two elements, two blocks, three switches, and three burners. Since the stated warranty was for only one year, I, the consumer, had to bear the brunt of the expense and inability to use the product, not to mention all the frustration.

← **Explanation and facts**

Last week--less than one year after we had the range repaired--one of the replaced burners would not work. What recourse do I have now? Since I hardly used the range, I believe Parker should send a service person to repair it without further cost to us.

← **Adjustment and confidence**

Figure 12-7
Persuasive Letter for Service After Warranty Date

Figure 12-7 represents a letter written to an appliance consumer action panel for help in correcting problems with an electric appliance. Even though the guarantee had expired, the appliance was serviced within three weeks at no extra charge to the consumer. The company did not reimburse the writer for the $123.69 paid two years previously to repair the appliance; the consumer did not request reimbursement.

CHAPTER SUMMARY

Persuasive requests and claims should be written with the inductive or indirect approach. Begin with a reader-centered attention-getter that is related to the subject and continue with persuasive explanatory or informative data that will convince the reader to comply with your request. Then, state the request clearly and concisely. If asking for an adjustment, be sure to request a fair adjustment. Include the necessary details and close with confidence.

In addition to following the basic guidelines for persuasive requests, persuasive letters to congressional representatives should state the bill number and name and be mailed while effective action is possible. They should be concise, objective, and nonthreatening. Facts should be based on research; the request should be stated clearly.

For persuasive letters, summon your greatest letter-writing skill and understanding of human nature. Make it easy for the reader to act.

The typical persuasive letter is longer than routine and good-news letters. It is also more challenging because the writer must convince the reader that he or she will benefit by complying with the stated request.

STUDY QUESTIONS

1. What is the difference between a routine request and a persuasive request?
2. How is a refusal letter similar to a persuasive letter?
3. Why is the persuasive claim longer than the routine claim?
4. Why should a persuasive claim request a fair adjustment?
5. Do companies ever grant adjustments when they are not at fault? Explain.
6. What are the basic steps for writing persuasive requests?
7. Why should the attention-getter be reader centered?
8. Why should persuasive data precede the request in a persuasive letter?
9. Why should you make the action easy in a persuasive letter? How can you do this?
10. When should you write a persuasive, rather than a routine, letter to a member of Congress?
11. State at least five special pointers you would give the writer of a persuasive letter to a congressional representative.

ACTIVITIES

1. Why is the following opening unsatisfactory for a persuasive inquiry letter:

   > The Beta Beta Lambda Fraternity at Central State University would like you to give an informal speech on your profession. We would like to know the opportunities available in public accounting and what the job is actually like for the new college graduate entering the field.

2. What is the purpose for the following letter? Which characteristics of effective writing are violated? (Use the boldface numbers to identify serious errors.) Rewrite an appropriate outline for the letter you would suggest writing. Then write your rough draft.

1. April 10, 19__

2. Central State Faculty
Central State University

3. Dear Faculty:

4. As you probably know, the Central State Flying Club was formed last Autumn. Since then you may not have heard too much about us. However, we have not been idle.

5. As friends and members of the Central State Flying Club, you will realize more mobility and enjoyment than ever thought possible. Your own ambition is the limit and ambition knows no limit. Of course, everything cannot be explained to you in this letter, so we invite you to meet with us.

6. We do realize that you have a busy Spring schedule; however, we want you to be with us Wednesday evening at 7:30 p.m. on April 15th in room B-2 of the Student Union.

7. We want to get to know you. We want you to get to know flying with the Central State Flying Club.

8. Watch for our promotion week on campus May 4-9.

9. Yours truly,

10. President, Central State Flying Club

11. A famous entertainer once said: "Flying broadens my horizons. It makes it possible for me to visit exciting places, meet interesting people, and escape the humdrum of everyday life. It is my inspiration. I wish everyone could share my joy."

3. You have just read a newspaper article, "Courting Customs are Curious," which reports an interview with Mr. Walter Raymond, a speaker for the platinum industry. Mr. Raymond began studying weddings as a hobby. He studied their history and customs and the part rings and gems play in nuptials. Mr. Raymond has lectured before civic clubs and has been a guest on radio talk shows. Write a persuasive letter inviting Mr. Raymond to talk to the members of your club. You can pay him a small amount—enough to cover his travel costs. Address your letter to Mr. Raymond at P.O. Box 001, New York City.
4. You need Dr. Bowers' help to complete your research project under the direction of Dr. Ann A. Wilson of the Special State University. Write a persuasive letter to Dr. Virginia Bowers, a leader in Business Education, as determined by a

nationwide sample of 200 classroom business teachers. Send her a checksheet of fifty-eight major issues and ask her to select the fifteen issues she considers most important and to rank the fifteen in order of importance, listing the most important issue first. Tell her that she can revise any issue if she believes that doing so will make the issue more complete or more accurate. Enclose a reply envelope and specify the day by which you need the information—about a month later.

5. Almost a month has passed since you wrote Dr. Bowers (Activity 4) and you have not received the information requested. Since you mailed the inquiry letter and checksheet to only thirty-one business education leaders, you very much want and need Dr. Bowers' reply. Write Dr. Bowers enclosing the following postal card for her completion and return:

☐ The questionnaire is on its way to you. I have selected and ranked the issues as you requested.

☐ The completed questionnaire will be sent to you on ____________________.

☐ I cannot participate in your study at this time.

☐ I would like another copy of the questionnaire.

Name ____

Follow-up Postal Card

6. With your Quality camera, you are taking pictures of the happy children at your nephew's birthday party. Suddenly, the shutter does not work. The dealer later explains that he cannot repair it. You plan to return the camera to the manufacturer to be repaired. Write a letter to Quality Camera Company in Chicago, Illinois, to accompany your camera. The camera was purchased slightly more than a year ago so that the warranty has expired.
7. Write a persuasive claim to Thermos Division, King-Seeley Thermos Co., Norwich, Connecticut. Persuade the reader to send you Stopper No. 722 for Bottle No. 2442/75. You believe the horizontal split across the threads of the stopper are a product defect. Tell them that you purchased the thermos several months ago and ask them whether they want the defective stopper returned to them? If so, ask for mailing instructions. You would like to have the stopper before you leave for a vacation in six weeks.

EDITING

Rewrite these sentences so that they will be more effective in persuasive letters.

1. A writers objective is to be clear and consice.
   Correct the grammar, spelling, and punctuation in this opening for a persuasive letter.
2. Why don't you sell good products like you used to do?
   Opening for a persuasive claim letter
3. Our budgeted amount for guest speakers is only $50.00.
4. We can provide a delicious dinner, an enthusiastic audience, and $50 for your visit.
5. I hope that you will send me a new tape recorder to replace the one that got broken in shipment.
   Adjustment request
6. Please send me a duplicate watch immediately; yours is the worst service ever.
   Adjustment request
7. Unless we receive a favorable adjustment, we'll never order another thing from you.
   Adjustment request
8. The linings of both shoes of pair of $64.50 Strollers of which I purchased last month in your store show signs of deterioration; they have not given me the wear which I am used to getting from Stroller shoes.
   Wordy explanation of the problem
9. We trust that we will not be inconvenienced again and would appreciate the refund by the end of this month.
   Ending statement
10. I am sure that under the circumstances, you will want to make a fair adjustment and send me a replacement pair of Strollers.
    Adjustment request

IN-BASKET SIMULATION

1. While you were visiting Mr. Gene Saxon, Public Relations, at Waltere Supermarkets, Inc., he mentioned that many of the business letters he receives are not clear or concise. He often has to follow up letters with a telephone call, mailgram, or letter to determine the writer's wishes.

   Using your best persuasive writing style, ask Mr. Saxon to speak to members of the University Management Club. As the Club's Corresponding Secretary, tell him something about the members so that he can prepare an appropriate talk. Even though the budget for speakers is necessarily limited, offer him a nominal amount for speaking. Mr. Saxon has a busy work schedule so give him a choice of speaking dates far in advance.

13 Writing Credit and Collection Letters

After studying Chapter 13, you should be able to:

- Describe the role of credit in the free-enterprise system
- Define the basic principles for writing effective credit and collections communications
- Write collection letters at the reminder, inquiry, appeal, and ultimatum stages of the collection process
- Write form collection notices

Our free-enterprise system depends upon the use of credit. **Credit** allows individuals and business firms to secure money, goods, or services by promising to pay for them at a later date. Companies use credit to borrow for expansion, to increase inventories, to receive cash discounts for early payments to suppliers, to pay for goods and services, and so on. Businesses encourage the use of credit, even though some people and some firms do not keep their promises to pay. Because of credit, sales increase, which frequently offsets the uncollectible accounts.

The word "credit" comes from the Latin *credo*, which means *I believe.* When you ask someone to grant credit, you are asking that person to believe in your willingness and ability to pay later.

Terms of credit vary with the parties involved, with the amounts of time and money, with the reason for credit, and so on. One of the most important considerations, however, is the borrower's ability to pay on time. The person getting the loan or goods must agree to make the regular payment by the stipulated due date. The institution granting the credit must then see to it that the correct payments are made at the agreed-upon time.

Credit offices within businesses are set up to handle routine credit plans. They have procedures for approving credit, processing payments, and soliciting overdue payments.

CREDIT REQUESTS

The **credit request** need not be long or complex; its purpose is to convince the reader that your intentions are honorable and that you will be able to fulfill the purchase contract by paying when due. When requesting credit, you should:

1. Make your request in the first sentence (deductive approach)
2. Give specific information to support your ability and willingness to pay
3. Close with confident expectation of receiving credit

The tone of your letter should reveal your sincerity. You can maintain this tone by supplying references. This openness helps the reader determine that you are able and willing to pay for the credit transaction. Generally, you should indicate the names and addresses of banks in which you have checking or savings accounts. You should also indicate names and addresses of businesses that have successfully granted you credit, either as a cash loan or as merchandise or service paid for later.

Directly and briefly, indicate the type of credit account you desire (currently a variety of open accounts are available). The company receiving Kevin Dolen's letter (Figure 13-1) will mail him a credit application form. Mr. Dolen should carefully and honestly complete the form and return it promptly.

Dear Credit Manager:

Credit request → May I open a 30-day charge account at Dover Furniture Company?

Supporting information → I have accepted the position of Chief Accountant at Turner and Turner Company; therefore, my family and I will be moving to Dallas next month and will be purchasing additional furnishings for our new home.

Action desired → Please mail me an application for credit.

Very truly yours,

Kevin Dolen

Figure 13-1
Letter Requesting Credit Application Form

Order → Please send by Railway Express prepaid the following chair on a 90-day charge account:

> One Model KK-109 A Early American Chair as advertised in your May catalog for $399.99

Credit request → These firms will vouch for my prompt payment of charge purchases:

> May Brothers Department Store
> One Public Square
> Houston, TX 77018
>
> American Furniture Company
> 99 Meadowlark Boulevard
> Houston, TX 77001
>
> Martin Furniture Company
> 111 Euclid Avenue
> Houston, TX 77020

Supporting data →

I have a checking account, savings account, and a $5,000 saving certificate at the Houston Savings and Loan Corporation, 312 Superior Avenue, Houston, TX 77020.

My employer is the Houston Stamping Company at 2010 Market Street, where I have been Office Manager for five years.

Action → Please let me know when the chair will arrive.

Very truly yours,

Henry Parker

Henry Parker

Figure 13-2
Letter Giving Credit Information and Ordering a Chair

Please send by Railway Express prepaid the following chair on a 90-day charge account: ← **Order** ← **Credit request**

One Model KK-109A Early American Chair as advertised in your May catalog for $399.99

The completed credit application that is enclosed should provide you with sufficient information to grant me credit. ← **Data**

Please let me know when the chair will arrive. ← **Action**

Figure 13-3
Letter Enclosing Completed Credit Application and Ordering a Chair

Sometimes it is possible to open a credit account at the time the first order is placed. In the letter in Figure 13-2 Henry Parker gives adequate information to prove that he has the character (willingness to pay), capital (money and property), and capacity (ability to earn) to pay for credit purchases.

Even though the letter in Figure 13-3 combines an order and credit request, the writer has enclosed a completed credit form to confirm that she is a good credit risk.

COLLECTION NOTICES

If all purchases were on a cash basis, there would be no need for collection reminders. Because credit transactions are extensive and payments are not always made on time, collection notices have become a common part of today's business activities. They do keep some accounts from becoming bad debts; therefore, many businesses use a variety of collection notices.

There is no one pattern used by all firms to collect past-due amounts. The collection process takes on the following dimensions:

Brief reminders → Inquiries → Persuasive appeals → Final action

Usually, a few days after the due date the creditor mails a simple **reminder notice** that the bill or invoice has not been paid. Often this form is a duplicate copy of the bill or invoice stamped with such statements as *Duplicate* or *Please Remit* or *Second Notice* or *Past Due*. Such reminders allow customers an opportunity to request corrections and adjustments since shipping or invoicing errors occasionally are made. From time to time, a normally prompt-paying customer may be short of immediate funds. Customers should be given ample time to express any dissatisfaction or pursue an alternate payment plan.

Many companies use automated equipment to help prepare repetitive messages in the collection process. Telephone calls,

Purpose →
Details →
Action desired →

Dear Friend:

Occasionally we need a friendly reminder to do something we had intended to do--but just forgot. That is why we are reminding you that the amount shown on the enclosed statement, $______, is past due.

Won't you please take a moment to mail your check today? If you have mailed your check, please disregard this notice.

Sincerely,

J & J INCORPORATED

B.A Smith

Credit Department

Figure 13–4
Collection Reminder Note (15 Days After Due Note)

personal visits, and telegrams are also used to request payment for past-due amounts. Many collection notices contain addressed and postage-paid envelopes to expedite payment.

The collection letter should leave no questions. Spell out the facts in simple unmistakable language:

1. *State purpose of letter or notice early* (deductive approach). Use the inductive approach beginning with inquiry stage.
2. *Give details, make inquiries, present appeals, and/or suggest final action.* Use accurate and specific language, and avoid negatives, sarcasm, anger, contempt, or rudeness. Be clear and concrete by restating the amount owed in each notice.
3. *Express action desired from customer*—endeavor to maintain goodwill.

Figures 13–4 through 13–7 are brief reminder collection notices. These notices—on cards, note paper, or letterhead—are often form messages reproduced in quantity with the help of word-processing equipment. Probably the simplest and least costly reminder notice is a copy of the original invoice or statement stamped with a notation indicating that it is a duplicate. Some business people send the duplicate form printed on colorful paper; others rubber stamp the document or affix attention-getting stickers.

No matter what form the reminder notice takes, the customer should see the device as a routine, business-like thing to do. Be as positive as possible and avoid insinuations.

Dear Customer:

We would appreciate your prompt payment of the following account balance which is past due our net terms of sale: ← **Purpose**

Date	Invoice Number	Amount

← **Details**

If you have paid the amount stated, please disregard this notice. ← **Action**

Credit Department

Figure 13-5
Collection Reminder Card (15 to 30 days After Due Date)

Dear (Name):

Again we remind you that your charge account is past due. ← **Purpose**

Please mail us your check for the amount shown under "minimum amount due" on the enclosed statement. ← **Details and action**

Perhaps your check is already enroute. If not, please mail or bring in your check today. ← **Action**

Sincerely,

MAY BROTHERS DEPARTMENT STORE

(Name)
Collection Department

Figure 13-6
Collection Reminder Form Letter

IMPORTANT . . . ← **Quick attention-getter**

Your account has been referred to our department because we have not received a scheduled payment for at least 60 days. ← **Purpose** ← **Details**

Please mail us your check so that we can restore your account to a current status. ← **Action**

MAY BROTHERS DEPARTMENT STORE

Collection Department

Telephone (317) 162-2500

Figure 13-7
Collection Reminder Note (60 days After Due Date)

Dear Mr. Jones:

SUBJECT: May Purchase

Reference → Your first order for Capco products was shipped to you last April, followed by a similar order in May. We are pleased to ship you orders on an open account basis.

Inquiry → Is there some reason why you cannot pay for your May purchases? Perhaps we can offer you a plan.

Action → Please mail us your check for $225.75 today or telephone us. We know some plan can be arranged to help you bring your account up to date again.

Cordially,

Thomas Marek

Figure 13-8
Collection Inquiry Letter

Dear Policyholder:

Reference → Today, we learned that your premium payment has not been received. Has it just slipped your mind? Even though the grace period has expired, you can still make your payment without red tape—if it is sent to us promptly.

Inquiry → Is there some reason why you have hesitated to mail us your check? We would like to hear from you. Perhaps working together we can find a solution.

If it is inconvenient for you to mail your check now, please let us know. Because of the flexibility built into your policy, we may be able to find a way to enable you to keep the valuable coverage it provides.

Action → Please telephone our Client Service Department, collect at (313) 471-6272, and we will do our best to help you. If that is inconvenient, please write us a brief note and we will contact you.

Anytime you need assistance, please write or telephone us.

Sincerely,

P. A. Wilcox

Client Service Department

Our toll free number for Michigan residents is 1-800-521-3600.

Figure 13-9
Collection Inquiry Form Letter

March 1, 19--

Ms. Geraldine Smith
71 Park Avenue
Indianapolis, IN 46208

Your record, Ms. Smith, for paying your invoices within the terms of sale has been excellent. We know you want to keep your good credit rating; therefore, we urge you to mail us your check to cover the following purchases:

6 lbs. assorted cheeses	$18.00
10 lbs. sliced ham	25.00
4 party loaves, rye and white	3.60
	$46.60

Until your account balance has been paid, we will not be able to send additional orders on an open credit basis.

Ms. Smith, will you help us maintain your preferred status? Please mail your check today.

Sincerely,

H. G. Wilson

Credit Department

HGW:cet

← Reference

← Appeal to keep good credit rating

← Action

Figure 13-10
Collection Appeal Letter—Keep Your Good Credit Rating

If the customer has not taken positive action after one or two reminder notices, then you must find out why (Figures 13-8 and 13-9). At the **inquiry stage**, you can use reproduced messages that have been made as personalized as possible to get some action from the customer. Although you cannot forget debts, you can offer a helpful plan to encourage a reply and repayment.

If your inquiry notice does not produce satisfactory results, apply your knowledge of human relations. Select a **suitable appeal** for the individual customer. For best results, emphasize just one appeal in a collection notice. For many customers, you can appeal to their desire to maintain their credit standing—to

April 10, 19--

Mrs. Jennifer Parsons
2124 Eaglecreek Drive
Indianapolis, IN 46224

Dear Mrs. Parsons:

Reference → Several months ago, we were pleased to welcome you as a new charge customer. **Commitment** → We agreed to fill your orders accurately and promptly with the understanding that you would mail us your remittance within 30 days after the date of our invoice.

It has been 60 days since we mailed you our invoice for your charge purchases. **Action** → Won't you cooperate with us by mailing us your check?

Please use the enclosed addressed and stamped envelope for mailing your $135.50 check today.

Sincerely,

H. G. Wilson

Credit Department

HGW:cet

Enclosure

Figure 13-11
Collection Appeal Letter—Keep Your Commitment

continue purchasing on an open-account basis. You can also appeal to the customer's desire to be fair and to cooperate or to be businesslike. If you realize that your positive appeals are not working, begin demanding payment (Figures 13-10 through 13-12). Note that banks can help in the collection process (see Figure 13-12).

At the **final** or **ultimatum stage**, you can assume that the customer does not intend to pay. Formally notify your intentions to pursue "legal avenues"; make no threats against any person's reputation (Figures 13-13 through 13-15). Consider using a form letter that has been typed as an original and sending it by certified mail with a return receipt request (Figures 13-13 and 13-14). Form mailgrams (Figure 13-15) sometimes have greater

Figure 13-12
Collection Appeal Letter—Form Letter

Dear

We have not received your payment in reply to our previous letter. Therefore, unless we hear from you by **Two weeks**, we must assume that you have no intention of meeting your obligations in a normal businesslike manner.

← **Appeal to do the correct thing**

We will proceed to draw a sight draft for $________, which will be forwarded to your bank for collection. If the draft is returned to us unpaid, your account will be automatically turned over to an outside agency for collection.

Because of the seriousness of this action, please make arrangements to pay for the draft when presented by your bank.

← **Action**

Waltere Supermarkets, Inc.
220 Michigan Avenue • P.O. Box 1785
Indianapolis, IN 46206 • 317-115-3502

May 15, 19--

Mr. Morton Alexander
2035 West Main Street
Bedford, IN 47421

Dear Mr. Alexander:

During the past several months, we have made numerous attempts to arrange for payment of your past-due amount of $353.88.

← **Reference**

Naturally, we do not like to submit any customer to the embarrassment of a collection process, but your lack of concern over this matter leaves us little alternative.

Unless the entire amount due is paid by May 29, 19--, we shall be forced to use those legal avenues available to us. Please make this unnecessary by mailing your check now.

← **Ultimatum**

Sincerely,

H. G. Wilson

Credit Department

HGW:cet

Figure 13-13
Collection Ultimatum—Form Letter 1

Dear

Reference ⟶ Since we have not received your reply to our letter of **Date**, we must assume that you have no intention of meeting your obligations in a normal businesslike way. Consequently, we have decided that the only alternative you have left us is to turn your account over to an outside agency for collection.

Ultimatum ⟶ Because of the seriousness of this action, please consider this letter our formal notice of intent. Unless we receive your check for $________ by **Fifteen days after date**, your account will be turned over to an outside collection agency.

Sincerely,

Figure 13-14
Collection Ultimatum—Form Letter 2

Reference ⟶ SINCE YOUR ACCOUNT IS CONSIDERABLY PAST OUR TERMS, WE ARE USING THIS FORM OF COMMUNICATION TO BRING IT TO YOUR ATTENTION.

Ultimatum ⟶ PLEASE MAIL US YOUR CHECK FOR $598.35; OTHERWISE, WE MUST ASSUME THAT YOU HAVE NO INTENTION OF MEETING YOUR OBLIGATIONS IN A NORMAL BUSINESSLIKE MANNER.

JOHN E. ABLE

NEWTON PRODUCTS COMPANY

Figure 13-15
Collection Ultimatum—Form Mailgram

impact than other communications. As a last resort, you might have to enlist a collection agency to collect past-due accounts (Figure 13-16).

If at some point during the collection process, a customer promises to pay the past-due amount but does not follow through, you must resume the collection process.

When you write collection notices, remember that working to keep all customers happy is important. However, your primary consideration is making sure that your employer collects the accounts that are past due. A company needs to pay its bills and make a reasonable profit to please its creditors and shareholders.

Time is critical when writing collection notices. Avoid vague phrases, such as *at your earliest convenience*, *as soon as possible*, *soon*, or *at an early date*. Use specific time periods or dates (for example, *within 10 days* or *by March 15*). The purpose of the collection notice is to get customers to pay, not to encourage them to delay payments at their convenience.

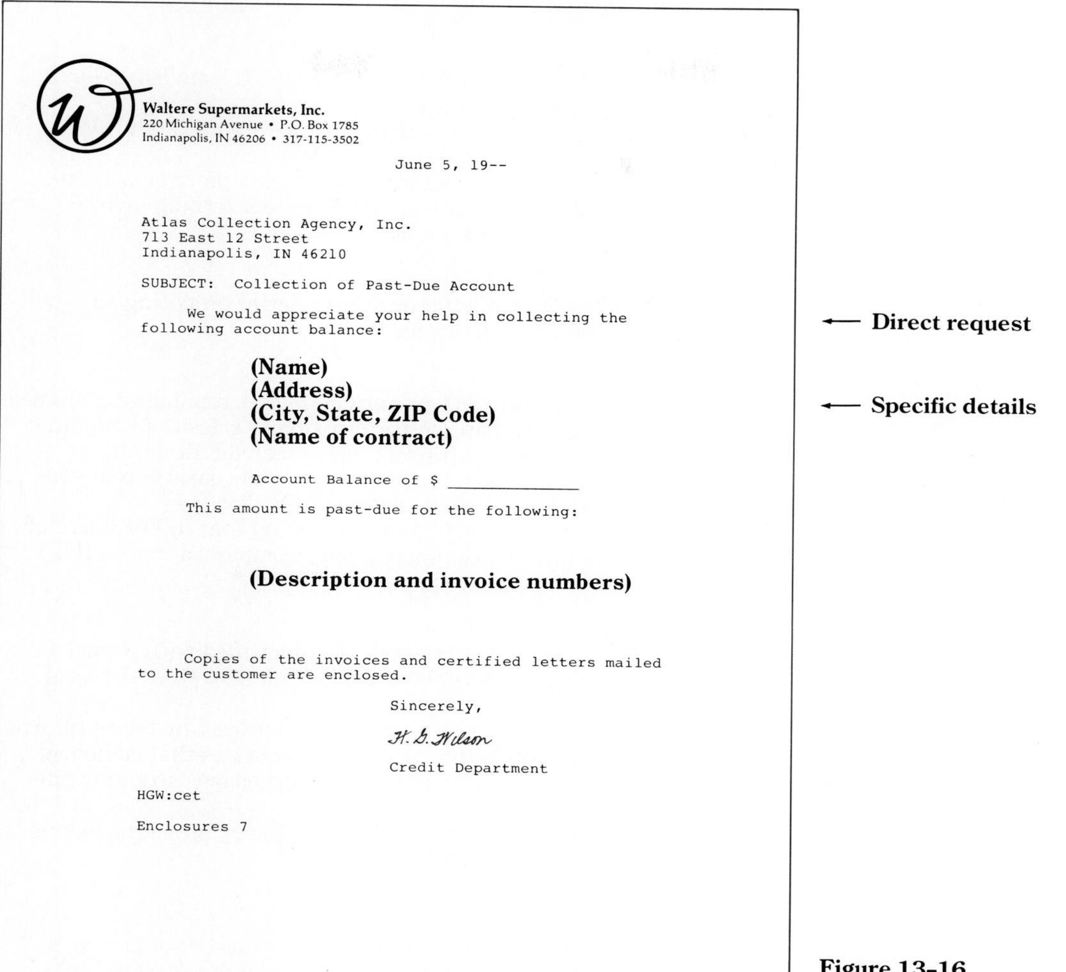

Waltere Supermarkets, Inc.
220 Michigan Avenue • P.O. Box 1785
Indianapolis, IN 46206 • 317-115-3502

June 5, 19--

Atlas Collection Agency, Inc.
713 East 12 Street
Indianapolis, IN 46210

SUBJECT: Collection of Past-Due Account

We would appreciate your help in collecting the following account balance:

(Name)
(Address)
(City, State, ZIP Code)
(Name of contract)

Account Balance of $ ____________

This amount is past-due for the following:

(Description and invoice numbers)

Copies of the invoices and certified letters mailed to the customer are enclosed.

Sincerely,

H. G. Wilson

Credit Department

HGW:cet

Enclosures 7

Figure 13-16
Letter to Collection Agency

Figure 13-17 illustrates one basic plan for the written collection series. Here the time interval at the beginning of the collection process is 15 days. As the final stage is reached, the time interval becomes shorter. However, the time between the collection notices should be flexible to fit specific circumstances. You may alter the time spans or omit any of the steps to meet the needs of the situation. Always adapt the plan to the company's policy or the customer's circumstances. Between communications, creditors should allow time for customers to receive collection notices and to act. However, the time lag should not be so long that customers forget their obligations.

Reminder Stage

1. Copy of original invoice stamped "DUPLICATE," mailed 15 days after due date—envelope enclosed.
2. 15 days later, second copy of original invoice stamped "PLEASE REMIT"—envelope enclosed.
3. 15 days later, form note or letter reminding customer of past-due amount and inquiring if there are problems concerning invoice, shipment, etc.—envelope enclosed.

Inquiry Stage

4. 15 to 30 days later, form letter or original letter proposing an alternate payment plan if desired.

Appeal Stage

5. 15 to 30 days later, form letter or original letter reminding customer of past-due amount and appealing to customer's desire to maintain good credit reputation, get future orders on credit, desire to cooperate, desire to be businesslike. Use the one basic appeal you believe will work best for that customer.
6. 15 to 30 days later, form mailgram requesting that full payment of past-due amount be mailed immediately. Company assumes that customer does not intend to pay amount owed.*

Ultimatum Stage

7. 7 days later, form letter or original letter (certified with return receipt) requesting entire amount paid within two weeks or legal avenues will be used to seek payment.*
8. Two weeks later, form letter or original letter (certified with return receipt) as formal notice of intention. Letter states that customer will have 15 days before account will be turned over to an outside agency for collection.*
9. Two weeks later, form letter to collection agency providing details and enclosing copies of all correspondence.*

*A blind copy of this communication can be sent to the salesperson or district manager. A notation of action taken should be recorded in the customer's file. After collection notice 6, future orders should be on a cash basis unless special circumstances exist for the delayed payment.

Figure 13–17
Plan for Written Collection Series

The customer may ignore the notice, pay the amount due, or explain why it has not been paid promptly. Many companies wait at least 60 days before refusing to extend credit to delinquent customers because they want to keep customers and maintain goodwill. Then they may allow another 30 or 60 days to pass before giving the account to an outside agency for collection.

Thank you for your check for your recent order shipped under Invoice No. ______________. The invoice totals $______________ which consists of $______________ for merchandise and $______________ for transportation charges. ← Agreeable idea

Since your check was for $______________, your account shows a balance of $______________, representing freight charges on your shipment. ← Explanation

We would appreciate your check for the amount due. ← Action

Sincerely,

M. J. Wilson

M. J. Wilson
Credit Department

Figure 13-18
Collection Notice for Freight Payment (Form Letter)

OTHER COLLECTION LETTERS

Collection letters may deal with problems other than nonpayment. They may request payment for additional amounts, such as freight charges (Figure 13-18) or unearned discounts (Figure 13-19). Requesting payment for an unearned discount can be touchy, especially if the customer represents a large account. The cash discount, a small percentage off the invoice amount, is granted to some customers if payment is made quickly (for example, five or ten days after the invoice date). Thus, businesses use the cash discount as an incentive for early payment.

A cash discount of 1 percent on a $3700 invoice amounts to $37. Sometimes the customer deducts the cash discount even after the discount is void. Some companies deliberately overlook the abuse, rather than forfeit that customer's goodwill. Other firms seek to recover the unearned discount, maintaining that the cash discount is a reward for early payment, not an automatic deduction from the invoice amount.

To collect for unearned discounts, follow a procedure similar to the one used for collecting past-due amounts. Early correspondence tactfully requesting payment should detail specific facts regarding the invoice and the unearned cash discount. Later correspondence should use persuasive appeals and an inductive approach (Figure 13-19).

Attention getter →

Explanation →

Action →

Dear Customer:

Pennies make dollars--in profits or losses.

Cash discounts--even very small ones--contribute to profit. Therefore, they are of mutual interest to us. To you, they represent added profit on your use of Waltere products. To us, they represent the prompt return of our capital investment in goods shipped and services provided.

We believe it is good business for our customers to earn additional profits by paying invoices within the cash discount period. Our customers can deduct ½% from the net invoice price--if the invoice is paid within ten days after date of invoice. After that period, the cash discount has not been earned.

Invoices requiring adjustment should be paid--less the adjustment--within the cash discount period to earn the discount. A memo for the adustment amount claimed should accompany the payment.

We are convinced that it is desirable to earn cash discounts. However, after the cash discount period, invoices should be paid on a net basis within 30 days after the invoice date. Most of our customers agree with us on these points, and we are grateful.

Please cooperate by mailing us your check for $_____ in the addressed and stamped envelope.

Sincerely,

H. G. Wilson

Credit Department

HGW:cet

Enclosure

Figure 13-19
Collection Notice for Unearned Discount (Form Letter)

CHAPTER SUMMARY

Credit has become an integral part of our economic system and permits individuals and organizations to acquire material items and services without immediate payment. This widespread practice necessitates special practices in credit and collection departments—practices that have become routine procedures. Credit requests and collection notices are common.

Use precise, direct, courteous wording for all letters and notices requesting payment. In letters requesting credit, indicate the type of credit account desired and give evidence supporting your ability to pay for credit purchases when due.

Creditors generally grant open credit—even to customers who turn out to be lax about making payments. However, creditors pursue those who do not pay their bills.

The stages in the collection process are reminder, inquiry, appeal, and ultimatum (final). Early notices are usually duplicate copies of the bills or invoices stamped with a reminder to pay the past-due amount. If the past-due amount is not paid after several reminders, the creditor continues sending its collection series—form notices and original letters. Mailgrams, telephone calls, and personal visits may all be part of the collection process. When working through the collection process, keep a careful record of all communication. Even though the collection process may spread over several months, positive language should be used throughout in an effort to keep a customer and maintain goodwill.

STUDY QUESTIONS

1. What is credit? Why is it important in the business world?
2. What type of data should you include in the credit request letter?
3. Why are collection notices necessary? What are the stages in the collection process?
4. What is the purpose of the first collection notice? Describe the possible forms it might take.
5. How does the inquiry collection notice differ from the reminder notice?
6. What appeals can you use to encourage debtors to pay past-due amounts? Why shouldn't you use more than one basic appeal in a notice?
7. What actual words might you find in each of the following types of collection notices:
   a. Reminder
   b. Inquiry
   c. Appeal
   d. Ultimatum (final)
8. From whom can you seek help for collecting past-due accounts? How much help will they be?
9. How much time should you allow between collection notices? Explain.

ACTIVITIES

1. As credit manager, you have been asked to answer Kevin Dolen's letter requesting credit (Figure 13-1). Write the letter enclosing a credit application form and a reply envelope.

2. Order a large and expensive item on credit. Assume that this is your first purchase from the company. Suggest how you might pay for the item (for example, in eight equal payments with no down payment, a down payment with the balance in four equal installments, cash within 90 days, or a personal note payable in several months). Your order should include information that will encourage the company to consider you a good credit risk.
3. Ms. C. E. Palace purchased an item on the installment plan. She regularly made payments for five months, but then stopped without any explanation. Two payments are now past due. What kind of collection notice should you send to Ms. Palace? Write an appropriate notice, addressing it to her at 100 East Adams Street, Los Angeles, California 90040.
4. Write an original collection letter at the final action or ultimatum stage of collection. Refer to Figures 13–13 through 13–15 for ideas. The letters should have a positive, businesslike tone.
5. Write a letter to your customer noting that his or her account will be turned over to a collection agency unless you receive an immediate check to pay for Invoice No. 213456-A ($320.50) and Invoice No. 315813-A ($125.25).
6. One year after her account was turned over to an outside agent for collection, a customer writes explaining that she is on sound footing and would like to activate her account and make purchases on open credit. Do you believe you should grant her credit now? Write an appropriate and tactful letter.
7. About two months ago, one of your previous customers voluntarily declared himself bankrupt. He has begun his business anew and is asking you for purchases between $600 and $1000 on open account. Will you allow him purchases on credit? Is there any difference between this case and the situation in Activity 6? Write an appropriate letter.
8. Ms. Janice Furnish mailed you a check for $5568.25—payment for Invoice No. 11305 after deducting a 1 percent cash discount of $56.25. Invoice No. 11305 stated:

Cost of items purchased	$4999.50
Sales tax	400.00
Shipping cost	225.00
	$5624.50

Since the discount can only be taken on the cost of the items (excluding taxes and transportation), calculate the unearned amount and write a tactful and explanatory letter to Ms. Furnish. The unearned amount will be added to her account.

EDITING

Rewrite the following sentences for credit and collection letters.

1. We would appreciate receiving your personal check for $458.75 as soon as possible.
2. Why don't you send us your check to pay for the catering service you ordered and received.
3. If you wish to order items on a credit basis, fill out the enclosed questionnaire and send it in the pre-addressed envelope which we are enclosing herein.
4. Since we have fulfilled our part of the bargain, how about fulfilling your part of the bargain and cooperate by sending us your check.
5. Unless we receive your check for $395.50 by May 10, we will sue you.
6. We want your check for the minimum amount due now.
7. What's the reason for you not paying your invoice on time?
8. Just to remind you that your account is past due.
9. Enclosed herewith is a addressed and stamped envelope for you to mail to us your check for $501.75.
10. Pay us what you owe us NOW!
11. We have not received your remittance for our invoices (No. 2190 for $49.50 and No. 3265 for $79.80) dated April 10th and April 30th. Nor have you advised us when they would be paid, as requested in our letter of June 20th. If your remittance is not already in the mail, please do so. If something is wrong, let us know. We trust to avoid any unpleasantness, you will submit your check by return mail.

IN-BASKET SIMULATIONS

1. One of Waltere's customers has been purchasing goods and services averaging $25 a month. The customer—Batten, Barker, and Bailey—now requests a special $600 catering job. As Credit Manager, write the company (attention of Mrs. Alice C. Barker) thanking them for their order and telling them that the credit department has approved it for processing now. Because this order is for an amount significantly higher than for past orders, ask the customer to complete a credit questionnaire which you are enclosing. Also enclose an addressed business envelope. All information will be kept strictly confidential.
2. A new customer has requested Waltere's Supermarkets to ship them an order on an open credit basis. You, the Credit Manager, have not had an opportunity to check the company's credit reputation. You need some credit information before you can send the order without payment.

Therefore, write the customer a letter enclosing a credit questionnaire and a return envelope. Ask him or her to complete and return the form so that it can be reviewed quickly and the order sent. All information will be kept confidential. You propose to the customer that quick shipment of the order is possible by mailing you a check (specify an amount equal to cost of entire order). You can then release the order immediately. Prepare a blind copy for the salesman.

3. The Able Company is one of Waltere's usually prompt paying customers. They owe Waltere's $135.59 for food catered for one of their special meetings. You have mailed two reminder notices, but have not heard from them. Write a third notice inquiring if there is a problem and proposing a possible way out. You want to keep the goodwill of this customer.
4. You are not pleased with the following collection letter appealing to the customer's desire to cooperate. Rewrite the letter.

Dear

Again we must ask your cooperation on your past-due account.

Receipt of your remittance for $_____ at this time will make it possible for us to serve your future requirements.

We expect to hear from you immediately.

Sincerely,

---

5. Another customer has mailed you a check for $1470.58 on a $1500.59 invoice which allowed a 2% cash discount if paid within ten days. The check is received ten days beyond the cash discount period. Write the customer a tactful letter requesting the amount of the unearned cash discount because payment was received after the cash discount period.
6. Write an appropriate letter to fit the following situation: As Credit Manager, you granted credit to Mr. Herbert A. Burkhart, employed by the Martin Supply Co. for ten years. Mr. Burkhart was granted credit on the basis of his promise to pay, recommendations from references, and employment. Although still employed, he has not made any effort to make the scheduled payments for the family room furniture (purchased for $925.50). You are at a loss to understand what the problem is. Appeal to his desire to cooperate and preserve

his credit rating. Ask him to make at least a partial payment and explain how he plans to pay the amounts owed.

7. You received a speed letter from Don Minuti, Meat Manager for Store No. 40. Write a letter to Customer Accounts, Chicago Meat Packing Company, 1010 La Salle Avenue, Chicago, IL 60607. Inform them of the mislabeled box and request a credit to Waltere's account (56.4 times 20¢).

SNAP-A-WAY AND RETAIN YELLOW COPY, SEND WHITE AND PINK COPIES WITH CARBON INTACT

GrayLine "Snap-A-Way" GrayLine "Snap-A-Way" GrayLine "Snap-A-Way" GrayLine "Snap-A-Way"

SPEED LETTER®

TO (You) FROM Don Minuti, No. 40 Meat Manager

SUBJECT Mislabeled Box from Chicago Meats

— NO. 9 & 10 FOLD

MESSAGE DATE August 4 19

On my perishable truck on Wednesday, August 1, I received four boxes labeled boneless rounds. One box contained semi-boneless rounds. The box weighted 56.4 pounds. I think the semi-boneless is 20¢ per pound less than the boneless.

SIGNED Don

REPLY DATE 19

— NO. 9 FOLD

— NO. 10 FOLD

SIGNED

GrayLine "SNAP-A-WAY" FORM 44-905 3 PARTS
WILSON JONES COMPANY • © 1963 • PRINTED IN U.S.A.

RETAIN WHITE COPY, RETURN PINK COPY

676

Speed Letter

14 Writing Sales Letters

After studying Chapter 14, you should be able to:

- Write effective solicited sales letters
- Write effective unsolicited sales letters using the concept of AIDA (attention, interest, desire, action)
- distinguish among the three different types of sales systems (continuous, wear-out, and campaign)
- Compile a mailing list

Businesses compete with one another for the sale of goods and services. Competition is keen. As a result, a well-prepared sales letter can stimulate sales, increase profits, and encourage goodwill among buyers and sellers. It can be a valuable asset to the business.

A **sales letter** is a persuasive letter that promotes the sale of goods or services. There are many attention-getting approaches and plans you can follow, but your letter's success will depend upon your understanding of its objectives. Every word must play an important role: to attract the reader's attention, to convince the reader through explanation, and to move the reader to action.

Before you successfully do this, you must know the product and the market. Learn all you can about the product or services you sell, determine the basic sales area for your product or service, and analyze the personality of consumers in the sales area. In writing the letter, use your knowledge of human nature to choose words that will appeal to the reader. Always remember, successful sales letters are written with the buyer in mind. The reader must believe that it is to his or her benefit to buy the specific product or service offered.

PRODUCT AND MARKET ANALYSIS

Writers of successful sales letters know the characteristics and components of the products they sell, as well as their competitors. They know, for example:

1. The special features of the products or services offered, as well as the competitors'
2. The ingredients or materials in the products, relative importance of each, and the manufacturing process
3. Research and development background
4. The way the products or services should be used for best results
5. Specific cleaning or care requirements
6. Repair and service facilities available
7. Price and guarantee information

To learn about products and services, read product and service information furnished by the company, manufacturers, and government regulators; visit the manufacturing concern and see how the product is made; talk to manufacturing representatives, service technicians, and sales personnel; talk to past and present users of the product or service; conduct tests and experiments; and/or use the product or service. Your product analysis should reveal features which make the product **special**. A special feature can become the **central selling point** (basic emphasis) for the sales letter.

After analyzing the products or services, direct sales communications to potential customers in the profitable market area. Generally, market research is done by skilled professionals. Results of this research is available in company records, government statistics, trade journals, and other publications. First-hand research is possible by observing users or by conducting interviews or analyzing survey instruments received from a representative sample of potential buyers.

READER ANALYSIS

Writers of sales communications should analyze the needs and personality of potential customers. Buyers are interested in products or services that supply physical needs (for example, food, drink, clothing, or shelter). To varying extents, buyers want to satisfy desires for affection, recognition, approval, security, wealth, prestige, respect, pleasure, education, and other social or ego-centered motivations. What are the common characteristics of the group (sex, age, income, occupation, lifestyle, education, special interest, geographic location, and so on)? What can the product or service do for the individual or for the group? Answering these questions will help you write reader-centered sales letters.

SALES APPEALS

Sales letters should stress a central selling point. Therefore, the writer should emphasize one or two special attributes of the product or service that will appeal to the readers. Choosing the best appeal may not be easy. The results of market studies can be helpful, as can studies of human nature.

Consumers may purchase automobiles, for example, to satisfy transportation needs; however, other appeals may include brand name reputation, specific features available (for example, cruise control or sun roof), ease of operation, appearance and style, size and comfort, price competitiveness, prestige possibilities, popularity of model, nonconformity with other buyers, service or repair record, and warranty.

It is difficult to write one letter that will entice all potential buyers of the product. The sales letter to would-be executives might stress the prestige possibilities. While sales letters to new high school graduates might use price competitiveness or economy of operation as the central selling theme, letters to individuals earning high salaries might stress uniqueness of product or service, price being of little or no consequence to them. Dealers and wholesalers are interested in turnover possibilities and profits. The smaller the group and the more **homogeneous** or similar the members are, the easier it is to select a specific, personal sales approach. Sales letters to large heterogeneous groups may be more impersonal because of the varying make-up of the market.

Solicited and Unsolicited Sales Letters

Solicited sales letters answer a request from a prospective client or customer. Begin by answering the individual's question. Since the reader has shown interest, your letter should answer the questions in a context that also extols the special features of your product or service:

1. Answer the reader's questions (deductive approach) with positive words
2. Give details and information so as to create a desire for the particular product or service
3. Suggest a definite action for the reader

The letter in Figure 8–19 is a **bid** (quotation) for pest control service. It is a solicited sales letter that answered an inquiry. The reader had already indicated interest in the supplier's service, so a special attention-getting statement not only would have been unnecessary, it would have been inappropriate and distracting.

Unsolicited sales letters should be sent to those who have not expressed an interest in your products or services. First, you must capture an audience and create an interest in what you have to sell. Such letters may be long—four or more pages. Many are folded in book form, with printing on both sides. The reproduced forms are attractive and feature appropriate use of blank areas and a variety of printing sizes and types. Along with the letter, many firms enclose descriptive brochures and reply cards or envelopes.

Sometimes letters are addressed specifically to the reader. This adds a personalized touch and stimulates reader interest. The named individual is encouraged to at least scan the communication even though it is obvious that the writer is attempting to sell something. Such letters appear more important than letters that are not personally addressed or are addressed to occupant.

Advertisers have coined the term AIDA (pronounced eye-ee-da) for formulating strong sales appeals: Attention, Interest, Desire, Action. It is a natural and logical plan that makes it easy for the reader to decide in favor of the product. The unsolicited sales letter should:

1. Get the reader's *attention* with an intriguing statement, question, quotation, or attention-getting device (inductive approach)
2. Stimulate *interest* in the product or service
3. Create a *desire* for the product or service
4. Suggest a definite *action* for the reader

Getting the Reader's Attention

The unsolicited sales letter should begin with a thought-provoking device that appeals to the market you are seeking. You must **catch the reader's attention** with both content and form. Techniques of **content** include questions, proverbs, quotations, and startling statements or facts. **Form** can be manipulated by using such devices as prominent type sizes or designs, underscores, bright colors, and small gifts. Note how both content and form are combined in the following attention-getters:

Question: Are you familiar with all of the services provided by the First National Trust Bank?

Can you imagine your home with a thick, green lawn in early spring?

Proverb: Better to light one candle than to curse the darkness.

Quotation: "All work and no play makes Jack a dull boy."

"The California Vinyl Soffit on our house," says Mrs. A. R. Jordan, "is as beautiful as it was thirty years ago."

Forceful statement: Cut window heat loss up to 79% and add comfort to every room.

a guaranteed lifetime protection feature is written into every policy.

SUBSCRIBE TODAY.

Each year as a special Christmas offer Masterson offers you an outstanding buy on all pipes. Solve your gift-buying problems early with big savings on all our hand-made, cool-smoking pipes.

Statistical fact: Each year, 26,000 Americans die and 1.5 million are injured by drunk drivers.

There are 22,000,000 accidents every year—mostly minor, but almost all costing money.

Split sentence: You made Christmas merrier last year . . . do it again this year—and save money too!

You can have a $3000 loan for less than $95 a month . . . without a second mortgage or collateral.

Split sentence and underline: <u>You just can't find</u> more inspiring Christmas gifts . . . than the magnificent books we have just packaged at a handsome 20% discount.

Split sentence and symbol: We invite you to help . . . with your contribution . . . the breath-saving service for you and your loved ones made possible by Christmas ✝ Seals.

Capitalization and split sentence: Here's a Promise:
SIX MONTHS FROM TODAY . . .
You can have money in the bank and be on sounder financial footing . . . without increasing your family income.

Handwritten with colored ink: *Would you throw away hard cash or valuable gifts if they were given to you absolutely FREE?*

Income tax information and service is our only business.

Descriptive case: I wish you could meet Antone. You would like him. He has big brown eyes, shiny black hair, a winning smile, and an infectious giggle. To see him in action, you would never know that early in his life—before he was six months old—he suffered not one, but two strokes!

Slogan with small gift attached: Only a nickel a day.
Shiny nickel attached beneath letterhead

Usually the attention-getter identifies the product or service; sometimes it does not. The best attention-getters are those that inspire the reader to continue reading, are related to the sales product or service, are reader centered, and are relatively concise.

Creating Interest and Desire

Getting the reader's attention is just the beginning. You must now **create interest and desire** for the products or services sold. Show the reader that the item has special merit, make him or her feel a personal desire for it by:

1. Concentrating on a few outstanding features of the product or services. You do not want to overwhelm the reader by using more than one main selling point throughout the letter.
2. Providing convincing evidence of excellence of product or service. Use statistics, guarantees, testimonials, or free samples.

3. Using believable, specific, and concrete language and avoiding superlatives or exaggerated praise, which might induce doubt. Consider inviting comparison with similar goods or services but be realistic and truthful.
4. Working prices in after the other merits have been presented. Unless price is used as one of the outstanding features, do not present it until the central part of the letter. This allows the reader to become interested in and develop a desire for the outstanding features before he or she has to consider cost. If possible, state the price as a small unit. A price of $8.99 a month for six months sounds less expensive than $53.80. Similarly, using the price in figures—$100, for example—is usually better than stretching it out with words—one hundred dollars. Advertisers often use odd-amount prices to soften a cost figure. Psychologically, $10.95 seems closer to $10, even though it's actually closer to $11. When comparing prices, use *less expensive* rather than *cheap*. Less expensive refers to price; cheap refers to quality.
5. Stating any bonuses or other advantages.

   The following kinds of statements will encourage interested buyers to order with minimum delay.
   Bonus statement: If you order *Tax Guide* now, you will receive a year's free subscription to *The Newsletter*. *The Newsletter* will inform you of important changes and developments in the current tax law.
   Trial period statement: Just for trying our portable color television, you will get a beautiful, radiant yellow electric kitchen clock absolutely free!

6. Making it easy for the reader. You may invite the reader to charge the cost, enclose order forms, business reply cards, business envelopes, or toll-free telephone numbers.
7. Calling attention to pertinent facts and ideas. Use illustrations, varied print sizes, underlining, capitalization, two colors of ink, postscripts, and blank space to highlight. Be careful. If attention-getters are used haphazardly or excessively, they will detract from the sales appeal.

Sales letters need **concrete language**—vivid, picture-inspiring words to create interest in and a desire for the product or service. A letter promoting a cookware set should describe the outstanding features that would be most attractive to the buyer. Remember that the buyer is likely to be the person who prepares daily meals for the household.

> It's a whole new way to cook.
>
> Tight-fitting lids lock in the food's natural moisture and keep it from escaping in steam. This allows foods to cook in their own flavorful juices, preserving their goodness.

> The carbon steel core in this cookware distributes heat quickly and evenly. Therefore, foods cook faster with minimum shrinkage of today's increasingly expensive meats and vegetables.
>
> Cook with each piece . . . put them in your freezer . . . in the oven (up to 350°F) . . . in the dishwasher. . . .
>
> Glistening, pure white porcelain is decorated with bright, country-kitchen design—permanently fired on—to last the life of the cookware.

The writer might further describe the cookware with terms that would appeal to the reader's emotions and logic. Notice the force carried by a few well-chosen words. The words create images that are desirable to prospective buyers:

Ideal Perfect for you

Decorative Multipurpose: visual as well as functional

Shiny new Qualities we all appreciate

Glistening Reinforces shiny new

Versatile Multipurpose

Beautiful A visual asset

Porcelain-on-steel Durable

Easy-cleaning Efficient

Tough, long-lasting Durable

Kitchen-brightening Visual

Store-and-serve Multipurpose; efficient

Action Statements

The very end of the letter should confidently **present an action** for the reader to take. This action should be simple and fast. Refer to an added stimulus—if it is available—for quick action.

> Mail your order before November 15 and save 20% to 30%.
>
> Please sign and return the enclosed business reply card, and you will receive your personalized handbag within fifteen days.
>
> Your permanent and personal identification card will be mailed to you as soon as we receive your first order.
>
> Make yours one of the "lucky families" and plan to visit us this summer. You will enjoy the short drive and you and your family will find a natural retreat.

Avoid demanding or negative statements, such as *Act now* and *Don't delay another moment.* Instead, stress some special features about the product or service that provide a reason for not delaying (free gifts, discounts, special terms). Then give a definite and reasonable time for positive action.

Dear Mr. and Mrs. Smith:

Attention-getter → Are you familiar with all of the services provided by the First National Trust Bank?

Interest and desire → You are probably familiar with our convenient U.S. Post Office substation . . . but did you know that we have safety deposit boxes at low yearly rental rates, regular savings accounts paying 6 percent interest, savings certificates for even higher rates, checking accounts that give you detailed monthly statements, low interest rates on auto loans, direct payment of utility bills, automatic teller banking, Master Card/VISA credit, and much, much more.

Miss Cathy A. Peterson will be your special banker at the First National Trust Bank.

Action → Do plan to visit our friendly banking center and introduce yourself to Cathy who will help you enjoy the convenience of one-stop banking.

Sincerely,

FIRST NATIONAL TRUST BANK

Beatrice Sailors

Mrs. Beatrice Sailors
Vice-President

tro

We are open Monday through Thursday from 9:30 a.m. until 4:30 p.m. and Friday from 9:30 a.m. until 7:00 p.m.

Figure 14-1
Sales Letter for Banking Services

The sales letter in Figure 14-1 is short but effective. The attention-getter specifies the sales item—bank services. This central selling point is stressed throughout the letter. After getting the readers' attention, Beatrice Sailors develops interest by identifying the individual services offered. The services are made more attractive by modifiers such as *low, yearly, regular, detailed,* and *direct*. Her message ends in a positive action statement with an added stimulus—personal attention. Finally, the postscript shows Mrs. Sailors' confidence by providing the reader with additional useful information—banking hours—to spur quick action.

The sales letter in Figure 14-2 is an excerpt from a sales letter in which the attention-getter does not identify the product or service. It does, however, lead smoothly into the succeeding paragraph, which reveals the product. The central selling theme—

Dear Friend:

Here's a Promise: ← **Attention**

SIX MONTHS FROM TODAY . . .

You can have money in the bank and

be on sounder financial footing

. . . without increasing your family income.

You can do these things as millions of other families have done. They have followed the sound, easy-to-understand money management advice presented each month in Spending Wisely, the consumers' magazine. ← **Interest**

For example, here are titles of several articles from just one recent single issue of the magazine:

Titles of various articles listed for the reader

Try Spending Wisely and see for yourself how valuable it can be to you. Enclosed is a card that entitles you to the next six issues of Spending Wisely and a copy of Planning Your Future. This invaluable 56-page book contains many practical and profitable ideas for saving and investing and for getting the most from your income. You will be amazed at the genuine down-to-earth help you will get. ← **Desire**

In order to get your free book and start your subscription to Spending Wisely, just check and return the enclosed card with your $8 check in the postpaid envelope. ← **Action**

If at any time you do not believe that Spending Wisely has helped you get on a better financial footing--actually saving you money--just tell us and you will get a refund for the undelivered copies of your subscription. Planning Your Future is yours to keep.

Please give us an opportunity to keep our promise--do mail your order today. ← **Action**

Sincerely,

Jane K. Woo

Jane K. Woo
Vice President, Marketing and Sales

Figure 14-2
Sales Letter for Magazine Subscription

Dear Customer:

Attention → You are invited to a CLOSED DOOR SALE on Sunday, November 12, 6:00 P.M. to midnight.

DAILEY is having a private closed door sale for YOU while the doors are closed to the general public.

Interest and desire → YOU MUST BRING THIS LETTER FOR ADMITTANCE TO THE STORE.

> This is a Sale of Sales. Prices will be greatly reduced for you on famous makes of televisions, stereo systems, and kitchen appliances. You will find well-known brand names such as General Electric, Admiral, Motorola, RCA, Capehart, and Hoover--to name just a few.
>
> Our suppliers have given us special permission to reduce prices during this sale.
>
> We will have a wide selection of models on hand for this big event.

Credit personnel will be on hand for immediate approvals. As always at DAILEY'S, you will receive full warranties; free delivery service is available.

Action → Come to the closed door sale on November 12 and enjoy outstanding buys, free coffee and donuts. And while you are here, register for our great door prize--a brand new portable color TV!

Sincerely,

Wayne Brittenden

Wayne Brittenden
Sales Manager

Figure 14-3
Invitation to Special Retail Sale

money management advice—is stressed throughout the letter. The bonus—a helpful book for planning investments—and the trial offer encourage the potential customer to act positively and quickly.

The sales letter in Figure 14-3 is meant for customers of a large retail store, inviting them to a special private sale of several well-known brand lines. The writer promises genuine savings, wide selection, full warranties, free delivery, credit terms, free coffee and donuts, and a "great" door prize.

Some companies find it profitable to send promotional messages occasionally, instead of sales letters, on cards of various sizes and colors (see Chapter 16).

SALES SYSTEM

Basically, there are three types of sales systems: the continuous system, the wear-out system and the campaign system.

Continuous System

The **continuous system**, which has no end, sends periodic messages to advertise the existence of a firm, its products, or its services. It is an effective way to maintain customer or public relations. Letters or notices in the continuous sales system might be mailed to sell a product or service, but they are basically aimed at inviting present or prospective customers to visit the firm or to introduce a new line of merchandise, a new or expanded department, or a new branch office. At times, letters are intended to extend good wishes or to solicit advice or inquiries.

Banks, utilities, retail stores, insurance companies, and industrial firms are among those using the continuous sales system. The letters in Figure 14–1 and 14–3 could have been part of a continuous sales system.

The sales letter in Figure 14–4 encourages readers to purchase products from the distributor (Dorsch Tool & Engineering Company). The writer explains what the distributor can do for the readers.

Wear-Out System

The **wear-out system** is used to sell low-priced items. One letter or three or four different letters all may be sent to the same mailing list, which generally becomes shorter and shorter until it is finally abandoned when the returns no longer seem to justify the cost of additional mailings. Each letter is a complete sales presentation. The letters may be mailed two weeks to several months apart. Campaigns to sell magazine subscriptions, books, records, and other low-priced items are often conducted through the wear-out system. The letter in Figure 14–2 could have been the first letter in a wear-out series.

Campaign System

The **campaign system** is used to sell relatively high-priced items or unusual items. Unlike letters in the wear-out system, each letter in the campaign system adds a little more information or persuasion to the previous message. The campaign is incomplete until a predesignated number of letters—possibly three or four—are mailed to each name on the list. The series usually extends over several months, each communication timed for an appropriate arrival. Real estate promoters and firms enticing individuals to use their products or services rely on the campaign system.

R & D

Established 1941

TOOL COMPANY, INC.

P.O. Box 416 • Farmington Hills, Michigan 48024 • (313) 474-1181
25820 Orchard Lake Road • Farmington Hills, MI 48018 • (313) 537-4820

August 1, 19--

Dear Friends:

Attention → We are pleased to announce the appointment of Dorsch Tool and Engineering Company as a distributor for our product line of flat replacement blades and cutting tools both in carbide-tipped and solid high speed designs.

Interest and desire → Dorsch Tool and Engineering will be able to fill your cutting tool needs not only for the standard style blades and wedges but also for your special blueprint designed cutting tool requirements. We are currently one of the nation's largest stockers of the Goddard & Goddard style blades and wedges and we also stock many of the other standard style blades. Dorsch Tool and Engineering can also now offer you substantial savings on your replacement wedge needs as we are now stocking the standard style replacement wedges for the VR/Wesson style and Valenite style indexable cutters.

Action → Please direct your quotation requests and requests for product information to the following address:

Dorsch Tool & Engineering Company
3419 Georgetown Road
Indianapolis, Indiana 46224
Phone: (317) 213-6722

Goodwill → We will be looking forward to helping you with your tooling and wedge needs in the future.

Very truly yours,

Ed.L. Latendresse

Edward L. Latendresse
Sales Manager

ELL/hjc

Figure 14-4
Sales Letter to Encourage Purchase of Product

The letters in Figures 14-5 and 14-6 could have been part of campaign systems. Mature motorists with safe-driving records are the target readers for Figure 14-5. The central selling features are guaranteed auto protection for low prices and quick service. The letter in Figure 14-6 is directed to individuals who might be in the market for recreation-resort property. Readers are urged to bring their families and visit the recreation-resort community; one or more valuable gifts or cash are used to encourage the *short drive* to the *natural retreat.*

Unsolicited sales letters to customers who have made no purchases for six months or longer are part of the campaign system.

Save $20 - $40 - $80 or more a year! ← **Attention-getter**

Dear Motorist:

Policyowners throughout the United States have realized significant savings on their automobile insurance coverage with Auto & Home Insurance Company. ← **Start of interest and desire**

We have a unique way to determine rates for automobile insurance. Your annual premium depends on the number of miles you drive for pleasure and business in combination with your age, the areas you live and drive in, the type and number of cars you drive, and your individual driving record. Auto & Home Insurance Company tries hard to favor the good driver who is 55 or older.

You have the security of knowing that your automobile insurance will never be dropped because you are getting older or because you have an auto accident. Each person is treated as an individual.

When you have a question, problem, or claim, just telephone us regardless of where you are in the United States--toll free or collect. Your personal claims representative will see your claim through to its satisfactory conclusion. In many cases, you will receive a check within five days. Our customer service representatives will answer your questions about premium notices, changes in coverage, or policy protection features. ← **Quick service**

Please take two minutes to complete the enclosed request-for-quotation card. You will be glad you did. This easy action can save you at least $20 each year, and you will have guaranteed lifetime protection with quick, individual service. ← **Action**

Figure 14-5
Sales Letter to Motorists 55 or Older for Auto Insurance Protection

They include an appeal to win back the customers. Writers use statements similar to:

1. We miss you. What happened?
2. Please consider this letter your personal invitation to return to . . .
3. You can use the enclosed $____ certificate toward your next purchase.
4. Even if you return the ____, the calculator is yours to keep.

The letters should indicate reader benefits in a friendly, sincere tone. Customers should sense the goodwill and believe it beneficial (to them) to resume the customer-seller relationship. Some customers will need much inducement. If the customer has a grievance, it must be resolved to his or her satisfaction.

Attention-getter → *Would you throw away hard cash or valuable gifts if they were given to you absolutely free?*

Interest and desire → Each year, many thousands of dollars in cash and awards are given away to families just like yours . . . and that is less than one tenth of the amount sponsors, like ours, are willing to give away absolutely free . . . no strings attached . . . after you visit us and pick up your gifts.

Let me explain. A local community developer is very interested in informing the public about his resort community. He has budgeted thousands of dollars for cash gifts, prizes, and advertising. We realize that the best and most effective form of advertising is through "word of mouth." However, to initiate this form of advertising, a select group of families must be aware of the integrity and superiority of the product--a recreation-resort community.

You and your family have been selected from many others to receive valuable gifts and/or cash, in the belief that, after seeing the resort area, you will want to tell all your friends and neighbors about it. This is our way of inviting you to visit a lovely community and see the property available. Believe me, this is not a gimmick! If you toss this notification into the trash, you will be throwing money away!

Action → Make yours one of the "lucky families" and plan to visit us this summer. You will enjoy the short drive, and you and your family will find a natural retreat.

Figure 14-6
Sales Letter to Encourage Real Estate Purchase

Writing an effective unsolicited sales letter requires considerable creative ability, human relation know-how, and written language skill. Each situation is unique. Examples of sales writing can be helpful, but they are not the complete answer. Commit yourself to developing effective sales letters. With commitment and experience you will write better sales letters.

MAILING LISTS

Mailing lists are names of those individuals or companies who might be interested in what you are selling. A few possible sources for mailing lists follow:

City directories
City records—automobile licenses; marriage licenses; various permits, such as those for fishing and hunting; corporate charters; births; deaths; divorces

Club rosters
College and university directories—faculty, staff, students
Commercial agencies selling specific mailing lists—classified in various ways
Company records—customers, sales personnel, executives
Convention rosters
Education directories—names of schools, administrators
Mercantile directories
Newspapers (local and national)—society and sports columns
Standard and Poor's Register of Corporations, Directors, and Executives
Telephone directories—alphabetical and classified sections
Thomas Register of American Manufacturers
Trade directories
The Value Line Investment Survey

Business firms can also develop mailing lists from suggested names furnished by satisfied customers. It is not unusual for a company to request information such as the following:

> If you are satisfied with your _______ won't you tell us the names and addresses of two friends who might also enjoy using this product.
>
> We will mail to them, without any obligation, descriptive literature and current prices.
>
> NAME ______________________________
>
> ADDRESS ______________________________
>
> CITY ______________ STATE _______ ZIP _______
>
> NAME ______________________________
>
> ADDRESS ______________________________
>
> CITY ______________ STATE _______ ZIP _______

Some businesses and fraternal organizations offer prizes to customers or members who furnish them with names and addresses of potential customers or members.

CHAPTER SUMMARY

Businesses rely upon sales letters to produce sales. Sales letters play an important role in creating new business and retaining existing customers. They must be expertly constructed, however, if they are to win the customer over.

To write an effective sales letter, you must know well the product or service to be sold, understand human nature, and frame the sales message around the reader's interests, needs, and wants. Sales letters must get the reader's attention, stimulate interest, create a desire for the product or service, and ultimately stir the reader to buy. The solicited sales letter should directly and positively answer the readers' questions. A special attention-getting statement would detract from the message.

These three sales systems are common: the continuous system, featuring periodic sales messages to maintain customer or public relations; the wear-out system for selling low-priced items, each letter a complete sales pitch; and the campaign system for selling relatively high-priced or unusual items, each letter adding more persuasive features about the product or service.

STUDY QUESTIONS

1. What is a sales letter? What is the difference between a solicited and an unsolicited sales letter?
2. What special knowledge should you have about the products, market, and reader in order to write an effective sales letter?
3. Why should you stress one central selling point throughout the sales letter?
4. What does AIDA mean with respect to sales letters?
5. What are the different techniques writers use to get the attention of the potential customer? Give examples.
6. What suggestions can you give to create an interest and desire for a product or service?
7. Why should your sales letter have a positive action ending?
8. What are the three types of sales systems? Explain when each should be used.
9. What sources are available to business people for compiling a mailing list of potential customers?

ACTIVITIES

1. Make a list of appropriate active and concrete terms for selling a product (for example, a video cassette recorder).
2. Examine an advertisement for a product or service and explain:
   a. How the advertiser achieves (1) attention, (2) interest, (3) desire, and (4) action.
   b. The type of audience you believe the advertisement is directed to. Describe the advertisement and write an attention-getter for a sales letter promoting the product or service.
3. Look at an actual sales letter, and:
   a. Determine the audience to whom the advertisement is directed.

   b. Explain how you believe the writer has used AIDA.
   c. State the kind of sales campaign you believe the letter represents.
   d. Rewrite the letter using a different attention-getter and varying the appeal.
4. Write attention-getting and action statements for these products:
   a. *Adding machine*: Convenient household adding machine that adds and subtracts figures up to 9,999,999. Automatic fingertip action—not a cheap spring-type model. Push-pull lever to clear machine. Checks bank statements. Has protective vinyl cover. Measures 4 in. × 4½ in. $12.50 plus $1.25 postage.
   b. *Bartender's plaque*: Wood-grained plaque with personal caricature for a bartender's bar. Hand-lettered name on the plaque. Measures 10 in. × 15 in. $15 postpaid. Send a photograph—state color of hair and eyes. Also print name you desire on plaque. The photograph will be returned to you.
   c. *Casual men's shoes*: Genuine deerskin leather uppers. Crepe soles and heels. An attractive and comfortable addition to your shoe wardrobe. Your foot rests on a thick cushion covered with glove leather. Easy to slip into because of the complete glove leather lining. Sizes 7 to 13, Widths B, C, D, E, EE, EEE. $59.50 postpaid.
5. Write a sales letter for the television set described below. Supply any descriptive or promotional ideas you wish.
   a. 10-in. screen
   b. 100% solid-state chassis
   c. Portable
   d. Color—clear, brilliant, true to life, up-to-the-minute color technology
   e. Space saving—15¾ in. wide × 11¾ in. high × 15¼ in. deep
   f. UHV tuner clicks in place for each channel
   g. Self-contained, high-powered, twin-telescoping antennas so that there is minimum need for other antennas
   h. Warranties—2 years on picture tube; 90 days for parts and labor on everything else in the set
   i. Free 15-day trial
   j. $148.50 cash price ($137.50 plus transportation) or $7.35 a month for 24 months, no down payment—this includes a finance charge of $27.90.
6. Write an attention-getter for each of the following products or services. Choose a different opening technique (question, proverb, quotation, statement, split sentence, and so on) for each.

   a. Electric kitchen clock
   b. Imported suit
   c. New catering service
   d. Piece of jewelry
   e. Snowmobile
   f. Accounting service
   g. Adding machine or other mechanical office machine
   h. Lawnmower

7. Write a sales letter for the dishwasher described below; give it a fancy name and realistic price $(398). Supply any other promotional ideas you wish.
   a. Portable Model DW-CIM
   b. Fully convertible to use under the counter
   c. Super Surge washing action—Designed with the help of a computer, it drenches washing surfaces with hot water. It is powerful, yet gentle enough to protect china and crystal.
   d. Holds the day's dishes for a family of four with room for pots and pans
   e. Racks pull all the way out to load easily
   f. Easy-to-fill automatic detergent dispensers
   g. Spots-Away rinse injection to condition water in final rinse
   h. Separate cycles for almost every situation
   i. Other models available at your dealer
8. As part of your sales promotion program, several employees scan newspaper advertisements for names and addresses of newly engaged women. Write a sales letter for persons on this mailing list. Your company sells wedding invitations, thank you notes, and other stationery items.
9. You want to start your own service business (such as tax preparation, auditing, interior decorating, messenger or delivery service, baby sitting, or landscape painting). Your service is expert, personalized, professional, efficient, prompt. Write a sales letter.
10. Choose a very special product you would like to have. List all the qualities you want the product to have. Assume you are the seller, rather than prospective buyer. Write the sales letter.

EDITING

1. Correct these phrases:
   a. Your invited
   b. Most unique
   c. First priority
   d. Entirely complete
   e. Green in color
   f. Appointed to the post

2. Change these to request positive action:
   a. I hope you will not delay.
   b. If you agree, send your money today.
3. Revise these opening statements to be more descriptive and appropriate for sales letters:
   a. It's a bright, tough, easy-to-wipe shine.
      To sell floor wax
   b. You can have a better lawn.
      Write a paragraph which helps the reader visualize a "better" lawn—a thick, green lawn.
   c. Thanks for your letter inquiring about our stock of fine, quality suits. We have just the one you are looking for.
4. Revise these ending statements to be more appropriate for sales letters:
   a. Please return the enclosed card now. Don't wait another minute.
   b. Nationwide Transportation Company makes moving anywhere a pleasure. So telephone us at 614-5042. Ask our rep to call on you and to discuss our low rates and to determine your packing needs.
5. Revise these statements for sales letters:
   a. Your money back if you aren't satisfied. We'll come back as often as necessary.
   b. This travel luggage comes in several colors to brighten up your travel appearance and make a fashion statement.
   c. The price for this luggage is $199.95 for the set which sells for $300 in retail stores.

IN-BASKET SIMULATIONS

1. Waltere Supermarkets wants to prepare a sales campaign promoting its new drugstore. As part of the publicity, you are asked to write a letter for publication in a local newspaper advertising the store's opening.

   Waltere Drugs will be opening in two weeks. The self-service store will have at all times a reputable pharmacist available for filling doctor's prescriptions quickly, correctly, and completely. Three cashiers will be on hand to expedite paying for purchases. Major credit cards will be honored.

   In addition to the pharmacy, other departments include film processing, camera equipment, cosmetics, greeting cards, jewelry, auto supplies, and various over-the-counter medicines and supplies.

   On opening day, a lovely carnation will be given to the first 100 women customers, small toys will be given to all children all day, a piece of specially made cake will be served to everyone (lots of special bargains available on opening day and every day). Write an appealing sales letter to be printed in the newspaper.

2. Write a sales letter to be sent to a list of local doctors announcing the opening of Waltere Drugs, the hours when drug purchases can be made, and the names of the two registered pharmacists. Waltere Drugs believes it is responsible for providing the most current therapeutic agents for physicians and their patients under the U.S. Food & Drug Administration regulations. Medicines and drugs will be available in both brand and generic names.
3. Peter Waltere wrote a memorandum to Thomas Leonard, President of Drug Operations, urging him to seek a definite entity for the drug division. He suggested writing letters to three advertising firms: (1) a well-established firm, (2) a growing firm, and (3) a new firm. Write a letter that could be sent to each firm requesting them to propose a total advertising and merchandising program based on their research and ideas. You are interested in their putting together a total program using television, radio, and newspapers, and submitting it to you within five weeks.
4. Peter Waltere got another idea: Would it be feasible to have gasoline pumps placed at various Mini Mart sites? He explained his idea to Jeffrey J. Jackson, President, Convenience Foods. Mr. Jackson asked you to do the necessary research.

   Research indicates that several locations might be profitable areas for the gasoline pumps. Thus, you decide to write letters to several large oil companies asking them to submit figures for installing and maintaining four gasoline pumps at the three specific Mini Marts you mention. You think that the oil companies can furnish other useful data and suggestions; you request the information within two weeks.
5. A customer has written that she does not trust electronic scanning used at the checkout lane at Waltere Supermarket where she shops. Write a convincing letter explaining that electronic-scanning technology speeds customers through checkout lanes at 35 Waltere Supermarkets—three added this year. The scanner picks up the price code faster and more accurately than the best cashier can do using conventional methods. You are so convinced about the merits of the electronic scanner that you tell the customer that any product incorrectly priced will be hers free. The store's manager will give her a refund immediately.

   Waltere uses the scanner at its Indianapolis warehousing and distribution facility. Conveyor belts from six areas of the warehouse merge into one lane leading to an electronic scanner. It picks up the code on the tag on each case and directs it to the station for each store's order.

Writing Interoffice Memoranda

15

After studying Chapter 15, you should be able to:

- Define the difference between letters and interoffice communications
- Write an effective interoffice memorandum
- Distinguish between an interoffice memorandum and a memorandum report

The **interoffice memorandum** (also shortened to memo) is a routine, concise, brief message transmitted within an organization to help the business operate smoothly at minimum cost. It is the most widely used written business communication for internal communication. Occasionally, the memorandum form is used for routine external communications. The idea is to convey messages quickly and easily, not to be creative. Nonetheless, the message should be written carefully.

Compared to other forms of written business communication, the memorandum is relatively inexpensive. Even though the form is printed, it is less expensive than company letterhead and envelopes, both of which include quality printing and/or embossing on good bond paper that has a watermark.

Interoffice memorandum forms come in two sizes: 8½″ x 11″ (standard size) and 8½″ x 5½″ (half sheet). The former is preferable since it will ensure that all file correspondence is of uniform size. Sometimes a handwritten note on an interoffice memorandum form may suffice in less formal situations, especially when a quick response to an enquiry is necessary.

PURPOSE FOR USING INTEROFFICE MEMORANDA

Interoffice memoranda are best used for routine messages that:

1. Confirm or remind someone of an oral message (Figure 15-1)
2. Inform in writing (for example, meeting dates and places, simple explanations and/or instructions, or routine details) (Figure 15-2)
3. Announce personnel appointments, products, news—Some firms post the message on bulletin boards or include the memorandum with employee's paycheck (Figure 15-3).
4. Suggest or advise in writing (Figure 15-4)

Memoranda are *not* useful for persuading or conveying complicated data. If the receiver is likely to have questions or needs additional information or advice, use a more formal method of communication.

Each memorandum is brief and concise, yet the necessary information is clearly and completely stated. Instead of listing names of all sales representatives (Figure 15-2), the memorandum can be directed to *All Sales Representatives* (Figure 15-1) or *Sales Representatives* (Figure 15-4). If understood, incomplete company names can be used (Figure 15-2); dates can be abbreviated (Figure 15-2); and commands can be used (Figures 15-2, 15-3, and 15-4).

DATE: September 1, 19--

TO: All Sales Representatives

FROM: M. E. Richards *M.E.R.*

SUBJECT: Meeting, September 7, 19--

Confirming today's telephone conversation, please attend the special sales meeting: ← **Purpose**

Date: September 7, 19--

Place: Conference Room, Second Floor ← **Details**

Time: 2:30 to 3:30 p.m.

Sales reps. from Anderson Supply Co., will be introducing you to a new and "improved" fumigant. The product sounds like a good one, and the price seems right.

I'd like your opinion. ← **Action**

pt

Figure 15-1
Interoffice Memorandum Confirming Telephone Message

DATE: September 1, 19--

TO: J. T. Avery
B. Dale Flowers
Mary J. Lacey
Jeanne Lafollette
Bill Martin
Henry A. Parker

FROM: M. E. Richards *M.E.R.*

SUBJECT: Meeting on September 7, 19--

Please attend the special meeting scheduled for September 7 in the second floor conference room, 2:30 to 3:30 p.m. ← **Purpose and details**

James Ball and Mildred V. Sims from Anderson Supply will introduce a new fumigant. The product seems to be worth our time and attention; the price seems right. ← **Details**

Give me your opinion. ← **Action**

pt

Figure 15-2
Interoffice Memorandum Informing Employees of Meeting

September 1, 19--

TO: ALL SALES REPRESENTATIVES

FROM: M. E. RICHARDS *Richards*

SUBJECT: SPECIAL MEETING, SEPTEMBER 7, 19--

Purpose and details →

IT IS IMPERATIVE THAT YOU ATTEND THE SALES MEETING ON MONDAY, SEPTEMBER 7, 19--, CONFERENCE ROOM, 2:30 TO 3:30 P.M.

Details →

ANDERSON SUPPLY CO. SALES REPS. WILL BE ON HAND TO ANSWER YOUR QUESTIONS ON CHEMAL FUMIGANTS. WE WILL BE THE SOLE SUPPLIERS FOR THEM IN THIS DISTRICT.

pt

Bulletin Board: 9/1-9/7/--

Figure 15-3
Bulletin Board Message

DATE: September 1, 19--

TO: SALES REPRESENTATIVES

FROM: M. E. Richards *M.E.R.*

SUBJECT: CHEMAL FUMIGANT SALES

Purpose and details →

Effective September 14, 19--, we will be handling all Chemal fumigant sales in this area. Attached are samples of labels and a copy of the current price list. This list also indicates available trade discounts for buyers purchasing large quantities.

pt

Attachments

Figure 15-4
Interoffice Memorandum
Conveying Information

COMPARISON WITH LETTERS

Format and terminology used in memoranda are less formal and less polished than they are for letters, for example:

Memorandum	**Letter**
Informal and brief format to define the intended receivers, writer, date, and subject	Basic and special letter parts always used
No courtesy titles before names of sender and receiver	Appropriate courtesy title used (for example, Miss Mary J. Lacey)
No business title after sender's name	Correct business title after person's name (for example, Henry A. Parker, Sales)
Sender's signature or initials without complimentary close	Complimentary close with sender's signature
Conversational language:	Formal language:
sales reps. (Figure 15-1)	sales representatives
price seems right (Figure 15-1)	price is competitive
I'd like your opinion. (Figure 15-1)	I would like your opinion.
Give me your opinion. (Figure 15-2)	Please give me your opinion.

ADVANTAGES OF USING MEMOS

There are several advantages for using memoranda to communicate within an organization.

1. *The memo provides an economical written record for either the writer, the reader, or both individuals.* Formal written communications require relatively expensive letterhead and envelopes, as well as postage.
2. *The memo can save time, energy, and expense* that might otherwise be needed to communicate with co-workers individually, by telephone, or in person. One message can be typed with copies for all individuals involved.
3. *The co-workers will receive the exact message at approximately the same time.*
4. *The co-workers do not have to remember specifics.*
5. *A written message is less likely than an oral message to be misinterpreted*—especially if it is technical or complicated.
6. *The memo can follow up an oral conversation*, reminding co-workers.

APPEARANCE OF MEMORANDA

Content and Format

Sometimes memoranda are typed on forms including the company letterhead (on much less expensive paper, however); all memos will contain a printed heading that provides specific space for:

1. The name of the person or persons for whom the message is intended (unlike letters, courtesy titles are omitted)
2. The name of the writer (courtesy title omitted)
3. The topic of the memo stated in a few well-chosen words
4. The date

The uniform heading makes it easy for the reader to identify the sender and the topic of the communication. Senders save time using the printed form; company officials are pleased with the easy-to-use, consistent format for routine internal communication.

Typically, memos are just a few paragraphs, but some can extend to a second page. Half-sheet forms are sometimes used for short messages; however, full-sheet forms are less likely to be lost or misfiled. Even though the message can be single- or double-spaced with blocked or indented paragraphs, you should always double-space between paragraphs. Blocked paragraphs can save typing time, but double-spaced messages should be indented.

Begin the message a triple space after the printed heading. The message should be concise and carefully worded. It should comply with the characteristics for effective business communications. When writing interoffice memoranda, use the deductive (direct) approach and:

1. State the purpose clearly
2. Supply necessary details, information, or instructions
3. Close courteously, indicating action desired

Unlike typical business letters, the memorandum never includes an inside address, salutation, or complimentary close. Like letters, the memo indicates names and possibly business titles of individuals receiving copies of the communication.

Copies to: Mary Therman, Purchasing Agent; John A. Barlow, Purchasing Agent

Copy to: John Cramer, Sales Manager

Usually, memo writers will personalize their communications by initialing or signing them (usually after the *FROM* line). Some writers will sign their names below the message, as done for business letters.

All Sales Representatives
Page 2
April 5, 19--

← Heading

Additional information is available from Mary Palmer, District Sales Manager for the Baltimore area. You can telephone her at 301-771-2138.

← Rest of message

pt

Figure 15-5
Second Page of Interoffice Memo

First- and Second-Page Headings

Although the order of printed headings may vary somewhat, they are usually double-spaced and consist of the words *TO, FROM, SUBJECT*, and *DATE* placed about one inch from the top of the page and one inch from the left margin. The required information is usually typed two spaces after the colon:

TO: Luis Rivera, Accounting
FROM: Dana Martinez, Sales
SUBJECT: Model L-1115
DATE: April 5, 19--

April 5, 19--

TO: Luis Rivera
FROM: Dana Martinez
SUBJECT: Model L-1115

TO: Luis Rivera
FROM: Dana Martinez
DATE: April 5, 19--
SUBJECT: Model L-1115

Second-page memos do not repeat the printed headings; instead, they include data similar to multiple-page letters (see Chapter 5). The proper heading includes the name of the intended receiver, the page number, and the date. Begin the heading 1 in. from the top of the sheet at the left margin; triple-space after the heading and continue your message.

These are three appropriate multiple-page headings:

Luis Rivera -2- April 5, 19--

Luis Rivera, April 5, 19--, page 2

Luis Rivera
Page 2
April 5, 19--

If the three-line heading is chosen, single-space the lines.

Figure 15-5 illustrates the second page of an interoffice memorandum.

DISBURSEMENT

The completed memo may be posted on a bulletin board as an announcement to all or certain employees or sent to the addressed employee in a routing envelope. Only memoranda intended for external business communication are placed and mailed in regular stationery envelopes.

COMPARISON OF INTEROFFICE MEMORANDUM AND MEMORANDUM REPORT

The **memorandum report** is an informational report used among employees of the same company. Like the interoffice memorandum, the memorandum report should be informal, brief, concise, and complete. Since it often indicates the results of research, it is more structured than the interoffice memo and includes subdivisions to guide the reader. The report is subdivided to include an **introduction** to the information, the **body** to provide necessary facts, and the **conclusion**, or **summary**, and/or recommendations.

Both the interoffice memorandum and the memorandum report have the *TO*, *FROM*, *SUBJECT*, and *DATE* headings. Multiple pages are handled in the same way. See Chapter 18 for more information about the content of the report.

The memorandum report is discussed more completely in Chapter 20.

CHAPTER SUMMARY

Internal written communication can be effectively and inexpensively accomplished by using the interoffice memorandum, often a preprinted form that designates specific places for stating the sender's and receiver's names, the date, and the subject. Although the form may include all or part of the company's letterhead, the paper is poor quality when compared to letterhead stationery.

Besides saving paper costs, the interoffice form saves writer and reader time, thus also reducing labor costs. The sender merely completes the *TO*, *FROM*, *SUBJECT* and *DATE* captions and states the message simply and concisely. Formal letter parts are omitted, but the sender personalizes the message by adding his or her initials. Messages can be read quickly.

The memorandum is useful for routine, simple written messages—especially within the organization. However, some business firms use the interoffice memorandum form to mail routine, noncomplicated data to customers and suppliers.

Most interoffice messages can be stated on one page (generally single-spaced with double spacing between the block style paragraphs). If two pages are needed, the second page should have a special heading similar to those used for multiple-page letters.

As with any other business communication, interoffice memoranda should be written carefully so that the message will be easily understood, complete, and concise.

The memorandum is similar to the memorandum report (an informational report).

STUDY QUESTIONS

1. Why is the interoffice memorandum the most widely used written business communication?
2. Which types of messages are best conveyed with a memorandum? Give several specific examples.
3. For which types of messages would a letter be more appropriate than a memo? Give several examples.
4. How is the memorandum similar to business letters?
5. How is the memorandum unlike business letters?
6. What plan should you follow for writing the memorandum message?
7. How is the second-page heading for memoranda similar to headings for multiple-page letters?
8. Since memoranda are necessarily brief and concise, how do writers personalize them?
9. How are memoranda disbursed?
10. What is a memorandum report?

ACTIVITIES

1. Write a memo to your teacher advising the advantages of using memoranda for internal communications.
2. Write a memo confirming an appointment made by telephone (supply necessary information).
3. As a district sales manager, write a memo to all salespersons in your district. Indicate that a special meeting will be held in two weeks (give the specific date) to discuss methods to promote sales of a specific product (choose the product). Encourage the sales personnel to bring their ideas to the meeting which will be at 3 p.m. in Conference Room A.
4. You are a personnel manager. Write a memo for the bulletin board announcing a job vacancy for Communication Specialist I in the Administrative Services Department. Your memo should include (1) job responsibilities, (2) desirable qualifications, and (3) application procedures. Interested individuals should submit a current resume and request an interview. A summary of job responsibilities follow: to prepare correspondence, articles, reports, speeches, outlines, charts and graphs, tables, and business forms from longhand

and rough draft copy; to compose appropriate internal and external communications. Applicants should be able to type rapidly and accurately, proofread for typing and content errors, use reference materials, make quick decisions, take the initiative and follow through, choose and compose appropriate communications, follow instructions, perform basic mathematical operations, and spell and use accurate English.

EDITING

Correct the following information for memoranda:

1. TO: Mr. Donald Minute, Advertising Specialist
   FROM: Mrs. Margaret Caronite, District Manager
   SUBJECT: Advertising schedule for custom draperies
   DATE: April 6, 19--.
2. Won't be long before summer will be here.
3. Until April 30th when you purchase beautiful custom draperies, I'll line them for you—free.
4. Draperies lined with Nu-Lining:
   a. Keep homes warmer in winter and cooler in summer.
   b. Protect room interiors from unnecessary window drafts.
   c. Sun deterioration and fading protection.
   d. Help prevent oil or water stains and streaking even after repeated launderings.
   e. Are completely dry cleanable or washable—shrinkage controlled to 2%.
   f. Grease resistant.
5. Why not give me a call today.
6. Our employees need to make important on-the-job decisions.
7. Supplementary reproducible materials are included in addition such as handouts.
8. Please write Seminar Planning, Huntington Beach, California 92647, P. O. Box 1170.
9. If any defects develop within a period of 30 days from the date of the invoice, they will be replaced free of charge.
10. Statistics prove that people remember 70% of what they hear after 3 hours and 10% after 3 days.

IN-BASKET SIMULATIONS

1. Write a memo to all office employees of Waltere Supermarkets, Inc. Advise that all letters are to be typewritten in full block (or modified block) as illustrated in the company manual No. A-111, Forms. This is to start immediately. You are the administrative assistant for Mr. Peter Waltere, Vice-President and General Manager.

2. You have created what you believe to be an appropriate and distinctive letterhead for Waltere Drugs (see In-Basket Simulation 2 for Chapter 5). Write a memo to Mr. Raymond Waltere, President of Waltere Supermarkets, Inc. Attach a copy of your proposal and explain why you believe the letterhead should be chosen. Also elaborate on the logo and slogan you developed. Request an appointment. Your suggestion may be worth a special bonus.
3. As Director of Employee Relations, prepare a memorandum that will be posted on the bulletin board and used as a payroll insert. Waltere Supermarkets, Inc., in cooperation with a dealer, is offering its employees certain electronic products (such as video recorders and computer equipment) at special prices and for a limited time only. Employees who are interested should order items through their supervisors who have the special order forms. A 10 percent down payment is required; the balance (including sales tax) is due within 30 days.
4. As Director of Salaried Personnel, write an interoffice memorandum to salaried employees informing them that the Board of Directors approved a college-credit reimbursement plan, effective next year. Eligible employees will be reimbursed as follows:

   100% tuition reimbursement for *A* grades
   75% tuition reimbursement for *B* grades
   50% tuition reimbursement for *C* grades
   No tuition reimbursement for grades below *C*

   Employees must be enrolled in approved courses and complete the appropriate forms prior to enrolling. For reimbursement, proof of grades is needed. Complete details are available upon request.

16 Writing Other Communications

After studying Chapter 16, you should be able to:

- Write an effective news release
- Differentiate between international and domestic correspondence
- Differentiate between postal and post cards
- Use preprinted and specially designed forms such as note-o-grams, routing slips, and message forms

If expertly constructed, letters provide a monumental service to the benefit of sales and management. There are other written formats that do not adhere to the standards of our letter styles but do, nevertheless, assume a monumental share of the volume of business correspondence. These documents may be isolated for study simply on the basis that they have one thing in common: they do not follow our established letter formats and standards. Yet they are responsible for conveying timely and vital information.

The purpose of these communications is understood; they do not need lengthy introductions, persuasive details, or summaries. And the formats are accepted; they provide convenience, speed, economy, and instant recognition. If you are to be actively involved in business, you should be able to recognize when and how to use these alternate forms of communication.

NEWS RELEASES

News releases are planned news or publicity given to news outlets—company publications or mass media (especially newspapers, radio, and television). They inform customers, employees, and the general public. They also promote goodwill among the parties involved. Even unfavorable news can be presented in a positive light.

News releases announce events or developments (for example, meeting information, employee promotions and transfers, new products or services, financial information, plant openings, company celebrations, management and union contracts, social and cultural programs, special offers, special awards and honors, and employee contests). To increase the chances of publication, the message should be newsworthy, timely, and properly formatted.

Large companies will have public relations departments to handle news releases; small firms may delegate the responsibility to a specific employee. The releases may be channeled through a specific individual to prevent publication of confidential, inaccurate, or untimely information.

Businesses that issue many news releases will use a preprinted form to save reading and writing time. This form includes letterhead data (the company name, address, and telephone number) and the name of an individual to contact for additional information. Generally, this data is prominently displayed at the top of the form, but it may be placed at the bottom.

The first paragraph is the most important part of the news release. Subsequent paragraphs should provide additional information in descending order of importance. Use a tightly worded, straightforward style, summarizing the highlights of the story first. Your plan is both to capture the reader's interest and to protect the essential information. If an editor shortens the story, or if the reader does not read the entire message, the most important elements remain intact in the initial paragraph (Figures 16-1 and 16-2). Use a deductive approach:

1. State the most important facts first (deductive approach).
2. Continue with the additional information giving the facts in descending order of importance. Be sure to answer, as necessary, the *who*, *what*, *why*, *where*, *when*, and *how*.

Writing

If your objective is to announce the appointment of an individual, the first paragraph might read:

> Dale A. Krause was appointed President and Chief Operating Officer of Convenience Foods, a division of Waltere Supermarkets, Inc., reported Raymond Waltere, Waltere Supermarkets' President and Chief Executive Officer.

Notice that the lead paragraph emphasizes the appointee, Dale A. Krause, rather than Raymond Waltere, the person announcing the appointment. Continue the news item by bringing in secondary information, for example:

> Krause, 25-year Waltere Supermarkets associate, was Director of Corporate Planning and Development. According to Katherine Waltere, Vice-President for Personnel, he will continue to be a member of the corporate board of directors and be involved in overall corporate activities, but will have primary responsibilities in the Convenience Foods division.
>
> Krause has held a variety of positions with the company including manager trainee, market analyst, Indianapolis employment manager, and director of real estate.
>
> He was graduated from Central High School and earned his bachelor's degree in economics from DePauw University and a master's degree in business administration from Indiana University.
>
> He has been involved in numerous civic and professional organizations and currently serves on the Board of Directors of the National Association of Convenience Stores.

If the editor decides to omit ("kill") part of the release because of space limitations, the last paragraph would be deleted first; the second-last paragraph, next; and so on. Thus, the most important information would remain.

FOR RELEASE:

February 10, 19--

Acme, Inc.
4311 Industrial Park
Springfield, IL 62703
Contact: John Smith
183-3209 (office)
189-8311 (home)

The United Workers of America will seek a guaranteed annual wage for its 240,000 members across the nation when contract negotiations begin in Detroit on Monday (February 14), according to a union spokesman. ← **Primary facts**

Union negotiators met last weekend to draft into contract language their latest demands, which labor sources say will center upon job protection and income security. The experimental contract now in force is due to expire on July 31 and labor leaders have indicated that a nationwide walk-out will be called unless their demands are met by that date. ← **Secondary information**

Unresolved national issues will be submitted to arbitration by April 20, but workers still have the right to strike over local plant issues.

-30-

Figure 16–1
News Release Announcing Negotiations Between Management and Union Leaders

FOR IMMEDIATE RELEASE:

Sportsleague Athletic Association
2200 Connecticut Avenue, N.W.
Washington, DC 20018
Contact: Sarah Jones
515-5480 (office)
711-3084 (home)

Jim Shane, Steve Newman, and Claude Gallot have been voted professional rookies of the year by the Sportsleague Athletic Association, according to an announcement today (January 29) by Andrew Baxter, President. ← **Primary information**

The rookies will be honored at a dinner on March 12, co-sponsored by Sportsleague and National Machinists. All except Newman will be present to receive their awards. ← **Secondary information**

XXX

Figure 16–2
News Release Announcing Special Recognition

Formatting

News releases may be written on letterhead or standard-size plain paper. You should, whenever possible, limit the release to a single page, even if you must use legal-size paper. Follow the typing and copy rules established by the media.

If the release is longer than a page, type the word *more* at the bottom of each page (except the last one). To indicate the end, type three X's (XXX) or -30- (which means "the end") centered on the page several blank lines after the last line of the story. Fasten the pages together with a paper clip or staple to ensure that the pages do not become separated in the newsroom.

Type all news releases with double spacing and five-space paragraph indentions. To allow ample room for copy editing, use side margins of at least 1 in. Leave a 1-in. blank area after the heading and before the first line of the story to allow space for the editor to write the headline above the copy.

The heading for a news release should consist of the release date and company information. The data at the left margin may be typewritten as follows:

FOR RELEASE
February 10, 19--

If possible, do not declare a specific release date, thus freeing the medium to use the news release at the most convenient time. In such cases, the date information would be:

FOR IMMEDIATE RELEASE

You may type the company information as follows:

The General Mfg. Co.
2121 East Main Street
Bismarck, ND 58501
Contact: J. C. Martin 213-9983 (Office)
151-2182 (Home)

It is a good idea to include the home telephone number of a person who can be contacted for additional information, if the editor wishes to contact the individual after business hours.

Preparing and Forwarding

Before distributing any news release, check for the following points:

1. *Make certain that your story contains timely and genuine news* that is important and interesting to the anticipated audience. The story that is a day or week late is not news—it is history. Unless your release meets these basic standards, your chances of getting the message publicized are slim and your efforts may be in vain.
2. *Keep stories* local *in nature to the greatest extent possible.* Names make the news, as do places and events, especially if they are within the circulation or the broadcast area of the mass medium.

3. *Double check every detail for accuracy* (the cardinal rule in any news room). Pay special attention to spelling, names, addresses, figures, and factual data. Once an editor detects even a small error, the entire story becomes suspect. If time is insufficient to check all of the story thoroughly, the editor may delete it altogether, rather than risk carrying an inaccurate story.
4. *Use precise dates and avoid confusion*; rather than saying, *today*, *tomorrow*, or *yesterday*, refer to the day and the month. For example: "The meeting will be held in the school auditorium on March 1."
5. *Identify photographs properly* so that they may be acceptable. A brief description of the event and the names of persons in the picture, from left to right, should be typed on a plain piece of paper and taped to the back of the photograph, at the bottom. Photographs add greatly to any news story—if properly identified.
6. *Use simple, understandable language for news releases to newspapers*. If more precise scientific and technical terms are used, then perhaps your story should be released to a specialized magazine or journal that caters to a more sophisticated, technical, or professional audience.

Type *NEWS RELEASE ENCLOSED* in the lower left-hand corner of the envelope containing your news release to ensure that your release is not misdirected in the mail after it has reached the newspaper office or broadcasting station. Releases to newspapers should be addressed to the editor of the department, using the editor's name whenever possible. Releases to radio and television stations should be directed to the news director, with the proper name.

Mr. John Doe, Sports Editor
The Hartford Daily Bugle

Ms. Jane Doe, News Director
Station WXYZ

INTERNATIONAL CORRESPONDENCE

International mail includes letters, aerogrammes, postal cards, and small packages sent either by parcel post or by air parcel post. **Aerogramme** stationery folds into an envelope and travels by air. It is convenient and less expensive than most other international mail, but no enclosures are permitted. Army Post Office (APO) and Fleet Post Office (FPO) mail are not considered international mail.

When writing letters to individuals or businesses in foreign countries, use the standard letter styles and procedures as explained in Chapters 5 and 6. In naming measurements, however, include metric designations, which are used worldwide.

The letters you receive from a foreign correspondent may not look or read like the standard letter you might write in this country. Appearance may not be a priority of the foreign letterwriter. Because of the relatively high cost for producing a letter and an emphasis on speed, foreign writers may mail letters that are not perfectly typewritten or perfectly balanced on the page. This does not mean that the correspondent wishes to create a poor impression, show negligence, or offend the reader. The accepted practice is to send the letter as is, rather than retype and increase costs. In addition, the letter may be on lightweight onion skin paper, or it may be a photocopy or a carbon copy.

Style

International letters often appear in modified block style (rarely are they full-block) and with mixed or closed punctuation (a mark after each line in inside address, salutation, complimentary close, and typed name of writer). See Figure 16–3.

Date

The dateline is usually in military style.

6th August, 1987 or 6.8.1987
8 de septimbre de 1987
Marzo 25 de 1987

Inside Address

Write the company name and address exactly as given you. The following address might be the inside address for a letter addressed to a company in Italy:

Spett. Ditta Nuccio & Figli S.p.A
Via Italiano 31
16103--GENOVA

Many Latin American letterheads state both a street address and a postal address. Use the postal address.

Apartado Postal 81 or Caiza Postal

A letter number may precede the inside address. (See Figure 16–3.) Addresses may include both the name of the province (or territory) and the country. For example:

ON
Canada K6J2L5
ON refers to Ontario

Letter No. 1505/81 5.7.19--

Mr. Allen M. Warren,
2020 Phillips Road,
Macon, GA 31202,
USA

Dear Sir,

Thank you very much for your letter dated 25th June, 19--. We are pleased to quote you the prices for the items desired by you:

1. G.E.C. 7.6 cu. ft.	95.00
2. Bosch 8.4 cu. ft.	125.00
3. Pye 7.5 cu. ft.	82.00

Delivery will be effected approximately in 10 to 12 weeks from date of order. For the order we require the following information:

1. Full name as in passport
2. Address in Pakistan
3. Amount of the goods, of course

Assuring you of our best services at all times.

Yours faithfully,
for Giftal Business, Ltd.,

C. H. Lopez

Figure 16-3
Foreign Letter Answering Request for Prices and Delivery Information

Body

The international letter is straightforward, brief, and courteous—often mixing formal with informal writing. It may contain traditional phrases, alternate spellings, accent marks, punctuation before and after a question or exclamation, and punctuation marks in long sentences.

British English—slightly different from American English—is taught and used abroad. British English uses some different words and phrases, as shown in the following table:

British English	American English
book a room	make a reservation
booking office	ticket office
lift	elevator
shop	store
Limited (Ltd.)	Incorporated (Inc.)

British English	**American English**
labour	labor
cheque	check
inclosed	enclosed

Ideas are often expressed differently. For example, *We inclose a cheque for the amount due you.* In American English, the statement would be: *Enclosed is a check for the amount we owe you.* The American writer might also write: *Enclosed is our $255.75 check for March purchases.*

> **British English:** We should be obliged if you would send us your latest catalogue and price-list together with new samples and patterns to enable us to show customers the latest fabrics.
> **American English:** Please send us a copy of your current catalog and price list. Also send us the new samples so that we can show our customers the latest fabric selection.

> **British English:** Further to our telephone conversation of today's date, we have pleasure in inclosing herewith our latest catalogue of bicycles, all of which can be supplied from stock immediately.
> **American English:** As requested in today's telephone conversation, enclosed is a copy of our current catalog of bicycles in stock. We can ship orders immediately.

> **British English:** We received your request for motor accessories, and hereby confirm that these have been sent 15th of March by separate post, together with publicity materials and price-lists.
> **American English:** On March 15, we mailed you the motor accessories you ordered, publicity information, and current price lists.

Telephone Numbers

Telephone numbers may be written in various ways, depending on the district:

781042	27.932	66.03.38
640.580	27.93	689.0.658

The letters in Figures 16-3 through 16-5 reveal the writer's style of writing and desire to be helpful and courteous to the reader. Instead of *TO WHOM IT MAY CONCERN*, Figure 16-5 might have been addressed to *Dear Prospective Employer.*

POSTAL AND POST CARDS

A **postal card** is sometimes appropriate for sending brief and informal messages (for example, to relay information about meetings, to make and confirm hotel-motel reservations, to notify the recipient of forthcoming sales, to record purchases for warranties, and to supply other routine information).

Re.: Letter 30 March 19--

Gentlemen:

We acknowledge with thanks receipt of your letter of 30 March, requesting our latest catalogue and a sample of our new soap. Enclosed, please find the catalogue. The soap follows under separate cover.

We hope to serve you, and look forward to the pleasure of receiving your order.

Yours very truly,

Figure 16–4
Foreign Letter Acknowledging Letter

TO WHOM IT MAY CONCERN:

Miss Maria Menoca has been employed by this company for three years, during which time her services as a secretary have been very satisfactory. She is efficient, punctual, and in every way a model employee. It is with regret that we accept her resignation. We recommend her unhesitatingly.

Sincerely yours,

Figure 16–5
Foreign Letter to an Anonymous Person Recommending an Employee

Because of limited space, the inside address is omitted from postal cards. Otherwise, the postal card message has all the standard parts included in a letter. In fact, it looks like a miniature personal-business letter. Figure 16–6 illustrates a postal card message regarding a business conference. Postal cards measure 5½ in. × 3½ in., can be purchased at U.S. postal stations, and require no additional postage.

Double postal cards, also purchased at postal stations, are really two standard-size postal cards that can be, and are meant to be, separated easily. One card is used for the message; the other for the return reply. Usually, the sender prepares the return card so that the receiver can simply check answers or write brief statements on the return card, detach and mail it. The receiver keeps the message card for reference.

Post cards are similar to postal cards but are generally used for nonbusiness communication. A picture, scene, or other display is on one side of the form, thus limiting the space for writing

29 Johnson Circle
Miami, FL 33134
August 1, 19--

Dear Mr. Simon:

Deductive (direct) approach →

The conference will begin on Monday, August 15, at 9 a.m. We are expecting representatives from every branch office.

As you requested, we have reserved a room for you at the Holiday Hotel. Please telephone us if there is more we can do to make your visit comfortable.

Sincerely,

Figure 16-6
Postal Card Message

a message. Post cards are printed by private firms and the purchase price does not include postage. A stamp must be purchased at a postal station and placed appropriately before mailing. The limited writing space and cost for the card and postage contribute to making post cards impractical for business communication.

OTHER CARDS

Cards and papers of various sizes and colors are used by business firms to replace costly letterheads, especially for communications related to advertising or public relations.

Retail establishments often mail promotional messages on cards of various sizes and colors. Figure 16-7 illustrates a card message to preferred customers. Since the card informs about an after-Christmas sale, a green or red background would be appropriate. The card might measure 4 in. x 5 in. Such a card would reflect the season and would stand out in the mail.

A business person who routinely mails specific information, catalogs, brochures, or descriptive literature might do so with a card message, instead of a letter. Figure 16-8 illustrates a card forwarding a copy of an article requested. See Chapters 8 and 9 for other possible communications with cards.

PREPRINTED AND SPECIALLY DESIGNED FORMS

Types of communication forms used in normal business operations are too numerous to illustrate in this book. Most are designed to expedite routine functions and ensure the transfer of complete information. Federal, state, and local government offices also require businesses to furnish some forms with numerous reports.

MALLOY'S
"First in Fashion"

Announces a Preferred Customer Sale for December 26-31. We want you to have first choice of our tremendous year-end savings. ← **Purpose**

Sale hours will be:

Sunday, December 6	–Noon to 5:00 p.m.
Monday-Thursday December 27-30	–10:00 a.m. to 9 p.m.
Friday, December 31	–10:00 a.m. to 5:00 p.m.

← **Details**

Come and see the usual "unusual" values in men's suits, sport coats, slacks, and other outerwear.

We look forward to seeing you at our special sale for preferred customers and we wish you and yours the VERY BEST HOLIDAY SEASON. ← **Goodwill action**

Figure 16–7
Card Message to Announce Preferred Customer Sale (4 in. × 5 in.)

Here is a copy of the article, "Using Credit Wisely." It should answer most of your questions on how to make credit work for you.

We are glad to furnish you with this helpful information. ← **Purpose**

Delores Cooper

Mrs. Delores Cooper
Public Relations Services

Attachment

Figure 16–8
Card Message Enclosing Information

Some forms are universally used and so can be purchased ready-made; other forms must be specially designed and printed to fit the specific needs of a particular business.

Business forms are used individually or in sets. The note-o-gram, for example, comes in a carbonized set. Copies of a form may be prepared in different colors for distribution and use by individuals in several departments or areas. For a form to be practical, it must be easy to use.

Forms frequently used for daily routine messages are note-o-grams, interorganizational memoranda (Chapter 15), routing slips, and while-you-were-out message forms.

FIRST INSURANCE COMPANY, INC.
1701 NORTH DRIVE ARLINGTON, VA 22209
Telephone: (703) 527-0000

MESSAGE	REPLY
TO Ms. Mary Martin 101 Northwest Towers Temple, TX 76503	DATE July 1, 19__
DATE June 21, 19__	I am enclosing the form with the requested information.
Dear Ms. Martin	
Purpose → Please complete and return the enclosed request	
Facts → for change in beneficiary form. An addressed and stamped envelope is enclosed for this purpose.	
Goodwill action → If we can help further, please let us know.	
BY *Pam Snider*	SIGNED *Mary Martin*
INSTRUCTIONS TO SENDER 1. KEEP YELLOW COPY 2. SEND WHITE AND PINK COPIES INTACT	INSTRUCTIONS TO RECEIVER 1. WRITE REPLY 2. DETACH STUB, KEEP PINK COPY, RETURN WHITE COPY TO SENDER.

Figure 16-9
Note-o-gram messages

Date *5/15/—*

✓ Please pass along in turn as numbered.
____Please take care of this item.
____Please give your reaction.
____Please prepare reply for my signature.
____Please discuss this with ________
____Please read and return.
____Please keep this for your file.

① Allenby	③ Nottingham	____Thompson
____Barger	____O'Neil	____Udalle
____Dover	____Pasco	____Unger
____Draper	④ Patrick	⑤ Yeager
② Le Boi	____Pringle	____
____Martin	____Smith	____

Comments *I would like your comments by 5/31.*

From *C. E. Jackson*

Figure 16-10
Routing Slip

MESSAGE

For Jack Miller Date 8/9/—

Caller's Name Joan Hays Time 3 p.m.

Company Ellison

Telephone No. 212-5834

✓ Telephoned ✓ Please telephone ___ Wants to see you

___ Came in to see you ___ Will call or come again

Other Message Needs more info.

Receiver A. Sampson

Figure 16–11
Message Form

Note-o-Gram

The **note-o-gram** can be very useful for writing simple, routine messages and their respective replies. It is an 8½ in. × 7 in. form purchased in carbonized sets of three pages, each sheet a different color. The form instructs the sender to keep the yellow (second) copy and mail the white (top) and pink (third) copy intact. After writing the reply, the receiver detaches and keeps the pink copy and returns the white one to the sender. Thus, both sender and receiver have a copy indicating the message and its reply. In Figure 16–9 a specific space is designated for the addressee's name and address. This allows for use of a window envelope, which also saves time and money.

Routing Slip

The **routing slip** forwards data to one or more co-workers, negating the need for a more involved memorandum. Basically the user of a routing slip need only check names of intended receivers and the action desired. Very little writing is needed. Figure 16–10 illustrates an abbreviated routing slip.

Message Form

The **message form** in Figure 16–11 can be used by a person who takes a message for someone else while the individual is away. The form can be used to record messages from telephone callers and from visitors. It is easy to use because the message-taker can quickly record the basic information while talking with the caller.

CHAPTER SUMMARY

Business communications serve many varied purposes. Letter formats are not always necessary or appropriate to the purpose or source of correspondence. Alternative methods are available and can be used effectively for speed, economy, and efficiency. Routine office information or special announcements, for example, may be passed to the reader in formats that are identifiable, acceptable, economical, and convenient.

Postal cards, note-o-grams, routing slips, and while-you-were-away message forms are used instead of formal letters to serve successfully a large volume of routine communication. News releases are expected to be presented in a straightforward journalistic style (they can be on letterhead). They should be newsworthy, timely, and in a format ready for publication.

Letters from foreign correspondents should be accepted on their own merit and not compared to American standards for spelling, format, phrasing, or appearance. These letters may exhibit different priorities and styles. Many are written in modified block style with mixed or closed punctuation. Because speed and economy are important, a letter may be typed on lightweight paper and may be mailed even if it is not perfectly typed or balanced on the page. However, when you write letters to individuals or businesses in foreign countries, use the American standard formats (Chapters 5 and 6). Remember to provide metric measurements when measurements are needed.

STUDY QUESTIONS

1. What is the purpose for using each of the following communication forms:
   a. News releases
   b. Postal cards
   c. Odd-size cards
   d. Note-o-grams
   e. Routing slips
   f. Message forms
2. With respect to news releases, what are the basic principles for:
   a. Order of presentation
   b. Heading information
   c. Dates
   d. Format
   e. Language used
   f. Timeliness
   g. Accuracy

3. "Accuracy is a cardinal rule in the news room." Why is this principle important? What might be the consequences of inaccuracies in reporting?
4. What differences might you find between American letters and foreign letters with respect to:
   a. Letter appearance
   b. Letter style
   c. Language
   d. Dates
   e. Telephone numbers
5. Does the postal card contain all letter parts? Explain.
6. Why might a company use a card instead of letterhead to communicate?
7. Why is the note-o-gram produced in a carbonized set?
8. How can business forms such as the note-o-gram, routing slip, and message form help business operate efficiently?

ACTIVITIES

1. As a representative for the U.S. Postal Service, issue a news release on Wednesday, October 6 indicating:

   Monday, October 11, will be the official date for observing Columbus Day and the holiday mail schedule will be in effect. The holiday schedule is:

   No regular residential or business area mail delivery during the day. No window service or special delivery service available. Lock box and caller firm mail will be available. Lock box service will be available on Sunday schedule. Mail will be collected from U.S. mail boxes designated with either one or two white stars as late in the day as possible to meet established first-class mail service standards.

   Normal weekend mail service will be provided on Saturday and Sunday.

2. As Campaign Chairperson for the Youth Operating Fund Campaign, issue a news release indicating that the campaign will begin with a meeting of local business, civic, and industrial leaders on Friday at a large, local motel. The goal is $58,500. Over 175 people are expected to attend.

   All solicitors will be urged to spread the message of youth's achievements—effectively developing in young people an understanding of the economic system by allowing them to operate their own small-scale businesses. Funds raised this year will be used for the operation and development of the Youth program in the eastern part of the state. The local program currently boasts that 376 teenagers have organized and are operating 16 companies.

3. Write a news release supplying the necessary details and color and indicating that according to Linda Pearson, Director of Personnel, Melinda Dickerson was appointed General Manager of Operations, including retail operations. Dickerson has worked for the company for 20 years and has held these positions: Marketing Manager (most recent); Coordinator of Marketing Functions, including the buying, merchandising, advertising and developing of new product categories. She was graduated from a local high school and attended two local colleges.
4. One of your customers has indicated that he paid the amount due for your Invoice No. 1010. You cannot find any record of payment. Using a note-o-gram, write the customer asking for the date and amount of his check and the name of the bank the check was drawn on. Your customer is Mr. Alex Perrodine, 21254 Cedar Avenue, Apartment 23, Cleveland, Ohio 44120.
5. As Alex Perrodine, reply to Activity 4 on the reply side of the note-o-gram.
6. Write a suitable postal card message informing the recipient of the details about a future club meeting.
7. Write a postal card message to your customer thanking him for taking advantage of the Bargain Day sale. Tell him that you are temporarily out of the garden tools ordered, but that shipment should be made by the end of the month. For information, the customer can telephone 212-7590, customer service.
8. Write a postal card message announcing a store-wide clearance sale of men's winter or summer clothing: suits, sport coats, slacks, and outerwear. You want to make room for spring or fall merchandise. Urge the customer to come early for a wider selection.
9. Write a postal card message to your congressional representative urging either a vote for or against a particular issue. Indicate the bill number and express reasons for your belief.
10. What is the English term for each of the following British expressions? (A dictionary may be helpful.)
    a. Ground floor
    b. Head office
    c. Tram
    d. Sweets
    e. Situations vacant
    f. Post

g. Petrol
h. Letter of complaint
i. To let
j. Shop assistant

11. What is the American spelling for each of the following British English terms?
    a. Centre
    b. Litre
    c. Instalment
    d. Woollen
    e. Jewellery
    f. Labour
    g. Programme
    h. Licence

EDITING

1. Rewrite the following news release:

    The directors serve for two years. Offices are held for one year. The Downtown Business Council has moved to an office at 213 West Charles Street. The office is open from 9 to 4 p.m. weekdays. Elected today were new directors and officers for the Downtown Business Council, according to William Hartley, again serving as president. Jane Murray is vice president for administration, and Robert Henderson is vice president for retail. Other officers were Arthur Hughes, secretary; Don Myers, treasurer. Other directors were Gary Holt, Katharine Reid, Ann Johnson, and Gene Sylvester.

2. Rewrite the following statements to reflect modern American English:
    a. In the letter from Messr. Jones which was sent to you yesterday, mention was made of the inclosure of two of our pamphlets on public relations.
    b. We hope you will visit our spacious new offices in the near future.
    c. We wish to call the attention of our valued customers and friends to our new location as of September 1.
    d. The classified lists you request have not yet been published, but you may be sure that they will be sent to you as soon as they come off the press.
    e. Would you be so kind as to acknowledge receipt of these important papers once they are in your hands?
    f. Please accept our congratulations on the celebration of your firm's twenty-fifth anniversary.
    g. Should you need further information or assistance, please let us know.
    h. The inclosed cheque covers your invoice of 1 novembre.

i. You will note that we have deducted the amount of US$584, in accordance with your credit memo of 15 August.
j. Reference is made to your letter of 8 March, requesting information regarding the company mentioned therein.

IN-BASKET SIMULATIONS

1. Write a news release. According to Mr. Peter Waltere, Vice-President and General Manager of Waltere Supermarkets, Inc., Duncan Builders Company will begin construction next week of the Waltere Drugs adjacent to an existing Waltere Supermarket at the popular intersection of Market and Main Streets. The present supermarket is being remodeled. The addition will be completed by March. It will be 15,000 square feet, making the total area for the supermarket and drug store 36,000 square feet. The parking area should accommodate 320 parked cars.

   The drug store will feature a complete, full-service pharmacy with a registered pharmacist on duty at all hours, a camera department with a film-processing section, a jewelry-cosmetic area, and greeting cards' section. Of course, customers can also purchase candies, tobacco items, housewares, and so on.

   The supermarket-drug store combination unit should be a pleasing facility for Waltere's customers. Waltere Supermarkets, Inc., has 50 large retail units and 120 convenience stores in 38 communities in Indiana; two warehouses serve the stores. This is the first drug store.
2. Write a news release (immediate release). According to Peter Waltere, Vice-President and General Manager of Waltere Supermarkets, Inc., Richard R. Mayes was appointed to the position of Real Estate Director for the Supermarket Division. His responsibilities include site selection and lease negotiations for both new and remodeled supermarkets. Other facts: Parker Central High School graduate; Bachelor in Business Administration from Indiana University ten years ago; real estate broker's license; 18 years employee; previous jobs were Assistant Store Manager, Property Manager, Director of Real Estate for the convenience Foods Division, Assistant Real Estate Director. Waltere Supermarkets, Inc., has 50 large retail units and 120 convenience stores in 38 communities in Indiana; two warehouses serve the stores.

3. Rewrite this short foreign order letter:

   Please accept our thanks for the sample assortment which you sent in prompt response to our recent request.

   We inclose an order for freight shipment at the C.I.F. prices quoted by you.

   Payment of your invoice will be sent you upon its receipt.

   Note: *C.I.F. is the abbreviation for cost insurance and freight.*

4. Write a postal card message to be mailed to all buyers for Waltere Supermarkets, Inc. The card announces the opening of Waltere Drugs and welcomes the employees and their spouses to a special closed-door sale on Sunday which is two weeks from today. Many items will be specially priced for the occasion. There will be surprises and door prizes.
5. Waltere Supermarkets, Inc., uses a speed letter instead of the usual interorganizational memorandum or note-o-gram. This form is similar to the memorandum with a reply section (see In-Basket Simulation 7 in Chapter 13).

   As Joe Manning from Store No. 38, send a speed letter dated December 23, to Jeffrey Mills, Buyer. The subject is: Billing to B & L Corporation. Advise Mr. Mills that he can bill B & L Corporation for the 220 hams purchased for the holiday season. The total weight for the semi-boneless hams was 3200 lb at a cost of $1.40/lb making a total price of $4,480.
6. As Jeffrey Mills, reply to the speed letter in In-Basket Simulation 5 advising that you have billed the customer. Attach a copy of the billing.
7. As Arthur Park, Meat Manager for Store No. 15, write a speed letter to Marie Gillespie, Meat Buyer. Explain that you received four boxes from the Chicago Meat Packing Co. all labeled boneless rounds. Two boxes contained semi-boneless rounds—total weight 127 lb. An adjustment should be made because the semi's cost $.20/lb less than boneless.
8. As Marie Gillespie reply to Arthur Park's speed letter (In-Basket Simulation 7). Ask Chicago Meat for a $25.40 credit and forward them a copy of Art's speed letter.

Applications of Writing Ideas—Reports

PART 4

17 Overview of the Report-Writing Process

After studying Chapter 17, you should be able to:

- Differentiate between an internal and an external report
- Analyze both the subject and the audience before preparing your report
- Determine whether a report is objective
- Gather, organize, and analyze data for a report
- Select the direct or indirect approach to presenting your data

The principles of effective writing are as essential to reports as they are to other written communications. A **report** is a planned presentation of data written to accomplish a particular purpose. A good report requires skillful planning, organizing, writing, and revising because its purpose is to present essential information clearly and concisely in a format that is logically sequenced and easy to read. Reports are prepared in similar ways, whether they are long or short. Once you understand the basic principles of writing a report, you can apply them to both long and short reports.

A report should convey information objectively, accurately, and reliably. Reports may be **informational** (written to inform the reader), **analytical** (written to analyze a situation), or **persuasive** (written to persuade the reader). In every one of these instances, a report is written to aid in decision making. Primarily, a report relates the facts about a situation or event that the intended reader may not be able to observe personally.

Reports may range from simple to complex. A sheet of paper bearing figures or words that is given to someone to provide information might be considered a report—such as a daily enrollment count handed by a teacher to an administrator. A report may be presented orally as well as in written form. If the teacher says to the administrator, "Susan Williams and Michael Goodson are absent today," the teacher is giving an oral report in its simplest form.

Business situations, however, often call for more detailed and complex information. This information must be adapted to a suitable format that is quickly and easily comprehended by all parties reading the report.

INTERNAL AND EXTERNAL REPORTS

The larger the organization, the more it depends upon reports to accomplish tasks. Reports that stay within an organization are called **internal reports**. Most of the reports that you will write in an entry-level position stay within the organization. Internal reports can travel upward, laterally, or downward to people on the company's organizational chart. Most reports, however, travel **upward**. Within the organization, reports pass from a person or committee up to a policymaker who uses the information to make decisions. Most managers cannot directly participate in everything that occurs, even in their own administrative areas. They do not have enough time to observe all activities personally, and they may not have the technical expertise to make personal assessments in all areas. The internal report advises the manager and allows the manager to act, based on the technical opinions and observations of other people.

Reports may also travel **laterally** or go to peers or to other employees in the organization. These internal reports help to coordinate the activities of the organization; they inform employees of activities and ideas outside their immediate areas. These reports contribute to good morale; employees have a better image of themselves and their organization when they are being informed of company activities.

Internal reports may travel from the policymaker **down** to subordinates to inform them of decisions to be implemented. They provide a permanent documented resource that the subordinate may refer to with confidence.

Reports that are sent outside an organization are called **external reports**. These reports may go to stockholders, customers, or the general public. They are particularly useful as public relations instruments—to inform or persuade. A company's annual report is an external report. It is used not only to inform stockholders of the status of the company but also to advertise or recruit for hiring new employees.

FORMAT

Choose the report format that will effectively present your ideas in the most attractive way. Some companies have their own requirements (Company Procedures Manuals) for report forms. But if you must provide a suitable format, base your selection on these factors:

Purpose of report
Your position within the organization
Policies of the organization

Complete instructions for formatting a report are found in Chapter 24.

AUDIENCE ANALYSIS

Reports usually go to both primary and secondary readers. The **primary reader** is the person who directly receives and reads the report; **secondary readers** might also read the report, at the suggestion of the primary reader, but they are not the audience to whom the report is addressed. When writing a report, though, you must use language that both primary and secondary readers will understand and will react to positively.

Know Your Audience

In some cases, it is not possible to know your audience personally. If possible, though, try to describe the audience in physical terms. How old are they? Are they predominantly males or females?

What is their educational background? What is their level of expertise? Will the report go inside or outside the organization? Is the reader your superior, subordinate, or peer? How much do they already know about the subject? How will they use the report or what information is needed from the report? How will they react to the information in the report—positively, negatively, or neutrally?

Choose Your Words

An accountant who is writing to other accountants might use the jargon of the accounting profession. However, when writing to people in other occupations, the accountant must select terms that will be easily understood. Technical language might slow down, or limit, the understanding of the reader. Occasionally, you may need to use technical words. If you have to use words that the reader may not know, define them in the introduction, the body, or glossary of the report so the reader does not have to look them up.

Define the Educational Level

When more than one person reads the report, the language should be suitable to the lowest educational level represented in the reading audience. If a report is directed to the supervisors of an organization in which the supervisors must have a high school education, the writing should be no higher than 12th grade level. But, in an organization in which a minimum educational level is not required, the language of the report should be appropriate for the supervisor with the lowest educational level. If you are in doubt about how low a level to use, write in simple, clear language, selecting words you are certain all readers will know. You can maintain dignity in simple language, without giving the impression that you are talking down to your reader.

Another alternative that might be used for a technical report that will be read by an audience with varying levels of expertise is to write more than one report, gearing the language to the particular groups that will read them. In this case, the language may be changed in the different reports. You might also consider sending only specific sections of the report to particular audiences. Every audience may not be interested in every part of the report. Some people, for example, may be interested in the conclusions only, whereas another group of people might be more interested in the methodology section. The report could then be tailored to the readers' interests and knowledge of the subject matter.

OBJECTIVE WRITING

Writing objectively means you will present the information accurately and in an unbiased manner. Writers sometimes have difficulty keeping personal opinions and biases out of their reports. This bias can even show itself by the sources you use to research a topic. If you use only sources that support your point of view, you are biasing the findings. Or, if you use sources that are not current, you might not present all the up-to-date facts about the problem and thus bias the findings of the report.

If you have already formed an opinion about the particular topic, take extra care to present the information objectively. Do not allow personal biases to influence your selection of facts or the way you present them.

Writing objectively does not necessarily mean that you will not use first and second person (*I, we, you*). Writing objectively does mean that you will present the information in the report in such a manner that the reader is not influenced by your personal opinions and biases. Because the primary purpose is to assist management in decision making, reports must be factual and objective. The two sentences below illustrate the difference between a biased sentence and an unbiased sentence:

Biased	**Unbiased**
It is my opinion that the four-day work week will not be good for our company.	A study of the advantages and disadvantages of the four-day work week supports the conclusion that we should not adopt this practice.

The formality of the language you choose will depend upon the purpose of the report, the audience, and the company policy. Most business people write in the informal personal tone, using *I*, *we*, and *you*. Some companies, however, require that all reports be written in as formal a style as possible—without the use of first or second person. Their opinion is that formality lends itself to objectivity. However, the choice of first, second, or third person does not create objectivity in a report. Just because you write in the third person does not mean you are writing objectively because you may not present the facts in an unbiased manner.

One disadvantage of using third person (*the writer*, *the author*, *the researcher* instead of *I* or *we*) is tone; the writing may be stiff, formal, stilted, and awkward. Using the third person often results in excessive use of the passive voice, which also contributes to a stilted tone. If you choose to write in third person, give special attention to editing your language to avoid excessive use of the passive voice and awkward, wordy sentences.

Objectivity comes more from how you choose and present the facts in the report rather than the use of third person. You must be careful to distinguish between statements of facts and your own value judgments. Include all relevant facts, not just those that support your own personal opinions.

Give the impression that you are presenting the facts as a bystander might, with no personal opinions on either side. Avoid emotional terms and excessive adjectives and adverbs. Too many adjectives and adverbs make your writing seem emotional rather than logical.

Objectivity also stems from describing your methods of gathering information. Explain the basis of your conclusions and recommendations; show that they are not affected by your own biases. Support all statements with facts. Avoid such statements as *In my opinion*, *I think*, and *I feel*. Instead, use such statements as *Analysis of the questionnaire shows* . . . or *The data show*. . . .

Being objective in your writing also means providing adequate documentation for your statements so the reader can follow up on any other needed research. Use sources that are accurate, reliable, objective, and up to date.

You can also achieve objectivity in the way you present recommendations. Recommendations are value judgments; base them on sufficient evidence. Examine all cause–effect statements for completeness before basing a recommendation on the statement. Ask yourself if the effect could have more than one cause.

You can write objectively in either a formal or informal style of writing. But you must present the information from an impartial point of view, avoiding preconceptions that can cause you to ignore some facts and overvalue others. Distinguish between **facts** (concrete, verifiable data), **inferences** (judgments arrived at through reasoning), and **opinions** (judgments made through informal procedures).

CONTENT

Every organized project, whether it is building a bridge, baking a cake, or writing a report, proceeds according to a logical plan. That plan should be obvious to the reader. Before presenting your data, consider the following two factors:

1. *The subject matter.* Are the data strictly informational or are they also persuasive? Will the reader react positively or negatively to the material? Are the data highly technical or is the reader fairly familiar with the topic?
2. *The audience.* Does the reader receive a large number of reports? Is the reader familiar with the background of the

problem and technical words found in the report? Does the reader usually want to know all the facts before making a decision?

In the chapters on letters, you learned that you can use organization or placement of data to emphasize certain points in the letter. The same principles apply to reports. The beginning and ending of the report receive the most attention. The reader will remember the last paragraph or sentence, but without a strong beginning, the reader may not get as far as the ending.

The purpose of a report determines its structure. You may present the most important information first (direct approach) or last (indirect approach), depending on how you expect the reader to react to the data.

Direct Approach

Also called the **deductive method**, the **direct approach** (most important information first) is most helpful when:

1. The reader is a busy person
2. The report is long
3. The reader prefers the direct approach

You may sequence the sections in either of the following two ways:

Ending Introduction Text	**OR**	Introduction Ending Text

Note that each plan presents the text last. The direct approach saves time for the reader by making it unnecessary to read through the text if the reader prefers not to. The essential information (summary, conclusions, and/or recommendations) appears at or near the beginning of the report.

Indirect Approach

Sometimes called the **inductive approach**, the **indirect approach** (most important information last) is helpful when the audience is not familiar with the subject. All facts precede the terminal section. The indirect approach is also helpful when the report is controversial. It allows the audience to read the entire report before reaching the terminal section. The discussion allows the writer to explain or support the conclusions or recommendations before the reader gets to them.

The indirect approach would present information as follows:

Introduction
Text
Ending

CHAPTER SUMMARY

Reports are an integral part of all organizations. The particular format you choose depends upon the purpose of your report, your position in the organization, and the policies of the organization.

Remember that the format itself is only a vehicle. The effectiveness of the message depends not only upon your ability to analyze the audience but also on your ability to communicate your ideas: to gather, organize, analyze, and present data. You must be able to write specifically, concisely, and correctly. You must write with a positive tone, as objectively as possible.

The text of the report must follow a clear and logical plan that is obvious to the reader. Consider the subject of the report and the audience to determine whether you should use a direct or indirect approach.

STUDY QUESTIONS

1. Write a definition of a report.
2. Name two reasons why reports are written.
3. What is the difference between an internal and an external report?
4. What factors determine the format to use in presenting information in a report?
5. What is the difference between primary and secondary readers of a report?
6. What factors determine the objectivity of a report?
7. What factors determine how a report is organized?
8. Name the points within a report where emphasis can best be achieved. Which place in a report is most effective for emphasis?
9. Name two examples of times when the direct approach would be appropriate for organizing a report.
10. What is the outline for the indirect approach for presenting data?

ACTIVITIES

1. Describe your audience if you are writing a report to be sent to your classmates.
2. Attend a public meeting (school, church, community) and write a short informational report summarizing the meeting.
3. Read the sports page of your local newspaper. Write a short report summarizing one article of major interest in the paper. Identify the audience to whom the article is written. Submit your summary to a classmate for editing; then revise the report.

4. Rewrite the following statements, using first or second person:
   a. Further research is recommended to determine the relationship between writing ability and attitude.
   b. The researcher conducted the study at State University during the spring.
   c. The total sample from whom data were collected and analyzed was 217.
   d. It was necessary to collect data from the academic records of all students.
   e. The writer found no significant difference in three of the five hypotheses.
5. Ask five of your classmates about their opinions about your school library. Write a report to your instructor giving the findings of your study.
6. Determine whether to use the direct or indirect approach for these report situations:
   a. Report asking your supervisor to increase travel funds for your department
   b. Results of a survey
   c. 100-page informational report
   d. Analytical report sent to someone who receives a large number of reports
   e. Report giving disappointing information

LANGUAGE SKILLS DEVELOPMENT

1. Rewrite the following sentences to avoid sexist language:
   a. The flight requires three flightcrew members, each intent on the details of his own job.
   b. In most cases, an aircraft owner's insurance protects him, not you.
   c. Even though a secretary can be excused from work to attend the seminar, she must pay the registration fee.
   d. The stewardess who works on this flight must stand for five hours.
   e. After interviewing seven candidates, the Personnel Department recommended three of them: Joe Aaron, Fred Miller, and Miss Sandra Collins.
   f. The appliance store offers an extensive training program for its salesmen.
   g. Can you recommend a doctor? He must be someone I can rely on.
   h. A construction worker must wear his hat at all times.

2. Divide the following words in the preferred place:
   a. delegated
   b. dependable
   c. cabbage
   d. forth
   e. juror
   f. $1,000
   g. business
   h. self-sufficient
   i. shredded
   j. venting

IN-BASKET SIMULATIONS

1. Using the direct approach, write a persuasive report (with recommendations) to Mr. Raymond Waltere, President, to convince him to keep a few of the supermarkets open 24 hours a day on a trial basis. List the advantages and disadvantages of this plan.
2. Using the indirect approach, write a report from Mr. Dale A. Krause, President of Convenience Foods, to Mr. Raymond Waltere, President, informing him of the status of shoplifting in the 110 marts. In addition to giving updated information, comment on what some of the Mini Marts are doing to lower the shoplifting rate. Mr. Waltere does not expect recommendations for this report.

18 Contents of the Report

After studying Chapter 18, you should be able to:

- Determine when each part of an introduction should be used
- Determine which organizational plan to use
- Set up the correct headings for a report
- Decide when to use a summary, conclusions, or recommendations in a report

What are the parts of a report and how should they be arranged? Once you can answer these questions, you have mastered a fundamental skill in writing effectively—identifying the necessary ingredients and organizing them in a logical plan that can be easily comprehended. Even the most complex material can be worked into a simple format.

To fully examine a problem, even the simplest of written reports should have an introduction, a discussion, and an ending (not necessarily in that order in the report). These parts are essential to stating the purpose, conveying the facts, and leaving the points firmly in the reader's mind. As the report grows in complexity, these three sections can incorporate many features to accomplish the purpose of the report.

INTRODUCTION

The **introduction** leads the reader into the body of the report. It is a telescopic look at the entire report; it sets the stage and tells the reader what you have done, why you did it, and what you plan to do in the remainder of the report. It can be as short as one paragraph or as long as several pages and presented in a separate chapter. For a short memorandum report, the introduction would probably be only a few sentences; however, the longer report might require several paragraphs or several pages to prepare the reader adequately for the text of the report.

The information to be included in an introduction can be subdivided into several sections: authorization statement, statement of the problem, purpose, background, scope, limitations, methodology, definitions, and presentation plan. Include as many parts as are needed to orient the reader to the problem; however, only one section is mandatory—the purpose of the report.

Authorization Statement

The **authorization statement** tells the reader who asked you to complete the report. If no one authorized you, omit this statement.

Use conversational language to present the authorization. If James Anderson asked you to do the report and Mr. Anderson is also the primary reader of the report, the statement might read, *As you requested, here is the* . . . or *Here is the report you asked me to complete on* . . . . If Ms. Harriet Diamond, the president of the organization, asked you to complete a report to be read by several people in the organization, the authorization statement might read, *Ms. Diamond asked me to* . . . or *As Ms. Diamond requested, this* . . . .

The authorization statement can lend credibility to your report. When someone with authority requested the report, the readers know the contents should be read carefully. This is especially important if the writer of the report is unknown.

If a report is authorized in a written format (letter or memo), you might include this letter as a prefatory part of the report so the reader knows exactly what is requested. This letter of authorization serves as a reminder for both the reader and the writer of the report. If a letter of authorization is included with a report, omit the authorization statement in the introduction.

Statement of the Problem

The **statement of the problem** identifies the global problem or question that will be dealt with in the report. You may already know the facts in a problem or you may need to do some preliminary research to learn about the problem. For example, you might be requested to find a solution to the paper problem (files) in your company. The problem in this case is records management or how to handle the files. If you are not already familiar with the latest records management systems, you might need to survey the literature or vendors to determine what equipment is available and what other companies are currently doing about their paper problems. This preliminary research helps you to understand the problem and gives guidance on how to proceed with your particular study. When writing this section of the report, write about the large problem, paper management, and what you know about it in your company.

Purpose

The **purpose** identifies why you are doing the research or writing this particular report and how the data will be used. The purpose is a small portion of the problem. You may not be able to solve the entire problem, but your purpose is to tackle a small part of it. The purpose is the only essential part of every introduction. State it early so the reader knows exactly why you did the report and what you plan to accomplish. The purpose may be stated as a statement, in the infinitive, or as a question; either way, use specific wording:

> The purpose of this report is to present the findings from the . . . .
>
> This report will present the findings and a recommendation from . . . .
>
> To determine the most profitable location in the Southeast for a branch . . . .
>
> What are the reasons for the high absentee rate for Group IV?

What are the trends of absenteeism in the company since January 1?

If the purpose is complex and you cannot accurately reflect it in one conclusive statement or question, subdivide it into as many parts as you need.

The purpose could be stated as objectives:

The objectives of this study are to determine:

1. Why Group IV has a higher absentee rate than Group II.
2. Why employees under 25 years of age have a higher absentee rate than those employees over 25 years of age.
3. Which incentives might work to decrease absenteeism in the company.

The purpose of a report might also be to report on the tests of certain **hypotheses** (tentative explanations of the problem). Hypotheses are used in research studies to test statistically two or more conditions under a controlled environment. These statements predict the outcome of a research study. The purpose of the research is to either support or not support the hypotheses. Evidence in a study never proves or disproves the hypotheses, but it supports or does not support the statements.

Hypotheses are stated only after you have thoroughly reviewed the literature and thought about the problem. Hypotheses should be stated as simply and concisely as possible. Stay away from vague words that cannot be defined. Be sure that each statement tests only one variable so your findings can support or not support each of the hypotheses separately.

Most of the time, hypotheses are stated in the negative or null form because the positive statement leaves the impression that the researcher has already decided the outcome of the results. Some examples of hypotheses stated in the null form are:

1. There is no significant difference between the computer science grades of those students who have personal computers at home and those students who do not have access to home computers.
2. No difference exists between the salary levels of accounting students who graduated from public universities and accounting students who graduated from private universities.

The hypotheses are tested by collecting data relevant to the statements and analyzing it to determine whether evidence exists to support or reject the hypotheses. In the terminal section of the report (summary or conclusions), make either supporting or rejecting statements about each of the hypotheses stated in the introduction.

Background

Include background information if the reader is not familiar with the problem situation. Background information sets the stage and brings readers up to date so they can grasp the overall picture of the problem. Perhaps the situation requires no more than a brief history of the problem; other situations might call for a detailed description of facts to summarize what has transpired up to the time of the report.

Scope

The scope refers to the boundaries you as a writer build around the topic. It narrows the topic so the reader knows what will be and will not be covered. By stating them early, you make clear to the reader exactly what you plan to cover and what you do not include in the report.

Try to reduce the problem to reasonable proportions; build a fence around the topic by omitting aspects you do not think are necessary or that you are not prepared to handle in depth. The result should be a topic that you can adequately handle in this particular study. One of the best ways to narrow the subject of a report is to present only the information that is needed to make a well-reasoned decision.

In a study on absenteeism for Groups II and IV, the scope restricts the study to only two work groups. Or, if you were studying records management procedures, you might narrow the topic to companies of a particular size (number of employees or amount of sales) located in a particular geographic area that manufacture or sell certain kinds of products. If you wanted to research pollution in a study, you might narrow the topic as shown in Figure 18-1.

Pollution is a topic much too broad to handle in one report. Reject areas you do not wish to discuss; narrow the subject down to manageable proportions until you have a topic you can adequately cover in the time available. Keep narrowing until you can state your purpose in one sentence. The topic should then be narrow enough to solve in one study: "The purpose of this report is to research the rules and regulations governing water pollution in Cleveland, Ohio, in 1985."

Limitations

The limitations are items over which you had no control but which prohibited your making investigations. Limitations usually refer to such things as too little time and money.

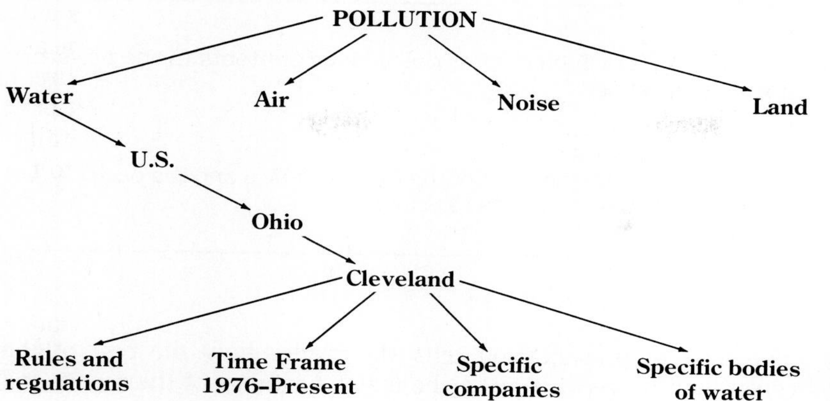

Figure 18-1
Narrowing Topics

Methodology

The methodology section of the introduction tells how you gathered the data. It describes the sources and the methods used to collect information. The methodology provides credibility to the study and permits anyone to repeat the study by following the procedures described in the methodology section of the report. More specific details on gathering information are provided in Chapter 19.

Definition of Terms

You may wish to define some words by explaining how you are using them in your particular study. Defining terms ensures against misunderstanding and loss of clarity in the report. The definitions might cover not only unfamiliar words but words that have a specific meaning for this report. The definition of terms is especially helpful if a term has several possible interpretations. The definitions may appear in several places in the report:

1. Use the introduction to define terms if only a few words need to be defined.
2. Use the text to define words that might be misunderstood in the context of the report. When defining words in the text, they may be defined at the point they are used in the sentence or they may be defined in a footnote reference called an explanatory footnote. Figure 18-2 illustrates an explanatory footnote.
3. Use the **glossary** (located at the end of the report in the appendix) when several words need to be defined. The glossary is useful for defining words that are used many times throughout the report.

Place the Table of Tables* after the Table of Contents in the prefatory section of a report.

*A Table of Tables is a list of the titles of tables and the page numbers on which the tables are found.

Figure 18-2
Explanatory Footnote

Plan of Presentation

The plan of presentation tells the reader how the rest of the report will proceed. It gives the major headings of the report and the order in which they are presented. This plan provides an **overview**, or an outline, to help the reader follow the organizational pattern of the remainder of the report.

TEXT

The **text** contains the bulk of the report body; it is the meat of the report. The text presents the data and, in analytical reports, an analysis of the data. The text, sometimes called the discussion or findings, constitutes the largest part of the report. The findings in a research report must be interpreted in light of the sample used. Any inconsistent findings must be discussed to try to account for the inconsistencies.

In a research report that uses library sources for most of the information, most of the paragraphs of the text are footnoted to document other people's ideas and thoughts.

All the principles for effective writing covered in earlier chapters should be applied when writing a report. It is especially important in report writing that you use topic sentences; transitional words, phrases, and sentences; and an orderly presentation of data. A well-written report will flow smoothly from one part to the next, keeping the interest of the reader.

Headings

The effectiveness of a report may be enhanced by the way you present the data—how attractive the report is, how the data are arranged, how easy it is to find information, and how easy it is to follow the content. **Headings** are used to make the report easier to read. Its organization and content become clearer.

Headings and subheadings are set off from the text to identify the content that follows. They help the reader locate information, and they make the report easier to read and understand. In addition, they organize the material and help the reader follow your arguments and keep track of important items.

LEVEL ONE HEADING

Center the first level of headings in all caps, on a line by itself. Triple space before and after the heading.

Level Two Heading

Begin the Level Two heading at the left margin, on a line by itself. Underscore, capitalizing only the principal words. A triple space precedes the heading and a double space follows the heading.

Level Three Heading. Indent the third level of heading as many spaces as you indent paragraphs. Capitalize principal words and underscore the heading. Place a period following the last word in this heading, but do not place the heading on a separate line. Follow immediately with the first sentence in the text. Do not use extra space above this heading.

Level four heading leads into the first sentence of the paragraph. Underline the beginning words of the sentence. Use the same spacing and capitalization for this heading as you used for all other sentences in the paragraph.

Figure 18-3
Headings

The various levels of headings in a report are called degrees. These degrees follow the levels found in an outline. You may use all the levels in a long report, but most short reports require only two or three levels of headings.

Figure 18-3 shows the correct spacing and location of headings in a report.

You may number the headings (I., II., III.A., III.B.) as you do in outlining, or the numbers may be omitted.

To develop headings, first develop a comprehensive outline of your topic; the outline becomes the major headings you use in a report; then the headings become the Table of Contents. Note how the outline in Figure 18-4 becomes the headings in Figure 18-5.

Headings are used according to the same basic rules that apply to outlining. Before listing a subheading, tell the reader what subheadings you are going to include in your discussion and include no less than two subheadings for any one level. Use parallel grammatical structure for headings of the same level. This means that if a second-degree heading is a complete sentence, then the next second-degree heading should also be a sentence. Or, if a heading of one level starts with an infinitive, then all the

I. Types of Office Environments
  A. Conventional Office
  B. Open Office
II. Office Lighting
  A. Fluorescent
  B. Task and Ambient
    1. Advantages of Task Lighting
    2. Disadvantages of Task Lighting
III. Summary

Figure 18-4
Outline of Report

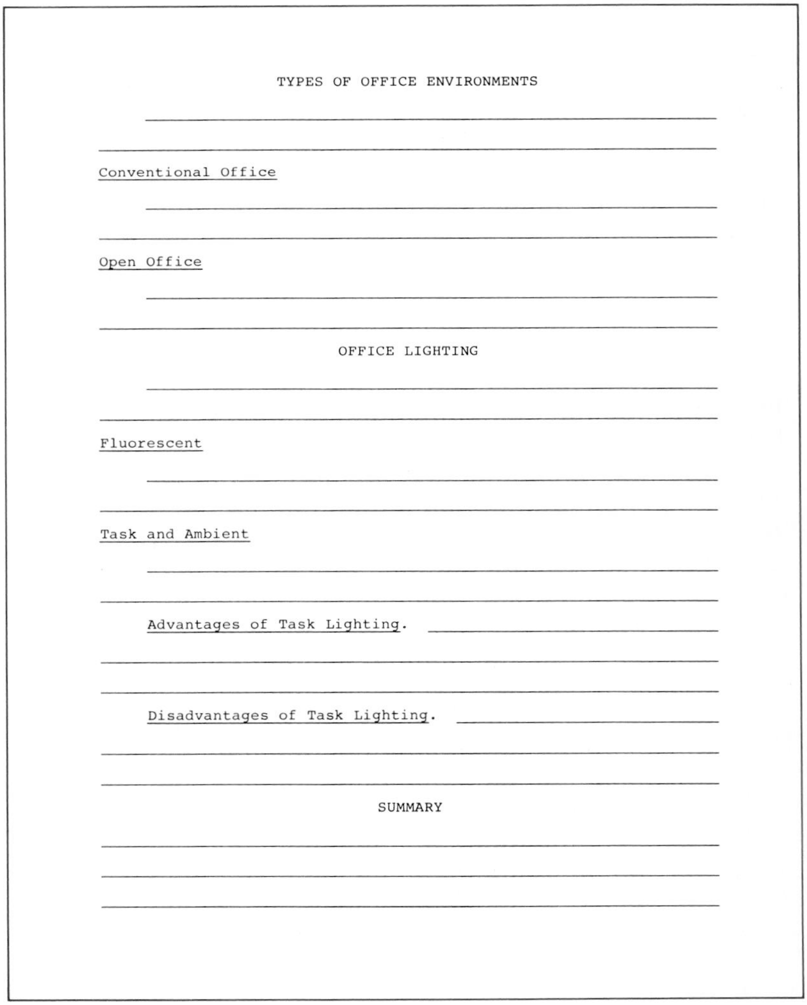

TYPES OF OFFICE ENVIRONMENTS

Conventional Office

Open Office

OFFICE LIGHTING

Fluorescent

Task and Ambient

Advantages of Task Lighting.

Disadvantages of Task Lighting.

SUMMARY

Figure 18-5
Outline Becomes the Headings in a Report

other subheadings in the same section should also start with infinitives. Suppose you have the following second-degree headings:

Choosing a Topic
Outlining the Information
Gathering the Data
Writing the Report

Notice that they all have parallel grammatical structure because the first word for each heading ends with "ing." These headings could be developed into complete sentences or they could start with the "you" understood, as shown in the following examples:

You should choose a topic that interests you.	**OR**	Choose a Topic
You need to outline the information.	**OR**	Outline the Information
You should spend a lot of time gathering the data.	**OR**	Gather the Data
You should write the report in one sitting.	**OR**	Write the Report

At least one paragraph should separate a major heading from its subheadings. You should not go from one heading to the next subheading without some writing (an introduction to the subheadings) between the heading and its subheadings. Headings are not a part of the text, so the information under the headings should be able to stand alone. The content should make sense if the headings were removed from the report. Under the heading, "War of 1812," the first sentence should not begin with "It" because the reader would not know what "It" refers to without looking at the heading; therefore, the first sentence after the heading will usually repeat the words found in the heading.

ENDING

The **ending** of a report presents the major results of the study. It depends upon the data collected, analyzed, and presented in the text portion of the report. You should not introduce new information in the terminal section.

Three kinds of information are appropriate for the terminal section: summary, conclusions, and/or recommendations. One, two, or all three parts may be used. Which of the three parts you use and how many of them you include depend on the purpose of the report and whether the person who authorized the report expects one, two, or all three sections.

Summary

The **summary** presents a condensed version of the important facts (concrete, verifiable data) and findings. It helps the reader to grasp quickly and easily the main points of the report. In fact, many people will read the summary first to get an overview of the report or to determine whether to read the entire report. Use the summary for informational reports or any report in which you are not presenting personal opinions or are not building a strong case for action.

Conclusions

Conclusions are objective statements that evaluate the reported findings of the report. From this analysis, conclusions are drawn. Conclusions are also called **inferences** (judgments arrived at through reasoning). Suppose you state the following facts in the summary.

1. Fifteen percent of the students own personal computers.
2. Seventy-five percent of the students who own personal computers made *A*'s in their mathematics classes.

The conclusion to these summary facts might be:

> Those students who own personal computers do well in their mathematics classes.

You are going one step beyond summarizing; you are drawing a conclusion, based on the facts in your study. But you are not making a recommendation.

Recommendations

Recommendations are based on the conclusions in the report and are more subjective than conclusions. The recommendations represent what you think should be done, based on the conclusions you have drawn. They allow some freedom since you can suggest possible uses of the conclusions. Since recommendations can be a sensitive area, be sure the reader wants the recommendations before you include them as a part of the report.

Your recommendation for the above conclusion might be to recommend that the university provide personal computers for all the students.

If you have several summary statements, conclusions, or recommendations, include them as enumerations. Enumerations are easier to read, and each of them can be evaluated separately. These enumerations should be preceded by a lead-in statement, such as: "The following conclusions are based on the findings of this report."

CHAPTER SUMMARY

The three parts of a report are the introduction, the text, and the ending.

In the introduction, give enough information to orient the reader to the problem, but omit the unnecessary elements. Your objective is to lead the reader into the report by giving the necessary information to prepare the reader for the text.

The text of the report must follow a clear and logical plan that is obvious to the reader. Headings make it easier for a reader to follow the discussion. Your ability to organize and express the findings will determine whether you accomplish the purpose of the report.

Your responsibility in the ending is to finish the report in a strong and positive way. The terminal section should drive home the major points or purpose of the report. Depending on the purpose of the report and the audience, you may include a summary, conclusions, and/or recommendations.

A summary restates the major points or facts of the text; informational reports end with a summary. Conclusions interpret the findings as objectively as possible. Recommendations present personal opinions, based on the conclusions, on how to solve the problem.

STUDY QUESTIONS

1. Name the three sections of a report.
2. Does the introduction have to be the first part presented in a report? Why or why not?
3. Define in sentence format five parts that might be included in an introduction.
4. Why should the purpose always be included in the introduction?
5. What are hypotheses? State a hypothesis in null form.
6. Where would you most likely define a few words in a report?
7. Why are headings important in a report?
8. Define each of the three parts that may be included in the ending section of a report.
9. Should recommendations always be included in an analytical report? Give reasons for your answer.
10. Is there any place in a formal report where you can give your personal opinions and value judgments? If yes, where?

ACTIVITIES

1. Narrow one of the following research topics until you can state the purpose of the study in one sentence:
   a. The Civil War
   b. Advertising
   c. Private schools
2. Write the procedures section for a report in which you would use library references for all your information.
3. Rewrite the following hypothesis in null form:

   College students who read below the 10th grade educational level will express less satisfaction with college than those who read at or above 10th grade level.

4. Label each of the following statements as summary, conclusion, or recommendation:
   a. A similar investigation should be conducted using a new sample.
   b. Collegiate schools of business should periodically evaluate their major curriculum to ascertain the extent to which it meets the needs of organizations.
   c. Opportunities for middle management employees in the next decade appear to be very strong in the textile mill products industries.
   d. There is an interest in consumer affairs professional positions among firms who do not presently employ CAPs.
   e. Gaining consumer affairs experience as part of preparation for consumer affairs careers is important.
   f. A factor analysis revealed four factor dimensions: job extrinsics, self-actualization, interpersonal relations, and independence.
   g. Parental occupations seem to be related to intrinsic work values, such as management, creativity, and the problem-solving elements of jobs.
5. Assume you are going to write a report on the evolution of microcomputers. Go to the library and find background information on the development of the first microcomputers. Write the background to the problem.
6. Label the following statements as scope or limitations:
   a. No up-to-date sources available
   b. Study will focus on male employees
   c. Survey companies in four southern states only
   d. Must be completed by August 1
   e. Study of evening students
   f. Limited budget
   g. No computer assistance available
   h. Study of middle management females

7. Use parallel construction as you revise the following report headings:
   a. Values Claimed for Information Analysis
      Benefits Associated with Information Analysis
      Assessing the Value of Information
   b. What is Cybernetics?
      What are the Characteristics of Cybernetics?
      The Fundamental Concept of Feedback
      What is the Difference Between Cybernetics and Systems Theory?
   c. The Channel Used
      Timing
      Editing
      Abstracting

LANGUAGE SKILLS DEVELOPMENT

1. Choose the correct usage of the words shown in parentheses:
   a. The dealer contributions may (affect, effect) customer savings.
   b. Dealers stand behind (their, there) work.
   c. The company sets high standards for everything (accept, except) price.
   d. The book shows you exactly what each project will look like when (its, it's) finished.
   e. This game is for (everyone, every one) who enjoys sports.
   f. Our people, products, and pricing consistently (bring, brings) us repeat business.
   g. It was the people themselves (who's, whose) contributions financed the building's construction.
   h. We just could not afford to (lose, loose) that contract.
   i. Joan's (principle, principal) civic work is the Girl Scouts.
   j. The tour group spent (too, to) much time at the Art Museum.
   k. I appreciate (you, your) sending the package on time.
2. Divide the following words in the preferred place:
   a. Grasshopper
   b. Epigram
   c. Enjoyable
   d. Charm
   e. Donor
   f. Fraudulent
   g. Nonbinding
   h. Product
   i. Ruggedness
   j. Scholarly

IN-BASKET SIMULATIONS

1. Write a report from Mr. Joseph Anthony, Director of Operations, to Mr. Raymond Waltere, President of Waltere Supermarkets, Inc., describing the energy conservation measures the supermarkets are now practicing. Include in the introduction the authorization statement, purpose, background, scope, and presentation plan. The energy conservation measures practiced include:
   a. Lowering the thermostats 3°F
   b. Opening stores one hour later on Monday, Tuesday, and Wednesday
   c. Using less lighting in nonhazardous areas.
2. Assume that you, the personnel director, had three applicants for the job of Office Manager at corporate headquarters. Analyze the three candidates and write a report to Mr. Peter Waltere, Vice-President and General Manager, making your recommendation for the job. Some of the criteria you considered are:

Audrey Ashburn, B.S. degree in Business Education, with six years of experience as an administrative assistant and two years of experience as an office manager; her letters of recommendation were good.

Mildred Wells, with an MBA degree, and one year of work experience in a management trainee position with a major department store in the area; recommendations were good.

Steve Hege, age 42, with a high school education, twenty years of work experience with the last twelve years as an office manager in a large industrial office; recommendations were excellent.

Collection and Organization of Data

19

After studying Chapter 19, you should be able to:

- Differentiate between primary and secondary data
- Describe the need for using surveys, interviews, observations, and experimental methods when collecting data
- Use library sources
- Take notes efficiently

The content and arrangement of data should be an outgrowth of your purpose in writing the report. Once you have a plan and an outline, you are ready to begin your search for data to make your point. One of the most important aspects of report writing is gathering, analyzing, and verifying information. One of the first steps, of course, is to know exactly what you want to learn or what you are looking for. This search process develops from the stating of your purpose and the outlining of your topic. In researching business information, you must constantly be aware of your objectives, and you must stay within the bounds of these objectives. The next step is to explore the resources that are available, such as the library and company records. Once the data are complete, you are in a position to choose the best means of presentation.

Data are either primary or secondary.

PRIMARY DATA

Primary Data refers to data collected firsthand; in other words, it is data that is not already printed or published by someone else. You may collect primary data through a variety of ways: surveys, interviews, observations, and experimental methods.

Surveys

You can conduct **surveys** through mailed questionnaires (or other printed means), through personal interviews, or sometimes over the telephone. The most frequent survey method is the questionnaire.

In surveys, you assume that the people asked to respond either are representative of a larger group or constitute the entire group to be studied. A **population** is all the people in a particular group who could have been surveyed; a **sample** is a group of people picked at random to represent the total population. The sample must either be representative of the entire population or be composed of the entire population. Since most populations are too large to be surveyed, researchers usually use a smaller number of people that fairly represent the entire group. If you surveyed all the members of the local community club on their occupations, you used the entire population. As long as you do not plan to generalize the findings to other community clubs, your results are reliable.

Several sampling methods are available:

1. *Random sampling* gives everyone in the population an equal chance of being surveyed. If you had a fishbowl and selected names from that bowl, every person would have an equal

chance to be chosen. Another common method of random sampling is to use a **table of random numbers** (a table usually generated by a computer to assure a random order).

2. *Stratified random sampling* means that the sample is composed of the same percentage of particular groups. For example, you might want the same number of males and females in the study or the same number of people under 40 years of age and over 40 years of age. Or, if the population is composed of 40 percent males and 60 percent females, you might want the sample to be composed of the same percentages. In these cases, you select names until the quotas for each group are filled.

The survey instrument must be **valid**; that is, it must measure what it is intended to measure. And it must also be **unbiased**—not constructed in such a way to force a particular conclusion. The instrument may be structured or unstructured.

Structured questionnaires. When planning a questionnaire, you have two goals:

1. To secure a satisfactory rate of return
2. To secure accurate answers

The **structured questionnaire** obtains objective replies to a standard set of questions. The questions should be designed to elicit answers that can be easily analyzed and summarized. Notice how easily the following question could be analyzed and summarized:

Your age: ______ 18–25
______ 26–40
______ 41–55
______ 56–65

From the responses to the above question, you can easily group the respondents into four age groups and analyze the data according to these four groups. Had you left one blank space for age, you might have obtained as many ages as you had people filling out the questionnaires.

Often the respondents rate items or answer questions using a scale such as the following, which facilitates tabulation and analysis:

	(Large variety) 1	2	3	4	(Small variety) 5
How would you evaluate the extracurricular activities at the university?	____	____	____	____	____

Before formulating the items for the structured questionnaire, try to visualize how you can assemble and include the data in the final report. You need to know in advance how you will analyze the raw data (for example, which computer software programs you will use) because it will make a difference in how you phrase the questions and what questions you ask.

Some other guidelines to follow when constructing a structured questionnaire are:

1. *Construct questions that the reader will be able to understand easily*; avoid ambiguous wording. The vocabulary should be nontechnical and geared to the least-educated respondent. Use short, simple sentences. Whenever possible, responses should be quantified (number of times per week instead of using responses like *sometimes* and *never*) because your readers might define the responses in different ways. For example, you might ask the following question:

How many times do you eat out each week?	**Often**	**Sometimes**	**Never**
	________	________	________

   The respondents to the question then have to define what *often*, *sometimes*, and *never* means. But, you could rephrase the question in this way:

   How often do you eat out each week?

   ________ 0

   ________ 1–2 times

   ________ 3–4 times

   ________ More than 4 times

   For this question, it is easy for the reader to respond to the question, and all the readers should interpret the question the same way. The question could be improved further by defining whether you are talking about the total times or just lunch or just dinner or if the fast food restaurants would be included if you bought the food there and took it home to eat. It is difficult to write a question that everyone interprets in the same way.

2. *Make sure the questionnaire does not take the respondent too long to answer* or your response rate will not be as high. Eliminate unnecessary items, especially when those answers are available some other place; don't ask respondents to do your research for you.

3. *Include a cover letter with the questionnaire*; make sure the letter is addressed to the respondent by name and title. It should explain the purpose of the survey, the value of the study, and the reason why the respondent was included in the sample. It should also promote the study so that the respondent will be motivated to reply. As in the sales letter, show benefits to the reader for answering the questionnaire. The signature on the cover letter is important; it may be helpful for a person well known to the respondents to sign the cover letter. Enclose a stamped, addressed envelope for returning the questionnaire, especially if the survey is sent to nonprofit organizations or to a private home.
4. *Assure the respondent that his or her replies to the questions will be confidential.* Rather than have the respondents put their names on the questionnaires, you might code them to help guard the anonymity of the responses.
5. *Group together items that concern the same subject.* This grouping makes it easier for the person filling out the questionnaire, and it also makes tabulations of replies much easier.
6. *Provide a space for any additional comments the respondent may want to add to the questionnaire.* You may glean information you had not anticipated.
7. *Test the wording of items with some people before preparing a final survey instrument.* Test the survey instrument with a small number of people and revise the questionnaire based on their suggestions.
8. *Arrange the questions so the easiest-to-answer items come at the beginning.* The respondent is more likely to finish it once he or she has started answering the questions, even if the final questions require more time or thinking. If both general and specific questions are asked on a topic, ask the general questions first. For example, first, ascertain if respondents are satisfied with working conditions before asking for changes they would recommend.
9. *Construct the questionnaire in such a way that it reflects quality and looks professional.* A questionnaire that appears to have been thrown together quickly will not elicit high returns.
10. *Phrase items so as to avoid bias or prejudice that might predetermine a respondent's answer.* A question that asked why college students should live in dormitories presupposes that the respondent agrees with the basic premise.

11. *Be sure that the alternatives to the various items are exhaustive.* If you asked a respondent what his or her marital status was and gave only two alternatives—single, married—you may not get as accurate a response as you might if you gave all the alternatives.
12. *Plan a follow-up for nonrespondents.* A postcard is usually used. After that, a second mailing of the questionnaire with a new cover letter can help you reach the maximum number of returns.

A structured questionnaire has many advantages. The administration and scoring are straightforward and the results lend themselves readily to analysis. The biggest disadvantage is it forces the respondents to choose one of a number of preselected alternative answers to questions. This restriction may increase its realiability but decrease its depth.

Unstructured questionnaires. The **unstructured questionnaire** does not include suggested answers; it gives respondents the freedom to reveal their opinions and attitudes. The unstructured questionnaire has open-ended questions, such as

What was your salary last year? ________________

How would you describe the food in the cafeteria? ________________

____

In the preliminary stages of a study, many researchers use an unstructured questionnaire at first to determine how respondents will answer particular questions. Then, the structured questions are formulated using responses gleaned from the trial run.

The biggest disadvantage to unstructured questionnaires is that the answers to open-ended questions are sometimes difficult to summarize and report. Another disadvantage is that respondents may omit important points or emphasize things that are of no interest to you and of no importance to the purpose of the research. The advantage, however, is that you may obtain more complete information, and you may obtain answers not anticipated in the questionnaire.

Some guidelines for developing unstructured questionnaires follow:

1. *Provide sufficient space for the respondents to record their answers.*
2. *Word the questions in such a way that you get the answers you need.* Suppose you wanted to know what specific qualities are

needed for a person to obtain a job in management, and you asked the following open-ended question:

> Are there particular personality traits needed for a person to obtain a job in management? ____________

The answer you get might be *yes* or *no* with no discussion or listing of the necessary traits. The question might better be phrased:

> What particular personality traits are needed for a person to obtain a job in management? ____________

3. Use verbs, such as *compare*, *describe*, and *explain*, that elicit amplified responses.

   Some studies require a questionnaire in which part of it is structured and part of it is unstructured.

Interviews. **Interviews** can be conducted either face to face or over the telephone. Personal interviews are more effective since you can pick up on more nonverbal communication. Interviews, as survey tools, still present problems.

Questionnaires, whether they are structured or unstructured, are typically more efficient and practical than interviews for a number of reasons:

They allow you to use a larger sample
Standard instructions are given to all subjects
The personal appearance or conduct of the interviewer will not influence the results
They help in getting information on sensitive matters that a respondent may not be willing to give in an interview
They can be completed in the privacy of the home or office, which assures more anonymity and gives more time to answer

The disadvantages of using questionnaires follow:

The response rate may be low
You never know when the respondents will return them
The respondents may misinterpret the questions

Questionnaires that are vague or confusing will produce a report containing these same weaknesses. A good questionnaire requires a great deal of time and effort.

Observations

Collecting data by observation means simply that you recognize and note the facts. These observations may be casual and informal, or planned, controlled, and scientific. In a report on the parking problem at your organization, you might report on your own personal parking problems—a casual observation. However, a scientific observation would require observing the parking situation at critical times of the day over a specified period of time. You could observe the number of people exiting and entering the parking lot, the number of available parking spaces and cars, or the times of the day when spaces are available.

Keep accurate and complete records while collecting the data. The observations can be done all the time, at specified times, or on an impromptu basis. Then analyze and interpret the data objectively.

Other information sources for observation are records in the files of the organization, assembly line observations, laboratory data, and market trends.

Some disadvantages of observations follow:

They are not useful for determining feelings, attitudes, and plans
They are more subjective because they frequently involve interpretation (the observer's own feelings might influence the assessment of the findings)
Sometimes changes occur just because of the observation (especially when people are being observed)

Observation is a costly, slow method of research that needs careful controls. Some of the controls include:

1. *Decide ahead of time what you plan to observe and what you plan to ignore*, since it is not possible for you to observe everything that happens.
2. *Train observers on what to look for;* they should practice ahead of time. The form should be trial tested to make sure it works.
3. *Decide ahead of time the procedures for recording the observations and the time segments for the observations.* The memory of most people is not adequate for remembering events and data.

Experimental Methods

To use an experimental method of research means that you conduct a test. If you wanted to know the effect of the number of parking attendants on the rate of parking, you could conduct a test by changing the number of attendants each week and measuring the rate of parking at specified times of each day.

The experimental design is usually considered the purest form of research. The experimental method, correctly used, is more precise than any other research method. It is somewhat limited in its application in business because you cannot control and manipulate the study variables, especially when people are used as variables.

The experimental method uses at least two groups: experimental and control groups. The **experimental group** is used to manipulate variables, and the **control group** is not subjected to manipulation.

You work with dependent and independent variables. The **dependent variable** is the phenomenon that is the object of the study; the **independent variable** is the variable that is manipulated. For example, to evaluate the use of a study guide on class grades, divide the class into two groups: those students who use a study guide (experimental group) and those students who do not use a study guide (control group). The dependent variable is the students' grades, and the independent variable is the use of the study guide. At the end of a specified time period, determine if the grades are higher for those students who used the study guide. Any significant difference between the two groups is attributed to the effect of the special treatment (study guide).

A modified version of an experimental design is to use just one group and subject this group to the special treatment. Measurements are taken before and after the treatment to determine if a difference exists because of the special treatment.

All methods of experimentation are outside the scope of this book, but several excellent research books that give a thorough coverage of experimental designs are available.

SECONDARY DATA

Secondary data are compiled by someone else. They are often obtained through library research. When using secondary sources, be certain to give credit to the author of the information through a footnote. You must footnote not only when using direct quotes but also when summarizing and paraphrasing. By not footnoting your sources, you are guilty of **plagiarism**. Footnoting secondary data is covered later in this chapter.

Of primary consideration in using secondary data is to decide whether the author is reliable and whether what he or she has to say is topical. Ask yourself if the author has discriminated between fact and opinion. Another important element is the date of the publication—especially if you are researching a current topic.

Library sources, government documents, business sources, and computer searches are some examples of secondary data.

Library Sources

A rich source of information is your school or public library. If a company is large, it may have its own library. These company libraries are seldom open to the general public. If a company library is available, you are fortunate to have business literature at your fingertips.

The library is carefully and logically organized. To use the library effectively, discover its wide variety of research materials and services. Reference librarians can save you hours of work in helping to find your materials. Many librarians answer telephone inquiries, as long as the request does not require extensive research, and many libraries provide instruction in the use of the library and its resources.

The first place to start looking for information is usually the card catalog, which is an index of the books (as well as cassettes, films, microforms, and periodicals), categorized by author, title, and subject. The card catalogs in some libraries have been replaced with computerized catalogs. Librarians shelve each book according to its reference number given in the card catalog. For a **book** by a particular author, go to the alphabetical listing of the authors to see if the library has that book. Or, if you know the title, look in the title section of the card catalog.

If, however, you are looking for information about a particular topic and you do not know any titles or you do not know who may have written on the subject, you can usually find what you need under the subject listings. If there is no subject heading in the catalog for your particular topic, look under a more general heading.

If you need current information, the best place to look is in the **periodicals** (journals). The periodical indexes and abstracts provide the names and sources of magazine articles that have been written on various subjects. Some popular indexes and abstracts are:

American Statistical Index
Business Education Index
Business Periodicals Index
Economic Abstracts
Education Index
Employment Relations Abstracts
New York Times Index
Personnel Management Abstracts
Psychological Abstracts
Reader's Guide to Periodical Literature
Social Science and Humanities Index
Wall Street Journal Index
Women Studies Abstracts
Work Related Abstracts

Magazine articles generally relay more recent information than that found in books because of the time necessary for book publication. Books, however, can explore a subject more thoroughly than can magazine articles. A book, however, usually requires more time to write. It takes an author at least 10 to 12 months to prepare the manuscript for a book. After the manuscript is complete, approximately 9 months are needed to get the book on the shelf. So, from the time an author gets an idea until the book appears on the shelf, a minimum of two years has passed.

Newspapers are another important source of information. In addition to local papers, nationally recognized papers, such as *The New York Times* and the *Wall Street Journal* provide a great deal of information. To help you locate the information you need, both of these national newspapers have indexes.

Many other sources are available in a library (for example, dictionaries, encyclopedias, almanacs, atlases, bibliographies, and yearbooks). Besides the traditional collections of books and journals, most libraries make use of the new technology: microfilm and microfiche collections and readers/printers, audio materials, and teaching machines, to name a few.

Several sources are available that contain periodic lists of all in-print books published by commercial publishing firms and university presses. These lists can be found in your local library or bookstore.

Government Documents

Many **government documents and publications** are found in local libraries. Most of those not available in libraries can be ordered from the Government Printing Office in Washington, D.C. You can obtain publications relating to a specific government agency by writing to that agency (for example, the Department of Commerce). A general publications listing is available from the government: *Selected List of U.S. Government Publications*, published ten times a year. Each publication lists the titles of at least 150 government publications that are available for a small charge.

Business Sources

Many libraries house **business sources** (such as annual reports or statements to stockholders from major corporations). If the annual report you are seeking is not in the library, write directly to the corporate secretary or obtain the report from a local stockbroker's office.

Directories are other important reference tools. Directories are time saving when you need brief data on companies, organizations, and individuals. They can be very helpful when researching manufacturers of a specific product, checking companies located in a particular area, or verifying company names, addresses, and telephone numbers.

Other information about businesses can be obtained from the following sources, which you can usually find in libraries:

F & S Index of Corporations and Industries
F & S International
Moody's Industrial Manual
Standard & Poor's

Computer Search

A **computer search** can also help to locate available materials. Most large libraries now have a computer terminal in which you can input key words to produce listings of books, periodicals, reports, or other sources for a particular subject. Millions of articles, reports, books, and current or completed research projects are stored in the data bases of the computer terminal.

Commercial Data Base Systems

Commercial data base systems or **electronic information systems** give users access to information stored in various data bases in remotely located computers. The equipment needed to access this information is a terminal or personal computer and a modem (the means of interfacing terminal equipment to the telephone system).

Data base searching is usually offered on a subscription or fee basis. The user obtains information from a data base by means of a structured searching procedure. Information is located by using key words or phrases describing the subject being researched. The user simply dials up the data base to which he or she subscribes and the information then appears on the display screen or is printed out in hard copy. Reprints of articles and papers can be ordered directly from a user's terminal.

A generic term to describe a one-way (computer to user) system is **teletext**. If the user wants to request specific information or interact with the computer system, he or she must use **videotex**, a two-way (computer to user and user to computer) system. Videotex provides color and graphics capabilities as well as text.

Three categories of data bases are available:

1. Current information and services (such as stock quotes and news wire services)
2. Information banks offering a collection of data banks that are accessed through a single organization

3. Specialized data bases offering concentrated information on a subject or profession (such as law)

Some existing U.S. information systems are The Source, CompuServe, Bibliographic Retrieval Services, Inc., New York Times Information Service, and Dialog Information Retrieval Service.

On-line banks make published information sources convenient. They can be used effectively with modest training. More than 1500 data bases are now available; during the next several years the number and scope of on-line data banks and their applications should expand significantly.

NOTETAKING

Having determined what kinds of data are available, you are ready to start taking notes. Your report requires documentation so that the information can be traced and validated. Expect to take more notes than you will eventually use in the report. First notations usually are rather full, becoming more brief as you encounter fewer new facts and opinions. Get all the information you think you will need the first time so you do not have to go back and relocate the source.

For ease of sorting and arranging the data, use 4 in. × 6 in., 5 in. × 8 in., or another convenient size of cards to record your data. Cards have an advantage because they are easy to shuffle, and they automatically control the number of notes.

Include three kinds of information on the note cards (Figure 19-1).

1. Key to the outline (name topic and give letter and number of the outline)
2. Key to the working bibliography (give author's last name and the page number of the source)
3. Content of the note

The notes you take can be in one of three formats: direct quote, summary, or paraphrase.

Direct Quote

Direct quotes should be used sparingly and only for special reasons: because the author has said it much better than you could do or when the material is of interest in itself. Make sure you use quotation marks around the item to show that the material is a direct quote.

Summary

A **summary** is a condensed statement of the findings from that source.

Miller, p. 11 II B. Education
Frost attended public schools for her early education but enrolled in a private institution for her secondary education.

Figure 19-1
A Completed Note Card

Paraphrase

To **paraphrase** means to restate an idea or sentence in your own words. You need to be careful not to change the meaning intended by the author when you paraphrase or summarize.

You may use photocopying machines to copy small passages for the purpose of gathering notes. Photocopying paragraphs saves time otherwise spent making notes, and you have the original copy accessible when you are writing your report.

When you feel that your research is complete, test it by drawing conclusions. If you have the complete picture, the conclusions should almost shape themselves. Do not waste your time taking a lot of unnecessary notes.

1. Before attempting to take a single note, read the source first for its general sense. If you plan to use only a section of the data, glance over the remainder of the data to make sure you know how your section fits into the overall picture.
2. As you reread the data, make notes of the important ideas; put only one note on each card.
3. As ideas occur to you, make notes of them. Identify these notes as your own and classify them under one of the sections of your outline.

SOURCE DOCUMENTATION

Always credit any material written by other persons, whether you are quoting this material verbatim, paraphrasing, or just summarizing. Never use someone else's ideas unless you give credit by documenting your source of information. No one expects you to document **general knowledge**. For example, you can state that George Washington was the first president of the United States without using a footnote. But if you are giving new or unusual information about George Washington that you read in a specific book, you are using that author's research and ideas, and you must provide a footnote. The use of material without giving credit is called **plagiarism** and it can have legal—as well as other—ramifications.

Footnotes serve two main purposes:

1. To give credit to writers whose words and ideas you have used
2. To refer the reader to the sources you have used

Business reports use few footnotes because they usually discuss only the writer's own research. Research reports, on the other hand, discuss other research and require frequent use of footnotes.

Footnotes may appear in two places—individually at the bottom of text pages or together at the end of the report. In the traditional method, the footnote appears at the bottom of the same page on which the quote, summary, or paraphrase appears. If the direct quote appears on page 4, the footnote appears at the bottom of page 4. To identify the footnote, a superior Arabic number appears at the end of the quote and preceding the note.

Type a 1½-in. solid rule over the top footnote and under the last line of text on that page. Single space the notes, inserting a blank line between each footnote. Indent the same number of spaces for the note as you indented paragraphs. Figure 19–2 uses these steps for correct spacing:

1. A typewritten rule separates the footnotes from the body with a blank line before and after; rule is 1½ in. long.
2. Footnotes are single-spaced with a blank line separating the footnotes.
3. Footnotes are indented the number of spaces the paragraphs are indented.
4. Superior numbers precede the footnotes.

Forms for proper footnoting for some of the most common references follow. For **books**, the sequence should be: *author* (first and last name), *book title* (underlined), (*City of publication: Publishing Co., date of publication*), *page number.*

[1]J.E. Brown, How to Improve Your Gardening (Trenton: Green Publishing Co., 1978), pp. 9-11.

The two primary requirements of modern ski bindings are safety and performance. To meet the safety requirements, a binding must release the skier from the ski before the forces acting on the ski can cause injury.[1]

According to Dr. Sikora, "A significant number of skiing injuries occur after a skier has released from his ski and is injured in the act of falling."[2]

---

[1]Eugene Sikora, Ski Bindings for Safety (New York. Release Publishing House, 1978), p. 35.

[2]Sikora, p. 23.

Figure 19-2
Format for Footnote Placement

If you refer to the Brown book again later in the report, you may use a version that gives the author's name and the exact page number:

[2]Brown, p. 51.

If you should quote two books by the same author, include an abbreviated title of the book:

[2]Brown, Gardening, p. 51.

Or, if you should quote books by two different authors whose last names are Brown, give a first initial in the shortened version:

[2]J. Brown, p. 51.

For **periodicals**, the sequence should be: *author* (first and last name), *"Title of Article," Name of Publication* (underlined), *date, page number.*

[4]James E. Brown, "Gardening at its Best," Horticulture Today, Spring, 1984, p. 54.

Interviews can be documented in this way:

[5]Statement by Edward E. Brown, Assistant Professor, personal interview, Cleveland, Ohio, August 25, 1985.

The other method of footnoting is to place all the footnotes together at the end of the report on a separate sheet of paper. This method uses a shortened version of the footnote after the quotes and paragraphs. Several methods are available for this identification of the footnote, but one of the most commonly used forms includes the last name of the author and the page number of the reference used. These two items are shown in parentheses immediately after the reference; no superior figures are given with this style of footnote. For example, if you wanted to put a footnote after this statement, it would be shown as follows:

(Adams, p. 7)

At the end of the report, then, is a complete listing of each of the references used in the report. This listing is arranged in bibliographical style (see Chapter 23 for the correct format for a bibliography).

CHAPTER SUMMARY

The more skilled you become in collecting business information, the more valuable you become. You need to know where to look for information and whom to ask for help in finding it.

Data that you collect for reports may be primary or secondary. Primary data are those you gather firsthand through surveys, observations, or experimental methods. Secondary data are those that already exist, that have been published by someone else.

Your notes may include direct quotes, summaries, or paraphrases, but you should not expect to use all of the notes you take. Any sources you use for compiling your report should be footnoted. You can use the traditional style of footnotes (located at the bottom of the page) or references cited footnotes (located on a page at the end of the report).

STUDY QUESTIONS

1. What information normally appears on note cards?
2. When would direct quotes be appropriate in a report?
3. Label each of the following sources as primary or secondary data:
    a. Newspaper
    b. Telephone interview
    c. Government report
    d. Dictionary
    e. Observation
    f. Filmstrip
    g. Magazine article
    h. Experiment
    i. Questionnaire findings
    j. Book
4. What are the characteristics of a structured questionnaire?
5. What are the usual sources of information for observations?
6. How are most card catalogs divided?

7. Name three periodical indexes and abstracts.
8. You plan to do reports on the following topics. To produce a literature review, what would be the key words to feed into the computer?
   a. The future of women as small business owners
   b. The admissions standards of state colleges in Oregon
   c. A survey of coffee pot cleaners
   d. Changes in children's sleepwear since 1980
   e. Trends in accountancy for large companies

ACTIVITIES

1. Paraphrase and summarize the following direct quote:

   > The length of a ski is determined more by the speed at which you ski and your strength than by your height and weight. Fast skiers need long skis. Heavy skiers need skis with a high spring rate and a relatively stiff bending flex. Mogul skiers need easy-flexing, quick-turning skis and never in lengths over 200 cm—unless they are strong and very expert. If you can ski the steep moguls well, you probably have the right skis for you and the bumps.

2. From one of the business reference sources in your library, find the following information about a corporation located in your geographic area:
   a. Gross sales for last year
   b. Chief executive officer
   c. Geographic locations of other plants
   d. Price per share of common stock

3. Develop and administer a structured questionnaire to determine the age, sex, major, year of study, and hobbies of the members of your class. Summarize the findings of your study.

4. Select an annual report from some organization or corporation in your geographic area. List all the major areas covered in the report and write a short summary of each part.

5. Critique the following survey questions:
   a. What is your present yearly salary?
   b. How would you evaluate your summer school experience?
   c. Check your educational level:
      _______ high school _______ college
   d. Do you go to the dentist once or twice a year?
   e. Do you outline and take notes of new chapters?
      _______ yes _______ no

6. Determine which primary research method would be most appropriate for the following situations:
   a. To determine the behavior of students taking an exam
   b. To determine the attitudes of shoppers to advertising
   c. Follow-up study of 250 graduates
   d. Comparison of ability of students who use word processing to write reports and those who do not.
   e. Comparison of amount of time males and females spend talking in class
   f. In-depth follow-up of 15 honor students
   g. Comparison of driving test scores of those who had formal training and those who did not

LANGUAGE SKILLS DEVELOPMENT

1. Rewrite the following sentences, using parallel structure.
   a. A question that commonly arises when talking about roses is which varieties are the most popular and can be relied on.
   b. The characteristics of these traditional groups of roses are increasingly difficult to identify and are hard to describe.
   c. There are many excellent varieties to choose from when planting new roses or to replace old varieties.
   d. Long-term VFR pilots obey these three basic rules:
      1. Remain VFR at all times.
      2. Recognize critical or deteriorating conditions.
      3. You should continue only so long as an alternative route exists.
   e. The center offers a course on management, implementing, and application of CAD/CAM.
2. Capitalize any of the following words that should be capitalized:
   a. harlem globetrotters
   b. joe edwards, team vice president
   c. speak english and spanish
   d. world war II
   e. vice president edwards
   f. easter weekend
   g. windy city
   h. american team
   i. shaker boulevard
   j. continental breakfast
   k. maple festival
   l. memorial day picnic

IN-BASKET SIMULATIONS

1. Develop a questionnaire that Waltere Supermarkets, Inc., could use to survey customers about their preferences on the following two items:
   a. Giving stamps (with purchases) that could be cashed in for gifts
   b. Stocking health foods in the supermarkets
2. Assume that Waltere's has been unhappy with the training procedures used in the past for store managers. You are authorized to determine better training procedures.
   a. Where would you go for information?
   b. Write a paragraph on the procedures you would use to solve this problem.
3. You want to observe the behavior of children who shop with their parents at Waltere. Develop a checklist to use for observation.

20

Short Reports

After studying Chapter 20, you should be able to:

- Differentiate between formal and informal reports
- Determine when to use informational, analytical, and persuasive reports
- Format a short report
- Use letter and memorandum reports as routinely as standardized and preprinted reports

One way to classify reports is by their length. Most of the reports you will write in business will be short reports. Many of the same procedures, though, are followed for long reports. Thus, once you can write an effective short report, you will be able to move on to longer reports. Short reports are called **informal reports** because they usually do not contain the prefatory and supplemental parts that formal reports need. These prefatory and supplemental parts are added for the convenience of the reader. If, for example, you have a 30-page report, you may need to add such pages as a table of contents, a bibliography, and an appendix. The more parts you add, the more formal the report becomes. These parts are discussed in Chapter 23.

Several formats are available for the informal report. Four frequently used formats are memorandum report, letter report, printed form report, and standardized report.

The length of a report does not necessarily determine the formality of the language used. Formal language can be used in both short and long reports or informal language is appropriate for either short or long reports. With **formal language**, you would not use contractions (*wouldn't, haven't*) and you would avoid first and second person (*I, we, you, our*). Formal language normally uses third person. Instead of writing, *Twenty-five professionals expressed their opinions about* . . . , you might use third person to say *The researcher interviewed* . . . or *The writer interviewed* . . .

The primary disadvantage of formal writing is that it is easy for the writer to lapse into passive voice so that the language can sound too stilted or awkward. As a result, formal language is usually reserved for such documents as theses and dissertations. However, formal language is sometimes used in business for longer reports and reports that will be read by top management.

Informal language, on the other hand, is usually the language of business, especially short reports, memoranda, and letters. The language written sounds the same as the language spoken.

MEMORANDUM REPORT

A **memorandum report** is a short, informal message that is usually sent between employees of the same company. It is also the format (whether it is a memo or memo report) used most frequently in businesses because it is fast, efficient, and convenient. Other advantages of the memorandum report follow:

It saves time because you can announce a message to many people at the same time. (You don't have to play telephone tag and find people in their offices to give them a message.)

MEMORANDUM

DATE: August 15, 19--

TO: Bill Pauless, Ext. 441

FROM: R. H. Dunbar, Ext. 321

SUBJECT: TRIP TO STANFORD RESEARCH INSTITUTE

On August 2, I visited Stanford Research Institute (SRI), Menlo Park, California, to discuss with Dr. Donald Vargo, Research Engineer, his work on nonmechanical means of controlling fluid flow. This report will give you an overview of my discussion with Dr. Vargo.

Research Work at SRI

1. Three fluid flow systems have been developed by SRI. Two of these systems are hydraulic-powered vibrators and the other system is a clutch. Tests show that these systems are capable of extremely high response rates.

2. Mechanically the systems are very simple. The result is a simple rugged mechanical system of high mechanical reliability.

3. One experimental device would cost between $8,000 and $10,000.

Conclusions

From my observations I believe that nonmechanical means of fluid control are still in infancy. Further major improvements should be available in the near future. We should definitely keep informed of the progress in this field.

eb

Figure 20-1
Memorandum

It aids memory because you are able to restate or clarify instructions given orally and to keep track of jobs to be completed.

It provides access to people you do not normally see or talk to.

The memo is the message format that is most frequently sent electronically (using a computer terminal to send and receive messages). The memo in Figure 20-1 is typical of a memorandum report.

As mentioned earlier, readers of memorandum reports are usually employees of the same organization. Because of this, the writer will often have personal and professional relationships with the reader or readers. A memo may be sent to only one or two people, or it may be a **broadcast message** (sent to several people in the organization). When you write a broadcast message, you need to write so everyone understands and so that the message is politically acceptable (prudent and diplomatic) to all of your readers. A message that is politically acceptable refers not only to the content of the message but also to the format chosen. The format should consider such things as the status of the people receiving the message. You should address the memo to the person with the most status first and then to the others in descending order. Or, if you are unsure of the status of the readers, be sure to alphabetize the last names of the readers. This rule would also apply to a copy notation at the bottom of the memo. Either place the names in order of importance or in alphabetical order.

A memo report flows in all directions in an organization—upward, downward, and sideways. For political reasons again, make sure that you route the communication through the proper channels if it is sent upward through the organizational chart of the company. If the memo report is sent downward, it may not always follow the channels on the organizational chart; sometimes a level or two in the organization may be skipped. The president of a company, for example, might write a memo report directly to employees of a company and skip the managerial and supervisory levels in between.

You need to decide who should receive a copy of the memorandum report. Two groups of readers might be interested in the content: those who must do something as a result of your report and those who need to know what you have said. Therefore, a memo report will usually have many readers, not just the person or persons who will be part of the decision-making process.

Primarily, memo reports provide information for decision making. Because they usually remain inside the organization, they may be less formal in tone and format; the writer may assume that the reader is familiar with many of the facts and terms. Brevity is one of the characteristics of the memo report. To hold down the total length of the report, be selective in choosing and presenting the pertinent data. Do not, of course, sacrifice clarity or completeness for conciseness.

Companies usually have memorandum forms preprinted. Most companies have a variety of sizes of paper printed (8½ in. × 11 in., half size, three-quarters of a page). The page may have a special heading (Memo, Memorandum, Interoffice Mail) printed on the page. Because the memo report remains within an organization, a cheaper grade of paper is often used, and an interoffice envelope

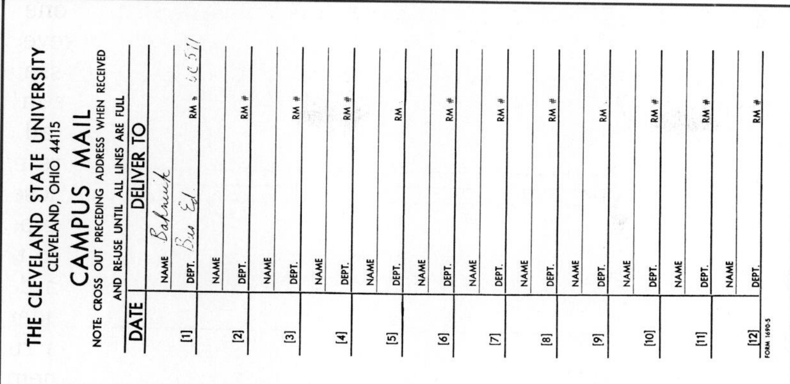
THE CLEVELAND STATE UNIVERSITY
CLEVELAND, OHIO 44115
CAMPUS MAIL
NOTE: CROSS OUT PRECEDING ADDRESS WHEN RECEIVED
AND RE-USE UNTIL ALL LINES ARE FULL

DATE	DELIVER TO	
[1]	NAME	
	DEPT.	RM #
[2]	NAME	
	DEPT.	RM #
[3]	NAME	
	DEPT.	RM #
[4]	NAME	
	DEPT.	RM #
[5]	NAME	
	DEPT.	RM #
[6]	NAME	
	DEPT.	RM #
[7]	NAME	
	DEPT.	RM #
[8]	NAME	
	DEPT.	RM #
[9]	NAME	
	DEPT.	RM #
[10]	NAME	
	DEPT.	RM #
[11]	NAME	
	DEPT.	RM #
[12]	NAME	
	DEPT.	RM #

FORM 1690-S

Figure 20-2
Interoffice Envelope

(See Figure 20-2) is used to mail the memo. This envelope does not require postage because it is mailed via intercompany mail, and it is used over and over again. You simply mark through the last name on the envelope and add the name of the new addressee.

Because the memo report is staying within the organization, you can dispense with many of the formalities of reports or letters that would be sent outside the organization. Rather than an inside address, special headings, such as *TO*, *FROM*, *SUBJECT*, and *DATE*, are used. Many memos have no signature, but the writer can initial or sign his or her name in ink after the typed name following "From."

The *TO* in the heading refers to the addressee, the *FROM* refers to the writer, the *DATE* refers to the current date, and the *SUBJECT* refers to the topic of the memo report. Other headings, such as location and copies, may be used on the preprinted form. The subject line becomes the title for the report. It should be short and descriptive. The subject line should contain key words that describe the content of the report, such as:

RECOMMENDATIONS FOR OFFICE MANAGER POSITION
ANALYSIS OF LOCATIONS FOR NEW BRANCH SITE
ANALYSIS OF HIRING PRACTICES FOR STAFF AT CSU

The memo report should include an introduction, a discussion, and an ending. Headings are helpful, even in short memoranda, in guiding the reader through the sections of the report.

A second page of a memo report should have a designation similar to that used in letters (see Chapter 5) and other memos (see Chapter 15). The second-page heading should contain the name of the addressee, the page number, and the date. The sub-

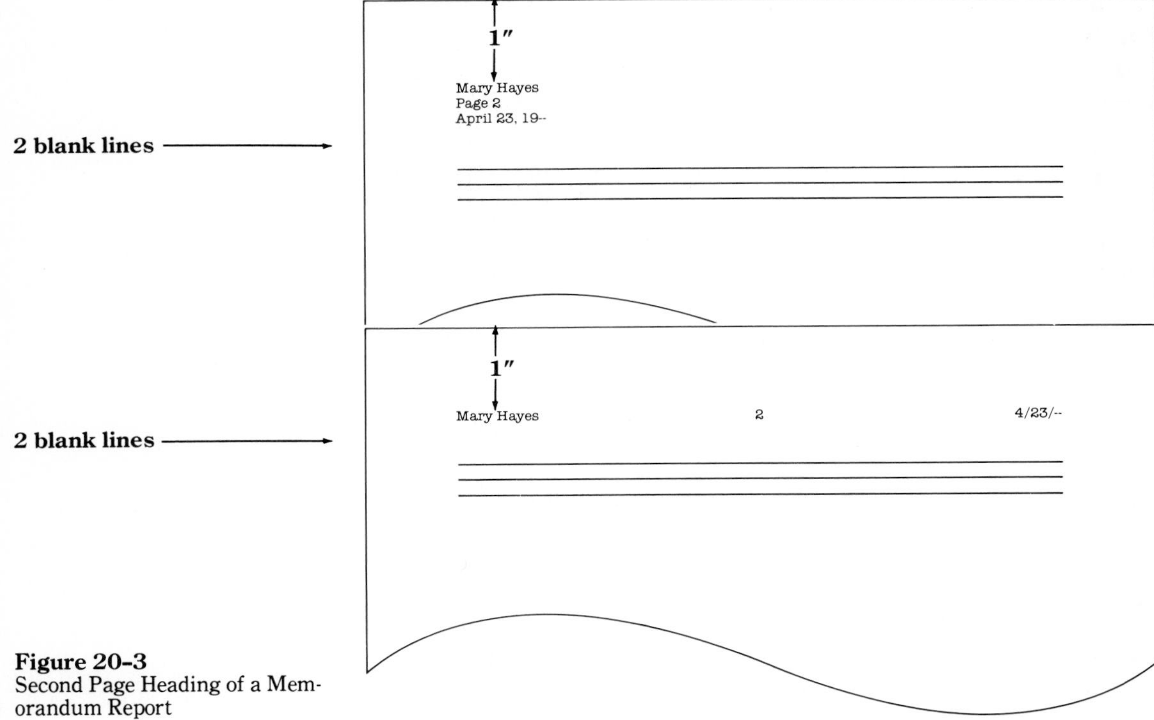

Figure 20-3
Second Page Heading of a Memorandum Report

ject may also be a part of the second-page designation. This heading may be placed single-spaced at the left margin about 1 in. from the top of the page, or it may be spread across the page. Figure 20-3 shows two ways to place this heading.

Most report writers receive specific assignments: to pass along information, to solve a problem, or to analyze two or more methods or materials. If you have been asked to provide information only, you would write the informational report. If, however, your suggested solutions are expected, you would write the analytical report. If you are in a position to build a strong case and call for action, you would write the persuasive report.

Informational Reports

The **informational report** passes on information or data without analysis, interpretation, or recommendations for action. It normally contains an introduction, a text, and a summary. It might be a one-time only report, dealing with a specific problem or event (such as the bicentennial advertising promotion). Or, it could be a routine report submitted at regular intervals, such as a progress report, budget report, or conference report.

Informational reports vary widely in content, depending upon the type of business, the purpose of the report, the topics discussed, and the reader's needs. Notice how the report in Figure 20-4 is organized and written.

1. The memo report format is appropriate because the report is short and is staying within the organization.
2. The report does not attempt to persuade or analyze; the purpose of the report is to present information.
3. Although the report is short, the headings help to guide the reader through the report.
4. The introduction of the report—the first paragraph—sets the stage by telling the reader why the report was written; the text gives the findings of the study; and the last section of the report contains the summary. The report is written using the indirect approach discussed in Chapter 17 (beginning, middle, and ending).
5. The introduction contains a statement of authorization, a statement of the problem, the purpose, the methodology, and the plan of presentation.
6. The findings are presented using enumerations to make it easier for the reader to follow.
7. Because this is an informational report, the ending contains a summary of the findings of the study.

Analytical Reports

All reports provide information. **Analytical reports**, however, go beyond that to analyze a particular situation and suggest solutions or even urge to action. The more opinions you include in the report, of course, the greater responsibility you assume. Hence, it is important to know, from the beginning, how much information you are expected to present and whether you should include recommendations.

When writing an analytical report, you need to determine some criteria to use for comparing services, products, or solutions to problems. These criteria are usually the headings you use in your report. If you were going to compare three minicomputers, you would not just present information first on Computer A, then Computer B, and finally Computer C. If you did this, you would have an informational report. If, instead, you compare the three computers on hardware features, software available, ease of use, and expandability, these criteria would become your headings in the analytical report, and you could compare all three computers under each of them. The three computers could be ranked under each of the criteria, or you could wait and rank them in your ending.

MEMORANDUM

DATE: October 5, 19--

TO: Neal Macky

FROM: Bob Wallace

SUBJECT: PARKING SITUATION IN LOTS A AND B

As you requested, I conducted a study, to determine if a parking problem exists in our two parking lots, Lot A and Lot B. This report contains the findings of this study. The study took place during the week of September 15-19, 19--.

Phase One of the Study

For the first portion of the study, I found the number of available parking spaces in the two lots and the approximate number of cars using the two lots at specified times of the day. The survey of the lots was conducted on Monday, September 15, at the following times:

Lot A, 8:30 a.m. and 3 p.m.
Lot B, 9 a.m. and 3:30 p.m.

Phase Two of the Study

In the second phase of the study, I interviewed a random sample of the employees who drive to work to determine if they think a parking problem exists. I interviewed 83 employees in Lot A on Tuesday and Wednesday, September 16 and 17, and 51 employees in Lot B Thursday and Friday, September 18 and 19.

Findings

Based on the two surveys, here are the findings:

Lot A

1. In Lot A, 240 parking spaces are available for employee parking; 12 spaces are available for visitor parking.

2. At 8:30 a.m. on September 15, all of the employee parking spaces were occupied; 11 cars were parked illegally in spaces reserved for visitors.

Figure 20-4
Informational Report
(Two Pages)

One example of an analytical report is the **justification report**, used to justify an expenditure or a change in procedure, that follows. To organize and write an effective justification report, you must first be able to analyze the situation correctly, as the following situation demonstrates. (More complete information about research methods is covered in Chapter 19.)

Situation. A parking problem exists (based on a survey conducted at an earlier time and the opinions of employees). You can approach the analysis in several ways:

1. Talk informally to employees or formally survey them to

Macky 2 October 5, 19--

3. At 3 p.m., 6 empty spaces were available for employee parking; 7 cars were parked illegally in the visitor's parking area.

4. Approximately 82% of the employees interviewed on September 16 and 17 said a parking problem does exist.

Lot B

1. In Lot B, 190 parking spaces are available for employee parking; no spaces are reserved for visitors.

2. At 9 a.m., all of the parking spaces were occupied, 5 cars were parked illegally, blocking other cars and creating driving hazards.

3. At 3:30 p.m., 188 of the 190 parking spaces were occupied, and no cars were parked illegally.

4. Of the employees interviewed in Lot B, 69.3% felt a parking problem exists in that lot.

Summary

1. For Lots A and B, 430 parking spaces are available for employees.

2. In the morning, all parking spaces were filled, and several cars were parked illegally in the two lots.

3. In the afternoon, the two parking lots were filled.

4. More than 69% of the employees surveyed said a parking problem exists.

determine if they have any suggestions for improvement; make a list of their suggestions.

2. Observe how other companies are solving similar parking problems or conduct a formal study of what other organizations are doing.
3. Interview the planning department of your organization to determine what long-range plans are being considered for improving the parking problem.
4. Do a cost analysis study to determine the feasibility of expansion.
5. Determine what public transportation is available in the area.

MEMORANDUM

DATE: 10/12/--

TO: Neal Macky

FROM: Bob Wallace

SUBJECT: RECOMMENDATION FOR PARKING PROBLEMS

This report contains alternatives for handling the parking problems in Lots A and B and reducing the parking congestion that exists during the rush periods (beginning and end of the work day). My recommendation is included after discussion of the three alternatives.

Stagger the Working Hours

One solution to the parking problem would be to stagger the working hours for the office employees. The 225 office employees could be divided into three groups. Each of these groups would begin and end work at three different times. For example, Group I might begin work at 7:30 a.m. and finish at 4:30 p.m. Group II would begin at 8 a.m. and finish at 5:00 p.m., and Group III would begin at 8:30 a.m. and finish at 5:30 p.m.

This alternative would cut down considerably on the congestion that occurs every working day in the parking lot between 7:45 and 8 a.m. when all the employees are arriving and at 5 and 5:30 p.m. when the employees leave work. One of these schedules might appeal to some of the employees, and another of the schedules might appeal to a different group; therefore, employee morale could be improved by giving the employees the option of when to arrive at work and when to leave at the end of the day.

Even though this plan would cut down on the congestion in the parking lots, it would not solve the problem of too few parking spaces available. Those employees arriving at 8:30 a.m. each morning would find too few spaces available for parking. Also, the flexible schedule might interfere with those employees who are currently riding in car pools.

Add Parking Attendants

Another suggestion for handling the parking problem is to use two additional parking attendants to work just during the rush periods or to work all day.

Figure 20-5
Analytical Report
(Two Pages)

6. Study the feasibility of setting up car pools and rewarding employees who participate in these car pools.

Facts. After considering all the alternatives, narrow the choices to the ones you consider the best for your organization at this time. In narrowing the choices, you need to consider:

1. The company has no plans at this time for adding to the number of parking spaces available.
2. Public transportation does not extend to where your company is located; the public transportation companies have no plans to expand their lines at this time.

Macky
Page 2
October 12, 19--

These two attendants would keep the traffic flowing into and out of the lots. They would also help to eliminate the problem of cars parking illegally and blocking other cars. The attendants could also recommend alternative parking areas for when the lots get filled.

However, this alternative would not give any additional parking spaces in Lots A and B.

Encourage Car Pooling

A third alternative is to encourage the employees to ride in car pools as much as possible to reduce the number of cars parking in Lots A and B.

If car pools are utilized, fewer cars will be driven to work and therefore, fewer spaces needed. Not only will the car pools solve the problem of too few spaces for the number of cars, but the smaller number of cars will help eliminate congestion during rush hours. The car pools will also help conserve energy used by employees on their way to work.

A disadvantage is that car pools might discourage employees from working overtime during the occasional times when extra people are needed. Another disadvantage would be the amount of time and effort involved in arranging car pools for the various sections of the city and then convincing the employees to try car pooling.

Recommendation

We should form a committee to study car pooling for the employees. The committee should also propose incentives that might be used to entice the employees to ride to and from work in car pools.

3. Approximately $30,000 is available in the budget for improving the parking problem.
4. The staggered hours theory (employees start and finish work at different times during the day) has been used successfully in a few organizations.

Report. After narrowing the possibilities to three alternatives, you are ready to write the report and present the choices with your recommendation for solving the parking problem. Notice the elements of the analytical report in Figure 20-5.

1. The indirect approach is used, with the introduction given first followed by the findings and a recommendation. A recommendation is not always given in an analytical report; including it depends upon whether the reader is expecting one.
2. The introduction includes a statement of the purpose of the report and the plan of presentation.
3. The headings are second-degree headings; they are parallel (complete sentences with "you" understood).
4. The report does more than present information; it analyzes the three alternatives. The three alternatives (criteria) are used as the headings in the report.
5. The recommendation is strong and positive. The reader has the option of following through on the recommendation, but you as the writer should not hedge in making a proposal.

Persuasive Reports

The **persuasive report** is an important instrument in effecting changes in such areas as company policy, budget, and departmental affairs. It is the most common means of presenting a proposal, the rationale for the proposal, and a call for action on the proposal. This kind of report is expected of authorized personnel who have the explicit responsibility of exploring situations and seeking solutions, then urging the reader of the report to act.

The persuasive report not only implies responsibility on the part of the writer, but in a business setting it often suggests authority as well, since the two are frequently related. Like other reports, the persuasive report has an introduction and text followed by a summary, conclusions, and recommendations. Its conclusions, however, do not present themselves merely as alternatives or solutions to a problem. Presented with conviction, they represent your best possible ideas for providing a much-needed solution. They may imply urgency—to the extent that the purpose of the report is to get action.

In creating the persuasive report, be certain of your purpose, the circumstances, and your position. It would be pointless to write a strong appeal if your audience is aware of the problem and has already initiated action to correct it—unless you think your solution needs to be given new consideration. Be certain, also, of all facts and information surrounding your report. And, especially with this kind of report, be certain that the language you use is positive, considerate, and appropriate.

One example of the persuasive report is usually written to seek authorization or funds for some project or course of action (See Figure 20–6).

INTEROFFICE CORRESPONDENCE

DATE: October 21, 19--

FROM: Bob Wallace

TO: Neal Macky

SUBJECT: COSTS OF TWO NEW PARKING ATTENDANTS

As you requested, I looked into the costs involved in hiring two additional parking attendants. These two attendants would be used to help relieve the congestion in Lots A and B during the rush parking hours.

Cost for Full-Time Employees

The cost (salaries, fringe benefits, training) for hiring a full-time parking attendant would be approximately $18,000 per year. Therefore, a budget of $36,000 per year would be needed to hire two additional employees for parking Lots A and B.

Cost for Part-Time Employees

An alternative to hiring full-time employees would be to hire two part-time workers to handle the parking problem. Part-time employees would be just as effective for the following reasons:

...ly during the rush traffic hours
... Parking attendants

Macky, Page 2, October 21, 19--

Recommendations

I recommend we hire two part-time employees for the present time to handle the parking congestion during the rush periods of the day. This plan would give us the most help when we need it, at the greatest economic savings; it should relieve the problem that now exists. We should also look into the possibility of expanding the parking facilities to handle the growing number of cars that are driven to work by the employees.

Figure 20-6
Persuasive Report

LETTER REPORT

The advantage of the **letter report**, which combines the features of the report and the letter, is that your presentation can be substantive, while your tone is personal and informal. Usually sent to someone outside the organization, the letter report follows the format of a business letter with the standard parts included: letterhead, date, inside address, salutation, closing, and signature. It usually includes a subject line that describes the contents of the report.

The body of the letter report, though, is presented as a report, using either the direct or indirect approach to present information. The first paragraph of the letter report serves as an intro-

miller engineering CONSULTING COMPANY
101 Lake Boulevard
Cleveland, OH 46080
(216)555-2022

July 18, 19--

Mr. Bruce H. Inman
Inman Law Assoc.
621 Forest Acres Building
Webster Lane
Cleveland, OH 44115

Dear Mr. Inman:

MR. VICTOR BROWN, File No. S221-78

On July 7, 19--, I tested the physical strength of Mr. Victor Brown. This report will give you the findings of these tests.

Strength Test

The tests suggest that there is a significant reduction from standard norms in the strength in Mr. Brown's extremities.

Following are Mr. Brown's force measurements:

	Right	Left
Arm pull	12 lbs. (max)	16 lbs. (max)
Arm lifting	12 lbs. (max)	8 lbs. (max)
Arm depression	12 lbs. (max)	16 lbs. (max)
Leg extension	28 lbs. (max)	50 lbs. (max)

Conclusions

I do not believe that Mr. Brown's present physical condition is such that he should or could work at his former job as an operator of a triaxle dump truck.

Sincerely,

Dennis Miller

Dennis Miller

Figure 20-7
Letter Report

duction and includes such parts as an authorization statement, the purpose, and the plan of presentation. It might also include a statement of the results. Headings may be used for the discussion portion of the report; an ending (summary, conclusions, and/or recommendations) concludes the presentation. The letter in Figure 20-7 is a letter report. The first paragraph serves as the introduction and includes the purpose of the report. After the findings (Strength Tests) are presented, the writer presents the conclusions. Note the use of headings throughout this short one-page report.

PRINT NAME & TITLE HERE—SIGN BELOW

LOCATION (TERRITORY-DISTRICT-REGION-DEPT.)

WEEK ENDING / /

EXPENSE ITEM	SUNDAY / /	MONDAY / /	TUESDAY / /	WEDNESDAY / /	THURSDAY / /	FRIDAY / /	SATURDAY / /	TOTALS DOLLARS CENTS
1 BREAKFAST								
2 LUNCH								
3 DINNER								
4 HOTEL								
5								
6 TAXI & LIMO.								
7 TIPS								
8 TEL. & TEL.								
9								
10 TRANSPORTATION								
11								
12 ENTERTAINMENT								
13								
14								
15								
TOTALS ▶								▶

TRANSPORTATION DETAIL (SUPPORTING ITEM 10)

TRAVEL FROM								ADVANCE
TRAVEL TO								
ENDING SPEEDOMETER READING								DUE COMPANY
BEGINNING SPEEDOMETER READING								
TOTAL MILEAGE								DUE EMPLOYEE
TRANSPORTATION TICKET NUMBER								

APPROVAL 1	APPROVAL 2	APPROVAL 3	APPROVAL 4	ACCOUNT NUMBER

EXPLAIN BY ITEM NUMBER ANY UNUSUAL EXPENSE THAT MAY BE QUESTIONED. (OTHER THAN ENTERTAINMENT EXPENSES)

PURPOSE OF TRIP:

DETAIL EXPLANATION OF ENTERTAINMENT EXPENSES (ITEMS 1, 2, 3, AND 12)

DATE	BREAKFAST LUNCH, DINNER, OTHER	ITEM NO.	NAME OF PERSON (S) ENTERTAINED - WHERE ENTERTAINED - NATURE & PURPOSE OF ENTERTAINMENT	AMOUNT

COMPANY CREDIT CARD & DIRECT CHARGES NOT INCLUDED IN TOTAL WKS. EXPENSES

DATE	ITEM #	AMOUNT

PERSONAL CREDIT CARD & DIRECT CHGS. INCLUDED IN TOT. WKS. EXPENSES

DATE	ITEM #	AMOUNT

ZO-21
REV-12-76

PRINTED BY THE STANDARD REGISTER COMPANY, U.S.A. ZIPSET®

X ____________________
SIGNATURE

WEEKLY EXPENSE REPORT

Figure 20-8
Printed Form Report

PREPRINTED FORM REPORT

The most routine of reports can be entered on a **preprinted form**. Other routine reports may be standardized according to a format that the organization provides. If the same type of information is reported at frequent intervals, most organizations devise a printed form. This form provides blank lines and spaces for each element to be considered. The person filling out the form adds the necessary figures, words, or sentences to the blanks.

The printed form report saves time because the writer does not have to repeat information that is constant for every report. Figure 20-8 is a common example of a printed form report.

STANDARDIZED REPORT

Reports that are written at regular intervals and that require standard information each time are called **standardized reports**. The standardized reports are sometimes called maintenance, progress, or periodic reports because they are frequently used to monitor and regulate.

The standardized format ensures that the periodic reports are uniform and complete. It also gives the receiver a convenient means for comparing data, because the same kinds of information are given each time and in approximately the same order. The headings themselves should be standard. The writer normally formats the report by using a blank sheet of paper and adding the appropriate headings while writing the report. Such a format eliminates the need for a printed form.

Because standardized reports usually are written to the same person about the same topic, the introduction and terminal section often are not necessary. Reports commonly standardized are the daily, weekly, or monthly sales reports; the annual corporate report; the monthly departmental report; and the weekly or monthly progress report.

CHAPTER SUMMARY

Reports are an integral part of all organizations. Formal reports usually concern matters of major substance. Informal reports are the most frequently used, and the memorandum report is the most popular kind of informal report. Both the memorandum and the letter reports add a personal tone. The standardized or preprinted form may be more efficient for routine information.

Informational, analytical, and persuasive memo reports require an introduction, text, and summary. The analytical reports additionally present alternatives and solutions. The persuasive reports provide conclusions and recommendations and sometimes a call to action. The circumstances, your position, and the responsibility assigned will determine if your report is to be strictly informational, analytical, or persuasive. But you should know from the beginning which type is expected of you. For example, an analytical report is on target only if you were asked to give recommendations. If you were asked to write a strictly informational report, you would be presumptuous in adding your opinions about how to solve the problem. All of these types of reports convey information and are commonly used in management to provide a basis for policymaking or simple transaction of work.

STUDY QUESTIONS

1. When would a memorandum report be used most effectively?
2. If printed reports are considered expensive, how can they also be defined as "money savers"?
3. Name two advantages of a memorandum report.
4. Name three formats available for the short report.
5. Why is the subject line so important in a memorandum report?
6. What are the advantages of standardized report forms?
7. What is the biggest difference between informational and analytical reports?
8. Which report normally includes recommendations?
9. Would you recommend headings for an informal report? Why or why not?

ACTIVITIES

1. Write an analytical memo report comparing two brands of cereal, commenting on at least three criteria. You may want to consider cost, availability, nutritional value, taste, size of container, versatility, advertising gimmicks, and prizes included with the cereal.
2. Write a persuasive report to the president of your school to convince him or her that classes should not be scheduled between noon and 2 p.m. on Wednesdays. This time could then be used for tutoring, relaxing, seminars, committee meetings, or whatever other good reasons you can invent.
3. You are a member of a student organization whose objective this year is to help the members of the group save money in buying school supplies. You are chairing the committee to survey the prices of school supplies in the area. After surveying three stores in the area, your committee is ready to report to the members of the organization. Write a report giving the findings.
   a. *Bracken Supply Store* gives a 10% discount to students with I.D. cards. The store is located about two miles from the school, but a bus runs from the school and stops almost directly in front of the store. The store has a large variety of items and a high quality of merchandise.
   b. *Nettles Book Store* is located right on campus. The store has high quality merchandise and a large variety. Nettles also readily exchanges items if a mistake is made in the purchase.
   c. *Deal Discounts* is located about four miles from the school, and no public transportation is available to the store. The store does not have the highest quality

merchandise, but a large variety of school supplies are available.

The prices of some common items at the stores are:

	Bracken	Nettles	Deal
1. Ream of typing paper	$11.00	$11.00	$ 9.00
2. 100 small white envelopes	1.15	1.02	.80
3. Pocket dictionary	2.80	2.65	2.50
4. Standard notebooks	1.79	1.65	.89

LANGUAGE SKILLS DEVELOPMENT

1. Choose the correct usage of numbers in the following sentences:
   a. The exhibit will be open through (April 30, April 30th).
   b. The artist is displaying (forty, 40) works.
   c. The museum is open every day from (4 to 9 p.m., 4:00 to 9:00 p.m.).
   d. Cleveland will be the (2nd, second) stop on the tour this year.
   e. Lynn spent (three years, 3 years) perfecting the recipe.
   f. The tickets can be ordered from the box office for ($12, twelve dollars).
   g. Tune in to Channel (eight, 8) for the latest news and weather.
   h. The price list contained the following new items: (4, four) shirts, (15, fifteen) pairs of slacks, and (11, eleven) sweaters.
   i. ($25, Twenty-five dollars) is too much to pay.
   j. They lost (three, 3) out of (fifteen, 15) games last season.
2. Choose the correct spelling of the words in parentheses:
   a. The (calendar, calender) sales improved the image of the company.
   b. Financial planners help you build long-term (capital, capitol).
   c. The plan that is prepared for you gives step-by-step (recommendations, recomendations).
   d. We have the professional expertise we need to (analyse, analyze) your company.
   e. The new car has all the great qualities that have helped it (develope, develop) a tradition of resale.
   f. More than 1.5 million (copys, copies) of the book are in print.
   g. We (receive, recieve) more mail on Mondays than on other days.

h. Truly new (ideas, ideals) are as risky as they are rare.
i. At least 30 states are considering a (similar, similiar) move.
j. The company plans to (aquire, acquire) at least three more subsidiaries.

IN-BASKET SIMULATIONS

1. Mr. Peter Waltere, Vice-President and General Manager, asked you, the Personnel Director, to design a standardized form report to be used by Waltere Supermarkets, Inc., for evaluating the performance of cashiers at the forty retail stores in Indiana. The forms will be used annually by supervisors in each of the stores. The results of the evaluations are to be used for such things as salary increases, promotions, and terminations. Each supervisor will discuss the results of the evaluation with the employees, and the results will then be placed on file in the corporate offices. Some of the items Mr. Waltere asked you to include on the evaluation form are:
   a. Customer relations
   b. Accuracy
   c. Facility on cash registers
   d. Knowledge of prices and products in store
   e. Promptness and absenteeism
   f. Personal appearance
2. The new Waltere Drug Store needs a printed form for employees to use for reporting travel expenses. Devise the printed form report. Consider the following items when developing the form:
   a. Include a line for the signature of the supervisor of the employee, as well as the employee's signature.
   b. Make the form easy to read, to fill out, to tabulate, and to analyze.
   c. Make sure the form is no longer than one page.
   d. Include a section for the purpose of the trip and the date of the trip.
3. As Mr. Raymond Waltere, President of Waltere Supermarkets, Inc., write a letter report to all the stockholders of the corporation. The purpose of the letter is to keep the stockholders informed of the operations of the corporation. Include in the report such items as the new drug store and short- and long-range plans for new stores.
4. Write a memo report from Joe Marion, Director of Drug Operations, to Thomas Leonard, President of Drug

Operations, giving him information on advertising methods and techniques. In the report you will answer such questions as:

a. How often should the store advertise?
b. Where should the advertising occur?
c. How much should be allocated for the advertising budget?

In compiling the information for this report you have consulted two advertising agencies, a local agency, and a national chain of advertisers.

5. Design a printed report form to be filled out by companies that want to establish credit with Waltere Supermarkets, Inc. The form will be called "Credit Questionnaire" and will need to include such things as credit references, amount of credit requested, bank account balances, and method of payment requested.
6. As Joe Marion, Director of Drug Operations, Waltere Supermarkets, Inc., write an analytical report to Mrs. Ruth Munson, Treasurer, giving the results of your survey of available copiers. Waltere needs a copier to reproduce a light load—approximately 200 copies a day. You have narrowed the choices to three possibilities:

a. the Grapo, Model 2142A
b. the Logan, Model 142R
c. the Representative, Model 11124-H

Each of the models is a middle-line copier, not designed for heavy duty copying. The Grapo and the Logan are very easy to operate and require minimum instructions for such things as replenishing the paper and making minor adjustments. The Representative, however, is a little more difficult to operate and the manufacturer recommends that only an experienced operator make adjustments on the machine. The Representative appears to be the sturdiest of the three machines, though, and should require a minimum amount of servicing. The space requirements for each of the copiers are:

a. Grapo, 25 in. wide and 50 in. long
b. Logan, 25 in. wide and 46 in. long
c. Representative, 28 in. wide and 53 in. long

The cost of the Grapo is $1775, the Logan is $1925, and the Representative sells for $2500. The service contracts for the three copiers are about the same. In rating the quality of the copiers, the Representative would be rated the highest, with the Grapo the next highest, and the Logan would be rated the lowest for the quality of copies.

7. Write a persuasive report from Mr. David Summer, Director of Sales, to Mr. Raymond Waltere, President, to convince him to consider stocking the store's own brand of merchandise. Use any reasons that might help to persuade Mr. Waltere. Some suggested reasons are:
   a. Several other grocery chains in Indiana carry their store labels on their merchandise.
   b. The store brand merchandise could be offered at a cost reduction to the customers of Waltere.
   c. A larger profit for the store could be made by selling its own brand name.

21 Long (Formal) Reports—Planning

After studying Chapter 21, you should be able to:

- Determine the need for and write a work plan
- Prepare both a solicited and unsolicited proposal
- Prepare a literature review
- Establish the relationship among outlines, headings, and table of contents
- Prepare both a topic and a sentence outline
- Compile a working bibliography
- Determine whether sources are appropriate

Long reports need additional features to help the reader comprehend the information. How many of these features you add depends upon the complexity and length of the report. The term "formal" implies that supplemental parts are included with the content of the report. A two-page report would not need many, if any, supplemental parts to make the material more quickly and easily readable. But in longer reports, the additional parts guide the reader through the content.

Most formal reports have at least a title page, a table of contents, and a bibliography, in addition to the other parts appropriate to the particular subject. Chapter 23 describes the supplemental parts of a report and where and when they should be used. (See the abbreviated version of a formal report in Appendix I.)

Once you know the purpose of the report and the type of report to write, you must determine how much and what kind of data to include. Good planning is essential to good report writing. First, devise a plan for collecting data. Then, construct an outline for the presentation of the data you have collected. These two plans not only help you see the problem clearly, but they also enable you to relate your findings concisely and clearly in a logical sequence.

WORK PLANS

Reports usually result from a request by management: a problem exists, and you—as report writer—are assigned to assess and report on the problem. Thus, management defines the problem. Many times assignments are given orally, and it then becomes incumbent on you to clarify the purpose of the report. If you cannot state the problem in a precise and brief sentence, you do not have a clear definition. Consequently, you must go back to the originator to determine the exact problem. By submitting a **work plan** that initially states the problem and how you plan to approach the problem, you are documenting the plan and giving the originator an opportunity to approve it as well. The work plan provides the opportunity to receive feedback on the plan before you spend a lot of time and find that the plan is ineffective.

Whatever the problem, you should approach it first with a plan for collecting data. The work plan is a preliminary statement, a check point, of what you plan to do to observe or assess the problem. For complex problems, a work plan saves time and money, as well as prevents misunderstandings. Submitted to the person who assigned the report, your plan tells that person specifically what you are going to do and how you are going to do it. It may be changed, of course, several times during the research process.

A comprehensive work plan might include:

1. Statement of the problem and purpose (what you plan to do)
2. Methods of procedures (how you plan to do it)
3. Tentative plan of presentation (what major topics will be covered)
4. Scope and limitations (what topics will be included; what topics will be excluded)
5. Bibliography (what tentative sources will be used)
6. Time table (when you plan to finish each section)
7. Budget (if the project requires funding, what expenditures should be explained)

The main idea of the work plan is to confirm for the person who authorized the report how you defined the problem and how you will approach the report, to make sure there is no misunderstanding. A work plan is especially beneficial if you are working with other people on a project. It sets priorities, dates, and budget restrictions, and everyone has a written record of the project and how it should proceed.

PROPOSALS

A problem may also be defined and initiated by the report writer. If you have an idea to improve operations, if you want to make a change, or if you want to carry out research, you will usually need to get approval to do these kinds of things if they involve a lot of time, labor, and/or money. To get approval and funds, a **proposal** is usually written.

Proposals can go up, down, or outside an organization. They are used to ask for external funds for a project, especially if you work for a nonprofit organization, and are also written to submit recommendations and bids on an external project. Depending on the source of the problem, there are two major kinds of proposals:

1. *Solicited proposals* (responding to a request). In this type of proposal, you do not spend a lot of time talking about the problem because the customer already knows about it. Most of the proposal is spent selling the solution to the problem.
2. *Unsolicited proposals* (initiated by the writer). In this type of proposal, you spend more time on the problem trying to convince the reader that something needs to be done.

Assume, for example, you work for a telecommunications consulting company. A local firm is planning to revise its telecommunications system and asks consulting firms to submit proposals on how they would change the system and how much they would charge to make these changes. Solicited proposals are written to answer this Request for Proposal (RFP).

Almost all proposals have the same format (the parts are similar to those included in a work plan), which can be divided into four principal sections:

1. *Problem identification.* In this section you convince the reader that the problem is important and that you understand it. A literature search may be a part of this section.
2. *Method of attack.* In this section you explain how you plan to solve the problem. This is usually the part that is most carefully read.
3. *Justification.* In this section you convince the reader that you should be the one to solve the problem and why it should be done now.
4. *Cost/time factors.* In this section you itemize the costs (facilities, equipment, and personnel) and give a time schedule when each part will be completed.

The format you follow in putting the proposal together depends on how long it is and who the audience is. It could be a memorandum, a letter, or a formal report with supplementary parts. Some guidelines to follow in writing the proposal so it will be more likely to be approved include:

1. Follow published guidelines exactly (number of pages, number of copies submitted, sequence of content, time frame, appropriate signatures).
2. Use headings and good visuals to guide the reader through the text. Make sure the content flows logically from section to section. If the proposal is long, provide an abstract.
3. Package it attractively. Make sure the typing and proofreading are flawless. Provide appendixes for supplementary material.
4. Use the language of the reader. Make sure the language is clear and the tone is objective.

PRELIMINARY RESEARCH

A **preliminary research** of the literature helps to determine what other people have discovered about your problem and may save you from investigating a problem that has already been solved. Duplication of research is costly and unnecessary; you may uncover, instead, other areas of needed research. You may find that what others have done in similar situations can help you solve your particular problem, while you obtain a general overview of the entire problem. The library should be the first place to start in gathering data; reference librarians usually know where to find particular information.

The **literature review**, or survey of materials already written about your problem, might include books, periodicals, computer searches, and theses, dissertations, and abstracts. The preliminary research should tell you if the problem has already been solved in a method that can be helpful to you or if you must continue your own research.

The literature review is often included as a part of a formal report. It shows the need for your study, gives background for your study, and shows how your study fits in with related research and findings. This section demonstrates your scholarship because it shows the extent to which you build on the research of others.

The literature review should include not only the most recent literature content and methodology, but it should also refer to classic studies in the area. How much you include or what research you include depends on the purpose of the report and how it will be used. Discuss other studies in sufficient detail to aid the nonspecialist to understand them. Indicate how your study moves beyond the others or will improve the company.

REPORT OUTLINE

Your next step is to determine what areas to investigate to sufficiently explore the problem. If you can, break the problem into subquestions: Who? What? When? Where? and How? An outline divides the report into its main parts, showing the relationship of each. Organization is the key to writing a successful report because it anticipates and answers the reader's questions. By dividing the topic into approximately equal, logical subdivisions, you can see and emphasize the most important points.

Outlining saves writing time. It points out, early in the process, areas that may be over- or underdeveloped. Submitting an outline also allows for feedback from others about the soundness and completeness of the plan. Think of outlining as an arrangement of your ideas.

1. *Write down all the major areas you plan to cover.* Then ask yourself: Have I listed all necessary topics? Are there irrelevant items I should omit? Revise the outline to incorporate additions or deletions.
2. *Further define each of the major topics by listing subtopics.* What are the items within each topic that require discussion? Are there "major" areas listed that would be more appropriate as a subtopic under a different heading? Rearrange, add, or delete ideas as you review your list.

I. Definition of Reports
II. Creation of Good Public Relations
  A. Employees
  B. Customers
III. Format of Reports
  A. Informal Reports
    1. Memo Report
    2. Letter Report
    3. Printed Form Report
    4. Standardized Report
      a. Monthly
      b. Quarterly
      c. Annual
  B. Formal Reports
  C. Oral Reports

Figure 21-1
Correct Format for the Use of Numbers and Letters in an Outline

3. *Put the topics in the order in which you plan to discuss them.* Give the most important ideas prominence in headings.
4. As the analysis evolves, *revise the outline as needed.*

The major listings in the final outline usually become the headings in the report and the headings become the Table of Contents in the finished report. A good outline should make sense on the basis of its major headings alone. The following mechanical procedures are standard in outlining:

1. *A numerical or alphabetical designation may or may not have a division under it,* but when divisions are shown, at least two or more must be listed. If you use an A, you must additionally use a B. If you have a number 1, you should also have a number 2.
2. *Parallel grammatical structure should be used within each division.*
3. *Divisions are designated by standard symbols*: Roman numerals for the major topics; capital letters for the first-degree subheadings; Arabic numbers for third-degree subheadings; and small letters are used to define the fourth-degree subheading. Figure 21-1 illustrates the correct format for an outline.

Start with a general outline, then develop a specific outline. Outlines can be in two formats: topic outline and sentence outline. The **topic outline** (Figure 21-2) is the fastest and probably the first outline you will put together for your report. It consists

I. Training
  A. Why
  B. How
  C. Where
II. Incentives

Figure 21-2
Topic Outline

I. Training in the company first started in 1960.
  A. Why did the company start in-house training?
  B. How is the training accomplished?
  C. Where is the training performed?
II. The incentives have improved 100 percent since 1975.

Figure 21-3
Sentence Outline

of single words, groups of words, or phrases and serves as a guide for organizing data.

Once you have developed the topic outline, you may define it further as a **sentence outline** (Figure 21-3). More complete than a topic outline, the sentence outline takes longer to develop, but it forces you to say something specific about each topic. The sentences often become the first sentence in each of the sections.

WORKING BIBLIOGRAPHY

A **working bibliography** is a tentative listing of the sources you plan to use in your report. Select about twice as many sources as you think you will use. Many of the references that appear pertinent will duplicate other sources and not provide new information when you read through them.

When searching for references, first check the Table of Contents to see if the reference applies to your subject. If you cannot tell from the Table of Contents, quickly glance over the contents of the book paying attention to headings and the first sentence in each paragraph. Do not, however, attempt to read every word during your initial review.

Compiling a working bibliography requires not only a knowledge of available library resources but also a system to record these sources of information and the ability to evaluate the sources once they are found. In evaluating references, consider:

1. Whether the source is firsthand or secondhand information
2. The objectivity of the author of the source
3. The author's qualifications (reputation, education, experience)
4. The date of publication

355.1
N33N

Nelson, William J. Finance for You. Chicago: Cairn Publishing Co., 1978. 332 pp.

Figure 21-4
Completed Bibliography Card

Most people use cards of a uniform and convenient size in compiling the working bibliography. List only one reference to each card, which should contain the author, title of publication, publishing information, page numbers, and library catalog number (Figure 21-4). Recording the library call number helps in locating the reference rapidly. The working bibliography cards can later be used in compiling your bibliography. Fill out the cards completely so you do not have to waste time later going back to get a page number or a date of publication.

CHAPTER SUMMARY

Before writing the report, complete the initial planning steps. Submit a statement that clearly defines what you plan to do and how you plan to accomplish your objective. Then both you and the person who authorized the report will know exactly what is being done. Some organizations require a work plan before a substantial amount of time and effort are committed to solving a problem.

Solicited proposals respond to a request. If you were to write this type of proposal, you would emphasize the solution rather than the problem. However, if you initiate a study, you may need to write an unsolicited proposal to obtain permission to complete the study and spend more time talking about the problem. The proposal contains many of the same parts as the work plan.

A literature review is an initial planning step that can save a great deal of time and effort. This survey will tell you what has already been done in your particular research area.

You can then outline the topic so you have a clear idea of how to proceed in your notetaking. Initially, the outline can be either a topic or a sentence outline.

A final planning step is to compile a working bibliography of possible references to use in solving your problem and writing the final report.

STUDY QUESTIONS

1. How would a work plan be used in an organization?
2. What parts are usually found in a work plan?
3. What is the difference between how you would write a solicited proposal and an unsolicited proposal?
4. Describe three parts that may be included in a proposal.
5. What is the purpose of surveying the literature before you begin your problem?
6. Describe the steps you would follow in your preliminary literature survey.
7. How do outlines, headings, and tables of contents differ?
8. What is the difference between the topic and the sentence outline?
9. What is the difference between a working bibliography and the bibliography used in a report?
10. Name three ways to evaluate whether a source would be appropriate for a report.

ACTIVITIES

1. Consult the periodical indexes and abstracts in your library and develop a list of five available sources for one of the following topics:
   a. Famous marketing errors
   b. Recent management theories
   c. Trends in corporate annual reports
   d. Electronic communications
2. Develop a work plan for the following situation:

   You are the president of the student government in your school. The president of the school reports that next year the school is considering changing from the quarter to the semester system. The president authorized you to study student opinions and reactions to the proposed changes and report back to him by the end of the quarter.

3. List three subjects you think would make good research topics. Do a working bibliography for one of them.
4. From the list of topics in Activity 3, choose one of these topics and make a topic outline of how you would approach the problem.
5. Expand the topic outline from Activity 4 into a sentence outline.
6. Some of the following parts of outlines have one or more errors. Correct the errors.
   a. I. Difference in Lasers
         A. Materials
         B. Construction
      II. The cost of lasers is not significant.

b. I. Submarine Warfare
   A. Lusitania is sunk
   B. Other ships with Americans involved
      1. Falaba
      2. Cushing
   C. French steamer Sussez is sunk.

c. III. Atomic Bomb
   A. Cost of the bomb
      1. $2,000,000,000
   B. Use of the bomb

d. II. Substandard Housing
   (A) Definition of Substandard Housing
   (B) Problems of Substandard Housing

e. I. Introduction
   A) Leo—the lion
      1. Explain sign
   B) How to recognize a Leo

LANGUAGE SKILLS DEVELOPMENT

1. Choose the correct word in the following sentences:
   a. Everyone in the group received (complimentary, complementary) tickets.
   b. Twelve people is too large (a number, an amount) of people to invite.
   c. Everybody in the family except (myself, me) went to bed early last night.
   d. The elevator was (all ready, already) full by the time it left the first floor.
   e. Ms. Jenkins types all my (personal, personnel) correspondence for me at home.
   f. The announcement of a four-day weekend boosted the employee (moral, morale).
   g. We have narrowed the location to three (sites, cites, sights).
2. For the following words, form their plurals and their plural possessives:
   a. Lady
   b. Business
   c. Child
   d. Company
   e. Sister-in-law
   f. Mary
   g. Fox
   h. Salesman
   i. Student
   j. Family

IN-BASKET SIMULATIONS

1. Mr. Peter Waltere, Vice-President and General Manager of Waltere Supermarkets, Inc., authorized you to write a report on one of the following topics:
   a. Authority and control of the Zone Manager (a manager over several stores in a particular geographical area)
   b. Procedures in policing other supermarkets
   c. Training new employees
   d. Electronic funds transfer systems
   e. Allocation of shelf space
   f. Feasibility of opening a new store in a particular location

   Write a statement of the problem; list some possible sources of information; compile a tentative outline of the topic.
2. Develop a work plan for one of the following areas:
   a. Feasibility of adding gasoline pumps at Mini Marts
   b. Feasibility of adding health food counters at supermarkets
   c. Feasibility of adding snack bars at supermarkets
3. Compile a working bibliography of at least five sources for one of the following topics:
   a. Growth of retail clerks union
   b. Inventory control methods
   c. Safety laws affecting retail establishments
4. Write a persuasive report to Mr. Waltere to convince him to add video screens in each of the Mini Marts to help combat shoplifting. After checking the costs of the video system, you find the screens would pay for themselves after three years if the shoplifting rate is reduced by only 20 percent in each of the Mini Marts.

22

Visual Aids

After studying Chapter 22, you should be able to:
- Use visual aids in a report
- Construct visual aids
- Recognize the value of computer graphics

Visual aids play an important part in data presentation and should be selected and developed carefully. "A picture is worth a thousand words" is frequently applied to the use of visual aids in reports. Visuals should be used any time your material can be conveyed more clearly in a table, graph, or other aid than with words. A visual aid can supplement a paragraph of text, but it is not a substitute for words; it should not be expected to do the job by itself. It should be used to enhance a point, to illustrate an explanation, to help the reader get an overview, or to compare facts and figures. Visual aids add clarity and can keep a report from becoming cluttered with statistics and lengthy descriptions.

Visual aids are available for a variety of purposes such as showing relationships, giving precise figures, or depicting models and charts. Your choice of one depends on your plan or purpose.

The appearance of a visual aid should appeal to the reader. It should tell the whole story, but it should not appear crowded or complex. The visual aid should be attractively presented with adequate white space surrounding it, and all the variables should be labeled clearly.

Visual aids are usually classified as tables and figures. If it is not a table, it is a figure. Figures include graphs, diagrams, and pictograms. Both tables and figures may be numbered with Arabic numerals, or a separate numbering system may be used for tables and figures (Roman numerals and Arabic numerals). Tables and figures are numbered separately. A report may include Table 1, 2, and 3 and Figures 1, 2, 3, and 4. The visuals may be numbered consecutively throughout the report; however, if the report is long enough to be divided into chapters, the visuals may be numbered sequentially by chapter. If the visuals are numbered by chapter, the first number refers to the chapter number and the second number refers to the visual number. Chapter 1 may include Figures 1.1, 1.2, and 1.3; Chapter 2 may include Figures 2.1, 2.2, 2.3, and 2.4.

Some other guidelines for including visual aids in a report follow:

1. *Introduce it before you show it.* A reader can get frustrated when encountering a visual aid before an explanation is included. The introduction is usually a sentence that refers the reader to the visual aid, gives its location, and refers to it by name or title. A sentence to introduce a table might read: *Students take more business courses than any other courses, as shown in Table 3.1 on Page 41.*
2. *Present a visual aid as soon as possible after its introduction.* If it is short enough to be included on a page with text, present

	Yes	No
At age 65, as is currently the law	52%	48%
At age 60	33%	67%
At age 68	08%	92%
Other age	07%	93%
(Number of respondents)	(1,006)	

Source: The Hearst Corporation, 959 Eighth Avenue, New York, N.Y. 10019.

Table 22-1
Should Retired Americans Be Eligible for Full Social Security Payments?

it immediately after the text. If it is long enough to be presented on a separate page, present it on the next page after its introduction. If, for example, you give the introduction to Table 1.3 on Page 12, then show the long table on Page 13.

3. *Avoid catchy or cute titles that are not descriptive of the content in the visual aid.* The title should accurately and succinctly summarize the content of a visual aid. The visual aid should make sense if it were removed from the content surrounding it. The title and number of a visual aid may be centered over the visual aid, located at the top left margin, or placed at the bottom of the visual aid.
4. *Do not discuss everything included in the visual aid.* Refer to a highlight, a high figure, a low figure, or an average; then refer the reader to the visual aid for the remainder of the information.
5. *If possible, design visual aids so they can be viewed upright rather than sideways.* The reader should not have to turn the page sideways.
6. *Indicate the source for the aid directly beneath the visual aid.* The word "source" precedes the footnote notation (See Table 22-1).
7. *Place a visual aid in the appendix if it is not an integral part of the text, if it is especially long, or if it is referred to in several places in the report.* If a visual aid is long and referred to in several places in the text, you might consider dividing it into several smaller visual aids and presenting them in the appropriate places in the text, rather than in one place. Tell the reader when a visual is found in the appendix and where it is located:

   A list of participating companies and their gross sales are found in Appendix B, page 58.

GROSS SALES IN MILLIONS OF DOLLARS
1984-1985

Month	1984	1985
January	3.7	4.5
February	3.6	4.5
March	3.9	4.6
April	4.0	4.2
May	4.2	4.3
June	3.4	4.1
July	3.7	4.2
August	3.7	4.5
September	3.4	4.3
October	3.5	4.3
November	3.5	4.4
December	3.6	4.4

Figure 22-1
Formal Table

Plane	Type
Cessna	172
Cessna	182
Piper	Cherokee
Piper	Dakota

Figure 22-2
Informal Table

TABLES

If you need to depict precise or exact facts and figures, use a table. A **table** arranges information in tabulated rows and columns (See Figure 22-1). Keep tables as simple and uncluttered as possible to present accurate, precise, and complete data in easy-to-read form. This enables the reader to grasp material readily and easily.

The columns in tables should be clearly identified with headings and subheadings if they are needed. In Figure 22-1 the column headings are *Month*, *1984*, and *1985*. In the same table, the column heading might be *Sales in millions* and the subheadings might be the years:

Sales in millions				
1982	**1983**	**1984**	**1985**	**1986**

Tables may be formal or informal. **Informal tables** are usually short and simple; they are an integral part of the content that precedes them. Informal tables (see Figure 22-2) do not have numbers or titles. They have no framing or vertical or horizontal lines. They are not included in a Table of Tables (a prefatory part after the Table of Contents that identifies the tables found in the report). A section of text and an informal table follow:

Over 50 percent of the students are enrolled in accounting courses. The percentages of students enrolled in business courses are:

Course	**Percentage**
Accounting	53
Finance	32
Marketing	10
Management	05

Formal tables are more complex than informal tables. They are usually numbered and titled. Whether they are included on a page with text depends on their size and their importance. A short table that takes up less than half a page may be included on a page with text, if there is enough room. The visual aid should be separated from the text with sufficient white space. It should not appear crowded. In fact, any visual aid that takes up a half page or more should be included on a page by itself.

Tables should be able to stand alone; that is, if they are removed from the content of the report, they are clear to the reader. They should have a title that clearly identifies the content. "Income" as the title of a table is not specific enough to give the reader an overview of the table. Does *income* refer to *gross income* or *net sales*? For what years does *income* refer?

A few rules for constructing tables follow:

1. Identify every row and column.
2. Align decimal points in the columns:

    1.041
    0.03
    10.11

3. Use *n.a.* (not applicable) or hyphens if information is not available. The use of zeros in the columns may confuse the reader.
4. Present tables as attractively as possible with lots of white space around them. Make sure you do not extend the table beyond the margins of the text.
5. Arrange data in a logical order (that is, descending order, ascending order, or alphabetical order) so they are readable and clear.

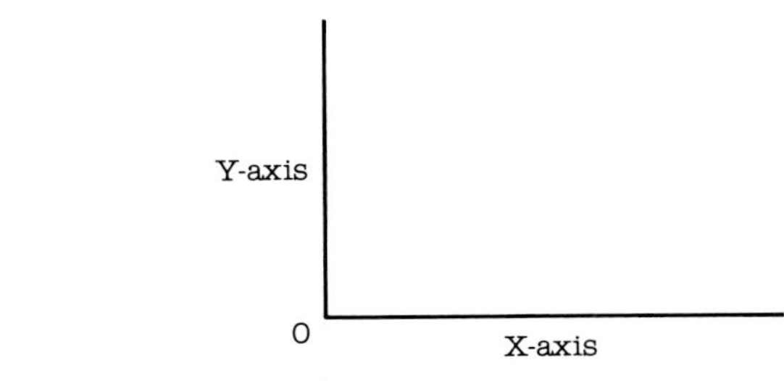

Figure 22-3
X- and Y-Axes for Line Graphs

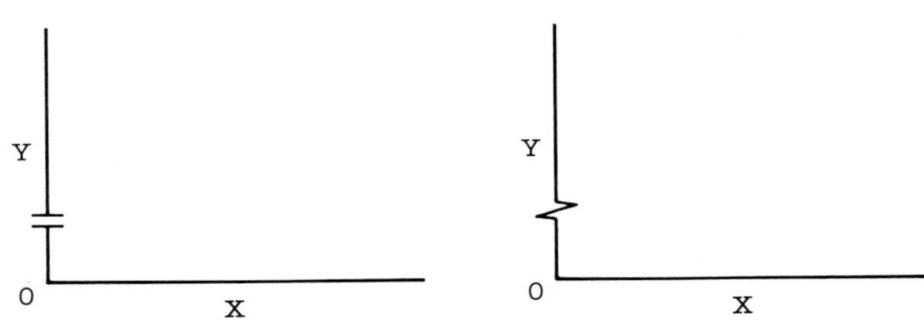

Figure 22-4
Examples of Broken Y-Axes

FIGURES

Figures include all visual aids except tables. Figures usually do not give exact values, but they are more pictorial. They show such things as relationships and trends.

Graphs

Graphs are used to give a general picture quickly and vividly. The kind of graph you choose depends upon what you intend to show. The main types of graphs are line, bar (horizontal and vertical), and pie (circle).

Line graphs. **Line graphs** are effective when you need to show changes over time or when you want to show trends or relationships. Line graphs have two axes: Y-axis (vertical) and X-axis (horizontal), as shown in Figure 22-3. The Y-axis should start at zero on the scale, but the Y-axis can be broken to show that parts have been omitted, as shown in Figure 22-4. All the vertical and horizontal gradations should be equal (equal spaces for equal amounts) so the data are not misrepresented. Both the Y- and X-axes should be labeled. Multiple lines may be used to distinguish variables.

In the line graph shown in Figure 22-5, the total number of marriages is shown for several years. The same graph may be used to show the total number of marriages for those people under 30 and those over 30 years of age (Figure 22-6) by distinguishing between the different lines. The lines could be presented in different ways or colors. A legend should identify each line.

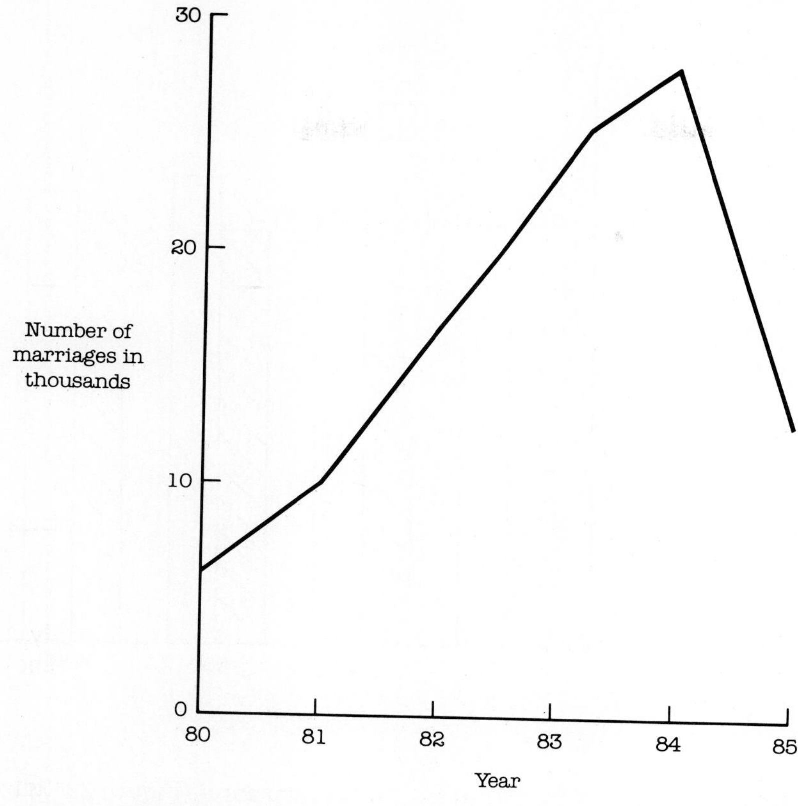

Figure 22-5
Line Graph

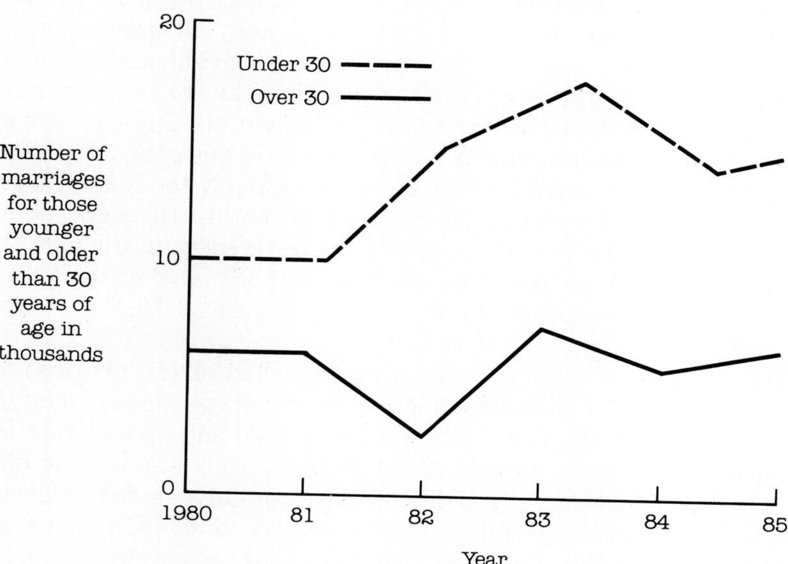

Figure 22-6
Line Graph

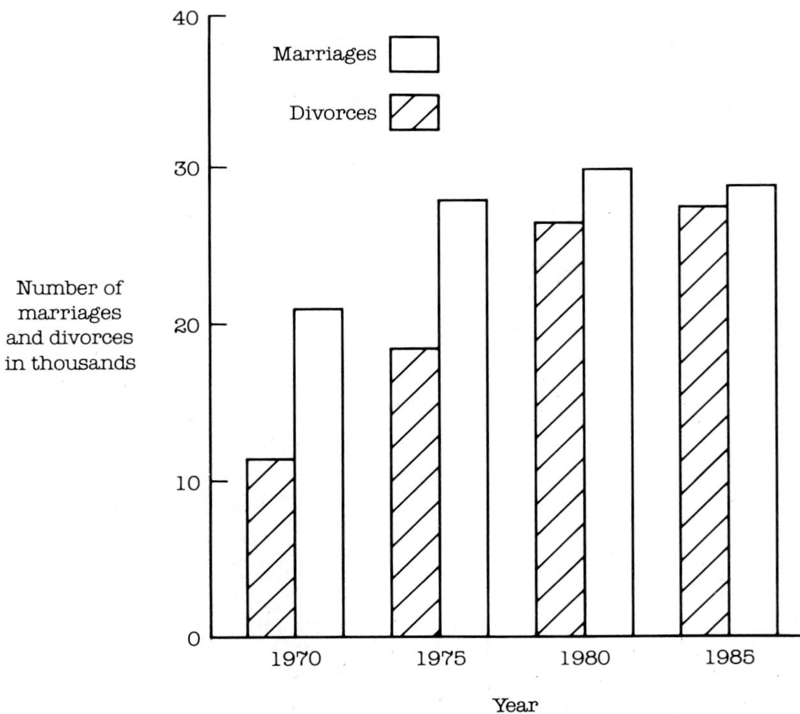

Figure 22-7
Vertical Bar Graph

Bar charts. **Bar charts** can be horizontal (Figure 22-7) or vertical (Figure 22-8). Horizontal and vertical graphs are primarily used for comparisons; they usually focus on quantity and changes in quantity. It is important to keep all bars equal to avoid distortion of data. The width between bars should be equal, too. Figure 22-9 shows the distortion that can occur if the bars are not equal. Multiple bar charts, as shown in Figure 22-7, can be used to compare two or more quantities in one chart. The bars can be distinguished from each other through the use of color shading and cross-hatching. Somewhere within the figure, you should include a legend to explain the differences in the bars. If you want to show exact figures, they may be placed at the top of each bar or within the bars, as shown in Figure 22-10.

Pie charts. Use **pie charts** (also called **circle graphs**) to depict parts of a whole (see Figure 22-11). Show the pie chart in percentages or fractions. These parts should add up to 100%. To label the pie chart, include descriptions for each segment within the circle if possible. If you do not have room to include the labels within the circle, use guide lines or arrows to identify each segment. Also include the percentage figures for each segment.

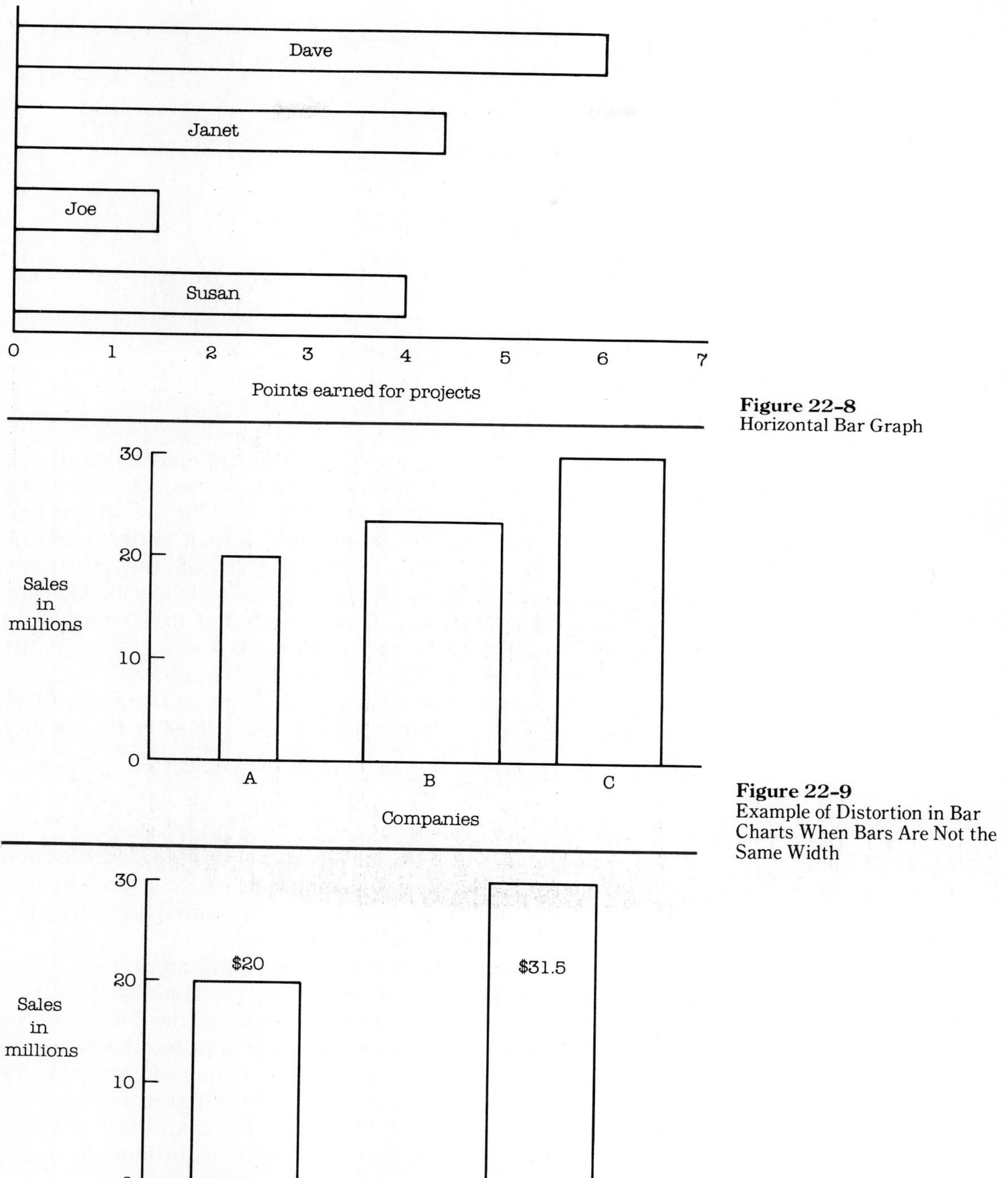

Figure 22-8
Horizontal Bar Graph

Figure 22-9
Example of Distortion in Bar Charts When Bars Are Not the Same Width

Figure 22-10
Examples of Label Positions on Bar Charts

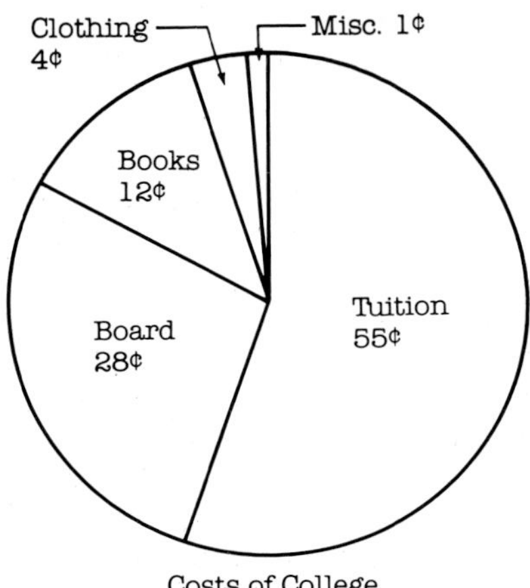

Figure 22-11
Pie Chart

To construct a pie chart, make the first radial line at the 12 o'clock position and continue in a clockwise motion (toward the right), as shown in Figure 22-12. Start with the largest segment and move clockwise in descending order. The first segment might be 54%; the second, 33%; the third, 10%; and the fourth, 3%. The last segment, regardless of its size is usually labeled *Other* or *Miscellaneous* and includes all the parts that are too small to include in a wedge by themselves. Include a description of the items covered in *Other* or *Miscellaneous* for the reader.

Include at least three segments but no more than seven segments in a pie chart. If necessary, combine some of the smaller segments.

Pictograms

A **pictogram** is a pictorial representation of data, a dressed-up bar graph. It is attention getting and is, therefore, especially useful when the report will be read by a lay or general audience. (See Figure 22-13).

Use pictures and symbols that are easily recognized. Show the quantities by the number of units rather than by the difference in sizes. This helps prevent distortions of the data and does not mislead the reader. If you wanted to use pictorial representatives of planes to show the monthly production of airplanes, the figures might look like Figure 22-14. This figure is distorted, though, because the 1985 figure looks more than three times as big as the 1984 figure, not because of the height but because of the volume in the figure. If you use figures that are equal in size, the reader gets a more accurate impression of the facts. The plane figures would look like those in Figure 22-15.

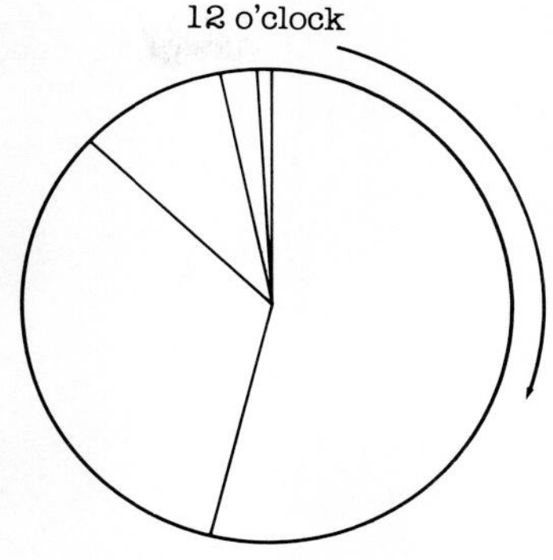

Figure 22-12
First Step in Constructing a Pie Chart

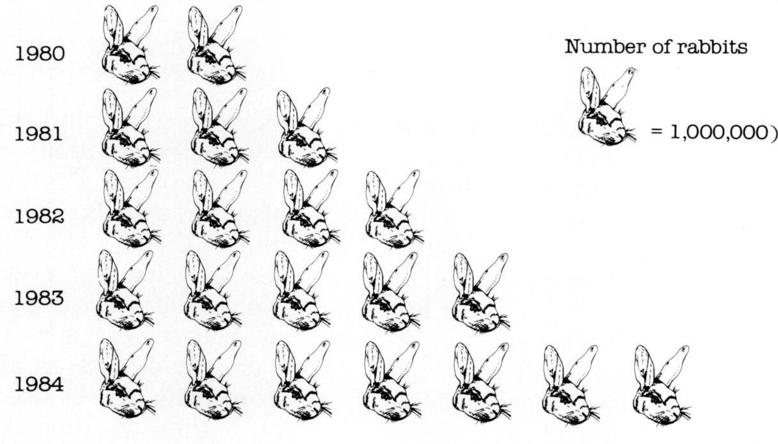

Figure 22-13
Pictogram

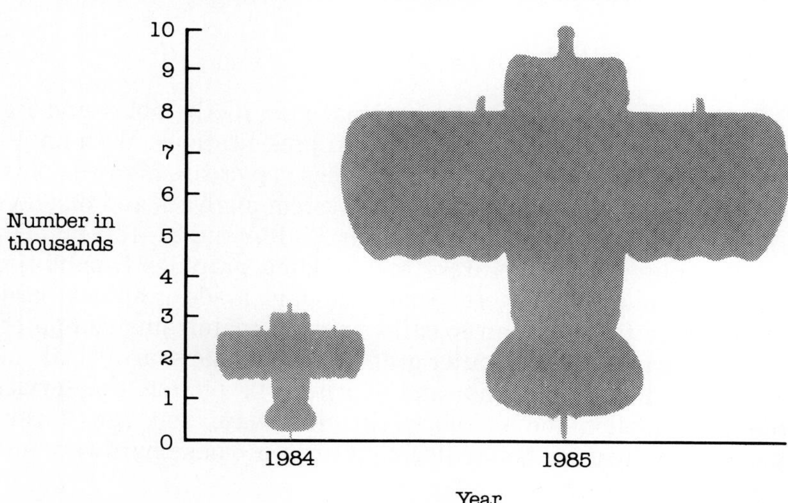

Figure 22-14
Example of Distortion in Pictogram Where Total Area is Not Considered

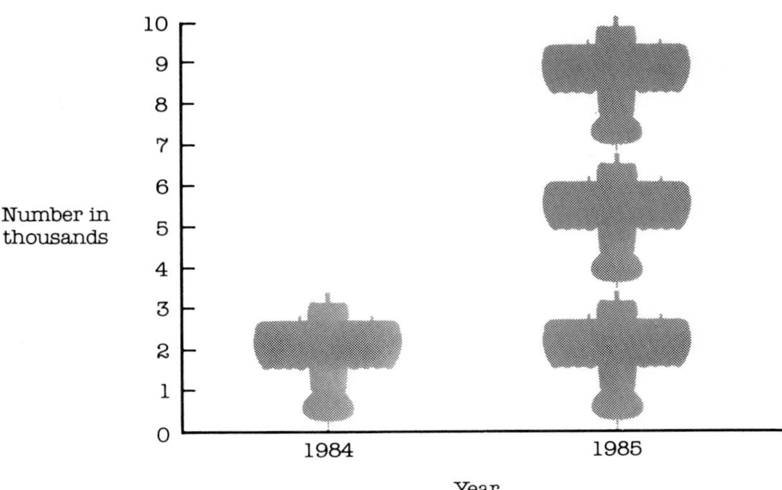

Figure 22-15
Distortion Removed from Pictogram in Figure 22-14

Other Figures

Many other types of visual aids can be used effectively in business reports. Many are used to show geographical locations or spatial relationships. A **diagram** is used for explaining rather than reproducing photographically. A diagram usually shows only a part of the whole picture. For example, if you wanted to show various sections of the library, you could photograph every section and try to fit them together, or you could draw a floor plan that shows the various sections and their relationships to each other. A **model** (See Figure 22-16) usually depicts an abstract set of ideas. For visual appeal, **photographs** may be used. **Organizational charts** (See Figure 22-17) show positions of formal authority in an organization and the relationships of each position.

COMPUTER GRAPHICS

The computer can help create visual aids (both tables and figures) to use in written reports or oral presentations. With only a few commands, many computer systems can create highly sophisticated, multicolored graphics. The system analyzes and displays the data within seconds. (See Figures 22-18A and 22-18B.)

Computer manufacturers are building graphics capabilities into their microcomputers. Some companies add graphics hardware and software to an existing mini or mainframe computer. Another way to use computer graphics is by time sharing. All you need is a display terminal and a printer or plotter; the service bureau supplies the software. In this way, you can experiment with graphics before deciding upon in-house hardware and software.

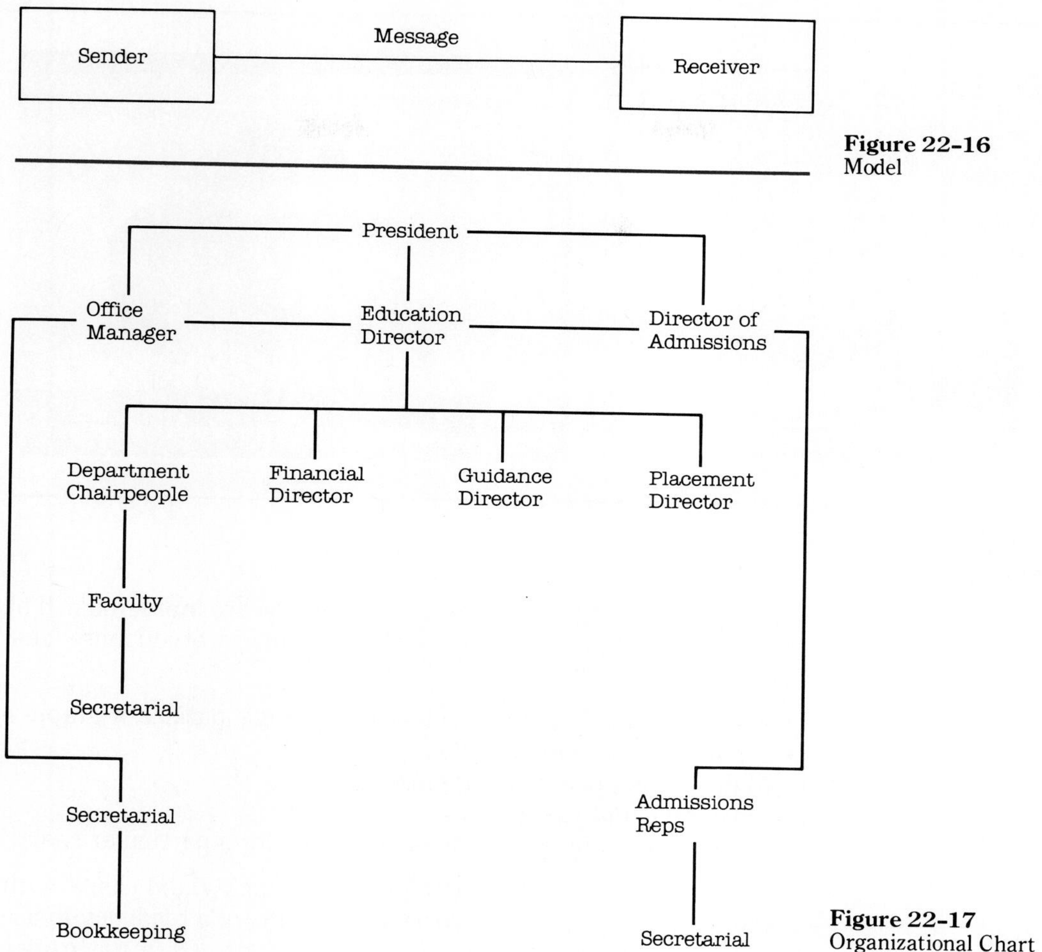

Figure 22-16
Model

Figure 22-17
Organizational Chart

Graphics systems range from the simple to the elaborate. Software packages are available for use with various computers and are distributed by all the major companies. Most of these packages are not interchangeable with different computers. Nevertheless, all of them operate similarly; that is, they offer menu selection options for such items as capitals, spacing, color, lines, bars, and size. Format choices include a wide range of choices from conics (such as arcs, circles, and ellipses) to shaded or patterned areas of any shape. The most common use of computer graphics programs are for bar or column charts, pie charts, scatter diagrams, curves, layouts, organizational charts, and flowcharts. The choice should be based on the kinds of information to be displayed and the relationships to be analyzed.

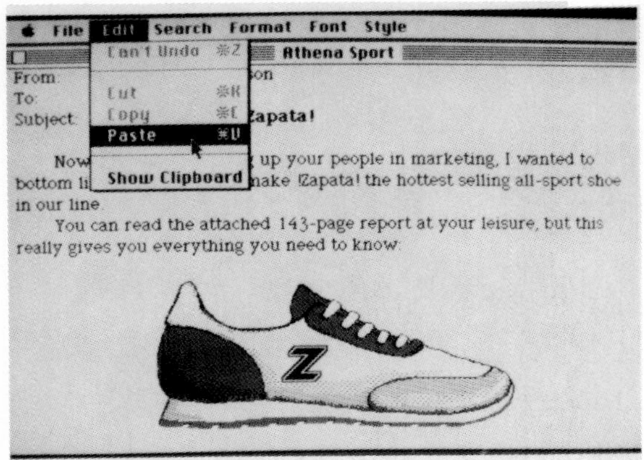

Figure 22-18A & B
Examples of Computer Graphics
Courtesy of Apple Computer, Inc.

The advantages of computer graphics are numerous. The biggest advantage is that you can save time in producing visual aids. In addition, you can:

- Reduce unwieldy amounts of data to a single picture or graph
- Interpret data more quickly
- Make professional-looking presentations
- Make revisions easily
- Experiment to determine the best design for a particular chart

Because visual aids can be produced quickly and easily with computer graphics, some experts are warning of a tendency to use graphics at the expense of content (referred to as **chart junk**). Graphics do not fit every application. You need to make sure that you do not substitute a picture for hard thinking. Another cautionary note has to do with the colors available. Color graphics make visuals more attractive; they make the relationships easier to see; and they have a greater impact on the reader. The problem is that too many colors can be distracting. (Some systems offer as many as 256 choices of colors.) Most experts advise a maximum of four to five colors in one chart so the reader is not overwhelmed with the number of colors.

Computer graphics provide a flexible and sometimes cost effective means for creating, manipulating, storing, and retrieving pictorial information. Even though the computer creates the visual aids, you, in addition to selecting which one to use, need to be aware of the mechanical details necessary for presenting the visuals in reports.

CHAPTER SUMMARY

Visual aids refer to tables and figures included in a report to simplify and to clarify text. They are not substitutes for words, but they should be used to complement the text.

Choosing and developing the appropriate visual aids are integral parts of the report-writing process. Since several types of visual aids are available, you should be able to choose one that is appropriate for the type of data you are presenting.

A table consists of rows and columns of data arranged systematically. Figures refer to all other types of visual aids, such as graphs, pictograms, photographs, diagrams, and charts.

Computer graphics, both figures and tables produced by a computer, can aid in developing sophisticated, multicolored charts. Computers can save time and labor in condensing text and developing professional and useful visuals.

STUDY QUESTIONS

1. When would you use a visual aid in a written report?
2. Name two methods to number visual aids in a report.
3. Where do the title and number appear on a visual aid?
4. When would you place a visual aid in the appendix rather than in the text of the report?
5. Name two ways companies use the computer to develop graphics.
6. What are three advantages of using the computer for developing graphics?
7. Why would you *not* use a large number of colors in a graph?
8. Name four kinds of figures that might be used in a report and list examples of times when each would be appropriate.
9. When would an informal table be used in a report?
10. What is the most effective graphic means of presenting each of the following:
    a. Number of graduates and undergraduates in the college of business for the past five years.
    b. The percentage of freshmen, sophomores, juniors, and seniors in the college of business for the present year.
    c. The increase or decline of the American dollar in Europe for the past decade.
    d. The number of births and deaths of males and females in the U.S. for the past three years.
    e. The steps in the registration process at your school.
    f. The eating facilities located on campus.
    g. The number of traffic accidents for all fifty states, comparing 1975 and 1985.

ACTIVITIES

1. Write an introduction for the following visual aid:

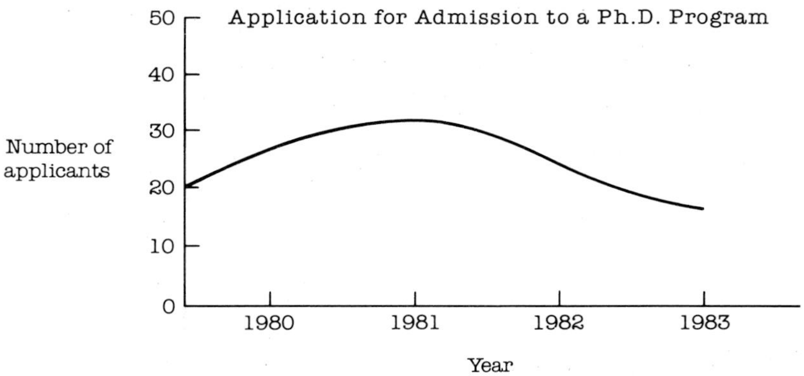

2. Prepare a visual aid for the following paragraph:

   The growth in enrollments brought increased budgetary support and an increased faculty size. In 1979–80 there were 71 faculty members who were distributed in the following way: 20 professors, 17 associate professors, 21 assistant professors, and 13 instructors. In 1981–82 we had 23 professors, 17 associate professors, 20 assistant professors, and 21 instructors. And in 1983–84 we had 79 faculty members with 18 professors, 18 associate professors, 26 assistant professors, and 17 instructors.

3. Write a letter to a software company and ask for information on its computer graphics software.
4. Develop a multiple line chart for the following information:

   Percent of TV Households Viewing Primetime Shows

Year	ABC	NBC	CBS
1978	21%	18%	18%
1980	19%	17%	19.8%
1982	17.3%	15%	17.5%
1984	16%	17.2%	18.6%

5. Develop an organizational chart for your school.
6. Collect from books, newspapers, or periodicals examples of three types of visual aids. Write an introduction for each example.
7. Develop a pie chart for the following information:

Major Divisions by Revenue for 1985

Broadcasting, 89%
Publishing, 9%
Video enterprises, 1%
Motion pictures, 1%

8. Develop a visual aid for the following information:

Average Prices of New Cars for Next Year

3 door, $11,850
4 door, $12,170
Turbo 3 door, $18,150
Turbo 4 door, $18,620

LANGUAGE SKILLS DEVELOPMENT

1. *Proofreading exercise.* Two of the three listed numbers are identical; one is different. Identify the different number.

a.	(615) 233-9537	(615) 233-9537	(615) 233-9357
b.	413-68-1007	412-68-1007	412-68-1007
c.	$100,563.24	$100,563.24	$100,653.24
d.	$125,447.12	$125,477.12	$125,447.12
e.	600,833,241	600,833,214	600,833,214
f.	(216) 423-4323	(261) 423-4323	(216) 423-4323
g.	(212) 950-0010	(212) 950-0010	(212) 590-0010
h.	323-44-8773	323-44-7873	323-44-7873
i.	02997x4xy	02977x4xy	02997x4xy
j.	273.346255	273.364255	273.346255

2. *Punctuation Exercise.* Insert the correct punctuation in the following sentences:
   a. Even though newspapers magazines and radio stations have been hard at work meeting this demand I am still frequently surprised by just how broad public interest in business seems to be.
   b. At this very moment hundreds of stories about crime are being written or videotaped by our nations media for publication or broadcast.
   c. I look at the amount of information being communicated by us and all the others and to be candid I am often overwhelmed by the quantity of it all.
   d. Younger Americans 18 to 24 years old are just as concerned about the possible reduction of Social Security benefits as Americans over 65 years of age.
   e. The three objectives of this study were to measure the current level of knowledge to determine where Americans get their information and to document public opinion.
   f. About 30 percent say they are concerned about a corporate takeover or merger of their company and 40 percent are concerned about their employer moving away from their area.

IN-BASKET SIMULATIONS

1. Develop a visual aid that will be used in the annual report of Waltere Supermarkets, Inc. It should show the growth of the corporation since 1950.
2. Assume that you observed for two days and two evenings in five of Waltere's supermarkets to determine who does the family shopping—the wife, the husband, the children, or a combination of them. Develop a visual aid that shows your findings.
3. Assume you will be including the visual aid you developed in In-Basket Simulation 2 in a report; write a paragraph that introduces the visual aid.
4. You were authorized to develop a promotional piece that describes the new drug store. Describe the types of visuals you would recommend for use in this brochure.

23

Supplemental Sections

After studying Chapter 23, you should be able to:

- Establish the difference between a formal report and formal writing
- Determine when each prefatory part should be used
- Determine when each terminal part should be used

Informal reports usually are brief and include only the text of the report (Chapter 20 discusses the short report.). Long reports are more complex and require more parts to help the reader to keep track of the information. The more parts a report has, the more formal it becomes. For example, a short three- or four-page report might have only a title page attached to it. As the report expands, it may become necessary to add other prefatory and supplemental parts. Some of these report parts are used to present a more attractive report, whereas other parts are added to assist the reader in finding and using information.

A list of all the prefatory and terminal parts that might be added to a formal report and the order in which they would be presented follows:

- I. Prefatory Parts
  - A. Cover
  - B. Title Fly
  - C. Title Page
  - D. Letter of Authorization
  - E. Letter of Transmittal
  - F. Abstract
  - G. Table of Contents
  - H. Table of Visual Aids (Graphs, Tables, and so on)
- II. Text
  - A. Introduction
  - B. Discussion
  - C. Ending
    - 1. Summary
    - 2. Conclusions
    - 3. Recommendations
- III. Terminal Parts
  - A. Bibliography
  - B. Appendix
  - C. Index

You will not need every one of these parts in every formal report. The level of formality of the report and the information readers require will determine your choice.

PREFATORY PARTS

Prefatory parts appear at the beginning of a report and introduce the reader to the contents of the report.

Cover

The **cover** is the first thing a reader sees of a report. Most business reports have a combined cover and title page, but you can embellish a formal report by adding a cover page separate from the title page. A clear plastic cover allows the title page to show through, so that you do not need to label the cover in any way. Covers are used to:

1. *Present the report title.* If you are not using clear plastic, place the title on the cover—in addition to the title page—to identify the topic of the report.
2. *Bind the report.* Longer reports may require more security than a staple or paper clip can provide; therefore, the cover keeps the report intact. Also, it protects the paper from damage and soiling.
3. *Present an attractive appearance.* The cover is the first part of a report the reader sees and should immediately create a favorable impression just as wrapping paper might enhance a gift. An attractive cover entices the reader and creates a good first impression. Choose a cover that will be appealing to the reader.

A cover design may help to convey the topic of the report. For example, assume you are writing a report analyzing two products. The cover might contain, in addition to the title, a drawing or photograph of the two products, as long as it does not appear garish or too showy.

Title Fly

The **title fly** is a sheet of paper inserted between the cover and the title page to protect the other pages of the report. The title fly, if not blank, contains no more than the title of the report. It appears only if you are using both a cover and a title page, and it is used primarily with hard-bound reports and books. When using a transparent cover, omit the title fly since it would cover the title page.

Title Page

The **title page** normally identifies the report title, the report author, the submission date of the report, and the recipient of the report. Other pieces of information, such as the name of the school or company, the titles of the receiver and sender and their office numbers, class name for which the report is prepared, and the meeting time of the class, might appear on the title page. What you include on the page depends upon the procedures at your school or company.

The balance, symmetry, neatness, and correctness of a title page are very important. Each line should be centered horizontally on the page. The most important element of the title page—the report title—should be typed in all capitals. Only the principal words in subtitles and all other typewritten material should be capitalized. For titles more than one line long, the inverted pyramid style is appropriate.

THE EFFECT ON READER COMPREHENSION

OF ORGANIZATION OF REPORT PARTS

AND USE OF HEADINGS

IN REPORTS

A good title is the key to a report. When deciding on the title of the report, strive to make it attractive, interesting, and useful to the reader and researchers. Some other suggestions are:

1. *Use key words to describe the content of the report.* Researchers should be able to insert these words into a computer to search the topic. For example, a report on the absenteeism rate of students in the public schools who have working mothers should contain *absenteeism*, *public schools*, and *working mothers* in the title.
2. *Keep the title as concise as possible, without sacrificing completeness or clarity.* Use a subtitle if extra details are needed to expand on the title. The following example illustrates how shortening the title and breaking it into a title and a subtitle combination increases its clarity:

   A STUDY TO DETERMINE THE RELATIONSHIP

   BETWEEN THE SOCIAL SECURITY SYSTEM

   AND PRIVATE RETIREMENT FUNDS FOR

   THE PERIOD COVERING 1980 TO 1990

   This title could be changed to:

   THE RELATIONSHIP BETWEEN THE SOCIAL SECURITY SYSTEM

   AND PRIVATE RETIREMENT FUNDS: 1980 TO 1990

   Leave out any unnecessary words in a title. You can shorten the titles *A Report on Microcomputers* and *An Investigation of Microcomputers* by omitting the first three words, *A Report on* and *An Investigation of.* But does the remaining title *Microcomputers* give enough information about the content of the report? Adding specific information, such as *The Growth of Microcomputers Since 1982* or *A Comparison of Microcomputers in 1983 and 1985*, also adds clarity.
3. *Avoid mystery in giving the report a title.* Remember that you are trying to inform, not keep the reader guessing about the content of the report. The title, *What People Are Dying to*

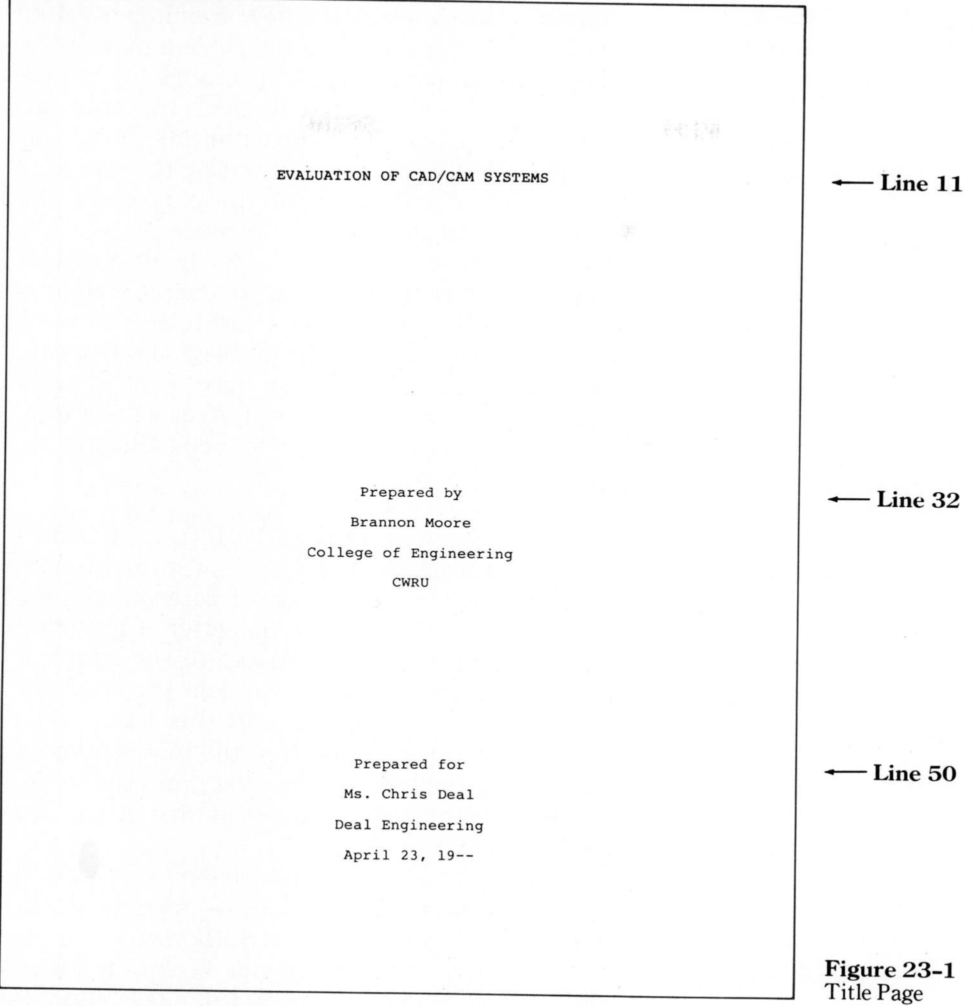
EVALUATION OF CAD/CAM SYSTEMS

Prepared by

Brannon Moore

College of Engineering

CWRU

Prepared for

Ms. Chris Deal

Deal Engineering

April 23, 19--

Figure 23-1
Title Page

Know, does not say that the report examines the high cost of funerals. *Fly-by-Night Organizations* does not adequately describe a report on the low cost of plane fares for evening flights.

4. *Consider the scope of the report when choosing a title.* A report on the salaries of female certified public accountants in Ohio would need to contain *female* and *Ohio* in the title because these words describe how the report is limited to these two areas.

Figure 23–1 demonstrates the correct spacing and capitalization of a Title Page.

Letter of Authorization

If you received a **letter of authorization**, memorandum or letter authorizing the report, you might include a copy as a part of the report. The authorization letter usually is the charge to the person or committee to perform the study. It gives the problem, scope, and limitations of the report. The letter protects the person authorizing the report, as well as the person writing the report. It can help prevent misunderstandings about the purpose of the report. The letter also can lend authority to the report.

If instructions were given orally for a study that would require a large investment of time or money, you might prepare a work plan before you actually start the investigation. The work plan is a statement of how you perceive the problem and how you plan to tackle the problem. A work plan can save a lot of problems by ironing out misunderstandings before the report is begun. A more detailed description of a work plan is found in Chapter 21.

Letter of Transmittal

Sometimes referred to as a **cover letter**, the **letter of transmittal** accompanies the report. It is a letter or memorandum from the author of the report to the person or persons who are receiving the report. Say the same thing in the letter of transmittal as you would say if you handed the report to the recipient personally, including a statement about why you prepared the report. You may include personal opinions in this letter, even though you have avoided them in presenting the information in the report. Avoid repeating the same statements you used in the introduction or in the abstract, but you may summarize the key findings or recommendations.

Use the direct approach in writing this letter. In the first paragraph give the reason for writing the letter—to transmit the report. You might also include a statement of authorization in the first paragraph. In the middle paragraphs give backup information—explanations, comments, ideas not included in the report. A statement of recommendations would also be appropriate. Make the last paragraph a courteous closing. You might include a statement of appreciation for the opportunity to work on the report, and you might offer to meet with the recipient or answer any questions about the report. You might also acknowledge anyone who assisted with the report.

Any acceptable letter style is appropriate or use a memorandum format (See Figure 23–2) for the letter of transmittal. Follow appropriate spacing, paragraphing, capitalization, and punctuation. (See preceding chapters on letters for more information on the mechanics of writing this letter.)

MEMORANDUM

DATE: April 23, 19--

TO: Ronald Peterson, Ext. 216

FROM: Paige Anderson, Ext. 345

SUBJECT: LETTER STYLES FOR THE SMALL BUSINESS OWNER

Here is the report on appropriate letter styles for the small business owner that you asked me to complete.

I had no idea so many different styles of letters are available for use in business correspondence. The most popular style is the full-blocked letter because it is both a time and money saver. I recommend that all our office personnel use the full-blocked letter style in the future. I would also recommend that we include a full description of the letter in the Office Procedures Manual.

If you have any questions about the various letter styles presented in the report, please call me. I was pleased to work on the report; it helped refresh my memory on the appropriate letter styles being used in business today.

aa

Figure 23-2
Letter of Transmittal

The letter of transmittal may be attached to the cover of the report, or it may follow the title page.

Abstract

The **abstract**, also called a **summary** or **synopsis**, gives an overview of the report. The abstract should be no more than one or two pages long. Some companies have specific standards about the length of the abstract, insisting that it be kept to one page, regardless of how long the complete report is. You should prepare the abstract after you have completed the content of the report.

The abstract is helpful for long, complicated reports; it also helps the very busy reader who has only a moment to review the findings. Because the abstract is sometimes reproduced and distributed to persons who do not read the entire report, it should present sufficient facts and findings to orient the reader. It

ABSTRACT

The purpose of this study was to determine if there were significant differences in students' attitudes toward the office management course when the traditional teaching method or the self-paced method was used. In addition, the study was to ascertain whether the traditional method developed a higher level of cognitive achievement.

It was concluded that there was no differential effect upon the attitude toward the course by students as a result of being taught by the traditional method or the self-paced method. There was no significant difference between treatment groups relative to the cognitive achievement objective posttest. A significant difference did exist between treatment groups on the combined mean scores of the test problems favoring the group taught by the self-paced method.

Figure 23-3
Informative Abstract

should be able to stand alone in meaning. A general audience, in addition to the primary audience, may read the abstract. Be sure that the content can be understood by all the readers. Do not include visual aids or bibliographic references in the abstract.

The **informative abstract** normally contains the statement of the problem, the purpose, the methodology, and a summary of the important findings of the report. It is imperative that you do not distort the findings or change the emphasis of the content in your abbreviated abstract. Figure 23-3 gives an example of an informative abstract.

Another type of abstract is the **descriptive abstract**. It lists the topics covered in the report but gives no results of the study. The descriptive abstract is normally used to help readers determine if they want to read the report.

In preparing an abstract, make it lean and useful. Read the material once to get an overall impression of what it is all about; reread it for notetaking and underlining; pay attention to the first and last sentences of each paragraph. Use your own words to write the abstract. Exclude remarks that indicate you are writing a summary.

Table of Contents

The **table of contents**, also called **contents**, helps the reader to locate information in the report, but it also serves as an outline guide to the topics and presentation of material. The table of contents precedes the text, but it is one of the last parts to be prepared because it must reflect the final format—the major headings and the page numbers on which these headings appear. The table of contents also contains headings for sections that appear after the text of the report, such as the bibliography and appendix, and the page numbers for these sections. The table of contents should be complete, accurate, and easy to read. The following guidelines will help you format the table of contents and make it more readable and useful:

1. Use a heading at the top: *Contents* or *Table of Contents*.
2. List the exact wording of the headings (first-, second-, and third-degree headings) with their text page numbers.
3. List only the first page numbers on which a section of text begins. The Introduction may be found on pages 1–4, but the Contents would indicate only that it began on page 1.
4. Use the exact words of the headings and present them in the order in which they are found in the text.
5. Use Roman numerals or numbers in front of your headings in the Contents only if you used them in the report.
6. Use leaders (periods and spaces alternately) to guide the reader's eye from the title of the heading to the page number if a lot of blank space separates the heading from the page number. If you use leaders, make sure they align vertically.
7. If a heading runs over to a second line, indent the second line.

Create an attractive style for your contents. You have several options available in preparing the page. You may capitalize every word or only the first-degree headings, with secondary headings having only the initial letters capitalized. You may use double spacing throughout or insert extra spacing only to separate major headings. A sample table of contents page appears in Figure 23–4.

Table of Visual Aids

If your report contains several visual aids, you may include a table of tables, table of figures, table of charts, table of graphs, or whatever other title might be appropriate. Like the table of contents, each of these parts helps the reader locate the visual aids by listing their titles and the page numbers on which they are found.

The table of visual aids may be placed on a page by itself that follows the table of contents. If your table of visual aids is short and you have sufficient space, you may place it on the same page as the table of contents. (See Figure 23–5.) The rules for titling, spacing, indenting, and capitalizing are the same as those used for the table of contents page. If you do place both on the same page, give each section a title and leave plenty of room between them so they do not appear crowded.

CONTENTS Page

iv

Figure 23-4
Table of Contents

TABLE OF CONTENTS

TABLE OF TABLES

Figure 23-5
Combined Table of Contents and Table of Tables

TERMINAL PARTS

Terminal parts appear at the end of a report. They allow the reader access to additional information without cluttering the text.

Bibliography

Since proper credit must always be given for any word or idea that is someone else's, we use both footnotes and bibliographies. Footnotes are used in the body of a report to give credit to someone else's words or ideas. The **bibliography** is an alphabetical listing of all the sources used in compiling the report. It includes not only the references for footnotes you used but also any references you used to compile the report but didn't actually footnote. Place the bibliography either immediately after the text or after the appendix. You can make the bibliography one complete alphabetical listing of all the sources used, or, if you've included a large number of different kinds of sources, you may subdivide entries according to the type of source. For example, if you are citing a large number of interviews, you may group the entries as books, periodicals, and interviews. You may group entries that are government or business publications, as well.

The bibliography does not indicate exactly which material in the text is being cited. It lists all sources consulted, including those not quoted directly in the report. Adhere to the following specific guidelines in styling the bibliography:

1. Use a heading, *Bibliography* or *References*, to precede the list of sources.
2. Single-space each of the references, using a double space to separate the entries. Start the first line of each entry at the left margin; indent the subsequent lines of the listing two spaces under the first line.
3. Arrange the sources alphabetically, with the author's last name first. If there is no author, use the title of the article or book to alphabetize the listing.
4. Present book references in the following order: author, title of publication, and facts of publication (city, publishing company, and date of publication).
5. Present the data for a periodical in the following order: author, title of article, publication title, date of publication.
6. Use periods to separate the items in a listing.

Figure 23-6 is an example of a bibliography that contains the correct format, spacing, and capitalization. Figure 23-7 is an example of a bibliography that is divided into subparts.

BIBLIOGRAPHY

Andrews, Stuart. Techniques of Letters. Boston: Grizer Publications, 1981.

Campbell, Olive. Dimensions of Reports. Chicago: Steiner Press, 1983.

Hatchley, Reba. Supervision. New York: Green Publishers, 1974.

Howe, Allen and Jane Schaum. "Writing that First Letter," The Monthly Reader. January 1984.

Lambert, Robert. Cases in Organizational Behavior. New York: Worldwide Publishers, 1976.

Figure 23-6
Bibliography Page

REFERENCES

Books

Hatchley, Reba. Supervision. New York: Green Publishers, 1974.

Lambert, Robert. Cases in Organizational Behavior. New York: Worldwide Publishers, 1976.

Needham, Lea. Solving Problems in the Public Schools. Chicago: Claret Publishing Co., Inc., 1978.

Periodicals

Alex, Mitchell. "Trees and How They Evolved." Environmental Design. March, 1972.

Match, Eleanor. "The World and Work and Christopher Stevens." The New Zealand Weekly. April 12, 1973.

Figure 23-7
Bibliography Page Divided into Subparts

Appendix

The **appendix** serves as an adjunct for the reader. It contains materials that are important to support your findings but are not necessary to the discussion and, therefore, do not have to appear within the text. For example, if you have used a mailed survey, you might include a copy of the cover letter and questionnaire in the appendix. The reader could refer to these documents, but they need not interrupt the text. Mention in the appropriate places in the text the items that are found in the appendix and on what pages they can be found.

The appendix gives details that might be cumbersome in the body of the report but are necessary to support the facts given in the text. Listed in the appendix, these details do not slow down the reader in the text and, thus, do not detract from its orderly flow. A copy of an extensive table or a computer printout might appear in the appendix rather than in the body of the report. If the material relates directly to the text and is essential to discussion, it should appear with the text; if it is additional and supplementary, place it in an appendix.

You may group supplementary material together as one appendix, or you may divide the material into separate sections—Appendix A, Appendix B, and so on, each containing separate pieces of data or attachments. If the appendix is divided, give each section a title (Appendix A: List of Companies) and list each title in the table of contents as an appendix. Sometimes a sheet of paper with the word "Appendix" on it separates the body of the report from the material in the appendixes.

Index

The **index** rarely appears in reports. It is an alphabetical listing of the subject matter in the report with the corresponding text page numbers. The index is useful in locating material in extensive reports.

CHAPTER SUMMARY

As reports increase in length, you may need to add supplemental parts to help the reader locate the information. The more parts that a writer adds to the report, the more formal the report becomes. An informal report might have few, if any, of the supplemental parts; but a long report might require many of them to organize and categorize the material sufficiently.

The prefatory parts can include a cover, title fly, title page, letters of authorization and transmittal, abstract, and tables of contents and visual aids. The cover not only binds a long report, but it can create a good first impression. The title page identifies the who, what, and when of the report. The authorization letter lends credibility to the report, and the letter of transmittal gives the author an opportunity to give explanations or personal opinions about the report. If a report is long, an abstract gives a brief summary of the important findings of the report. The table of contents identifies the important topics covered in the report, and the table of visual aids identifies the visual aids used in the report.

The terminal parts include the bibliography, appendix, and index. The bibliography is a listing of sources used in compiling the report. The appendix houses supplementary material that might clutter the content of the report. Indexes are not frequently included at the end of business reports.

STUDY QUESTIONS

1. Describe the difference between formal writing and formal reports.
2. Why would a title fly not be used in a report in which a transparent cover is used?
3. Why are the use of key words in a title important?
4. What is the difference between a letter of transmittal and a letter of authorization?
5. How could the letter of authorization be considered a protection for the writer?
6. What is the purpose of an abstract?
7. What is the difference between footnotes and bibliographies?
8. Why would a ten-page abstract not be desirable?
9. When would a table of tables be appropriate in a report?
10. If a lengthy table is to be presented in a report, what would be the best place for it?
11. Define a table of graphs.
12. Arrange the following information into the correct bibliographical entries:
    a. *Modern Business: A Systems Approach* by Rosenblatt, S. Bernard, Bonnington, Robert L. and Needles, Belverd E.; published in 1983 by Houghton Mifflin Company in Boston, Atlanta, Dallas, and Geneva
    b. *Administrative Office Management* by Lewis Keeling, Norman Kallaus, and John Neuner; published in 1978 by South-Western Publishing Co. in Cincinnati
13. Arrange the following information into a correct title page:
    Author: Bruce Baron
    Completion date of report: September 1985
    Report completed for the Commission on Higher Education, Washington, D.C.
    Title: Women Doctorates Conferred by Washington, Oregon, California, and Texas from 1978–1983

14. Improve the following titles of reports:
    a. A Study to Determine if There Is a Relationship between the Hiring Practices of Large and Small Companies
    b. An Investigation of the Status of Female Certified Professional Secretaries
    c. A Report on the Use of Training Films in Education
    d. Current Problems of Salesmen
    e. Income Tax Changes for 1980, 1981, 1982, and 1983

ACTIVITIES

1. Prepare a bibliography of at least five sources for one of the following topics:
    a. Women in management
    b. A career in computers, banking, or sales
    c. Regulations for driving
2. Defend or dispute the following statements in a paragraph. After you have written the paragraphs, revise and edit the paragraphs and have someone else check them for clarity and correctness.
    a. You should edit and revise a report immediately after the first draft has been written because the content is still fresh in your mind.
    b. Since you know more about the report than anyone else, you should do your own proofreading.
    c. All the sentences in a report should be approximately 18 words.
    d. Writing objectively means you will avoid the use of first and second person.
    e. A report written in third person sounds stilted and awkward.
3. Write a letter of transmittal to accompany a research report to be turned in to your instructor.
4. Read a journal article; write an abstract of it.
5. Construct a title page for a report to be turned in to your instructor.

LANGUAGE SKILLS DEVELOPMENT

1. Each of the following sentences contains a dangling modifier. Rewrite each sentence, correcting it.
    a. Before buying new towels, the bathroom should be painted.
    b. To prepare for the trip, the suitcase was repacked three times by Gene.
    c. While visiting Japan, the Ambassador asked Jerry to speak.

d. When hungry, my lunch seems to beckon.
e. Before leaving for work, the driveway needs to be shoveled.
f. Troubled by so many absences, the students were lectured by the professor.
g. To develop a good outline, a lot of thinking needs to be done.

2. The following sentences use passive voice. Rewrite them using active voice.
   a. Members who have experience in this area are being encouraged to contact the association office.
   b. Extensive tests have not been revealed to the public.
   c. Our plans are to leave work early.
   d. The president's refusal was a blow to everyone in the organization.
   e. The cookies were sold by over 75 percent of the members.
   f. The rejection by the university was a disappointment to David.
   g. A significant contribution was made to the society by neighbors.
   h. Discussions were held between the participants and the press.
   i. Precautions can be taken simply by prechecking the equipment.
   j. Additional tests are planned for next year.

IN-BASKET SIMULATIONS

1. Refer to In-Basket Simulation 1 in Chapter 21. Develop a title page, a letter of transmittal, and a table of contents to accompany your report.
2. Write a letter of authorization from the President of the Corporation, Mr. Waltere, to Mr. David Summer, Director of Sales, to have him study the problems involved with the shopping carts. Some of the problems are:
   a. The high theft rate of the carts left in the parking lots
   b. The damage occurring to carts when customers leave carts in the parking lots and cars accidentally hit the carts.

24

Presentation of the Report

After studying Chapter 24, you should be able to:

- Defend the report as a public relations tool
- Write a rough draft
- Edit and proofread your final draft until it is complete, concise, clear, and adapted to the audience who will receive it
- Apply a readability formula to what you have written
- Format a report

You are ready to write the first draft of the report when you have completed each of the preliminary steps: defined the problem; outlined the problem; collected, sorted, interpreted data; developed visual aids; and selected the format for the report.

The first draft establishes the general shape of the report, based on the outline. It provides a quick transition from outline form to text form, without attention to mechanical details (such as spelling, punctuation, and grammar).

Edit in subsequent drafts to smooth out rough phrases, inaccuracies in spelling or grammar, and points that need expansion or revision. The final draft should be error-free and typewritten after all text changes are final. The final draft should be neat, appropriately styled, and correct to give the report its best possible image.

PUBLIC RELATIONS

Reports can promote public relations, as well as dispense information and help solve problems. When the reader does not know you personally and must rely upon your report for an impression of you and the organization, the report takes on the responsibility for image. First impressions are important and lasting. An impression is formed from the moment the reader first sees the report. If the report does not have an attractive cover, if the name of the recipient is spelled incorrectly, or if the report is typed on a cheap grade of paper, a negative impression may be formed.

A poorly written report can have the opposite effect you are seeking. It can infuriate the reader if it is so unorganized and unclear that it taxes his or her mental powers or if it approaches the problem in unfriendly terms or from a biased viewpoint. Common problems in report writing occur:

In the tone—The report may insult the reader by the language used or the implications in the message.

In the organization—The report may be difficult to understand because of the order in which ideas and paragraphs are presented.

In believability—The writer may not have been objective in presenting the content, or the conclusions may not be based on the facts presented.

Positive and well-written reports, on the other hand, promote good relations because they are easy to read and understand and the reader forms a positive impression of both the writer and the company represented. Reports that are well written reflect positively not only on you but on your supervisor or company as well. They are the stepping stones to promotability and positions of leadership.

READABILITY FORMULAS

Several valid methods are available for analyzing the reading difficulty and level of your writing. Some of these tests are the SMOG Index, the FOG Index, and the Fry Readability Graph. (These tests are mentioned in Chapter 2.) These methods give the approximate reading difficulty of your writing.

To determine the readability level based on the SMOG Index, select three passages of ten sentences each—one at the beginning, one in the middle, and one at the end of the text. Count the polysyllables in the thirty-sentence sample. Take the nearest even square root of the number of polysyllabic words and add 3 to the approximate square root as shown in the following table:

Number of polysyllabic words in thirty sentences	**Square root**	**SMOG grade level**
1–2	1	4
3–6	2	5
7–12	3	6
13–20	4	7
21–30	5	8
31–42	6	9
43–56	7	10
57–72	8	11
73–90	9	12
91–110	10	13
111–132	11	14
133–156	12	15
157–183	13	16
184–210	14	17

This is the approximate grade level at which a person must read to be able to understand the material. The SMOG Index assumes that only word length affects reading difficulty.

The FOG Index makes the assumption that both sentence length and word length affect reading difficulty. To determine the readability level based on the FOG Index, again select three passages of ten sentences each—one from the beginning, one in the middle, and one toward the end of the text. Count the total number of words in the thirty-sentence sample and divide this by the total number of sentences. Then count the number of words that are three or more syllables long. From this, calculate the percent of polysyllables in the three passages by dividing the total number of words into the number of polysyllables and multiplying by 100. Finally add the average sentence length to the percent of polysyllables to determine the readability index based on the following table:

Readability index (sum of average sentence length plus percent of polysyllables)	**FOG grade level**
Under 20	Grade School
20–25	Junior High School
25–30	High School
30–35	Junior College
35–40	College
Over 40	Doctorate

To get an accurate picture of the readability of the entire report, apply either formula to several sections of the report as suggested. If the educational level is higher than the audience can comfortably handle, revise, substituting appropriate language:

1. Use simple words.
2. Keep the average sentence length between 17 and 20 words.
3. Use only one thought for each sentence.

EDITING AND PROOFREADING

Quickly write the first draft, or at least one complete section of the report, from the outline you have constructed. Write without stopping to check mechanical things, such as spelling, word division, and word choice. If you use visual aids, draft a preliminary copy of them before starting the actual writing. Or if certain points need to be checked or clarified, do so before starting the writing. After completing the rough draft of the report, read for the finer points, improving word choice, spelling, punctuation, and word division. Put in headings and footnote references, if you need any, after the first draft has been written.

Because the report is made up of distinct sections, it is not necessary to start at the beginning of the report and work to the end. Do the section first that is easiest for you to write. If the conclusions seem the easiest to get into, write them first or present your findings first and do your introduction last. Once the writing has started, it becomes easier, and the more difficult sections fall into place.

In the first draft, leave wide margins and plenty of space between the lines to make insertions or changes. Say as much as you can in the first draft; it is easier to delete extra wording later than add to the report at a later time.

After you have finished the first draft, put it aside for a day or so, then come back to revise and edit. Writers are more subjective and less critical of their work immediately after completing it. Try reading the report aloud because it is easier to pick out awkward sentences. Editing the first draft of the report requires cool objectivity.

In reading your first draft, edit for the following points:

1. *Completeness.* Check the statement of the problem to make sure you have answered all the stated questions. Make sure you have left no room for misunderstanding in the report.
2. *Correctness.* Check spelling, punctuation, word division, margins, spacing, paragraphing, and other mechanical points to make sure they are correct.
3. *Conciseness.* Avoid cluttering the report with irrelevant details. Be cautious about keeping to the point and avoiding deadwood and unnecessary words and phrases.
4. *Clarity.* Check the report to make sure you have used the correct word to convey a particular idea. Write simply; do not try to impress your reader with an extensive vocabulary. Incorporate the techniques for achieving readability through arrangement and format: spacing, listings, headings, and visual aids.

You can take additional steps to ensure that your report reads smoothly. As finishing touches, these simple practices give a professional quality to your writing:

1. *Sentence length.* Vary the length of sentences, avoiding extremely long and complex sentences and also short choppy sentences. Even though most sentences should average around 17–20 words, the final length depends on the complexity of your idea as well as intended audience.
2. *Paragraph length.* The maximum number of lines in a report paragraph should not exceed 15. One helpful rule is to divide paragraphs so that you do not include more than one topic sentence per paragraph.
3. *Headings.* Use headings throughout the report to help guide the reader through the various sections.
4. *Transitional words and phrases.* Transitional words and phrases link sentences and paragraphs to create a smooth flow of thoughts. Avoid beginning sentences with a slow expletive opening such as *there are* and *it is.*
5. *Tense.* The verb tense used in a report varies. Use **past tense** (for example, *A survey instrument was developed and administered*) to describe anything done before you began to write the report. Present the findings and conclusions in the **present tense** (for example, *Telecommunications technology requires educators to retool*). Occasionally, you may use the **future tense** to tell the reader that a particular point is

These suggestions can help you to become a better dictator:
1. Select a quiet location.
2. Schedule dictation early in the day.
3. Try to prevent interruptions.
4. Gather appropriate materials.
5. Outline your points.
6. Visualize the reader.
7. Practice dictating.

Figure 24–1
Enumerations Aid Clarity

discussed later in the report (for example, *A literature review on the types of information managers need will be presented in the next chapter*).

6. *Direct quotes.* Use direct quotes sparingly—only when a summary or paraphrase might be misinterpreted. A much better way to present information in a report is to paraphrase or summarize the information.

   Before presenting a direct quote, lead into the quote—either with a reference to the author or the source of information or something similar to identify the source of the quote. For example, when referring to a statement Adams made, the lead-in might be:

   > Adams, in his first speech on the subject, said this about air pollution: "Air polution is the No. 1 environmental problem facing the nation today."[1]

   Treat short direct quotes (three or fewer lines) just like the rest of the report. Double-space and insert quotation marks before and after the quote to indicate that it is a direct quote.

   Single-space long quotes (four or more typed lines), indenting from the left and right margins the same number of spaces that you indented text paragraphs. Do not use quotation marks for long quotes; indenting and single-spacing shows the reader that it is a direct quote.
7. *Enumerations.* Use listings or enumerations whenever you have more than two points to give. The listings help the reader follow your discussion with greater ease and understanding (Figure 24–1).
8. *Topic sentences.* Topic sentences should begin each section; clearly tell the reader what you intend to do in that section. Conclude each section with a summarizing statement that shows what you did and how it relates to the material that follows.

9. *Title, introduction, and terminal sections.* Look critically at the title, introduction, and supplemental parts to make sure they are clear and complete. Remember that the purpose of editing is to correct and improve the final copy of the report.

WRITING MECHANICS

For the very formal report, you may wish to consult a style manual. Most business reports, however, follow specific guidelines for typing. By following these guidelines you can expect your report to have a suitable appearance.

Paper and Type

Your report should be typed on a good quality, white, 8½-in. × 11-in. size sheet of paper. The paper should have at least 25 percent rag content and be 16- or 20-lb. bond paper. Refrain from using the erasable paper; it does not make a professional presentation.

Make sure the type on your typewriter is even and clean, especially the o, a, and e, which have a tendency to ink up. Use a standard business type (elite, pica) for your reports; script type is not considered an appropriate business type.

Any device that makes professional corrections is appropriate. If a correction is noticeable, it needs to be redone. Correcting typewriters and word processors have made corrections an easy task for the report writer. If you need to make copies of the report, be sure to use a high-quality printer or reproduction device. If the report will be sent outside the company, a letter-quality printer is recommended over a dot matrix printer.

How attractive the report is makes an impression on the reader. One of the criteria used for attractiveness is how the paper, type, and corrections appear. Be sure the content of the report does not suffer because the presentation is of poor quality.

Margins

Provide margins all around the content, just as you would frame a picture. Make the two side margins at least 1 in. wide. If you plan to bind the report, allow an additional ½ in. for the left margin for the binding. The side margin settings for pica and elite machine type (if the report is bound at the left margin) follow:

	Left margin	*Right margin*
Pica type	1½ in., 15	1 in., 75
Elite type	1½ in., 18	1 in., 90

The bottom margin should be approximately 1 in. deep. If you are placing footnotes at the bottom of the page, keep them above

Figure 24-2
Lines Per 8½ in. × 11 in. Page

the 1 in. bottom margin. A standard 8½-in. × 11-in. page holds 66 single-spaced vertical lines. One vertical inch on most typewriters is 6 lines. One good method is to place a light pencil mark about 1½ in. above the bottom of the page to warn you that you are nearing the bottom. A guide sheet similar to the one shown in Figure 24-2 is also helpful. It shows the number of lines remaining on the sheet of paper. This guide sheet is placed behind your typing paper so you always know how many lines are left on the page.

The top margin varies depending on whether the page is the first page of a major section or a continuation page. The first

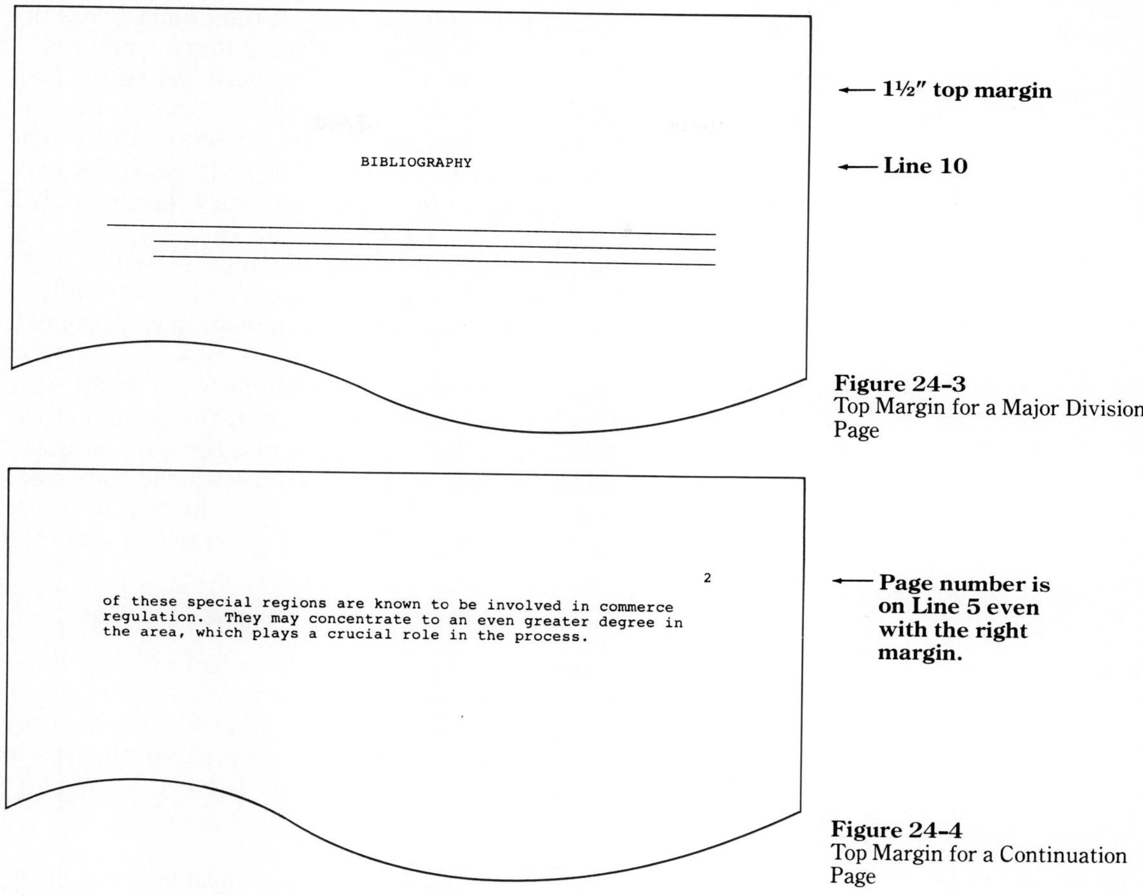

← 1½″ top margin
BIBLIOGRAPHY
← Line 10
2
of these special regions are known to be involved in commerce regulation. They may concentrate to an even greater degree in the area, which plays a crucial role in the process.
← Page number is on Line 5 even with the right margin.

Figure 24-3
Top Margin for a Major Division Page

Figure 24-4
Top Margin for a Continuation Page

page of a major section, such as the first page of the Table of Contents, the first page of the body of the report, or the first page of the Bibliography, has a 1½-in. top margin. The titles of these pages appear in all capitals on line 10 from the top of the sheet of paper (See Figure 24-3).

The continuation pages—page 2 and those pages that follow—have about a ¾-in. top margin. The page number appears on the fifth line from the top of the sheet of paper (Figure 24-4).

Spacing and Paragraphing

Double-space the formal report, indenting paragraphs from 5 to 15 spaces. Typists usually indent paragraphs 5 spaces, starting the first letter on the sixth space. If you single-space the report, leave a blank line between the paragraphs. A single-spaced report does not need to have the paragraphs indented; this is the writer's prerogative.

Paging

Each page has an assigned number, even if the number does not appear on the page. The title page is always Roman numeral i, even though it is not actually typed on the page. All subsequent preliminary pages (acknowledgments, table of figures, table of contents, and so on) have lowercase Roman numerals. If the table of contents is the next page to follow the title page, its page number would be ii, typed on the page, centered, approximately 1 in. from the bottom.

The text—the content portion of the report—begins with Arabic number 1. The numbering then progresses sequentially to the last page of the report, including the bibliography, appendix, and index.

Center the page numbers for major sections (such as the table of contents and bibliography) about 1 in. from the bottom of the page (Figure 24-5). Place the other page numbers in the upper right-hand corner of the page on line 5, even with the right margin. It is not necessary to put *page* in front of the numbers, nor should you use periods, hyphens, or parentheses around the numbers.

Proofreading

Proofread each page of the report several times before you submit it. You might consider asking someone else to proofread it also to catch any errors you might have missed. Someone who has not worked on the project is more likely to see errors than the person closely involved with it.

ORAL REPORTS

Long reports or reports involving complex problems or extensive research normally are prepared first in typweritten form. Then, a shortened version may be presented orally. Oral reports usually are intended to inform or persuade an audience. Many of the same principles used for written reports apply also to oral reports. In fact, the oral report requires much of the same preparation as a written report. The presenter needs to be able to define the problem, to organize the material, to use effective methods of research, and to state what was found, efficiently and effectively. A strong opening and closing, in addition to the well-prepared discussion, are essential.

To deliver the report well, the presenter needs to know his or her subject thoroughly and strive to inform and explain, not to impress. Audience awareness is important in planning the presentation. A presenter must analyze the audience and the probable reaction to the findings.

TABLE OF CONTENTS

	Page
INTRODUCTION	1
LETTERS.	4
REPORTS.	21
SUMMARY.	27
BIBLIOGRAPHY	29

ii

Page number centered ← 1″ from bottom of page

Figure 24-5
Placement of Page Number on a Major Section Page

In delivering the report, all effective communicators keep in mind that their bodies are also communicating through their posture, facial expressions, gestures, and eyes. For this reason, visual aids in an oral report are even more important than they are in a written report. Slides, charts, transparencies, and the chalkboard are invaluable aids in maintaining interest and driving home the points. Chapter 25 gives more details about making oral presentations.

CHAPTER SUMMARY

Writing the report is the final stage of preparing any report. It now becomes your responsibility to communicate your findings in a way that achieves the purpose of the report. First, concentrate on one task—developing the topic in your first draft. Then return to the rough copy to polish your work—to edit and revise until the writing reflects all of the qualities that make it a professional and impressive report. Apply a readability formula to what you have written if you doubt whether you have written it at an appropriate level. No matter how short or long the report, revise it until you are satisfied that it is complete, correct, concise, clear, and adapted to the audience that will receive the finished product.

Only after you are content with what you have said and how the report reads should you concern yourself with the mechanics and what the report will look like. You can either consult a style manual or follow widely accepted guidelines.

Reports can promote public relations as well as help in decision making. A first impression may influence the reader of a report. Writing mechanics are also important to help readers form a positive first impression.

Written reports may be presented in oral form as well as in written form. Many of the same principles used in written reports apply also to oral reports.

STUDY QUESTIONS

1. How can reports be considered public relations tools?
2. Will using a readability formula cure poor writing?
3. Why is script type not appropriate for most business reports?
4. Name three criteria that can be used to form a positive first impression in a report.
5. If you are a careful writer, is it possible for you to skip the editing and proofreading stage? Why or why not?
6. What are some effective techniques for helping the reader speed up reading a report?
7. If you are summarizing someone else's ideas, is it necessary to footnote that summary?
8. What are the approximate top, side, and bottom margins for a formal report?
9. Describe how a guide sheet makes typing reports easier.
10. Define what is meant by clarity in a report.

ACTIVITIES

1. Assume that the following paragraph was in the first draft of a formal report. Revise the paragraph for spelling, punctuation, grammar, and word choice.

   In comparing Typewriter X and Typewriter Y I found the following differences; cost and Durability. Typewriter X is guaranted by the supplyer for 1 year, and cost $600.00 whereas Typewriter Y has a guarante of 2 years. and cost $675. Not really much difference in costs. However, the longer guarante makes typewriter Y the best choice for our companies use.

2. Rewrite the following sentences, changing them from passive to active voice.
   a. Reservations for the vacation were made three months in advance.
   b. The race car was driven by an 18-year-old person.
   c. On Friday evening computer crime will be discussed by authorities in crime prevention.
   d. Access to the building was made possible by the campus patrol.
   e. A new generation of computers is being made available to the public by the company.
3. Write the opening statement for the following oral reports:
   a. A Comparison of Hot and Cold Cereals
   b. Developing an Effective Résumé
   c. A Review of Management Theories
4. You are typing a 12-page report. What numbers would be assigned to each of the following pages?
   a. Title Page
   b. First page of the body of the report
   c. Bibliography

LANGUAGE SKILLS DEVELOPMENT

1. Complete the following sentences by choosing the correct word in the parentheses.
   a. (Whose, Who's) the person working on the project with Melanie?
   b. The captain, (whose, who's) job is uncertain, plans to retire.
   c. Ms. Moore and (I, me) plan to redecorate the room.
   d. Did the supervisor complain about (you, your) leaving early today?
   e. (Its, It's) a known fact that the company plans to close.
   f. Mr. Thomas briefed (us, we) operators about the proper procedures.

g. Tim tries harder than (he, him).
h. Sarah gave the report to Chris and (I, me).
i. Kim, Sandy, and (I, myself) will organize the seminar.
j. The company planned (its, it's) advertising promotion for the first week in June.

2. Choose the correct verb for the following sentences:
   a. The audience (are, is) going to be admitted after the press.
   b. The committee (meet, meets) every Thursday afternoon.
   c. The department (are, is) planning to teach four sections of the course next year.
   d. The corporation (are, is) located only three blocks away.
   e. The team (has, have) lost three games so far.
   f. Either Paige or Christy (are, is) going to collect the newspapers.
   g. None of the faculty (are, is) changing office locations.
   h. All the airplane owners (are, is) planning to fly in formation.
   i. The sister, not the brothers, (repair, repairs) the equipment.
   j. One of the cars (has been, have been) sold.

IN-BASKET SIMULATIONS

1. As the new Office Manager for Waltere Supermarkets, Inc., you must develop an office manual outlining the mechanical items associated with writing and typing letters and reports. Outline the items you wish to include in this office manual.
2. The President of Drug Operations plans to write an article for a trade publication on the principles of communication in an organization. Write a brief report of items to include in the article. Proofread and edit the report.

Oral and Nonverbal Communications

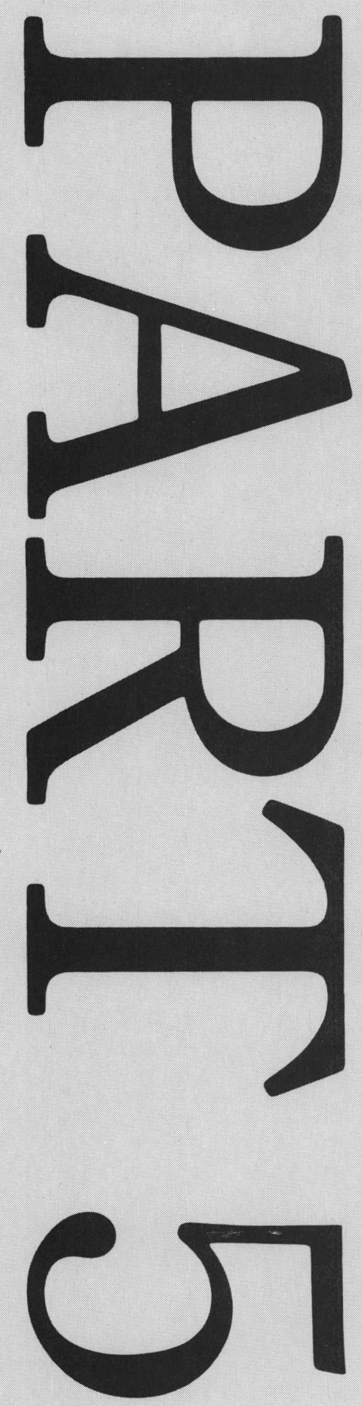

25

Oral Communication

After studying Chapter 25, you should be able to:

- Recognize the importance of good interpersonal communications
- Discuss the role of planning skills, human relations skills, and communications skills in effective oral communications
- Differentiate between formal and informal person-to-person communications
- List the responsibilities of a conference leader
- Recognize a skilled public speaker
- Recognize a skilled dictator
- Improve your listening skills

Oral communication—speaking and listening—is the most common form of communication. Approximately 75 percent of all communication is oral. Thus, the skilled oral communicator is welcome in society and in business. In business, oral internal and external communications must be accurate and based on corporate policy.

By its very nature, oral communication must be a two-way communication; it requires both a speaker and at least one listener. Each participant uses nonverbal communication. Each needs to be an effective listener and hold up her and his end of the conversation, whether in a face-to-face encounter or in a group or meeting.

The effective communicator recognizes the multifaceted nature of communication and the skills it requires: planning, language use, and human relations.

INTERPERSONAL COMMUNICATION

Oral communication is **interpersonal communication**. Employees at all levels—general workers to top administrators—use oral communication to inform, to instruct, and to reach decisions. In addition, business people communicate orally with persons outside the firm (for example, customers, stockholders, governmental units, and the public). Business cannot function without oral communication.

Successful oral business communication requires:

1. A plan
2. Human relation skills (both general and specific knowledge about the situation and the individuals involved)
3. Good speaking and listening skills
4. Nonverbal communication skills

Importance of Planning

When communicators plan, they identify objectives; determine the proper procedure, information, materials, and equipment to facilitate achieving those objectives; and recognize the need to consider **who** should be involved, **how** each individual is to participate, and **when** and **where** activities should take place. A good plan helps achieve effective communication because it is based on a specific purpose; considers the feelings and philosophies of those involved; and ensures completeness and correctness of facts in a logical sequence and without waste of time, energy, and money.

Although some informal oral business settings are not planned or structured, technical business situations should be planned.

Importance of Good Human Relation Skills

Good human relation skills encourage goodwill and high employee morale. **Morale** is a composite of employee attitudes, feelings, and sentiment toward the work environment. It is revealed by employees' consideration of the best interests of the organization. Workers with high morale enjoy working with other employees toward the common good of the business.

Workers with low morale do not reflect this attitude. Indeed, such employees may take unnecessary time away from the job, work below potential, have poor safety records, request transfers or quit, complain about minor problems, or strike. Quality may decline; customers may become dissatisfied. Costs will increase; profits, decrease. The individuals involved need to feel special, necessary, and important.

It is easier to accomplish planned objectives when the unique backgrounds, beliefs, and ideas of individuals involved have been considered. Some psychologists believe that humans need a proper amount of oral "stroking" (recognition). This need varies from person to person and situation to situation. Some instances demand only one stroke (such as a "Hello" to a friend one sees daily) while others require several strokes (such as when the friend has been vacationing for several weeks). Judging the proper amount of oral stroking is a fine art. If too little stroking is given, the strokee may think he or she is being treated as an insignificant and unimportant person. Too much stroking may be regarded as evidence of insincerity. A great deal of human sensitivity is needed to judge each situation.

Because each individual is unique, successful oral business communicators contemplate basic human needs and wants and the particular background, interests, and philosophies of the participants.

Importance of Speaking and Listening Skills

Speaking coherently, correctly, clearly, and concisely helps an individual convey the message intended. If the intended message is not received, the communicator must restate the message. Time, energy, and money are wasted, and morale and goodwill may be affected.

Listening attentively is an important attribute for both speakers and listeners. Individuals listen to receive information—information about people, the subject matter, and the situation. This information may generate new ideas to make intelligent decisions and to resolve problems.

Listening is important for employee morale. Employees want to be heard. Supervisors must listen attentively (not superficially) to what workers say. Likewise, subordinates should listen attentively to superiors.

Importance of Nonverbal Communication

Nonverbal communication, always present, can confirm or deny oral communication. Thus, the effective oral communicator realizes that nonverbal cues affect the message. The intended purpose may not be achieved if the nonverbal cues contradict the verbal. Effective oral communicators acknowledge, understand, and use appropriate nonverbal language.

For additional information on nonverbal communication, refer to Chapters 1, 2, 26, and 29, as well as to ideas expressed later in this chapter (nonverbal communication and the public speaker).

Business Settings for Interpersonal Communication

In a business atmosphere, interpersonal oral communication is used in various situations (for example, in person-to-person or telephone conversations, interviews, conferences, meetings, public speaking, and dictation). Some people experience these activities daily; few do them well. The following data should help you improve your business oral communication in typical business situations.

Person-to-person conversations. Person-to-person conversations (also called face-to-face or one-to-one conversations) can be either informal or formal meetings with two or more persons.

The **informal person-to-person meeting** may be limited to spur-of-the-moment planning: the initiator may plan a few basic questions or statements, but basically the conversation develops as the participants speak and listen to one another.

Unless the participants use language understood by all and really listen to one another, person-to-person conversations are actually **talking experiences**. Person *A* talks; Person *B* talks. *A* talks again; then it is *B*'s turn to comment. Each person is concentrating on his or her sound qualities, a specific viewpoint, or the desire to use powerful or impressive words. Very little (if any) genuine communication takes place in such encounters.

Formal face-to-face conversations may be internal (such as evaluation and counseling) or external (such as sales and purchase). To be successful, formal business person-to-person conversations must be planned; the participants must understand the language and listen carefully. Each participant should be involved in the communication process: speaking and listening attentively and at appropriate times.

Telephone conversations. Telephone communication is a commonly misused form of oral communication. This may be because telephone communication is relatively economical, readily available, easy to use, and fast. The telephone has become so commonplace that toddlers to senior citizens use it with little thought or effort. Within a few minutes, communication almost anywhere is possible. Business conference calls (several people in different cities engaging in one telephone conversation) are daily occurrences.

As commonplace as the telephone is, some people find it difficult to use for securing information or discussing solutions to specific problems. The telephone conversation is basically a short, planned person-to-person conversation. Users should get to the point and avoid wasting time and money on idle chatter.

Before dialing (be sure the number is correct!), list in appropriate order the questions and important points you want to discuss. During the conversation, listen carefully and take notes. Avoid rude mannerisms (such as rattling papers, monopolizing the conversation, interrupting, talking to others, shouting, whistling, playing music, eating, drinking, chewing gum, or smoking while conversing).

Make a good impression and maintain goodwill by being pleasant and courteous.

Identify yourself immediately. No busy person appreciates a "guess who's calling" routine.

Be ready to speak when the call is placed. Do not keep someone waiting unnecessarily.

Speak directly into the telephone mouthpiece using words and expressions understood by the listener and pronouncing them clearly and correctly.

Avoid slang and offensive sexist expressions.

Speak at an appropriate rate and volume (not too fast or slow, too loud or soft), varying your voice to add emphasis where needed.

Avoid prolonging your conversation. You can telephone again if your business cannot be completed in one telephone call.

If you have listened carefully and taken notes, you can write a memorandum summarizing the important points covered after the call. Business people dealing with the public, buyers, and suppliers write telephone memoranda for future reference. Often, telephone communications are confirmed with written communications (a letter, for example). Message forms are available for recording telephone messages for "while you are out" times. (See a sample form in Chapter 16.)

You may wish to devise a special message form to guide telephone conversations—especially if you have many similar telephone communications involving technical information (for example, purchases and sales orders, engineering data) or complaints.

To curtail wasted time and effort and maintain good human relations, at least one telephone system has circulated publications explaining exactly where to hold the mouthpiece, good telephone etiquette, and ways to communicate various messages. Teletraining equipment, public speakers, and software to educate and train business people on telephoning properly and efficiently are also available.

Interviews, conferences, and meetings. The most common interview, the employment interview, is discussed in Chapter 29. Other types of interviews include the exit interview (when an individual leaves a company) and a problem-solving interview (personal interview to gather information from a specific group, often for research purposes).

The **interview** is usually planned and may be **structured** (planned so as to follow established guidelines with definite sequences of questions and comments) or **unstructured** (planned so as to follow established guidelines, but flexible to allow natural flow of questions and comments).

At business conferences and meetings, a planned agenda is necessary for getting the proposed business done efficiently and effectively. Each participant should understand clearly his or her part in the proceedings. When no plan for the order of business has been adopted, the usual agenda follows the format outlined by *Robert's Rules of Order.*

During interviews, conferences, meetings, and similar group situations, listen carefully and remember the effect of various nonverbal cues; the importance of good human relations; and the need to present ideas clearly, completely, and correctly. Each participant should know the precise purpose for the meeting and plan the presentation of important facts. All individuals should listen to viewpoints expressed and make comments and criticisms respecting the rights and feelings of everyone involved.

The physical setting for an interview, conference, or meeting can affect the end results. Insofar as possible, the room should be private; have comfortable seating and working space; be uncluttered; be free from noises and distractions; have appropriate lighting and temperature controls; and contain necessary word processing, electronic, and visual aids (chalkboards, flip charts, flannel boards, overhead projectors, film projectors, and screens). A photocopy machine can be available to provide copies of technical or complicated data.

Interviews, conferences, and meetings are usually summarized in a written report. Tape recorders, dictation machines, stenographers, and secretaries may be present to help record proceedings and prepare minutes and reports. The proceedings may be reported as suggested by company policies or *Robert's Rules of Order*.

The presiding officer for an interview, conference, or meeting should be chosen carefully, for the success of the meeting is the leader's responsibility. The leader should:

1. Prepare an agenda based on established guidelines and preset goals
2. Provide each participant with a copy of the agenda with adequate time for study and analysis before the meeting
3. Choose an appropriate meeting time and location
4. Invite knowledgeable and interested participants
5. Arrange transportation, lodging, meals, visual and technical aids, and refreshments as necessary and advisable
6. Determine who is to record the proceedings and how it is to be done
7. Make each participant feel necessary, important, and relatively at ease (but not overpowering others)
8. Bring out varying viewpoints and ideas
9. Guide and summarize discussions to reach relevant decisions based on logic
10. Open and close meetings on time

•

PUBLIC SPEAKING

Your success in the business world may depend on your public speaking ability. If the idea of speaking before an audience frightens you—as it does many people—remember that public speakers develop their ability to speak well. It is a rewarding accomplishment. Besides possible monetary rewards, effective public speakers are rewarded by feeling good about their achievements.

Becoming an accomplished public speaker involves studying your subject matter, your nonverbal and verbal abilities, and your intended audience. In addition, time must be spent practicing effective communication skills. Specifically, public speakers must reach their listeners with their voices, verbal and nonverbal expressions, and speech organization and content. They are presenters of information meant to inform, persuade, or entertain.

Voice

Analyze your voice qualities. Is your voice easily heard, but not loud and overpowering? Is the voice pitch low, rather than high? High-pitched voices can be irritating and suggest lack of confidence. Does your voice evidence changes in thought and mood, or is it monotonous and dull? You can create audience enthusiasm by changing the volume, tone, or tempo of your voice. Do you join words smoothly, or are they interlaced with meaningless and distracting *you knows*, *uhs*, and *okays*? Do you drop word beginnings or endings? Do you pronounce words correctly and appropriately for the audience?

Video equipment and tape recorders can help the would-be public speaker define and develop good speaking techniques. However, even without the aid of technical equipment, you can rehearse your speech and time your delivery rate. Practice your *entire* speech over and over. This will help you relate to the whole message with enthusiasm.

Speech Format

Public speakers must do more than speak well. They must know thoroughly their subject matter and related data. Effective listening is likely when public speakers know what they are talking about and can relate it with ease. The speech should fit the occasion and be logically organized and interesting to the listeners. Start with a simple, basic format, for example:

- I. Introduction
  - A. Attention-getter
  - B. Topic and purpose
  - C. Brief outline of text
- II. Major Point I
  - A. Details, facts, and examples
  - B. Supporting evidence
    1. Sources
    2. Statistics and/or
    3. Quotations or testimonials

(Repeat Section II as many times as necessary to cover all major points)

- III. Summary and concluding statements
- IV. Question time

A brief outline for a speech entitled "Hidden Communication of the Face and Hands" follows:

- I. Nonverbal communication
  - A. Display "smiles" and "monkey" transparencies as attention-getter
  - B. Define nonverbal communication
  - C. Point out key factors
  - D. Explain importance

II. Facial expressions
    A. Display transparencies (quiz approach)
    B. Explain and comment
        1. Eye language
        2. Smiles and their meanings
        3. Liar cues
    C. State sources
III. Hand communication
    A. Display transparencies
    B. Explain and illustrate hand communications
        1. Normal handshake
        2. Nonverbal cues
            a. Weak, lazy, unenthusiastic
            b. Strong, power plays
            c. Sportsmanship
            d. Narrow-mindedness
            e. Authority
    C. State sources
IV. Summary and implications
    A. "Read" nonverbal communication carefully
    B. Remember that meaning is based on
        1. Situation
        2. Listeners
        3. Context
        4. Cultural influences
    C. State sources
V. Questions from listeners

Keep within your time limit and cover major points adequately. Covering too many major points will confuse listeners. If you can talk for just five minutes, bring out just one major idea. Within a half hour, you might adequately and realistically speak about two or three major points.

Speech Content

After deciding the major topics for your speech, you can begin writing. As you write,

Be aware of your intended audience
Be sure your facts and supporting data are accurate

The final speech draft should be well organized, contain relevant ideas backed by realistic research and accurate data, and be free from English errors.

During the introduction, get your audience's attention and establish a rapport with them. Some speakers secure attention with a joke or short story related to the subject. You can tell a personal experience or use an appropriate anecdote from a book or magazine. It is important to use only appropriate humor and stories and to limit the amount of time spent in such activity. Listeners generally want to hear about the subject matter, not numerous stories or off-color jokes. If you like, you can also start your speech with a provocative statement, question, or quotation.

Successful public speakers will neither talk "up" nor "down" to their audiences. They will use technical words in a meaningful context and explain them when necessary. They also avoid slang and English idioms (expressions with special meanings, such as *run for office* or *buy a pig in a poke*). You will need to edit your speech until you find the best words to accomplish your purpose. Words and actions can create feelings of joy, disgust, amazement, resentment, disbelief, delight, anger, or other powerful emotions. Some speakers deliberately plan to evoke strong emotions. This practice can be useful—or detrimental—to the purpose of the speech. Remember to use correct English, including the correct person and tense, the active voice, and parallel expressions.

Conclude your speech with a few well-planned summary statements. This is the time to draw ideas together, but not to repeat the speech. You can use the conclusion to challenge listeners or propose a solution.

Allow time for verbal feedback. You may choose either to

1. Entertain questions throughout your talk
2. Ask your listeners to hold questions until the formal question time. (You might tell your audience that you have scheduled five or ten minutes for answering questions.)

Generally, listeners prefer asking questions and making comments during the presentation.

Answering valid questions directly will improve your credibility. To make sure that the audience has heard the question, repeat it briefly. This procedure will ensure that you are answering the question asked. Give brief, complete, and concise answers, letting your eyes float around the audience as you speak. Give everyone a chance to ask one question before answering several questions from the same person and ignoring other hands raised for recognition. Avoid embarrassing yourself or your audience. Try to determine what the questioner really wants to know. When answering hostile questions, speak slowly and distinctly in a normal voice.

If the speech time allotted you is insufficient for answering questions adequately, tell the listeners where more information is available or make arrangements to handle individual problems.

Speech Delivery

It is normal for even the most experienced speaker to have stage fright. Feeling a little nervous may be an advantage; you will be alert and more apt to consider audience reaction. Your nervousness may not be obvious. To help you relax, breathe deeply and slowly before speaking. In-depth preparation and numerous speech rehearsals will help you build your confidence.

Instead of memorizing your entire speech, memorize just the beginning and the ending. This practice will get you off to a good start and make it possible for you to end quickly if you must. You can memorize major topics or refer to your note cards.

Note cards will help you remember and support your main ideas. If you use note cards, place just one major idea on a card. Write with big letters and underline (with colored ink) the words you wish to emphasize. Mark punctuation (with another color ink) so that you will naturally pause or change your voice pattern. Smile stickers will remind you to smile occasionally.

Nonverbal communication. A well-planned and rehearsed speech can be ineffective if the speaker ignores nonverbal forces (such as environment, listeners' actions and nonactions, and the speaker's dress, grooming, and body language). In addition, the location of the room and its size, color, lighting, temperature, and seating arrangement will affect both speaker and listeners. Other factors to consider are the availability of a podium or lectern and visual and audio equipment. If a speaker has planned to use a stand to hold notes and visual aids (and perhaps hide nervous actions) or technical equipment (for example, overhead projectors and movie or slide projectors) to illustrate and explain major points, she or he can be thrown off guard without these props.

Public speakers should dress and groom themselves neatly, appropriately, and comfortably; maintain occasional eye contact; and use well-chosen, significant gestures to convey the message quickly and easily. The speaker's verbal communication should agree with the nonverbal.

Paralanguage (how something is said) is often more significant than what is said. The listener's interpretation of the message may be affected by the speaker's voice tone and volume; pronunciation, articulation, and inflection of words; number and length of pauses between words; and vocal mannerisms (such as, throat clearing and repeated *uh*s and *okay*s). Even the most common word can portray a different meaning by the way it is said.

Research Information

First, check the library's card catalog, the key to most library holdings. If you need help finding a source, ask a librarian. The appendix also lists possible library sources to help you research your speech topic. Another helpful source is *Vital Speeches*. This magazine identifies speech topics and includes information from well-known speakers.

DICTATION

Few business people prepare their business communications in longhand. Many use word processors or other technical equipment. At times, they may dictate to an individual using a shorthand writing system or a typewriter, or they may use dictation equipment. Knowing how to dictate written communications can make you a better communicator. The skillful dictator is organized and skilled in verbal communication. Skillful dictation to either person or machine takes preplanning and practice. Very few persons dictate well instinctively. Dictating is complex. While thinking what to say next, the dictator must be able to hear the words spoken and spot incorrect or unclear statements and also make necessary corrections and additions.

Dictation to an Individual

When dictating to an individual, skillful dictators:

1. *Have pertinent information and materials before them or readily available.* Sometimes necessary data and materials are stored in nearby files or illustrated in company manuals. This would include addressee names, addresses, and telephone numbers; style illustrations; special preprinted forms; and stationery.
2. *Dictate when they are not smoking, chewing gum, or apt to be distracted by noises and other people.* Having an object in the mouth (especially cigar or cigarette) changes the sounds of words. In addition, smoke or the smell of smoke may annoy or harm the individual taking dictation.
3. *Face the individual taking dictation, and avoid constant walking.*
4. *Indicate immediately specific information needed:*
   a. Name, business title, department, telephone number
   b. Requirements (for example, date desired, rough draft, final copy, quantities, kinds of copies, names and addresses of receivers, or format desired)
   c. Communication need (for example, memorandum, letter, special message form, minutes of meeting, or agenda)
5. *Speak naturally and enunciate clearly.* Your locale (part of the United States or World) affects word choice and pronunciation.

6. *Plan to spell proper names and common, unusual, difficult, or sound-alike words.* The transcriber can experience problems with such terms. For example, Mr. Smith may spell his name *Smith, Smithe, Smythe,* or even *Schmidt.* Technical and professional vocabularies may be particularly difficult for the new employee.
7. Use the phonetic alphabet to clarify spellings:

   A as in Alice
   B as in Bertha
   C as in Charles
   D as in David
   E as in Edward
   F as in Frank
   G as in George
   H as in Henry
   I as in Ida
   J as in James
   K as in Kate
   L as in Lewis
   M as in Mary
   N as in Nellie
   O as in Oliver
   P as in Peter
   Q as in Quaker
   R as in Robert
   S as in Samuel
   T as in Thomas
   U as in Utah
   V as in Victor
   W as in William
   X as in X-ray
   Y as in Young
   Z as in Zebra

   Carol is spelled *C* as in Charles, *A* as in Alice, *R* as in Robert, *O* as in Oliver, and *L* as in Lewis.

8. *Dictate in thought groups:*

   Thank you for your letter [pause] of May 10. *Say* **10** *instead of* **10th**.

9. *Always state the following punctuation marks: semicolon, colon, dash, quotation marks, exclamation point, question mark, parentheses, and brackets.* Stipulate special items such as, centerings, indentations, tables, new paragraphs, capitalizations, signature information, and special closing parts.

tables, new paragraphs, capitalizations, signature information, and special closing parts.

> Indent, Quote To err is human, to forgive comma divine unquote.
> New paragraph
> **Note:** *You might pause for the first comma.*

10. *Express a thank you to the person taking dictation.*

Dictation to a Machine

When dictating to a machine, skillful dictators follow the basic rules. They are especially careful to specify special instructions before starting and to state corrections immediately. In addition, they know how to operate the dictation equipment before using it, and endeavor to dictate in as noise-free a setting as possible. Even the slightest sound is amplified on dictating equipment.

Dictation over the Telephone

When dictating over the telephone, skillful dictators keep the individual taking the dictation in mind. She or he may have to manipulate the telephone while writing or typing. They also allow for catch-up time and ask that the message be read back before concluding the telephone conversation.

Dictation Skills

You can develop your dictation skill by:

1. *Preparing a rough outline of the important points you wish to cover and in the order of presentation.* This will help ensure coherence, clarity, completeness, and correctness.
2. *Practicing dictation privately.* If possible, record your voice as you dictate. Then analyze the play-back realistically and critically. In the long run, you will be using your time wisely. Time spent this way is far better than time spent plodding through dictation to an individual.
3. *Enrolling in available seminars that will help you learn to dictate with proper voice inflection, diction, phrasing, volume, and speed.*
4. *Asking the transcriber to tell you any problems he or she experienced with your dictation.* Then, take steps to correct the situation.

Courtesy

As a final word, remember that dictation involves at least two people. Consider the particular needs and feelings of the other person. By doing so, you will organize your work, be helpful, be courteous, and save time and energy.

LISTENING

An advantage to oral communication is that speakers can change their verbal and nonverbal language to fit responses from listeners. This advantage, however, is lost when the speaker does not listen attentively to verbal and nonverbal answers.

Barriers to Effective Listening

The ability to listen varies from person to person and time to time. Nonetheless, the following factors affect how much individuals really hear:

1. *Noises and distractions.* A cough, baby's cry, shout, telephone ring, or visitor entering the room are among the common noises that interrupt listening.
2. *Acts of God.* An unexpected event (such as a thunderstorm) may temporarily or permanently stop listening.
3. *Listener's physical hearing ability.* Some people are deaf to certain tones and sounds. Regardless of how well the physically impaired concentrate, they will not hear a dull tone, soft voice, or piercing sound.
4. *Listener's physical condition.* Listening is more than a simple, passive exposure to sound. Listeners who are tired, bored, ill, or sleepy may not have the willpower effective listening requires.
5. *Listener's physical comfort.* Listeners bothered by room arrangements, too warm or too cold conditions, uncomfortable seats, color schemes, inadequate or nonworking equipment, and similar environmental factors may have little desire to listen.
6. *Listener's emotional comfort.* Words can cause powerful emotions (such as, anger, contempt, pleasure, or unhappiness). Such emotional digression will keep the listener from hearing at least some portion of the speaker's message.
7. *Listener's attitude.* If the listener has preconceived ideas about the topic or speaker, he or she may block out the speaker.
8. *Listener's and speaker's vocabularies.* If the speaker uses an unfamiliar word, the listener may spend several seconds trying to determine the meaning of the term. If many unknown expressions are used, the listener will not receive the message.
9. *Listener's concentration on words alone.* Listeners should concentrate on ideas, rather than actual words spoken. Since many words have alternate meanings, listening to just the words may raise questions and confuse the listener. The listener should listen for meaning.

10. *Listener's talking while speaker talks.* This should be self-explanatory. You cannot be a speaker and a listener at the same time and expect to get the message.
11. *Listener's awareness of nonverbal cues.* Everyone speaks without actually expressing words. The listener's ability to observe and interpret the speaker's nonverbal communication will affect the message received.
12. *Listener's daydreaming, doodling, or dozing.* Obviously the daydreamer, the doodler and the dozer are not listening attentively. A speaker can inspire (unfortunately) listeners to daydream, doodle, or doze.

Are You a Good Listener?

The belief that listening requires mental effort and attention is revealed in the following self-examination encouraged by the Christophers:

ARE YOU A GOOD LISTENER?

Are you eager to learn about other persons, places, and things?
Can you put yourself in the other person's shoes?
Do you tune in on the speaker's feelings as well as the words being spoken?
Do you try to overcome your own emotional attitudes and prejudgments?
Do you work to identify the main ideas, attitudes and feelings being communicated?
Do you avoid interrupting? Especially, do you curb the impulse to complete the other person's sentences?
Do you ever ask for "feedback" on how people rate you as a listener?
Do you consciously practice listening skills?*

How to Be a Better Listener

If you want to be a better listener, you must work at it.

Do what you can to be informed and knowledgeable: improve your vocabulary, read, study, research
Avoid self-instigated distractions (for example, inattention, talking, doodling, or dozing)
Strive to relate to the speaker's objectives and listen attentively for ideas and meaning, rather than just words
Listen to the speaker's nonverbal communication

**Christopher News Notes*, New York, New York 10017.

CHAPTER SUMMARY

Technical oral business communications should be planned carefully. Effective oral communicators are organized, use good speaking and listening skills, understand human behavior, and know and use nonverbal language correctly.

Person-to-person conversations can be informal with little or no structure. Formal person-to-person conversations require extensive planning. Telephone conversations are actually short, planned, one-to-one conversations, even though the parties are not visible to each other. Interviews can be structured or unstructured. Business meetings and conferences should follow an agenda planned by a presiding officer. Conference leaders are also responsible for choosing knowledgeable participants; setting meeting time and location; arranging physical requirements; opening and closing the meeting on time; and guiding discussions so that all viewpoints are heard and logical decisions made.

Speakers are presenters of information, and they basically rely on nonverbal feedback. Whenever possible, speakers should allow time for verbal feedback (questions and comments, for example). Public speakers are challenged to speak well; know their subject matter; choose and organize words suitable for the intended audience; be skilled nonverbal communicators; and project confidence, know-how, and enthusiasm.

Skilled dictators achieve this distinction by outlining what they want to say and then speaking so that the transcriber will hear and understand precisely. Thus, the skilled dictator will choose appropriate words and speak them at a reasonable speed and volume using proper voice inflection, diction, and phrasing. The dictation environment should be free from distractions and other noises. To develop an effective dictating style, you can attend specific seminars or tape and analyze your dictation. Then practice repeatedly using correct dictation techniques.

Listening is an integral part of oral communication. Both speakers and listeners must listen attentively. Barriers to effective listening include sounds and distractions; acts of God; listener's physical hearing and health, comfort, attitude, actions, ability to discern verbal and nonverbal ideas; and listener's and speaker's vocabulary. To improve your listening ability, become informed and knowledgeable about the subject matter, identify with the speaker's objectives and philosophy, concentrate on listening, and avoid self-instigated distractions.

STUDY QUESTIONS

1. Why is listening an integral part of oral communication?
2. Why are planning skills, human relation skills, and communication skills important for effective oral communication?
3. What are the guidelines for effective telephone conversations?
4. What are the responsibilities of the presiding officer of a business meeting or conference?
5. What is the basic organizational format for public speech?
6. What advice would you give a business person desiring to cultivate good dictation skills?
7. What factors affect our ability and desire to listen attentively?

ACTIVITIES

1. To encourage the need for attentive listening, on the first class day, play this listening-retention game: Player 1 (seat 1) states clearly his or her full name. Player 2 (seat 2) repeats first player's name and adds his or her name. Player 3 (seat 3) must repeat names of player 1 and 2 and add his or her name. Each player in turn would repeat this process until all players have participated. After the game, each player can silently analyze his or her feelings and ability to recall names.

   Note: Players should ask other players to repeat names they have not heard or understood. Players should not take notes during the game.

2. As accurately as you can, for one week keep a daily record of the time you spend reading, writing, speaking, and listening. Total the hours and determine to the nearest percent what part of each day you spend in each activity. Are you surprised at the results?
3. Choose a topic that interests you (perhaps a special interest, hobby, or recreational activity) and prepare an outline for a 15- to 30-minute informative talk. Use the basic format and ideas stated in this chapter. Be sure your outline is limited to one or two ideas you can cover adequately.
4. Without planning, role play a common business telephone transaction; for example, taking a customer's order, ordering supplies from a company vendor, explaining terms of a contract, conveying a complaint, or refusing or accepting a request. Afterward, analyze the good and bad points. Would a planned approach have helped achieve your objective more easily?

   Note: Two students could volunteer or be appointed to role play; the rest of the class should listen attentively to critique the unstructured telephone conversation.

5. If your instructor so directs, follow through with the talk discussed in Activity 3. What attention-getter will you use? What visual aids?
6. You are scheduled to give the speech outlined on pages 451 and 452; however, the Program Committee reduced your speech time to 20 minutes. Revise the outline to comply with this request. You may change the title of the speech.
7. As a classmate gives a short oral talk, interject a barrier to effective listening. Afterward, discuss the effects of your behavior on the speaker.

   Note: Teacher should select or ask for a volunteer to do this. The barrier should be decided upon before the talk. An alternative might be to request a visitor to provide the barrier.

8. Prepare an official agenda for a meeting (business or social group).
9. Record and analyze your dictation voice. (This could be a private recording.)
10. Using the dictation guidelines, dictate a letter from Chapter 8 or 9. (Two students can be selected to participate while classmates listen for factors such as thought groups, word and voice usage, and the dictator's desire to consider the transcriber's needs and ability.)
11. If possible, video tape an oral presentation. Analyze the verbal and nonverbal communication.

LANGUAGE SKILLS DEVELOPMENT

Rewrite each of the following sentences in accordance with the elements of effective writing:

1. Business people, dealing with customers on a large scale, need good communication skills.
2. Oral communication is common in business firms, 75 percent is oral communication.
3. A well-planned speech can be ineffective, if the speaker uses inadequate nonverbal communication.
4. He said a good oral communicator is a good listener."
5. Some speakers deliberately plan to evoke strong emotions, such can be useful.
6. If you want to improve your oral communication ability become a good listener.
7. Lack dynamic opening and closing lines in their presentations.
8. As quick, stop stores, Convenience Foods operatons were not effected by the food price war.

9. During the fiscal year ended June 30, 1985 the corporation sold 9 drug stores in the Indianapolis Area.
10. In the highly automated retailing business, there is still one on one contact between customers and staff.
11. The company's loan agreements provide for the maintenance of minimum working capitals as well as limitations on cash dividends, purchases of common stock, and future lease obligations.
12. Future minimum annual lease payments will be as follows in 1988, $3,963,000, 1989, $3,701,000, and 1990, $3,400,000.

IN-BASKET SIMULATIONS

1. As a spokesperson for Waltere Supermarkets, Inc., prepare an outline for a talk to convince your listeners (customers and potential customers) that the corporation contributes to strong community relations. Supporting evidence includes:
   a. Allowing advertising and in-store ticket sales for local attractions and events. Most tickets are available at discounted prices.
   b. Providing high school students (through distributive education) with on-the-job work experience. The students earn and learn. Presently, many young people are learning how to use electronic scanning equipment.
   c. Holding shopping sprees for organizations to raise funds for the special projects.
   d. Donating funds for research to combat debilitating and other diseases.
   e. Recognizing employees who assume leadership roles in community service.
   f. Offering shoppers consumer goods (such as china, crystal, silverware, and cookware) at little or no cost.
   g. Conducting tours (including free transportation) to special events.
   h. Donating goods to local organizations for charitable or money-making projects.
2. As an advertising executive for Waltere Supermarkets, Inc., prepare an outline and dictate a form letter to potential customers. (As the instructor suggests, dictate to an individual using a shorthand system, to an individual at a typewriter or other machine, or to a dictation machine.) Describe Waltere's del-bakeries:
   a. Del-bakeries are in 66 stores (first one opened 12 years ago).
   b. Sizes range from 100 to 2000 square feet.

c. Items include approximately 200 bakery items and 600 deli items; 150 imported and domestic cheeses are available in ten del-bakeries. Hot entrees for ready-made meals and various sizes and types of cakes baked and decorated for special occasions are other specialty items.
d. New items are continually developed.
e. Racks full of baking pans can be rolled directly into modern rack ovens.
f. One-on-one customer service, even though the retail stores are highly automated.
g. Various size and content party trays to save work for the busy party giver.

Nonverbal Communication

After studying Chapter 26, you should be able to:

- Identify the impact of nonverbal communications
- Identify nonverbal communications in both written and oral communications
- Decode nonverbal cues in context
- Describe why nonverbal communications create a greater credibility than verbal communications

Like verbal language, nonverbal communication provides information. The information is principally about the sender. Every one transmits nonverbal messages, and everyone is influenced by those messages. No one can stop nonverbal communication. Thus, for successful interpersonal relations, everyone should develop nonverbal communication skills.

An estimated 90 percent of the messages communicated are nonverbal. However, most people do not realize how much or what they are communicating to others nonverbally. While verbal communication may be planned, nonverbal communication is often unconscious and unplanned. Because of this, the listener (or reader, since written communications also speak nonverbally) may believe nonverbal language more readily than verbal.

Although many nonverbal symbols have recognized meanings, a nonverbal symbol should not be isolated or overemphasized. Even skilled interpreters of nonverbal language do not take this liberty. It is too easy to disagree on the nonverbal message. Since nonverbal communication is complex, isolated factors should not be taken out of context. Indeed, it is unwise to interpret any language—verbal or nonverbal—without considering the specific situation, the individuals involved, and the specific environment or culture.

NONVERBAL COMMUNICATION DEFINED

Very simply, **nonverbal communication** is all human communication other than verbal. Typically, nonverbal communication is evidenced by body movements: posture, fingers, hands, arms, legs, eyes, and facial expressions. However, nonverbal communication includes silence, appearance, use of space, use of possessions, grooming, clothing, touching behavior, smelling sensitivity, cultural practices, the environment, and body movements.

NONVERBAL COMMUNICATION TERMINOLOGY

The study of human nonverbal communication still needs to be defined and structured; however, some vocabulary is widely recognized.

Cues are the symbols used to convey nonverbal messages. Thus, a gesture, body movement, silence, or any of the signals mentioned earlier have recognized meanings. Some nonverbal cues have more than one meaning. For example, a wink can say *Keep this information secret* or *Don't believe what I am saying* or *I think you are attractive* or *I'd like to know you better*. In addition, the wink may really be an eye reflex—the winker may have dust in the eye or a medical problem with the eye. Thus, it is not wise to take a symbol out of context. Meaning should be established on the basis of the specific situation, the individuals involved, and the culture.

When individuals talk with gestures, they are using **sign language**. When they move their bodies to fulfill a personal need, they are using **action language**. As they eat dinner, drink a beverage, smoke a cigarette, walk, or sleep, they may (perhaps, innocently) be communicating more than the need for food, drink, transportation, exercise, or sleep. A myriad of meanings have been attached to these everyday actions. Some researchers believe, for example, that the way a person walks speaks nonverbally to a would-be rapist.

Another category of nonverbal communication is **object language**. This language is evidenced by the intentional or unintentional display and use of the body and things (for example, color and choice of style of clothing, automobiles, and other possessions; the interior decorations in homes; the jewelry selected and worn; the fragrances emitted; and the occupations pursued). Things are talking daily.

Kinesics is the study and classification of body movements. Prime examples of kinesics are posture and eye, facial, and hand movements. Dr. Ray Birdwhistell was one of America's first psychologists to research body communication.

Proxemics is the use of personal and social space. Like animals, humans have a physical and psychological need for space. The amount of necessary space depends on the individuals involved, the situation, and the culture.

Paralanguage (discussed in Chapter 25) is a nonverbal language that stresses the importance of how an individual speaks, rather than what is said.

Metacommunication is a message received from spoken words but not expressly stated in those words. For example, *I am busy* may communicate *Don't ask me to do the work* or *Ask someone else to help you.* Or, bragging about yourself or poking exaggerated fun at yourself by pointing out your weaknesses, vices, embarrassments, or setbacks may communicate *I have no confidence in myself.*

NONVERBAL COMMUNICATION IN INTERNAL BUSINESS SETTINGS

As mentioned in Chapter 25, conversations, interviews, meetings, and conferences are typical business settings for internal oral communication. However, they are also settings for nonverbal communication. The nonverbal communication can reveal confidence, interest, sincerity, openness, honesty, dependability, or lack of any of these desirable traits. Nonverbal cues can reinforce or contradict verbal symbols.

Common meanings for the nonverbal communication are encouraged by an individual's posture, hands, eyes, facial expressions, and space requirements. The nonverbal communication may be oversimplified, but an understanding of the possible messages is important for effective communication.

Posture and Body Movements

To show confidence and assertiveness, individuals should stand erect, but not rigid. They should walk with a deliberate and easy gait (rather than stiffly like a tin soldier). Research indicates that superiors tend to keep their heads raised while talking and are more relaxed than their subordinates who nod often and lower their heads when speaking.

Sitting slightly forward shows interest in the situation; however, gradually sitting back shows confidence. It is advisable to sit straight (but not stiff) with legs toward another. Turning the body away from a person may indicate dislike or disinterest in that person. Legs can be crossed above the knees or at the ankles, but wrapping them around chair legs is an unsightly distraction. Tapping a foot indicates boredom, overeagerness, or high nervousness.

Hand Communication

The hands explain and emphasize verbal communication as well as the nonverbal communication of the body and face. Hands welcome individuals; they control and adapt conversations through gestures.

A handshake suggests personal attributes and the mutual reaching out for approval and acceptance. Ideally, the handshake is a brief clasping of right hands—with equal pressure by both persons—followed by one, two, or three up-and-down movements. Hands should be clasped in a firm grip; the bone-crushing grip suggests masochism or insecurity. A hand offered limply suggests neither fellowship nor respect. Such individuals may be judged weak, indifferent, lazy, undependable, sullen, forgetful, or unhealthy. The other person feels let down.

Hands continue talking even when motionless. Individuals fearing incorrect moves will inhibit hand and body movements. Motionless hands may reveal a dull personality. Hands tightly grasping chair arms imply nervousness and insecurity.

Excessive hand movements can reveal anxiety or below-average intelligence or confidence. While two-handed gestures emphasize ideas and suggest confidence, used excessively they weaken the message. Hands should be moved three or four times a minute. Finger tapping and inappropriate arm waving should be avoided. Marking each point with the down motion of the fingers can be a positive way to enumerate ideas. It reveals know-how and confidence.

Hand gestures considered as power plays cause some people to feel threatened. Such gestures include making a steeple with the hands, shaking a pointed finger, pounding on the desk, clasping hands behind the head and thrusting the chest forward, placing hands on hips, or crossing them across your chest.

Research studies indicate that successful liars display excessive hand-to-face gestures: covering their mouths as if to conceal the truth or to avoid speaking; touching their chins or noses; rubbing their cheeks; scratching their eyebrows; and tugging or fussing with their ears, beards, or hair. The inference is that people who want to appear open and honest will avoid touching any part of their faces or hair. Such nervous actions communicate the negative.

Certain finger or hand mannerisms are always considered offensive in a business atmosphere: combing or brushing hair; filing, polishing, or cleaning finger nails; using a toothpick or fingers to pick teeth; yawning; toying with pencils, jewelry, eyeglasses, or any object; obscene gestures; straightening papers on someone's desk (without permission); smoking (especially in a nonsmoking area); and brushing real or imagined lint from another's clothes.

Eye and Facial Communication

Like the body and hands, the face communicates an individual's intentions, outlook, emotions, and personality. Most people cannot hide completely their true feelings and attitude.

The eyes are considered the most expressive part of the body. Open and alert eyes reveal interest and enthusiasm, but eyes open very wide reveal astonishment or surprise. The pupils of the eye will dilate (widen) when an individual is interested; contract (become narrow) when the person is uninterested or dislikes something. A person may temporarily close the eyes to see or think through a situation. On the other hand, the person may be shutting out or ignoring everyone.

Eye movements are conversation regulators; conversationalists take brief, alternating turns speaking and listening. The listener's eyes can reveal the depth of understanding and interest in the conversation. Certain eye movements suggest lack of interest, boredom, or tact: gazing about the room while someone speaks, checking watch or wall clock, or reading another's personal papers without permission.

Americans expect occasional eye contact. They trust those who can look them in the eye. The length of time spent looking can indicate whether the gazer is interested or uninterested. Direct eye contact for more than ten seconds makes others feel uncomfortable and anxious. Staring eyes seem to overpower and stress authority.

A smile may indicate pleasure, humor, ridicule, friendliness, good manners, doubt, acceptance, equality, superordination, or subordination. Its meaning depends on the situation and the culture. Accoring to Dr. Ray Birdwhistell, one of America's first psychologists to study body motion communication, the smile is not a natural gesture but a mass of contradictions. He learned that some subjects smiled when subjected to a positive environment; others smiled in a repugnant environment. A smile in one society depicted friendliness; in another, embarrassment. In some cases, a smile is a warning that hostility will follow unless tension is reduced or eliminated.

Space

In many business situations (for example, interviews, conferences, and meetings) the acceptable interpersonal distance is approximately 4 ft. However, the public speaker standing on a raised platform at least 12 ft. from the audience feels secure and important.

Direct eye contact has the effect of shortening the amount of needed personal space. In a conversation, individuals seated opposite each other will feel more comfortable with direct eye contact than individuals who are seated side by side, especially if the conversation is considered very personal.

Business people often use their desks to separate them from employees or visitors. The desk provides the needed space to "protect" their territory. A business person who shortens this distance by standing at the side (rather than behind) the desk reveals a deeper interest in the other individual.

The culture affects space requirements. It is said that individuals in certain foreign countries (for example, Italy and South America) will allow a closer proximity than do North Americans in the same situation.

Appearance, Grooming, Color, and Time

You are what you appear to be. This is a common conception of many people, including business people. Individuals who want to give the impression that they can be or are successful office or professional employees will dress and groom appropriately. A conservative business suit or a basically styled (not ultra frilly or flashy) dress is considered appropriate by numerous executives employed by the Fortune 500 corporations. The casually dressed person communicates a desire for leisure and relaxation, rather than *I am ready to work on the company team.* Even jeans with a famous name stated on the back pocket or a shirt with an animal figure on its front pocket are not considered traditional clothing for the business or office employee who wants to climb the corporate ladder of success.

Cleanliness and neatness are important nonverbal communicators. Everyone should have a clean body and wear neatly pressed and clean clothing. Since odors communicate nonverbally, avoid using cosmetics or fragrances with strong, conflicting odors. A little fragrance goes a long way in a business setting.

Men and women should choose simple and attractive hair styles. A man's hair should not be longer than the top of his collar; women can have longer hair. Neatly trimmed mustaches and beards are gaining acceptance, but too much (or unkempt) facial hair nonverbally communicates that the individual will not listen to authority, has something to hide, or is sloppy or careless.

Colors create moods and can affect the business setting. Blue is considered calm and soothing; brown, protective; black, masterful; red, defiant or stimulating; white, open. The more vibrant the color, the deeper the feeling.

Have you ever known someone who is always late for appointments? Such individuals are communicating nonverbally, and the message is unfavorable. Prompt individuals reveal their interest in others and the situation.

NONVERBAL COMMUNICATION OF THE PUBLIC SPEAKER

Public speakers usually rely on nonverbal communication for feedback, and the audience will relate to the verbal and nonverbal symbols speakers use. Thus, it is extremely important for speakers to know what they are communicating nonverbally and to understand the nonverbal language of the audience.

Public speakers want to communicate subject know-how with confidence and enthusiasm. This is possible with timely and appropriate verbal and nonverbal language. Chapter 25 includes ideas on improving verbal communication. Appropriate nonverbal communication for public speakers includes:

1. *Dressing to fit the occasion.* The conservative business suit is appropriate for most situations. In an informal atmosphere, speakers should dress neatly, but informally. At presidential fireside chats, a president sat erect (but comfortably) and wore a sweater instead of the typical suit jacket.

2. *Standing erect with hands at one's sides or behind one's back.* The hands can be placed on the sides of the lectern but not too tightly to suggest insecurity and nervousness. Seated public speakers can show authority by placing their chairs on a raised platform at least 12 ft. from the audience.
3. *Allowing the eyes to float around the room so as to have frequent eye contact with many listeners.* The audience will consider such speakers open and honest; the speakers can observe nonverbal cues. Even public speakers who read their talks and use visual and audio aids should look at the audience occasionally.
4. *Maximizing audience attention by moving toward the listeners (if possible).*
5. *Using meaningful and appropriate gestures.* (See *Hand Communication* in this chapter.)
6. *Smiling appropriately to communicate pleasure, humor, friendliness, and acceptance.*

NONVERBAL COMMUNICATION OF WRITTEN COMMUNICATIONS

Written communications speak nonverbally to the reader. The company or writer choosing a full block or AMS simplified letter style (see Figures 6–2 and 6–3) nonverbally communicates the desire to save time and motion. These letter styles can be typed more easily and more quickly than other traditional business styles. However, since the AMS letter style does not include a salutation, letter writers using the style may communicate that a salutation is unnecessary or that no salutation is better than one that might offend.

The appearance of written communications speak nonverbally. Personnel managers advise that poorly organized, sloppy, or carelessly written résumés and cover letters influence their decision not to interview potential candidates. Such unattractive employment forms nonverbally communicate that the applicant is poorly organized, sloppy, or careless and that his or her work will be too.

The mechanical features used in letters, reports, and other business communications speak nonverbally. For example, writers can emphasize data by using headings, capital letters, colors, underlines, illustrations, graphs, charts, tables, and pictures. The placement of information and the amount of space devoted to it nonverbally communicate the importance attached to the topic. Consequently, several pages about a subject tells the reader that the writer believed the topic more important than a topic buried in the middle of a large paragraph. (See Chapter 3, "Developing Language Skill," for more information.)

Tone (the way a statement sounds) is communicated nonverbally. Negative words and ideas emphasize the negative; however, writers can use positive and cheerful words and still arouse negative feelings in the reader. The reader may read between the lines and not like the message. Writers using many ego-centered words (*I*, *we*, *me*, *us*, *mine*, *our*, the company name) suggest an overwhelming self-interest.

The timing of a communication speaks nonverbally. Unnecessary delays may nonverbally communicate that either the reader or the communication is not important. Correspondence should be answered promptly. Most correspondence can be answered within two weeks. Prompt replies help readers feel important. However, the reader should not think decisions were made without careful consideration of all facts.

CHAPTER SUMMARY

Everyone constantly communicates nonverbally with gestures, face and body actions, possessions, appearance, grooming, color, time, space, touch, smell, and paralanguage.

Nonverbal communication can have a significant impact on both private and professional lives. It can make a difference between a successful and unsuccessful business person, an effective or ineffective speech, and an acceptable or unacceptable written communication.

Nonverbal cues should be decoded in context with the situation, people involved, and culture. Otherwise the meaning may differ and the message may be distorted. Because nonverbal communication is usually spontaneous, it usually has greater credibility than verbal communication.

STUDY QUESTIONS

1. Why should business people be skilled nonverbal communicators?
2. Write a definition for each of the following nonverbal communications terms:
   - a. Kinesics
   - b. Proxemics
   - c. Paralanguage
   - d. Metacommunication
   - e. Nonverbal cues
   - f. Sign language
   - g. Action language
   - h. Object language
3. For each of the following, specify one or more nonverbal cues and the messages conveyed:
   - a. Gestures
   - b. Face
   - c. Posture
   - d. Space
   - e. Clothing
   - f. Colors
   - g. Grooming

4. How do public speakers communicate nonverbally?
5. How do letters and reports communicate nonverbally?
6. How can your clothing, appearance, and time usage impress your business associates?
7. How can metacommunication influence your verbal message?

ACTIVITIES

1. Specify ten do's and ten don'ts of nonverbal communication at a business meeting.
2. Observe two individuals in a public place (such as a restaurant or bus station). What nonverbal communication do you see in the facial expressions? Bodily movements? Physical appearance? Clothing? Possessions? Other? Write your observations and ideas.
3. Devise a slogan or statement to fit the nonverbal communication evidenced by an individual illustrated in a magazine or newspaper advertisement.
4. Write a short critique on a phase of nonverbal communication that interests you. Include complete bibliography data.
5. In an informal face-to-face situation with a friend (for example, dining, studying, or talking), set an object (for example, your book, purse, or watch) near him or her. While you continue the informal activity and use the item as needed, gradually place the object closer and closer to your friend. Try to be nonchalant, but deliberately invade his or her territory. How is your friend reacting?
6. Watch the nonverbal language of a political speaker. What is she or he communicating with gestures, facial expressions, posture, and appearance? Does the nonverbal agree with the verbal communication? Explain.
7. Try this experiment with a friend. Agree to the friend's suggestion (for example, watch a specific television program; go to a party, dance, or sporting event; or join him or her for dinner) but use nonverbal communication that negates your voice. How did the other person react?

LANGUAGE SKILLS DEVELOPMENT

1. What might be the metacommunication for each of the following?
   a. It's time for class to begin. (Teacher's statement at the beginning of class.)
   b. Come any time.
   c. I'm the greatest.
   d. I'm sure you will agree with our proposal.
   e. Did you proofread the report carefully?
   f. You are the only person to mention this problem.

2. What might be the kinesic message (or messages) for each of the following actions?
   a. A person usually arrives on time for appointments
   b. A person usually arrives late for appointments
   c. A sales representative arrives on time for an appointment but must wait to see the potential buyer
   d. A person looks at his or her wristwatch during an interview
   e. A person shakes hands limply
   f. A person does not answer several questions on a form
   g. A letter writer mails a communication with just one spelling error
   h. An individual avoids eye contact
   i. An individual reads a newspaper while you are talking
   j. A professor ties his necktie incorrectly and has unshined shoes
   k. A student misses several classes (Would your answer be different if the student told the teacher before missing class?)
   l. An employee misses several days of work and doesn't telephone employer

IN-BASKET SIMULATIONS

Mr. Raymond Waltere, President of Waltere Supermarkets, Inc., called a special meeting of officers to discuss the possibility of opening another store in Indianapolis. State the possible communication message portrayed by each of the following:

1. One officer arrived ten minutes late with uncombed hair and no suit jacket.
2. One officer arrived two minutes late. He was neatly dressed and groomed.
3. Two officers arrived five minutes early.
4. One officer did not attend, but she sent a note explaining that she was attending another scheduled meeting.
5. These statements were made:
   a. As soon as convenient, please get out a news release.
   b. Rush this item a little bit.
   c. I'm sure I can handle that matter.
   d. Perhaps I can take care of that before the month ends.
   e. Harry can do that.
   f. I'll remind you tomorrow.
   g. I waited two hours for him.
   h. If you want to get something done, you better do it yourself.

Career Applications

27

Writing the Data Sheet

After studying Chapter 27, you should be able to:

- Analyze yourself, potential employers, and the job market
- Recognize the difference between data sheets (personal data sheets, résumés, and vita)
- Categorize and word information to best present yourself
- Prepare your own data sheet

A written communication may be the first contact you have with a potential employer. It paints the first picture of you. Before contacting an employer, however, you are going to need the single most important document in your career file: your data sheet.

The **data sheet** may take one of three forms: the personal data sheet, résumé, or vita. Each gives facts that the prospective employer would want to know about you. The amount and style of information differs with each of these forms. For example, the **personal data sheet** lists selected information in abbreviated form. The **résumé** explains the details in descriptive paragraphs. The **vita** elaborates on the applicant's formal education and work experience and is especially useful for the highly technical or professional worker.

The purpose of any data sheet is to present your most marketable information in a format that will appeal to the prospective employer. First, ask yourself, what do I want the employer to know? Then ask, what will the employer want to know about me?

While preparing your data sheet, you are preparing (at least in part) for your employment interview. You analyzed the job characteristics and requirements; the company—its organization, procedures, products or services, and possible opportunities; and yourself in relation to the job and to the company.

YOU AND THE JOB MARKET

To prepare an informative data sheet projecting the most marketable you, conduct three analyses: self-analysis, job or market analysis, and company analysis. The more thorough the analyses, the more apt you are to make the best career decisions and to create an effective data sheet and **application** (also called **cover**) **letter**. (An application letter would accompany your data sheet. For specific ideas on writing application letters, see Chapter 28.)

Self-Analysis

Before trying to sell yourself, know yourself. Conduct a self-inventory or self-assessment by evaluating your past and present life (for example, your personal characteristics, interests, needs, values, aptitudes, formal education and training, and work experience).

You can begin by listing enjoyable activities, personal priorities, and long- and short-range goals. List specifically all special courses, jobs, awards, special interests, major areas of study, special study groups or committees, and languages, as well as extra-curricular activities including memberships in social and professional organizations, athletics, and other groups.

Analyze your marketable skills:

1. Specific content or technical skills
2. Functional skills
3. Adaptive skills

Content and **technical skills** are generally achieved through vocational or on-the-job training. Most jobs require certain specialized, technical skills. **Functional skills** are nontechnical and can be transferred from job to job. They include oral and written communication skills (including listening), computation skills, problem-solving and analytical skills, organizational skills, and interpersonal skills. **Adaptive skills** are the personal and social traits that help employees adjust to the work environment. Employers prefer professional and technical workers who are tactful, assertive, outgoing, industrious, well groomed, motivated, self-promoting, flexible, persevering, and creative. They also want employees who are fast learners and positive thinkers. An applicant's nontechnical and personal attributes may make the critical difference in getting (or not getting) the professional or technical job.

After you have recorded everything you can think of (even though not every item will become part of the final data sheet), categorize the items under such general headings as Personal Data; Formal Education and Training; Work Experience; Special Skills, Activities, and Interests; Miscellaneous. The result should be a picture of you—your accomplishments, interests, talents, and priorities up to this point in your life.

Special aids are available to help with this analysis. You can consult with librarians, career specialists, counselors, teachers, and friends; use reference sources and self-assessment exercises in the library and in college placement offices; and study results from interest inventories, value or personality surveys, and aptitude tests. Specific information sources are included in the bibliography at the end of this chapter.

Job Analysis

If you have not yet decided what field to pursue, make that your next step. After you do decide on a specific job, expand your thinking. What other possibilities are open to you? For example, besides being a personnel manager, can you qualify for other managerial or professional positions? Check into employment opportunities, the work atmosphere, the nature of the position, the training needed, the estimated earnings, and so on.

Explore possible careers by reading career pamphlets and books, occupational reference books, trade and professional publications, and newspapers. Talk with friends, relatives, placement personnel, and business and professional persons. Review career films. Excellent career publications include the *Dictionary of Occupational Titles*, *Occupational Outlook Handbook*, and the *Occupational Outlook Reprint Series*, all published by the U.S. Bureau of Labor Statistics. Other information sources are listed in the bibliography at the end of this chapter.

Company Analysis

Once a general career area has taken priority in your plans, learn what you can about specific companies that can further your career ambitions. Determine their organizational structure, procedures, products or services, financial status, executives' names and job titles, possible job opportunities, and so on. The more you know about a company's policies, practices, and personnel, the easier it is to write creative, original, and you-centered data sheets and application letters. Consult references in libraries, publications and videos housed in placement offices, telephone and business directories, employment advertisements, or any other sources that might be helpful. Personal visits to business companies can be very enlightening. Several specific sources of information are listed in the bibliography at the end of this chapter.

After you have researched yourself, career fields, and possible businesses and organizations that may hire you, you are ready to assemble the information in a concise format that will appeal to prospective employers. You are going to turn that information into marketable assets directed to the company of your choice.

Which data sheet will best serve your needs—the personal data sheet, résumé, or vita? For the new college graduate, a data sheet in detailed form (sometimes called a personal data sheet) or descriptive form (résumé) gives the facts needed to encourage employment interviews. As your career achievements increase, the vita (described later) becomes necessary.

PERSONAL DATA SHEET

If you were to write an application letter including all the information that a prospective employer might want to know before the interview, the letter would probably have two or more pages. Therefore, the common practice is to present details about yourself in a data sheet, accompanied by a short, concise, creative, you-centered letter.

Federal and state laws prohibit prospective employers from requesting initial information about an applicant's sex, date of birth or age, marital status, race, color, religion, national origin (in the case of women, maiden name or parent's name), or any other data that would directly or indirectly furnish such knowledge. However, laws do not prohibit applicants from volunteering any particular type of information. The self-analysis and company analysis should help you determine which facts are pertinent to the data sheet.

Basic sections of the data sheet include Personal Information, Formal Education and Training, Work Experience, Special Interests and Activities, and, in some cases, References. The sections can be arranged to suit the writer, but information such as your name, address, and telephone number should be prominently placed on the first page. All facts should be arranged to impress the employer favorably.

Personal Information

You may center your name, address, and telephone number as the heading (at least one-half inch from the top of the page):

Steven J. Parks
9918 Euclid Street, N.E.
Cleveland, OH 44123
(216) 617-7120

Or you may type the information flush with the left margin (full-block style) along with other personal data:

Personal Data

Name:	Steven J. Parks
Address:	9918 Euclid Street, N.E.
	Cleveland, OH 44123
Telephone Number:	(216) 617-7120
Job Interest:	Office Supervisor
Career Objective:	Director of Personnel

I am willing to relocate and/or travel.

Be sure to specify your job interest; many employers also want to know your career objective. Some organizations, especially large and international ones, stipulate that travel or transfer is likely. The transfer may be a much-desired promotion. Therefore, initially indicate your willingness (or lack of it) to relocate or travel.

After the personal data section, you may list specific details relating to your formal education and/or training or your work experience. List the strongest area first. Generally, formal education is listed first because the anticipated applicant's knowledge and training is directly related to the career choice. On the other hand, work experience is often limited to part-time work for funds to cover tuition or living expenses.

Education or Training

List your general and specific educational qualifications in chronological order. Eliminate language that the reader would not understand and avoid abbreviations. The education section might look like this:

Formal Education

Glenville High School Cleveland, OH 44110	Academic Course	June, 19--
Clark College Toronto, Ontario Canada	Associate of Arts	June, 19--
Ball State University Muncie, IN 47306	Bachelor of Arts Major--Management Minor--English	May, 19--
	Grade Point Average 3.2 on a 4.0 scale	

Some employers show little interest in knowing the name of the high school attended by the college applicant or the applicant's high school scholastic standing. If space is a premium, omit high school information. Data relative to post-high school education is very important. A commendable grade point average listed on the data sheet may enhance your chances for an employment interview.

If you have attended college but have not earned a degree, you may choose to list specific college classes. Usually it is neither necessary nor wise to list every college class or to include the course numbers or grades earned. Your transcript of college credits will reveal complete information. On the data sheet, briefly list only subjects related to the job interest.

Formal Education

Indiana State University 19-- to 19--
Terre Haute, IN 46139

Job-related Business Classes:

Accounting (two years)	Marketing
Personnel Management	Money and Banking
Business Law	Business Organization
Life Insurance	Human Relations

Work Experience

Account for all time since high school even though your career may have been interrupted by service in the armed forces or by responsibilities toward your family. The prospective employer is certain to question time omissions. Usually, the most recent experience is shown first. Indicate the name, address, and telephone number (if known) of each employer; dates worked for each company; notation if job was part time or full time; job titles or brief descriptions of job duties; and reasons for leaving previous jobs. You might include the salary or wages earned at each job. The work experience section might look like this:

Work Experience

April, 19-- to Present Full Time	Office Supervisor (8 people) at Johnson Smith Corporation 193 Market Street Akron , OH 44301 Telephone No. (216) 121-5438 Supervisor--Mrs. Anne L. Marks
October, 19-- to April, 19-- Part Time	General Office Clerk at Mann and Mann, Inc. 231 Broad Street Columbus, OH 43201 Telephone No. (216) 311-1782 Supervisor--Mr. Jack Morgan, Office Manager Left company for advancement purposes
Summer, 19-- Full Time	Retail Clerk at Solomon's Fine Foods 313 Maple Avenue Terre Haute, IN 46138 Telephone No. (317) 212-9757 Supervisor--Mr. George O. Solomon, Owner Left company to continue formal education
July, 19-- to March 19--	United States Navy Last Rank--Lieutenant Stationed in Chicago, San Diego, and Guam Honorable Discharge

You can omit your military status and type of discharge (honorable or dishonorable) received.

Activities and Interests

List only those activities and interests that you believe help employers in employee selection. This includes memberships and offices in community, academic, and professional organizations; leadership activities; and special honors (scholarships and awards, including dates received). If the organization's name does not suggest the fundamental purpose of the group, include the information rather than leave the reader in doubt. For the same reason, avoid using acronyms, initials, or Greek symbols.

Consider the following examples:

Example 1: Activities and Interests

High School

Valedictorian
Rotary Club Citizenship Award, 19--
National Honor Society (Grades 10, 11, 12)
Class President (Grades 10, 12)
Student Council Vice President (Grade 11)
Baseball (Grades 9, 10, 11, 12; Captain in Grade 12)

College

Student Volunteer Services (Freshman)
Student Orientation Corps (Senior)
Society for Advancement of Management (Senior)
"Hoosier" State Scholar, 19--
Dr. George R. Blake Management Scholarship, 19--
Junior-of-the-Year in the College of Business, 19--
Intramural Softball

Example 2: Activities and Interests

High School Valedictorian
Class President (Grades 10, 12)
Society for Advancement of Management (College Senior)
"Hoosier" State Scholar, 19--
Dr. George R. Blake Management Scholarship, 19--
Junior-of-the-Year in the College of Business, 19--

Some employers would find Example 1 overly long and complex; Example 2, a condensed and representative sample of an applicant's activities and interests.

References

The data sheet may contain a section that lists names, addresses, and telephone numbers of three or four persons who can vouch for your formal education, work experience, and character. Preferred references include prior supervisors, previous teachers in your professional field (particularly those you have had for more than one class), and employees of the firm where the data sheet is being sent. Do not list relatives or members of the clergy.

Before listing anyone as a reference, ask the individual if you may do so. You will want to list only those references who agree to be so named. By doing so, you are more apt to receive prompt and very favorable recommendations. Keep in mind that every individual who writes a letter of recommendation for you is doing you a special favor.

When listing the reference, be sure to list all information accurately. Record names, titles, and telephone numbers carefully. People prefer certain courtesy titles; business titles and department names vary with the institution.

A reference entry may take the following form:

Dr. Henry A. Mull, Professor
Department of Finance and Management
Ball State University
Muncie, IN 47306
Telephone No. (317) 216-5439

Also, see "Inside Address and Courtesy Title" in Chapter 5 for additional information on stating addresses.

Other Data

If you have special skills in connection with the job being sought, you should include a section in the data sheet that spells out these skills.

<u>Office and Related Skills</u>

Office Machines:	Practical skill on computer and duplicating, collating, dictating, mimeographing, and copier machines
Computer Languages:	BASIC, COBOL, FORTRAN languages
Foreign Language:	Conversational and written Spanish ability
Typewriting:	70 net words a minute
Shorthand:	120 words a minute
Telephone:	Job experience receiving salesperson's calls

Executives ask about finances: How was your college education financed? What salary do you desire? If you worked your way through college or received scholarship funds for paying part or all of your formal education and training, you may want to indi-

May 1, 19--

PERSONAL DATA SHEET
of
Martin J. Flowerson
1101 North Plum Street
Springfield, OH 45504

Telephone Number: (513) 141-7704		Job Interest:	Management Trainee
I am willing to relocate.		Career Goal:	Personnel Supervisor

Formal Education

Central High School Springfield, OH 45501	Academic Course	June, 19--
The Ohio State University Columbus, OH 43210	Business Subjects	19-- to 19--
Ball State University Muncie, IN 47306	Bachelor of Science Degree Major--Management Minor--English	May, 19--
	Grade Point Average--3.3 on a 4.0 scale	

Work Experience

April, 19-- to present Part time	Office Assistant at Johnson Smith Corporation 193 Main Street Muncie, IN 47302 Telephone--(317) 121-6971 Supervisor--Mr. A. J. Hill, Office Manager
September, 19-- to April, 19-- Part time	General Office Clerk at Mann and Mann, Inc. 231 Broad Street Columbus, OH 43202 Telephone--(614) 121-2259 Supervisor--Mrs. Mary Smith, Office Supervisor Left company for advancement purposes
June, 19-- to September, 19-- Full time	Lifeguard for City of Columbus Columbus, OH 43202 Telephone--(614) 181-1414 Left to begin formal education

Activities and Awards

Coach for Boy's Little League since 19--
Treasurer of Senior Class at Central High School, 19--
"Hoosier" State Scholar, 19--
Member of Management Club at Ball State University, 19-- and 19--

Other Data

Salary is open.
References are on file in the Ball State University Placement Office.

Figure 27-1
Personal Data Sheet—Example 1

cate this information on the data sheet. Many employers are favorably impressed by applicants whose desire for a college education and initiative inspire them to work at least part time—regardless of the job held. A scholarship may reveal special aptitudes or favorable character traits. Knowing the salary to expect may show that you have surveyed the market situation. Financial information may be included with the personal information, or in a miscellaneous information section. Figures 27-1 and 27-2 illustrate complete personal data sheets.

DATA SHEET — JANELLE T. YOUNGE — September 1, 19--

Address until November 25, 19--:
308 First Street
Amherst, MA 01002

Telephone: 617-189-6674

Permanent Address:
1145 Poplar Street
Newton, MA 02158

Telephone: 617-417-2983

Career Objective: Marketing Management or Marketing Analysis

Work Experience

September, 19-- to July, 19--	Administrative Assistant for Graduate Senate University of Massachusetts Amherst, MA 01002 20 hours weekly
Summers, 19-- and 19--	Operations Aide at J. B. Hendrick & Co. 23 Center Street Waltham, MA 02154 Full time

Education

University of Massachusetts Amherst, MA 01002	Bachelor of Business Administration, 19-- Major: Marketing Minor: Management Information Systems Graduated Magna Cum Laude

Extracurricular Activities

Member of American Marketing Association, 19-- to 19--
  Speaker Committee, 19--
  Participant at several workshops and seminars
Dormitory Treasurer, University of Massachusetts, 19--
Treasurer of Mortar Board (National Honorary Sorority), 19-- to 19--
Sports Participant (golf, water skiing)

References (with permission)

Dr. George A. Penny, Professor of Marketing — Telephone No.: 617-412-2857
University of Massachusetts
Amherst, MA 01002

Dr. Helen A. Oliveri, Management Consultant — Telephone No.: 617-317-9781
J. B. Hendrick & Co.
Waltham, MA 02154

Mr. Samuel Ross, Attorney-at-Law — Telephone No.: 617-412-7689
Carnegie Building, Room 404
Amherst, MA 01002

Dr. George Aaron Nelson, Faculty Advisor — Telephone No.: 617-412-6645
University of Massachusetts
Amherst, MA 01002

Other Data

I financed my own education. I am willing to relocate or to travel.
Salary desired: $19,000 to $21,000 with opportunities for advancement.

Figure 27-2
Personal Data Sheet—Example 2

PERSONAL DATA SHEET VERSUS THE RÉSUMÉ

All that has been said about the personal data sheet can be said about the résumé. Do not be overly concerned with the label you give your data sheet. Some employers use the terms personal data sheet, data sheet, and résumé interchangeably. The important thing is to prepare an attractive, complete, concise, and accurate description of you and your accomplishments. The following examples illustrate technical differences between a personal data sheet entry and a résumé entry for the same job:

Summer, 19-- Full Time	Staff Reporter Marion Chronicle-Tribune 8354 South Adams Street Marion, IN 46952 Telephone No. (317) 114-2117 Supervisor--Mr. Richard Martin, Editor

Resume Entry:

Summer, 19-- Full Time Staff Reporter	Marion Chronicle-Tribune 8354 South Adams Street Marion, IN 46952 Telephone No. (317) 114-2117 Supervisor--Mr. Richard Martin, Editor I reported police and courthouse news and reviewed performances by local summer theatre groups. In the three months, 72 of my features were published.

The résumé supplies a job description, whereas a personal data sheet does not.

Use active rather than passive language. Say, *I reported police and courthouse news* instead of *My responsibilities included reporting police and courthouse news*. Other good action verbs include *coordinated*, *created*, *developed*, *established*, *implemented*, *initiated*, *planned*, and *supervised*.

Employers expect both a data sheet and an application (cover) letter. A data sheet can be submitted without the letter, but it is not a good idea. The résumé, because of its explanatory data (Figure 27-3), is more readily acceptable without an accompanying letter. However, employers prefer receiving both letter and résumé. Chapter 28 explains how to write a successful application (cover) letter.

VITA

Vita means *life*. A vita may be required from the highly qualified technical or professional person. In addition to giving personal facts, names, types of degrees, and titles of theses, the vita may include a list of the applicant's publications, patents, or copyrights. It may describe the individual's research experiments, consulting work, and travels. The document is necessarily longer than other data sheets, but you should not expect a prospective employer to read more than six pages.

OTHER CONSIDERATIONS

In addition to the information needed for the data sheet, consider the length of the data sheet and the color of the stationery. Also, decide whether to include a college transcript of grades and/or photograph.

Length of Data Sheet

Employers are explicit in their requests for concise, straightforward data sheets. Many executives prefer one- or two-page data sheets. Because they often must read hundreds of data sheets for

RESUME

PERSONAL DATA — March 1, 19--

Name:	Tracy B. Stanford
Address:	2020 Main Street, Racine, WI 53401
Telephone Number:	414-148-1783

CAREER OBJECTIVE . . . . My ultimate goal is to achieve a position in administrative management at the corporate level.

Options: Corporate planning and development
Financial and systems management
Technical management
Consulting

My business career began in my family's business, where I managed the sales and accounting functions.

I am willing to relocate and travel.

FORMAL EDUCATION . . . . Bachelor of Arts degree from Wellesley College, Wellesley, Massachusetts, June, 19--. Major in Economics with concentration in Finance and Mathematics.

WORK EXPERIENCE . . . . . Research Assistant at Wellesley College, October, 19-- to March, 19-- for C. A. Grover, Associate Professor, Economics Department (617-185-7484). Responsibilities included the collection, preparation, interpretation, and review of data to be used in a publication. Part time

Manager, Racine Plumbing and Heating Company, Racine, Wisconsin, June, 19-- to August, 19-- for Clifford Ball, Owner (414-148-0128). Responsibilities dealt primarily with the coordination of main office activities, including purchasing, pricing, selling, accounting, and organizing new product acceptance policies. Full time, summers

INTERESTS . . . . Outside interests include travel, tennis, skiing, and all spectator sports. I also enjoy reading and listening to music.

REFERENCES . . . . References can be furnished upon request.

Figure 27-3
Resume

a single job opening, they especially appreciate receiving a short, but complete, one-page form. Reveal your job know-how and language skill by including only appropriate and useful job-related information in your data sheet.

Color of Stationery

Most employers prefer either white or off-white stationery. Understandably, job applicants want their data sheets to be unique and stand out, especially in a tight job market. Tinted stationery can help the data sheet stand out, but it will not make up for any deficiencies.

College Transcript of Grades

Although scholastic rating is important information to an employer, an official transcript of grades is seldom required with the data sheet. However, a transcript may be requested later—especially from the college graduate seeking a first technical or professional position.

Photograph of Applicant

Sending a photograph with your data sheet appears unimportant—perhaps unwise and costly. Many employers do not object to receiving the applicant's photograph with the data sheet; however, some personnel managers state that laws emphasizing equal employment opportunities prohibit employers from requesting photographs prior to the interview. In addition, they stress that a photograph adds nothing to the application and that it is not necessary.

IMPORTANCE OF NEATNESS AND CORRECTNESS

To increase your chances for getting an interview, always submit a neat, grammatically correct, and well-arranged data sheet. Type the original on good quality (16 or 20 lb.) bond paper. You may send a good printed copy but never a carbon copy.

Allow NO misspelled words. Spell and punctuate all names of individuals, companies, and organizations correctly and in the form preferred. State exact business titles and departments. Include complete addresses and telephone numbers.

You want your data sheet to say: *I am precise, organized, accurate, neat, reliable, and thorough. I want to do a very good job.* Without a doubt, executives are influenced by your command of language.

Many employers, however, are unhappy with the inadequate written communication skills college graduates reveal through their data sheets and application letters. The most common communication problems include hazy job objective, incorrect spelling, incorrect punctuation, incomplete information, incorrect sentence structure, long résumés, lack of concise wording, difficult-to-read communications, poor organization, long letters, sloppy documents, unattractive format, and incorrect address or salutation. Lack of parallelism is also a common English error in employment documents. Be sure all parts of the sentence are equal.

See Chapter 3 for ideas on how you can develop your written communication skills.

CHAPTER SUMMARY

Within 2 or 3 minutes, the prospective employer should be able to learn much significant career-centered information about you.

Since the data sheet represents you, plan and prepare it so that it will present the best picture of you. It will have to speak for you until you can get an interview and speak for yourself. Make the data sheet portray a neat, interested, well-organized, informed, educated, capable, and reliable person.

The recent graduate may prepare the data sheet as a personal data sheet (listed format) or résumé (descriptive format). The highly technical or professional applicant should prepare a vita because it will give the prospective employer a more comprehensive picture.

In addition to personal information (name, address, and so on), prospective employers want specific data about your formal education, work experience, special skills, outside interests and activities, and references. Before arranging the information on good quality (16 or 20 lb) bond paper, do your homework. Learn all you can about yourself, the job market, and potential employers. Then type a complete and concise data sheet that will favorably impress the reader. Remember, the data sheet is the most important document in your career file. It is you on paper.

STUDY QUESTIONS

1. Why is the data sheet the most important document in your career file?
2. What three analyses should you make before preparing a data sheet (or application letter)? What aids are available to you for making each analysis?
3. What specific information should you advise prospective employers relative to
   a. Yourself
   b. Your work experience
   c. Your formal education
   d. Your awards, activities, and special interests
   e. Your references?
4. What are the basic differences between the types of data sheets described in this chapter?

ACTIVITIES

1. Conduct a self-analysis to determine your personal characteristics, needs, interests, values, talents, abilities, formal education, and work experience.
2. Determine available career opportunities that suit your particular background, abilities, and goals. Which sources of information did you use?

3. Make a list of potential employers and carefully analyze one; use available library references, conversations with employees, or visits to the firm.
4. Assume that you are about to graduate from college. Prepare a data sheet (preferably one page) for the company of your choice. Assume that you have the necessary academic background, training, and work experience. Be sure your data sheet is complete but concise, neat, attractive, well-organized, and typewritten. Use good quality bond paper.

LANGUAGE SKILLS DEVELOPMENT

Rewrite the following data sheet statements:

1. Job Objective: Entry level position as Sales Representative for a well-managed company producing technical or consumer products.
2. Member of S.A.M.
3. Self motivated
4. Possess the following attributes:
   dependable
   hard working
   good personal habits
   take initiative
   work well under pressure
   seek responsibility
5. Worked independently without supervision
6. Gained valuable first hand experience in managing the pressures and responsibilities of management
7. Duties included painting, scraping, wallpaper removal, patching and general cleanup
8. Financed 25% of educational expenses through work experience
9. B.A. in Management Information Systems
10. Phone Number (317) 181-4752

IN-BASKET SIMULATION

Assume that you are well qualified for a secretarial, office manager, or supervisory position at Waltere Supermarkets, Inc. Prepare a data sheet to be mailed to Karen Todd, Personnel Director. Ms. Todd believes the following information should be included on a one-page data sheet:

1. Personal data—full name, address, telephone number
2. Special job or career interest
3. Salary desired (very important)
4. Willingness or lack of willingness to relocate
5. Formal education—names and addresses of schools

6. Dates and types of diplomas and degrees earned
7. Major and minor study areas
8. Grade-point average in post-high school studies
9. Major source of financing formal education
10. List of special skills
11. Previous employers—names, addresses, telephone numbers (very important)
12. Dates worked for each employer
13. Notation if job was part time or full time
14. Job title or description
15. Names and titles of supervisors
16. Reasons for leaving previous jobs (very important)
17. Salary or wages earned at previous jobs
18. List of hobbies, recreational interests
19. List of awards and dates received
20. References included in résumé (no relatives or neighbors)

Ms. Todd believes that the applicant should take the proper time and trouble to prepare a neat and correct data sheet. A transcript of college grades and your photograph are not required with the data sheet.

SPECIAL REFERENCES FOR CAREER PLANNING

Austin, Margaret F. *Bridges to Success: Finding Jobs and Changing Careers*. New York, John Wiley & Sons, Inc., 1983. Practical suggestions on self-analysis and job searching techniques.

Barron's Profiles of American Colleges. New York: Barron's Educational Series. Gives information about specific career curricula in American colleges and universities and describes individual schools.

Bolles, Richard. *What Color is Your Parachute?* Berkeley, Calif.: Ten Speed Press, annual. Includes self-assessment exercises. It is a practical and humorous publication for getting to know yourself better.

Career Employment Opportunities Directory. Santa Monica, Calif.: Ready Reference Press. Describes corporations, government agencies, and professional organizations offering employment to college graduates.

The College Blue Book. New York: CCM Information Corporation. Lists occupational schools in each state, curricula offered, accredited schools in various areas of study, occupational descriptions, and financial aid.

Collegiate Summer Employment Guide. Los Angeles, Calif.: American Collegiate Employment Institute. Lists recreational jobs (summer camps, National parks, resorts;

career training programs; overseas jobs; government positions; guides to collegiate summer employment.

The CPC Annual. Bethlehem, Penn.: College Placement Council. Lists corporations and government agencies and their occupational recruiting needs (one paragraph about the company).

The Dictionary of Occupational Titles. Washington, D.C.: Bureau of Labor Statistics, Employment Service. Lists thousands of occupations and contains comprehensive, current occupational information on job duties and requirements in the United States. It is an excellent source for career guidance and long range planning.

Directory of Overseas Summer Jobs. Oxford, England: Vacation-Work. Cincinnati, Ohio: National Directory Service. Lists full-time summer work for youth in United States and Canada. It specifies organizations and agencies that arrange jobs with other employers.

Encyclopedia of Associations. Detroit, Mich.: Gale Research Company. Includes data on professional and occupational associations.

The Encyclopedia of Careers and Vocational Guide. Chicago: J. G. Ferguson Publishing Co., 1981. 2 vols. Offers specific information on careers and provides guidance for career planning.

Figler, Howard. *The Complete Job Search Handbook—All the Skills You Need to Get Any Job and Have a Good Time Doing it*. New York: Holt, Rinehart, and Winston, 1979. Discusses career search skills for the complete career search process.

Flusser, Alan. *The Insider's Guide to Buying and Wearing Men's Clothes*. New York: Simon & Schuster. Down-to-earth guidebook on how to dress with style.

Gale, Barry. *Discover What You're Good At: The National Career Aptitude System and Career Directory*. New York: Simon and Schuster, 1982. Helpful guide to aptitude tests and career planning.

Gootnick, David. *Getting a Better Job*. New York: McGraw-Hill, 1978. Practical ideas to get you ready for effective job interview, includes sample résumés, employment letters.

Guide for Occupational Exploration. Washington, D.C.: U.S. Department of Labor, Employment and Training Administration. Relates aptitudes and interests (arranged by general interest area) to the skills and requirements of a group of jobs.

Lewis, Adale Beatrice. *How to Choose, Change, Advance Your*

Career. Woodbury, N.Y.: Barron's Education Series, Inc., 1983. Career planning guide.

Lovejoy's College Guide. New York: Simon and Schuster. Gives information about special programs and careers in American colleges and universities.

Molloy, John T. *Dress for Success*. New York: Warner Books, 1975.

Molloy, John T. *Woman's Dress for Success Book*. New York: Warner Books, 1977.

Occupational Outlook Handbook. (U.S. Bureau of Labor Statistics)—tells how to enter an occupation, job duties, working conditions, training or education needed, future availability of jobs, and where to get more data. It will help you determine national employment trends and your chances for employment in an occupation.

Occupational Outlook Quarterly. Washington, D.C.: U.S. Bureau of Labor Statistics. Supplements quarterly the *Occupational Outlook Handbook*. Every two years it features "The Occupational Outlook Handbook in Brief" projecting the growth of occupations.

Peterson's Annual Guide to Graduate Study. Princeton, N.J.: Peterson's Guides, annual. Each volume presents data on a major graduate study discipline.

Peterson's Annual Guide to Undergraduate Study. Princeton, N.J.: Peterson's Guides, annual. Lists colleges and universities geographically, alphabetically, and by major study areas. Includes comparative information and profiles of individual schools.

Standard and Poor's Register of Corporations, Directors, and Executives. New York: Standard and Poor's Corporation. Provides much corporate data and gives names and addresses of executives.

Summer Employment Directory of the United States. Cincinnati, Ohio: National Directory Service. Specifies actual summer job openings for high school seniors, college students, teachers, nurses, foreign students, and retirees.

Thomas' Register of American Manufacturers and Thomas' Register Catalog File. New York: Thomas Publishing Co. Lists companies by products or services and includes company names, addresses, and catalogs.

von Furstenberg, Egon. *The Power Look*. Practical tips on choosing color-coordinated, stylish men's clothing.

World-Wide Summer Placement Directory. Brooklyn, N.Y.: Advancement and Placement Institute. Details summer jobs available in the United States and in foreign countries.

Writing the Application and Other Employment Letters

28

After studying Chapter 28, you should be able to:

- Write solicited and unsolicited application letters
- Write reader-centered openings
- Write logical, informative, and supportive middle paragraphs
- Write ending paragraphs that inspire
- Write reference letters
- Write notification letters (acceptance, refusal, and resignation)
- Write follow-up letters

Letters that have to do with securing or terminating employment all concern one important product: ourselves. The general principles of letter writing apply to these letters. In addition, there are specific characteristics and courtesies that can improve your employment letters.

The **application letter** serves as your introduction to the prospective employer. It is a sales letter to promote yourself. It is not merely to inform or inquire but also to persuade—to convince the reader that you should be granted an interview. In order to persuade, however, your letter must first be read.

When an application letter is mailed with a data sheet, it is called a **cover letter**. The letter is placed on top; therefore, it covers the data sheet.

Prospective employers receive hundreds of letters regarding a single job opening. Some letters are glanced at; some are never read. If your letter is to accomplish its goal, its mission will be twofold: to attract the eye of the reader and to persuade the reader to grant you an interview. You can follow specific steps to optimize your chances for success.

Another important employment letter is the **reference letter**. This letter is written to acquaintances who can comment on the applicant's character traits, skills, and knowledge. The letter seeks permission to use the reader's name as a source of pertinent information.

Other employment letters are written to accept or reject job offers, to resign from a position, and to follow up application letters. Employment follow-up letters generally thank the reader for an interview and often offer additional data to enhance the opportunity for a job offer. Whether or not a job offer is made, the follow-up letter is a courtesy to the interviewer.

APPLICATION LETTERS

Appearance

Type your application letter so that it is well centered on one page, attractive, and neat. The physical appearance of your letter will make a first impression on the prospective employer. It must be an original—not even a well-produced copy will do. Unless you have been asked to submit a handwritten letter, type your letter on good white bond paper (8½ in. × 11 in.). Use the personal-business letter style illustrated in Chapter 6. Never use company letterhead or club stationery.

Keep the letter short. A long letter will not attract a busy executive who has stacks of mail to scan every day. Keep the lengthy details in the data sheet that accompanies your letter.

Current research reveals that employers complain that application letters are illogically organized, overly long, very wordy, and sloppily and carelessly typed. Such letters are discarded or placed at the bottom of the stack. Retype the letter rather than mail it with even one spelling error. Allow no strikeovers, obvious corrections, smudges, wrinkles, tears, or other distractions.

Content

Employers want personalized letters that show that the applicant knows something about the company, the job, and how he or she would fit into the employment setting. They are also looking for letters that are unique, creative, and positive. In as few words as possible, present yourself as capable and enthusiastic. Use reader-centered and relevant language, but do not confuse enthusiasm with aggressiveness (or wordiness with selling power). Your application letter should:

1. *Indicate your job interest* (for example, sales representative), *your sources of information* (a specific newspaper advertisement, *CPC annual*, etc.), *and your interest in the company*. If you are not applying for a specific job, indicate your interest in the company and the kinds of positions that would interest you.
2. *Introduce your data sheet with an enclosure statement.* Use traditional wording such as, *Enclosed is* . . . rather than *Here is*. . . .
3. *Expand on your strong points*—personal qualities, formal education, skills, and work experience. Show how they relate to company needs and your job interest and/or career goal. (Amplify the information in your data sheet; do not merely repeat it.)
4. *Request action.* You can give your telephone number, if desired. Many employers appreciate knowing the applicant's availability date.

Address the letter to a specific person and it will have greater likelihood of being read. Include the person's business title, as well as the person's name. Many application letters are directed to a personnel manager; sometimes it is wise to address your letter to another area (Engineering, for example), where the final decision to hire will be made. This is particularly true for the highly technical or professional candidate.

Before preparing a rough draft of your letter, think through your approach and write an appropriate outline. Write the rough draft, revising it as often as necessary to ensure that it includes all the necessary information but no extra words. It must also be interesting, reader-centered, positive but not overly aggressive, and logically sequenced. It should flow, not jog.

Beginning statements. When you are applying for an advertised vacancy, indicate the job you are interested in and the source of your information. Your reply may be the result of either an oral or a written solicitation. Some examples of opening statements for the solicited application letter follow:

> Mrs. Robert Hall advised that an executive secretarial position is open at Springfield Corporation. Please consider me a candidate for the position.

> Mr. Kenneth Schneider indicated that you have an accounting position open. Since my training and interest are in this particular area, please consider my qualifications for this position.

> The Placement Office at the University of Colorado Medical Center indicated a vacancy at Western Reserve Hospital for an individual holding a Master of Arts degree in Hospital Administration. I believe I am qualified for the position and would like to apply for it.

> In response to your advertisement in this morning's STAR, I am applying for the marketing position which will be available next month.

Be tactful when opening your first paragraph with a person's name. Some employers may feel that you are name dropping. Others consider the named individual as a possible reference source and react favorably, especially when they respect the opinion of the person named.

When you write an unsolicited letter of application, you must write your letter based on what you believe the company will consider important for hiring new employees.

> Lafayette's international involvement in pharmaceuticals, animal health products, and agricultural products prompts my inquiry into possible career opportunities at Lafayette.

> I would like to be considered as an applicant for an elementary school teaching position.

> Do you have an opening for a thoroughly qualified executive secretary?

Humorous statements may be appropriate in some application letters but generally should be avoided. Humor written to an unknown reader may be interpreted as sarcasm or flippancy.

Middle paragraphs. The middle paragraphs for all letters of application should expand (not repeat) details in the data sheet based on the prospective employer's needs and the job specifications. The information should reveal your personality, self-confidence, enthusiasm, and sincerity. Avoid writing numerous *I* and ego-centered statements, exaggerations, and negative ideas. A few examples of well-written paragraphs follow:

> In addition to the information listed in the enclosed résumé, my experience at Schenley included work in the cap plant, shipping department, and bottling area. The varied activities and honors in high school and college are evidence of my aggressiveness and self-motivation.
>
> While working as a technician at Haag Drug, I became familiar with generic and specific drug names; the cleaning, filling, and repairing of pharmacy counting machines; and the expectations of some drugs.
>
> Enclosed is a data sheet listing complete details about my education and work-related experience. During the last two years, I have tutored voluntarily several second and third grade students during lunch periods and some evenings. In addition, I tutored elementary level students my entire four years of high school.

Notice that each writer is avoiding qualitative statements such as *I am just the person you want.* Instead, each gives pertinent explanatory facts on which the reader can conclude that the applicant is exceptional: *I shall ask this person to come in for an interview. She or he sounds like a good candidate for the job.*

Negative statements do not effectively stress your qualification for a job:

> Your recent strike has probably put you behind in your output and my training has given me the means to cope with the situation and solve the problem. As a trained administrative assistant, I have been instructed in the methods of getting the most production from a labor force even following a strike as large as yours. Throughout my college career, I worked closely with both management and the general labor force and, therefore, know each one's wants, needs, and breaking points.

The writer of this statement presumes to be capable of resolving a serious problem that persons knowing all the details were unable to resolve. This "savior" attitude is sure to meet with disfavor.

Statements such as *I have had only part-time jobs* are negative. State your information as assets: *The following part-time jobs have increased my skills in sales, as well as office work.* Remember that any experience is usually better than none and may have been valuable in a number of ways. Stress those experiences that may make you a probable candidate for the job vacancy.

Concluding statements. The final sentence or paragraph should encourage the reader to act or should stress what the writer intends to do. Here are some appropriate endings for an application letter. You can modify them to suit your situation.

> I would welcome an opportunity to discuss my qualifications with you. You can telephone me at (219) 413-5304 between 9 a.m. and 2 p.m.
>
> May I come for an interview? Please telephone me at 159-9773 any weekday.
>
> I will be available for full-time employment on May 24. You can reach me at the address shown on my resume, or by telephoning 187-6320.
>
> I would welcome the opportunity to review my qualifications with you at your convenience.
>
> I will telephone you for an appointment to discuss my credentials.
>
> I have completed and enclosed your application blank for office employment. In a few days, I will telephone you for an employment interview.
>
> Please give me an opportunity to discuss the possibility of beginning my career with Franklin Life and Casualty Company. You can telephone me at 181-7782. I look forward to hearing from you.

Even though your telephone number appears on the data sheet, you can repeat it in the cover letter. Most employers appreciate having the telephone number easily accessible. If you follow up with a telephone call, telephone after the prospective employer has had an opportunity to receive your letter. Avoid telephoning just before and during the lunch hour, near closing time, on Monday mornings, on Friday afternoons, or at times when the employer may be deeply involved with company business.

Solicited and unsolicited application letters. If your letter is answering an advertisement or announcement for a specific job, it is a **solicited application letter**. The prospective employer is looking for applicants and wants letters concerning that vacancy. You should open your letter with a reference to the job and advertisement and indicate that you want to be considered for the vacancy. The letter in Figure 28–1 is a solicited application letter. The first paragraph indicates that the writer learned about the secretary–receptionist opening from a knowledgeable and capable employee.

9223 Barkley Square
Overland Park, KS 66204
July 15, 19--

Mrs. A. Louise Williamson
Director of Personnel
American Products, Inc.
P. O. Box 2135
Topeka, KS 66601

Dear Mrs. Williamson

Mrs. Helen Marvino (Purchasing Department) recently informed me that American Products, Inc. will have an opening for a secretary-receptionist on August 1. Please consider me for this position. ← **Job interest**

The enclosed data sheet lists my formal work experience and educational qualifications. Central State College will furnish a transcript of my college grades if you desire it. ← **Data sheet**

As a receptionist for the Johnson Smith Company, I worked consistently with the general public in telephone and in face-to-face situations and became skillful with various secretarial procedures, including the filing system which I reorganized. ← **Persuasion**

May I discuss my qualifications with you? You can telephone me at 451-7520. ← **Action**

Sincerely

Sherry Talbott

Ms. Sherry Talbott

Enclosure

Figure 28-1
Solicited Letter of Application—Example 1

A solicited letter answering a newspaper or trade journal advertisement might have begun with the following paragraph:

> Answering your advertisement in Computer News and Reports (January 10), I would appreciate your considering me for the Senior Computer Operator position, which will be available on February 12.

If you are writing to a company that has not advertised a vacancy, your letter is an **unsolicited application letter**. You are not answering a request; you are merely hoping that a posi-

Dear Ms. Barnes:

Job interest →

Do you have an opening for a buyer in MiLady's Department Store?

Data sheet →

Persuasion →

I believe the enclosed resume shows that my education and retail store experience qualify me as a buyer of women's clothing for a store such as yours. FASHIONNAIRE'S customers are discerning women who enjoy dressing well and who want to get the most for their money.

Action →

Please give me an opportunity to discuss my qualifications and express my ideas. My telephone number is 176-8671.

Sincerely,

Figure 28–2
Unsolicited Letter of Application—Example 1

Dear Mr. Kohl:

Job interest →

Are you approaching employee vacation time
--when you work overtime to keep routines on schedule?
--when workers on hand assume additional responsibilities?
--when errors start increasing because of volume?

Persuasion →

Then for you there is someone
--who is a competent stenographer, typist, and bookkeeper.
--who adapts easily to new situations.
--who enjoys office work.
--who can follow instructions.
--who is alert and accurate.
--who is seeking temporary employment.

Data sheet →

I am enclosing a resume to verify my abilities and education.

Action →

In a few days, I will telephone you for an appointment; if you prefer, you can telephone me at 317-716-5427.

Sincerely,

Figure 28–3
Unsolicited Letter of Application—Example 2

tion might be available. Consequently, you must give special attention to your approach and write your letter based on what you believe the reader would consider important for hiring new employees.

Sometimes cleverness, used cautiously, impresses the reader. In Figure 28–2 the writer has used a sales approach to apply for a sales job. In Figure 28–3, the writer has devised an unusual format to stimulate interest. And in Figure 28–4, the writer believed that the credentials should be prominent and has reinforced the

Dear Mr. Atkins

This summer I would enjoy being a children's counselor at Harris' Summer Camp. ← **Job interest**

Presently, I am a junior at Central State University with a grade point average of 3.24 on a 4.0 scale. The following courses have provided me with helpful guides for working with children: ← **Persuasion**

Child Guidance ← **Data**
Art for Elementary Teachers
Health Education for Elementary Teachers
Creative Physical Education for Elementary Teachers
Educational Sociology

Most of my work experience has been with children from six to twelve years old. Last summer, I worked in a private nursery school.

These people will vouch for my character, education, and ability:

Mrs. Mary Lewis, Director ← **Data**
Crestview Nursery School
1010 Farmington Drive
Denver, CO 80205
Telephone: (303) 213-3217

Doctor William Collins, Professor
Department of Elementary Education
Central State University
Boulder, CO 80303
Telephone: (303) 314-9714

Mr. Robert Wilson, Manager
Gates Mills Day Camp
121 Center Road
Colorado Springs, CO 80901
Telephone: (303) 613-8779

May I have a personal interview before May 15? Please write or telephone me at (303) 218-5412. ← **Action**

Sincerely

Figure 28–4
Unsolicited Letter of Application—Example 3

letter by including a built-in, abbreviated résumé. Note that the information has been selectively chosen to reinforce qualifications for the job; that the material has been attractively and conveniently arranged; and that the information is brief and to the point. If the writer had decided to conserve space or believed that the references were not immediately crucial to securing an interview, the writer could have omitted them entirely and substituted: *The placement office at Central State University will furnish you with my complete credentials, including references, upon request.*

In general, a direct approach works best. Decide, first of all, on your purpose: *to secure a personal interview.* Next, determine the tone of your letter: *enthusiastic and capable.* Next, devise a topic outline that tells the reader that you are informed about the company and interested in working for that company:

Paragraph one. Begin with reader-oriented thought that includes a statement of the purpose for the letter.

Middle paragraphs. Introduce your data sheet and expand on purpose of letter by giving in logical sequence facts that support your purpose. Include explanations when they are necessary and comparisons or examples if they are helpful.

Concluding paragraphs. End with a positive, action thought that reinforces the purpose of the letter and inspires the reader to act in your interest.

Answers to Want Ads

If your application letter is a reply to an advertisement, be sure to answer the specific questions stated in the advertisement and avoid a "canned" letter. A **blind advertisement** is one that does not specify the names of individuals or firms offering jobs.

The letter in Figure 28–5 is an answer to the following blind newspaper advertisement:

> PUBLIC ACCOUNTANT
> Recent college graduate with high academic standing required by rapidly expanding CPA firm. Submit resume to Box FA 58, Plain Dealer.

Notice that the advertisement specifically requests a résumé from a college graduate with a high grade-point average. In addition to including a résumé and evidence that she was graduated from college with a high grade-point average, Sara Fiorentin might have offered to mail her potential employer an official transcript of her grades. She could have said:

> Enclosed is a résumé detailing my formal education, including an accounting internship. You can readily note that I was graduated with honors from Cleveland State University; you can request an official transcript of my grades.

Her work experience reflects a working relationship with public accounting. Also, the reader will appreciate the short and informative letter.

4289 Springwood Trail
Cleveland, OH 44132
June 14, 19--

Plain Dealer
Box FA-58
Cleveland, OH 44113

Ladies and Gentlemen:

I would like to apply for the accounting position advertised in the Plain Dealer on June 13. ← **Job interest**

Enclosed is a resume detailing my formal education, including an accounting internship. ← **Data sheet** You can readily note that I was graduated with honors from Cleveland State University. As an intern at Edwards, Smith, and Partens, I audited financial papers for General Marketing Corporation and for Brass and Bolts Company. ← **Persuasion**

May I come in for an interview? If so, please telephone me at 441-0049 between 10 a.m. and 3 p.m. ← **Action**

Sincerely,

Sarah Fiorentin

Miss Sarah Fiorentin

Enclosure

Figure 28-5
Solicited Letter of Application

If the advertisement had stated, *Send resume and salary requirement*, the third paragraph of the letter might have read one of these two ways:

> I am interested primarily in establishing myself with a growing firm so as to learn and work in my chosen field. However, I would be happy to discuss salary considerations with you at our interview.
>
> I am primarily interested in establishing myself with a growing firm such as yours, but I would like a starting salary of $20,000 to $21,000.

REFERENCE LETTERS

The list of references on the data sheet tells an interested employer that the persons are willing to vouch for the applicant's character, educational background, or classroom or on-the-job performance. The prospective employer might contact the references—orally or in writing.

It is not courteous to use someone's name as a reference without first getting express permission. If you like, you can approach the persons and tactfully ask if you could use their names as references. The written request is sometimes more practical; it can be less embarrassing.

There are two basic reasons for writing the **reference letter**:

1. To ask permission to use the reader's name as a reference on a data sheet
2. To request the reader to write a letter recommending you for a particular job or position on the basis of your character, educational background, and/or ability

Use the following plan for the reference letter:

1. If the reader will recognize your name, begin the letter with your request. If the reader may not recognize your name, begin letter with background data about yourself and then state your request.
2. State your interest in the particular job (or job area) and perhaps give reasons why you believe you qualify.
3. Give desired action.

Because the reference letter asks the reader to do something or supply information, it is very much like an inquiry letter.

When you write the reference letter, be sure the reader knows who you are. You cannot expect an individual to vouch for you without recognizing you—your name, your personality, your background, your achievements. Most often, people chosen as references are previous employers and professionals (such as doctors, lawyers, and teachers). These are people who meet many persons and a variety of persons every year. Mentioning only your name may not be very enlightening. The reader may not realize that Martin Lewan was once known to him as Martin Lewandowsky. Likewise, the reader may remember student Marilyn J. Galina, but who is Mrs. George Ryan?

If yours is a very common name or if several years have passed since your last communication with the reader, you may need to jog the reader's memory. As a reminder, perhaps you can relate something unique about yourself. Specify the exact purpose for writing. Tell the reader whether you are seeking a recommendation for your character, your educational background, your on-the-job performance, or a combination of these traits. If you want the letter of recommendation based on one, some, or all of these characteristics, say so.

Dear Mr. Anderson:

May I use your name as a reference for a job as a junior accountant? ← **Request**

Since I am eager to complete my resume and begin job hunting, ← **Reasons** please give me your answer by telephone. You can reach me at ← **Action** 417-7123 any afternoon.

Respectfully yours,

Figure 28-6
Requesting a Reference Letter—Example 1

Dear Mr. Anderson:

Rual and Turner recently advertised for a junior accountant to ← **Reason for writing** assist with audits and to handle accounts. They want someone who is eager and willing to learn. I believe that I have the personal and educational requirements for the position.

If you agree that I do have the necessary qualifications, please ← **Request** recommend me, addressing your letter to:

Mr. Adam Turner
Rual and Turner
Professional Building, Room 221
Des Moines, IA 50309

To learn your decision, I will telephone you by March 12. ← **Action**

Respectfully yours,

Figure 28-7
Requesting a Reference Letter—Example 2

Tell the reader your occupational desires so that an intelligent decision can be made and an appropriate letter written. After considering your personality, ability, and education, the reader may believe you more suited for one occupation and thereby be willing to give you a good reference in one instance, but not in another. For example, the reader may vouch for your ability as a social worker, but not for a business job; as a secretary, but not as a teacher of business subjects or office skills; as a bookkeeper, but not as an accountant; or as a typist, but not as a receptionist.

If you are well acquainted with the reader, you might write a letter similar to the one in Figure 28-6 requesting permission to use the reader's name as a job reference. You might refer to Figure 28-7 to request a letter of recommendation. And you might send a letter similar to that in Figure 28-8 to a former teacher you last saw several years ago.

Dear Mr. Anderson

Explanation → During the Winter, 19-- quarter, I was enrolled in your auditing class (AC-385). Because of my sincere interest in accounting, you generously answered my many questions and loaned me your file copies of Journal of Accountancy.

Request → You are well qualified to judge the value of my educational background--especially in the study of accounting procedures. May I, therefore, list your name as a reference?

Action → To learn your decision, I will telephone you by March 12.

Respectfully yours

Figure 28-8
Requesting a Reference Letter—Example 3

If you are asked to write a letter of recommendation, write a truthful letter without malice or deliberately trying to injure the named individual. Truthful letters of recommendation can be very helpful to prospective employers, but the letters should not intentionally or carelessly mislead the inquirer. In good faith, you can state what you know. Indicate that you are answering a request and ask that the information be kept confidential. You can use such wording as: *In my opinion, . . .*

NOTIFICATION LETTERS

If a job offer is not extended at the interview, an offer may be made later. If this is the case, you will need to let the prospective employer know whether you accept or reject the offer. If you accept the position, you will have to let your present employer know of your decision.

Letter Accepting the Position

A written **letter of acceptance** is not always necessary, but like the written thank you, it creates a feeling of goodwill and makes a good impression. Use this plan for writing the letter of acceptance:

1. Accept the job
2. Explain any particulars about the job
3. Indicate preferred starting date

The letter should briefly, but enthusiastically, confirm the specific facts about the job, such as the name or type of position, salary, and starting date. Of course, the reader should recognize immediately that you are accepting the job (deductive approach). The letter in Figure 28-9 is a brief letter of acceptance.

Dear Mrs. Miley

I accept happily the position of secretary to Mr. George Allison, Director of Purchasing. As agreed, my beginning salary will be $1,000 a month, and I shall remain with my present employer to train another employee for my secretarial job.

← **Acceptance**

← **Particulars**

On October 8, you will find me very eager to accept the challenges of my new position at General Electric Mfg. Co.

← **Starting date (goodwill)**

Sincerely yours

Figure 28-9
Letter of Acceptance

Thank you, Miss Applegate, for offering me the position of manager of the Pittsburgh office. Your offer is very enticing; the work should be challenging and rewarding.

← **Job interest**

As mentioned during our talks, I once lived in the New England area and enjoyed it immensely. Therefore, I shall accept an offer with a large retail firm in Connecticut. The position also offers new challenges and opportunities for growth. It is my opportunity to return to a locality my family likes.

← **Explanation (refusal)**

I shall read with special interest any news items on developments in Pittsburgh.

← **Goodwill**

Sincerely yours,

Figure 28-10
Letter of Refusal

Letter Refusing the Position

Just as company representatives hire only one person for a specific vacancy, the applicant can accept only one position of considerable authority and responsibility. Use this plan for writing the **letter of refusal**:

1. Specify the job offered
2. Refuse politely giving reason(s) for refusing the job
3. End with a goodwill thought

The letter of refusal need not specify the alternative you have chosen, but it should briefly and graciously explain why you are refusing the job offer. Figure 28-10 illustrates a letter of refusal that begins by thanking the reader for the job offer.

Letter of Resignation

It seems appropriate also to discuss here the **letter of resignation**. The usual practice is to discuss the decision to leave your job orally with your superior two weeks before your resignation date. However, some professional positions require a written

---

Dear Dean Blake:

Resignation → It is with mixed emotions that I am resigning effective May 13.

Explanation → After much consideration, I accepted a teaching position at the University of California, beginning in September. The position offers many attractive factors such as location, promotion in rank, and opportunities to specialize in advising and teaching graduate students.

I have enjoyed being a part of the University of Alabama and shall remember my years here with pride, respect, and appreciation for my growth as an instructor.

Goodwill → Finally, I shall always be listening for news about this university and my many friends here.

Respectfully,

Figure 28-11
Letter of Resignation

resignation several weeks or months before the actual time. The more difficult it is for the employer to find a replacement, the longer the needed notice period. Some contracts stipulate the exact date by which the resignation must be submitted. Teacher contracts are an example of such a contract. Resignations after a set date will be accepted by some employers. Nonetheless, the responsible person avoids leaving employment without sufficient notice.

Include the following information in your letter of resignation:

1. Give resignation date and job from which you are resigning
2. Explain briefly reason for resigning
3. End with a goodwill message

The letter of resignation should briefly but sincerely explain why you wish to leave your present position. Realistic employers understand an employee's desire to seek new challenges, a higher job status, more income, or a better or more glamorous work environment. No matter what your reason may be, resign gracefully. The letter in Figure 28-11 illustrates a tactful letter of resignation.

Even though you may be very happy or excited about the prospect of new challenges, your letter of resignation should express some unhappiness for leaving your present job. A resignation implies a desire for bigger or better things, but your employer should not be made to feel guilty or overwhelmed by your newly found pleasure.

Perhaps the shortest notice of resignation was written by the 37th President of the United States, Richard M. Nixon. Possibly, the publicity preceding this important announcement lessened the need for any explanations:

I hereby resign the Office of President of the United States.

FOLLOW-UP LETTERS

If, after reading the application letter and studying the résumé, the prospective employer concludes that the applicant may qualify for the vacancy, he or she may contact the applicant for a personal interview. The employer may interview several applicants for the same position. Only one will be hired, but the entire process may take several months.

An applicant interested in the job might mail a follow-up letter thanking the interviewer for the interview. If possible, the applicant should furnish additional information that would interest the prospective employer. The follow-up letter might also confirm acceptance or refusal of a job offer.

Generally, the most difficult positions to fill are those requiring special personal characteristics, much formal education, and related work experience. It may take months of searching and screening among candidates to find the right person.

Use this plan for writing the follow-up letter:

1. If you are writing shortly after the interview, thank the reader for the interview, identifying the particular job. If you are writing several months after the interview, give the date of the interview and identify the job.
2. Express continued interest and, if possible, supply more information or materials.
3. Give desired action.

Soon after the job interview, you may write a letter thanking the prospective employer for the interview and reviewing facts of particular interest. If possible, include additional factors that may place you in a more favorable position. The letter in Figure 28–12 illustrates a short follow-up letter.

Keep in mind that society and business are in a constant state of flux. Present jobs must be refilled because employees die, retire, resign, accept a promotion, and so on. New vacancies result from organizational changes, increased sales, technological changes, new laws, new plants, and new products.

If you are genuinely interested in working for a particular company, send a follow-up letter several months after your application letter. Include additional information to increase your chances for employment. The letter in Figure 28–13 is an example of such a follow-up letter.

Dear Mrs. Miller:

Thank you →

Thank you for interviewing me yesterday for the sports reporting job. I believe I am well qualified for it.

Persuasion →

The enclosed samples of my work for the Bay City Times reveal the depth of my experience reporting sports events.

Action →

I am available for work immediately. Please telephone me at 178-2582.

Sincerely yours,

Figure 28-12
Follow-up Letter Enclosing Work Samples—Example 1

Dear Mrs. Miller:

Job interest →

On April 14, you interviewed me for a secretarial position in the Purchasing Department. You were looking for someone with several years experience, so I did not get the job.

Persuasion →

Since the interview, I have been doing secretarial work for the J & L Foundry. I enjoy my work and my co-workers but would prefer working for General Insurance Co. because of the advancement opportunities you offer.

Action →

Will you please review my application and let me know if you need someone with my qualifications? Please telephone me at 311-6123.

Sincerely,

Figure 28-13
Follow-up Letter—Example 2

CHAPTER SUMMARY

Application letters (called cover letters when accompanied by data sheets) serve as screening instruments for the prospective employer. If yours is to achieve its purpose—succeed in getting you an interview—you must use every available means to prepare and mail a good letter.

Make your application letter speak well for you. Keep it attractive and short. Use the personal-business format. In this framework, sell yourself, avoiding a canned letter.

Always use a reader-centered approach and make your letter easy to read, interesting, positive, and concise. Tell the prospective employer what you think she or he wants to know. Begin by stating your purpose. Use the middle paragraphs to give key information that supports your candidacy for the position. Conclude your letter with a positive thought that includes your request for action. If your application letter is a reply to an advertisement, be sure to answer the questions stated in the advertisement specifically and accurately.

All employment letters become your ambassadors of goodwill toward employers. This includes reference letters, notification letters (acceptance, refusal, resignation), and follow-up letters. Follow guidelines for application letters: state the purpose, include only relevant and interesting information, and instill a positive tone. Be original, be considerate, and be concise.

Before using someone's name as a reference, be sure to request permission, orally or with a reference letter. This may save you embarrassment.

Your letter of acceptance should briefly and enthusiastically confirm the specific facts about the job. The letter of refusal need not specify the alternative chosen, but it should briefly and pleasantly explain why you are refusing the job offer. If you need to write a letter of resignation, give your employer ample notice and write a gracious letter. Do not give up too soon on a job you would like to have. Write a follow-up letter giving the potential employer additional, pertinent information.

STUDY QUESTIONS

1. Why should you be able to write an effective letter of application?
2. What are the key principles for writing effective application letters?
3. What do the following terms mean:
   a. Cover letter
   b. Solicited application letter
   c. Unsolicited application letter
   d. Blind advertisement
   e. Reference letter
4. What are the key principles for writing an effective reference letter?
5. How can a follow-up letter help an applicant?
6. Why is the letter of acceptance sometimes considered a goodwill letter?
7. When is the letter of refusal an important employment communication?
8. When is it important to write a letter of resignation?

ACTIVITIES

1. Rewrite the following statements so they will represent good opening sentences for a letter of application:
   a. This letter is in answer to the advertisement on television requesting qualified summer counselors for Camp Quaker Haven.
   b. Mr. James Clinton, President of Lincoln Insurance Co. in Indianapolis, informed me this morning of a secretarial position opening as of June 1, 19-- in your office.
   c. Referring to your advertisement in the TRADE JOURNAL, wish to advise you that I'm just the person you are looking for.
2. Rewrite the following statements regarding the applicant's formal education and work experience:
   a. I am sending along the enclosed data sheet of my business background so that you may have it on your desk for consideration when you choose your staff.
   b. The only jobs I have had are part-time and summer jobs.
   c. I gained a lot of experience and knowledge as a counselor for two summers at Camp Crossley, Oswego, Ontario.
   d. I am 29 years old and have been married and divorced and have worked for several large firms and in two small offices.
   e. At the present, I am a graduate of the University of Denver.
   f. I feel that my experience qualifies me for a sales position in your company.
3. Rewrite the following statements so they will represent better concluding statements for the application letter:
   a. I would appreciate an interview at an early date.
   b. During Christmas vacation, I will be spending the holidays with my grandparents in Los Angeles. Would it be possible to obtain an interview during that time of December 21 and January 4? My telephone number is VIking 3-7006.
   c. Hoping to hear from you at your earliest convenience, I am,
   d. Thank you for your cooperation.
   e. I hope that you will favor me with an interview. I assure you that it will pay you to interview me.
4. Rewrite the following statements so that they will represent better communication of thanks for an interview or for a letter of recommendation.
   a. I would like to take this opportunity to thank you for the interview.
   b. Thank you for taking the time to write a letter of recommendation to Mr. Wilson at Hooks Drug Store.

c. Please accept my thanks for your efforts to recommend me for the job.

5. Write a topic outline for Figure 28–1. The following example is an outline for Figure 28–5:
   Apply for acctg. job. adv. in Plain Dealer yesterday
   Enclose resume
   Graduate honors
   Internship at Edwards, Smith, and Partens
   Auditing for General Mkg., Brass and Bolts
   Desire interview
   Telephone 441–0049, 10–3.

   Notice that preparation of such an outline makes writing the letter easier.
6. Prepare the outline for a cover letter to your data sheet (Activity 4 in Chapter 27).
7. Using your outline as a guide, write the cover letter for Activity 6. Be sure your work is neat and typewritten on good quality paper. Prepare the envelope.
8. Assume that you are applying for a summer job. Prepare a letter of application, which includes information usually found in a data sheet. (Be sure to write a brief outline first.)
9. Select a business or professional person who knows your educational background or ability. Write a reference letter, requesting use of that person's name in a data sheet to accompany your letter of application. Consider telling the reader the type of position you intend to apply for.
10. Write Dr. Henry Madison, your former teacher, requesting him to write the U.S. Automobile Co. recommending you for a position you want. Supply all necessary details.
11. You did not get an answer to your application letter (Activity 7). Write a follow-up letter.
12. Suppose you did get an interview in answer to your application letter (Activity 7). You have heard nothing further. Write a follow-up letter. Although you really want the job, you do not want to appear overeager.
13. In answer to the letter you wrote for Activities 11 or 12, you were granted an interview. Several days after the interview, the Personnel Director offered you the position. Write your letter accepting the position.
14. Suppose you got a better offer (see Activity 13) and decided to refuse the job. Write a letter refusing the position.
15. Secure and complete an application blank. Which items duplicate information stated in a data sheet?

SPECIAL CASES

1. Prepare an answer for this advertisement:

    PERSONNEL CAREER PERSONS
    National company with exclusive fashion products has unusual opportunity for aggressive person with home party plan experience. Person selected will be trained for top local sales management position. Will consider applicant with limited prior experience. Base salary plus commission and bonus. Wire collect name, address, and phone number to PRESIDENT, 111 Derby Street, New Haven, Connecticut.

2. Write an outline for the application letter to answer one of the following blind advertisements:
    a.
        CHIEF ENGINEER
        for
        Sheet Metal Fabrication. Must be graduate mechanical engineer. BOX FW41, THE PRESS.
    b.
        LEGAL STENOGRAPHER
        To work for one lawyer in law firm, downtown, modern office, exp. required, Box FJ129, The Press.
    c.
        CREDIT MANAGER
        For national leasing company. Must have ability to analyze corporate financial statements and breakdown ratios, supervise collections, handle correspondence and control office internally. Good starting salary and benefits. BOX FE213, THE PRESS.
3. Write your letter for an advertisement in Problem 2 or one of the following:
    a.
        EXECUTIVE SECRETARY
        An excellent opportunity for an executive secretary seeking a challenging position at the corporate staff level.
        3–5 years experience as executive secretary required. Good typing and shorthand skills a necessity. State salary desired. Send resume to Mrs. Betty Feller, Employment Supervisor.
        AVISTON AIRCRAFT
        20111 Chagrin Blvd.
        An Equal Opportunity Employer

b.

CORPORATE ATTORNEY
$15–20,000

Prominent, large, multi-division manufacturer with local headquaters, seeks attorney with general corporation experience, to join its small legal staff. Broad areas of responsibilities in all other areas. Position opening is a result of promotion to Corporate Management Position. Excellent salary and benefits. Send resume and present income to: Box FH43, THE PRESS.

c.

QUALITY CONTROL MANAGER

Manager is desired to implement and maintain quality assurance program for a Southeast suburban company engaged in assembly and manufacture of all construction equipment. Responsible for all inspection product quality control in warranty inspection. Send resume and salary requirements to: P.O. Box 39261, SOLON, OHIO 44139.

d.

ASSISTANT OFFICE MANAGER

Assistant to office manager needed in large local auto dealership. Bookkeeping experience required. This is not a single desk type position but is highly interesting because of the variety of work. Opportunity to work with electronic accounting. We desire a person with a potential to develop to the management level. State desired salary. For interview send your resume to BOX FW274, THE PRESS.

e. Cut or copy an actual job advertisement in the "Help Wanted" section of the newspaper, a trade journal, or the college placement records. Be sure that you will qualify for the job after graduation and that the job seems interesting. Write the appropriate cover letter.

f.

DIRECTOR OF NURSING

Modern convalescent facility of 100 beds needs sharp R.N. who knows the State and Federal regulations. Must be able to supervise staff and get along with other department heads. This is a challenging and rewarding position. Salary negotiable. References required. Send resume to: STAR AND PRESS, BOX 862.

g.

Instructor—Office Careers Cluster. Position open for experienced business teacher in adult vocational training program. Subjects may include typing, business English, accounting, office procedures, office machines and employment preparation. Experience in developing and using individualized curriculum. A base salary: $18,776 per year, higher with experience and training. Reply to Mr. Robert D. Booher, Project Director, Alaska Skill Center, Box 615, Seward, AK 99664.

h.

SENIOR COMPUTER OPERATOR

Position available for individual with recent data processing and computer operation experience. Applicant must be able to effectively manage staff. Send resume to STAR AND PRESS, Box TO-835.

4. A friend has told you about a position open in a company that interests you. Write a letter to apply for the job and include your friend's name in the opening paragraph.
5. Write a want ad for a position for which you might qualify.

LANGUAGE SKILLS DEVELOPMENT

Rewrite the following statements for employment letters:

1. Leonard Walker
   Personal Director
   Container Corporation
   One Butterfield Road
   Muncie, Ind. 47303

   Sir:
2. Director of Salaried Employment
   Welsh & Associates
   261 S. Walnut Street
   Bloomington, IN 47401

   Ladies and Gentlemen
3. My thorough education in finance plus williness to learn, should enable me to succeed as an bank manager with your company.
4. After researching the prospective job market, I am interested in being considered for an accounting position with Haskins & Sells.

5. If after evaluating the enclosed data sheet, you find you would like additional information, my credentials are on file at The Placement Office of Central State University.
6. The enclosed data sheet indicates the education and office experience I have gained which has prepared me to assume a responsible position in your organization.
7. I have enclosed a résumé that lists my experiences and my educational qualifications.
8. A transcript of my college credits and some other relevant information may be obtained by contacting the Center State University Placement Services at Center State University, Detroit, Michigan, 48233, or by telephoning (313) 117-4029.
9. This work exposed me to the general public and aloud me to develop excellent communication skills and taught me to present myself in a professional manner.
10. Because I am trained in many areas of data processing, this enhances my abilities to learn quickly and efficiently.
11. I would genuinely welcome the opportunity to review my qualifications with you at a time that is convenient for you.
12. Would it be possible for me to come in for an interview next week?
13. You can reach me by telephoning 128-0731 before noon on any weekday.
14. A personal interview can be arranged at your convenience.
15. I can be contacted at the address shown on my résumé, or by telephone; 317-111-7440.
16. May I use your name as a reference for a job?
17. Thank you. I accept the job offer of Operations Manager.
18. Thank you for the job offer of Sales Manager, but I must decline in order to accept a much higher paying job at L & L Imported Products.
19. I am resigning with this letter.

IN-BASKET SIMULATION

Prepare the cover letter to accompany your data sheet to Karen Todd at the Waltere Supermarkets, Inc. (see In-Basket Simulation in Chapter 27). Ms. Todd believes the application letter should include reasons for contacting the company or how you found out about the job. Include your telephone number in the letter, but avoid limiting dates for a possible interview. If your data sheet does not include salary information (range or specific amount), be sure to specify your expectations in your application letter.

29

The Employment Interview

After studying Chapter 29, you should be able to:

- List the steps in the employment interview
- Use your data sheet to fill out an application blank
- Dress appropriately for an interview
- Follow an interviewer's lead
- Anticipate the kinds of questions that will undoubtedly be asked in an interview and be aware of those that should not be asked or are "illegal"
- Discuss the reasons employers cite for rejecting an applicant

While preparing your successful data sheet (Chapter 27), you were preparing (at least in part) for your job interview: You analyzed the job characteristics and requirements; the company organization, procedures, products or services, and possible opportunities; and yourself in relation to the job and to the company.

Think of the interview time as a genuine opportunity to explain your data sheet, to bring out your immediate and future desires, and to emphasize your strong points. With confidence in yourself and your abilities, follow the interviewer's lead. An interviewer will initiate the dialogue and will give you clues (oral, visual, or both) when the interview is to end. Express your thanks for the interview and leave with positive feelings. Even if you do not get the job, you have learned more about yourself and the business world. Subsequent employment interviews should be easier and perhaps more enjoyable.

Bring a copy of your data sheet to the interview so that you can easily record certain facts on the application blank, a form furnished by employers. You should not try to remember important dates, telephone numbers, addresses, and other specific information included on data sheets and required by employers.

STEPS IN THE EMPLOYMENT INTERVIEW

The following step-by-step outline indicates what an applicant might expect at a job interview. The first few minutes of the interview are the most crucial; they establish that important first impression.

Preliminary activities

- Applicant greets interviewer by name (pronouncing it correctly).
- Applicant accepts interviewer's outstretched hand for a friendly, firm handshake.
- Applicant sits at interviewer's invitation to do so.

Actual interview

- Applicant completes application blank (may have been done outside the office or some time before the interview).
- Interviewer asks casual questions or makes comments to put applicant at ease.
- Interviewer reviews applicant's credentials by asking applicant:
    - easy to answer and general questions
    - specific questions relating to the company, the job, the applicant
- Interviewer invites applicant to ask questions:
    - about the job
    - about the company

- Interviewer closes interview.
- Applicant thanks interviewer for the opportunity to review her or his credentials.
- Interviewer (1) offers job to candidate, (2) explains that applicant will be considered for the job, or (3) advises that applicant will be called if a vacancy for which she or he is qualified should occur.

All applicants should be prepared to take various tests applicable to successful job performance. These tests can include skills tests (for example, typewriting, shorthand, or machines); intelligence tests; judgment (logic) tests; personality tests; aptitude tests; inventory of attitudes and values; mathematics tests; grammar or language usage tests; and physical examination. They should also be prepared to show samples illustrating specific job ability (for example, journal articles, arts, crafts, or printing).

During the interview, an interviewer will notice applicant's appearance, voice, gestures, behavior, and manner and may record brief notes. After the interview, the interviewer may complete various interview forms and reports.

THE APPLICATION BLANK

Generally before a prospective employer will hire you, you will be asked to complete a preprinted form called an **application blank**. Application blanks differ to some extent, but all companies will request data similar to that included in data sheets.

Application forms require specific information regarding your formal education, work experience, special abilities, personal information (for example, your name, address, telephone and social security number), and references. The form might include these questions:

1. Whom shall we notify in case of an emergency?
2. When will you be available for employment?
3. Have you applied for work here before? When?
4. Are you willing to work overseas?
5. Do you have a chauffeur's driving license?
6. Why are you interested in employment with **Company name** ?
7. What do you consider your greatest strengths?
8. Can you speak or write any foreign languages? Which? Explain your ability.
9. What was your salary when you left each previous job?

10. What starting salary do you expect?
11. Do you have any relatives (first cousin or closer) employed with this company or any of its divisions? If so, give names, relationships, places of employment, and business titles.

Write (print or type if asked to do so) neatly and be sure to complete each blank accurately. If a question does not apply to you, write *not applicable* or *N/A* in the space provided for the answer. You can use standard abbreviations where space is too meager for complete words. Most often you will be asked to use a pen and to print at least your name.

Since an application blank is a pre-employment form, it will often include a comment such as "An Equal Opportunity Employer" and will cover only data which is not in violation with the Equal Employment Opportunities Commission (EEOC), state and federal laws.

Employers reserve the right to discharge employees who knowingly furnish pre-employment information that is incorrect or not true. The applicant may be asked to sign a statement on the application blank that verifies the authenticity of information given.

NONVERBAL MESSAGES

Much communication at the employment interview is nonverbal. Before the interview begins, prepare yourself—be clean, dress neatly and appropriately, and be on time.

Be Neat and Clean

The importance of neatness and cleanliness cannot be stressed too much. Your clothes should be free from wrinkles and stains; your shoes shined. Your hands, fingernails, teeth, and hair should be clean. A trimmed, attractive hair style will favorably impress the interviewer. On the other hand, long hair may negatively distract.

Dress for the Business World

Visualize yourself on the job; dress to look the part. Jeans, leisure wear, sneakers, and loafers may be comfortable, but they do not suggest business or work. The successful job applicant should be interested in style, but not in fashion fads. Avoid designer labels and flashy or bulky accessories. Men should wear business suits. Women should wear business suits with plain blouses or tailored simple dresses. The female job applicant is not expected to wear a tie or look or dress like a male. On the other hand, her attire should not overplay her sexuality.

Like clothes, color can influence the interviewer. While women can successfully wear a variety of colors, the male job applicant shouts "executive material" by wearing conservative colors.

See Chapter 26 for more information on how grooming and appearance influence interviewers.

Be on Time for the Interview

Some interviewers will not even speak with you if you are late without good reason. Promptness to the interview reveals a desire to continue the good impression the prospective employer experienced after reading your application letter and data sheet. Many employers equate promptness to the interview with interest and motivation on the job and applicant's habits with respect to promptness. To allow for the unexpected, plan to arrive at least 15 minutes before the scheduled interview time.

INTERVIEW QUESTIONS

The interviewer may ask questions related to:

Your character and your personal interests
Your ability to get along well with others, especially those with whom you might be working
Your activities since graduation
Your educational background
What you consider to be your strengths and your weaknesses
Your willingness to relocate or to travel
Your previous jobs (duties, what you learned, why you left, and salary earned)
Your future career plans
Your knowledge about the company
Your expected contributions to the company
Your ideas on a suitable salary
Your ability as related to the job vacancy

While preparing for your interview, rehearse answers to questions you are likely to be asked. Be sure to answer questions completely and correctly. Strive to speak enthusiastically and to use good English, avoiding slang. Numerous *uh*s and *okay*s can be distracting. Just pause briefly before answering.

Specifically, the interviewer might ask:

1. What led you to choosing ______________________ University?
2. Why did you select ______________________ course of study?
3. How do you see your education contributing to your employment?
4. What have you been doing since graduation?
5. In what activities have you participated?
6. If you were to begin college again, what courses would you take?
7. How did you finance your college education?
8. Why did you leave (previous jobs)?
9. What do you see as your specific strengths and weaknesses as they relate to this job?
10. What experience have you had that would be helpful in performing the responsibilities we have talked about?
11. Why should we hire you?
12. How does your past experience contribute to successful employment?
13. What suggestions, innovations, or accomplishments did you make at ______**Previous jobs**______?
14. What things were you unable to achieve? Why?
15. To which professional organizations do you belong?
16. How much salary do you expect?
17. How do you feel about working with ______**Groups of people (for example, children)**______?
18. Relative to the position, what do you like most? Least?
19. Do you prefer working with others or by yourself?
20. How much do you expect to be earning ten years from now?
21. Are you willing to move to another city?
22. Do you own a car? Are you willing to travel on the job?
23. Have you ever been bonded?
24. How do you perceive yourself?
25. Tell me about yourself.
26. Who has been most influential in your life? Why?
27. What are your short-term and long-term objectives?
28. What is your expected timetable to reach your goals?
29. What do you expect to be doing ten years from now?
30. Why did you choose to interview with us?
31. How do you think you will contribute to the company?
32. How do you feel we can meet your career objectives?
33. What do you know about our company?
34. What led you to pursue a career in ______________________?
35. What did you do between ______**Date**______ and ______**Date**______?

The applicant should feel free to ask questions relating to the company or the job. Ask concrete questions that will reveal your interest in the position and the company and impress the interviewer. Avoid questions that suggest you have not done your homework—employment research. At the first interview, do not ask salary or fringe-benefit questions; they imply that money and benefits are your prime interests. You can ask such questions at a second interview. Here are suggestions for questions at the initial employment interview:

1. What is the nature of the training program and supervision during the first and second years of employment?
2. Would I report to more than one supervisor during the training program?
3. What will be expected of me as a new employee?
4. What is your success record with graduates from ______________________ College (or University)?
5. Will I need my car for traveling between job sites? How will travel expenses be paid?

ILLEGAL QUESTIONS—PRIOR TO THE JOB OFFER

Federal and state laws and the Equal Employment Opportunity Commission (EEOC) prohibit prospective employers from requesting information relating to job equality, race, religion, color, sex, national origin, or ancestry because it may lead to unlawful discrimination. Applicants can volunteer pertinent job information on the data sheet or during the interview. Information that employers cannot legally request *prior to the job offer* includes:

1. *Race or color.*
2. *Religion or religious customs*; however, an employer can ask an applicant if he or she is willing to work a required work schedule.
3. *Marital status.*
4. *Maiden or previous name*; however, an employer might ask if applicant's work records are recorded under another name than the one on the application blank, application letter, or data sheet.
5. *Housing information that reveals whether applicant owns or rents, lives in an apartment or house.* However, an employer can request your home address and how long you have lived there.
6. *Ages of applicant and applicant's children.*
7. *Number of children and whether applicant plans to have or adopt additional children, as well as data regarding child care.*
8. *Sex of applicant*—except for rare instances (a supervisor of a restroom, for example, may be required to be a certain sex).

9. *Physical data*—unless job related. An applicant may be hired on condition that he or she passes a physical examination. Handicapped persons cannot be excluded from employment unless the handicap hinders job performance.
10. *Names of relatives working for the company.*
11. *Military service records or type of discharge*; however, the employer can request applicant to indicate branch of service and rank attained prior to discharge.
12. *Academic information solely for the purpose of revealing the applicant's nationality, racial, or religious affiliation*; however, the employer can ask for names and addresses of schools attended.
13. *References from clergy or anyone else specifically to determine applicant's race, religion, sex, national origin, or ancestry.*
14. *Organizational memberships that reveal the applicant's race, religion, sex, national origin, or ancestry*; however, applicant may be requested to list memberships and offices held in professional and social organizations.
15. *Arrests*; however, applicant may be asked to list convictions.
16. *Photograph of applicant.*

In some cases, questions that directly (or indirectly) solicit illegal information are difficult to establish. Sometimes only the courts can interpret what constitutes unlawful inquiry.

REASONS FOR REJECTING APPLICANTS

During the interview, an applicant may display behavior traits offensive to the interviewer, thereby resulting in a rejection for the vacancy or for a subsequent opening. The following items (listed from most to least offensive) are acknowledged by job interviewers as reasons for rejecting applicants.

1. Poor personal appearance
2. Inadequate knowledge of specialty
3. Indifferent or unenthusiastic attitude
4. Overbearing (superiority complex)
5. Ill-mannered
6. Unable to express views clearly
7. Late to interview without good reason
8. Little (or no) interest in the company
9. Inadequate planning for career (no goals)
10. Sloppy application blank
11. Condemnatory of previous employers
12. Insufficient (or no) questions related to the job
13. Tactless
14. Evasive answers to questions
15. Immature behavior

16. Unwilling to start at bottom (if applicable)
17. Indefinite responses to questions
18. Short-term employment (for permanent job)
19. Constant name-dropper
20. Intolerant
21. Insufficient eye contact
22. Poor scholastic record
23. Insufficient belief in herself or himself
24. Uninformed about the company
25. Job shopper
26. Low moral standards
27. Limp handshake

The limp handshake has been equated with shaking hands with a dead fish. Even though *limp handshake* is the last item on the list of offensive behavior traits, a handshake may be the first action at the interview. Thus, it becomes the basis for an early reaction from the interviewer. It is best to begin the interview in a positive manner.

SUGGESTIONS FOR A SUCCESSFUL INTERVIEW

The list of offensive behavior traits suggests the following list of things to do for a successful interview:

1. Be neat and wear appropriate clothes.
2. Be on time—better yet, plan to be early.
3. Complete the application blank by answering all questions completely, truthfully, neatly, and as indicated.
4. Shake an offered hand with a firm, but not bone-crushing, grip.
5. Look the interviewer in the eye—at least do not avoid occasional eye contact.
6. Be enthusiastic about the job and the interview. Perhaps explain why the new job will fulfill your objectives.
7. Consider the feelings of all persons present (in other words, follow the Golden Rule).
8. Be cheerful and courteous during the interview and express thanks at its conclusion.
9. Be interested in the company and your possible role within it.
10. Answer questions honestly, clearly, and distinctly.
11. Ask relevant questions.
12. Emphasize what you know, not whom you know.
13. Say only positive things about previous employers and co-workers.

Besides a copy of your data sheet and a list of questions to ask the interviewer, bring to the interview your social security card or card number, working pen and pencils, a note pad, and examples of work for quick reference. These tools show your interest in the company. Do not take notes during the interview.

FOLLOW-UP INTERVIEWS

Most often, the applicant will be interviewed by one interviewer and just once. Occasionally, the applicant will be asked to return for a second interview. Applicants for executive positions may be interviewed three, four, or more times in different cities and by different people. The applicant's spouse may be included in one or more of the interviews. Sometimes interviews are in the form of social events in a private home or some place other than within the office, with prospective co-workers present. The successful applicant prepares for each interview.

If a job offer is not extended at the interview, it may be made at a later date. An applicant interested in an available job might mail a follow-up letter to thank the interviewer and to submit additional information that would interest the prospective employer. (See Chapter 28.)

CHAPTER SUMMARY

Refer to your data sheet to complete the application blank, a pre-employment form provided by prospective employers. Be sure to answer all questions as requested. State the information neatly and accurately.

Dress neatly and appropriately for the business world and be on time to show genuine interest in the job opportunity.

The employment interview is structured so that the applicant and the interviewer can ask suitable questions and discuss the company—and the applicant in relation to the job and the company.

Applicants should consider employment interviews (there may be more than one) as opportunities to explain the data sheet, to bring out immediate and future desires, and to emphasize strong points. With confidence in yourself and your abilities, follow the interviewer's lead. Interviewers will initiate the dialogue and give clues when the interview is to end.

Prior to the job offer, employers should not ask questions that may lead to unlawful discrimination. This would include questions relating to job equality, race, religion, color, sex, national origin, or ancestry. Applicants, however, can volunteer pertinent job information on the data sheet or during the interview. It is important for applicants to refrain from any verbal or nonverbal behavior that might lead to rejection for the vacancy or for a subsequent opening.

Express your thanks for the interview and leave with positive feelings. Even if you do not get the job, you have learned more about yourself and the business world. Subsequent job interviews should be easier and perhaps more enjoyable.

STUDY QUESTIONS

1. What pointers should you give someone about to complete an application blank?
2. What kinds of information does the typical application blank contain?
3. Why might an employer want to know if you can speak and/or write any foreign languages?
4. Why is the interviewer's first impression of an applicant important?
5. Why is the handshake important to the interviewer and to the interviewee?
6. What does it mean to be neat, clean, and dressed for the business world?
7. Studies have revealed that it is best for job applicants to wear conservative business clothes. Specifically, how should the would-be executive dress for a job interview?
8. What is your career objective? Name several specific questions an interviewer might ask you. What questions might you ask an interviewer?
9. Why are several questions considered illegal? Name specific illegal information an applicant might volunteer before a job offer. Why would an applicant do this?
10. What suggestions would you give job applicants desiring successful interviews?
11. What is the purpose of the initial interview? The follow-up interview?

ACTIVITIES

1. Secure an application form. Study the questions and complete the form as requested. It should be totally, correctly, and carefully filled in.
2. Compare two application forms (from same type of industry or from different industries—retailing, service, or manufacturing) as your teacher suggests. What specific similarities do you see? What differences?
3. Prepare a list of specific questions a job interviewer might ask you. Write your detailed answers.
4. Prepare a list of questions to ask an interviewer.
5. Prepare a checksheet listing recommended steps to get ready for a successful employment interview.
6. Prepare a script for an employment interview situation—allow time for unstructured questions.
7. How can you let a prospective employer know that you get along well with people without appearing boastful?
8. What should you say to sell your formal education to an interviewer?

9. What should you say to sell your work experience to an interviewer?
10. Role play a job interview. If possible, videotape the interview and critique it. What were your strengths? What were your weaknesses? How will you strive to eliminate your weaknesses?
11. Critique an available film (depicting an employment interview) in the college placement office.

EDITING

1. Revise the following statements included in application forms:

EDUCATION

School Name & Address	Date of Graduation	Degree	Class Standing
a. Baker Jr. College	June, 19--	A.A.	Upper 1/10
b. Rochester High School Rochester, N.Y. City	June, 19--	Degree	85%
c. Tucson College of Business Tucson, Arizona	19-- to 19--	Degree	2/3

PREVIOUS EMPLOYMENT

Date (Mo., Year)	Name and Address	Position	Salary	Reason for Leaving
a. Racine Plumbing	Jan., 19-- to July, 19--	Operations Aide	$100	Begin College
b. 8/19__- 7/19__	Johnson Smith Co.	Office Clerk	$1,000 Month	Advance-ment
c. 8/19__- 12/'__	Mann & Mann, Inc. Columbus, O.	Office Supvr.		

REFERENCES

a. Name: Mary Mills
Occupation: Secretary
Company: Johnson & Johnson Co.
Street Address: Main Street
City, State, ZIP: Amherst, MA 01001

b. Name: Paul Rover
Occupation: V-P
Company:
Street Address: 385 E. 25th Street
City, State, ZIP: Amherst, MA 01001

c. A. Sally Golden — Company: (216) 188-6537
Street Address: Central State Univ.
Occupation: Prof. — City, State, ZIP: Waltham, MA 02152

HOBBIES: Member of Travel Club, photography, riding

2. Revise the following replies to interviewers questions and explain why the answer stated originally is not satisfactory:
   a. **Question:** What salary do you expect?
      Answer: Whatever you want to pay me.

   b. **Question:** Why should I hire you?
      Answer: I have friends in the company.

   c. **Question:** Does your grade point average reveal your ability?
      Answer: No.

   d. **Question:** Do you have a valid driver's license?
      Answer: Why do you need to know?

IN-BASKET SIMULATION

With joy, you agree to an employment interview with Ms. Karen Todd, Personnel Director for Waltere Supermarkets, Inc. List the questions you think Ms. Todd might ask you. Write answers to the questions. List several questions you might ask Ms. Todd.

Selected Pages of a Formal Report

APPENDIX I

The University of Tennessee

WOMEN IN THE LABOR MARKET

by

Eugene Schlosser

Presented to

Dr. Nancy Deal

Spring 19--

TABLE OF CONTENTS

ii

WOMEN IN THE LABOR MARKET

Introduction

The labor force participation rate has changed dramatically over the past 20 years; the reason for this change is the upward trend of the employment of women into the work force.

The participation rate of women in the labor force in the United States has doubled since 1900. The composition of these jobs has shifted from agricultural and industrial to white collar and service occupations.[1]

The number of women seeking a college education is rising at both the undergraduate and graduate levels. Women are preparing themselves to adjust to the labor requirements of the 1980s.

Purpose

The purpose of this report is to determine which factors influenced the increase of women into the labor market.

Scope

This paper will be limited to a brief history of women who have entered the labor market and a discussion of the major reasons why women enter the work force.

---

[1]Gilbert Sandal. Women Today. Columbus: Human Resources Press, 1985, p. 57.

The work load for women shifted from home to factory. However, women had always produced goods for the family. The difference was that these home-produced goods became a product of the labor market for pay.

Workload changes for women have been fairly recent. As late as 1890, nearly half of all American women lived on farms. The jobs performed by women were never ending. They included making all the clothing for the family, keeping a garden, milking, churning, canning fruits and vegetables, and cooking.[2]

World War II, which created a labor shortage, greatly improved women's economic opportunities and contributed to an understanding of women's abilities and usefulness. Women helped fill the demand in such jobs as personnel management, transportation, and other technical fields. Since World War II, larger business organizations and expanded activities of both commerce and communication have required the use of new labor resources and have helped to change traditional attitudes concerning women's status in the labor force.[3]

<u>Factors Influencing Female Entry</u>

American women of all classes have entered the labor market. Prolonged education, expanding job opportunities,

---

[2]Gladys E., Harbeson. <u>Choice and Challenge for the American Woman</u>. Cambridge: Schenkman Publishing Co., 1982, pp. 30-32.

[3]Harbeson, p. 35.

10

Conclusion

The image of women is changing. The old picture of the retiring, self-sacrificing, and completely domestic woman is a thing of the past. The new image is a woman who is more dynamic and intelligent about the world outside her home; and she is a participant in it.

In spite of any apparent improvement in the occupational status of women within the past few years, however, they still have a long way to go before their vocational opportunities will be as wide and as unrestricted as those of men.

Bibliography

Darling, Margaret. The Role of Women in the World. New York: Paris Publishing Company, 1983.

Harbeson, Gladys E. Choice and Challenge for the American Woman. Cambridge: Schenkman Publishing Co., 1982.

Sandal, Gilbert. Women Today. Columbus: Human Resources Press, 1985.

Sweet, James A. Women in the Labor Force. New York: Seminar Press, 1984.

How to Use the Library

APPENDIX II

The library is a special place where you can find and read a book on almost any subject—fiction or nonfiction. Or you can browse through a magazine or newspaper from a distant location; listen to fine music; study for a test; or research a subject you are curious about. You can borrow (free) publications and even framed pictures for a week, two weeks, or longer.

The card catalog is the key to most of the library's holdings. If you cannot locate the information you seek or need help using references or equipment (such as a microform reader), a trained attendant will help you. But you should know the facilities and resources available to you.

REFERENCE MATERIALS

If you are searching for information in the library, you can get direct personal assistance, which includes help in using the main card catalog, reference works, and indexes. A well-selected reference book collection includes dictionaries, encyclopedias, almanacs, atlases, directories, handbooks, guidebooks, *Who's Who* books, newspapers, and other general and special reference works. If you do not know which reference book to use, consult the *Guide to Reference Works*. Generally, reference books do not circulate, but you can use the books in the reference area for several hours.

Dictionaries (See Appendix III)

Abridged—Shortened content of vocabulary
Special—Various languages and various fields of study, such as business and law.
Unabridged—Comprehensive content of vocabulary.

Thesaurus (See Appendix IV)

A list of synonyms, antonyms, and related words.

Encyclopedias

General—Information on various subjects; one or several volumes.
Special—Information covers various fields such as business, sports, education.

Statistics

Statistical information (numerical data) on many subjects; many are published annually. Examples include: *People's Almanac*, *Information Please Almanac*, *Sports Almanac*, *The World Almanac*, *Guinness Book of World Records*, *Statistical Abstract of the United States*, and *Census Reports*.

Atlases

A collection of maps and information on the history, population, products, agriculture, and business of specific areas.

Directories

Listed information on various subjects. Examples include telephone directories (for popular cities and towns), city directories (gives names, addresses, and occupations of residents and names and addresses of businesses, social, and civic institutions), governmental directories (such as the *Congressional Directory*), educational directories, and special directories issued by businesses (trade directories), clubs, and newspapers.

Guidebooks and Handbooks

Available on many topics; for example, *Hotel and Motel Red Book*, *Official Airline Guide*, *Accountant's Handbook*, *Financial Handbook*, *Official Baseball Guide*, *U.S. Postal Service Manual* (see Chapter 7), and *Reference Guide for Consumers*.

Government Publications

The United States Government Printing Office in Washington, D.C., has numerous publications on various subjects of general and special interest to the public. Individual governmental units publish other publications. The *United States Government Organization Manual* provides information on the functions, services, and publications of various governmental agencies.

Newspapers

Popular daily newspapers, including local newspapers, *Wall Street Journal*, *Chicago Tribune*, and *The New York Times*.

Educational Resources

Materials and equipment for the teacher; including textbooks, curriculum guides, framed prints, career resources, films, and curriculum media (standardized tests, pamphlets, maps, transparencies, textiles, units of work, picture post cards, and mounted pictures).

College Catalog Collection

A selective collection of university, college, and junior college catalogs for reference use in the library. The collection is useful if you want to learn more about a specific post-high school.

Special Collections

Materials of significant price or value (rare books, archives, manuscripts, autographed items, map collections, drama collections) may be housed in a special section of the library and listed in the main card catalog. Generally, the materials are available for in-room use, with special permission needed for photocopying. The archives may consist of various college or university and student publications (for example, catalogs, newspapers, and original research papers), county records (for example, histories, records of vital statistics, tax duplicates, and deed and estate records), maps, photographs, and diaries.

Unpublished Research

Theses, dissertations, creative projects, and various research papers are available, including the opportunity to borrow others by using the Interlibrary Loan Service.

Biographical

Brief abstracts about famous or specialized people (living or dead) are contained in resources such as the *People's Almanac* and various *Who's Who's* (such as, *Who's Who*, *Who's Who in America*, *Who's Who in Commerce and Industry*, *Who's Who in American Education*, *Who's Who in the Midwest*, *Who's Who Among Students in American Universities and Colleges*, and *Who's Who in Sports*).

Occupational

Many publications are available to guide you in your career choice and give specific and detailed information on various occupations. Best known sources are *The Dictionary of Occupational Titles* and the *Occupational Outlook Handbook*. These and others are described in the Other Readings for Chapter 27.

INDEXES

An index to articles written in many popular general and special interest magazines. Articles are listed by subject and by author.

Reader's Guide to Periodical Literature

Special Fields

Specific indexes are available for particular trades and professions; for example, *Business Education Index*, *Industrial Arts Index*, and *Education Index*.

EQUIPMENT

Microform Readers and Printers

Equipment such as the microcard, microfiche, and microfilm readers and printers is available for reading and making copies of various microforms. The microforms and equipment must be handled carefully so that the microforms are not smudged, scratched, or torn. A library attendant will be on hand for help.

Photocopiers

For a nominal charge, pages from books and periodicals can be reproduced quickly. The copyright laws must be observed.

Typewriters

Some libraries provide typewriters for a nominal charge.

Film and Slide Projectors

Available to preview films and slides.

SPECIAL AREAS

Educational Resources Information Center (ERIC)

A library can be a subscriber to the services of this nationwide information system designed and supported by the United States Office of Education. ERIC provides abstracts of documents on many aspects of education, usually on 4-in. × 6-in. microfiche. You will need a fiche reader (available in the library) to read the documents. A monthly abstract journal, *Resources in Education*, contains a synopsis of each document included and indexes: institution, author, and subject. (Prior to January, 1975, the publication was called *Research in Education*.) To use the ERIC collection, get the "ED" number from the journal and give it to the librarian.

Interlibrary Loan Service

Libraries can borrow materials owned by other libraries, usually for two weeks. The lending library sets restrictions on the use of their materials and the loan period, but loan procedures are regulated by a National Interlibrary Loan Code. To use the interlibrary loan service, a student need only complete an interlibrary loan request form and give it to the librarian. Giving all information requested will expedite receipt of borrowed materials. Some interlibrary materials are on film, for which there is a charge.

The Vertical File

A collection of pamphlets and brochures on topics of current interest: abortion, aged, diseases, birth control, child abuse, drug abuse, equal rights, alcoholism, family life education, physiological effects of tobacco, euthanasia, and so on. To use, simply follow usual checkout procedure.

Other Areas

A library may designate certain areas for study or special use (for example, faculty study rooms, student study rooms, group study rooms, seminar rooms, and typewriting rooms).

How to Use the Dictionary

APPENDIX III

If you master the use of the dictionary, you will find it easier to write smoothly and more quickly. Choosing the right words for a particular thought you wish to express can best be done by using the dictionary. Some tips to help you get acquainted with this valuable tool follow:

1. Use a recent edition of a dictionary that is recommended by your school librarian or other reliable source. Several thousand new words are added to the dictionary each year; you need a contemporary edition for all the current words and their meanings.
2. Read the preface of your dictionary to determine the method used for defining words. Learn the symbols that are used to show correct pronunciation.
3. Practice the pronunciation of a word several times aloud before you use it so you will feel at ease the first time you use it in public.
4. Acquire the habit of using the dictionary to learn new words. Develop a plan for learning a predetermined number of new words each week. As you become familiar with a new set of words, you will find it much easier to write smoothly and to use the right words for the particular thought you wish to express.

Dictionaries are designed to help you learn to use words effectively:

1. Words are divided into syllables to help with pronunciation and word division.
2. Pronunciations are given after the correct spelling of the word is presented. When two or more pronunciations for a single word are listed, the most common form is usually given first.
3. Parts of speech (noun, verb, adverb, adjective) are usually given for each word.
4. Plurals, past tense, and other word endings are usually given for each word.
5. Definitions, of course, are also included. Supplementary information (such as whether the term is vulgar or slang) is often given after the definition.
6. Synonyms and antonyms for each word are often listed.
7. Word etymology (background or origin of the word) is given to help you understand how the word became part of the English language.

APPENDIX IV

How to Use a Thesaurus

A thesaurus can help you choose the right word for the occasion; it helps you avoid the repetitious use of the same word. A thesaurus is a list of synonyms (words having the same meaning), antonyms (words having the opposite meaning), and related words (words having similar meanings). The thesaurus:

1. Lists words alphabetically.
2. Lists other words of related meaning but of different parts of speech.
3. Gives words and phrases to show how the listed word might be used in a sentence.
4. Tells the parts of speech (noun, verb, adjective).

To use a thesaurus, look up the word for which you wish to have a synonym, antonym, or word related in some other way, and the thesaurus will list one or more words to use.

A thesaurus is not a dictionary and does not give definitions of words. If you need the meaning of a word, consult the dictionary.

Ten Hints for Increasing Your Spelling Vocabulary

APPENDIX V

1. Concentrate on a limited number of words each week—perhaps ten.
2. Ask a friend to dictate the words before studying them. This should reveal words you need to study. In the process, your friend may also become a better speller.
3. Study each word for spelling clues. For example, *bookkeeping*, which relates to keeping books, includes the words "book" and "keep," and *stationery*, a type of paper, ends in *er* as does the word "paper."
4. Check the spelling rules. For example, *believe* and *receive* comply with the rule: *i* before *e* except after *c*. Some words, however, follow exceptions to rules.
5. Refer to the most complete dictionary available to you. Check to see if the word is spelled similar to a foreign word or if the word is spelled as it is pronounced. It has been said that about 80 percent of American words conform to regular phonetic spelling patterns.
6. Study the chosen words for about 10 minutes daily. A short study period should be more useful than one or two long study periods during the same timespan.
7. Ask a friend to dictate the words you have studied.
8. Make a list of the words you find most troublesome.
9. Review periodically the troublesome words—as you add new words to your spelling vocabulary.
10. Be positive! You will increase your spelling vocabulary if you honestly strive to improve your spelling ability.

APPENDIX VI

275 Troublesome Spelling Words

ac cept
ac cept ance
ac ces sory
ac com mo date
ac com mo da tion
ac cu mu late
ac cu rate
achieve ment
ac quaint ance
ad journ ment
ad van ta geous
ad ver tise ment
af fect (verb)
af fili ate
a gree a ble
all right
al lot ment
al lot ted
al most
al ready
amend ment
a mong
a nal y sis
ana lyze
ap par ent
ap pear ance
ap point ment
ap pro pri ate
ar chi tect
ar range ment
as sign ment
as sist ance
ath let ics
at tend ance
at tor neys
auc tion eer
aux il iary
avi ator
bal lot
bank ruptcy
ban quet
bat tery
be gin ning
be hav ior
be liev able
bene fi cial
bene fited
bro chure
budget
bul le tin
bu reaus
busi ness
cal endar
cam paign
can cel la tion
ca reer
cen sus
change able
clien tele
col lege
com mit ment
com mit tee
com peti tor
con cede
con fi dence
con fi dent
con grat u la tions
con science
con sci en tious
con secu tively
con sen sus
con trib ute
con trol ling
con ven ience
con ven ient
cor re spond ent
coun cil (an assembly)
counsel
cus tom er
de ci sion
de duct i ble
de fend ant
de ferred
defi nite
dele gate
de lin quent
de scrip tion
de velop
de vel op ment
di ag no sis
dis burse ment
dis tinct
ef fect (result)
elec tron ic
eli gi ble
emi nent
en cy clo pe dia
en dorse ment
en ter prise
e quip ment
equip ped
evi dently
ex ceed
ex cel lent
ex hi bi tion
ex ten sion
ex traor di nary
fac sim ile
fa mil iar
fea si ble
Feb ru ary
flexi ble
for eign
forty
fran chise
ful fill
gauge
gen uine
ges ture
gov ern ment

gov er nor
gram mar
gra tu ity
gro cery
guar an tee
guid ance
height
il le gal
imi ta tion
im me di ately
in au gu rate
in ci den tally
in de pend ence
in stal la tion
is suing
its (ownership)
it's (it is)
jew elry
jour ney
jus ti fi able
jus ti fied
kin der gar ten
knowl edge
labo ra tory
ledger
le giti mate
lei sure
li ai son
li brary
li cense
lien
lik able
liq uefy
lis ten
live li hood
loose (adj.)
lose (verb)
lovely
main te nance
man age able
man age ment
man ual
manu fac turer
manu script
mathe ma tics

mile age
mis cel la ne ous
mis spell
mod ern
mort gage
mov able
nec es sary
ne ces sity
ninety
ninth
no tice able
oc ca sion
oc ca sion ally
oc curred
oc cur rence
omis sion
omit ted
op por tu ni ty
op po site
or di nance (law)
pam phlet
par al lel
par cel
par lia men tary
par tial
per form ance
per ma nent
per mis si ble
per se ver ance
per son al
per son ally
per son nel
per suade
phy si cian
plan ning
pos ses sion
prac ti cal
pre cede
pre ced ing
pre ferred
pre cious
pref er able
pre limi nary
preva lent
prin ci pal (main)

prin ci ple (rule)
privi lege
pro ce dure
pro ceed
pro fes sor
promi nent
prom is sory
psy chol ogy
pub licly
quan tity
ques tion naire
rap port
re ceipt
re ceive
re cipi ent
rec om mend
rec om men da tion
rec on cile
ref er ence
re ferred
rele vant
re mit tance
rep re sent a tive
re plies
re scind
res tau rant
re veal
safety
sal able
scho las tic
sec re tary
sen si ble
sepa rate
se rial
ship ment
ship ping
simi lar
si mul ta ne ous
since
siz able
spe cifi cally
speech
sta tion ary (fixed)
sta tion ery (paper)
sta tis tics

suc ceed
suc ces sor
suf fi cient
su ing
su per in tend ent
super sede
sur prise
tai lor
tan gi ble
tech ni cal
tech nique
tem po rary
tend ency
ter ri tory
their (ownership)
theory
trag edy
trans ferred
unani mous
unique
us able
use ful
visi ble
visi tor
vi ta min
vol ume
waiver
war ranty
weather (air)
whether (conj.)
yes ter day
you're (you are)

Function of Words

APPENDIX VII

This brief section reviews the basic functions of words. For more details, refer to an English handbook or dictionary.

NOUNS

Nouns are words which name persons, places, or things. If the noun names a specific person, place, or thing, it is called a **proper noun** and is capitalized (for example, John Jackson, America, and Kellogg's corn flakes). The noun is often either the subject or an object in the sentence. The plural of most nouns is formed by adding an *s*. Adding an *'s* to most nouns shows ownership.

PRONOUNS

Pronouns are substitutes for nouns. Therefore, the pronoun is often the subject or an object in the sentence. A pronoun following a linking verb (*to be*) is always in the **nominative case**. You would say, for example, *It is I* rather than *It is me*. Use the **objective case** pronoun as a direct object of other verbs, indirect object, object of a preposition or infinitive, and subject of an infinitive. (An infinitive is the word *to* with an action verb; for example, *to meet*, *to tell*, and *to analyze*.) Use the **possessive case** to show ownership.

Table A-1 lists the singular and plural forms of personal pronouns in the nominative case, objective case, and possessive case.

Person	**Nominative case** (subject acts)		**Objective case** (subject is acted upon)		**Possessive case** (ownership)	
	Singular	*Plural*	*Singular*	*Plural*	*Singular*	*Plural*
First	I	we	me	us	my, mine	our, ours
Second	you	you	you	you	you, your	your, yours
Third	he, she, it, who, whoever	they who, whoever	he, him, it, whom, whomever	them whom, whomever	his, her, hers, its, whose, whosoever	their, theirs, whose, whosoever

Table A-1
Personal Pronouns

Other classes of pronouns include:

Indefinite pronouns refer to an indefinite person or thing (for example, *each*, *every*, *either*, *neither*, *someone*, *anyone*, and *no one*).
Demonstrative pronouns point out something (for example, *this*, *that*, *these*, and *those*).
Relative pronouns introduce a clause that modifies the noun preceding the pronoun. Use *who*, *whom*, and *whose* to refer to people; use *that* and *which* to refer to things.
Reflective pronouns emphasize the doer, so that the subject of the verb is also its object (for example, *myself*, *yourself*, *himself*, *herself*, and *itself*).

A pronoun must agree with its antecedent (word it refers to) in number, gender, and person. Two subjects joined by *and* require a plural pronoun; two subjects joined by *or* or *nor* require a singular pronoun.

VERBS

Verbs show either action or condition. If the verb shows condition, it is called a **linking verb**. All forms of the verb *to be* (for example, *am*, *are*, *is*, *was*, *were*, *be*, and *been*) are linking verbs. Verbs that can be replaced by the word "is" are also considered linking verbs. Since the verb is the power plant of the sentence, use **action verbs** as much as possible. The action can take place in the present, in the past, or in the future. If the action is just completed or continuing into the present, use *have* or *has* with the past tense of the verb (*have talked*, *has talked*). If the action was completed at a definite past time, use *had* with the past tense of the verb (*had talked*). If the action will be completed in a definite future time, use *shall have* or *will have* with the past tense of the verb (*shall have talked*, *will have talked*).

If the action is progressing at the present time, use the *ing* form of the word with the appropriate helper (*I am talking*, *He is talking*, *They are talking*). If the action is progressing in the past, say *I was talking*, *He was talking*, *They were talking*. Future progressive action would be: *I will be talking*.

Most verbs form the past tense by adding *d* or *ed* to the present tense.

For more information, see the section entitled "Active and Passive Voice" in Chapter 3.

ADJECTIVES

An **adjective** is a modifier. It is used with a noun or pronoun to explain, describe, or limit. Descriptive adjectives add color; limiting adjectives impose boundaries. The effective communicator skillfully uses adjectives.

Sentence without adjectives	**Sentence with adjectives**
Secretary wrote report.	The young, energetic, polished secretary wrote one brief, concise, and complete report.

The and *one* are **limiting adjectives**, as are *a*, *an*, *many*, and *several*. They restrict the nouns they modify. *Young*, *energetic*, *polished*, *brief*, *concise*, *complete* are **descriptive adjectives**, which further elaborate on quality, kind, or condition of the nouns they modify.

To show comparison with one item, most adjectives end in *er*. To show comparison with two or more items, *est* is commonly added.

> She is *younger* than he.
> She is the *youngest* employee.

Long (most two- or three-syllable) adjectives show comparison by using *more* or *most*.

> Her report is *more complete*.
> She wrote the *most complete* report.

Most adjectives precede the noun or pronoun they modify, but the adjective sometimes follows. This happens when linking verbs are used.

> She is *younger* than he.
> Her report is *more complete*.
> This book is *good*.

When two or more adjectives used to describe a noun are so closely related that to consider each word as a separate adjective would change the meaning, they are called **compound adjectives**. Generally compound adjectives before the noun are hyphenated; compound adjectives after the noun are not hyphenated.

> This is an up-to-date book.
> This book is up to date.
> The well-known lady gave a speech.
> The lady is well known.
> John organized a ten-year plan.
> John organized a plan of four years.
> An executive must have problem-solving ability.
> An executive does problem solving.
> The package needed a fifty-cent stamp.
> Income tax is a pay-as-you-go tax.

ADVERBS

Like adjectives, **adverbs** are modifiers. However, adverbs modify the action or condition of verbs, adjectives, or other adverbs. Adverbs answer the when, where, how, and how much.

He wrote the report **yesterday**.
When
Please speak **softly**.
How
They are **seldom here**.
Where and how often
Papers were **everywhere** in the room.
Where
The secretary was **very** tired.
How much

Some common adverbs follow:

again	much	seldom
almost	near	since
better	nevertheless	then
consequently	no	there
early	nonetheless	therefore
ever	often	twice
fair	once	well
far	only	when
here	quite	where
how	rather	wrong
however	right	yes
late		

Most adjectives can be changed to adverbs by adding *ly*.

Adjective	**Adverb**
brief	briefly
concise	concisely
effective	effectively
beautiful	beautifully
unusual	unusually
personal	personally
prompt	promptly
careful	carefully

Sometimes the spelling changes slightly.

Adjective	**Adverb**
considerable	considerably
gentle	gently
satisfactory	satisfactorily

The words "just" and "only" should be placed close to the words they modify. If not, the sentence meaning can change drastically. See section entitled "Dangling or Misplaced Modifiers" in Chapter 3.

PREPOSITIONS

Prepositions show relationships. Each preposition connects a noun or pronoun (its object) to the sentence. The object of the preposition is never the sentence subject; therefore, recognizing prepositional phrases should help you distinguish the main parts of a sentence. A partial list of the approximately seventy prepositions follows:

aboard	behind	down	of	to
above	below	during	off	toward
about	beneath	except	on	under
across	beside	for	over	underneath
after	besides	from	regarding	until
against	between	in	respecting	up
along	beyond	inside	since	upon
around	but	into	through	with
at	by	like	throughout	within
before	concerning	near	till	without

Even though some words have other functions, only prepositions have objects and function as connectives. A few prepositional phrases follow:

after the meeting
between John and Mary
in the adjacent room
on Friday
to us
within thirty days

It is important that you choose the prepositions that express the relationship you desire. Changing the preposition will change the meaning:

after the meeting	before the meeting	during the meeting
on Friday	by Friday	except Friday
to us	besides us	against us
within two weeks	about two weeks	beyond two weeks
in the office	across from the office	behind the office

Some word groups function as prepositions.

as to	by way of	in reference to
as for	contrary to	on account of
as regards	instead of	to the extent of
apart from	in place of	with respect to
	in regard to	

Specific prepositions are used with certain words.

aware **of**
adhere **to**
conform **to**
consistent **with**
results **of**
capable **of**
comply **with**
find fault **with**
coincide **with**
different **from**
inconsistent **with**
independent **of**
infer **from**
in accordance **with**
come **to**
interested **in**
object **to**
interfere **with**
profit **by**

CONJUNCTIONS

Conjunctions connect two or more ideas and show a relationship between them. **Coordinate conjunctions** connect equal parts, two predicates, or two independent clauses. Common coordinate conjunctions are *and*, *yet*, *nor*, *but*, and *or*.

Arthur and James
read and write
She read the book, but he wrote the book.

Subordinate conjunctions begin incomplete clauses—clauses dependent upon the rest of the sentence for their meaning.

Because she was the chairperson, she called the meeting to order.

She called the meeting to order because she was the chairperson.
Notice that the comma is omitted when the dependent clause follows the independent clause.

Other examples of subordinate conjunctions are *since*, *as soon as*, *if*, *when*, *because*, *though*, *otherwise*, *unless*, *than*, *that*, and *although*. There are many others.

Correlative conjunctions come in pairs and show comparisons: *either . . . or*, *both . . . and*, *neither . . . nor*, *as . . . as*, and *not only . . . but also*.

Please mail **either** your note **or** your letter in ten days.

Miss Smith is **as** nice **as** Miss Jones.

INTERJECTIONS

An **interjection** is a word or several words that express strong emotion. Usually, interjections are not part of a sentence and are followed with an exclamation point.

Oh, my!
Good grief!
Surprise!
Very good!
Help!

A mild interjection may begin a sentence. If so, the interjection would be followed by a comma.

Indeed, I can hardly wait.
Oh well, send the bill.

Business communications contain few interjections. They are more appropriate in speeches and personal communications.

APPENDIX VIII

Punctuation

Can you imagine what a letter would look like without any punctuation marks? As examples, here are two paragraphs written without the benefit of punctuation marks:

> As you can see from the resume I am enclosing Accounting was my college major My grade point average was 3015 on a 40 scale if you would like a copy of my official transcript of credits I can ask the College Registrar to send you one
>
> Several well known personalities will be at the convention this year They include Dr J L Halenstein Dean of Academic Studies Bowling Green State University Bowling Green Ohio Dr Esther A Madison Duke University Durham North Carolina and Dr Martin A Stevenson Columbia University New York New York

Each paragraph would have been even more difficult to understand if capital letters had been omitted also.

BASIC USES OF PUNCTUATION IN BUSINESS LETTERS AND REPORTS

The Period (.)

The **period** is used at the end of imperative and declarative sentences, after initials and abbreviations, and as a decimal point.

1. Use a period at the end of a sentence that is not a question or an exclamation. A statement cannot be a sentence unless it has both a subject and a verb.

   I am enclosing a copy of the letter.

2. Use a period at the end of a statement that sounds like a request but is not meant as one. Sometimes the last statement of a letter is used this way.

   May I expect your check by April 15.

3. Use a period at the end of a statement that is only mildly exclamatory.

   Ship the materials immediately.

4. Use a period after an accepted abbreviation.

   Please send me one No. 891 stapler on a C.O.D. basis.

5. Use a period after an initial.

   Dr. H. A. Washington will be the guest speaker.

6. Use a period as a decimal point. No typewriting space follows.

   The price for 1.5 tons would be $76.50.

Notes

Miss is not an abbreviation; therefore, no period is necessary. The abbreviation *Ms.* is not a shortened form for *Miss*, but a courtesy title used by some women.

Miss Geraldine Kramer **Ms.** Sandra Saber

Quantities are not abbreviations; therefore, no periods are necessary.

He bought these items: 12 apples, 10 peaches, 10 pears.

Certain business letter parts do not use periods:

JLK:abc	(not JLK:abc.)
Encl. 2	(not Encl. 2.)
pc	(meaning photocopy--Periods might lead the reader to believe that the letters stand for initials.)
PS	Abbreviation for Postscript

The Comma (,)

The **comma** acts as a separator. Ultimately, the comma helps clarify the meaning of the sentence.

1. Use a comma to join two thoughts that can stand alone but that are joined by a coordinate conjunction (*and*, *but*, *or*, *nor*).

   I enjoy my work, but I would prefer working for your firm.

   The comma may be omitted in a very short compound sentence.

   He offered the job and I accepted it.

2. Use a comma to separate the parts of a series. The series might be expressed in letters or symbols, in words, in figures, or in short phrases or clauses.

   Her scores were 90, 99, 87, and 93.

   The speaker has given talks in New York, Chicago, and Los Angeles.

   The guests ordered ham and eggs, bacon and eggs, or eggs.

   The comma before the last item in the series is optional, but this comma can help clarify the items in the series. If you must use the abbreviation *etc.* (avoid it whenever you can be specific), do not place a comma after it. Never use *and etc.* because *etc.* (et cetera) means *and so forth*.

   To write effective business letters, you should understand the reasons for using periods, commas, dashes, etc.

Usually the comma before the ampersand in a company's name is omitted.

The name of the firm was Johnson, Johnson & Johnson.

If a conjunction is used between the series, the commas are omitted.

His scores were 90 and 88 and 87.

3. When it will aid the reader, add commas to break up large numbers.

The items sold for $33,398.75.

The policy number was M88776.
Generally, no commas

4. Use commas to set off a name used in direct address.

Thank you, Mr. Smith, for remembering me.

Congratulations, Jim!

5. Use commas to set off more than one word used in apposition. (An appositive identifies the word or words preceding it.)

Our representative, Mr. Zoe Clark, will be in your office on Monday morning.

I myself will supervise the installation.

6. Use commas to set off words or clauses that interrupt the sentence and are *not necessary to the meaning* of that sentence.

Dr. A. C. Smith, who is a leader in the field, will be the guest speaker.

The salesman wrote that Model L100, an improved version of Model L90, is available.

The man who seemed to be most effficient was hired.

The report that he submitted was complete and correct.

7. Use a comma after introductory words, phrases, and clauses.

Therefore, I will be happy to visit you.

Because of my interest in accounting, I am eager to work.

If you agree, I would appreciate an interview.

If the dependent clause is at the end of the sentence, the comma is not used unless it is necessary for the sentence meaning.

I am interested in the position because of my interest in accounting.

I will resign today, since this is what you want.

8. Use a comma after *Yes* or *No* at the beginning of the sentence.

Yes, I will be pleased to be the guest speaker.

9. Use commas to separate words and phrases such as *for example*, *that is*, *namely*, and *for instance*. If the words introduce a series, then use a semicolon before the word(s) and a comma after the expression.

The meeting date, namely, January 25, will be the date my vacation starts.

The meetings will be on the fourth Friday of each month; for example, January 24, February 28, March 28, and April 25.

10. Use a comma to separate the person's name from abbreviations such as *Jr.*, a title, or a degree. A comma should follow *Jr.* or *Sr.*

Mr. Chester Mills, Sr., was a member of our firm.

Dorothy Jones, M.D.

11. Use commas to separate the week day from the month, the month and the day of the month, the day from the year, and after the date.

On Monday, July 20, 1980, I started the bookkeeping job.

12. Use commas to separate the city from the state or the country. Place a comma after the state or country if more of the sentence follows.

She lived in Los Angeles, California, last year.

My cousin lives in Los Angeles, California, United States of America.

13. Use commas between parallel adjectives—adjectives of equal rank that call for a short pause. Omit the comma if the adjectives are of unequal rank and meaning would be altered by adding the comma.

The speaker was direct, emphatic, forceful.

We are seeking a young emphatic speaker.

14. Use a comma to indicate the omission of an understood verb.

She attends Northwestern University; her brother, Columbia.

15. Use a comma to show that a statement has been turned into a question and requires a change in voice tone.

    All business people are interested in effective letters and reports, are they not?

    You want the job, or do you?

16. Use a comma to separate contrasting ideas.

    The problem must be handled with understanding, not bitterness.

17. Use a comma before the direct quotation.

    He said, "Now is the time to begin the meeting."

18. Use commas to set off direct quotes within a sentence—unless a period, question mark, or exclamation mark is necessary.

    "This," she replied, "is what I ordered yesterday."

    "Are you planning to attend the meeting?" he asked.

19. Use commas also to set off indirect quotes:

    He would attend the meeting, he said, if he was in town.

    If *that* follows *he said*, the expressions are no longer parenthetical; therefore, omit the commas.

    He answered that he would attend the meeting if he was in town.

20. If a reader's first name is used in the salutation—informal letter—a comma may be used (unless open punctuation style is desired).

    Dear John, Dear Uncle John, Dear Mary,

21. Use a comma after the complimentary close of a letter (unless open punctuation style is desired).

    Very truly yours, Sincerely yours, Cordially,

22. Do not use a comma to separate units designating weight, measure, or time.

    The boy was 5 feet 6 inches tall.

    The crate weighed 90 lb. 14 oz.

Common mistakes with commas. Confusion, rather than clarification, is the result when too many commas are used.

1. The comma should never separate the verb from the subject or the object.

He ignored his friends and wrote the letter.

He said that he would try to come.

2. The comma should not precede *but* when it is being used as a preposition.

No one but the president knows the combination for the safe.

3. Too many commas may result in choppy sentences difficult to understand. Revise the sentence to read smoothly without excessive commas.

Consequently, it is not, in my opinion, desirable.
Excessive commas

Consequently, I do not believe the plan is desirable.
Sentence revised for conciseness

The Semicolon (;)

The **semicolon** is used when a comma cannot provide enough separation between thoughts.

1. Use a semicolon to take the place of the conjunction between two independent clauses.

You may be satisfied with your sales record; the manager is not.

2. Use a semicolon before the connecting adverb that follows an independent clause in a compound sentence. Common adverbs include *accordingly*, *also*, *besides*, *consequently*, *finally*, *further*, *furthermore*, *hence*, *in addition*, *indeed*, *likewise*, *meanwhile*, *moreover*, *nevertheless*, *surely*, *otherwise*, *so*, *still*, *thus*, *then*, and *yet*.

I would like to speak before the group; however, I must be in Detroit at that time.

He said he was pleased with the invitation; yet, he did not accept it.

3. Use a semicolon between complete thoughts that contain commas.

As we told you last month, your sales are far behind the quota; yet you do not seem to be making any changes.

4. Use semicolons in a complex sentence that contains commas, especially if several subordinate clauses depend on one clause.

After studying your plan in great detail, we suggest that you add additional electrical outlets; that you lower the ceilings; that you reroute the water lines; that you increase the size of the master bedroom.

5. Use a semicolon before expressions such as *for example, that is, namely, for instance* if a list of items follows.

   The meetings will be held on the fourth Friday of each month; for instance, February 28, March 28, April 25, and May 23.

6. Use a semicolon after each item in a series containing commas.

   The members live in Columbus, Ohio; Pittsburgh, Pennsylvania; Detroit, Michigan; and Grand Rapids, Michigan.

   The delegates came from several countries: 3 from America; 2, France; 2, Russia; 3, London; 2, Germany; and 3, Switzerland.

The Colon (:)

The **colon** precedes a list of items or a quotation and acts as a separator.

1. Use a colon to introduce a series or phrase.

   I have had courses in these areas: education, law, English, accounting, science, and history.

   Effective letter writing requires: first, planning and organizing the letter; and second, complying with the basic elements of writing such as clarity, completeness, conciseness, concreteness, correctness, and coherence.

   Copies to: Mr. John Smith, Dr. J. R. Thomas

   Attention: Mrs. Janet Mason

2. Use a colon to introduce a tabulated series.

   Please ship the following items by railway express:

   10 yds. No. 103 silk
   10 yds. No. 201 facing
   5 yds. No. 101 leather

3. Use a colon to introduce a long quotation:

   Lincoln said: "Four score and seven years ago, our fathers brought forth upon this continent a new nation conceived in liberty and dedicated to the proposition that all men are created equal."

   The letter read in part:
   As I mentioned in our talks, I have always wanted to live in the New England area. Therefore, I shall be accepting a position with a large retail firm in the northern part of Connecticut.

4. Use a colon after formal salutations in business letters (unless open punctuation style is desired).

   Dear Mr. Smith: My dear Miss Jones:

   Ladies and Gentlemen: Dear Sir:

5. A colon may be used to separate the dictator's initials from the typist's initials or identification number.

   HHH:ABC

   HHH:abc

   HHH:c

   HHH:5

6. Use a colon to separate chapter and verses in the Bible.

   The Biblical reference is John 9:1-38.

7. Use a colon to separate hours and minutes when the time is written in figures.

   The airplane will depart from Gate A at 10:05 a.m. today.

8. Use a colon to show relationships—the colon stands for the word "to."

   The current ratio for the Star Company is $600,000 to $260,000 or 2.31 to 1 (2.31:1).

The Exclamation Point (!)

The **exclamation point** adds emphasis.

1. Use an exclamation point to express *strong* emotion (such as fear, surprise, sarcasm, disbelief, and joy). The mark can be used after a word, phrase, or sentence.

   Congratulations! You won!

   What a beautiful day!

   Help! Help!

   Oh, happy day!

2. Use an exclamation point after an emphatic interjection. The first word following the exclamation point must be capitalized.

   Alas! The day is done.

The Question Mark (?)

The **question mark** is generally used after a statement requiring an answer.

1. Use a question mark after a direct interrogation (question).

   May I come in for an interview next week?

   Use a period after an indirect question.

   She asked if she might come in for an interview.

2. Use a question mark after a question followed by a series of words or phrases meant as additional questions.

   May I see you on Monday? on Tuesday? on Wednesday?

   Who are you? Mary Smith? Margaret Adams?

3. Use a question mark in parentheses to show that you question the accuracy of the preceding word, phrase, or figure.

   This is a copy of the current (?) catalog.

Quotation Marks (“ ”)

Quotation marks are used to enclose direct quotations or to emphasize certain words.

1. Use quotation marks to indicate the exact spoken or written words.

   He wrote, “I shall arrive on Saturday, May 29, at 1 p.m.”

   Sometimes the quotation is interrupted by words that are not part of the quotation. If the continued quotation completes a sentence, then the first word is not capitalized.

   “I shall be there,” he said, “on Saturday, May 29.”

   If a new sentence begins or if an exclamation point precedes the continued quotation, then the first word is capitalized.

   “I will be there at 1 p.m.” he said, “Meet me at the airport, please.”

   “Congratulations!” he shouted, “You won the match.”

   Quotation marks are not used with indirect quotations. The word “*that*” usually precedes the indirect quotation.

   He said that he would be here at 1 p.m.

2. Use single quotation marks around words quoted within a quotation.

   These are the words she said to me: “I cannot return to work because my husband said, ‘I need you to help me complete a project.’”

   If the quoted material is interrupted by words or expressions requiring quotation marks, single quotation marks (an apostrophe) should be used within the quotation.

   He said, “The word ‘analyze’ is difficult to spell correctly.”

3. Use quotation marks around titles of pictures, reports, poems, plays, songs, chapters and sections of books, movies, and speeches.

   We would like to hear your talk, "Management—The Ultimate Career."

4. Use quotation marks sparingly around words that you are using in a special way. (Do not overdo this.)

   The speaker asked the "dummy" to come to the stage.

5. Use quotation marks around words and phrases that follow these introductory words: *the word*, *so-called*, *termed*, *marked*, *entitled*, *named*, and *known as*.

   The word "order" can be used in several ways.

   Abraham Lincoln is known as "The Great Emancipator."

   Slang expressions may be placed in quotation marks. However, avoid using slang in business letters. Instead of quotation marks, an underscore can be used to indicate italicized words.

   The word *receive* has the *e* before the *i* to comply with the spelling rule: "Use the *i* before *e* except after *c*."

6. If you are quoting several paragraphs and do not wish to indent or center the quote, you can use quotation marks at the beginning of each new paragraph and at the end of the last paragraph.

   The Personnel Manager received this letter:

   "I am planning to be in Columbus the last two weeks of April and would like an appointment to discuss plans for earning a Master of Arts degree in Education.

   "The Registrar has agreed to mail you an official copy of my transcript of credits. You should receive it this week.

   "Please telephone me at 417-1712. I prefer a Monday or Tuesday appointment."

   Always place periods and commas *inside* quotation marks. Always place semicolons and colons *outside* quotations. Placement of other marks varies with sentence meaning.

The Apostrophe (')

The **apostrophe** is used to show ownership, omission of letters or numbers, or plurals.

1. Use an apostrophe to show possession.

   Singular and plural nouns that do not end in *s*: add an apostrophe and an *s*.

The child's toys were in the yard.

The children's toys are here.

Proper nouns and plural nouns ending in *s*: add an apostrophe only.

The family took three weeks' vacation.

The Jones' house is decorated well.

Compound nouns: add an apostrophe and *s* to the last word only.

My sister-in-law's piano needs tuning.

Two or more nouns that have joint possession: add an apostrophe and *s* to the last name only.

Rogers and Hammerstein's music is enjoyed by many people.

We went to see Mary and Jim's new house.

Two or more nouns that have individual possession: show each noun in possessive case:

We accepted Mr. Smith's letter and Mr. Henry's report.

The boys' and girls' toys are in the neighbor's yard.
Two or more toys, one neighbor

Two or more nouns that have joint possession and are preceded by the word "the": no apostrophe.

The Smith and Henry Report was accepted by their employer.

2. Use an apostrophe to show omission of letters or figures.

I'm sure that you will enjoy the meeting.

The class of '65 celebrated its twenty-fifth anniversary.

The supervisor O.K.'d the report.

3. Add an apostrophe and *s* to show plurals of letters, figures, symbols, and named words.

Children confuse the 6's and the 9's.

A table does not have to list all the $'s.

The Hyphen (-)

Use the **hyphen** with compound words or numbers and to divide words at the end of the writing line.

1. Hyphenate compound words that refer to individuals or names of organizations (proper nouns, capital letters)—if

preceded by prefixes (such as *anti-*, *pro-*, *pre-*, *ex-*, *ultra-*, *neo-*, and *post-*).

He is pro-British and anti-Communist.

2. Hyphenate words that begin with *self.*

   The self-made man was self-supporting, self-willed, and self-righteous.

3. Hyphenate compound nouns with the preposition *in.*

   The President is the commander-in-chief.

4. Hyphenate two or more adjectives that must be used as one word to describe the noun. (Using the adjectives individually would create a different picture.)

   The income tax is a pay-as-you-go tax.

   Please place a twenty-two-cent stamp on this envelope and send it by first-class mail.

   The well-known lady was wearing a blue-green dress with green accessories.

   Most people do not like someone who has an I-know-it-all attitude.

   Do not use a hyphen between an adverb which ends in *-ly* and a verb.

   The widely advertised booklet was readily available at all book stores.

5. Hyphenate compound numbers. Most numbers between twenty-one and ninety-nine are compound numbers.

   On his nineteenth birthday he was six feet tall and weighed one hundred seventy-five pounds.

6. Hyphenate fractions unless they are used as nouns.

   The recipe called for one and one-half cups of sugar.

   Two thirds of the people did not vote for the legislation.
   Two thirds *is a noun; therefore, we do not use a hyphen.*

7. Substitute a hyphen for the word "to" in a score.

   The score was 7–3 in favor of the Travelers.

8. A hyphen can be used to indicate the word "through" when indicating a span of years, pages, chapters.

   From 1935–1938 he wrote pages 1–500 or Chapters 1–10 of his autobiography.

9. Hyphenate words at the end of the writing line if you do not have space for the entire word. Consult the dictionary for correct syllable division. Words with hyphens should be divided only at the hyphen.

The Dash (—)

The **dash** is used to set off words that summarize, emphasize, or describe. This separation is more emphatic than separations using commas, semicolons, or parentheses.

1. Use a dash to set off words that summarize the thought of the sentence.

   Algebra, History, Mathematics, Psychology, English—all are subjects I have studied.

2. Use a dash to indicate a thought you do not intend to complete.

   I would come with you but—

3. Use a dash to set off an expression you want to stand out.

   A new shop—the Francine—will open on Wednesday.

4. Use a dash to emphasize words or phrases.

   Do it now—tomorrow may be too late.

The Underscore or Underline (_)

The **underscore** is used to show italicized words and words you want to emphasize.

1. Underscore the names of books, periodicals, ships, and airplanes.

   He read about the sinking of the <u>Titanic</u> in the <u>New York Times</u>.

   <u>Gone</u> <u>with</u> <u>the</u> <u>Wind</u> was a very popular book.

   The underline can be a full underscore (first example) or a broken underscore (second example), but be consistent throughout the letter or report.

2. Use an underscore to emphasize letters, words, or phrases.

   Some people believe <u>receive</u> is a difficult word to spell.

   You <u>will</u> visit Disneyland, won't you?

3. Underscore biological names and foreign words that are usually in italics.

   The French phrase <u>tres bien</u> means very good.

   The strawberry belongs to the <u>Rosaceae</u>, or the rose family.

The Parentheses ( )

Parentheses are used to enclose helpful, explanatory, or confirming information.

1. Use parentheses to enclose explanatory or helpful information.

   His wife (the former Mary Smith) is a native of Montreal.

   The advertisement in *Good Housekeeping* (see page 10) tells where you can purchase the china.

2. Use parentheses around numbers used to enumerate a series.

   The items on the order included: (1) home furnishings, (2) boys' clothing, (3) girls' clothing, and (4) household appliances.

3. Use parentheses around figures to confirm the written words.

   He sold more than five million (5,000,000) records.

Brackets ([ ])

Brackets are used to add information to or about quoted material.

1. Use brackets to explain or provide additional information to a quotation.

   He said, "I will be able to see you next month [August] to discuss your proposal."

2. Use [sic] to indicate that the quoted data is stated exactly as written, even though it is incorrect. *Sic* is a Latin word meaning *thus* and should be underlined (use no period).

   The historian wrote, "Columbus discovered America in the fourteenth [sic] century."

APPENDIX IX

Frequently Misused Words

Some words are frequently misused. Illustrations of some common problems in writing follow:

ability (noun)—talent
capacity (noun)—the power of receiving and holding knowledge

She has the **ability** to talk well.

He has a great **capacity** to talk well.

accept (verb)—to take willingly
except (preposition)—but

Please **accept** the offer.

All of the reports are ready **except** the progress report.

adapt (verb)—to make suitable
adopt (verb)—to take as one's own
adept (adj.)—highly skilled
adept (noun)—an expert

Please **adapt** the plan to suit the occasion.

Please **adopt** the proposal.

He was **adept** at using the carpenter's tools.

advice (noun)—an opinion or judgment
advise (verb)—to inform, to counsel

Your **advice** makes good sense.

Please **advise** the status of the Jones' account.

What do you **advise**?

affect (verb)—to influence, to bring about
effect (noun)—result

What would be the **effect** of accepting the Jones' proposal?

This regulation will **affect** sales.

agree to (verb, prep.)—terms, prices
agree with (verb, prep.)—an opinion

He will **agree to** the terms of sale.

Do you **agree with** Mr. Smith?

a lot (phrase)—many
allot (verb)—to allocate

A lot of people do engineering work.

Better: Ten thousand people build bridges.
More specific

Please allot each customer one gift.

amount (noun)—items referred to as a mass
number (noun)—items that can be counted individually

The **amount** of advertising space is limited.

The **number** of employees who desire raises is increasing.

angry (adj.)—a feeling of anger
mad (adj.)—insane

I am **angry** at his behavior.
Not **mad**

She had a **mad** dog.

Mad people are institutionalized.

anxious (adj.)—eagerly wishing, concerned (worry)
eager (adj.)—great enthusiasm (no worry)

Students should be **eager** for (desire) good grades, not **anxious** (worried) about getting good grades.

as (conj.)—used when comparing verbs
like (prep.)—used when comparing nouns; similar to

He will write the report **as** you requested.
Comparison of verbs, **write** *and* **request**

He did not write the report **as well as** he could.

Mr. Smith acts **like** an executive.
Comparison of nouns, **Smith** *and* **executive**

He writes **like** a professional writer.

because of (conj.)—caused by (use with nonlinking verb)
due to—caused by (use after linking verb)

Because of illness, they could not complete the inventory.

Her illness was **due to** insufficient rest.

believe (verb)—thought based on logic
feel (verb)—thought based mostly on emotion, state of feeling

I **believe** you can learn to write well.

I **feel** sad that the resolution failed.

biannual (adj.)—happening twice a year (semiannual)
biennial (adj.)—happening every two years

The **biannual** report was issued in January and July.

The next **biennial** budget will be due in 1988.
Two years from now

borrow (verb)—to accept something temporarily
lend (verb)—to loan something temporarily
loan (noun)—the item

You can **borrow** the money from a commercial bank.

The bank executive will **lend** you the money needed.

Ms. Smith borrowed the $500 **loan** from the commercial bank.

can (verb)—capable of
may (verb)—permission to

Can you write the letter?
Meaning: **Are you capable of writing the letter?**

May I write the reply tomorrow?
Requesting permission to write

capital (noun)—wealth, assets
capital (adj.)—principal, main, etc.
Capitol (noun)—home of the United States Congress
Always capitalized
capitol (noun)—state of being

He invested **capital** in the company.

Always begin sentences with a **capital** letter.

Columbus has been the **capital** of Ohio since 1788.

Murder is a **capital** offense.

You can write to your senator at the **Capitol**.

The meeting will be in the **capitol** in Columbus.
State capitol

cheap (adj.)—poor quality
inexpensive (adj.)—less money

This is a **cheap** machine.
A machine lacking quality

This is an **inexpensive** machine.
A machine that is low priced

cite (verb)—to quote
sight (noun)—ability to see
site (noun)—a location

He can **cite** several authorities.

You can **sight** the building in your telescope.

The building **site** will be chosen by the legislators.

complement—to complete
compliment—to praise

The dress and shoes **complement** each other.

"How nice you look" is a **compliment**.

continual (adj.)—on going (but stopping and starting)
continuous (adj.)—never stopping

He heard **continual** thunder for ten minutes.
Off and on thunder

Today, the rain is **continuous**.
Never stopping rain

differ from—comparison of things
differ with—people comparison

How does the Jones' contract **differ from** his contract?

How does Jones **differ with** Martin?

disinterested (adj.)—interested but impartial (*dis* means *away from*)
uninterested (adj.)—not interested (*un* means *not*)

He was a **disinterested** observer.

He was **uninterested** in a sales career.

fewer (adj.)—items that can be counted individually
less (adj.)—items referred to as a mass.

Fewer people are hired to supervise operations.

The assistant manager earns **less** money than the manager.

formally (adv.)—in customary form
former (adj.)—first in a series of two
formerly (adv.)—at a former time

He was **formally** introduced to Dr. Marilyn Pinkerton.

John and George are employees; the **former** has more seniority.

She was **formerly** known by her maiden name, Donna Sanders.

good (adj.)—general term of approval
well (adv.)—state of being

You should prepare **good** topic outlines before writing the letters.

Mr. Sims is not feeling **well** today.

imply (verb)—to suggest
infer (verb)—to conclude after analysis of facts

Did he **imply** that the meeting would be cancelled?

Did you **infer** from his letter that the meeting would be cancelled?

in (prep.)—a condition, within
into (prep.)—an action, one place to another

A copy of the letter is **in** the file cabinet.

He reached **into** the file cabinet to get the letter.

loose (adj.)—free, not fastened, not precise
lose (verb)—to suffer loss, to fail to keep
loss (noun)—state of being lost

This revision is a **loose** translation of the original.

She did not **lose** a single word of his lecture.

We sympathize with your **loss**.

may be (verb phrase)—possibly
maybe (adv.)—perhaps

Mr. Ryder **may be** out of town on May 15.

Maybe Mr. Ryder will be in town today.

of (prep.)
off (adv.)
off of (do not use)
from (prep.)

She received a copy **of** the report.

Painting is the type **of** work he does daily.

He might have begun the report.
Not **might of begun**

The report fell **off** the desk.
Not **off of**

He borrowed the capital **from** the bank.
Not **off of**

She received the report **from** me.
Not **off of**

personal (adj.)—refers to a person
personnel (noun)—employees

Writing is a **personal** business.

All **personnel** are expected to follow company policies and practices.

principal (noun)—chief school administrator, sum of money
principal (adj.)—main or most important
principle (noun)—a fundamental truth or law

Jean A. Carter is the **principal** of Lincoln High School.

His **principal** objective is to increase profits and provide services.

You must pay the **principal** and interest within thirty days.

Effective communicators follow the **principles** of business communication.

The **principle** of equality is important to men and women.

real (adj.)—actual, genuine
very (adv.)—to a great extent

The diamonds are **real**.

She is **very** efficient.

respectably (adv.)—worthy of respect to a certain degree
respectfully (adv.)—full of respect, a complimentary close
respectively (adv.)—in order named

They acted **respectably** at the formal dinner.

He spoke **respectfully** to his parents.

Respectfully yours,

Carol, James, and Barbara won the first, second, and third prizes **respectively**.

sometime (adv.)—a point in time
some time (adj.)—an amount of time
sometimes (adv.)—now and then

The promotion will be effective **sometime** later.

It will be **some time** before she receives her promotion.

Sometimes managers must work long hours.

stationary (adj.)—fixed position, not moving
stationery (noun)—paper and envelopes used for writing letters

The printing press was bolted to the floor to make it **stationary**.

Letterhead is quality **stationery**.

than (conj.)—introduces statements of comparison or preference
then (adv.)—time in the future or past

Written communication is more complex than oral communication.

The meeting is tomorrow; you can read your report then.

their (pronoun)—possessive
there (adv.)—tells where
they're (pronoun and verb)—contraction for they are

Their report is very detailed.

Please place the orders **there**.

They're expected to complete the building by next year.

Better: They are expected to complete the building by November 1.

to (prep. or part of an infinitive)—direction
too (adv.)—also, very
two (adj.)—refers to the number 2

The manager and his assistant went **to** the meeting.

"**To** be or not **to** be" is a famous phrase.

The clerk was **too** tired to go to the meeting, too.

He ordered **two** hundred copies.

Business Communications and the Law

APPENDIX X

We have encouraged communicators to follow the fundamental principles of communication: communicating an understood purpose in a tone that considers the reader and in language that is complete, clear, concise, concrete, correct, coherent, courteous, and positive. In addition, communicators must be aware of the legal implications of their communications.

This brief appendix is written to alert communicators to the legal risks of their communications. Volumes can be written; therefore, this section only highlights some basic ideas. When in doubt, take steps to be certain. Consult lawyers, state and federal laws, and court decisions for pertinent information.

Although state laws differ, a common philosophy exists, and ignorance of the law is never an acceptable excuse. Federal laws, of course, take precedence over state laws. What you say and write can initiate litigation; your communication can be evidence against you and the company. When using company stationery, writers are generally presumed to be acting for the company.

Several basic legal terms are described below, as well as procedures to help you avoid legal litigation.

LEGAL TERMINOLOGY

Libel is a complex concept, which consists of three elements:

1. *Existence of defamation*—a false and malicious written statement that injures an identifiable person's character or reputation. Oral defamation is called **slander**.
2. *Third party recognition*, whether by nickname, pseudonym, or circumstance
3. *Publication*—a third party reading the unconsented intentional or negligent statement

Under certain conditions, the elements of libel are allowed by the concept of privilege. **Privilege** is the legal right to defame under specific circumstances (for example, letters between attorneys relating to the case in dispute or dictation related to the ordinary conduct of business).

To guard against libel, ask yourself, Is the statement defamatory to an identifiable person? If your answer is *yes*, then ask yourself, Is the information privileged? If it is not, then ask yourself, Is the statement true? A true statement is generally not considered defamation.

Invasion of privacy is the unreasonable and unprivileged intrusion into another's private life without the individual's consent. This is possible even without defamation of character or reputation, the existence of a third party, or publication (the elements of libel). Two examples of invasion of privacy are (1) using, without the individual's permission, a person's name or photograph to promote sales (sales letter or advertisement communications) and (2) reading without the individual's permission the person's correspondence or records (for example, credit or medical records).

Fraud is the intentional deception to cause a person to give up property or some lawful right. Thus, it requires the following elements:

1. Communicator making statements with the intent to deceive
2. Communicator misrepresenting material facts—not merely statements of opinion or future conditions
3. Receiver justly relying on the statement
4. Receiver legally damaged by the false statement

The basic way to avoid fraud, it would seem, would be to reveal all pertinent facts completely and truthfully (especially in letters, reports, and sales warranties) and to be fair in all business transactions, including obligations under warranties and the use of mail (to avoid mail fraud). It is not lawful, for example, to mail false statements to sell real or fake products, stock, or services; to obtain funds; or to promote nonexisting business opportunities or worthless medical cures.

POINTERS FOR COMMUNICATORS

How can communicators avoid unwanted litigation? Here are several general suggestions:

1. Write only truthful statements and all facts related to the situation.
2. Avoid superlatives (the best) and terminology that carries a negative impact (even if true). Consider, for example, *blackmailer*, *Communist*, *deadbeat*, *dishonest*, *drunkard*, *incompetent*, *inferior*, *irresponsible*, *liar*, *negligent*, *quack*, *unworthy*, and *worthless*.
3. Make it difficult for a third party to hear or read statements that might be considered defamatory:
   a. Speak privately to the individual, making sure that no one else can overhear. Do not tape or record the conversation. Taped and written records of conversations can be used as evidence.

   b. Address mail and envelope to the specific person, adding a *Confidential* or *Personal* notation.
   c. Place a blank sheet of paper on top of the communication and/or fold it so that the message cannot be read through the envelope.
   d. Seal envelopes.
   e. Use a patterned or opaque envelope.
4. Use form messages prepared by individuals cognizant of the legal risks involved in certain messages (for example, collection letters, credit letters and reports, employment correspondence and agreements, and letters of recommendation). By using the prepared messages, uninformed employees can conduct company business and avoid legal complications resulting from stating defamatory or false information.
5. Use proper stationery: company letterhead for company business; personal stationery for personal matters.
6. Know state and federal laws regulating the communications you handle.
   a. *Credit and collection notices*—Refer to the Consumer Credit Protection Act, Federal Truth-in-Lending Act, Fair Credit Reporting Act, Equal Credit Opportunity Act, Uniform Common Code, Fair Credit Billing Act, Federal Trade Commission Improvement Act, Fair Debt Collection Practices Act, and so on.
   b. *Employment*—See legislation such as the National Labor Relations Act, Taft-Hartley Act, Equal Employment Opportunity Act, Vocational Rehabilitation Act, and so on. (Chapters 27 and 29 include specific legal risks relating to employment communications.)
   c. *Letters of recommendation*—Since 1974, the Family Education Rights and Privacy Act has allowed parents and students over 18 the right to see their education records housed by public schools, including colleges and universities. (See Chapter 28 for specific ideas.)
   d. *Product use and warranties*—The Environmental Protection Agency's laws are designed to protect health (for example, the Clean Air Act and the Noise Control Act). The Uniform Common Code and the Consumer Product Warranty Act stipulate guidelines regarding warranties.
   e. Employee evaluations—The Equal Employment Opportunity Commission monitors employers' practices involving hiring, training, promoting, and retiring employees.

   f. *Advertising*—Helpful data are available from the Council of Better Business Bureaus (Fair Practice Code), the Direct Mail/Marketing Association, and the U. S. Postal Service (pamphlets regarding mail fraud laws, unlawful mail, and unordered merchandise). The Fair Packaging and Labeling Act encourages language that accurately and adequately describes the product.

7. Read another's communications or records only with the person's permission—to protect the individual's right to privacy.
8. Seek legal counsel before preparing communications (such as those mentioned in this section) and/or when in doubt as to what the law stipulates.

Readings on Communication APPENDIX XI

Adelstein, Michael E., and W. Keats Sparrow. *Business Communications*. New York: Harcourt Brace Jovanovich, 1983.

Adler, Ronald B. *Communicating at Work*. New York: Random House, 1983.

Andrews, Deborah C., and Margaret D. Blickle. *Technical Writing*, 2nd Ed. New York: Macmillan, 1982.

Applbaum, Ronald L., and Karl W. E. Anatol. *Effective Oral Communications for Business and the Professions*. Chicago: SRA, 1982.

Aronoff, Craig E., Otis W. Baskin, Robert W. Hays, and Harold E. Davis. *Getting Your Message Across*. St. Paul: West Publishing Company, 1981.

Bateman, David N. *Business Communication Concepts Cases, Decisions, and Applications*. Glenview, Ill.: Scott, Foresman and Company, 1982.

Batteiger, Richard P. *Business Writing: Process and Form*. Belmont, Calif.: Wadsworth Publishing Company, 1985.

Baxter, Carol McFarland. *Business Report Writing*. Boston: Kent Publishing Company, 1983.

Bonner, William H. *Communicating in Business: Key to Success*, 3rd Ed. Houston, Tex.: Dame Publications, 1983.

Bowman, Joel P., and Bernadine P. Branchaw. *Business Report Writing*. Chicago: The Dryden Press, 1984.

Bowman, Joel P., and Bernadine P. Branchaw. *Successful Communication in Business*. San Francisco: Harper & Row, 1980.

Bromage, Marg C. *Writing for Business*. Ann Arbor: The University of Michigan Press, 1975.

Brown, Leland. *Communicating Facts and Ideas in Business*. 3rd Ed., Englewood Cliffs, N.J.: Prentice-Hall, 1982.

Brown, Leland. *Effective Business Report Writing*, 4th Ed. Englewood Cliffs, N.J.: Prentice-Hall, 1985.

Brusaw, Charles T., Gerald J. Alred, and Walter E. Oliu. *The Business Writer's Handbook*, 2nd Ed. New York: St. Martin's Press, 1982.

Camp, Sue C. *Developing Editing Skill*. New York: McGraw-Hill, 1985.

Campbell, William Giles and Stephen V. Ballou. *Form and Style*, 6th Ed. Boston: Houghton Mifflin Company, 1982.

Carr-Ruffino, Norma. *Writing Short Business Reports*. New York: McGraw-Hill, 1980.

Clarke, Peter, C. W. Wilkinson, and Dorothy Wilkinson. *Communicating Through Letters and Reports*, 8th Ed. Homewood, Ill.: Richard D. Irwin, 1983.

Conover, Hobart H., Milton K. Berlye, and Sanford D. Gordon. *Business Dynamics*. Indianapolis: Bobbs-Merrill Educational Publishing, 1982.

Donaghy, William C. *The Interview Skills and Applications*. Glenview, Ill.: Scott, Foresman and Company, 1984.

DuBrin, Andrew. *Effective Business Psychology*. Reston, Va.: Reston Publishing Company, 1980.

Dumont, Raymond A., and John M. Lannon. *Business Communications*. Boston: Little, Brown and Company, 1985.

Eisenberg, Abne M. *Understanding Communication in Business and the Professions*. New York: Macmillan, 1978.

Eisenberg, Anne. *Effective Technical Communication*. New York: McGraw-Hill, 1982.

Fear, David E. *Technical Communication*, 2nd Ed. Glenview, Ill.: Scott, Foresman and Company, 1981.

Feinberg, Lilian O. *Applied Business Communication*. Sherman Oaks, Calif.: Alfred Publishing Company, 1982.

Figgins, Ross, Steven P. Golen, and C. Glenn Pearce. *Business Communication Basics Application and Technology*. New York: John Wiley & Sons, 1984.

Flesch, Rudolph. *The Art of Readable Writing*. New York: Harper & Row, 1949.

Frank, Allan D. *Communicating on the Job*. Glenview, Ill.: Scott, Foresman and Company, 1982.

Gieselman, Robert D., Ed. *Readings in Business Communication*, 3rd Ed. Champaign, Ill.: Stipes Publishing Company, 1982.

Golen, Steven P., C. Glenn Pearce, and Ross Figgins. *Report Writing for Business and Industry*. New York: John Wiley & Sons, 1985.

Gunning, Robert. *The Technique of Clear Writing*. New York: McGraw-Hill, 1968.

Haggblade, Berle. *Business Communication*. St. Paul: West Publishing Company, 1982.

Hamilton, Cheryl, Cordell Parker, and Doyle D. Smith. *Communicating for Results*. Belmont, Calif.: Wadsworth Publishing Company, 1982.

Hanna, Michael S., and Gerald L. Wilson. *Communicating in Business and Professional Settings*. New York: Random House, 1984.

Hart, Andrew W., and James A. Reinking. *Writing for Career-Education Students*, 2nd Ed. New York: St. Martin's Press, 1982.

Hatch, Richard. *Business Communication*. Chicago: SRA, 1983.

Hawkins, Brian L., and Paul Preston. *Managerial Communication*. Scott, Foresman and Company, 1981.

Henze, Geraldine. *From Murk to Masterpiece: Style for Business Writing*. Homewood, Ill.: Richard D. Irwin, 1985.

Himstreet, William C., and Wayne M. Baty. *Business Communications*, 7th Ed. Belmont, Calif.: Kent Publishing Company, 1984.

Himstreet, William C., Gerald W. Maxwell, and Mary Jean Onorato. *Business Communications: A Guide to Effective Writing, Speaking, and Listening*. 2nd Ed. Encino, Calif.: Glencoe Publishing Company, 1987.

Houp, Kenneth W., and Thomas E. Pearsall. *Reporting Technical Information*, 5th Ed. New York: Macmillan, 1984.

Howard, C. Jeriel, and Richard F. Tracz. *The Essential English Handbook and Rhetoric*. Indianapolis: Bobbs-Merrill Educational Publishing, 1985.

Hugenberg, Lawrence W., and Donald D. Yoder. *Speaking in the Modern Organization: Skills and Strategies*. Scott, Foresman and Company, 1985.

Huseman, Richard C., James M. Lahiff, John M. Penrose, Jr., and John D. Hatfield. *Business Communication*, 2nd Ed. Chicago: The Dryden Press, 1985.

Hybels, Saundra, and Richard L. Weaver II. *Speech/Communication*, 2nd Ed. New York: Van Nostrand, 1979.

Iacone, Salvatore J. *Modern Business Report Writing*. New York: Macmillan, 1985.

Janis, J. Harold. *Writing and Communicating in Business*, 3rd Ed. New York: Macmillan, 1978.

Johnson, H. Webster, Anthony J. Faria, and Ernest L. Maier. *How to Use the Business Library*, 5th Ed. Cincinnati: South-Western, 1984.

Johnson, H. Webster, Ernest L. Maier, and A. J. Faria. *How to Use the Business Library—With Sources of Business Information*, 5th Ed. Cincinnati: South-Western, 1984.

Kakonis, Thomas E., and John Scally. *Writing in an Age of Technology*. New York: Macmillan, 1978.

Keithley, Erwin M., and Philip J. Schreiner. *A Manual of Style for the Preparation of Papers and Reports*, 3rd Ed. Cincinnati: South-Western, 1980.

Kell, Carl L., and Paul R. Corts. *Let's Talk Business*. Boston: Little, Brown and Company, 1983.

Kenny, Michael. *Presenting Yourself*. New York: John Wiley & Sons, 1982.

Koehler, Jerry W., and John I. Sisco. *Public Communication in Business and the Professions*. St. Paul: West Publishing Company, 1981.

Kolin, Philip C. *Successful Writing at Work*. Lexington, Mass.: D. C. Heath and Company, 1982.

Lannon, John M. *Technical Writing*, 3rd Ed. Waltham, Mass.: Little, Brown and Company, 1985.

Lee, LaJuana Williams, Sallye Starks Benoit, Wilma Collins Moore, and Celeste Stanfield Powers. *Business Communication*. Chicago: Rand McNally College Publishing Company, 1980.

Lesikar, Raymond V. *Basic Business Communication*, 3rd Ed. Homewood, Ill.: Richard D. Irwin, 1985.

Lesikar, Raymond V. *Business Communication: Theory and Application*, 5th Ed. Homewood, Ill.: Richard D. Irwin, 1984.

Lesikar, Raymond V. *Report Writing for Business*, 6th Ed. Homewood, Ill.: Richard D. Irwin, 1981.

Lewis, Phillip V. *Organizational Communications: The Essence of Effective Management*. Columbus: Grid, 1975.

Lewis, Phillip, and William H. Baker. *Business Report Writing*. Columbus: Grid, 1978.

Mathes, J. C., and Dwight W. Stevenson. *Designing Technical Reports*. Indianapolis: The Bobbs-Merrill Company, 1976.

McMahan, Elizabeth, and Susan Day. *The Writer's Handbook*. New York: McGraw-Hill, 1980.

Moyer, Ruth, Eleanour Stevens, and Ralph Switzer. *The Research and Report Handbook*. New York: John Wiley & Sons, 1981.

Murphy, Herta A. and Herbert W. Hildebrandt. *Effective Business Communications*, 4th Ed. New York: McGraw-Hill, 1984.

Nixon, Robert. *Practical Business Communications*. San Diego: Harcourt Brace Jovanovich, 1984.

Oliu, Walter E., Charles T. Brusaw, and Gerald J. Alred. *Writing That Works*, 2nd Ed. New York: St. Martin's Press, 1984.

Pearce, C. Glenn, Ross Figgins, and Steven P. Golen. *Principles of Business Communication Theory, Application, and Technology*. New York: John Wiley & Sons, 1984.

Persing, Bobbye Sorrels. *Business Communication Dynamics.* Columbus: Charles E. Merrill Publishing Company, 1981.

Poe, Roy W., and Rosemary T. Fruehling. *Business Communication: A Problem-Solving Approach*, 3rd Ed. New York: McGraw-Hill, 1984.

Robbins, Larry M. *The Business of Writing and Speaking: A Managerial Communication Manual.* New York: McGraw-Hill, 1985.

Robertson, Mary, and W. E. Perkins. *Effective Correspondence for College*, 5th Ed. Cincinnati: South-Western, 1982.

Roundy, Nancy. *Strategies for Technical Communication.* Boston: Little, Brown and Company, 1985.

Russell, J. Stephen. *Writing at Work.* Chicago: The Dryden Press, 1985.

Rutkoskie, Alice E., and Carolyn T. Murphree. *Effective Writing for Business.* Columbus: Charles E. Merrill Publishing Company, 1983.

Schachter, Norman, and Alfred T. Clark, Jr. *Basic English Review*, 3rd Ed. Cincinnati: South-Western, 1985.

Schutte, William M., and Erwin R. Steinberg. *Communication in Business and Industry.* New York: Holt, Rinehart, and Winston, 1983.

Shurter, Robert L., and Donald J. Leonard. *Effective Letters in Business*, 3rd Ed. New York: McGraw-Hill, 1984.

Sigband, Norman B. *Communication for Management and Business*, 3rd. Ed. Glenview, Ill.: Scott, Foresman and Company, 1982.

Sigband, Norman B., and David N. Bateman. *Communicating in Business*, 2nd Ed. Glenview, Ill.: Scott, Foresman and Company, 1985.

Sigband, Norman B., Theodore W. Hipple, and Lois J. Bachman. *Successful Business English.* Glenview, Ill.: Scott, Foresman and Company, 1983.

Slocum, Keith. *Business English: A Worktext with Reinforcement*, 3rd Ed. Indianapolis: Bobbs-Merrill Educational Publishing, 1985.

Spitzer, Michael, Michael W. Gamble, and Teri Kwal Gamble. *Writing and Speaking in Business.* New York: Random House, 1984.

Starzyk, Lawrence J., and John R. Jewell. *Effective Business Writing.* New York: Macmillan, 1984.

Stewart, Marie M., and Kenneth Zimmer. *College English and Communication*, 4th Ed. New York: McGraw-Hill, 1982.

Swenson, Dan H. *Business Reporting*. Chicago: SRA, 1983.

Swindle, Robert E., and Elizabeth M. Swindle. *The Business Communicator*, 2nd Ed. Englewood Cliffs, N.J.: Prentice-Hall, 1985.

Tacey, William S. *Business and Professional Speaking*, 3rd Ed. Dubuque: William C. Brown Company, 1980.

Treece, Malra. *Communication for Business and the Professions*, 2nd Ed. Boston: Allyn & Bacon, 1983.

Treece, Malra. *Effective Reports*. Boston: Allyn & Bacon, 1982.

Van Oosting, James. *Business Correspondence: Writer, Reader, and Text*. Englewood Cliffs: Prentice-Hall, 1983.

Walker, Melissa. *Writing Research Papers*. New York: W. W. Norton & Company, 1984.

Weeks, Francis W., Daphne A. Jameson, and Robert D. Gieselman. *Principles of Business Communication*. Champaign, Ill.: Stipes Publishing Company, 1984.

Whalen, Doris H. *Handbook of Business English*. New York: Harcourt Brace Jovanovich, 1980.

Wilkinson, C. W., B. Clarke, and Dorothy C. Wilkinson. *Communicating Through Letters and Reports*, 8th Ed. Homewood, Ill.: Richard D. Irwin, 1983.

Williams, Joseph M. *Style*. Glenview, Ill.: Scott, Foresman and Company, 1981.

Wolf, Morris Philip, and Shirley Kuiper. *Effective Communication in Business*, 8th Ed. Cincinnati: South-Western, 1984.

Zinsser, William. *On Writing Well*. New York: Harper & Row, 1980.

Zinsser, William. *Writing With a Word Processor*. New York: Harper & Row, 1980.

Sources of Public Information

APPENDIX XII

Accountants' index. American Institute of Certified Public Accountants, Inc., 1211 Avenue of the Americas, New York, NY 10036-8775.

Abridged readers' guide to periodical literature, July 1935–. Author and subject index to a selected list of periodicals, New York: Wilson.

American statistics index. A comprehensive guide and index to the statistical publications of the U.S. Government, 1973–. Washington: Congressional Information Service, 1973–.

Bell, Marion V., and Jean C. Bacon. *Poole's index, date and volume key*. Chicago: Association of College and Research Libraries.

Biography index. A cumulative index to biographical material in books and magazines. New York: Wilson, 1947–.

Brown, Everett Somerville. *Manual of government publications, United States and foreign*. New York: Appleton, 1950.

Business books in print, 1973–. New York: Bowker, 1973–.

Business periodicals index. Subject entries to business periodicals articles.

Chicago Center for Research Libraries, *The Center for Research Libraries Catalogue: Newspapers*. Chicago: The Center.

Childs, James Bennett. *Government document bibliography in the U.S. and elsewhere*, 3rd Ed. Washington: Government Printing Office.

Coman, Edwin Truman. *Sources of business information*, Rev. Ed. Berkeley, Los Angeles: University of California Press, 1964.

Contemporary Authors: A bio-bibliographical guide to current authors and their works. Detroit: Gale Research, 1962–.

Cumulative List of Organizations. List of organizations to whom contributions are deductible.

Dissertation Abstracts International. Ann Arbor, Mich.: University Microfilms, 1938–.

Dun & Bradstreet reference book of corporate management. New York: Dun & Bradstreet, 1967–.

Editorials on File, v. 1–. January 1970–. New York: Facts on File, 1970–.

Encyclopedia of business information sources. Paul Wasserman, managing Ed. Detroit: Gale, 1970.

F & S index of corporations and industries, 1960–. Detroit: Funk & Scott.

F & S index international, predicasts. Cleveland.

Guide to reference books, Ninth Ed. Compiled by Eugene P. Sheehy. Chicago: American Library Assoc., 1976.

Guide to U.S. government publications, 1973–. McLean, Va.: Documents Index, 1973–.

Harvard University Graduate School of Business Administration Baker Library Business Reference Sources. Compiled by Lorna M. Daniells. Boston: 1971.

International Federation for Documentation. Abstracting Services. The Hague: The Federation, 1969.

International Statistical Institute. Bibliography of basic texts and monographs on statistical methods. 1945–1960. 2nd Ed. by William R. Buckland and Ronald A. Fox. Edinburgh: Oliver & Boyd, 1963. New York: Hagner 1963.

Journalism Abstracts, v. 1–. 1963–. Minneapolis Assoc. for Education in Journalism, 1963–.

Kujoth, Jean Spealman. *Subject guide to periodical indexes and review indexes*. Meteuchen, N.J.: Scarecrow, 1969.

Moody's industrial manual. Covers companies listed on the New York and American stock exchanges as well as companies listed on regional American exchanges.

National Association of State Libraries. Public Document Clearing House Committee. Checklist of legislative journals of the states of the U.S. Compiled by Grace E. Macdonald. Providence, R.I.: Oxford Press.

National directory of newsletters and reporting services. Detroit: Gale.

New York Public Library. A checklist of cumulative indexes to individual periodicals in the New York Public Library. Compiled by Daniel C. Haskell. New York: New York Library.

New York Public Library. Research libraries, catalog of government publications in the research libraries. Boston: G.K. Hall, 1972.

Notable names in American history: A tabulated register, 3rd Ed. of *White's conspectus of American biography*. Clifton, N.J.: James T. White & Co., 1973.

Personnel literature. Published monthly by U.S. Office of Personnel Management Library; books, journal articles, and documents received in the OPM Library are included.

Personnel Management Abstracts. Lists articles from a large number of academic and trade journals that deal with the management of people and organizational behavior. Chelsea, Mich.

Pohle, Linda C. *A guide to popular government publications for libraries and home reference*. Littleton, Colo.: Libraries Unlimited, 1972.

Poor's register of corporations, directors, and executives, U.S. and Canada. New York: Standard and Poor's Corp., 1928–.

Population Index. v. 1–. 1935–. Princeton, N.J.: Office of Population Research, Princeton Univ. and the Population Assoc. of America.

Reader's guide to periodical literature, 1900–. New York: Wilson, 1905–.

SIE guide to business and investment books. New York: Select Information Exchange, 1974.

Social sciences and humanities index. New York: Wilson, 1916–74.

United Nations, statistical office. Statistical papers: Series M. New York: 1949–.

U.S. Bureau of the Census. *Catalog of U.S. Census Publications, 1946–*. Washington: Government Printing Office.

U.S. Congress Senate Library. *Index to congressional committee hearings*.

U.S. Library of Congress, Catalog Publication Division. Newspapers in microform: United States 1948–1972. Washington, D.C.: 1973.

U.S. Library of Congress, General Reference and Bibliography Division. Compiled by Ruth S. Freitag. Washington, D.C.: 1964.

U.S. presidents, A compilation of the messages and papers of the presidents. New York: Bureau of National Liberature.

Wall street journal index.

Who's who in america, a biographical dictionary of notable living men and women. Chicago: Marquis, 1899–.

Who's who in finance and industry. Chicago: Marquis, 1936–.

Wolf, William B. *An author's guide to business publications*. Los Angeles: Univ. of Southern California Research Institute for Business and Economics, 1967.

Work related abstracts. From over 250 management, labor, government, professional, and university periodicals.

Wynkoop, Sally. *Subject guide to government reference books*. Littleton, Colo.: Libraries Unlimited, 1972.

APPENDIX XIII

Special Readings on Oral Communication

Anatasi, Thomas E. *Listen! Techniques for Improving Communication Skills*. Boston: CBI Publishing Company, 1982.

Applbaum, Ronald L., and Karl W. E. Anatol. *Effective Oral Communication for Business and the Professions*. Chicago: SRA, 1982.

Barker, Larry L. *Listening Behavior*. Englewood Cliffs, N.J.: Prentice-Hall, 1971.

Carnegie, Dale. *Effective Speaking*. New York: Pocket Books, 1977.

Christopher News Notes. New York.

Classen, George. *Better Business English*. New York: ARCO, 1966.

Ehninger, Douglas, Bruce E. Gronback, and Alan H. Monroe. *Principles of Speech Communications*, 8th Ed. Glenview, Ill.: Scott, Foresman and Company, 1982.

Fellows, Hugh, and Fusaye Ikeda. *Business Speaking & Writing*. Englewood Cliffs, N.J.: Prentice-Hall, 1982.

Fisher, Roger, and William Ury. *Getting to Yes*. New York: Penguin Books, 1981.

Fletcher, Leon. *How to Design and Deliver A Speech*, 2nd Ed. New York: Harper and Row, 1979.

Frank, Ted, and David Ray. *Basic Business and Professional Speech Communication*. Englewood Cliffs, N.J.: Prentice-Hall, 1979.

Gruner, Charles R. *Plain Public Speaking*. New York: Macmillan, 1984.

Gwyn, Jack, Robert J. Gwyn, and Betty J. Sander. *The Business of Oral Communication*. Cincinnati: South-Western, 1980. (Audio Cassette and Study Guides)

Handley, Cathy. *10 Days to Miracle Speech Power*. West Nyack, N.Y.: Parker Publishing Company, 1978.

Hodnett, Edward. *Effective Presentations*. West Nyack, N.Y.: Parker Publishing Co., 1967.

Jay, Anthony. *The New Oratory*. AMA, 1971.

Kell, Carl L., and Paul R. Corts. *Let's Talk Business: Improving Communication Skills*. Boston: Little, Brown and Company, 1983.

Kenny, Michael (for Eastman Kodak Company). *Presenting Yourself*. New York: John Wiley & Sons, 1982.

Koehler, Jerry W., and John I. Sisco. *Public Communication in Business and the Professions*. St. Paul: West Publishing Company, 1981.

LeRoux, Paul. *Selling to a Group: Presentation Strategies*. New York: Harper & Row, 1984.

Lucas, Stephen. *The Art of Public Speaking*. New York: Random House, 1983.

Matthews, Ann L. *The Letter Clinic: How to Dictate*. Cincinnati: South-Western, 1982.

Meuse, Leonard F. *Mastering the Business and Technical Presentation*. Boston: CBI Publishing Company, 1980.

Michulka, Jean. *Let's Talk Business*, 2nd Ed. Cincinnati: South-Western, 1983.

Nichols, Ralph G., and Leonard A. Stevens. *Are You Listening?* New York: McGraw-Hill, 1957.

Quick, John. *A Short Book on the Subject of Public Speaking*. New York: McGraw-Hill, 1978.

Ries, Al, and Jack Trout. *Positioning: The Battle for Your Mind*. New York: McGraw-Hill, 1981.

Samovar, Larry A., Stephen W. King, and Myron W. Lustig. *Speech Communication in Business and the Professions*. Belmont, Calif.: Wadsworth Publishing Company, 1981.

Samuels, Mike, and Nancy Samuels. *Seeing with the Mind's Eye*. New York: Random House, 1975.

Simmons, S. H. *How to be the Life of the Podium*. New York: AMACOM, 1982.

Sommet, Robert. *The Mind's Eye*. New York: Dell, 1978.

Spitzer, Michael, Michael W. Gamble, and Teri K. Gamble. *Writing and Speaking in Business*. New York: Random House, 1984.

Tacey, William S. *Business and Professinal Speaking*, 3rd Ed. Dubuque: William C. Brown Company, 1980.

The ABCA Bulletin (a publication of the American Business Communication Association), 608 S. Wright Street, Urbana, Illinois 61801. Published monthly.

The Journal of Business Communication (a publication of ABCA. Published quarterly.

The Toastmaster (a publication of Toastmasters International), P. O. Box 10400, Santa Ana, CA 92711. Published monthly.

Thourlby, William. *You Are What You Wear*. New York: New American Library, 1980.

Timm, Paul R. *Functional Business Presentations*. Englewood Cliffs, N.J.: Prentice-Hall, 1981.

Townsend, Robert. *Further Up the Organization*. New York: Knopf, 1984.

Van Oech, Roger. *A Whack on the Side of the Head*. New York: Warner Communications, 1983.

Van Oosting, James. *The Business Speech: Speaker, Audience, Text.* Englewood Cliffs, N.J.: Prentice-Hall, 1985.

Vasile, Albert J., and Harold K. Mintz. *Speak with Confidence: A Practical Guide*, 2nd Ed. Cambridge, Mass.: Winthrop Publishers, 1980.

Walter, Otis M., and Robert L. Scott. *Thinking and Speaking*, 5th Ed. New York: Macmillan, 1984.

Welsh, James J. *The Speech Writing Guide*. New York: Robert E. Krieger Publishing Company, 1979.

White, Eugene E. *Basic Public Speaking*. New York: Macmillan, 1984.

Williams, J. Clifton. *Human Behavior in Organizations*, 2nd Ed. Cincinnati: South-Western, 1982.

Special Readings on Nonverbal Communication

APPENDIX XIV

Birdwhistell, Ray L. *Introduction to Kinesics*. Louisville, Ky.: University of Louisville Press, 1952.

________________________. *Kinesics and Context: Essays on Body Motion Communication*. Philadelphia: University of Pennsylvania Press, 1970.

Davis, Martha. *Understanding Body Movement: An Annotated Bibliography*. New York: Arno Press, 1972.

Fast, Julius. *Body Language*. New York: M. Evans and Company, 1970.

Hall, Edward T. *The Hidden Dimension*. New York: Doubleday, 1966.

________________________. *The Silent Language*. New York: Doubleday, 1959.

Knapp, Mark. *Nonverbal Communication in Human Interaction*, 2nd Ed. New York: Holt, Rinehart & Winston, 1978.

Molloy, John T. *Dress for Success*. New York: Warner Books, 1976.

________________________. *The Woman's Dress for Success*. Follett, 1977.

Ruesch, Jurgen, and Weldon Kees. *Nonverbal Communication*. Berkeley, Calif.: University of California Press, 1970.

APPENDIX XV

Proofreaders' Marks

Symbol	Meaning	Illustration
Punctuation marks		
ⅴ̓	insert apostrophe	proofreaders marks
:|	insert colon	1005 a.m.
^,	insert comma	Yes I will come
|=|	insert hyphen	one cent stamps
⊙	insert period	Please mail the letter ⊙
?	insert question mark	Will you come ?
“ ”	insert quotation marks	He said, Come.
;|	insert semicolon	Canton, Ohio ; Toledo, Ohio

Symbol	Meaning	Illustration
Operational marks		
⊂ or cl	close up, omit space	proofread er proof reader
ℓ	delete	proofread it well
#	add space	proofreadwell
∽ or tr	transpose	well proofread well proofread
cap or ≡	capitalize	cap bermuda bermuda note
stet	keep as it was	proofread (stet)
lc or /	lower case letters	lc Dictionary Words
[	move left	[dictionary
]	move right	letter]
(sp)	spell out	231 North St. (sp)
___ or ital	underline or italicize	Gone with the Wind
¶	begin new paragraph	¶ The report is ready for you.
no ¶	no new paragraph here	no ¶ The report is ready.

INDEX

A

B

C

D

E

F

G

H

I

J

L

M

N

O

Q

R

S

T

V

W

Y

Z